# GREATEST GREEK PHILOSOPHERS

**Plato • The Republic
Aristotle • Politics
Epictetus • The Enchiridion**

CLASSICS

**Published 2024**
**FiNGERPRINT! CLASSICS**
**An imprint of Prakash Books India Pvt. Ltd**

113/A, Darya Ganj,
New Delhi-110 002
Email: info@prakashbooks.com/sales@prakashbooks.com

Fingerprint Publishing
@FingerprintP
@fingerprintpublishingbooks
www.fingerprintpublishing.com

ISBN: 978 93 5856 853 0

"What is the first business of one who practices philosophy? To get rid of self-conceit. For it is impossible for anyone to begin to learn that which he thinks he already knows."

Ancient Greece, often regarded as the cradle of Western civilization, produced an astonishing array of philosophical thought that continues to shape our understanding of the world and our place within it. Three figures stand out among the countless thinkers of that era—Plato, Aristotle, and Epictetus. Each of these philosophers offered unique insights into a wide range of topics, from ethics and politics to metaphysics and the nature of knowledge.

Born in Athens around 427–428 BCE, Plato emerged from an aristocratic family but chose a path of intellectual pursuit over political prominence. His philosophy, deeply influenced by his mentor Socrates, covers a vast spectrum of topics, making him one of the most prolific thinkers in history.

One of Plato's most renowned works is *The Republic*, a dialogue that delves into the nature of justice, the ideal state, and the human soul. In this remarkable piece of philosophical literature, Plato introduces the allegory of the cave, a powerful metaphor illustrating his belief that most people live in ignorance, mistaking shadows for reality. Only those who actively seek knowledge can truly understand the world beyond superficial appearances. This seminal work also introduces the concept of the philosopher-king, advocating for a just society led by individuals with a profound understanding of truth and justice.

In *The Republic*, Plato articulates a hierarchical vision of society where citizens are categorized based on their innate abilities and virtues. This hierarchical structure mirrors the tripartite division of the soul into reason, spirit, and desire, highlighting the need for a harmonious balance within both the individual and the state.

Aristotle, born in 384 BCE in Stagira, a Greek colony in Macedonia, was a student of Plato. His intellectual pursuits spanned a wide array of subjects, including ethics, politics, biology, and metaphysics, establishing him as one of history's most versatile thinkers.

In *Politics*, Aristotle embarks on a comprehensive exploration of the organization and governance of human societies. Unlike his teacher Plato, Aristotle favors empirical observation and practicality in his political philosophy. He asserts that the ideal state is one that fosters the flourishing of its citizens, emphasizing the importance of the middle class and a balanced constitution. His analysis of different forms of government, including monarchy, aristocracy, and democracy, remains a foundational text for political science and philosophy.

Aristotle's emphasis on moderation, the pursuit of the common good, and his rejection of utopian ideals provide valuable insights into the complexities of real-world governance. His work continues to shape discussions on political theory and ethics, emphasizing the importance of virtuous leadership and the collective pursuit of human well-being.

Lastly, Epictetus, a Stoic philosopher, offers a practical and timeless approach to living a virtuous life. Born in Hierapolis, Phrygia, around 55 CE, his early life was marked by enslavement until he gained his freedom and dedicated himself to the study of philosophy.

*The Enchiridion,* or "The Handbook", stands as one of Epictetus's most enduring works. In this concise manual, he distills the core principles of Stoicism into a guide for daily living. Unlike many philosophers who dwell on abstract concepts, Epictetus provides actionable advice on how to achieve tranquility and moral excellence in the face of life's challenges.

At the heart of Epictetus's philosophy lies the Stoic belief that individuals have control over their thoughts, desires, and actions, while external events are beyond their control. This profound insight empowers individuals to find serenity by aligning their inner values with the Stoic virtues of wisdom, courage, justice, and temperance. *The Enchiridion* serves as a practical roadmap for those seeking inner peace and ethical living.

Epictetus's Stoic teachings emphasize the importance of focusing on what is within one's control, letting go of unnecessary worries about external events, and cultivating an unwavering commitment to virtue. This practical wisdom resonates strongly in today's world, where individuals grapple with numerous challenges and uncertainties.

Plato, Aristotle, and Epictetus, each a luminary in the world of philosophy, continue to inspire and challenge thinkers today. Their collective contributions span ethics, politics, and personal development, making them enduring figures in the intellectual history of humanity. Although they emerged from different times and philosophical traditions, their works remain timeless sources of wisdom, inviting us to engage in the age-old pursuit of understanding ourselves and the world in which we live.

# CONTENTS

# THE
# REPUBLIC

# Plato

# INTRODUCTION

*T*he *Republic* of Plato is the longest of his works with the exception of the *Laws*, and is certainly the greatest of them. There are nearer approaches to modern metaphysics in the Philebus and in the Sophist; the Politicus or Statesman is more ideal; the form and institutions of the State are more clearly drawn out in the Laws; as works of art, the Symposium and the Protagoras are of higher excellence. But no other Dialogue of Plato has the same largeness of view and the same perfection of style; no other shows an equal knowledge of the world, or contains more of those thoughts which are new as well as old, and not of one age only but of all. Nowhere in Plato is there a deeper irony or a greater wealth of humor or imagery, or more dramatic power. Nor in any other of his writings is the attempt made to interweave life and speculation, or to connect politics with philosophy. The Republic is the centre around which the other Dialogues may be grouped; here philosophy reaches the highest point to which ancient thinkers ever attained. Plato among the Greeks, like Bacon among the moderns, was the first who conceived a method of knowledge, although neither of them always distinguished the bare outline or form from the substance of truth; and both of them had to be content with an abstraction of science which was not yet realized. He was the greatest metaphysical genius whom the world has seen; and in him, more than in any other ancient thinker, the germs of future knowledge are contained. The sciences of logic and psychology, which have supplied so many instruments of thought to after-ages, are based upon the analyses of Socrates and Plato. The principles of definition, the law of contradiction, the fallacy of arguing in a circle, the distinction between the essence and accidents of a thing or notion, between means and ends, between causes and conditions; also the division of the mind into the rational, concupiscent, and irascible elements, or of pleasures and desires into necessary and unnecessary—these and other great forms of thought are all of them to be found in the Republic, and were probably first invented by Plato. The greatest of all logical truths, and the one of which writers on philosophy are most apt to lose sight, the difference between words and things, has been most strenuously insisted on by him, although he has not always avoided the confusion of them in his own writings. But he does not bind up truth in logical formulae,— logic is still veiled in metaphysics; and the science which he imagines to "contemplate all truth and all existence" is very unlike the doctrine of the syllogism which Aristotle claims to have discovered.

Neither must we forget that the Republic is but the third part of a still larger design which was to have included an ideal history of Athens, as well as a political and physical philosophy. The fragment of the Critias has given birth to a world-famous fiction, second only in importance to the tale of Troy and the legend of Arthur; and is said as a fact to have inspired some of the early navigators of the sixteenth century. This mythical tale, of which the subject was a history of the wars of the Athenians against the Island of Atlantis, is supposed to be founded upon an unfinished poem of Solon, to which it would have stood in the same relation as the writings of the logographers to the poems of Homer. It would have told of a struggle for Liberty, intended to represent the conflict of Persia and Hellas. We may judge from the noble commencement of the Timaeus, from the fragment of the Critias itself, and from the third book of the Laws, in what manner Plato would have treated this high argument. We can only guess why the great design was abandoned; perhaps because Plato became sensible of some incongruity in a fictitious history, or because he had lost his interest in it, or because advancing years forbade the completion of it; and we may please ourselves with the fancy that had this imaginary narrative ever been finished, we should have found Plato himself sympathizing with the struggle for Hellenic independence, singing a hymn of triumph over Marathon and Salamis, perhaps making the reflection of Herodotus where he contemplates the growth of the Athenian empire—" How brave a thing is freedom of speech, which has made the Athenians so far exceed every other state of Hellas in greatness!" or, more probably, attributing the victory to the ancient good order of Athens and to the favor of Apollo and Athene.

Again, Plato may be regarded as the "captain" ('arhchegoz') or leader of a goodly band of followers; for in the Republic is to be found the original of Cicero's De Republica, of St. Augustine's City of God, of the Utopia of Sir Thomas More, and of the numerous other imaginary States which are framed upon the same model. The extent to which Aristotle or the Aristotelian school were indebted to him in the Politics has been little recognized, and the recognition is the more necessary because it is not made by Aristotle himself. The two philosophers had more in common than they were conscious of; and probably some elements of Plato remain still undetected in Aristotle. In English philosophy too, many affinities may be traced, not only in the works of the Cambridge Platonists, but in great original writers like Berkeley or Coleridge, to Plato and his ideas. That there is a truth higher than experience, of which the mind bears witness to herself, is a conviction which in our own generation has been enthusiastically asserted, and is perhaps gaining ground. Of the Greek authors who at the Renaissance brought a new life into the world Plato has had the greatest influence. The Republic of Plato is also the first treatise upon education, of which the writings of Milton and Locke, Rousseau, Jean Paul, and Goethe are the legitimate descendants. Like Dante or Bunyan, he has a revelation of another life; like Bacon, he is profoundly impressed with the un unity of knowledge; in the early Church he exercised a real influence on theology, and at the Revival of Literature on politics. Even the fragments of his words when "repeated at second-hand" have in all ages ravished the hearts of men, who have seen reflected in them their own higher nature. He is the father of idealism in philosophy, in politics, in literature. And many of the latest conceptions of modern thinkers and statesmen, such as the unity of knowledge, the reign of law, and the equality of the sexes, have been anticipated in a dream by him.

# ARGUMENT

The argument of the Republic is the search after Justice, the nature of which is first hinted at by Cephalus, the just and blameless old man—then discussed on the basis of proverbial morality by Socrates and Polemarchus—then caricatured by Thrasymachus and partially explained by Socrates—reduced to an abstraction by Glaucon and Adeimantus, and having become invisible in the individual reappears at length in the ideal State which is constructed by Socrates. The first care of the rulers is to be education, of which an outline is drawn after the old Hellenic model, providing only for an improved religion and morality, and more simplicity in music and gymnastic, a manlier strain of poetry, and greater harmony of the individual and the State. We are thus led on to the conception of a higher State, in which "no man calls anything his own," and in which there is neither "marrying nor giving in marriage," and "kings are philosophers" and "philosophers are kings;" and there is another and higher education, intellectual as well as moral and religious, of science as well as of art, and not of youth only but of the whole of life. Such a State is hardly to be realized in this world and would quickly degenerate. To the perfect ideal succeeds the government of the soldier and the lover of honor, this again declining into democracy, and democracy into tyranny, in an imaginary but regular order having not much resemblance to the actual facts. When "the wheel has come full circle" we do not begin again with a new period of human life; but we have passed from the best to the worst, and there we end. The subject is then changed and the old quarrel of poetry and philosophy which had been more lightly treated in the earlier books of the Republic is now resumed and fought out to a conclusion. Poetry is discovered to be an imitation thrice removed from the truth, and Homer, as well as the dramatic poets, having been condemned as an imitator, is sent into banishment along with them. And the idea of the State is supplemented by the revelation of a future life.

The division into books, like all similar divisions, is probably later than the age of Plato. The natural divisions are five in number;—

(1) Book I and the first half of Book II down to the paragraph beginning, "I had always admired the genius of Glaucon and Adeimantus," which is introductory; the first book containing a refutation of the popular and sophistical notions of justice, and concluding, like some of the earlier Dialogues, without arriving at any definite result. To this is appended a restatement of the nature of justice according to common opinion, and an answer is demanded to the question—What is justice, stripped of appearances? The second division (2) includes the remainder of the second and the whole of the third and fourth books, which are mainly occupied with the construction of the first State and the first education. The third division (3) consists of the fifth, sixth, and seventh books, in which philosophy rather than justice is the subject of inquiry, and the second State is constructed on principles of communism and ruled by philosophers, and the contemplation of the idea of good takes the place of the social and political virtues. In the eighth and ninth books (4) the perversions of States and of the individuals who correspond to them are reviewed in succession; and the nature of pleasure and the principle of tyranny are further analyzed in the individual man. The tenth book (5) is the conclusion of the whole, in which the relations of philosophy to poetry are finally determined, and the happiness of the citizens in this life, which has now been assured, is crowned by the vision of another.

Or a more general division into two parts may be adopted; the first (Books I–IV) containing the description of a State framed generally in accordance with Hellenic notions of religion and morality, while in the second (Books V–X) the Hellenic State is transformed into an ideal kingdom of philosophy, of which all other governments are the perversions. These two points of view are really opposed, and the opposition is only veiled by the genius of Plato. The Republic, like the Phaedrus, is an imperfect whole; the higher light of philosophy breaks through the regularity of the Hellenic temple, which at last fades away into the heavens. Whether this imperfection of structure arises from an enlargement of the plan; or from the imperfect reconcilement in the writer's own mind of the struggling elements of thought which are now first brought together by him; or, perhaps, from the composition of the work at different times—are questions, like the similar question about the Iliad and the Odyssey, which are worth asking, but which cannot have a distinct answer. In the age of Plato there was no regular mode of publication, and an author would have the less scruple in altering or adding to a work which was known only to a few of his friends. There is no absurdity in supposing that he may have laid his labors aside for a time, or turned from one work to another; and such interruptions would be more likely to occur in the case of a long than of a short writing. In all attempts to determine the chronological he order of the Platonic writings on internal evidence, this uncertainty about any single Dialoguebeing composed at one time is a disturbing element, which must be admitted to affect longer works, such as the Republic and the Laws, more than shorter ones. But, on the other hand, the seeming discrepancies of the Republic may only arise out of the discordant elements which the philosopher has attempted to unite in a single whole, perhaps without being himself able to recognize the inconsistency which is obvious to us. For there is a judgment of after ages which few great writers have ever been able to anticipate for themselves. They do not perceive the want of connection in their own writings, or the gaps in their systems which are visible enough to those who come after them. In the beginnings of literature and philosophy, amid the first efforts of thought and language, more inconsistencies occur than now, when the paths of speculation are well worn and the meaning of words precisely defined. For consistency, too, is the growth of time; and some of the greatest creations of the human mind have been wanting in unity. Tried by this test, several of the Platonic Dialogues, according to our modern ideas, appear to be defective, but the deficiency is no proof that they were composed at different times or by different hands. And the supposition that the Republic was written uninterruptedly and by a continuous effort is in some degree confirmed by the numerous references from one part of the work to another.

The second title, "Concerning Justice," is not the one by which the Republic is quoted, either by Aristotle or generally in antiquity, and, like the other second titles of the Platonic Dialogues, may therefore be assumed to be of later date. Morgenstern and others have asked whether the definition of justice, which is the professed aim, or the construction of the State is the principal argument of the work. The answer is, that the two blend in one, and are two faces of the same truth; for justice is the order of the State, and the State is the visible embodiment of justice under the conditions of human society. The one is the soul and the other is the body, and the Greek ideal of the State, as of the individual, is a fair mind in a fair body. In Hegelian phraseology the State is the reality of which justice is the ideal. Or, described in Christian language, the kingdom of God is within, and yet develops into a Church or external kingdom; "the house not made with hands, eternal in the heavens," is reduced to the proportions of an earthly building. Or, to use a Platonic image, justice and the State are the warp and the woof which run through the whole texture. And when the constitution of the State is completed, the conception of justice is not dismissed, but reappears under the same or different names throughout the work, both as the inner law of the individual soul, and finally as the principle of rewards and punishments in another life. The virtues are based on justice, of which common honesty in buying and selling is the shadow, and justice is based on the idea of good, which is the harmony of the world, and is reflected both in the institutions of States and in motions of the heavenly bodies. The Timaeus, which takes up the political rather than the ethical side of the Republic, and is chiefly occupied with hypotheses concerning the outward world, yet contains many indications that the same law is supposed to reign over the State, over nature, and over man.

Too much, however, has been made of this question both in ancient and in modern times. There is a stage of criticism in which all works, whether of nature or of art, are referred to design. Now in ancient writings, and indeed in literature generally, there remains often a large element which was not comprehended in the original design. For the plan grows under the author's hand; new thoughts occur to him in the act of writing; he has not worked out the argument to the end before he begins. The reader who seeks to find someone idea under which the whole may be conceived, must necessarily seize on the vaguest and most general. Thus Stallbaum, who is dissatisfied with the ordinary explanations of the argument of the Republic, imagines himself to have found the true argument "in the representation of human life in a State perfected by justice and governed according to the idea of good." There may be some use in such general descriptions, but they can hardly be said to express the design of the writer. The truth is, that we may as well speak of many designs as of one; nor need anything be excluded from the plan of a great work to which the mind is naturally led by the association of ideas, and which does not interfere with the general purpose. What kind or degree of unity is to be sought after in a building, in the plastic arts, in poetry, in prose, is a problem which has to be determined relatively to the subject-matter. To Plato himself, the inquiry "what was the intention of the writer," or "what was the principal argument of the Republic" would have been hardly intelligible, and therefore had better be at once dismissed.

Is not the Republic the vehicle of three or four great truths which, to Plato's own mind, are most naturally represented in the form of the State? Just as in the Jewish prophets the reign of Messiah, or "the day of the Lord," or the suffering Servant or people of God, or the "Sun of righteousness with healing in his wings" only convey, to us at least, their great spiritual ideals, so through the Greek State Plato reveals to us his own thoughts about divine perfection, which is the idea of good—like the sun in the visible world;—about human perfection, which is justice—about education beginning in youth and continuing in later years—about poets and sophists and tyrants who are the false teachers and evil rulers of mankind—about "the world" which is the embodiment of them—about a kingdom which exists nowhere upon earth but is laid up in heaven to be the pattern and rule of human life. No such inspired creation is at unity with itself, any more than the clouds of heaven when the sun pierces through them. Every shade of light and dark, of truth, and of fiction which is the veil of truth, is allowable in a work of philosophical imagination. It is not all on the same plane; it easily passes from ideas to myths and fancies, from facts to figures of speech. It is not prose but poetry, at least a great part of it, and ought not to be judged by the rules of logic or the probabilities of history. The writer is not fashioning his ideas into an artistic whole; they take possession of him and are too much for him. We have no need therefore to discuss whether a State such as Plato has conceived is practicable or not, or whether the outward form or the inward life came first into the mind of the writer. For the practicability of his ideas has nothing to do with their truth; and the highest thoughts to which he attains may be truly said to bear the greatest "marks of design"— justice more than the external frame-work of the State, the idea of good more than justice. The great science of dialectic or the organization of ideas has no real content; but is only a type of the method or spirit in which the higher knowledge is to be pursued by the spectator of all time and all existence. It is in the fifth, sixth, and seventh books that Plato reaches the "summit of speculation," and these, although they fail to satisfy the requirements of a modern thinker, may therefore be regarded as the most important, as they are also the most original, portions of the work.

It is not necessary to discuss at length a minor question which has been raised by Boeckh, respecting the imaginary date at which the conversation was held (the year 411 B. C. which is proposed by him will do as well as any other); for a writer of fiction, and especially a writer who, like Plato, is notoriously careless of chronology, only aims at general probability. Whether all the persons mentioned in the Republic could ever have met at any one time is not a difficulty which would have occurred to an Athenian reading the work forty years later, or to Plato himself at the time of writing (any more than to Shakespeare respecting one of his own dramas); and need not greatly trouble us now. Yet this may be a question having no answer "which is still worth asking," because the investigation shows that we cannot argue historically from the dates in Plato; it would be useless therefore to waste time in inventing far-fetched reconcilements of them in order avoid chronological difficulties, such, for example, as the conjecture of

C. F. Hermann, that Glaucon and Adeimantus are not the brothers but the uncles of Plato, or the fancy of Stallbaum that Plato intentionally left anachronisms indicating the dates at which some of his Dialogues were written.

## CHARACTERS

The principal characters in the Republic are Cephalus, Polemarchus, Thrasymachus, Socrates, Glaucon, and Adeimantus. Cephalus appears in the introduction only, Polemarchus drops at the end of the first argument, and Thrasymachus is reduced to silence at the close of the first book. The main discussion is carried on by Socrates, Glaucon, and Adeimantus. Among the company are Lysias (the orator) and Euthydemus, the sons of Cephalus and brothers of Polemarchus, an unknown Charmantides—these are mute auditors; also there is Cleitophon, who once interrupts, where, as in the Dialogue which bears his name, he appears as the friend and ally of Thrasymachus.

Cephalus, the patriarch of house, has been appropriately engaged in offering a sacrifice. He is the pattern of an old man who has almost done with life, and is at peace with himself and with all mankind. He feels that he is drawing nearer to the world below, and seems to linger around the memory of the past. He is eager that Socrates should come to visit him, fond of the poetry of the last generation, happy in the consciousness of a well-spent life, glad at having escaped from the tyranny of youthful lusts. His love of conversation, his affection, his indifference to riches, even his garrulity, are interesting traits of character. He is not one of those who have nothing to say, because their whole mind has been absorbed in making money. Yet he acknowledges that riches have the advantage of placing men above the temptation to dishonesty or falsehood. The respectful attention shown to him by Socrates, whose love of conversation, no less than the mission imposed upon him by the Oracle, leads him to ask questions of all men, young and old alike, should also be noted. Who better suited to raise the question of justice than Cephalus, whose life might seem to be the expression of it? The moderation with which old age is pictured by Cephalus as a very tolerable portion of existence is characteristic, not only of him, but of Greek feeling generally, and contrasts with theexaggeration of Cicero in the De Senectute. The evening of life is described by Plato in the most expressive manner, yet with the fewest possible touches. As Cicero remarks (Ep. ad Attic. iv. 16), the aged Cephalus would have been out of place in the discussion which follows, and which he could neither have understood nor taken part in without a violation of dramatic propriety.

His "son and heir" Polemarchus has the frankness and impetuousness of youth; he is for detaining Socrates by force in the opening scene, and will not "let him off" on the subject of women and children. Like Cephalus, he is limited in his point of view, and represents the proverbial stage of morality which has rules of life rather than principles; and he quotes Simonides as his father had quoted Pindar. But after this he has no more to say; the answers which he makes are only elicited from him by the dialectic of Socrates. He has not yet experienced the influence of the Sophists like Glaucon and Adeimantus, nor is he sensible of the necessity of refuting them; he belongs to the pre-Socratic or pre-dialectical age. He is incapable of arguing, and is bewildered by Socrates to such a degree that he does not know what he is saying. He is made to admit that justice is a thief, and that the virtues follow the analogy of the arts. From his brother Lysias we learn that he fell a victim to the Thirty Tyrants, but no allusion is here made to his fate, nor to the circumstance that Cephalus and his family were of Syracusan origin, and had migrated from Thurii to Athens.

The "Chalcedonian giant," Thrasymachus, of whom we have already heard in the Phaedrus, is the personification of the Sophists, according to Plato's conception of them, in some of their worst characteristics. He is vain and blustering, refusing to discourse unless he is paid, fond of making an oration, and hoping thereby to escape the inevitable Socrates; but a mere child in argument, and unable to foresee that the next "move" (to use a Platonic expression) will "shut him up." He has reached the stage of framing general notions, and in this respect is in advance of Cephalus and Polemarchus. But he is incapable of defending them in a discussion, and vainly tries to cover his confusion in banter and insolence. Whether such doctrines as are attributed to him by Plato were really held either by him or by any other Sophist is uncertain; in the infancy of philosophy serious errors about morality might easily grow up—they are certainly put into the mouths of speakers in Thucydides; but we are concerned at present with Plato's description of him, and not with the historical reality. The inequality of the contest adds greatly to the humor of the scene. The pompous and empty Sophist is utterly helpless in the hands of the great master of dialectic, who knows how to touch all the springs of vanity and weakness in him. He is greatly irritated by the irony of Socrates, but his noisy and imbecile rage only lays him more and more open to the thrusts of his assailant. His determination to cram down their throats, or put "bodily into their souls" his own words, elicits a cry of horror from Socrates. The state of his temper is quite as worthy of remark as the process of the argument. Nothing is more amusing than his complete submission when he has been once thoroughly beaten. At first he seems to continue the discussion with reluctance, but soon with apparent good-will, and he even testifies his interest at a later stage by one or two occasional remarks. When attacked by Glaucon he is humorously protected by Socrates "as one who has never been his enemy and is now his friend." From Cicero and Quintilian and from Aristotle's Rhetoric we learn that the Sophist whom Plato has made so ridiculous was a man of note whose writings were preserved in later ages. The play on his name which was made by his contemporary Herodicus, "thou wast ever bold in battle," seems to show that the description of him is not devoid of verisimilitude.

When Thrasymachus has been silenced, the two principal respondents, Glaucon and Adeimantus, appear on the scene: here, as in Greek tragedy, three actors are introduced. At first sight the two sons of Ariston may seem to wear a family likeness, like the two friends Simmias and Cebes in the Phaedo. But on a nearer examination of them the similarity vanishes, and they are seen to be distinct characters. Glaucon is the impetuous youth who can "just never have enough of

fechting" (cf. the character of him in Xen. Mem. iii. 6); the man of
pleasure who is acquainted with the mysteries of love; the *"juvenis qui
gaudet canibus,"* and who improves the breed of animals; the lover of
art and music who has all the experiences of youthful life. He is full of
quickness and penetration, piercing easily below the clumsy platitudes
of Thrasymachus to the real difficulty; he turns out to the light the
seamy side of human life, and yet does not lose faith in the just and true.
It is Glaucon who seizes what may be termed the ludicrous relation of
the philosopher to the world, to whom a state of simplicity is "a city
of pigs," who is always prepared with a jest when the argument offers
him an opportunity, and who is ever ready to second the humor of
Socrates and to appreciate the ridiculous, whether in the connoisseurs
of music, or in the lovers of theatricals, or in the fantastic behavior
of the citizens of democracy. His weaknesses are several times alluded
to by Socrates, who, however, will not allow him to be attacked by his
brother Adeimantus. He is a soldier, and, like Adeimantus, has been
distinguished at the battle of Megara.

The character of Adeimantus is deeper and graver, and the
profounder objections are commonly put into his mouth. Glaucon
is more demonstrative, and generally opens the game. Adeimantus
pursues the argument further. Glaucon has more of the liveliness and
quick sympathy of youth; Adeimantus has the maturer judgment of
a grown-up man of the world. In the second book, when Glaucon
insists that justice and injustice shall be considered without regard to
their consequences, Adeimantus remarks that they are regarded by
mankind in general only for the sake of their consequences; and in a
similar vein of reflection he urges at the beginning of the fourth book
that Socrates falls in making his citizens happy, and is answered that
happiness is not the first but the second thing, not the direct aim but
the indirect consequence of the good government of a State. In the
discussion about religion and mythology, Adeimantus is the respondent,
but Glaucon breaks in with a slight jest, and carries on the conversation
in a lighter tone about music and gymnastic to the end of the book. It
is Adeimantus again who volunteers the criticism of common sense on

the Socratic method of argument, and who refuses to let Socrates pass lightly over the question of women and children. It is Adeimantus who is the respondent in the more argumentative, as Glaucon in the lighter and more imaginative portions of the Dialogue. For example, throughout the greater part of the sixth book, the causes of the corruption of philosophy and the conception of the idea of good are discussed with Adeimantus. Then Glaucon resumes his place of principal respondent; but he has a difficulty in apprehending the higher education of Socrates, and makes some false hits in the course of the discussion. Once more Adeimantus returns with the allusion to his brother Glaucon whom he compares to the contentious State; in the next book he is again superseded, and Glaucon continues to the end.

Thus in a succession of characters Plato represents the successive stages of morality, beginning with the Athenian gentleman of the olden time, who is followed by the practical man of that day regulating his life by proverbs and saws; to him succeeds the wild generalization of the Sophists, and lastly come the young disciples of the great teacher, who know the sophistical arguments but will not be convinced by them, and desire to go deeper into the nature of things. These too, like Cephalus, Polemarchus, Thrasymachus, are clearly distinguished from one another. Neither in the Republic, nor in any other Dialogue of Plato, is a single character repeated.

The delineation of Socrates in the Republic is not wholly consistent. In the first book we have more of the real Socrates, such as he is depicted in the Memorabilia of Xenophon, in the earliest Dialogues of Plato, and in the Apology. He is ironical, provoking, questioning, the old enemy of the Sophists, ready to put on the mask of Silenus as well as to argue seriously. But in the sixth book his enmity towards the Sophists abates; he acknowledges that they are the representatives rather than the corrupters of the world. He also becomes more dogmatic and constructive, passing beyond the range either of the political or the speculative ideas of the real Socrates. In one passage Plato himself seems to intimate that the time had now come for Socrates, who had passed his whole life in philosophy, to give his own opinion and not to be always repeating the notions of other men. There is no evidence that either the idea of good or the conception of a perfect State were comprehended in the Socratic teaching, though he certainly dwelt on the nature of the universal and of final causes (cp. Xen. Mem. i. 4; Phaedo 97); and a deep thinker like him in his thirty or forty years of public teaching, could hardly have failed to touch on the nature of family relations, for which there is also some positive evidence in the Memorabilia (Mem. i. 2, 51 foll.) The Socratic Method is nominally retained; and every inference is either put into the mouth of the respondent or represented as the common discovery of him and Socrates. But anyone can see that this is a mere form, of which the affectation grows wearisome as the work advances. The method of inquiry has passed into a method of teaching in which by the help of interlocutors the same thesis is looked at from various points of view.

The nature of the process is truly characterized by Glaucon, when he describes himself as a companion who is not good for much in an investigation, but can see what he is shown, and may, perhaps, give the answer to a question more fluently than another.

Neither can we be absolutely certain that, Socrates himself taught the immortality of the soul, which is unknown to his disciple Glaucon in the Republic; nor is there any reason to suppose that he used myths or revelations of another world as a vehicle of instruction, or that he would have banished poetry or have denounced the Greek mythology. His favorite oath is retained, and a slight mention is made of the daemonium, or internal sign, which is alluded to by Socrates as a phenomenon peculiar to himself. A real element of Socratic teaching, which is more prominent in the Republic than in any of the other Dialogues of Plato, is the use of example and illustration ('taphorhtika auto prhospherhontez'): "Let us apply the test of common instances." "You," says Adeimantus, ironically, in the sixth book, "are so unaccustomed to speak in images." And this use of examples or images, though truly Socratic in origin, is enlarged by the genius of Plato into the form of an allegory or parable, which embodies in the concrete what has been already described, or is about to be described, in the abstract. Thus the figure of the cave in Book VII is a recapitulation of the divisions of knowledge in Book VI. The composite animal in Book IX is an allegory of the parts of the soul. The noble captain and the ship and the true pilot in Book VI are a figure of the relation of the people to the philosophers in the State which has been described. Other figures, such as the dog in the second, third, and fourth books, or the marriage of the portion less maiden in the sixth book, or the drones and wasps in the eighth and ninth books, also form links of connection in long passages, or are used to recall previous discussions.

Plato is most true to the character of his master when he describes him as "not of this world." And with this representation of him the ideal State and the other paradoxes of the Republic are quite in accordance, though they cannot be shown to have been speculations of Socrates. To him, as to other great teachers both philosophical and religious, when they looked upward, the world seemed to be the embodiment of error and evil. The common sense of mankind has revolted against this view, or has only partially admitted it. And even in Socrates himself the sterner judgment of the multitude at times passes into a sort of ironical pity or love. Men in general are incapable of philosophy, and are therefore at enmity with the philosopher; but their misunderstanding of him is unavoidable: for they have never seen him as he truly is in his own image; they are only acquainted with artificial systems possessing no native force of truth—words which admit of many applications. Their leaders have nothing to measure with, and are therefore ignorant of their own stature. But they are to be pitied or laughed at, not to be quarrelled with; they mean well with their nostrums, if they could only learn that they are cutting off a Hydra's head. This moderation towards those who are in error is one of the most characteristic features of Socrates in the Republic. In all the different representations of Socrates, whether of Xenophon or Plato, and the differences of the earlier or later Dialogues, he always retains the character of the unwearied and disinterested seeker after truth, without which he would have ceased to be Socrates.

# PERSONS OF THE DIALOGUE

Socrates, who is the narrator
Glaucon
Adeimantus
Polemarchus
Cephalus
Thrasymachus
Cleitophon
And others who are mute auditors

The scene is laid in the house of Cephalus at the Piraeus; and the whole dialogue is narrated by Socrates the day after it actually took place to Timaeus, Hermocrates, Critias, and a nameless person, who are introduced in the Timaeus.

# BOOK I

I went down yesterday to the Piraeus with Glaucon the son of Ariston, that I might offer up my prayers to the goddess (Bendis, the Thracian Artemis.); and also because I wanted to see in what manner they would celebrate the festival, which was a new thing. I was delighted with the procession of the inhabitants; but that of the Thracians was equally, if not more, beautiful. When we had finished our prayers and viewed the spectacle, we turned in the direction of the city; and at that instant Polemarchus the son of Cephalus chanced to catch sight of us from a distance as we were starting on our way home, and told his servant to run and bid us wait for him. The servant took hold of me by the cloak behind, and said: Polemarchus desires you to wait.

I turned round, and asked him where his master was.

There he is, said the youth, coming after you, if you will only wait.

Certainly we will, said Glaucon; and in a few minutes Polemarchus appeared, and with him Adeimantus, Glaucon's brother, Niceratus the son of Nicias, and several others who had been at the procession.

Polemarchus said to me: I perceive, Socrates, that you and your companion are already on your way to the city.

You are not far wrong, I said.

But do you see, he rejoined, how many we are?

Of course.

And are you stronger than all these? for if not, you will have to remain where you are.

May there not be the alternative, I said, that we may persuade you to let us go?

But can you persuade us, if we refuse to listen to you? he said.

Certainly not, replied Glaucon.

Then we are not going to listen; of that you may be assured.

Adeimantus added: Has no one told you of the torch-race on horseback in honour of the goddess which will take place in the evening?

With horses! I replied: That is a novelty. Will horsemen carry torches and pass them one to another during the race?

Yes, said Polemarchus, and not only so, but a festival will be celebrated at night, which you certainly ought to see. Let us rise soon after supper and see this festival; there will be a gathering of young men, and we will have a good talk. Stay then, and do not be perverse.

Glaucon said: I suppose, since you insist, that we must.

Very good, I replied.

Accordingly we went with Polemarchus to his house; and there we found his brothers Lysias and Euthydemus, and with them Thrasymachus the Chalcedonian, Charmantides the Paeanian, and Cleitophon the son of Aristonymus. There too was Cephalus the father of Polemarchus, whom I had not seen for a long time, and I thought him very much aged. He was seated on a cushioned chair, and had a garland on his head, for he had been sacrificing in the court; and there were some other chairs in the room arranged in a semicircle, upon which we sat down by him. He saluted me eagerly, and then he said:—You don't come to see me, Socrates, as often as you ought: If I were still able to go and see you I would not ask you to come to me. But at my age I can hardly get to the city, and therefore you should come oftener to the Piraeus. For let me tell you, that the more the pleasures of the body fade away, the greater to me is the pleasure and charm of conversation. Do not then deny my request, but make our house your resort and keep company with these young men; we are old friends, and you will be quite at home with us.

I replied: There is nothing which for my part I like better, Cephalus, than conversing with aged men; for I regard them as travellers who have gone a journey which I too may have to go, and of whom I ought to enquire, whether the way is smooth and easy, or rugged and difficult. And this is a question which I should like to ask of you who have arrived at that time which the poets call the 'threshold of old age'—Is life harder towards the end, or what report do you give of it?

I will tell you, Socrates, he said, what my own feeling is. Men of my age flock together; we are birds of a feather, as the old proverb says; and at our meetings the tale of my acquaintance commonly is—I cannot eat, I cannot drink; the pleasures of youth and love are fled away: there was a good time once, but now that is gone, and life is no longer life. Some complain of the slights which are put upon them by relations, and they will tell you sadly of how many evils their old age is the cause. But to me, Socrates, these complainers seem to blame that which is not really in fault. For if old age were the cause, I too being old, and every other old man, would have felt as they do. But this is not my own experience, nor that of others whom I have known. How well I remember the aged poet Sophocles, when in answer to the question, How does love suit with age, Sophocles,—are you still the man you were? Peace, he replied; most gladly have I escaped the thing of which you speak; I feel as if I had escaped from a mad and furious master. His words have often occurred to my mind since, and they seem as good to me now as at the time when he uttered them. For certainly old age has a great sense of calm and freedom; when the passions relax their hold, then, as Sophocles says, we are freed from the grasp not of one mad master only, but of many. The truth is, Socrates, that these regrets, and also the complaints about relations, are to be attributed to the same cause, which is not old age, but men's characters and tempers; for he who is of a calm and happy nature will hardly feel the pressure of age, but to him who is of an opposite disposition youth and age are equally a burden.

I listened in admiration, and wanting to draw him out, that he might go on—Yes, Cephalus, I said: but I rather suspect that people in general are not convinced by you when you speak thus; they think that old age sits lightly upon you, not because of your happy disposition, but because you are rich, and wealth is well known to be a great comforter.

You are right, he replied; they are not convinced: and there is something in what they say; not, however, so much as they imagine. I might answer them as Themistocles answered the Seriphian who was abusing him and saying that he was famous, not for his own merits but because he was an Athenian: "If you had been a native of my country or I of yours, neither of us would have been famous." And to those who are not rich and are impatient of old age, the same reply may be made; for to the good poor man old age cannot be a light burden, nor can a bad rich man ever have peace with himself.

May I ask, Cephalus, whether your fortune was for the most part inherited or acquired by you?

Acquired! Socrates; do you want to know how much I acquired? In the art of making money I have been midway between my father and grandfather: for my grandfather, whose name I bear, doubled and trebled the value of his patrimony, that which he inherited being much what I possess now; but my father Lysanias reduced the property below what it is at present: and I shall be satisfied if I leave to these my sons not less but a little more than I received.

That was why I asked you the question, I replied, because I see that you are indifferent about money, which is a characteristic rather of those who have inherited their fortunes than of those who have acquired them; the makers of fortunes have a second love of money as a creation of their own, resembling the affection of authors for their own poems, or of parents for their children, besides that natural love of it for the sake of use and profit which is common to them and all men. And hence they are very bad company, for they can talk about nothing but the praises of wealth.

That is true, he said.

Yes, that is very true, but may I ask another question?—What do you consider to be the greatest blessing which you have reaped from your wealth?

One, he said, of which I could not expect easily to convince others. For let me tell you, Socrates, that when a man thinks himself to be near death, fears and cares enter into his mind which he never had before; the tales of a world below and the punishment which is exacted there of deeds done here were once a laughing matter to him, but now he is tormented with the thought that they may be true: either from the weakness of age, or because he is now drawing nearer to that other place, he has a clearer view of these things; suspicions and alarms crowd thickly upon him, and he begins to reflect and consider what wrongs he has done to others. And when he finds that the sum of his transgressions is great he will many a time like a child start up in his sleep for fear, and he is filled with dark forebodings. But to him who is conscious of no sin, sweet hope, as Pindar charmingly says, is the kind nurse of his age: "Hope," he says, "cherishes the soul of him who lives in justice and holiness, and is the nurse of his age and the companion of his journey;—hope which is mightiest to sway the restless soul of man."

How admirable are his words! And the great blessing of riches, I do not say to every man, but to a good man, is, that he has had no occasion to deceive or to defraud others, either intentionally or unintentionally; and when he departs to the world below he is not in any apprehension about offerings due to the gods or debts which he owes to men. Now to this peace of mind the possession of wealth greatly contributes; and therefore I say, that, setting one thing against another, of the many advantages which wealth has to give, to a man of sense this is in my opinion the greatest.

Well said, Cephalus, I replied; but as concerning justice, what is it?—to speak the truth and to pay your debts—no more than this? And even to this are there not exceptions? Suppose that a friend when in his right mind has deposited arms with me and he asks for them when he is not in his right mind, ought I to give them back to him? No one would say that I ought or that I should be right in doing so, any more than they would say that I ought always to speak the truth to one who is in his condition.

You are quite right, he replied.

But then, I said, speaking the truth and paying your debts is not a correct definition of justice.

Quite correct, Socrates, if Simonides is to be believed, said Polemarchus interposing.

I fear, said Cephalus, that I must go now, for I have to look after the sacrifices, and I hand over the argument to Polemarchus and the company.

Is not Polemarchus your heir? I said.

To be sure, he answered, and went away laughing to the sacrifices.

Tell me then, O thou heir of the argument, what did Simonides say, and according to you truly say, about justice?

He said that the repayment of a debt is just, and in saying so he appears to me to be right.

I should be sorry to doubt the word of such a wise and inspired man, but his meaning, though probably clear to you, is the reverse of clear to me. For he certainly does not mean, as we were just now saying, that I ought to return a deposit of arms or of anything else to one who asks for it when he is not in his right senses; and yet a deposit cannot be denied to be a debt.

True.

Then when the person who asks me is not in his right mind I am by no means to make the return?

Certainly not.

When Simonides said that the repayment of a debt was justice, he did not mean to include that case?

Certainly not; for he thinks that a friend ought always to do good to a friend and never evil.

You mean that the return of a deposit of gold which is to the injury of the receiver, if the two parties are friends, is not the repayment of a debt,—that is what you would imagine him to say?

Yes.

And are enemies also to receive what we owe to them?

To be sure, he said, they are to receive what we owe them, and an enemy, as I take it, owes to an enemy that which is due or proper to him—that is to say, evil.

34

Simonides, then, after the manner of poets, would seem to have spoken darkly of the nature of justice; for he really meant to say that justice is the giving to each man what is proper to him, and this he termed a debt.

That must have been his meaning, he said.

By heaven! I replied; and if we asked him what due or proper thing is given by medicine, and to whom, what answer do you think that he would make to us?

He would surely reply that medicine gives drugs and meat and drink to human bodies.

And what due or proper thing is given by cookery, and to what?

Seasoning to food.

And what is that which justice gives, and to whom?

If, Socrates, we are to be guided at all by the analogy of the preceding instances, then justice is the art which gives good to friends and evil to enemies.

That is his meaning then?

I think so.

And who is best able to do good to his friends and evil to his enemies in time of sickness?

The physician.

Or when they are on a voyage, amid the perils of the sea?

The pilot.

And in what sort of actions or with a view to what result is the just man most able to do harm to his enemy and good to his friend?

In going to war against the one and in making alliances with the other.

But when a man is well, my dear Polemarchus, there is no need of a physician?

No.

And he who is not on a voyage has no need of a pilot?

No.

Then in time of peace justice will be of no use?

I am very far from thinking so.

You think that justice may be of use in peace as well as in war?

Yes.

Like husbandry for the acquisition of corn?

Yes.

Or like shoemaking for the acquisition of shoes,—that is what you mean?

Yes.

And what similar use or power of acquisition has justice in time of peace?

In contracts, Socrates, justice is of use.

And by contracts you mean partnerships?

Exactly.

But is the just man or the skilful player a more useful and better partner at a game of draughts?

The skilful player.

And in the laying of bricks and stones is the just man a more useful or better partner than the builder?

Quite the reverse.

Then in what sort of partnership is the just man a better partner than the harp-player, as in playing the harp the harp-player is certainly a better partner than the just man?

In a money partnership.

Yes, Polemarchus, but surely not in the use of money; for you do not want a just man to be your counsellor in the purchase or sale of a horse; a man who is knowing about horses would be better for that, would he not?

Certainly.

And when you want to buy a ship, the shipwright or the pilot would be better?

True.

Then what is that joint use of silver or gold in which the just man is to be preferred?

When you want a deposit to be kept safely.

You mean when money is not wanted, but allowed to lie?

Precisely.

That is to say, justice is useful when money is useless?

That is the inference.

And when you want to keep a pruning-hook safe, then justice is useful to the individual and to the state; but when you want to use it, then the art of the vine-dresser?

Clearly.

And when you want to keep a shield or a lyre, and not to use them, you would say that justice is useful; but when you want to use them, then the art of the soldier or of the musician?

Certainly.

And so of all other things;—justice is useful when they are useless, and useless when they are useful?

That is the inference.

Then justice is not good for much. But let us consider this further point: Is not he who can best strike a blow in a boxing match or in any kind of fighting best able to ward off a blow?

Certainly.

And he who is most skilful in preventing or escaping from a disease is best able to create one?

True.

And he is the best guard of a camp who is best able to steal a march upon the enemy?

Certainly.

Then he who is a good keeper of anything is also a good thief?

That, I suppose, is to be inferred.

Then if the just man is good at keeping money, he is good at stealing it.

That is implied in the argument.

Then after all the just man has turned out to be a thief. And this is a lesson which I suspect you must have learnt out of Homer; for he, speaking of Autolycus, the maternal grandfather of Odysseus, who is a favourite of his, affirms that "He was excellent above all men in theft and perjury."

And so, you and Homer and Simonides are agreed that justice is an art of theft; to be practised however "for the good of friends and for the harm of enemies,"—that was what you were saying?

No, certainly not that, though I do not now know what I did say; but I still stand by the latter words.

Well, there is another question: By friends and enemies do we mean those who are so really, or only in seeming?

Surely, he said, a man may be expected to love those whom he thinks good, and to hate those whom he thinks evil.

Yes, but do not persons often err about good and evil: many who are not good seem to be so, and conversely?

That is true.

Then to them the good will be enemies and the evil will be their friends? True.

And in that case they will be right in doing good to the evil and evil to the good?

Clearly.

But the good are just and would not do an injustice?

True.

Then according to your argument it is just to injure those who do no wrong?

Nay, Socrates; the doctrine is immoral.

Then I suppose that we ought to do good to the just and harm to the unjust?

I like that better.

But see the consequence:—Many a man who is ignorant of human nature has friends who are bad friends, and in that case he ought to do harm to them; and he has good enemies whom he ought to benefit; but, if so, we shall be saying the very opposite of that which we affirmed to be the meaning of Simonides.

Very true, he said: and I think that we had better correct an error into which we seem to have fallen in the use of the words 'friend' and 'enemy.'

What was the error, Polemarchus? I asked.

We assumed that he is a friend who seems to be or who is thought good.

And how is the error to be corrected?

We should rather say that he is a friend who is, as well as seems, good; and that he who seems only, and is not good, only seems to be and is not a friend; and of an enemy the same may be said.

You would argue that the good are our friends and the bad our enemies?

Yes.

And instead of saying simply as we did at first, that it is just to do good to our friends and harm to our enemies, we should further say: It is just to do good to our friends when they are good and harm to our enemies when they are evil?

Yes, that appears to me to be the truth.

But ought the just to injure any one at all?

Undoubtedly he *ought* to injure those who are both wicked and his enemies.

When horses are injured, are they improved or deteriorated?

The latter.

Deteriorated, that is to say, in the good qualities of horses, not of dogs?

Yes, of horses.

And dogs are deteriorated in the good qualities of dogs, and not of horses?

Of course.

And will not men who are injured be deteriorated in that which is the proper virtue of man?

Certainly.

And that human virtue is justice?

To be sure.

Then men who are injured are of necessity made unjust?

That is the result.

But can the musician by his art make men unmusical?

Certainly not.

Or the horseman by his art make them bad horsemen?

Impossible.

And can the just by justice make men unjust, or speaking generally, can the good by virtue make them bad?

Assuredly not.

Any more than heat can produce cold?

It cannot.

Or drought moisture?

Clearly not.

Nor can the good harm any one?

Impossible.

And the just is the good?

Certainly.

Then to injure a friend or any one else is not the act of a just man, but of the opposite, who is the unjust?

I think that what you say is quite true, Socrates.

Then if a man says that justice consists in the repayment of debts, and that good is the debt which a just man owes to his friends, and evil the debt which he owes to his enemies,—to say this is not wise; for it is not true, if, as has been clearly shown, the injuring of another can be in no case just.

I agree with you, said Polemarchus.

Then you and I are prepared to take up arms against any one who attributes such a saying to Simonides or Bias or Pittacus, or any other wise man or seer?

I am quite ready to do battle at your side, he said.

Shall I tell you whose I believe the saying to be?

Whose?

I believe that Periander or Perdiccas or Xerxes or Ismenias the Theban, or some other rich and mighty man, who had a great opinion of his own power, was the first to say that justice is 'doing good to your friends and harm to your enemies.'

Most true, he said.

Yes, I said; but if this definition of justice also breaks down, what other can be offered?

Several times in the course of the discussion Thrasymachus had made an attempt to get the argument into his own hands, and had been put down by the rest of the company, who wanted to hear the end. But when Polemarchus and I had done speaking and there was a pause, he could no longer hold his peace; and, gathering himself up, he came at us like a wild beast, seeking to devour us. We were quite panic-stricken at the sight of him.

He roared out to the whole company: What folly, Socrates, has taken possession of you all? And why, sillybillies, do you knock under to one another? I say that if you want really to know what justice is, you should not only ask but answer, and you should not seek honour to yourself from the refutation of an opponent, but have your own answer; for there is many a one who can ask and cannot answer. And now I will not have you say that justice is duty or advantage or profit or gain or interest, for this sort of nonsense will not do for me; I must have clearness and accuracy.

I was panic-stricken at his words, and could not look at him without trembling. Indeed I believe that if I had not fixed my eye upon him, I should have been struck dumb: but when I saw his fury rising, I looked at him first, and was therefore able to reply to him.

Thrasymachus, I said, with a quiver, don't be hard upon us. Polemarchus and I may have been guilty of a little mistake in the argument, but I can assure you that the error was not intentional. If we were seeking for a piece of gold, you would not imagine that we were 'knocking under to one another,' and so losing our chance of finding it. And why, when we are seeking for justice, a thing more precious than many pieces of gold, do you say that we are weakly yielding to one another and not doing our utmost to get at the truth? Nay, my good friend, we are most willing and anxious to do so, but the fact is that we cannot. And if so, you people who know all things should pity us and not be angry with us.

How characteristic of Socrates! he replied, with a bitter laugh;—that's your ironical style! Did I not foresee—have I not already told you, that whatever he was asked he would refuse to answer, and try irony or any other shuffle, in order that he might avoid answering?

You are a philosopher, Thrasymachus, I replied, and well know that if you ask a person what numbers make up twelve, taking care to prohibit him whom you ask from answering twice six, or three times four, or six times two, or four times three, "for this sort of nonsense will not do for me,"—then obviously, if that is your way of putting the question, no one can answer you. But suppose that he were to retort, "Thrasymachus, what do you mean? If one of these numbers which you interdict be the true answer to the question, am I falsely to say some other number which is not the right one?—is that your meaning?"— How would you answer him?

Just as if the two cases were at all alike! he said.

Why should they not be? I replied; and even if they are not, but only appear to be so to the person who is asked, ought he not to say what he thinks, whether you and I forbid him or not?

I presume then that you are going to make one of the interdicted answers?

I dare say that I may, notwithstanding the danger, if upon reflection I approve of any of them.

But what if I give you an answer about justice other and better, he said, than any of these? What do you deserve to have done to you?

Done to me!—as becomes the ignorant, I must learn from the wise—that is what I deserve to have done to me.

What, and no payment! a pleasant notion!

I will pay when I have the money, I replied.

But you have, Socrates, said Glaucon: and you, Thrasymachus, need be under no anxiety about money, for we will all make a contribution for Socrates.

Yes, he replied, and then Socrates will do as he always does— refuse to answer himself, but take and pull to pieces the answer of some one else.

Why, my good friend, I said, how can any one answer who knows, and says that he knows, just nothing; and who, even if he has some faint notions of his own, is told by a man of authority not to utter them? The natural thing is, that the speaker should be some one like yourself who professes to know and can tell what he knows. Will you then kindly answer, for the edification of the company and of myself?

Glaucon and the rest of the company joined in my request, and Thrasymachus, as any one might see, was in reality eager to speak; for he thought that he had an excellent answer, and would distinguish himself. But at first he affected to insist on my answering; at length he consented to begin. Behold, he said, the wisdom of Socrates; he refuses to teach himself, and goes about learning of others, to whom he never even says Thank you.

That I learn of others, I replied, is quite true; but that I am ungrateful I wholly deny. Money I have none, and therefore I pay in praise, which is all I have; and how ready I am to praise any one who appears to me to speak well you will very soon find out when you answer; for I expect that you will answer well.

Listen, then, he said; I proclaim that justice is nothing else than the interest of the stronger. And now why do you not praise me? But of course you won't.

Let me first understand you, I replied. Justice, as you say, is the interest of the stronger. What, Thrasymachus, is the meaning of this? You cannot mean to say that because Polydamas, the pancratiast, is stronger than we are, and finds the eating of beef conducive to his bodily strength, that to eat beef is therefore equally for our good who are weaker than he is, and right and just for us?

That's abominable of you, Socrates; you take the words in the sense which is most damaging to the argument.

Not at all, my good sir, I said; I am trying to understand them; and I wish that you would be a little clearer.

Well, he said, have you never heard that forms of government differ; there are tyrannies, and there are democracies, and there are aristocracies?

Yes, I know.

And the government is the ruling power in each state?

Certainly.

And the different forms of government make laws democratical, aristocratical, tyrannical, with a view to their several interests; and these laws, which are made by them for their own interests, are the justice which they deliver to their subjects, and him who transgresses them they punish as a breaker of the law, and unjust. And that is what I mean when I say that in all states there is the same principle of justice, which is the interest of the government; and as the government must be supposed to have power, the only reasonable conclusion is, that everywhere there is one principle of justice, which is the interest of the stronger.

Now I understand you, I said; and whether you are right or not I will try to discover. But let me remark, that in defining justice you have yourself used the word 'interest' which you forbade me to use. It is true, however, that in your definition the words 'of the stronger' are added.

A small addition, you must allow, he said.

Great or small, never mind about that: we must first enquire whether what you are saying is the truth. Now we are both agreed that justice is interest of some sort, but you go on to say 'of the stronger'; about this addition I am not so sure, and must therefore consider further.

Proceed.

I will; and first tell me, Do you admit that it is just for subjects to obey their rulers?

I do.

But are the rulers of states absolutely infallible, or are they sometimes liable to err?

To be sure, he replied, they are liable to err.

Then in making their laws they may sometimes make them rightly, and sometimes not?

True.

When they make them rightly, they make them agreeably to their interest; when they are mistaken, contrary to their interest; you admit that?

Yes.

And the laws which they make must be obeyed by their subjects,— and that is what you call justice?

Doubtless.

Then justice, according to your argument, is not only obedience to the interest of the stronger but the reverse?

What is that you are saying? he asked.

I am only repeating what you are saying, I believe. But let us consider: Have we not admitted that the rulers may be mistaken about their own interest in what they command, and also that to obey them is justice? Has not that been admitted?

Yes.

Then you must also have acknowledged justice not to be for the interest of the stronger, when the rulers unintentionally command things to be done which are to their own injury. For if, as you say, justice is the obedience which the subject renders to their commands, in that case, O wisest of men, is there any escape from the conclusion that the weaker are commanded to do, not what is for the interest, but what is for the injury of the stronger?

Nothing can be clearer, Socrates, said Polemarchus.

Yes, said Cleitophon, interposing, if you are allowed to be his witness.

But there is no need of any witness, said Polemarchus, for Thrasymachus himself acknowledges that rulers may sometimes command what is not for their own interest, and that for subjects to obey them is justice.

Yes, Polemarchus,—Thrasymachus said that for subjects to do what was commanded by their rulers is just.

Yes, Cleitophon, but he also said that justice is the interest of the stronger, and, while admitting both these propositions, he further acknowledged that the stronger may command the weaker who are his subjects to do what is not for his own interest; whence follows that justice is the injury quite as much as the interest of the stronger.

But, said Cleitophon, he meant by the interest of the stronger what the stronger thought to be his interest,—this was what the weaker had to do; and this was affirmed by him to be justice.

Those were not his words, rejoined Polemarchus.

Never mind, I replied, if he now says that they are, let us accept his statement. Tell me, Thrasymachus, I said, did you mean by justice what the stronger thought to be his interest, whether really so or not?

Certainly not, he said. Do you suppose that I call him who is mistaken the stronger at the time when he is mistaken?

Yes, I said, my impression was that you did so, when you admitted that the ruler was not infallible but might be sometimes mistaken.

You argue like an informer, Socrates. Do you mean, for example, that he who is mistaken about the sick is a physician in that he is mistaken? or that he who errs in arithmetic or grammar is an arithmetician or grammarian at the time when he is making the mistake, in respect of the mistake? True, we say that the physician or arithmetician or grammarian has made a mistake, but this is only a way of speaking; for the fact is that neither the grammarian nor any other person of skill ever makes a mistake in so far as he is what his name implies; they none of them err unless their skill fails them, and then they cease to be skilled artists. No artist or sage or ruler errs at the time when he is what his name implies; though he is commonly said to err, and I adopted the common mode of speaking. But to be perfectly accurate, since you are such a lover of accuracy, we should say that the ruler, in so far as he is a ruler, is unerring, and, being unerring, always commands that which is for his own interest; and the subject is required to execute his commands; and therefore, as I said at first and now repeat, justice is the interest of the stronger.

Indeed, Thrasymachus, and do I really appear to you to argue like an informer?

Certainly, he replied.

And do you suppose that I ask these questions with any design of injuring you in the argument?

Nay, he replied, 'suppose' is not the word—I know it; but you will be found out, and by sheer force of argument you will never prevail.

I shall not make the attempt, my dear man; but to avoid any misunderstanding occurring between us in future, let me ask, in what sense do you speak of a ruler or stronger whose interest, as you were saying, he being the superior, it is just that the inferior should execute— is he a ruler in the popular or in the strict sense of the term?

In the strictest of all senses, he said. And now cheat and play the informer if you can; I ask no quarter at your hands. But you never will be able, never.

And do you imagine, I said, that I am such a madman as to try and cheat, Thrasymachus? I might as well shave a lion.

Why, he said, you made the attempt a minute ago, and you failed.

Enough, I said, of these civilities. It will be better that I should ask you a question: Is the physician, taken in that strict sense of which you are speaking, a healer of the sick or a maker of money? And remember that I am now speaking of the true physician.

A healer of the sick, he replied.

And the pilot—that is to say, the true pilot—is he a captain of sailors or a mere sailor?

A captain of sailors.

The circumstance that he sails in the ship is not to be taken into account; neither is he to be called a sailor; the name pilot by which he is distinguished has nothing to do with sailing, but is significant of his skill and of his authority over the sailors.

Very true, he said.

Now, I said, every art has an interest?

Certainly.

For which the art has to consider and provide?

Yes, that is the aim of art.

And the interest of any art is the perfection of it—this and nothing else?

What do you mean?

I mean what I may illustrate negatively by the example of the body. Suppose you were to ask me whether the body is self-sufficing or has wants, I should reply: Certainly the body has wants; for the body may be ill and require to be cured, and has therefore interests to which the art of medicine ministers; and this is the origin and intention of medicine, as you will acknowledge. Am I not right?

Quite right, he replied.

But is the art of medicine or any other art faulty or deficient in any quality in the same way that the eye may be deficient in sight or the ear fail of hearing, and therefore requires another art to provide for the interests of seeing and hearing—has art in itself, I say, any similar liability to fault or defect, and does every art require another supplementary art to provide for its interests, and that another and another without end? Or have the arts to look only after their own interests? Or have they no need either of themselves or of another?— having no faults or defects, they have no need to correct them, either by the exercise of their own art or of any other; they have only to consider the interest of their subject-matter. For every art remains pure and faultless while remaining true—that is to say, while perfect and unimpaired. Take the words in your precise sense, and tell me whether I am not right.

Yes, clearly.

Then medicine does not consider the interest of medicine, but the interest of the body?

True, he said.

Nor does the art of horsemanship consider the interests of the art of horsemanship, but the interests of the horse; neither do any other arts care for themselves, for they have no needs; they care only for that which is the subject of their art?

True, he said.

But surely, Thrasymachus, the arts are the superiors and rulers of their own subjects?

To this he assented with a good deal of reluctance.

Then, I said, no science or art considers or enjoins the interest of the stronger or superior, but only the interest of the subject and weaker?

He made an attempt to contest this proposition also, but finally acquiesced.

Then, I continued, no physician, in so far as he is a physician, considers his own good in what he prescribes, but the good of his patient; for the true physician is also a ruler having the human body as a subject, and is not a mere money-maker; that has been admitted?

Yes.

And the pilot likewise, in the strict sense of the term, is a ruler of sailors and not a mere sailor?

That has been admitted.

And such a pilot and ruler will provide and prescribe for the interest of the sailor who is under him, and not for his own or the ruler's interest?

He gave a reluctant "Yes."

Then, I said, Thrasymachus, there is no one in any rule who, in so far as he is a ruler, considers or enjoins what is for his own interest, but always what is for the interest of his subject or suitable to his art; to that he looks, and that alone he considers in everything which he says and does.

When we had got to this point in the argument, and every one saw that the definition of justice had been completely upset, Thrasymachus, instead of replying to me, said: Tell me, Socrates, have you got a nurse?

Why do you ask such a question, I said, when you ought rather to be answering?

Because she leaves you to snivel, and never wipes your nose: she has not even taught you to know the shepherd from the sheep.

What makes you say that? I replied.

Because you fancy that the shepherd or neatherd fattens or tends the sheep or oxen with a view to their own good and not to the good of himself or his master; and you further imagine that the rulers of states, if they are true rulers, never think of their subjects as sheep, and that they are not studying their own advantage day and night. Oh, no; and so entirely astray are you in your ideas about the just and unjust as not even to know that justice and the just are in reality another's good; that is to say, the interest of the ruler and stronger, and the loss of the subject and servant; and injustice the opposite; for the unjust is lord over the truly simple and just: he is the stronger, and his subjects do what is for his interest, and minister to his happiness, which is very far from being their own. Consider further, most foolish Socrates, that the just is always a loser in comparison with the unjust. First of all, in private contracts: wherever the unjust is the partner of the just you will find that, when the partnership is dissolved, the unjust man has always more and the just less. Secondly, in their dealings with the State: when there is an income-tax, the just man will pay more and the unjust less on the same amount of income; and when there is anything to be received the one gains nothing and the other much. Observe also what happens when they take an office; there is the just man neglecting his affairs and perhaps suffering other losses, and getting nothing out of the public, because he is just; moreover he is hated by his friends and acquaintance for refusing to serve them in unlawful ways. But all this is reversed in the case of the unjust man. I am speaking, as before, of injustice on a large scale in which the advantage of the unjust is most apparent; and my meaning will be most clearly seen if we turn to that highest form of injustice in which the criminal is the happiest of men, and the sufferers or those who refuse to do injustice are the most miserable—that is to say tyranny, which by fraud and force takes away the property of others, not little by little but wholesale; comprehending in one, things sacred as well as profane, private and public; for which acts of wrong, if he were detected perpetrating any one of them singly, he would be punished and incur great disgrace—they who do such wrong in particular cases are called robbers of temples, and man-stealers and burglars and swindlers and thieves. But when a man besides taking away the money of the citizens has made slaves of them, then, instead of these names of reproach, he is termed happy and blessed, not only by the citizens but by all who hear of his having achieved the consummation of injustice. For mankind censure injustice, fearing that they may be the victims of it and not because they shrink from committing it. And thus, as I have shown, Socrates, injustice, when on a sufficient scale, has more strength and freedom and mastery than justice; and, as I said at first, justice is the interest of the stronger, whereas injustice is a man's own profit and interest.

Thrasymachus, when he had thus spoken, having, like a bath-man, deluged our ears with his words, had a mind to go away. But the company would not let him; they insisted that he should remain and defend his position; and I myself added my own humble request that he would not leave us. Thrasymachus, I said to him, excellent man, how suggestive are your remarks! And are you going to run away before you have fairly taught or learned whether they are true or not? Is the attempt to determine the way of man's life so small a matter in your eyes—to determine how life may be passed by each one of us to the greatest advantage?

And do I differ from you, he said, as to the importance of the enquiry?

You appear rather, I replied, to have no care or thought about us, Thrasymachus—whether we live better or worse from not knowing what you say you know, is to you a matter of indifference. Prithee, friend, do not keep your knowledge to yourself; we are a large party; and any benefit which you confer upon us will be amply rewarded. For my own part I openly declare that I am not convinced, and that I do not believe injustice to be more gainful than justice, even if uncontrolled and allowed to have free play. For, granting that there may be an unjust man who is able to commit injustice either by fraud or force, still this does not convince me of the superior advantage of injustice, and there may be others who are in the same predicament with myself. Perhaps we may be wrong; if so, you in your wisdom should convince us that we are mistaken in preferring justice to injustice.

And how am I to convince you, he said, if you are not already convinced by what I have just said; what more can I do for you? Would you have me put the proof bodily into your souls?

Heaven forbid! I said; I would only ask you to be consistent; or, if you change, change openly and let there be no deception. For I must remark, Thrasymachus, if you will recall what was previously said, that although you began by defining the true physician in an exact sense, you did not observe a like exactness when speaking of the shepherd; you thought that the shepherd as a shepherd tends the sheep not with a view to their own good, but like a mere diner or banquetter with a view to the pleasures of the table; or, again, as a trader for sale in the market, and not as a shepherd. Yet surely the art of the shepherd is concerned only with the good of his subjects; he has only to provide the best for them, since the perfection of the art is already ensured whenever all the requirements of it are satisfied. And that was what I was saying just now about the ruler. I conceived that the art of the ruler, considered as ruler, whether in a state or in private life, could only regard the good of his flock or subjects; whereas you seem to think that the rulers in states, that is to say, the true rulers, like being in authority.

Think! Nay, I am sure of it.

Then why in the case of lesser offices do men never take them willingly without payment, unless under the idea that they govern for the advantage not of themselves but of others? Let me ask you a question: Are not the several arts different, by reason of their each having a separate function? And, my dear illustrious friend, do say what you think, that we may make a little progress.

Yes, that is the difference, he replied.

And each art gives us a particular good and not merely a general one—medicine, for example, gives us health; navigation, safety at sea, and so on?

Yes, he said.

And the art of payment has the special function of giving pay: but we do not confuse this with other arts, any more than the art of the pilot is to be confused with the art of medicine, because the health of the pilot may be improved by a sea voyage. You would not be inclined to say, would you, that navigation is the art of medicine, at least if we are to adopt your exact use of language?

Certainly not.

Or because a man is in good health when he receives pay you would not say that the art of payment is medicine?

I should not.

Nor would you say that medicine is the art of receiving pay because a man takes fees when he is engaged in healing?

Certainly not.

And we have admitted, I said, that the good of each art is specially confined to the art?

Yes.

Then, if there be any good which all artists have in common, that is to be attributed to something of which they all have the common use?

True, he replied.

And when the artist is benefited by receiving pay the advantage is gained by an additional use of the art of pay, which is not the art professed by him?

He gave a reluctant assent to this.

Then the pay is not derived by the several artists from their respective arts. But the truth is, that while the art of medicine gives health, and the art of the builder builds a house, another art attends them which is the art of pay. The various arts may be doing their own business and benefiting that over which they preside, but would the artist receive any benefit from his art unless he were paid as well?

I suppose not.

But does he therefore confer no benefit when he works for nothing?

Certainly, he confers a benefit.

Then now, Thrasymachus, there is no longer any doubt that neither arts nor governments provide for their own interests; but, as we were before saying, they rule and provide for the interests of their subjects who are the weaker and not the stronger—to their good they attend and not to the good of the superior. And this is the reason, my dear Thrasymachus, why, as I was just now saying, no one is willing to govern; because no one likes to take in hand the reformation of evils which are not his concern without remuneration. For, in the execution of his work, and in giving his orders to another, the true artist does not regard his own interest, but always that of his subjects; and therefore in order that rulers may be willing to rule, they must be paid in one of three modes of payment, money, or honour, or a penalty for refusing.

What do you mean, Socrates? said Glaucon. The first two modes of payment are intelligible enough, but what the penalty is I do not understand, or how a penalty can be a payment.

You mean that you do not understand the nature of this payment which to the best men is the great inducement to rule? Of course you know that ambition and avarice are held to be, as indeed they are, a disgrace?

Very true.

And for this reason, I said, money and honour have no attraction for them; good men do not wish to be openly demanding payment for governing and so to get the name of hirelings, nor by secretly helping themselves out of the public revenues to get the name of thieves. And not being ambitious they do not care about honour. Wherefore necessity must be laid upon them, and they must be induced to serve from the fear of punishment. And this, as I imagine, is the reason why the forwardness to take office, instead of waiting to be compelled, has been deemed dishonourable. Now the worst part of the punishment is that he who refuses to rule is liable to be ruled by one who is worse than himself. And the fear of this, as I conceive, induces the good to take office, not because they would, but because they cannot help—not under the idea that they are going to have any benefit or enjoyment themselves, but as a necessity, and because they are not able to commit the task of ruling to any one who is better than themselves, or indeed as good. For there is reason to think that if a city were composed entirely of good men, then to avoid office would be as much an object of contention as to obtain office is at present; then we should have plain proof that the true ruler is not meant by nature to regard his own interest, but that of his subjects; and every one who knew this would choose rather to receive a benefit from another than to have the trouble of conferring one. So far am I from agreeing with Thrasymachus that justice is the interest of the stronger. This latter question need not be further discussed at present; but when Thrasymachus says that the life of the unjust is more advantageous than that of the just, his new statement appears to me to be of a far more serious character. Which of us has spoken truly? And which sort of life, Glaucon, do you prefer?

I for my part deem the life of the just to be the more advantageous, he answered.

Did you hear all the advantages of the unjust which Thrasymachus was rehearsing?

Yes, I heard him, he replied, but he has not convinced me.

Then shall we try to find some way of convincing him, if we can, that he is saying what is not true?

Most certainly, he replied.

If, I said, he makes a set speech and we make another recounting all the advantages of being just, and he answers and we rejoin, there must be a numbering and measuring of the goods which are claimed on either side, and in the end we shall want judges to decide; but if we proceed in our enquiry as we lately did, by making admissions to one another, we shall unite the offices of judge and advocate in our own persons.

Very good, he said.

And which method do I understand you to prefer? I said.

That which you propose.

Well, then, Thrasymachus, I said, suppose you begin at the beginning and answer me. You say that perfect injustice is more gainful than perfect justice?

Yes, that is what I say, and I have given you my reasons.

And what is your view about them? Would you call one of them virtue and the other vice?

Certainly.

I suppose that you would call justice virtue and injustice vice?

What a charming notion! So likely too, seeing that I affirm injustice to be profitable and justice not.

What else then would you say?

The opposite, he replied.

And would you call justice vice?

No, I would rather say sublime simplicity.

Then would you call injustice malignity?

No; I would rather say discretion.

And do the unjust appear to you to be wise and good?

Yes, he said; at any rate those of them who are able to be perfectly unjust, and who have the power of subduing states and nations; but perhaps you imagine me to be talking of cutpurses. Even this profession if undetected has advantages, though they are not to be compared with those of which I was just now speaking.

I do not think that I misapprehend your meaning, Thrasymachus, I replied; but still I cannot hear without amazement that you class injustice with wisdom and virtue, and justice with the opposite.

Certainly I do so class them.

Now, I said, you are on more substantial and almost unanswerable ground; for if the injustice which you were maintaining to be profitable had been admitted by you as by others to be vice and deformity, an answer might have been given to you on received principles; but now I perceive that you will call injustice honourable and strong, and to the unjust you will attribute all the qualities which were attributed by us before to the just, seeing that you do not hesitate to rank injustice with wisdom and virtue.

You have guessed most infallibly, he replied.

Then I certainly ought not to shrink from going through with the argument so long as I have reason to think that you, Thrasymachus, are speaking your real mind; for I do believe that you are now in earnest and are not amusing yourself at our expense.

I may be in earnest or not, but what is that to you?—to refute the argument is your business.

Very true, I said; that is what I have to do: But will you be so good as answer yet one more question? Does the just man try to gain any advantage over the just?

Far otherwise; if he did he would not be the simple amusing creature which he is.

And would he try to go beyond just action?

He would not.

And how would he regard the attempt to gain an advantage over the unjust; would that be considered by him as just or unjust?

He would think it just, and would try to gain the advantage; but he would not be able.

Whether he would or would not be able, I said, is not to the point. My question is only whether the just man, while refusing to have more than another just man, would wish and claim to have more than the unjust?

Yes, he would.

And what of the unjust—does he claim to have more than the just man and to do more than is just?

56

Of course, he said, for he claims to have more than all men.

And the unjust man will strive and struggle to obtain more than the unjust man or action, in order that he may have more than all?

True.

We may put the matter thus, I said—the just does not desire more than his like but more than his unlike, whereas the unjust desires more than both his like and his unlike?

Nothing, he said, can be better than that statement.

And the unjust is good and wise, and the just is neither?

Good again, he said.

And is not the unjust like the wise and good and the just unlike them?

Of course, he said, he who is of a certain nature, is like those who are of a certain nature; he who is not, not.

Each of them, I said, is such as his like is?

Certainly, he replied.

Very good, Thrasymachus, I said; and now to take the case of the arts: you would admit that one man is a musician and another not a musician?

Yes.

And which is wise and which is foolish?

Clearly the musician is wise, and he who is not a musician is foolish.

And he is good in as far as he is wise, and bad in as far as he is foolish?

Yes.

And you would say the same sort of thing of the physician?

Yes.

And do you think, my excellent friend, that a musician when he adjusts the lyre would desire or claim to exceed or go beyond a musician in the tightening and loosening the strings?

I do not think that he would.

But he would claim to exceed the non-musician?

Of course.

And what would you say of the physician? In prescribing meats and drinks would he wish to go beyond another physician or beyond the practice of medicine?

He would not.

But he would wish to go beyond the non-physician?

Yes.

And about knowledge and ignorance in general; see whether you think that any man who has knowledge ever would wish to have the choice of saying or doing more than another man who has knowledge. Would he not rather say or do the same as his like in the same case?

That, I suppose, can hardly be denied.

And what of the ignorant? would he not desire to have more than either the knowing or the ignorant?

I dare say.

And the knowing is wise?

Yes.

And the wise is good?

True.

Then the wise and good will not desire to gain more than his like, but more than his unlike and opposite?

I suppose so.

Whereas the bad and ignorant will desire to gain more than both?

Yes.

But did we not say, Thrasymachus, that the unjust goes beyond both his like and unlike? Were not these your words?

They were.

And you also said that the just will not go beyond his like but his unlike?

Yes.

Then the just is like the wise and good, and the unjust like the evil and ignorant?

That is the inference.

And each of them is such as his like is?

That was admitted.

Then the just has turned out to be wise and good and the unjust evil and ignorant.

58

Thrasymachus made all these admissions, not fluently, as I repeat them, but with extreme reluctance; it was a hot summer's day, and the perspiration poured from him in torrents; and then I saw what I had never seen before, Thrasymachus blushing. As we were now agreed that justice was virtue and wisdom, and injustice vice and ignorance, I proceeded to another point: Well, I said, Thrasymachus, that matter is now settled; but were we not also saying that injustice had strength; do you remember?

Yes, I remember, he said, but do not suppose that I approve of what you are saying or have no answer; if however I were to answer, you would be quite certain to accuse me of haranguing; therefore either permit me to have my say out, or if you would rather ask, do so, and I will answer 'Very good,' as they say to story-telling old women, and will nod 'Yes' and 'No.'

Certainly not, I said, if contrary to your real opinion.

Yes, he said, I will, to please you, since you will not let me speak. What else would you have?

Nothing in the world, I said; and if you are so disposed I will ask and you shall answer.

Proceed.

Then I will repeat the question which I asked before, in order that our examination of the relative nature of justice and injustice may be carried on regularly. A statement was made that injustice is stronger and more powerful than justice, but now justice, having been identified with wisdom and virtue, is easily shown to be stronger than injustice, if injustice is ignorance; this can no longer be questioned by any one. But I want to view the matter, Thrasymachus, in a different way: You would not deny that a state may be unjust and may be unjustly attempting to enslave other states, or may have already enslaved them, and may be holding many of them in subjection?

True, he replied; and I will add that the best and most perfectly unjust state will be most likely to do so.

I know, I said, that such was your position; but what I would further consider is, whether this power which is possessed by the superior state can exist or be exercised without justice or only with justice.

If you are right in your view, and justice is wisdom, then only with justice; but if I am right, then without justice.

I am delighted, Thrasymachus, to see you not only nodding assent and dissent, but making answers which are quite excellent.

That is out of civility to you, he replied.

You are very kind, I said; and would you have the goodness also to inform me, whether you think that a state, or an army, or a band of robbers and thieves, or any other gang of evil-doers could act at all if they injured one another?

No indeed, he said, they could not.

But if they abstained from injuring one another, then they might act together better?

Yes.

And this is because injustice creates divisions and hatreds and fighting, and justice imparts harmony and friendship; is not that true, Thrasymachus?

I agree, he said, because I do not wish to quarrel with you.

How good of you, I said; but I should like to know also whether injustice, having this tendency to arouse hatred, wherever existing, among slaves or among freemen, will not make them hate one another and set them at variance and render them incapable of common action?

Certainly.

And even if injustice be found in two only, will they not quarrel and fight, and become enemies to one another and to the just?

They will.

And suppose injustice abiding in a single person, would your wisdom say that she loses or that she retains her natural power?

Let us assume that she retains her power.

Yet is not the power which injustice exercises of such a nature that wherever she takes up her abode, whether in a city, in an army, in a family, or in any other body, that body is, to begin with, rendered incapable of united action by reason of sedition and distraction; and does it not become its own enemy and at variance with all that opposes it, and with the just? Is not this the case?

Yes, certainly.

And is not injustice equally fatal when existing in a single person; in the first place rendering him incapable of action because he is not at unity with himself, and in the second place making him an enemy to himself and the just? Is not that true, Thrasymachus?

Yes.

And O my friend, I said, surely the gods are just?

Granted that they are.

But if so, the unjust will be the enemy of the gods, and the just will be their friend?

Feast away in triumph, and take your fill of the argument; I will not oppose you, lest I should displease the company.

Well then, proceed with your answers, and let me have the remainder of my repast. For we have already shown that the just are clearly wiser and better and abler than the unjust, and that the unjust are incapable of common action; nay more, that to speak as we did of men who are evil acting at any time vigorously together, is not strictly true, for if they had been perfectly evil, they would have laid hands upon one another; but it is evident that there must have been some remnant of justice in them, which enabled them to combine; if there had not been they would have injured one another as well as their victims; they were but half-villains in their enterprises; for had they been whole villains, and utterly unjust, they would have been utterly incapable of action. That, as I believe, is the truth of the matter, and not what you said at first. But whether the just have a better and happier life than the unjust is a further question which we also proposed to consider. I think that they have, and for the reasons which I have given; but still I should like to examine further, for no light matter is at stake, nothing less than the rule of human life.

Proceed.

I will proceed by asking a question: Would you not say that a horse has some end?

I should.

And the end or use of a horse or of anything would be that which could not be accomplished, or not so well accomplished, by any other thing?

I do not understand, he said.

Let me explain: Can you see, except with the eye?

Certainly not.

Or hear, except with the ear?

No.

These then may be truly said to be the ends of these organs?

They may.

But you can cut off a vine-branch with a dagger or with a chisel, and in many other ways?

Of course.

And yet not so well as with a pruning-hook made for the purpose?

True.

May we not say that this is the end of a pruning-hook?

We may.

Then now I think you will have no difficulty in understanding my meaning when I asked the question whether the end of anything would be that which could not be accomplished, or not so well accomplished, by any other thing?

I understand your meaning, he said, and assent.

And that to which an end is appointed has also an excellence? Need I ask again whether the eye has an end?

It has.

And has not the eye an excellence?

Yes.

And the ear has an end and an excellence also?

True.

And the same is true of all other things; they have each of them an end and a special excellence?

That is so.

Well, and can the eyes fulfil their end if they are wanting in their own proper excellence and have a defect instead?

How can they, he said, if they are blind and cannot see?

You mean to say, if they have lost their proper excellence, which is sight; but I have not arrived at that point yet. I would rather ask the question more generally, and only enquire whether the things which fulfil their ends fulfil them by their own proper excellence, and fail of fulfilling them by their own defect?

Certainly, he replied.

I might say the same of the ears; when deprived of their own proper excellence they cannot fulfil their end?

True.

And the same observation will apply to all other things?

I agree.

Well; and has not the soul an end which nothing else can fulfil? for example, to superintend and command and deliberate and the like. Are not these functions proper to the soul, and can they rightly be assigned to any other?

To no other.

And is not life to be reckoned among the ends of the soul?

Assuredly, he said.

And has not the soul an excellence also?

Yes.

And can she or can she not fulfil her own ends when deprived of that excellence?

She cannot.

Then an evil soul must necessarily be an evil ruler and superintendent, and the good soul a good ruler?

Yes, necessarily.

And we have admitted that justice is the excellence of the soul, and injustice the defect of the soul?

That has been admitted.

Then the just soul and the just man will live well, and the unjust man will live ill?

That is what your argument proves.

And he who lives well is blessed and happy, and he who lives ill the reverse of happy?

Certainly.

Then the just is happy, and the unjust miserable?

So be it.

But happiness and not misery is profitable.

Of course.

Then, my blessed Thrasymachus, injustice can never be more profitable than justice.

Let this, Socrates, he said, be your entertainment at the Bendidea.

For which I am indebted to you, I said, now that you have grown gentle towards me and have left off scolding. Nevertheless, I have not been well entertained; but that was my own fault and not yours. As an epicure snatches a taste of every dish which is successively brought to table, he not having allowed himself time to enjoy the one before, so have I gone from one subject to another without having discovered what I sought at first, the nature of justice. I left that enquiry and turned away to consider whether justice is virtue and wisdom or evil and folly; and when there arose a further question about the comparative advantages of justice and injustice, I could not refrain from passing on to that. And the result of the whole discussion has been that I know nothing at all. For I know not what justice is, and therefore I am not likely to know whether it is or is not a virtue, nor can I say whether the just man is happy or unhappy.

# BOOK II

With these words I was thinking that I had made an end of the discussion; but the end, in truth, proved to be only a beginning. For Glaucon, who is always the most pugnacious of men, was dissatisfied at Thrasymachus' retirement; he wanted to have the battle out. So he said to me: Socrates, do you wish really to persuade us, or only to seem to have persuaded us, that to be just is always better than to be unjust?

I should wish really to persuade you, I replied, if I could.

Then you certainly have not succeeded. Let me ask you now:—How would you arrange goods—are there not some which we welcome for their own sakes, and independently of their consequences, as, for example, harmless pleasures and enjoyments, which delight us at the time, although nothing follows from them?

I agree in thinking that there is such a class, I replied.

Is there not also a second class of goods, such as knowledge, sight, health, which are desirable not only in themselves, but also for their results?

Certainly, I said.

And would you not recognize a third class, such as gymnastic, and the care of the sick, and the physician's art; also the various ways of money-making—these do us good but we regard them as disagreeable; and no one would choose them for their own sakes, but only for the sake of some reward or result which flows from them?

There is, I said, this third class also. But why do you ask?

Because I want to know in which of the three classes you would place justice?

In the highest class, I replied,—among those goods which he who would be happy desires both for their own sake and for the sake of their results.

Then the many are of another mind; they think that justice is to be reckoned in the troublesome class, among goods which are to be pursued for the sake of rewards and of reputation, but in themselves are disagreeable and rather to be avoided.

I know, I said, that this is their manner of thinking, and that this was the thesis which Thrasymachus was maintaining just now, when he censured justice and praised injustice. But I am too stupid to be convinced by him.

I wish, he said, that you would hear me as well as him, and then I shall see whether you and I agree. For Thrasymachus seems to me, like a snake, to have been charmed by your voice sooner than he ought to have been; but to my mind the nature of justice and injustice have not yet been made clear. Setting aside their rewards and results, I want to know what they are in themselves, and how they inwardly work in the soul. If you, please, then, I will revive the argument of Thrasymachus. And first I will speak of the nature and origin of justice according to the common view of them. Secondly, I will show that all men who practise justice do so against their will, of necessity, but not as a good. And thirdly, I will argue that there is reason in this view, for the life of the unjust is after all better far than the life of the just—if what they say is true, Socrates, since I myself am not of their opinion. But still I acknowledge that I am perplexed when I hear the voices of Thrasymachus and myriads of others dinning in my ears; and, on the other hand, I have never yet heard the superiority of justice to injustice maintained by any one in a satisfactory way. I want to hear justice praised in respect of itself; then I shall be satisfied, and you are the person from whom I think that I am most likely to hear this; and therefore I will praise the unjust life to the utmost of my power, and my manner of speaking will indicate the manner in which I desire to hear you too praising justice and censuring injustice. Will you say whether you approve of my proposal?

Indeed I do; nor can I imagine any theme about which a man of sense would oftener wish to converse.

I am delighted, he replied, to hear you say so, and shall begin by speaking, as I proposed, of the nature and origin of justice.

They say that to do injustice is, by nature, good; to suffer injustice, evil; but that the evil is greater than the good. And so when men have both done and suffered injustice and have had experience of both, not being able to avoid the one and obtain the other, they think that they had better agree among themselves to have neither; hence there arise laws and mutual covenants; and that which is ordained by law is termed by them lawful and just. This they affirm to be the origin and nature of justice;—it is a mean or compromise, between the best of all, which is to do injustice and not be punished, and the worst of all, which is to suffer injustice without the power of retaliation; and justice, being at a middle point between the two, is tolerated not as a good, but as the lesser evil, and honoured by reason of the inability of men to do injustice. For no man who is worthy to be called a man would ever submit to such an agreement if he were able to resist; he would be mad if he did. Such is the received account, Socrates, of the nature and origin of justice.

Now that those who practise justice do so involuntarily and because they have not the power to be unjust will best appear if we imagine something of this kind: having given both to the just and the unjust power to do what they will, let us watch and see whither desire will lead them; then we shall discover in the very act the just and unjust man to be proceeding along the same road, following their interest, which all natures deem to be their good, and are only diverted into the path of justice by the force of law. The liberty which we are supposing may be most completely given to them in the form of such a power as is said to have been possessed by Gyges, the ancestor of Croesus the Lydian. According to the tradition, Gyges was a shepherd in the service of the king of Lydia; there was a great storm, and an earthquake made an opening in the earth at the place where he was feeding his flock. Amazed at the sight, he descended into the opening, where, among other marvels, he beheld a hollow brazen horse, having doors, at which he stooping and looking in saw a dead body of stature, as appeared to him, more than human, and having nothing on but a gold ring; this he took from the finger of the dead and reascended. Now the shepherds met together, according to custom, that they might send their monthly report about the flocks to the king; into their assembly he came having the ring on his finger, and as he was sitting among them he chanced to turn the collet of the ring inside his hand, when instantly he became invisible to the rest of the company and they began to speak of him as if he were no longer present. He was astonished at this, and again touching the ring he turned the collet outwards and reappeared; he made several trials of the ring, and always with the same result—when he turned the collet inwards he became invisible, when outwards he reappeared. Whereupon he contrived to be chosen one of the messengers who were sent to the court; whereas soon as he arrived he seduced the queen, and with her help conspired against the king and slew him, and took the kingdom. Suppose now that there were two such magic rings, and the just put on one of them and the unjust the other; no man can be imagined to be of such an iron nature that he would stand fast in justice. No man would keep his hands off what was not his own when he could safely take what he liked out of the market, or go into houses and lie with any one at his pleasure, or kill or release from prison whom he would, and in all respects be like a God among men. Then the actions of the just would be as the actions of the unjust; they would both come at last to the same point. And this we may truly affirm to be a great proof that a man is just, not willingly or because he thinks that justice is any good to him individually, but of necessity, for wherever any one thinks that he can safely be unjust, there he is unjust. For all men believe in their hearts that injustice is far more profitable to the individual than justice, and he who argues as I have been supposing, will say that they are right. If you could imagine any one obtaining this power of becoming invisible, and never doing any wrong or touching what was another's, he would be thought by the lookers-on to be a most wretched idiot, although they would praise him to one another's faces, and keep up appearances with one another from a fear that they too might suffer injustice. Enough of this.

Now, if we are to form a real judgment of the life of the just and unjust, we must isolate them; there is no other way; and how is the isolation to be effected? I answer: Let the unjust man be entirely unjust, and the just man entirely just; nothing is to be taken away from either of them, and both are to be perfectly furnished for the work of their respective lives. First, let the unjust be like other distinguished masters of craft; like the skilful pilot or physician, who knows intuitively his own powers and keeps within their limits, and who, if he fails at any point, is able to recover himself. So let the unjust make his unjust attempts in the right way, and lie hidden if he means to be great in his injustice: (he who is found out is nobody:) for the highest reach of injustice is, to be deemed just when you are not. Therefore I say that in the perfectly unjust man we must assume the most perfect injustice; there is to be no deduction, but we must allow him, while doing the most unjust acts, to have acquired the greatest reputation for justice. If he have taken a false step he must be able to recover himself; he must be one who can speak with effect, if any of his deeds come to light, and who can force his way where force is required by his courage and strength, and command of money and friends. And at his side let us place the just man in his nobleness and simplicity, wishing, as Aeschylus says, to be and not to seem good. There must be no seeming, for if he seem to be just he will be honoured and rewarded, and then we shall not know whether he is just for the sake of justice or for the sake of honours and rewards; therefore, let him be clothed in justice only, and have no other covering; and he must be imagined in a state of life the opposite of the former. Let him be the best of men, and let him be thought the worst; then he will have been put to the proof; and we shall see whether he will be affected by the fear of infamy and its consequences. And let him continue thus to the hour of death; being just and seeming to be unjust. When both have reached the uttermost extreme, the one of justice and the other of injustice, let judgment be given which of them is the happier of the two.

Heavens! my dear Glaucon, I said, how energetically you polish them up for the decision, first one and then the other, as if they were two statues.

I do my best, he said. And now that we know what they are like there is no difficulty in tracing out the sort of life which awaits either of them. This I will proceed to describe; but as you may think the description a little too coarse, I ask you to suppose, Socrates, that the words which follow are not mine.—Let me put them into the mouths of the eulogists of injustice: They will tell you that the just man who is thought unjust will be scourged, racked, bound—will have his eyes burnt out; and, at last, after suffering every kind of evil, he will be impaled: Then he will understand that he ought to seem only, and not to be, just; the words of Aeschylus may be more truly spoken of the unjust than of the just. For the unjust is pursuing a reality; he does not live with a view to appearances—he wants to be really unjust and not to seem only:—"His mind has a soil deep and fertile, Out of which spring his prudent counsels."

In the first place, he is thought just, and therefore bears rule in the city; he can marry whom he will, and give in marriage to whom he will; also he can trade and deal where he likes, and always to his own advantage, because he has no misgivings about injustice; and at every contest, whether in public or private, he gets the better of his antagonists, and gains at their expense, and is rich, and out of his gains he can benefit his friends, and harm his enemies; moreover, he can offer sacrifices, and dedicate gifts to the gods abundantly and magnificently, and can honour the gods or any man whom he wants to honour in a far better style than the just, and therefore he is likely to be dearer than they are to the gods. And thus, Socrates, gods and men are said to unite in making the life of the unjust better than the life of the just.

I was going to say something in answer to Glaucon, when Adeimantus, his brother, interposed: Socrates, he said, you do not suppose that there is nothing more to be urged?

Why, what else is there? I answered.

The strongest point of all has not been even mentioned, he replied.

Well, then, according to the proverb, 'Let brother help brother'— if he fails in any part do you assist him; although I must confess that Glaucon has already said quite enough to lay me in the dust, and take from me the power of helping justice.

*Nonsense, he replied. But let me add something more: There is another side to Glaucon's argument about the praise and censure of justice and injustice, which is equally required in order to bring out what I believe to be his meaning. Parents and tutors are always telling their sons and their wards that they are to be just; but why? not for the sake of justice, but for the sake of character and reputation; in the hope of obtaining for him who is reputed just some of those offices, marriages, and the like which Glaucon has enumerated among the advantages accruing to the unjust from the reputation of justice. More, however, is made of appearances by this class of persons than by the others; for they throw in the good opinion of the gods, and will tell you of a shower of benefits which the heavens, as they say, rain upon the pious; and this accords with the testimony of the noble Hesiod and Homer, the first of whom says, that the gods make the oaks of the just—*

*"To bear acorns at their summit, and bees in the middle;*
*And the sheep are bowed down with the weight of their fleeces,"*

and many other blessings of a like kind are provided for them. And Homer has a very similar strain; for he speaks of one whose fame is— "As the fame of some blameless king who, like a god, Maintains justice; to whom the black earth brings forth Wheat and barley, whose trees are bowed with fruit, And his sheep never fail to bear, and the sea gives him fish."

Still grander are the gifts of heaven which Musaeus and his son vouchsafe to the just; they take them down into the world below, where they have the saints lying on couches at a feast, everlastingly drunk, crowned with garlands; their idea seems to be that an immortality of drunkenness is the highest meed of virtue. Some extend their rewards yet further; the posterity, as they say, of the faithful and just shall survive to the third and fourth generation. This is the style in which they praise justice. But about the wicked there is another strain; they bury them in a slough in Hades, and make them carry water in a sieve; also while they are yet living they bring them to infamy, and inflict upon them the punishments which Glaucon described as the portion of the just who are reputed to be unjust; nothing else does their invention supply. Such is their manner of praising the one and censuring the other.

Once more, Socrates, I will ask you to consider another way of speaking about justice and injustice, which is not confined to the poets, but is found in prose writers. The universal voice of mankind is always declaring that justice and virtue are honourable, but grievous and toilsome; and that the pleasures of vice and injustice are easy of attainment, and are only censured by law and opinion. They say also that honesty is for the most part less profitable than dishonesty; and they are quite ready to call wicked men happy, and to honour them both in public and private when they are rich or in any other way influential, while they despise and overlook those who may be weak and poor, even though acknowledging them to be better than the others. But most extraordinary of all is their mode of speaking about virtue and the gods: they say that the gods apportion calamity and misery to many good men, and good and happiness to the wicked. And mendicant prophets go to rich men's doors and persuade them that they have a power committed to them by the gods of making an atonement for a man's own or his ancestor's sins by sacrifices or charms, with rejoicings and feasts; and they promise to harm an enemy, whether just or unjust, at a small cost; with magic arts and incantations binding heaven, as they say, to execute their will. And the poets are the authorities to whom they appeal, now smoothing the path of vice with the words of Hesiod;—"Vice may be had in abundance without trouble; the way is smooth and her dwelling-place is near. But before virtue the gods have set toil," and a tedious and uphill road: then citing Homer as a witness that the gods may be influenced by men; for he also says:—"The gods, too, may be turned from their purpose; and men pray to them and avert their wrath by sacrifices and soothing entreaties, and by libations and the odour of fat, when they have sinned and transgressed."

And they produce a host of books written by Musaeus and Orpheus, who were children of the Moon and the Muses—that is what they say—according to which they perform their ritual, and persuade not only individuals, but whole cities, that expiations and atonements for sin may be made by sacrifices and amusements which fill a vacant hour, and are equally at the service of the living and the dead; the latter sort they call mysteries, and they redeem us from the pains of hell, but if we neglect them no one knows what awaits us.

He proceeded: And now when the young hear all this said about virtue and vice, and the way in which gods and men regard them, how are their minds likely to be affected, my dear Socrates,—those of them, I mean, who are quickwitted, and, like bees on the wing, light on every flower, and from all that they hear are prone to draw conclusions as to what manner of persons they should be and in what way they should walk if they would make the best of life? Probably the youth will say to himself in the words of Pindar—"Can I by justice or by crooked ways of deceit ascend a loftier tower which may be a fortress to me all my days?"

For what men say is that, if I am really just and am not also thought just profit there is none, but the pain and loss on the other hand are unmistakeable. But if, though unjust, I acquire the reputation of justice, a heavenly life is promised to me. Since then, as philosophers prove, appearance tyrannizes over truth and is lord of happiness, to appearance I must devote myself. I will describe around me a picture and shadow of virtue to be the vestibule and exterior of my house; behind I will trail the subtle and crafty fox, as Archilochus, greatest of sages, recommends. But I hear some one exclaiming that the concealment of wickedness is often difficult; to which I answer, Nothing great is easy. Nevertheless, the argument indicates this, if we would be happy, to be the path along which we should proceed. With a view to concealment we will establish secret brotherhoods and political clubs. And there are professors of rhetoric who teach the art of persuading courts and assemblies; and so, partly by persuasion and partly by force, I shall make unlawful gains and not be punished. Still I hear a voice saying that the gods cannot be deceived, neither can they be compelled. But what if there are no gods? or, suppose them to have no care of human things—why in either case should we mind about concealment? And even if there are gods, and they do care about us, yet we know of them only from tradition and the genealogies of the poets; and these are the very persons who say that they may be influenced and turned by 'sacrifices and soothing entreaties and by offerings.' Let us be consistent then, and believe both or neither. If the poets speak truly, why then we had better be unjust, and offer of the fruits of injustice; for if we are just, although we may escape the vengeance of heaven, we shall lose the gains of injustice; but, if we are unjust, we shall keep the gains, and by our sinning and praying, and praying and sinning, the gods will be propitiated, and we shall not be punished. "But there is a world below in which either we or our posterity will suffer for our unjust deeds." Yes, my friend, will be the reflection, but there are mysteries and atoning deities, and these have great power. That is what mighty cities declare; and the children of the gods, who were their poets and prophets, bear a like testimony.

On what principle, then, shall we any longer choose justice rather than the worst injustice? when, if we only unite the latter with a deceitful regard to appearances, we shall fare to our mind both with gods and men, in life and after death, as the most numerous and the highest authorities tell us. Knowing all this, Socrates, how can a man who has any superiority of mind or person or rank or wealth, be willing to honour justice; or indeed to refrain from laughing when he hears justice praised? And even if there should be some one who is able to disprove the truth of my words, and who is satisfied that justice is best, still he is not angry with the unjust, but is very ready to forgive them, because he also knows that men are not just of their own free will; unless, peradventure, there be some one whom the divinity within him may have inspired with a hatred of injustice, or who has attained knowledge of the truth—but no other man. He only blames injustice who, owing to cowardice or age or some weakness, has not the power of being unjust. And this is proved by the fact that when he obtains the power, he immediately becomes unjust as far as he can be.

The cause of all this, Socrates, was indicated by us at the beginning of the argument, when my brother and I told you how astonished we were to find that of all the professing panegyrists of justice—beginning with the ancient heroes of whom any memorial has been preserved to us, and ending with the men of our own time—no one has ever blamed injustice or praised justice except with a view to the glories, honours, and benefits which flow from them. No one has ever adequately described either in verse or prose the true essential nature of either of them abiding in the soul, and invisible to any human or divine eye; or shown that of all the things of a man's soul which he has within him, justice is the greatest good, and injustice the greatest evil. Had this been the universal strain, had you sought to persuade us of this from our youth upwards, we should not have been on the watch to keep one another from doing wrong, but every one would have been his own watchman, because afraid, if he did wrong, of harbouring in himself the greatest of evils. I dare say that Thrasymachus and others would seriously hold the language which I have been merely repeating, and words even stronger than these about justice and injustice, grossly, as I conceive, perverting their true nature. But I speak in this vehement manner, as I must frankly confess to you, because I want to hear from you the opposite side; and I would ask you to show not only the superiority which justice has over injustice, but what effect they have on the possessor of them which makes the one to be a good and the other an evil to him. And please, as Glaucon requested of you, to exclude reputations; for unless you take away from each of them his true reputation and add on the false, we shall say that you do not praise justice, but the appearance of it; we shall think that you are only exhorting us to keep injustice dark, and that you really agree with Thrasymachus in thinking that justice is another's good and the interest of the stronger, and that injustice is a man's own profit and interest, though injurious to the weaker. Now as you have admitted that justice is one of that highest class of goods which are desired indeed for their results, but in a far greater degree for their own sakes—like sight or hearing or knowledge or health, or any other real and natural and not merely conventional good—I would ask you in your praise of justice to regard one point only: I mean the essential good and evil which justice and injustice work in the possessors of them. Let others praise justice and censure injustice, magnifying the rewards and honours of the one and abusing the other; that is a manner of arguing which, coming from them, I am ready to tolerate, but from you who have spent your whole life in the consideration of this question, unless I hear the contrary from your own lips, I expect something better. And therefore, I say, not only prove to us that justice is better than injustice, but show what they either of them do to the possessor of them, which makes the one to be a good and the other an evil, whether seen or unseen by gods and men.

I had always admired the genius of Glaucon and Adeimantus, but on hearing these words I was quite delighted, and said: Sons of an illustrious father, that was not a bad beginning of the Elegiac verses which the admirer of Glaucon made in honour of you after you had distinguished yourselves at the battle of Megara:—"Sons of Ariston," he sang, "divine offspring of an illustrious hero."

The epithet is very appropriate, for there is something truly divine in being able to argue as you have done for the superiority of injustice, and remaining unconvinced by your own arguments. And I do believe that you are not convinced—this I infer from your general character, for had I judged only from your speeches I should have mistrusted you. But now, the greater my confidence in you, the greater is my difficulty in knowing what to say. For I am in a strait between two; on the one hand I feel that I am unequal to the task; and my inability is brought home to me by the fact that you were not satisfied with the answer which I made to Thrasymachus, proving, as I thought, the superiority which justice has over injustice. And yet I cannot refuse to help, while breath and speech remain to me; I am afraid that there would be an impiety in being present when justice is evil spoken of and not lifting up a hand in her defence. And therefore I had best give such help as I can.

Glaucon and the rest entreated me by all means not to let the question drop, but to proceed in the investigation. They wanted to arrive at the truth, first, about the nature of justice and injustice, and secondly, about their relative advantages. I told them, what I really thought, that the enquiry would be of a serious nature, and would require very good eyes. Seeing then, I said, that we are no great wits, I think that we had better adopt a method which I may illustrate thus; suppose that a short-sighted person had been asked by some one to read small letters from a distance; and it occurred to some one else that they might be found in another place which was larger and in which the letters were larger—if they were the same and he could read the larger letters first, and then proceed to the lesser—this would have been thought a rare piece of good fortune.

Very true, said Adeimantus; but how does the illustration apply to our enquiry?

I will tell you, I replied; justice, which is the subject of our enquiry, is, as you know, sometimes spoken of as the virtue of an individual, and sometimes as the virtue of a State.

True, he replied.

And is not a State larger than an individual?

It is.

Then in the larger the quantity of justice is likely to be larger and more easily discernible. I propose therefore that we enquire into the nature of justice and injustice, first as they appear in the State, and secondly in the individual, proceeding from the greater to the lesser and comparing them.

That, he said, is an excellent proposal.

And if we imagine the State in process of creation, we shall see the justice and injustice of the State in process of creation also.

I dare say.

When the State is completed there may be a hope that the object of our search will be more easily discovered.

Yes, far more easily.

But ought we to attempt to construct one? I said; for to do so, as I am inclined to think, will be a very serious task. Reflect therefore.

I have reflected, said Adeimantus, and am anxious that you should proceed.

A State, I said, arises, as I conceive, out of the needs of mankind; no one is self-sufficing, but all of us have many wants. Can any other origin of a State be imagined?

There can be no other.

Then, as we have many wants, and many persons are needed to supply them, one takes a helper for one purpose and another for another; and when these partners and helpers are gathered together in one habitation the body of inhabitants is termed a State.

True, he said.

And they exchange with one another, and one gives, and another receives, under the idea that the exchange will be for their good.

Very true.

Then, I said, let us begin and create in idea a State; and yet the true creator is necessity, who is the mother of our invention.

Of course, he replied.

Now the first and greatest of necessities is food, which is the condition of life and existence.

Certainly.

The second is a dwelling, and the third clothing and the like.

True.

And now let us see how our city will be able to supply this great demand: We may suppose that one man is a husbandman, another a builder, some one else a weaver—shall we add to them a shoemaker, or perhaps some other purveyor to our bodily wants?

Quite right.

The barest notion of a State must include four or five men.

Clearly.

And how will they proceed? Will each bring the result of his labours into a common stock?—the individual husbandman, for example, producing for four, and labouring four times as long and as much as he need in the provision of food with which he supplies others as well as himself; or will he have nothing to do with others and not be at the trouble of producing for them, but provide for himself alone a fourth of the food in a fourth of the time, and in the remaining three fourths of his time be employed in making a house or a coat or a pair of shoes, having no partnership with others, but supplying himself all his own wants?

Adeimantus thought that he should aim at producing food only and not at producing everything.

Probably, I replied, that would be the better way; and when I hear you say this, I am myself reminded that we are not all alike; there are diversities of natures among us which are adapted to different occupations.

Very true.

And will you have a work better done when the workman has many occupations, or when he has only one?

When he has only one.

Further, there can be no doubt that a work is spoilt when not done at the right time?

No doubt.

For business is not disposed to wait until the doer of the business is at leisure; but the doer must follow up what he is doing, and make the business his first object.

He must.

And if so, we must infer that all things are produced more plentifully and easily and of a better quality when one man does one thing which is natural to him and does it at the right time, and leaves other things.

Undoubtedly.

Then more than four citizens will be required; for the husbandman will not make his own plough or mattock, or other implements of agriculture, if they are to be good for anything. Neither will the builder make his tools—and he too needs many; and in like manner the weaver and shoemaker.

True.

Then carpenters, and smiths, and many other artisans, will be sharers in our little State, which is already beginning to grow?

True.

Yet even if we add neatherds, shepherds, and other herdsmen, in order that our husbandmen may have oxen to plough with, and builders as well as husbandmen may have draught cattle, and curriers and weavers fleeces and hides,—still our State will not be very large.

That is true; yet neither will it be a very small State which contains all these.

Then, again, there is the situation of the city—to find a place where nothing need be imported is wellnigh impossible.

Impossible.

Then there must be another class of citizens who will bring the required supply from another city?

There must.

But if the trader goes empty-handed, having nothing which they require who would supply his need, he will come back empty-handed.

That is certain.

And therefore what they produce at home must be not only enough for themselves, but such both in quantity and quality as to accommodate those from whom their wants are supplied.

Very true.

Then more husbandmen and more artisans will be required?

They will.

Not to mention the importers and exporters, who are called merchants?

Yes.

Then we shall want merchants?

We shall.

And if merchandise is to be carried over the sea, skilful sailors will also be needed, and in considerable numbers?

Yes, in considerable numbers.

Then, again, within the city, how will they exchange their productions? To secure such an exchange was, as you will remember, one of our principal objects when we formed them into a society and constituted a State.

Clearly they will buy and sell.

Then they will need a market-place, and a money-token for purposes of exchange.

Certainly.

Suppose now that a husbandman, or an artisan, brings some production to market, and he comes at a time when there is no one to exchange with him,—is he to leave his calling and sit idle in the market-place?

Not at all; he will find people there who, seeing the want, undertake the office of salesmen. In well-ordered states they are commonly those who are the weakest in bodily strength, and therefore of little use for any other purpose; their duty is to be in the market, and to give money in exchange for goods to those who desire to sell and to take money from those who desire to buy.

This want, then, creates a class of retail-traders in our State. Is not 'retailer' the term which is applied to those who sit in the market-place engaged in buying and selling, while those who wander from one city to another are called merchants?

Yes, he said.

And there is another class of servants, who are intellectually hardly on the level of companionship; still they have plenty of bodily strength for labour, which accordingly they sell, and are called, if I do not mistake, hirelings, hire being the name which is given to the price of their labour.

True.

Then hirelings will help to make up our population?

Yes.

And now, Adeimantus, is our State matured and perfected?

I think so.

Where, then, is justice, and where is injustice, and in what part of the State did they spring up?

Probably in the dealings of these citizens with one another. I cannot imagine that they are more likely to be found any where else.

I dare say that you are right in your suggestion, I said; we had better think the matter out, and not shrink from the enquiry.

Let us then consider, first of all, what will be their way of life, now that we have thus established them. Will they not produce corn, and wine, and clothes, and shoes, and build houses for themselves? And when they are housed, they will work, in summer, commonly, stripped and barefoot, but in winter substantially clothed and shod. They will feed on barley-meal and flour of wheat, baking and kneading them, making noble cakes and loaves; these they will serve up on a mat of reeds or on clean leaves, themselves reclining the while upon beds strewn with yew or myrtle. And they and their children will feast, drinking of the wine which they have made, wearing garlands on their heads, and hymning the praises of the gods, in happy converse with one another. And they will take care that their families do not exceed their means; having an eye to poverty or war.

But, said Glaucon, interposing, you have not given them a relish to their meal.

True, I replied, I had forgotten; of course they must have a relish— salt, and olives, and cheese, and they will boil roots and herbs such as country people prepare; for a dessert we shall give them figs, and peas, and beans; and they will roast myrtle-berries and acorns at the fire, drinking in moderation. And with such a diet they may be expected to live in peace and health to a good old age, and bequeath a similar life to their children after them.

Yes, Socrates, he said, and if you were providing for a city of pigs, how else would you feed the beasts?

But what would you have, Glaucon? I replied.

Why, he said, you should give them the ordinary conveniences of life. People who are to be comfortable are accustomed to lie on sofas, and dine off tables, and they should have sauces and sweets in the modern style.

Yes, I said, now I understand: the question which you would have me consider is, not only how a State, but how a luxurious State is created; and possibly there is no harm in this, for in such a State we shall be more likely to see how justice and injustice originate. In my opinion the true and healthy constitution of the State is the one which I have described. But if you wish also to see a State at fever-heat, I have no objection. For I suspect that many will not be satisfied with the simpler way of life. They will be for adding sofas, and tables, and other furniture; also dainties, and perfumes, and incense, and courtesans, and cakes, all these not of one sort only, but in every variety; we must go beyond the necessaries of which I was at first speaking, such as houses, and clothes, and shoes: the arts of the painter and the embroiderer will have to be set in motion, and gold and ivory and all sorts of materials must be procured.

True, he said.

Then we must enlarge our borders; for the original healthy State is no longer sufficient. Now will the city have to fill and swell with a multitude of callings which are not required by any natural want; such as the whole tribe of hunters and actors, of whom one large class have to do with forms and colours; another will be the votaries of music—poets and their attendant train of rhapsodists, players, dancers, contractors; also makers of divers kinds of articles, including women's dresses. And we shall want more servants. Will not tutors be also in request, and nurses wet and dry, tirewomen and barbers, as well as confectioners and cooks; and swineherds, too, who were not needed and therefore had no place in the former edition of our State, but are needed now? They must not be forgotten: and there will be animals of many other kinds, if people eat them.

Certainly.

And living in this way we shall have much greater need of physicians than before?

Much greater.

And the country which was enough to support the original inhabitants will be too small now, and not enough?

Quite true.

Then a slice of our neighbours' land will be wanted by us for pasture and tillage, and they will want a slice of ours, if, like ourselves, they exceed the limit of necessity, and give themselves up to the unlimited accumulation of wealth?

That, Socrates, will be inevitable.

And so we shall go to war, Glaucon. Shall we not?

Most certainly, he replied.

Then without determining as yet whether war does good or harm, thus much we may affirm, that now we have discovered war to be derived from causes which are also the causes of almost all the evils in States, private as well as public.

Undoubtedly.

And our State must once more enlarge; and this time the enlargement will be nothing short of a whole army, which will have to go out and fight with the invaders for all that we have, as well as for the things and persons whom we were describing above.

Why? he said; are they not capable of defending themselves?

No, I said; not if we were right in the principle which was acknowledged by all of us when we were framing the State: the principle, as you will remember, was that one man cannot practise many arts with success.

Very true, he said.

But is not war an art?

Certainly.

And an art requiring as much attention as shoemaking?

Quite true.

And the shoemaker was not allowed by us to be a husbandman, or a weaver, or a builder—in order that we might have our shoes well made; but to him and to every other worker was assigned one work for which he was by nature fitted, and at that he was to continue working all his life long and at no other; he was not to let opportunities slip, and then he would become a good workman. Now nothing can be more important than that the work of a soldier should be well done. But is war an art so easily acquired that a man may be a warrior who is also a husbandman, or shoemaker, or other artisan; although no one in the world would be a good dice or draught player who merely took up the game as a recreation, and had not from his earliest years devoted himself to this and nothing else? No tools will make a man a skilled workman, or master of defence, nor be of any use to him who has not learned how to handle them, and has never bestowed any attention upon them. How then will he who takes up a shield or other implement of war become a good fighter all in a day, whether with heavy-armed or any other kind of troops?

Yes, he said, the tools which would teach men their own use would be beyond price.

And the higher the duties of the guardian, I said, the more time, and skill, and art, and application will be needed by him?

No doubt, he replied.

Will he not also require natural aptitude for his calling?

Certainly.

Then it will be our duty to select, if we can, natures which are fitted for the task of guarding the city?

It will.

And the selection will be no easy matter, I said; but we must be brave and do our best.

We must.

Is not the noble youth very like a well-bred dog in respect of guarding and watching?

What do you mean?

I mean that both of them ought to be quick to see, and swift to overtake the enemy when they see him; and strong too if, when they have caught him, they have to fight with him.

All these qualities, he replied, will certainly be required by them.

Well, and your guardian must be brave if he is to fight well?

Certainly.

And is he likely to be brave who has no spirit, whether horse or dog or any other animal? Have you never observed how invincible and unconquerable is spirit and how the presence of it makes the soul of any creature to be absolutely fearless and indomitable?

I have.

Then now we have a clear notion of the bodily qualities which are required in the guardian.

True.

And also of the mental ones; his soul is to be full of spirit?

Yes.

But are not these spirited natures apt to be savage with one another, and with everybody else?

A difficulty by no means easy to overcome, he replied.

Whereas, I said, they ought to be dangerous to their enemies, and gentle to their friends; if not, they will destroy themselves without waiting for their enemies to destroy them.

True, he said.

What is to be done then? I said; how shall we find a gentle nature which has also a great spirit, for the one is the contradiction of the other?

True.

He will not be a good guardian who is wanting in either of these two qualities; and yet the combination of them appears to be impossible; and hence we must infer that to be a good guardian is impossible.

I am afraid that what you say is true, he replied.

Here feeling perplexed I began to think over what had preceded.— My friend, I said, no wonder that we are in a perplexity; for we have lost sight of the image which we had before us.

What do you mean? he said.

I mean to say that there do exist natures gifted with those opposite qualities.

And where do you find them?

Many animals, I replied, furnish examples of them; our friend the dog is a very good one: you know that well-bred dogs are perfectly gentle to their familiars and acquaintances, and the reverse to strangers.

Yes, I know.

Then there is nothing impossible or out of the order of nature in our finding a guardian who has a similar combination of qualities?

Certainly not.

Would not he who is fitted to be a guardian, besides the spirited nature, need to have the qualities of a philosopher?

I do not apprehend your meaning.

The trait of which I am speaking, I replied, may be also seen in the dog, and is remarkable in the animal.

What trait?

Why, a dog, whenever he sees a stranger, is angry; when an acquaintance, he welcomes him, although the one has never done him any harm, nor the other any good. Did this never strike you as curious?

The matter never struck me before; but I quite recognise the truth of your remark.

And surely this instinct of the dog is very charming;—your dog is a true philosopher.

Why?

Why, because he distinguishes the face of a friend and of an enemy only by the criterion of knowing and not knowing. And must not an animal be a lover of learning who determines what he likes and dislikes by the test of knowledge and ignorance?

Most assuredly.

And is not the love of learning the love of wisdom, which is philosophy?

They are the same, he replied.

And may we not say confidently of man also, that he who is likely to be gentle to his friends and acquaintances, must by nature be a lover of wisdom and knowledge?

That we may safely affirm.

Then he who is to be a really good and noble guardian of the State will require to unite in himself philosophy and spirit and swiftness and strength?

Undoubtedly.

Then we have found the desired natures; and now that we have found them, how are they to be reared and educated? Is not this an enquiry which may be expected to throw light on the greater enquiry which is our final end—How do justice and injustice grow up in States? for we do not want either to omit what is to the point or to draw out the argument to an inconvenient length.

Adeimantus thought that the enquiry would be of great service to us.

Then, I said, my dear friend, the task must not be given up, even if somewhat long.

Certainly not.

Come then, and let us pass a leisure hour in story-telling, and our story shall be the education of our heroes.

By all means.

And what shall be their education? Can we find a better than the traditional sort?—and this has two divisions, gymnastic for the body, and music for the soul.

True.

Shall we begin education with music, and go on to gymnastic afterwards?

By all means.

And when you speak of music, do you include literature or not?

I do.

And literature may be either true or false?

Yes.

And the young should be trained in both kinds, and we begin with the false?

I do not understand your meaning, he said.

You know, I said, that we begin by telling children stories which, though not wholly destitute of truth, are in the main fictitious; and these stories are told them when they are not of an age to learn gymnastics.

Very true.

That was my meaning when I said that we must teach music before gymnastics.

Quite right, he said.

You know also that the beginning is the most important part of any work, especially in the case of a young and tender thing; for that is the time at which the character is being formed and the desired impression is more readily taken.

Quite true.

And shall we just carelessly allow children to hear any casual tales which may be devised by casual persons, and to receive into their minds ideas for the most part the very opposite of those which we should wish them to have when they are grown up?

We cannot.

Then the first thing will be to establish a censorship of the writers of fiction, and let the censors receive any tale of fiction which is good, and reject the bad; and we will desire mothers and nurses to tell their children the authorised ones only. Let them fashion the mind with such tales, even more fondly than they mould the body with their hands; but most of those which are now in use must be discarded.

Of what tales are you speaking? he said.

You may find a model of the lesser in the greater, I said; for they are necessarily of the same type, and there is the same spirit in both of them.

Very likely, he replied; but I do not as yet know what you would term the greater.

Those, I said, which are narrated by Homer and Hesiod, and the rest of the poets, who have ever been the great story-tellers of mankind.

But which stories do you mean, he said; and what fault do you find with them?

A fault which is most serious, I said; the fault of telling a lie, and, what is more, a bad lie.

But when is this fault committed?

Whenever an erroneous representation is made of the nature of gods and heroes,—as when a painter paints a portrait not having the shadow of a likeness to the original.

Yes, he said, that sort of thing is certainly very blameable; but what are the stories which you mean?

First of all, I said, there was that greatest of all lies in high places, which the poet told about Uranus, and which was a bad lie too,—I mean what Hesiod says that Uranus did, and how Cronus retaliated on him. The doings of Cronus, and the sufferings which in turn his son inflicted upon him, even if they were true, ought certainly not to be lightly told to young and thoughtless persons; if possible, they had better be buried in silence. But if there is an absolute necessity for their mention, a chosen few might hear them in a mystery, and they should sacrifice not a common (Eleusinian) pig, but some huge and unprocurable victim; and then the number of the hearers will be very few indeed.

Why, yes, said he, those stories are extremely objectionable.

Yes, Adeimantus, they are stories not to be repeated in our State; the young man should not be told that in committing the worst of crimes he is far from doing anything outrageous; and that even if he chastises his father when he does wrong, in whatever manner, he will only be following the example of the first and greatest among the gods.

I entirely agree with you, he said; in my opinion those stories are quite unfit to be repeated.

Neither, if we mean our future guardians to regard the habit of quarrelling among themselves as of all things the basest, should any word be said to them of the wars in heaven, and of the plots and fightings of the gods against one another, for they are not true. No, we shall never mention the battles of the giants, or let them be embroidered on garments; and we shall be silent about the innumerable other quarrels of gods and heroes with their friends and relatives. If they would only believe us we would tell them that quarrelling is unholy, and that never up to this time has there been any quarrel between citizens; this is what old men and old women should begin by telling children; and when they grow up, the poets also should be told to compose for them in a similar spirit. But the narrative of Hephaestus binding Here his mother, or how on another occasion Zeus sent him flying for taking her part when she was being beaten, and all the battles of the gods in Homer—these tales must not be admitted into our State, whether they are supposed to have an allegorical meaning or not. For a young person cannot judge what is allegorical and what is literal; anything that he receives into his mind at that age is likely to become indelible and unalterable; and therefore it is most important that the tales which the young first hear should be models of virtuous thoughts.

There you are right, he replied; but if any one asks where are such models to be found and of what tales are you speaking—how shall we answer him?

I said to him, You and I, Adeimantus, at this moment are not poets, but founders of a State: now the founders of a State ought to know the general forms in which poets should cast their tales, and the limits which must be observed by them, but to make the tales is not their business.

Very true, he said; but what are these forms of theology which you mean?

Something of this kind, I replied:—God is always to be represented as he truly is, whatever be the sort of poetry, epic, lyric or tragic, in which the representation is given.

Right.

And is he not truly good? and must he not be represented as such?

Certainly.

And no good thing is hurtful?

No, indeed.

And that which is not hurtful hurts not?

Certainly not.

And that which hurts not does no evil?

No.

And can that which does no evil be a cause of evil?

Impossible.

And the good is advantageous?

Yes.

And therefore the cause of well-being?

Yes.

It follows therefore that the good is not the cause of all things, but of the good only?

Assuredly.

Then God, if he be good, is not the author of all things, as the many assert, but he is the cause of a few things only, and not of most things that occur to men. For few are the goods of human life, and many are the evils, and the good is to be attributed to God alone; of the evils the causes are to be sought elsewhere, and not in him.

That appears to me to be most true, he said.

Then we must not listen to Homer or to any other poet who is guilty of the folly of saying that two casks

'Lie at the threshold of Zeus, full of lots, one of good, the other of evil lots,' and that he to whom Zeus gives a mixture of the two 'Sometimes meets with evil fortune, at other times with good;' but that he to whom is given the cup of unmingled ill, 'Him wild hunger drives o'er the beauteous earth.'

And again—"Zeus, who is the dispenser of good and evil to us."

And if any one asserts that the violation of oaths and treaties, which was really the work of Pandarus, was brought about by Athene and Zeus, or that the strife and contention of the gods was instigated by Themis and Zeus, he shall not have our approval; neither will we allow our young men to hear the words of Aeschylus, that "God plants guilt among men when he desires utterly to destroy a house."

And if a poet writes of the sufferings of Niobe—the subject of the tragedy in which these iambic verses occur—or of the house of Pelops, or of the Trojan war or on any similar theme, either we must not permit him to say that these are the works of God, or if they are of God, he must devise some explanation of them such as we are seeking; he must say that God did what was just and right, and they were the better for being punished; but that those who are punished are miserable, and that God is the author of their misery—the poet is not to be permitted to say; though he may say that the wicked are miserable because they require to be punished, and are benefited by receiving punishment from God; but that God being good is the author of evil to any one is to be strenuously denied, and not to be said or sung or heard in verse or prose by any one whether old or young in any well-ordered commonwealth. Such a fiction is suicidal, ruinous, impious.

I agree with you, he replied, and am ready to give my assent to the law.

Let this then be one of our rules and principles concerning the gods, to which our poets and reciters will be expected to conform,—that God is not the author of all things, but of good only.

That will do, he said.

And what do you think of a second principle? Shall I ask you whether God is a magician, and of a nature to appear insidiously now in one shape, and now in another—sometimes himself changing and passing into many forms, sometimes deceiving us with the semblance of such transformations; or is he one and the same immutably fixed in his own proper image?

I cannot answer you, he said, without more thought.

Well, I said; but if we suppose a change in anything, that change must be effected either by the thing itself, or by some other thing?

Most certainly.

And things which are at their best are also least liable to be altered or discomposed; for example, when healthiest and strongest, the human frame is least liable to be affected by meats and drinks, and the plant which is in the fullest vigour also suffers least from winds or the heat of the sun or any similar causes.

Of course.

And will not the bravest and wisest soul be least confused or deranged by any external influence?

True.

And the same principle, as I should suppose, applies to all composite things—furniture, houses, garments: when good and well made, they are least altered by time and circumstances.

Very true.

Then everything which is good, whether made by art or nature, or both, is least liable to suffer change from without?

True.

But surely God and the things of God are in every way perfect?

Of course they are.

Then he can hardly be compelled by external influence to take many shapes?

He cannot.

But may he not change and transform himself?

Clearly, he said, that must be the case if he is changed at all.

And will he then change himself for the better and fairer, or for the worse and more unsightly?

If he change at all he can only change for the worse, for we cannot suppose him to be deficient either in virtue or beauty.

Very true, Adeimantus; but then, would any one, whether God or man, desire to make himself worse?

Impossible.

Then it is impossible that God should ever be willing to change; being, as is supposed, the fairest and best that is conceivable, every God remains absolutely and for ever in his own form.

That necessarily follows, he said, in my judgment.

Then, I said, my dear friend, let none of the poets tell us that 'The gods, taking the disguise of strangers from other lands, walk up and down cities in all sorts of forms;' and let no one slander Proteus and Thetis, neither let any one, either in tragedy or in any other kind of poetry, introduce Here disguised in the likeness of a priestess asking an alms 'For the life-giving daughters of Inachus the river of Argos;'—let us have no more lies of that sort. Neither must we have mothers under the influence of the poets scaring their children with a bad version of these myths—telling how certain gods, as they say, "Go about by night in the likeness of so many strangers and in divers forms;" but let them take heed lest they make cowards of their children, and at the same time speak blasphemy against the gods.

Heaven forbid, he said.

But although the gods are themselves unchangeable, still by witchcraft and deception they may make us think that they appear in various forms?

Perhaps, he replied.

Well, but can you imagine that God will be willing to lie, whether in word or deed, or to put forth a phantom of himself?

I cannot say, he replied.

Do you not know, I said, that the true lie, if such an expression may be allowed, is hated of gods and men?

What do you mean? he said.

I mean that no one is willingly deceived in that which is the truest and highest part of himself, or about the truest and highest matters; there, above all, he is most afraid of a lie having possession of him.

Still, he said, I do not comprehend you.

The reason is, I replied, that you attribute some profound meaning to my words; but I am only saying that deception, or being deceived or uninformed about the highest realities in the highest part of themselves, which is the soul, and in that part of them to have and to hold the lie, is what mankind least like;—that, I say, is what they utterly detest.

There is nothing more hateful to them.

And, as I was just now remarking, this ignorance in the soul of him who is deceived may be called the true lie; for the lie in words is only a kind of imitation and shadowy image of a previous affection of the soul, not pure unadulterated falsehood. Am I not right?

Perfectly right.

The true lie is hated not only by the gods, but also by men?

Yes.

Whereas the lie in words is in certain cases useful and not hateful; in dealing with enemies—that would be an instance; or again, when those whom we call our friends in a fit of madness or illusion are going to do some harm, then it is useful and is a sort of medicine or preventive; also in the tales of mythology, of which we were just now speaking—because we do not know the truth about ancient times, we make falsehood as much like truth as we can, and so turn it to account.

Very true, he said.

But can any of these reasons apply to God? Can we suppose that he is ignorant of antiquity, and therefore has recourse to invention?

That would be ridiculous, he said.

Then the lying poet has no place in our idea of God?

I should say not.

Or perhaps he may tell a lie because he is afraid of enemies?

That is inconceivable.

But he may have friends who are senseless or mad?

But no mad or senseless person can be a friend of God.

Then no motive can be imagined why God should lie?

None whatever.

Then the superhuman and divine is absolutely incapable of falsehood?

Yes.

Then is God perfectly simple and true both in word and deed; he changes not; he deceives not, either by sign or word, by dream or waking vision.

Your thoughts, he said, are the reflection of my own.

You agree with me then, I said, that this is the second type or form in which we should write and speak about divine things. The gods are not magicians who transform themselves, neither do they deceive mankind in any way.

I grant that.

Then, although we are admirers of Homer, we do not admire the lying dream which Zeus sends to Agamemnon; neither will we praise the verses of Aeschylus in which Thetis says that Apollo at her nuptials

"Was celebrating in song her fair progeny whose days were to be long, and to know no sickness. And when he had spoken of my lot as in all things blessed of heaven he raised a note of triumph and cheered my soul. And I thought that the word of Phoebus, being divine and full of prophecy, would not fail. And now he himself who uttered the strain, he who was present at the banquet, and who said this—he it is who has slain my son."

These are the kind of sentiments about the gods which will arouse our anger; and he who utters them shall be refused a chorus; neither shall we allow teachers to make use of them in the instruction of the young, meaning, as we do, that our guardians, as far as men can be, should be true worshippers of the gods and like them.

I entirely agree, he said, in these principles, and promise to make them my laws.

# BOOK III

S uch then, I said, are our principles of theology—some tales are to be told, and others are not to be told to our disciples from their youth upwards, if we mean them to honour the gods and their parents, and to value friendship with one another.

Yes; and I think that our principles are right, he said.

But if they are to be courageous, must they not learn other lessons besides these, and lessons of such a kind as will take away the fear of death? Can any man be courageous who has the fear of death in him?

Certainly not, he said.

And can he be fearless of death, or will he choose death in battle rather than defeat and slavery, who believes the world below to be real and terrible?

Impossible.

Then we must assume a control over the narrators of this class of tales as well as over the others, and beg them not simply to revile but rather to commend the world below, intimating to them that their descriptions are untrue, and will do harm to our future warriors.

That will be our duty, he said.

Then, I said, we shall have to obliterate many obnoxious passages, beginning with the verses, "I would rather be a serf on the land of a poor and portionless man than rule over all the dead who have come to nought."

We must also expunge the verse, which tells us how Pluto feared, "Lest the mansions grim and squalid which the gods abhor should be seen both of mortals and immortals."

And again:—"O heavens! verily in the house of Hades there is soul and ghostly form but no mind at all!"

Again of Tiresias:—"(To him even after death did Persephone grant mind,) that he alone should be wise; but the other souls are flitting shades."

Again:—"The soul flying from the limbs had gone to Hades, lamenting her fate, leaving manhood and youth."

Again:—"And the soul, with shrilling cry, passed like smoke beneath the earth."

And,—"As bats in hollow of mystic cavern, whenever any of them has dropped out of the string and falls from the rock, fly shrilling and cling to one another, so did they with shrilling cry hold together as they moved."

And we must beg Homer and the other poets not to be angry if we strike out these and similar passages, not because they are unpoetical, or unattractive to the popular ear, but because the greater the poetical charm of them, the less are they meet for the ears of boys and men who are meant to be free, and who should fear slavery more than death.

Undoubtedly.

Also we shall have to reject all the terrible and appalling names which describe the world below—Cocytus and Styx, ghosts under the earth, and sapless shades, and any similar words of which the very mention causes a shudder to pass through the inmost soul of him who hears them. I do not say that these horrible stories may not have a use of some kind; but there is a danger that the nerves of our guardians may be rendered too excitable and effeminate by them.

There is a real danger, he said.

Then we must have no more of them.

True.

Another and a nobler strain must be composed and sung by us.

Clearly.

And shall we proceed to get rid of the weepings and wailings of famous men?

They will go with the rest.

But shall we be right in getting rid of them? Reflect: our principle is that the good man will not consider death terrible to any other good man who is his comrade.

Yes; that is our principle.

And therefore he will not sorrow for his departed friend as though he had suffered anything terrible?

He will not.

Such an one, as we further maintain, is sufficient for himself and his own happiness, and therefore is least in need of other men.

True, he said.

And for this reason the loss of a son or brother, or the deprivation of fortune, is to him of all men least terrible.

Assuredly.

And therefore he will be least likely to lament, and will bear with the greatest equanimity any misfortune of this sort which may befall him.

Yes, he will feel such a misfortune far less than another.

Then we shall be right in getting rid of the lamentations of famous men, and making them over to women (and not even to women who are good for anything), or to men of a baser sort, that those who are being educated by us to be the defenders of their country may scorn to do the like.

That will be very right.

Then we will once more entreat Homer and the other poets not to depict Achilles, who is the son of a goddess, first lying on his side, then on his back, and then on his face; then starting up and sailing in a frenzy along the shores of the barren sea; now taking the sooty ashes in both his hands and pouring them over his head, or weeping and wailing in the various modes which Homer has delineated. Nor should he describe Priam the kinsman of the gods as praying and beseeching, "Rolling in the dirt, calling each man loudly by his name."

Still more earnestly will we beg of him at all events not to introduce the gods lamenting and saying, "Alas! my misery! Alas! that I bore the bravest to my sorrow."

But if he must introduce the gods, at any rate let him not dare so completely to misrepresent the greatest of the gods, as to make him say—"O heavens! with my eyes verily I behold a dear friend of mine chased round and round the city, and my heart is sorrowful."

Or again:—"Woe is me that I am fated to have Sarpedon, dearest of men to me, subdued at the hands of Patroclus the son of Menoetius."

For if, my sweet Adeimantus, our youth seriously listen to such unworthy representations of the gods, instead of laughing at them as they ought, hardly will any of them deem that he himself, being but a man, can be dishonoured by similar actions; neither will he rebuke any inclination which may arise in his mind to say and do the like. And instead of having any shame or self-control, he will be always whining and lamenting on slight occasions.

Yes, he said, that is most true.

Yes, I replied; but that surely is what ought not to be, as the argument has just proved to us; and by that proof we must abide until it is disproved by a better.

It ought not to be.

Neither ought our guardians to be given to laughter. For a fit of laughter which has been indulged to excess almost always produces a violent reaction.

So I believe.

Then persons of worth, even if only mortal men, must not be represented as overcome by laughter, and still less must such a representation of the gods be allowed.

Still less of the gods, as you say, he replied.

Then we shall not suffer such an expression to be used about the gods as that of Homer when he describes how "Inextinguishable laughter arose among the blessed gods, when they saw Hephaestus bustling about the mansion."

On your views, we must not admit them.

On my views, if you like to father them on me; that we must not admit them is certain.

Again, truth should be highly valued; if, as we were saying, a lie is useless to the gods, and useful only as a medicine to men, then the use of such medicines should be restricted to physicians; private individuals have no business with them.

Clearly not, he said.

Then if any one at all is to have the privilege of lying, the rulers of the State should be the persons; and they, in their dealings either with enemies or with their own citizens, may be allowed to lie for the public good. But nobody else should meddle with anything of the kind; and although the rulers have this privilege, for a private man to lie to them in return is to be deemed a more heinous fault than for the patient or the pupil of a gymnasium not to speak the truth about his own bodily illnesses to the physician or to the trainer, or for a sailor not to tell the captain what is happening about the ship and the rest of the crew, and how things are going with himself or his fellow sailors.

Most true, he said.

If, then, the ruler catches anybody beside himself lying in the State, "Any of the craftsmen, whether he be priest or physician or carpenter," he will punish him for introducing a practice which is equally subversive and destructive of ship or State.

Most certainly, he said, if our idea of the State is ever carried out.

In the next place our youth must be temperate?

Certainly.

Are not the chief elements of temperance, speaking generally, obedience to commanders and self-control in sensual pleasures?

True.

Then we shall approve such language as that of Diomede in Homer, "Friend, sit still and obey my word," and the verses which follow, "The Greeks marched breathing prowess, . . . in silent awe of their leaders," and other sentiments of the same kind.

We shall.

What of this line, "O heavy with wine, who hast the eyes of a dog and the heart of a stag," and of the words which follow? Would you say that these, or any similar impertinences which private individuals are supposed to address to their rulers, whether in verse or prose, are well or ill spoken?

They are ill spoken.

They may very possibly afford some amusement, but they do not conduce to temperance. And therefore they are likely to do harm to our young men—you would agree with me there?

Yes.

And then, again, to make the wisest of men say that nothing in his opinion is more glorious than 'When the tables are full of bread and meat, and the cup-bearer carries round wine which he draws from the bowl and pours into the cups,' is it fit or conducive to temperance for a young man to hear such words? Or the verse

"The saddest of fates is to die and meet destiny from hunger?"

What would you say again to the tale of Zeus, who, while other gods and men were asleep and he the only person awake, lay devising plans, but forgot them all in a moment through his lust, and was so completely overcome at the sight of Here that he would not even go into the hut, but wanted to lie with her on the ground, declaring that he had never been in such a state of rapture before, even when they first met one another 'Without the knowledge of their parents;' or that other tale of how Hephaestus, because of similar goings on, cast a chain around Ares and Aphrodite?

Indeed, he said, I am strongly of opinion that they ought not to hear that sort of thing.

But any deeds of endurance which are done or told by famous men, these they ought to see and hear; as, for example, what is said in the verses, "He smote his breast, and thus reproached his heart, Endure, my heart; far worse hast thou endured!"

Certainly, he said.

In the next place, we must not let them be receivers of gifts or lovers of money.

Certainly not.

Neither must we sing to them of 'Gifts persuading gods, and persuading reverend kings.'

Neither is Phoenix, the tutor of Achilles, to be approved or deemed to have given his pupil good counsel when he told him that he should take the gifts of the Greeks and assist them; but that without a gift he should not lay aside his anger. Neither will we believe or acknowledge Achilles himself to have been such a lover of money that he took Agamemnon's gifts, or that when he had received payment he restored the dead body of Hector, but that without payment he was unwilling to do so.

Undoubtedly, he said, these are not sentiments which can be approved.

Loving Homer as I do, I hardly like to say that in attributing these feelings to Achilles, or in believing that they are truly attributed to him, he is guilty of downright impiety. As little can I believe the narrative of his insolence to Apollo, where he says, "Thou hast wronged me, O far-darter, most abominable of deities. Verily I would be even with thee, if I had only the power;" or his insubordination to the river-god, on whose divinity he is ready to lay hands; or his offering to the dead Patroclus of his own hair, which had been previously dedicated to the other river-god Spercheius, and that he actually performed this vow; or that he dragged Hector round the tomb of Patroclus, and slaughtered the captives at the pyre; of all this I cannot believe that he was guilty, any more than I can allow our citizens to believe that he, the wise Cheiron's pupil, the son of a goddess and of Peleus who was the gentlest of men and third in descent from Zeus, was so disordered in his wits as to be at one time the slave of two seemingly inconsistent passions, meanness, not untainted by avarice, combined with overweening contempt of gods and men.

You are quite right, he replied.

And let us equally refuse to believe, or allow to be repeated, the tale of Theseus son of Poseidon, or of Peirithous son of Zeus, going forth as they did to perpetrate a horrid rape; or of any other hero or son of a god daring to do such impious and dreadful things as they falsely ascribe to them in our day: and let us further compel the poets to declare either that these acts were not done by them, or that they were not the sons of gods;—both in the same breath they shall not be permitted to affirm. We will not have them trying to persuade our youth that the gods are the authors of evil, and that heroes are no better than men—sentiments which, as we were saying, are neither pious nor true, for we have already proved that evil cannot come from the gods.

Assuredly not.

And further they are likely to have a bad effect on those who hear them; for everybody will begin to excuse his own vices when he is convinced that similar wickednesses are always being perpetrated by— "The kindred of the gods, the relatives of Zeus, whose ancestral altar, the altar of Zeus, is aloft in air on the peak of Ida," and who have "the blood of deities yet flowing in their veins."

And therefore let us put an end to such tales, lest they engender laxity of morals among the young.

By all means, he replied.

But now that we are determining what classes of subjects are or are not to be spoken of, let us see whether any have been omitted by us. The manner in which gods and demigods and heroes and the world below should be treated has been already laid down.

Very true.

And what shall we say about men? That is clearly the remaining portion of our subject.

Clearly so.

But we are not in a condition to answer this question at present, my friend.

Why not?

Because, if I am not mistaken, we shall have to say that about men poets and story-tellers are guilty of making the gravest misstatements when they tell us that wicked men are often happy, and the good miserable; and that injustice is profitable when undetected, but that justice is a man's own loss and another's gain—these things we shall forbid them to utter, and command them to sing and say the opposite.

To be sure we shall, he replied.

But if you admit that I am right in this, then I shall maintain that you have implied the principle for which we have been all along contending.

I grant the truth of your inference.

That such things are or are not to be said about men is a question which we cannot determine until we have discovered what justice is, and how naturally advantageous to the possessor, whether he seem to be just or not.

Most true, he said.

Enough of the subjects of poetry: let us now speak of the style; and when this has been considered, both matter and manner will have been completely treated.

I do not understand what you mean, said Adeimantus.

Then I must make you understand; and perhaps I may be more intelligible if I put the matter in this way. You are aware, I suppose, that all mythology and poetry is a narration of events, either past, present, or to come?

Certainly, he replied.

And narration may be either simple narration, or imitation, or a union of the two?

That again, he said, I do not quite understand.

I fear that I must be a ridiculous teacher when I have so much difficulty in making myself apprehended. Like a bad speaker, therefore, I will not take the whole of the subject, but will break a piece off in illustration of my meaning. You know the first lines of the Iliad, in which the poet says that Chryses prayed Agamemnon to release his daughter, and that Agamemnon flew into a passion with him; whereupon Chryses, failing of his object, invoked the anger of the God against the Achaeans. Now as far as these lines, 'And he prayed all the Greeks, but especially the two sons of Atreus, the chiefs of the people,' the poet is speaking in his own person; he never leads us to suppose that he is any one else. But in what follows he takes the person of Chryses, and then he does all that he can to make us believe that the speaker is not Homer, but the aged priest himself. And in this double form he has cast the entire narrative of the events which occurred at Troy and in Ithaca and throughout the Odyssey.

Yes.

And a narrative it remains both in the speeches which the poet recites from time to time and in the intermediate passages?

Quite true.

But when the poet speaks in the person of another, may we not say that he assimilates his style to that of the person who, as he informs you, is going to speak?

Certainly.

And this assimilation of himself to another, either by the use of voice or gesture, is the imitation of the person whose character he assumes?

Of course.

Then in this case the narrative of the poet may be said to proceed by way of imitation?

Very true.

Or, if the poet everywhere appears and never conceals himself, then again the imitation is dropped, and his poetry becomes simple narration. However, in order that I may make my meaning quite clear, and that you may no more say, "I don't understand," I will show how the change might be effected. If Homer had said, "The priest came, having his daughter's ransom in his hands, supplicating the Achaeans, and above all the kings;" and then if, instead of speaking in the person of Chryses, he had continued in his own person, the words would have been, not imitation, but simple narration. The passage would have run as follows (I am no poet, and therefore I drop the metre), "The priest came and prayed the gods on behalf of the Greeks that they might capture Troy and return safely home, but begged that they would give him back his daughter, and take the ransom which he brought, and respect the God. Thus he spoke, and the other Greeks revered the priest and assented. But Agamemnon was wroth, and bade him depart and not come again, lest the staff and chaplets of the God should be of no avail to him—the daughter of Chryses should not be released, he said—she should grow old with him in Argos. And then he told him to go away and not to provoke him, if he intended to get home unscathed. And the old man went away in fear and silence, and, when he had left the camp, he called upon Apollo by his many names, reminding him of everything which he had done pleasing to him, whether in building his temples, or in offering sacrifice, and praying that his good deeds might be returned to him, and that the Achaeans might expiate his tears by the arrows of the god,"—and so on. In this way the whole becomes simple narrative.

I understand, he said.

Or you may suppose the opposite case—that the intermediate passages are omitted, and the dialogue only left.

That also, he said, I understand; you mean, for example, as in tragedy.

You have conceived my meaning perfectly; and if I mistake not, what you failed to apprehend before is now made clear to you, that poetry and mythology are, in some cases, wholly imitative—instances of this are supplied by tragedy and comedy; there is likewise the opposite style, in which the poet is the only speaker—of this the dithyramb affords the best example; and the combination of both is found in epic, and in several other styles of poetry. Do I take you with me?

Yes, he said; I see now what you meant.

I will ask you to remember also what I began by saying, that we had done with the subject and might proceed to the style.

Yes, I remember.

In saying this, I intended to imply that we must come to an understanding about the mimetic art,—whether the poets, in narrating their stories, are to be allowed by us to imitate, and if so, whether in whole or in part, and if the latter, in what parts; or should all imitation be prohibited?

You mean, I suspect, to ask whether tragedy and comedy shall be admitted into our State?

Yes, I said; but there may be more than this in question: I really do not know as yet, but whither the argument may blow, thither we go.

And go we will, he said.

Then, Adeimantus, let me ask you whether our guardians ought to be imitators; or rather, has not this question been decided by the rule already laid down that one man can only do one thing well, and not many; and that if he attempt many, he will altogether fail of gaining much reputation in any?

Certainly.

And this is equally true of imitation; no one man can imitate many things as well as he would imitate a single one?

He cannot.

Then the same person will hardly be able to play a serious part in life, and at the same time to be an imitator and imitate many other parts as well; for even when two species of imitation are nearly allied, the same persons cannot succeed in both, as, for example, the writers of tragedy and comedy—did you not just now call them imitations?

Yes, I did; and you are right in thinking that the same persons cannot succeed in both.

Any more than they can be rhapsodists and actors at once?

True.

Neither are comic and tragic actors the same; yet all these things are but imitations.

They are so.

And human nature, Adeimantus, appears to have been coined into yet smaller pieces, and to be as incapable of imitating many things well, as of performing well the actions of which the imitations are copies.

Quite true, he replied.

If then we adhere to our original notion and bear in mind that our guardians, setting aside every other business, are to dedicate themselves wholly to the maintenance of freedom in the State, making this their craft, and engaging in no work which does not bear on this end, they ought not to practise or imitate anything else; if they imitate at all, they should imitate from youth upward only those characters which are suitable to their profession—the courageous, temperate, holy, free, and the like; but they should not depict or be skilful at imitating any kind of illiberality or baseness, lest from imitation they should come to be what they imitate. Did you never observe how imitations, beginning in early youth and continuing far into life, at length grow into habits and become a second nature, affecting body, voice, and mind?

Yes, certainly, he said.

Then, I said, we will not allow those for whom we profess a care and of whom we say that they ought to be good men, to imitate a woman, whether young or old, quarrelling with her husband, or striving and vaunting against the gods in conceit of her happiness, or when she is in affliction, or sorrow, or weeping; and certainly not one who is in sickness, love, or labour.

Very right, he said.

Neither must they represent slaves, male or female, performing the offices of slaves?

They must not.

And surely not bad men, whether cowards or any others, who do the reverse of what we have just been prescribing, who scold or mock or revile one another in drink or out of drink, or who in any other manner sin against themselves and their neighbours in word or deed, as the manner of such is. Neither should they be trained to imitate the action or speech of men or women who are mad or bad; for madness, like vice, is to be known but not to be practised or imitated.

Very true, he replied.

Neither may they imitate smiths or other artificers, or oarsmen, or boatswains, or the like?

How can they, he said, when they are not allowed to apply their minds to the callings of any of these?

Nor may they imitate the neighing of horses, the bellowing of bulls, the murmur of rivers and roll of the ocean, thunder, and all that sort of thing?

Nay, he said, if madness be forbidden, neither may they copy the behaviour of madmen.

You mean, I said, if I understand you aright, that there is one sort of narrative style which may be employed by a truly good man when he has anything to say, and that another sort will be used by a man of an opposite character and education.

And which are these two sorts? he asked.

Suppose, I answered, that a just and good man in the course of a narration comes on some saying or action of another good man,—I should imagine that he will like to personate him, and will not be ashamed of this sort of imitation: he will be most ready to play the part of the good man when he is acting firmly and wisely; in a less degree when he is overtaken by illness or love or drink, or has met with any other disaster. But when he comes to a character which is unworthy of him, he will not make a study of that; he will disdain such a person, and will assume his likeness, if at all, for a moment only when he is performing some good action; at other times he will be ashamed to play a part which he has never practised, nor will he like to fashion and frame himself after the baser models; he feels the employment of such an art, unless in jest, to be beneath him, and his mind revolts at it.

So I should expect, he replied.

Then he will adopt a mode of narration such as we have illustrated out of Homer, that is to say, his style will be both imitative and narrative; but there will be very little of the former, and a great deal of the latter. Do you agree?

Certainly, he said; that is the model which such a speaker must necessarily take.

But there is another sort of character who will narrate anything, and, the worse he is, the more unscrupulous he will be; nothing will be too bad for him: and he will be ready to imitate anything, not as a joke, but in right good earnest, and before a large company. As I was just now saying, he will attempt to represent the roll of thunder, the noise of wind and hail, or the creaking of wheels, and pulleys, and the various sounds of flutes, pipes, trumpets, and all sorts of instruments: he will bark like a dog, bleat like a sheep, or crow like a cock; his entire art will consist in imitation of voice and gesture, and there will be very little narration.

That, he said, will be his mode of speaking.

These, then, are the two kinds of style?

Yes.

And you would agree with me in saying that one of them is simple and has but slight changes; and if the harmony and rhythm are also chosen for their simplicity, the result is that the speaker, if he speaks correctly, is always pretty much the same in style, and he will keep within the limits of a single harmony (for the changes are not great), and in like manner he will make use of nearly the same rhythm?

That is quite true, he said.

Whereas the other requires all sorts of harmonies and all sorts of rhythms, if the music and the style are to correspond, because the style has all sorts of changes.

That is also perfectly true, he replied.

And do not the two styles, or the mixture of the two, comprehend all poetry, and every form of expression in words? No one can say anything except in one or other of them or in both together.

They include all, he said.

And shall we receive into our State all the three styles, or one only of the two unmixed styles? or would you include the mixed?

I should prefer only to admit the pure imitator of virtue.

Yes, I said, Adeimantus, but the mixed style is also very charming: and indeed the pantomimic, which is the opposite of the one chosen by you, is the most popular style with children and their attendants, and with the world in general.

I do not deny it.

But I suppose you would argue that such a style is unsuitable to our State, in which human nature is not twofold or manifold, for one man plays one part only?

Yes; quite unsuitable.

And this is the reason why in our State, and in our State only, we shall find a shoemaker to be a shoemaker and not a pilot also, and a husbandman to be a husbandman and not a dicast also, and a soldier a soldier and not a trader also, and the same throughout?

True, he said.

And therefore when any one of these pantomimic gentlemen, who are so clever that they can imitate anything, comes to us, and makes a proposal to exhibit himself and his poetry, we will fall down and worship him as a sweet and holy and wonderful being; but we must also inform him that in our State such as he are not permitted to exist; the law will not allow them. And so when we have anointed him with myrrh, and set a garland of wool upon his head, we shall send him away to another city. For we mean to employ for our souls' health the rougher and severer poet or story-teller, who will imitate the style of the virtuous only, and will follow those models which we prescribed at first when we began the education of our soldiers.

We certainly will, he said, if we have the power.

Then now, my friend, I said, that part of music or literary education which relates to the story or myth may be considered to be finished; for the matter and manner have both been discussed.

I think so too, he said.

Next in order will follow melody and song.

That is obvious.

Every one can see already what we ought to say about them, if we are to be consistent with ourselves.

I fear, said Glaucon, laughing, that the word 'every one' hardly includes me, for I cannot at the moment say what they should be; though I may guess.

At any rate you can tell that a song or ode has three parts— the words, the melody, and the rhythm; that degree of knowledge I may presuppose?

Yes, he said; so much as that you may.

And as for the words, there will surely be no difference between words which are and which are not set to music; both will conform to the same laws, and these have been already determined by us?

Yes.

And the melody and rhythm will depend upon the words?

Certainly.

We were saying, when we spoke of the subject-matter, that we had no need of lamentation and strains of sorrow?

True.

And which are the harmonies expressive of sorrow? You are musical, and can tell me.

The harmonies which you mean are the mixed or tenor Lydian, and the full-toned or bass Lydian, and such like.

These then, I said, must be banished; even to women who have a character to maintain they are of no use, and much less to men.

Certainly.

In the next place, drunkenness and softness and indolence are utterly unbecoming the character of our guardians.

Utterly unbecoming.

And which are the soft or drinking harmonies?

The Ionian, he replied, and the Lydian; they are termed 'relaxed.'

Well, and are these of any military use?

Quite the reverse, he replied; and if so the Dorian and the Phrygian are the only ones which you have left.

I answered: Of the harmonies I know nothing, but I want to have one warlike, to sound the note or accent which a brave man utters in the hour of danger and stern resolve, or when his cause is failing, and he is going to wounds or death or is overtaken by some other evil, and at every such crisis meets the blows of fortune with firm step and a determination to endure; and another to be used by him in times of peace and freedom of action, when there is no pressure of necessity, and he is seeking to persuade God by prayer, or man by instruction and admonition, or on the other hand, when he is expressing his willingness to yield to persuasion or entreaty or admonition, and which represents him when by prudent conduct he has attained his end, not carried away by his success, but acting moderately and wisely under the circumstances, and acquiescing in the event. These two harmonies I ask you to leave; the strain of necessity and the strain of freedom, the strain of the unfortunate and the strain of the fortunate, the strain of courage, and the strain of temperance; these, I say, leave.

And these, he replied, are the Dorian and Phrygian harmonies of which I was just now speaking.

Then, I said, if these and these only are to be used in our songs and melodies, we shall not want multiplicity of notes or a panharmonic scale?

I suppose not.

Then we shall not maintain the artificers of lyres with three corners and complex scales, or the makers of any other many-stringed curiously-harmonised instruments?

Certainly not.

But what do you say to flute-makers and flute-players? Would you admit them into our State when you reflect that in this composite use of harmony the flute is worse than all the stringed instruments put together; even the panharmonic music is only an imitation of the flute?

Clearly not.

There remain then only the lyre and the harp for use in the city, and the shepherds may have a pipe in the country.

That is surely the conclusion to be drawn from the argument.

The preferring of Apollo and his instruments to Marsyas and his instruments is not at all strange, I said.

Not at all, he replied.

And so, by the dog of Egypt, we have been unconsciously purging the State, which not long ago we termed luxurious.

And we have done wisely, he replied.

Then let us now finish the purgation, I said. Next in order to harmonies, rhythms will naturally follow, and they should be subject to the same rules, for we ought not to seek out complex systems of metre, or metres of every kind, but rather to discover what rhythms are the expressions of a courageous and harmonious life; and when we have found them, we shall adapt the foot and the melody to words having a like spirit, not the words to the foot and melody. To say what these rhythms are will be your duty—you must teach me them, as you have already taught me the harmonies.

But, indeed, he replied, I cannot tell you. I only know that there are some three principles of rhythm out of which metrical systems are framed, just as in sounds there are four notes (i.e. the four notes of the tetrachord.) out of which all the harmonies are composed; that is an observation which I have made. But of what sort of lives they are severally the imitations I am unable to say.

Then, I said, we must take Damon into our counsels; and he will tell us what rhythms are expressive of meanness, or insolence, or fury, or other unworthiness, and what are to be reserved for the expression of opposite feelings. And I think that I have an indistinct recollection of his mentioning a complex Cretic rhythm; also a dactylic or heroic, and he arranged them in some manner which I do not quite understand, making the rhythms equal in the rise and fall of the foot, long and short alternating; and, unless I am mistaken, he spoke of an iambic as well as of a trochaic rhythm, and assigned to them short and long quantities. Also in some cases he appeared to praise or censure the movement of the foot quite as much as the rhythm; or perhaps a combination of the two; for I am not certain what he meant. These matters, however, as I was saying, had better be referred to Damon himself, for the analysis of the subject would be difficult, you know? (Socrates expresses himself carelessly in accordance with his assumed ignorance of the details of the subject. In the first part of the sentence he appears to be speaking of paeonic rhythms which are in the ratio of $3/2$; in the second part, of dactylic and anapaestic rhythms, which are in the ratio of $1/1$; in the last clause, of iambic and trochaic rhythms, which are in the ratio of $1/2$ or $2/1$).

Rather so, I should say.

But there is no difficulty in seeing that grace or the absence of grace is an effect of good or bad rhythm.

None at all.

And also that good and bad rhythm naturally assimilate to a good and bad style; and that harmony and discord in like manner follow style; for our principle is that rhythm and harmony are regulated by the words, and not the words by them.

Just so, he said, they should follow the words.

And will not the words and the character of the style depend on the temper of the soul?

Yes.

And everything else on the style?

Yes.

Then beauty of style and harmony and grace and good rhythm depend on simplicity,—I mean the true simplicity of a rightly and nobly ordered mind and character, not that other simplicity which is only an euphemism for folly?

Very true, he replied.

And if our youth are to do their work in life, must they not make these graces and harmonies their perpetual aim?

They must.

And surely the art of the painter and every other creative and constructive art are full of them,—weaving, embroidery, architecture, and every kind of manufacture; also nature, animal and vegetable,—in all of them there is grace or the absence of grace. And ugliness and discord and inharmonious motion are nearly allied to ill words and ill nature, as grace and harmony are the twin sisters of goodness and virtue and bear their likeness.

That is quite true, he said.

But shall our superintendence go no further, and are the poets only to be required by us to express the image of the good in their works, on pain, if they do anything else, of expulsion from our State? Or is the same control to be extended to other artists, and are they also to be prohibited from exhibiting the opposite forms of vice and intemperance and meanness and indecency in sculpture and building and the other creative arts; and is he who cannot conform to this rule of ours to be prevented from practising his art in our State, lest the taste of our citizens be corrupted by him? We would not have our guardians grow up amid images of moral deformity, as in some noxious pasture, and there browse and feed upon many a baneful herb and flower day by day, little by little, until they silently gather a festering mass of corruption in their own soul. Let our artists rather be those who are gifted to discern the true nature of the beautiful and graceful; then will our youth dwell in a land of health, amid fair sights and sounds, and receive the good in everything; and beauty, the effluence of fair works, shall flow into the eye and ear, like a health-giving breeze from a purer region, and insensibly draw the soul from earliest years into likeness and sympathy with the beauty of reason.

There can be no nobler training than that, he replied.

And therefore, I said, Glaucon, musical training is a more potent instrument than any other, because rhythm and harmony find their way into the inward places of the soul, on which they mightily fasten, imparting grace, and making the soul of him who is rightly educated graceful, or of him who is ill-educated ungraceful; and also because he who has received this true education of the inner being will most shrewdly perceive omissions or faults in art and nature, and with a true taste, while he praises and rejoices over and receives into his soul the good, and becomes noble and good, he will justly blame and hate the bad, now in the days of his youth, even before he is able to know the reason why; and when reason comes he will recognise and salute the friend with whom his education has made him long familiar.

Yes, he said, I quite agree with you in thinking that our youth should be trained in music and on the grounds which you mention.

Just as in learning to read, I said, we were satisfied when we knew the letters of the alphabet, which are very few, in all their recurring sizes and combinations; not slighting them as unimportant whether they occupy a space large or small, but everywhere eager to make them out; and not thinking ourselves perfect in the art of reading until we recognise them wherever they are found: True—Or, as we recognise the reflection of letters in the water, or in a mirror, only when we know the letters themselves; the same art and study giving us the knowledge of both: Exactly—Even so, as I maintain, neither we nor our guardians, whom we have to educate, can ever become musical until we and they know the essential forms of temperance, courage, liberality, magnificence, and their kindred, as well as the contrary forms, in all their combinations, and can recognise them and their images wherever they are found, not slighting them either in small things or great, but believing them all to be within the sphere of one art and study.

Most assuredly.

And when a beautiful soul harmonizes with a beautiful form, and the two are cast in one mould, that will be the fairest of sights to him who has an eye to see it?

The fairest indeed.

And the fairest is also the loveliest?

That may be assumed.

And the man who has the spirit of harmony will be most in love with the loveliest; but he will not love him who is of an inharmonious soul?

That is true, he replied, if the deficiency be in his soul; but if there be any merely bodily defect in another he will be patient of it, and will love all the same.

I perceive, I said, that you have or have had experiences of this sort, and I agree. But let me ask you another question: Has excess of pleasure any affinity to temperance?

How can that be? he replied; pleasure deprives a man of the use of his faculties quite as much as pain.

Or any affinity to virtue in general?

None whatever.

Any affinity to wantonness and intemperance?

Yes, the greatest.

And is there any greater or keener pleasure than that of sensual love?

No, nor a madder.

Whereas true love is a love of beauty and order—temperate and harmonious?

Quite true, he said.

Then no intemperance or madness should be allowed to approach true love?

Certainly not.

Then mad or intemperate pleasure must never be allowed to come near the lover and his beloved; neither of them can have any part in it if their love is of the right sort?

No, indeed, Socrates, it must never come near them.

Then I suppose that in the city which we are founding you would make a law to the effect that a friend should use no other familiarity to his love than a father would use to his son, and then only for a noble purpose, and he must first have the other's consent; and this rule is to limit him in all his intercourse, and he is never to be seen going further, or, if he exceeds, he is to be deemed guilty of coarseness and bad taste.

I quite agree, he said.

Thus much of music, which makes a fair ending; for what should be the end of music if not the love of beauty?

I agree, he said.

After music comes gymnastic, in which our youth are next to be trained.

Certainly.

Gymnastic as well as music should begin in early years; the training in it should be careful and should continue through life. Now my belief is,—and this is a matter upon which I should like to have your opinion in confirmation of my own, but my own belief is,—not that the good body by any bodily excellence improves the soul, but, on the contrary, that the good soul, by her own excellence, improves the body as far as this may be possible. What do you say?

Yes, I agree.

Then, to the mind when adequately trained, we shall be right in handing over the more particular care of the body; and in order to avoid prolixity we will now only give the general outlines of the subject.

Very good.

That they must abstain from intoxication has been already remarked by us; for of all persons a guardian should be the last to get drunk and not know where in the world he is.

Yes, he said; that a guardian should require another guardian to take care of him is ridiculous indeed.

But next, what shall we say of their food; for the men are in training for the great contest of all—are they not?

Yes, he said.

And will the habit of body of our ordinary athletes be suited to them?

Why not?

I am afraid, I said, that a habit of body such as they have is but a sleepy sort of thing, and rather perilous to health. Do you not observe that these athletes sleep away their lives, and are liable to most dangerous illnesses if they depart, in ever so slight a degree, from their customary regimen?

Yes, I do.

Then, I said, a finer sort of training will be required for our warrior athletes, who are to be like wakeful dogs, and to see and hear with the utmost keenness; amid the many changes of water and also of food, of summer heat and winter cold, which they will have to endure when on a campaign, they must not be liable to break down in health.

That is my view.

The really excellent gymnastic is twin sister of that simple music which we were just now describing.

How so?

Why, I conceive that there is a gymnastic which, like our music, is simple and good; and especially the military gymnastic.

What do you mean?

My meaning may be learned from Homer; he, you know, feeds his heroes at their feasts, when they are campaigning, on soldiers' fare; they have no fish, although they are on the shores of the Hellespont, and they are not allowed boiled meats but only roast, which is the food most convenient for soldiers, requiring only that they should light a fire, and not involving the trouble of carrying about pots and pans.

True.

And I can hardly be mistaken in saying that sweet sauces are nowhere mentioned in Homer. In proscribing them, however, he is not singular; all professional athletes are well aware that a man who is to be in good condition should take nothing of the kind.

Yes, he said; and knowing this, they are quite right in not taking them.

Then you would not approve of Syracusan dinners, and the refinements of Sicilian cookery?

I think not.

Nor, if a man is to be in condition, would you allow him to have a Corinthian girl as his fair friend?

Certainly not.

Neither would you approve of the delicacies, as they are thought, of Athenian confectionary?

Certainly not.

All such feeding and living may be rightly compared by us to melody and song composed in the panharmonic style, and in all the rhythms.

Exactly.

There complexity engendered licence, and here disease; whereas simplicity in music was the parent of temperance in the soul; and simplicity in gymnastic of health in the body.

Most true, he said.

But when intemperance and diseases multiply in a State, halls of justice and medicine are always being opened; and the arts of the doctor and the lawyer give themselves airs, finding how keen is the interest which not only the slaves but the freemen of a city take about them.

Of course.

And yet what greater proof can there be of a bad and disgraceful state of education than this, that not only artisans and the meaner sort of people need the skill of first-rate physicians and judges, but also those who would profess to have had a liberal education? Is it not disgraceful, and a great sign of want of good-breeding, that a man should have to go abroad for his law and physic because he has none of his own at home, and must therefore surrender himself into the hands of other men whom he makes lords and judges over him?

Of all things, he said, the most disgraceful.

Would you say 'most,' I replied, when you consider that there is a further stage of the evil in which a man is not only a life-long litigant, passing all his days in the courts, either as plaintiff or defendant, but is actually led by his bad taste to pride himself on his litigiousness; he imagines that he is a master in dishonesty; able to take every crooked turn, and wriggle into and out of every hole, bending like a withy and getting out of the way of justice: and all for what?—in order to gain small points not worth mentioning, he not knowing that so to order his life as to be able to do without a napping judge is a far higher and nobler sort of thing. Is not that still more disgraceful?

Yes, he said, that is still more disgraceful.

Well, I said, and to require the help of medicine, not when a wound has to be cured, or on occasion of an epidemic, but just because, by indolence and a habit of life such as we have been describing, men fill themselves with waters and winds, as if their bodies were a marsh, compelling the ingenious sons of Asclepius to find more names for diseases, such as flatulence and catarrh; is not this, too, a disgrace?

Yes, he said, they do certainly give very strange and newfangled names to diseases.

Yes, I said, and I do not believe that there were any such diseases in the days of Asclepius; and this I infer from the circumstance that the hero Eurypylus, after he has been wounded in Homer, drinks a posset of Pramnian wine well besprinkled with barley-meal and grated cheese, which are certainly inflammatory, and yet the sons of Asclepius who were at the Trojan war do not blame the damsel who gives him the drink, or rebuke Patroclus, who is treating his case.

Well, he said, that was surely an extraordinary drink to be given to a person in his condition.

Not so extraordinary, I replied, if you bear in mind that in former days, as is commonly said, before the time of Herodicus, the guild of Asclepius did not practise our present system of medicine, which may be said to educate diseases. But Herodicus, being a trainer, and himself of a sickly constitution, by a combination of training and doctoring found out a way of torturing first and chiefly himself, and secondly the rest of the world.

How was that? he said.

By the invention of lingering death; for he had a mortal disease which he perpetually tended, and as recovery was out of the question, he passed his entire life as a valetudinarian; he could do nothing but attend upon himself, and he was in constant torment whenever he departed in anything from his usual regimen, and so dying hard, by the help of science he struggled on to old age.

A rare reward of his skill!

Yes, I said; a reward which a man might fairly expect who never understood that, if Asclepius did not instruct his descendants in valetudinarian arts, the omission arose, not from ignorance or inexperience of such a branch of medicine, but because he knew that in all well-ordered states every individual has an occupation to which he must attend, and has therefore no leisure to spend in continually being ill. This we remark in the case of the artisan, but, ludicrously enough, do not apply the same rule to people of the richer sort.

How do you mean? he said.

I mean this: When a carpenter is ill he asks the physician for a rough and ready cure; an emetic or a purge or a cautery or the knife,—these are his remedies. And if some one prescribes for him a course of dietetics, and tells him that he must swathe and swaddle his head, and all that sort of thing, he replies at once that he has no time to be ill, and that he sees no good in a life which is spent in nursing his disease to the neglect of his customary employment; and therefore bidding good-bye to this sort of physician, he resumes his ordinary habits, and either gets well and lives and does his business, or, if his constitution fails, he dies and has no more trouble.

Yes, he said, and a man in his condition of life ought to use the art of medicine thus far only.

Has he not, I said, an occupation; and what profit would there be in his life if he were deprived of his occupation?

Quite true, he said.

But with the rich man this is otherwise; of him we do not say that he has any specially appointed work which he must perform, if he would live.

He is generally supposed to have nothing to do.

Then you never heard of the saying of Phocylides, that as soon as a man has a livelihood he should practise virtue?

Nay, he said, I think that he had better begin somewhat sooner.

Let us not have a dispute with him about this, I said; but rather ask ourselves: Is the practice of virtue obligatory on the rich man, or can he live without it? And if obligatory on him, then let us raise a further question, whether this dieting of disorders, which is an impediment to the application of the mind in carpentering and the mechanical arts, does not equally stand in the way of the sentiment of Phocylides?

Of that, he replied, there can be no doubt; such excessive care of the body, when carried beyond the rules of gymnastic, is most inimical to the practice of virtue.

Yes, indeed, I replied, and equally incompatible with the management of a house, an army, or an office of state; and, what is most important of all, irreconcileable with any kind of study or thought or self-reflection—there is a constant suspicion that headache and giddiness are to be ascribed to philosophy, and hence all practising or making trial of virtue in the higher sense is absolutely stopped; for a man is always fancying that he is being made ill, and is in constant anxiety about the state of his body.

Yes, likely enough.

And therefore our politic Asclepius may be supposed to have exhibited the power of his art only to persons who, being generally of healthy constitution and habits of life, had a definite ailment; such as these he cured by purges and operations, and bade them live as usual, herein consulting the interests of the State; but bodies which disease had penetrated through and through he would not have attempted to cure by gradual processes of evacuation and infusion: he did not want to lengthen out good-for-nothing lives, or to have weak fathers begetting weaker sons;—if a man was not able to live in the ordinary way he had no business to cure him; for such a cure would have been of no use either to himself, or to the State.

Then, he said, you regard Asclepius as a statesman.

Clearly; and his character is further illustrated by his sons. Note that they were heroes in the days of old and practised the medicines of which I am speaking at the siege of Troy: You will remember how, when Pandarus wounded Menelaus, they "Sucked the blood out of the wound, and sprinkled soothing remedies," but they never prescribed what the patient was afterwards to eat or drink in the case of Menelaus, any more than in the case of Eurypylus; the remedies, as they conceived, were enough to heal any man who before he was wounded was healthy and regular in his habits; and even though he did happen to drink a posset of Pramnian wine, he might get well all the same. But they would have nothing to do with unhealthy and intemperate subjects, whose lives were of no use either to themselves or others; the art of medicine was not designed for their good, and though they were as rich as Midas, the sons of Asclepius would have declined to attend them.

They were very acute persons, those sons of Asclepius.

Naturally so, I replied. Nevertheless, the tragedians and Pindar disobeying our behests, although they acknowledge that Asclepius was the son of Apollo, say also that he was bribed into healing a rich man who was at the point of death, and for this reason he was struck by lightning. But we, in accordance with the principle already affirmed by us, will not believe them when they tell us both;—if he was the son of a god, we maintain that he was not avaricious; or, if he was avaricious, he was not the son of a god.

All that, Socrates, is excellent; but I should like to put a question to you: Ought there not to be good physicians in a State, and are not the best those who have treated the greatest number of constitutions good and bad? and are not the best judges in like manner those who are acquainted with all sorts of moral natures?

Yes, I said, I too would have good judges and good physicians. But do you know whom I think good?

Will you tell me?

I will, if I can. Let me however note that in the same question you join two things which are not the same.

How so? he asked.

Why, I said, you join physicians and judges. Now the most skilful physicians are those who, from their youth upwards, have combined with the knowledge of their art the greatest experience of disease; they had better not be robust in health, and should have had all manner of diseases in their own persons. For the body, as I conceive, is not the instrument with which they cure the body; in that case we could not allow them ever to be or to have been sickly; but they cure the body with the mind, and the mind which has become and is sick can cure nothing.

That is very true, he said.

But with the judge it is otherwise; since he governs mind by mind; he ought not therefore to have been trained among vicious minds, and to have associated with them from youth upwards, and to have gone through the whole calendar of crime, only in order that he may quickly infer the crimes of others as he might their bodily diseases from his own self-consciousness; the honourable mind which is to form a healthy judgment should have had no experience or contamination of evil habits when young. And this is the reason why in youth good men often appear to be simple, and are easily practised upon by the dishonest, because they have no examples of what evil is in their own souls.

Yes, he said, they are far too apt to be deceived.

Therefore, I said, the judge should not be young; he should have learned to know evil, not from his own soul, but from late and long observation of the nature of evil in others: knowledge should be his guide, not personal experience.

Yes, he said, that is the ideal of a judge.

Yes, I replied, and he will be a good man (which is my answer to your question); for he is good who has a good soul. But the cunning and suspicious nature of which we spoke,—he who has committed many crimes, and fancies himself to be a master in wickedness, when he is amongst his fellows, is wonderful in the precautions which he takes, because he judges of them by himself: but when he gets into the company of men of virtue, who have the experience of age, he appears to be a fool again, owing to his unseasonable suspicions; he cannot recognise an honest man, because he has no pattern of honesty in himself; at the same time, as the bad are more numerous than the good, and he meets with them oftener, he thinks himself, and is by others thought to be, rather wise than foolish.

Most true, he said.

Then the good and wise judge whom we are seeking is not this man, but the other; for vice cannot know virtue too, but a virtuous nature, educated by time, will acquire a knowledge both of virtue and vice: the virtuous, and not the vicious, man has wisdom—in my opinion.

And in mine also.

This is the sort of medicine, and this is the sort of law, which you will sanction in your state. They will minister to better natures, giving health both of soul and of body; but those who are diseased in their bodies they will leave to die, and the corrupt and incurable souls they will put an end to themselves.

That is clearly the best thing both for the patients and for the State.

And thus our youth, having been educated only in that simple music which, as we said, inspires temperance, will be reluctant to go to law.

Clearly.

And the musician, who, keeping to the same track, is content to practise the simple gymnastic, will have nothing to do with medicine unless in some extreme case.

That I quite believe.

The very exercises and tolls which he undergoes are intended to stimulate the spirited element of his nature, and not to increase his strength; he will not, like common athletes, use exercise and regimen to develope his muscles.

Very right, he said.

Neither are the two arts of music and gymnastic really designed, as is often supposed, the one for the training of the soul, the other for the training of the body.

What then is the real object of them?

I believe, I said, that the teachers of both have in view chiefly the improvement of the soul.

How can that be? he asked.

Did you never observe, I said, the effect on the mind itself of exclusive devotion to gymnastic, or the opposite effect of an exclusive devotion to music?

In what way shown? he said.

The one producing a temper of hardness and ferocity, the other of softness and effeminacy, I replied.

Yes, he said, I am quite aware that the mere athlete becomes too much of a savage, and that the mere musician is melted and softened beyond what is good for him.

Yet surely, I said, this ferocity only comes from spirit, which, if rightly educated, would give courage, but, if too much intensified, is liable to become hard and brutal.

That I quite think.

On the other hand the philosopher will have the quality of gentleness. And this also, when too much indulged, will turn to softness, but, if educated rightly, will be gentle and moderate.

True.

And in our opinion the guardians ought to have both these qualities?

Assuredly.

And both should be in harmony?

Beyond question.

And the harmonious soul is both temperate and courageous?

Yes.

And the inharmonious is cowardly and boorish?

Very true.

And, when a man allows music to play upon him and to pour into his soul through the funnel of his ears those sweet and soft and melancholy airs of which we were just now speaking, and his whole life is passed in warbling and the delights of song; in the first stage of the process the passion or spirit which is in him is tempered like iron, and made useful, instead of brittle and useless. But, if he carries on the softening and soothing process, in the next stage he begins to melt and waste, until he has wasted away his spirit and cut out the sinews of his soul; and he becomes a feeble warrior.

Very true.

If the element of spirit is naturally weak in him the change is speedily accomplished, but if he have a good deal, then the power of music weakening the spirit renders him excitable;—on the least provocation he flames up at once, and is speedily extinguished; instead of having spirit he grows irritable and passionate and is quite impracticable.

Exactly.

And so in gymnastics, if a man takes violent exercise and is a great feeder, and the reverse of a great student of music and philosophy, at first the high condition of his body fills him with pride and spirit, and he becomes twice the man that he was.

Certainly.

And what happens? if he do nothing else, and holds no converse with the Muses, does not even that intelligence which there may be in him, having no taste of any sort of learning or enquiry or thought or culture, grow feeble and dull and blind, his mind never waking up or receiving nourishment, and his senses not being purged of their mists?

True, he said.

And he ends by becoming a hater of philosophy, uncivilized, never using the weapon of persuasion,—he is like a wild beast, all violence and fierceness, and knows no other way of dealing; and he lives in all ignorance and evil conditions, and has no sense of propriety and grace.

That is quite true, he said.

And as there are two principles of human nature, one the spirited and the other the philosophical, some God, as I should say, has given mankind two arts answering to them (and only indirectly to the soul and body), in order that these two principles (like the strings of an instrument) may be relaxed or drawn tighter until they are duly harmonized.

That appears to be the intention.

And he who mingles music with gymnastic in the fairest proportions, and best attempers them to the soul, may be rightly called the true musician and harmonist in a far higher sense than the tuner of the strings.

You are quite right, Socrates.

And such a presiding genius will be always required in our State if the government is to last.

Yes, he will be absolutely necessary.

Such, then, are our principles of nurture and education: Where would be the use of going into further details about the dances of our citizens, or about their hunting and coursing, their gymnastic and equestrian contests? For these all follow the general principle, and having found that, we shall have no difficulty in discovering them.

I dare say that there will be no difficulty.

Very good, I said; then what is the next question? Must we not ask who are to be rulers and who subjects?

Certainly.

There can be no doubt that the elder must rule the younger.

Clearly.

And that the best of these must rule.

That is also clear.

Now, are not the best husbandmen those who are most devoted to husbandry?

Yes.

And as we are to have the best of guardians for our city, must they not be those who have most the character of guardians?

Yes.

And to this end they ought to be wise and efficient, and to have a special care of the State?

True.

And a man will be most likely to care about that which he loves?

To be sure.

And he will be most likely to love that which he regards as having the same interests with himself, and that of which the good or evil fortune is supposed by him at any time most to affect his own?

Very true, he replied.

Then there must be a selection. Let us note among the guardians those who in their whole life show the greatest eagerness to do what is for the good of their country, and the greatest repugnance to do what is against her interests.

Those are the right men.

And they will have to be watched at every age, in order that we may see whether they preserve their resolution, and never, under the influence either of force or enchantment, forget or cast off their sense of duty to the State.

How cast off? he said.

I will explain to you, I replied. A resolution may go out of a man's mind either with his will or against his will; with his will when he gets rid of a falsehood and learns better, against his will whenever he is deprived of a truth.

I understand, he said, the willing loss of a resolution; the meaning of the unwilling I have yet to learn.

Why, I said, do you not see that men are unwillingly deprived of good, and willingly of evil? Is not to have lost the truth an evil, and to possess the truth a good? and you would agree that to conceive things as they are is to possess the truth?

Yes, he replied; I agree with you in thinking that mankind are deprived of truth against their will.

And is not this involuntary deprivation caused either by theft, or force, or enchantment?

Still, he replied, I do not understand you.

I fear that I must have been talking darkly, like the tragedians. I only mean that some men are changed by persuasion and that others forget; argument steals away the hearts of one class, and time of the other; and this I call theft. Now you understand me?

Yes.

Those again who are forced, are those whom the violence of some pain or grief compels to change their opinion.

I understand, he said, and you are quite right.

And you would also acknowledge that the enchanted are those who change their minds either under the softer influence of pleasure, or the sterner influence of fear?

Yes, he said; everything that deceives may be said to enchant.

Therefore, as I was just now saying, we must enquire who are the best guardians of their own conviction that what they think the interest of the State is to be the rule of their lives. We must watch them from their youth upwards, and make them perform actions in which they are most likely to forget or to be deceived, and he who remembers and is not deceived is to be selected, and he who fails in the trial is to be rejected. That will be the way?

Yes.

And there should also be toils and pains and conflicts prescribed for them, in which they will be made to give further proof of the same qualities.

Very right, he replied.

And then, I said, we must try them with enchantments—that is the third sort of test—and see what will be their behaviour: like those who take colts amid noise and tumult to see if they are of a timid nature, so must we take our youth amid terrors of some kind, and again pass them into pleasures, and prove them more thoroughly than gold is proved in the furnace, that we may discover whether they are armed against all enchantments, and of a noble bearing always, good guardians of themselves and of the music which they have learned, and retaining under all circumstances a rhythmical and harmonious nature, such as will be most serviceable to the individual and to the State. And he who at every age, as boy and youth and in mature life, has come out of the trial victorious and pure, shall be appointed a ruler and guardian of the State; he shall be honoured in life and death, and shall receive sepulture and other memorials of honour, the greatest that we have to give. But him who fails, we must reject. I am inclined to think that this is the sort of way in which our rulers and guardians should be chosen and appointed. I speak generally, and not with any pretension to exactness.

And, speaking generally, I agree with you, he said.

And perhaps the word 'guardian' in the fullest sense ought to be applied to this higher class only who preserve us against foreign enemies and maintain peace among our citizens at home, that the one may not have the will, or the others the power, to harm us. The young men whom we before called guardians may be more properly designated auxiliaries and supporters of the principles of the rulers.

I agree with you, he said.

How then may we devise one of those needful falsehoods of which we lately spoke—just one royal lie which may deceive the rulers, if that be possible, and at any rate the rest of the city?

What sort of lie? he said.

Nothing new, I replied; only an old Phoenician tale (Laws) of what has often occurred before now in other places, (as the poets say, and have made the world believe,) though not in our time, and I do not know whether such an event could ever happen again, or could now even be made probable, if it did.

How your words seem to hesitate on your lips!

You will not wonder, I replied, at my hesitation when you have heard.

Speak, he said, and fear not.

Well then, I will speak, although I really know not how to look you in the face, or in what words to utter the audacious fiction, which I propose to communicate gradually, first to the rulers, then to the soldiers, and lastly to the people. They are to be told that their youth was a dream, and the education and training which they received from us, an appearance only; in reality during all that time they were being formed and fed in the womb of the earth, where they themselves and their arms and appurtenances were manufactured; when they were completed, the earth, their mother, sent them up; and so, their country being their mother and also their nurse, they are bound to advise for her good, and to defend her against attacks, and her citizens they are to regard as children of the earth and their own brothers.

You had good reason, he said, to be ashamed of the lie which you were going to tell.

True, I replied, but there is more coming; I have only told you half. Citizens, we shall say to them in our tale, you are brothers, yet God has framed you differently. Some of you have the power of command, and in the composition of these he has mingled gold, wherefore also they have the greatest honour; others he has made of silver, to be auxiliaries; others again who are to be husbandmen and craftsmen he has composed of brass and iron; and the species will generally be preserved in the children. But as all are of the same original stock, a golden parent will sometimes have a silver son, or a silver parent a golden son. And God proclaims as a first principle to the rulers, and above all else, that there is nothing which they should so anxiously guard, or of which they are to be such good guardians, as of the purity of the race. They should observe what elements mingle in their offspring; for if the son of a golden or silver parent has an admixture of brass and iron, then nature orders a transposition of ranks, and the eye of the ruler must not be pitiful towards the child because he has to descend in the scale and become a husbandman or artisan, just as there may be sons of artisans who having an admixture of gold or silver in them are raised to honour, and become guardians or auxiliaries. For an oracle says that when a man of brass or iron guards the State, it will be destroyed. Such is the tale; is there any possibility of making our citizens believe in it?

Not in the present generation, he replied; there is no way of accomplishing this; but their sons may be made to believe in the tale, and their sons' sons, and posterity after them.

I see the difficulty, I replied; yet the fostering of such a belief will make them care more for the city and for one another. Enough, however, of the fiction, which may now fly abroad upon the wings of rumour, while we arm our earth-born heroes, and lead them forth under the command of their rulers. Let them look round and select a spot whence they can best suppress insurrection, if any prove refractory within, and also defend themselves against enemies, who like wolves may come down on the fold from without; there let them encamp, and when they have encamped, let them sacrifice to the proper Gods and prepare their dwellings.

Just so, he said.

And their dwellings must be such as will shield them against the cold of winter and the heat of summer.

I suppose that you mean houses, he replied.

Yes, I said; but they must be the houses of soldiers, and not of shop-keepers.

What is the difference? he said.

That I will endeavour to explain, I replied. To keep watch-dogs, who, from want of discipline or hunger, or some evil habit or other, would turn upon the sheep and worry them, and behave not like dogs but wolves, would be a foul and monstrous thing in a shepherd?

Truly monstrous, he said.

And therefore every care must be taken that our auxiliaries, being stronger than our citizens, may not grow to be too much for them and become savage tyrants instead of friends and allies?

Yes, great care should be taken.

And would not a really good education furnish the best safeguard?

But they are well-educated already, he replied.

I cannot be so confident, my dear Glaucon, I said; I am much more certain that they ought to be, and that true education, whatever that may be, will have the greatest tendency to civilize and humanize them in their relations to one another, and to those who are under their protection.

Very true, he replied.

And not only their education, but their habitations, and all that belongs to them, should be such as will neither impair their virtue as guardians, nor tempt them to prey upon the other citizens. Any man of sense must acknowledge that.

He must.

Then now let us consider what will be their way of life, if they are to realize our idea of them. In the first place, none of them should have any property of his own beyond what is absolutely necessary; neither should they have a private house or store closed against any one who has a mind to enter; their provisions should be only such as are required by trained warriors, who are men of temperance and courage; they should agree to receive from the citizens a fixed rate of pay, enough to meet the expenses of the year and no more; and they will go to mess and live together like soldiers in a camp. Gold and silver we will tell them that they have from God; the diviner metal is within them, and they have therefore no need of the dross which is current among men, and ought not to pollute the divine by any such earthly admixture; for that commoner metal has been the source of many unholy deeds, but their own is undefiled. And they alone of all the citizens may not touch or handle silver or gold, or be under the same roof with them, or wear them, or drink from them. And this will be their salvation, and they will be the saviours of the State. But should they ever acquire homes or lands or moneys of their own, they will become housekeepers and husbandmen instead of guardians, enemies and tyrants instead of allies of the other citizens; hating and being hated, plotting and being plotted against, they will pass their whole life in much greater terror of internal than of external enemies, and the hour of ruin, both to themselves and to the rest of the State, will be at hand. For all which reasons may we not say that thus shall our State be ordered, and that these shall be the regulations appointed by us for guardians concerning their houses and all other matters?

Yes, said Glaucon.

# BOOK IV

Here Adeimantus interposed a question: How would you answer, Socrates, said he, if a person were to say that you are making these people miserable, and that they are the cause of their own unhappiness; the city in fact belongs to them, but they are none the better for it; whereas other men acquire lands, and build large and handsome houses, and have everything handsome about them, offering sacrifices to the gods on their own account, and practising hospitality; moreover, as you were saying just now, they have gold and silver, and all that is usual among the favourites of fortune; but our poor citizens are no better than mercenaries who are quartered in the city and are always mounting guard?

Yes, I said; and you may add that they are only fed, and not paid in addition to their food, like other men; and therefore they cannot, if they would, take a journey of pleasure; they have no money to spend on a mistress or any other luxurious fancy, which, as the world goes, is thought to be happiness; and many other accusations of the same nature might be added.

But, said he, let us suppose all this to be included in the charge.

You mean to ask, I said, what will be our answer?

Yes.

If we proceed along the old path, my belief, I said, is that we shall find the answer. And our answer will be that, even as they are, our guardians may very likely be the happiest of men; but that our aim in founding the State was not the disproportionate happiness of any one class, but the greatest happiness of the whole; we thought that in a State which is ordered with a view to the good of the whole we should be most likely to find justice, and in the ill-ordered State injustice: and, having found them, we might then decide which of the two is the happier. At present, I take it, we are fashioning the happy State, not piecemeal, or with a view of making a few happy citizens, but as a whole; and by-and-by we will proceed to view the opposite kind of State. Suppose that we were painting a statue, and some one came up to us and said, Why do you not put the most beautiful colours on the most beautiful parts of the body—the eyes ought to be purple, but you have made them black—to him we might fairly answer, Sir, you would not surely have us beautify the eyes to such a degree that they are no longer eyes; consider rather whether, by giving this and the other features their due proportion, we make the whole beautiful. And so I say to you, do not compel us to assign to the guardians a sort of happiness which will make them anything but guardians; for we too can clothe our husbandmen in royal apparel, and set crowns of gold on their heads, and bid them till the ground as much as they like, and no more. Our potters also might be allowed to repose on couches, and feast by the fireside, passing round the winecup, while their wheel is conveniently at hand, and working at pottery only as much as they like; in this way we might make every class happy—and then, as you imagine, the whole State would be happy. But do not put this idea into our heads; for, if we listen to you, the husbandman will be no longer a husbandman, the potter will cease to be a potter, and no one will have the character of any distinct class in the State. Now this is not of much consequence where the corruption of society, and pretension to be what you are not, is confined to cobblers; but when the guardians of the laws and of the government are only seeming and not real guardians, then see how they turn the State upside down; and on the other hand they alone have the power of giving order and happiness to the State. We mean our guardians to be true saviours and not the destroyers of the State, whereas our opponent is thinking of peasants at a festival, who are enjoying a life of revelry, not of citizens who are doing their duty to the State. But, if so, we mean different things, and he is speaking of something which is not a State. And therefore we must consider whether in appointing our guardians we would look to their greatest happiness individually, or whether this principle of happiness does not rather reside in the State as a whole. But if the latter be the truth, then the guardians and auxiliaries, and all others equally with them, must be compelled or induced to do their own work in the best way. And thus the whole State will grow up in a noble order, and the several classes will receive the proportion of happiness which nature assigns to them.

I think that you are quite right.

I wonder whether you will agree with another remark which occurs to me.

What may that be?

There seem to be two causes of the deterioration of the arts.

What are they?

Wealth, I said, and poverty.

How do they act?

The process is as follows: When a potter becomes rich, will he, think you, any longer take the same pains with his art?

Certainly not.

He will grow more and more indolent and careless?

Very true.

And the result will be that he becomes a worse potter?

Yes; he greatly deteriorates.

But, on the other hand, if he has no money, and cannot provide himself with tools or instruments, he will not work equally well himself, nor will he teach his sons or apprentices to work equally well.

Certainly not.

Then, under the influence either of poverty or of wealth, workmen and their work are equally liable to degenerate?

That is evident.

Here, then, is a discovery of new evils, I said, against which the guardians will have to watch, or they will creep into the city unobserved.

What evils?

Wealth, I said, and poverty; the one is the parent of luxury and indolence, and the other of meanness and viciousness, and both of discontent.

That is very true, he replied; but still I should like to know, Socrates, how our city will be able to go to war, especially against an enemy who is rich and powerful, if deprived of the sinews of war.

There would certainly be a difficulty, I replied, in going to war with one such enemy; but there is no difficulty where there are two of them.

How so? he asked.

In the first place, I said, if we have to fight, our side will be trained warriors fighting against an army of rich men.

That is true, he said.

And do you not suppose, Adeimantus, that a single boxer who was perfect in his art would easily be a match for two stout and well-to-do gentlemen who were not boxers?

Hardly, if they came upon him at once.

What, now, I said, if he were able to run away and then turn and strike at the one who first came up? And supposing he were to do this several times under the heat of a scorching sun, might he not, being an expert, overturn more than one stout personage?

Certainly, he said, there would be nothing wonderful in that.

And yet rich men probably have a greater superiority in the science and practise of boxing than they have in military qualities.

Likely enough.

Then we may assume that our athletes will be able to fight with two or three times their own number?

I agree with you, for I think you right.

And suppose that, before engaging, our citizens send an embassy to one of the two cities, telling them what is the truth: Silver and gold we neither have nor are permitted to have, but you may; do you therefore come and help us in war, and take the spoils of the other city: Who, on hearing these words, would choose to fight against lean wiry dogs, rather than, with the dogs on their side, against fat and tender sheep?

That is not likely; and yet there might be a danger to the poor State if the wealth of many States were to be gathered into one.

But how simple of you to use the term State at all of any but our own!

Why so?

You ought to speak of other States in the plural number; not one of them is a city, but many cities, as they say in the game. For indeed any city, however small, is in fact divided into two, one the city of the poor, the other of the rich; these are at war with one another; and in either there are many smaller divisions, and you would be altogether beside the mark if you treated them all as a single State. But if you deal with them as many, and give the wealth or power or persons of the one to the others, you will always have a great many friends and not many enemies. And your State, while the wise order which has now been prescribed continues to prevail in her, will be the greatest of States, I do not mean to say in reputation or appearance, but in deed and truth, though she number not more than a thousand defenders. A single State which is her equal you will hardly find, either among Hellenes or barbarians, though many that appear to be as great and many times greater.

That is most true, he said.

And what, I said, will be the best limit for our rulers to fix when they are considering the size of the State and the amount of territory which they are to include, and beyond which they will not go?

What limit would you propose?

I would allow the State to increase so far as is consistent with unity; that, I think, is the proper limit.

Very good, he said.

Here then, I said, is another order which will have to be conveyed to our guardians: Let our city be accounted neither large nor small, but one and self-sufficing.

And surely, said he, this is not a very severe order which we impose upon them.

And the other, said I, of which we were speaking before is lighter still,—I mean the duty of degrading the offspring of the guardians when inferior, and of elevating into the rank of guardians the offspring of the lower classes, when naturally superior. The intention was, that, in the case of the citizens generally, each individual should be put to the use for which nature intended him, one to one work, and then every man would do his own business, and be one and not many; and so the whole city would be one and not many.

Yes, he said; that is not so difficult.

The regulations which we are prescribing, my good Adeimantus, are not, as might be supposed, a number of great principles, but trifles all, if care be taken, as the saying is, of the one great thing,—a thing, however, which I would rather call, not great, but sufficient for our purpose.

What may that be? he asked.

Education, I said, and nurture: If our citizens are well educated, and grow into sensible men, they will easily see their way through all these, as well as other matters which I omit; such, for example, as marriage, the possession of women and the procreation of children, which will all follow the general principle that friends have all things in common, as the proverb says.

That will be the best way of settling them.

Also, I said, the State, if once started well, moves with accumulating force like a wheel. For good nurture and education implant good constitutions, and these good constitutions taking root in a good education improve more and more, and this improvement affects the breed in man as in other animals.

Very possibly, he said.

Then to sum up: This is the point to which, above all, the attention of our rulers should be directed,—that music and gymnastic be preserved in their original form, and no innovation made. They must do their utmost to maintain them intact. And when any one says that mankind most regard 'The newest song which the singers have,' they will be afraid that he may be praising, not new songs, but a new kind of song;

and this ought not to be praised, or conceived to be the meaning of the poet; for any musical innovation is full of danger to the whole State, and ought to be prohibited. So Damon tells me, and I can quite believe him;—he says that when modes of music change, the fundamental laws of the State always change with them.

Yes, said Adeimantus; and you may add my suffrage to Damon's and your own.

Then, I said, our guardians must lay the foundations of their fortress in music?

Yes, he said; the lawlessness of which you speak too easily steals in.

Yes, I replied, in the form of amusement; and at first sight it appears harmless.

Why, yes, he said, and there is no harm; were it not that little by little this spirit of licence, finding a home, imperceptibly penetrates into manners and customs; whence, issuing with greater force, it invades contracts between man and man, and from contracts goes on to laws and constitutions, in utter recklessness, ending at last, Socrates, by an overthrow of all rights, private as well as public.

Is that true? I said.

That is my belief, he replied.

Then, as I was saying, our youth should be trained from the first in a stricter system, for if amusements become lawless, and the youths themselves become lawless, they can never grow up into well-conducted and virtuous citizens.

Very true, he said.

And when they have made a good beginning in play, and by the help of music have gained the habit of good order, then this habit of order, in a manner how unlike the lawless play of the others! will accompany them in all their actions and be a principle of growth to them, and if there be any fallen places in the State will raise them up again.

Very true, he said.

Thus educated, they will invent for themselves any lesser rules which their predecessors have altogether neglected.

What do you mean?

I mean such things as these:—when the young are to be silent before their elders; how they are to show respect to them by standing and making them sit; what honour is due to parents; what garments or shoes are to be worn; the mode of dressing the hair; deportment and manners in general. You would agree with me?

Yes.

But there is, I think, small wisdom in legislating about such matters,—I doubt if it is ever done; nor are any precise written enactments about them likely to be lasting.

Impossible.

It would seem, Adeimantus, that the direction in which education starts a man, will determine his future life. Does not like always attract like?

To be sure.

Until some one rare and grand result is reached which may be good, and may be the reverse of good?

That is not to be denied.

And for this reason, I said, I shall not attempt to legislate further about them.

Naturally enough, he replied.

Well, and about the business of the agora, and the ordinary dealings between man and man, or again about agreements with artisans; about insult and injury, or the commencement of actions, and the appointment of juries, what would you say? there may also arise questions about any impositions and exactions of market and harbour dues which may be required, and in general about the regulations of markets, police, harbours, and the like. But, oh heavens! shall we condescend to legislate on any of these particulars?

I think, he said, that there is no need to impose laws about them on good men; what regulations are necessary they will find out soon enough for themselves.

Yes, I said, my friend, if God will only preserve to them the laws which we have given them.

And without divine help, said Adeimantus, they will go on for ever making and mending their laws and their lives in the hope of attaining perfection.

You would compare them, I said, to those invalids who, having no self-restraint, will not leave off their habits of intemperance?

Exactly.

Yes, I said; and what a delightful life they lead! they are always doctoring and increasing and complicating their disorders, and always fancying that they will be cured by any nostrum which anybody advises them to try.

Such cases are very common, he said, with invalids of this sort.

Yes, I replied; and the charming thing is that they deem him their worst enemy who tells them the truth, which is simply that, unless they give up eating and drinking and wenching and idling, neither drug nor cautery nor spell nor amulet nor any other remedy will avail.

Charming! he replied. I see nothing charming in going into a passion with a man who tells you what is right.

These gentlemen, I said, do not seem to be in your good graces.

Assuredly not.

Nor would you praise the behaviour of States which act like the men whom I was just now describing. For are there not ill-ordered States in which the citizens are forbidden under pain of death to alter the constitution; and yet he who most sweetly courts those who live under this regime and indulges them and fawns upon them and is skilful in anticipating and gratifying their humours is held to be a great and good statesman—do not these States resemble the persons whom I was describing?

Yes, he said; the States are as bad as the men; and I am very far from praising them.

But do you not admire, I said, the coolness and dexterity of these ready ministers of political corruption?

Yes, he said, I do; but not of all of them, for there are some whom the applause of the multitude has deluded into the belief that they are really statesmen, and these are not much to be admired.

What do you mean? I said; you should have more feeling for them. When a man cannot measure, and a great many others who cannot measure declare that he is four cubits high, can he help believing what they say?

Nay, he said, certainly not in that case.

Well, then, do not be angry with them; for are they not as good as a play, trying their hand at paltry reforms such as I was describing; they are always fancying that by legislation they will make an end of frauds in contracts, and the other rascalities which I was mentioning, not knowing that they are in reality cutting off the heads of a hydra?

Yes, he said; that is just what they are doing.

I conceive, I said, that the true legislator will not trouble himself with this class of enactments whether concerning laws or the constitution either in an ill-ordered or in a well-ordered State; for in the former they are quite useless, and in the latter there will be no difficulty in devising them; and many of them will naturally flow out of our previous regulations.

What, then, he said, is still remaining to us of the work of legislation?

Nothing to us, I replied; but to Apollo, the God of Delphi, there remains the ordering of the greatest and noblest and chiefest things of all.

Which are they? he said.

The institution of temples and sacrifices, and the entire service of gods, demigods, and heroes; also the ordering of the repositories of the dead, and the rites which have to be observed by him who would propitiate the inhabitants of the world below. These are matters of which we are ignorant ourselves, and as founders of a city we should be unwise in trusting them to any interpreter but our ancestral deity. He is the god who sits in the centre, on the navel of the earth, and he is the interpreter of religion to all mankind.

You are right, and we will do as you propose.

But where, amid all this, is justice? son of Ariston, tell me where. Now that our city has been made habitable, light a candle and search, and get your brother and Polemarchus and the rest of our friends to help, and let us see where in it we can discover justice and where injustice, and in what they differ from one another, and which of them the man who would be happy should have for his portion, whether seen or unseen by gods and men.

Nonsense, said Glaucon: did you not promise to search yourself, saying that for you not to help justice in her need would be an impiety?

I do not deny that I said so, and as you remind me, I will be as good as my word; but you must join.

We will, he replied.

Well, then, I hope to make the discovery in this way: I mean to begin with the assumption that our State, if rightly ordered, is perfect.

That is most certain.

And being perfect, is therefore wise and valiant and temperate and just.

That is likewise clear.

And whichever of these qualities we find in the State, the one which is not found will be the residue?

Very good.

If there were four things, and we were searching for one of them, wherever it might be, the one sought for might be known to us from the first, and there would be no further trouble; or we might know the other three first, and then the fourth would clearly be the one left.

Very true, he said.

And is not a similar method to be pursued about the virtues, which are also four in number?

Clearly.

First among the virtues found in the State, wisdom comes into view, and in this I detect a certain peculiarity.

What is that?

The State which we have been describing is said to be wise as being good in counsel?

Very true.

And good counsel is clearly a kind of knowledge, for not by ignorance, but by knowledge, do men counsel well?

Clearly.

And the kinds of knowledge in a State are many and diverse?

Of course.

There is the knowledge of the carpenter; but is that the sort of knowledge which gives a city the title of wise and good in counsel?

Certainly not; that would only give a city the reputation of skill in carpentering.

Then a city is not to be called wise because possessing a knowledge which counsels for the best about wooden implements?

Certainly not.

Nor by reason of a knowledge which advises about brazen pots, I said, nor as possessing any other similar knowledge?

Not by reason of any of them, he said.

Nor yet by reason of a knowledge which cultivates the earth; that would give the city the name of agricultural?

Yes.

Well, I said, and is there any knowledge in our recently-founded State among any of the citizens which advises, not about any particular thing in the State, but about the whole, and considers how a State can best deal with itself and with other States?

There certainly is.

And what is this knowledge, and among whom is it found? I asked.

It is the knowledge of the guardians, he replied, and is found among those whom we were just now describing as perfect guardians.

And what is the name which the city derives from the possession of this sort of knowledge?

The name of good in counsel and truly wise.

And will there be in our city more of these true guardians or more smiths?

The smiths, he replied, will be far more numerous.

Will not the guardians be the smallest of all the classes who receive a name from the profession of some kind of knowledge?

Much the smallest.

And so by reason of the smallest part or class, and of the knowledge which resides in this presiding and ruling part of itself, the whole State, being thus constituted according to nature, will be wise; and this, which has the only knowledge worthy to be called wisdom, has been ordained by nature to be of all classes the least.

Most true.

Thus, then, I said, the nature and place in the State of one of the four virtues has somehow or other been discovered.

And, in my humble opinion, very satisfactorily discovered, he replied.

Again, I said, there is no difficulty in seeing the nature of courage, and in what part that quality resides which gives the name of courageous to the State.

How do you mean?

Why, I said, every one who calls any State courageous or cowardly, will be thinking of the part which fights and goes out to war on the State's behalf.

No one, he replied, would ever think of any other.

The rest of the citizens may be courageous or may be cowardly, but their courage or cowardice will not, as I conceive, have the effect of making the city either the one or the other.

Certainly not.

The city will be courageous in virtue of a portion of herself which preserves under all circumstances that opinion about the nature of things to be feared and not to be feared in which our legislator educated them; and this is what you term courage.

I should like to hear what you are saying once more, for I do not think that I perfectly understand you.

I mean that courage is a kind of salvation.

Salvation of what?

Of the opinion respecting things to be feared, what they are and of what nature, which the law implants through education; and I mean by the words 'under all circumstances' to intimate that in pleasure or in pain, or under the influence of desire or fear, a man preserves, and does not lose this opinion. Shall I give you an illustration?

If you please.

You know, I said, that dyers, when they want to dye wool for making the true sea-purple, begin by selecting their white colour first; this they prepare and dress with much care and pains, in order that the white ground may take the purple hue in full perfection. The dyeing then proceeds; and whatever is dyed in this manner becomes a fast colour, and no washing either with lyes or without them can take away the bloom. But, when the ground has not been duly prepared, you will have noticed how poor is the look either of purple or of any other colour.

Yes, he said; I know that they have a washed-out and ridiculous appearance.

Then now, I said, you will understand what our object was in selecting our soldiers, and educating them in music and gymnastic; we were contriving influences which would prepare them to take the dye of the laws in perfection, and the colour of their opinion about dangers and of every other opinion was to be indelibly fixed by their nurture and training, not to be washed away by such potent lyes as pleasure—mightier agent far in washing the soul than any soda or lye; or by sorrow, fear, and desire, the mightiest of all other solvents. And this sort of universal saving power of true opinion in conformity with law about real and false dangers I call and maintain to be courage, unless you disagree.

But I agree, he replied; for I suppose that you mean to exclude mere uninstructed courage, such as that of a wild beast or of a slave—this, in your opinion, is not the courage which the law ordains, and ought to have another name.

Most certainly.

Then I may infer courage to be such as you describe?

Why, yes, said I, you may, and if you add the words 'of a citizen,' you will not be far wrong;—hereafter, if you like, we will carry the examination further, but at present we are seeking not for courage but justice; and for the purpose of our enquiry we have said enough.

You are right, he replied.

Two virtues remain to be discovered in the State—first, temperance, and then justice which is the end of our search.

Very true.

Now, can we find justice without troubling ourselves about temperance?

I do not know how that can be accomplished, he said, nor do I desire that justice should be brought to light and temperance lost sight of; and therefore I wish that you would do me the favour of considering temperance first.

Certainly, I replied, I should not be justified in refusing your request.

Then consider, he said.

Yes, I replied; I will; and as far as I can at present see, the virtue of temperance has more of the nature of harmony and symphony than the preceding.

How so? he asked.

Temperance, I replied, is the ordering or controlling of certain pleasures and desires; this is curiously enough implied in the saying of 'a man being his own master;' and other traces of the same notion may be found in language.

No doubt, he said.

There is something ridiculous in the expression 'master of himself;' for the master is also the servant and the servant the master; and in all these modes of speaking the same person is denoted.

Certainly.

The meaning is, I believe, that in the human soul there is a better and also a worse principle; and when the better has the worse under control, then a man is said to be master of himself; and this is a term of praise: but when, owing to evil education or association, the better principle, which is also the smaller, is overwhelmed by the greater mass of the worse—in this case he is blamed and is called the slave of self and unprincipled.

Yes, there is reason in that.

And now, I said, look at our newly-created State, and there you will find one of these two conditions realized; for the State, as you will acknowledge, may be justly called master of itself, if the words 'temperance' and 'self-mastery' truly express the rule of the better part over the worse.

Yes, he said, I see that what you say is true.

Let me further note that the manifold and complex pleasures and desires and pains are generally found in children and women and servants, and in the freemen so called who are of the lowest and more numerous class.

Certainly, he said.

Whereas the simple and moderate desires which follow reason, and are under the guidance of mind and true opinion, are to be found only in a few, and those the best born and best educated.

Very true.

These two, as you may perceive, have a place in our State; and the meaner desires of the many are held down by the virtuous desires and wisdom of the few.

That I perceive, he said.

Then if there be any city which may be described as master of its own pleasures and desires, and master of itself, ours may claim such a designation?

Certainly, he replied.

It may also be called temperate, and for the same reasons?

Yes.

And if there be any State in which rulers and subjects will be agreed as to the question who are to rule, that again will be our State?

Undoubtedly.

And the citizens being thus agreed among themselves, in which class will temperance be found—in the rulers or in the subjects?

In both, as I should imagine, he replied.

Do you observe that we were not far wrong in our guess that temperance was a sort of harmony?

Why so?

Why, because temperance is unlike courage and wisdom, each of which resides in a part only, the one making the State wise and the other valiant; not so temperance, which extends to the whole, and runs through all the notes of the scale, and produces a harmony of the weaker and the stronger and the middle class, whether you suppose them to be stronger or weaker in wisdom or power or numbers or wealth, or anything else. Most truly then may we deem temperance to be the agreement of the naturally superior and inferior, as to the right to rule of either, both in states and individuals.

I entirely agree with you.

And so, I said, we may consider three out of the four virtues to have been discovered in our State. The last of those qualities which make a state virtuous must be justice, if we only knew what that was.

The inference is obvious.

The time then has arrived, Glaucon, when, like huntsmen, we should surround the cover, and look sharp that justice does not steal away, and pass out of sight and escape us; for beyond a doubt she is somewhere in this country: watch therefore and strive to catch a sight of her, and if you see her first, let me know.

Would that I could! but you should regard me rather as a follower who has just eyes enough to see what you show him—that is about as much as I am good for.

Offer up a prayer with me and follow.

I will, but you must show me the way.

Here is no path, I said, and the wood is dark and perplexing; still we must push on.

Let us push on.

Here I saw something: Halloo! I said, I begin to perceive a track, and I believe that the quarry will not escape.

Good news, he said.

Truly, I said, we are stupid fellows.

Why so?

Why, my good sir, at the beginning of our enquiry, ages ago, there was justice tumbling out at our feet, and we never saw her; nothing could be more ridiculous. Like people who go about looking for what they have in their hands—that was the way with us—we looked not at what we were seeking, but at what was far off in the distance; and therefore, I suppose, we missed her.

What do you mean?

I mean to say that in reality for a long time past we have been talking of justice, and have failed to recognise her.

I grow impatient at the length of your exordium.

Well then, tell me, I said, whether I am right or not: You remember the original principle which we were always laying down at the foundation of the State, that one man should practise one thing only, the thing to which his nature was best adapted;—now justice is this principle or a part of it.

Yes, we often said that one man should do one thing only.

Further, we affirmed that justice was doing one's own business, and not being a busybody; we said so again and again, and many others have said the same to us.

Yes, we said so.

Then to do one's own business in a certain way may be assumed to be justice. Can you tell me whence I derive this inference?

I cannot, but I should like to be told.

Because I think that this is the only virtue which remains in the State when the other virtues of temperance and courage and wisdom are abstracted; and, that this is the ultimate cause and condition of the existence of all of them, and while remaining in them is also their preservative; and we were saying that if the three were discovered by us, justice would be the fourth or remaining one.

That follows of necessity.

If we are asked to determine which of these four qualities by its presence contributes most to the excellence of the State, whether the agreement of rulers and subjects, or the preservation in the soldiers of the opinion which the law ordains about the true nature of dangers, or wisdom and watchfulness in the rulers, or whether this other which I am mentioning, and which is found in children and women, slave and freeman, artisan, ruler, subject,—the quality, I mean, of every one doing his own work, and not being a busybody, would claim the palm—the question is not so easily answered.

Certainly, he replied, there would be a difficulty in saying which.

Then the power of each individual in the State to do his own work appears to compete with the other political virtues, wisdom, temperance, courage.

Yes, he said.

And the virtue which enters into this competition is justice?

Exactly.

Let us look at the question from another point of view: Are not the rulers in a State those to whom you would entrust the office of determining suits at law?

Certainly.

And are suits decided on any other ground but that a man may neither take what is another's, nor be deprived of what is his own?

Yes; that is their principle.

Which is a just principle?

Yes.

Then on this view also justice will be admitted to be the having and doing what is a man's own, and belongs to him?

Very true.

Think, now, and say whether you agree with me or not. Suppose a carpenter to be doing the business of a cobbler, or a cobbler of a carpenter; and suppose them to exchange their implements or their duties, or the same person to be doing the work of both, or whatever be the change; do you think that any great harm would result to the State?

Not much.

But when the cobbler or any other man whom nature designed to be a trader, having his heart lifted up by wealth or strength or the number of his followers, or any like advantage, attempts to force his way into the class of warriors, or a warrior into that of legislators and guardians, for which he is unfitted, and either to take the implements or the duties of the other; or when one man is trader, legislator, and warrior all in one, then I think you will agree with me in saying that this interchange and this meddling of one with another is the ruin of the State.

Most true.

Seeing then, I said, that there are three distinct classes, any meddling of one with another, or the change of one into another, is the greatest harm to the State, and may be most justly termed evil-doing?

Precisely.

And the greatest degree of evil-doing to one's own city would be termed by you injustice?

Certainly.

This then is injustice; and on the other hand when the trader, the auxiliary, and the guardian each do their own business, that is justice, and will make the city just.

I agree with you.

We will not, I said, be over-positive as yet; but if, on trial, this conception of justice be verified in the individual as well as in the State, there will be no longer any room for doubt; if it be not verified, we must have a fresh enquiry. First let us complete the old investigation, which we began, as you remember, under the impression that, if we could previously examine justice on the larger scale, there would be less difficulty in discerning her in the individual. That larger example appeared to be the State, and accordingly we constructed as good a one as we could, knowing well that in the good State justice would be found. Let the discovery which we made be now applied to the individual— if they agree, we shall be satisfied; or, if there be a difference in the individual, we will come back to the State and have another trial of the theory. The friction of the two when rubbed together may possibly strike a light in which justice will shine forth, and the vision which is then revealed we will fix in our souls.

That will be in regular course; let us do as you say.

I proceeded to ask: When two things, a greater and less, are called by the same name, are they like or unlike in so far as they are called the same?

Like, he replied.

The just man then, if we regard the idea of justice only, will be like the just State?

He will.

And a State was thought by us to be just when the three classes in the State severally did their own business; and also thought to be temperate and valiant and wise by reason of certain other affections and qualities of these same classes?

True, he said.

And so of the individual; we may assume that he has the same three principles in his own soul which are found in the State; and he may be rightly described in the same terms, because he is affected in the same manner?

Certainly, he said.

Once more then, O my friend, we have alighted upon an easy question—whether the soul has these three principles or not?

An easy question! Nay, rather, Socrates, the proverb holds that hard is the good.

Very true, I said; and I do not think that the method which we are employing is at all adequate to the accurate solution of this question; the true method is another and a longer one. Still we may arrive at a solution not below the level of the previous enquiry.

May we not be satisfied with that? he said;—under the circumstances, I am quite content.

I too, I replied, shall be extremely well satisfied.

Then faint not in pursuing the speculation, he said.

Must we not acknowledge, I said, that in each of us there are the same principles and habits which there are in the State; and that from the individual they pass into the State?—how else can they come there? Take the quality of passion or spirit;—it would be ridiculous to imagine that this quality, when found in States, is not derived from the individuals who are supposed to possess it, e.g. the Thracians, Scythians, and in general the northern nations; and the same may be said of the love of knowledge, which is the special characteristic of our part of the world, or of the love of money, which may, with equal truth, be attributed to the Phoenicians and Egyptians.

Exactly so, he said.

There is no difficulty in understanding this.

None whatever.

But the question is not quite so easy when we proceed to ask whether these principles are three or one; whether, that is to say, we learn with one part of our nature, are angry with another, and with a third part desire the satisfaction of our natural appetites; or whether the whole soul comes into play in each sort of action—to determine that is the difficulty.

Yes, he said; there lies the difficulty.

Then let us now try and determine whether they are the same or different.

How can we? he asked.

I replied as follows: The same thing clearly cannot act or be acted upon in the same part or in relation to the same thing at the same time, in contrary ways; and therefore whenever this contradiction occurs in things apparently the same, we know that they are really not the same, but different.

Good.

For example, I said, can the same thing be at rest and in motion at the same time in the same part?

Impossible.

Still, I said, let us have a more precise statement of terms, lest we should hereafter fall out by the way. Imagine the case of a man who is standing and also moving his hands and his head, and suppose a person to say that one and the same person is in motion and at rest at the same moment—to such a mode of speech we should object, and should rather say that one part of him is in motion while another is at rest.

Very true.

And suppose the objector to refine still further, and to draw the nice distinction that not only parts of tops, but whole tops, when they spin round with their pegs fixed on the spot, are at rest and in motion at the same time (and he may say the same of anything which revolves in the same spot), his objection would not be admitted by us, because in such cases things are not at rest and in motion in the same parts of themselves; we should rather say that they have both an axis and a circumference, and that the axis stands still, for there is no deviation from the perpendicular; and that the circumference goes round. But if, while revolving, the axis inclines either to the right or left, forwards or backwards, then in no point of view can they be at rest.

That is the correct mode of describing them, he replied.

Then none of these objections will confuse us, or incline us to believe that the same thing at the same time, in the same part or in relation to the same thing, can act or be acted upon in contrary ways.

Certainly not, according to my way of thinking.

Yet, I said, that we may not be compelled to examine all such objections, and prove at length that they are untrue, let us assume their absurdity, and go forward on the understanding that hereafter, if this assumption turn out to be untrue, all the consequences which follow shall be withdrawn.

Yes, he said, that will be the best way.

Well, I said, would you not allow that assent and dissent, desire and aversion, attraction and repulsion, are all of them opposites, whether they are regarded as active or passive (for that makes no difference in the fact of their opposition)?

Yes, he said, they are opposites.

Well, I said, and hunger and thirst, and the desires in general, and again willing and wishing,—all these you would refer to the classes already mentioned. You would say—would you not?—that the soul of him who desires is seeking after the object of his desire; or that he is drawing to himself the thing which he wishes to possess: or again, when a person wants anything to be given him, his mind, longing for the realization of his desire, intimates his wish to have it by a nod of assent, as if he had been asked a question?

Very true.

And what would you say of unwillingness and dislike and the absence of desire; should not these be referred to the opposite class of repulsion and rejection?

Certainly.

Admitting this to be true of desire generally, let us suppose a particular class of desires, and out of these we will select hunger and thirst, as they are termed, which are the most obvious of them?

Let us take that class, he said.

The object of one is food, and of the other drink?

Yes.

And here comes the point: is not thirst the desire which the soul has of drink, and of drink only; not of drink qualified by anything else; for example, warm or cold, or much or little, or, in a word, drink of any particular sort: but if the thirst be accompanied by heat, then the desire is of cold drink; or, if accompanied by cold, then of warm drink; or, if the thirst be excessive, then the drink which is desired will be excessive; or, if not great, the quantity of drink will also be small: but thirst pure and simple will desire drink pure and simple, which is the natural satisfaction of thirst, as food is of hunger?

Yes, he said; the simple desire is, as you say, in every case of the simple object, and the qualified desire of the qualified object.

But here a confusion may arise; and I should wish to guard against an opponent starting up and saying that no man desires drink only, but good drink, or food only, but good food; for good is the universal object of desire, and thirst being a desire, will necessarily be thirst after good drink; and the same is true of every other desire.

Yes, he replied, the opponent might have something to say.

Nevertheless I should still maintain, that of relatives some have a quality attached to either term of the relation; others are simple and have their correlatives simple.

I do not know what you mean.

Well, you know of course that the greater is relative to the less?

Certainly.

And the much greater to the much less?

Yes.

And the sometime greater to the sometime less, and the greater that is to be to the less that is to be?

Certainly, he said.

And so of more and less, and of other correlative terms, such as the double and the half, or again, the heavier and the lighter, the swifter and the slower; and of hot and cold, and of any other relatives;—is not this true of all of them?

Yes.

And does not the same principle hold in the sciences? The object of science is knowledge (assuming that to be the true definition), but the object of a particular science is a particular kind of knowledge; I mean, for example, that the science of house-building is a kind of knowledge which is defined and distinguished from other kinds and is therefore termed architecture.

Certainly.

Because it has a particular quality which no other has?

Yes.

And it has this particular quality because it has an object of a particular kind; and this is true of the other arts and sciences?

Yes.

Now, then, if I have made myself clear, you will understand my original meaning in what I said about relatives. My meaning was, that if one term of a relation is taken alone, the other is taken alone; if one term is qualified, the other is also qualified. I do not mean to say that relatives may not be disparate, or that the science of health is healthy, or of disease necessarily diseased, or that the sciences of good and evil are therefore good and evil; but only that, when the term science is no longer used absolutely, but has a qualified object which in this case is the nature of health and disease, it becomes defined, and is hence called not merely science, but the science of medicine.

I quite understand, and I think as you do.

Would you not say that thirst is one of these essentially relative terms, having clearly a relation—

Yes, thirst is relative to drink.

And a certain kind of thirst is relative to a certain kind of drink; but thirst taken alone is neither of much nor little, nor of good nor bad, nor of any particular kind of drink, but of drink only?

Certainly.

Then the soul of the thirsty one, in so far as he is thirsty, desires only drink; for this he yearns and tries to obtain it?

That is plain.

And if you suppose something which pulls a thirsty soul away from drink, that must be different from the thirsty principle which draws him like a beast to drink; for, as we were saying, the same thing cannot at the same time with the same part of itself act in contrary ways about the same.

Impossible.

No more than you can say that the hands of the archer push and pull the bow at the same time, but what you say is that one hand pushes and the other pulls.

Exactly so, he replied.

And might a man be thirsty, and yet unwilling to drink?

Yes, he said, it constantly happens.

And in such a case what is one to say? Would you not say that there was something in the soul bidding a man to drink, and something else forbidding him, which is other and stronger than the principle which bids him?

I should say so.

And the forbidding principle is derived from reason, and that which bids and attracts proceeds from passion and disease?

Clearly.

Then we may fairly assume that they are two, and that they differ from one another; the one with which a man reasons, we may call the rational principle of the soul, the other, with which he loves and hungers and thirsts and feels the flutterings of any other desire, may be termed the irrational or appetitive, the ally of sundry pleasures and satisfactions?

Yes, he said, we may fairly assume them to be different.

Then let us finally determine that there are two principles existing in the soul. And what of passion, or spirit? Is it a third, or akin to one of the preceding?

162

I should be inclined to say—akin to desire.

Well, I said, there is a story which I remember to have heard, and in which I put faith. The story is, that Leontius, the son of Aglaion, coming up one day from the Piraeus, under the north wall on the outside, observed some dead bodies lying on the ground at the place of execution. He felt a desire to see them, and also a dread and abhorrence of them; for a time he struggled and covered his eyes, but at length the desire got the better of him; and forcing them open, he ran up to the dead bodies, saying, Look, ye wretches, take your fill of the fair sight.

I have heard the story myself, he said.

The moral of the tale is, that anger at times goes to war with desire, as though they were two distinct things.

Yes; that is the meaning, he said.

And are there not many other cases in which we observe that when a man's desires violently prevail over his reason, he reviles himself, and is angry at the violence within him, and that in this struggle, which is like the struggle of factions in a State, his spirit is on the side of his reason;—but for the passionate or spirited element to take part with the desires when reason decides that she should not be opposed, is a sort of thing which I believe that you never observed occurring in yourself, nor, as I should imagine, in any one else?

Certainly not.

Suppose that a man thinks he has done a wrong to another, the nobler he is the less able is he to feel indignant at any suffering, such as hunger, or cold, or any other pain which the injured person may inflict upon him—these he deems to be just, and, as I say, his anger refuses to be excited by them.

True, he said.

But when he thinks that he is the sufferer of the wrong, then he boils and chafes, and is on the side of what he believes to be justice; and because he suffers hunger or cold or other pain he is only the more determined to persevere and conquer. His noble spirit will not be quelled until he either slays or is slain; or until he hears the voice of the shepherd, that is, reason, bidding his dog bark no more.

163

The illustration is perfect, he replied; and in our State, as we were saying, the auxiliaries were to be dogs, and to hear the voice of the rulers, who are their shepherds.

I perceive, I said, that you quite understand me; there is, however, a further point which I wish you to consider.

What point?

You remember that passion or spirit appeared at first sight to be a kind of desire, but now we should say quite the contrary; for in the conflict of the soul spirit is arrayed on the side of the rational principle.

Most assuredly.

But a further question arises: Is passion different from reason also, or only a kind of reason; in which latter case, instead of three principles in the soul, there will only be two, the rational and the concupiscent; or rather, as the State was composed of three classes, traders, auxiliaries, counsellors, so may there not be in the individual soul a third element which is passion or spirit, and when not corrupted by bad education is the natural auxiliary of reason?

Yes, he said, there must be a third.

Yes, I replied, if passion, which has already been shown to be different from desire, turn out also to be different from reason.

But that is easily proved:—We may observe even in young children that they are full of spirit almost as soon as they are born, whereas some of them never seem to attain to the use of reason, and most of them late enough.

Excellent, I said, and you may see passion equally in brute animals, which is a further proof of the truth of what you are saying. And we may once more appeal to the words of Homer, which have been already quoted by us, 'He smote his breast, and thus rebuked his soul,' for in this verse Homer has clearly supposed the power which reasons about the better and worse to be different from the unreasoning anger which is rebuked by it.

Very true, he said.

And so, after much tossing, we have reached land, and are fairly agreed that the same principles which exist in the State exist also in the individual, and that they are three in number.

Exactly.

Must we not then infer that the individual is wise in the same way, and in virtue of the same quality which makes the State wise?

Certainly.

Also that the same quality which constitutes courage in the State constitutes courage in the individual, and that both the State and the individual bear the same relation to all the other virtues?

Assuredly.

And the individual will be acknowledged by us to be just in the same way in which the State is just?

That follows, of course.

We cannot but remember that the justice of the State consisted in each of the three classes doing the work of its own class?

We are not very likely to have forgotten, he said.

We must recollect that the individual in whom the several qualities of his nature do their own work will be just, and will do his own work?

Yes, he said, we must remember that too.

And ought not the rational principle, which is wise, and has the care of the whole soul, to rule, and the passionate or spirited principle to be the subject and ally?

Certainly.

And, as we were saying, the united influence of music and gymnastic will bring them into accord, nerving and sustaining the reason with noble words and lessons, and moderating and soothing and civilizing the wildness of passion by harmony and rhythm?

Quite true, he said.

And these two, thus nurtured and educated, and having learned truly to know their own functions, will rule over the concupiscent, which in each of us is the largest part of the soul and by nature most insatiable of gain; over this they will keep guard, lest, waxing great and strong with the fulness of bodily pleasures, as they are termed, the concupiscent soul, no longer confined to her own sphere, should attempt to enslave and rule those who are not her natural-born subjects, and overturn the whole life of man?

Very true, he said.

Both together will they not be the best defenders of the whole soul and the whole body against attacks from without; the one counselling, and the other fighting under his leader, and courageously executing his commands and counsels?

True.

And he is to be deemed courageous whose spirit retains in pleasure and in pain the commands of reason about what he ought or ought not to fear?

Right, he replied.

And him we call wise who has in him that little part which rules, and which proclaims these commands; that part too being supposed to have a knowledge of what is for the interest of each of the three parts and of the whole?

Assuredly.

And would you not say that he is temperate who has these same elements in friendly harmony, in whom the one ruling principle of reason, and the two subject ones of spirit and desire are equally agreed that reason ought to rule, and do not rebel?

Certainly, he said, that is the true account of temperance whether in the State or individual.

And surely, I said, we have explained again and again how and by virtue of what quality a man will be just.

That is very certain.

And is justice dimmer in the individual, and is her form different, or is she the same which we found her to be in the State?

There is no difference in my opinion, he said.

Because, if any doubt is still lingering in our minds, a few commonplace instances will satisfy us of the truth of what I am saying.

What sort of instances do you mean?

If the case is put to us, must we not admit that the just State, or the man who is trained in the principles of such a State, will be less likely than the unjust to make away with a deposit of gold or silver? Would any one deny this?

No one, he replied.

Will the just man or citizen ever be guilty of sacrilege or theft, or treachery either to his friends or to his country?

Never.

Neither will he ever break faith where there have been oaths or agreements?

Impossible.

No one will be less likely to commit adultery, or to dishonour his father and mother, or to fail in his religious duties?

No one.

And the reason is that each part of him is doing its own business, whether in ruling or being ruled?

Exactly so.

Are you satisfied then that the quality which makes such men and such states is justice, or do you hope to discover some other?

Not I, indeed.

Then our dream has been realized; and the suspicion which we entertained at the beginning of our work of construction, that some divine power must have conducted us to a primary form of justice, has now been verified?

Yes, certainly.

And the division of labour which required the carpenter and the shoemaker and the rest of the citizens to be doing each his own business, and not another's, was a shadow of justice, and for that reason it was of use?

Clearly.

But in reality justice was such as we were describing, being concerned however, not with the outward man, but with the inward, which is the true self and concernment of man: for the just man does not permit the several elements within him to interfere with one another, or any of them to do the work of others,—he sets in order his own inner life, and is his own master and his own law, and at peace with himself; and when he has bound together the three principles within him, which may be compared to the higher, lower, and middle notes of the scale, and the intermediate intervals—when he has bound all these together, and is no longer many, but has become one entirely temperate and perfectly adjusted nature, then he proceeds to act, if he has to act, whether in a matter of property, or in the treatment of the body, or in some affair of politics or private business; always thinking and calling that which preserves and co-operates with this harmonious condition, just and good action, and the knowledge which presides over it, wisdom, and that which at any time impairs this condition, he will call unjust action, and the opinion which presides over it ignorance.

You have said the exact truth, Socrates.

Very good; and if we were to affirm that we had discovered the just man and the just State, and the nature of justice in each of them, we should not be telling a falsehood?

Most certainly not.

May we say so, then?

Let us say so.

And now, I said, injustice has to be considered.

Clearly.

Must not injustice be a strife which arises among the three principles—a meddlesomeness, and interference, and rising up of a part of the soul against the whole, an assertion of unlawful authority, which is made by a rebellious subject against a true prince, of whom he is the natural vassal,—what is all this confusion and delusion but injustice, and intemperance and cowardice and ignorance, and every form of vice?

Exactly so.

And if the nature of justice and injustice be known, then the meaning of acting unjustly and being unjust, or, again, of acting justly, will also be perfectly clear?

What do you mean? he said.

Why, I said, they are like disease and health; being in the soul just what disease and health are in the body.

How so? he said.

Why, I said, that which is healthy causes health, and that which is unhealthy causes disease.

Yes.

And just actions cause justice, and unjust actions cause injustice?

That is certain.

And the creation of health is the institution of a natural order and government of one by another in the parts of the body; and the creation of disease is the production of a state of things at variance with this natural order?

True.

And is not the creation of justice the institution of a natural order and government of one by another in the parts of the soul, and the creation of injustice the production of a state of things at variance with the natural order?

Exactly so, he said.

Then virtue is the health and beauty and well-being of the soul, and vice the disease and weakness and deformity of the same?

True.

And do not good practices lead to virtue, and evil practices to vice?

Assuredly.

Still our old question of the comparative advantage of justice and injustice has not been answered: Which is the more profitable, to be just and act justly and practise virtue, whether seen or unseen of gods and men, or to be unjust and act unjustly, if only unpunished and unreformed?

In my judgment, Socrates, the question has now become ridiculous. We know that, when the bodily constitution is gone, life is no longer endurable, though pampered with all kinds of meats and drinks, and having all wealth and all power; and shall we be told that when the very essence of the vital principle is undermined and corrupted, life is still worth having to a man, if only he be allowed to do whatever he likes with the single exception that he is not to acquire justice and virtue, or to escape from injustice and vice; assuming them both to be such as we have described?

Yes, I said, the question is, as you say, ridiculous. Still, as we are near the spot at which we may see the truth in the clearest manner with our own eyes, let us not faint by the way.

Certainly not, he replied.

Come up hither, I said, and behold the various forms of vice, those of them, I mean, which are worth looking at.

I am following you, he replied: proceed.

I said, The argument seems to have reached a height from which, as from some tower of speculation, a man may look down and see that virtue is one, but that the forms of vice are innumerable; there being four special ones which are deserving of note.

What do you mean? he said.

I mean, I replied, that there appear to be as many forms of the soul as there are distinct forms of the State.

How many?

There are five of the State, and five of the soul, I said.

What are they?

The first, I said, is that which we have been describing, and which may be said to have two names, monarchy and aristocracy, accordingly as rule is exercised by one distinguished man or by many.

True, he replied.

But I regard the two names as describing one form only; for whether the government is in the hands of one or many, if the governors have been trained in the manner which we have supposed, the fundamental laws of the State will be maintained.

That is true, he replied.

# BOOK V

S uch is the good and true City or State, and the good and true man is of the same pattern; and if this is right every other is wrong; and the evil is one which affects not only the ordering of the State, but also the regulation of the individual soul, and is exhibited in four forms.

What are they? he said.

I was proceeding to tell the order in which the four evil forms appeared to me to succeed one another, when Polemarchus, who was sitting a little way off, just beyond Adeimantus, began to whisper to him: stretching forth his hand, he took hold of the upper part of his coat by the shoulder, and drew him towards him, leaning forward himself so as to be quite close and saying something in his ear, of which I only caught the words, 'Shall we let him off, or what shall we do?'

Certainly not, said Adeimantus, raising his voice.

Who is it, I said, whom you are refusing to let off?

You, he said.

I repeated, Why am I especially not to be let off?

Why, he said, we think that you are lazy, and mean to cheat us out of a whole chapter which is a very important part of the story; and you fancy that we shall not notice your airy way of proceeding; as if it were self-evident to everybody, that in the matter of women and children 'friends have all things in common.'

And was I not right, Adeimantus?

Yes, he said; but what is right in this particular case, like everything else, requires to be explained; for community may be of many kinds. Please, therefore, to say what sort of community you mean. We have been long expecting that you would tell us something about the family life of your citizens—how they will bring children into the world, and rear them when they have arrived, and, in general, what is the nature of this community of women and children—for we are of opinion that the right or wrong management of such matters will have a great and paramount influence on the State for good or for evil. And now, since the question is still undetermined, and you are taking in hand another State, we have resolved, as you heard, not to let you go until you give an account of all this.

To that resolution, said Glaucon, you may regard me as saying Agreed.

And without more ado, said Thrasymachus, you may consider us all to be equally agreed.

I said, You know not what you are doing in thus assailing me: What an argument are you raising about the State! Just as I thought that I had finished, and was only too glad that I had laid this question to sleep, and was reflecting how fortunate I was in your acceptance of what I then said, you ask me to begin again at the very foundation, ignorant of what a hornet's nest of words you are stirring. Now I foresaw this gathering trouble, and avoided it.

For what purpose do you conceive that we have come here, said Thrasymachus,—to look for gold, or to hear discourse?

Yes, but discourse should have a limit.

Yes, Socrates, said Glaucon, and the whole of life is the only limit which wise men assign to the hearing of such discourses. But never mind about us; take heart yourself and answer the question in your own way: What sort of community of women and children is this which is to prevail among our guardians? and how shall we manage the period between birth and education, which seems to require the greatest care? Tell us how these things will be.

Yes, my simple friend, but the answer is the reverse of easy; many more doubts arise about this than about our previous conclusions. For the practicability of what is said may be doubted; and looked at in another point of view, whether the scheme, if ever so practicable, would be for the best, is also doubtful. Hence I feel a reluctance to approach the subject, lest our aspiration, my dear friend, should turn out to be a dream only.

Fear not, he replied, for your audience will not be hard upon you; they are not sceptical or hostile.

I said: My good friend, I suppose that you mean to encourage me by these words.

Yes, he said.

Then let me tell you that you are doing just the reverse; the encouragement which you offer would have been all very well had I myself believed that I knew what I was talking about: to declare the truth about matters of high interest which a man honours and loves among wise men who love him need occasion no fear or faltering in his mind; but to carry on an argument when you are yourself only a hesitating enquirer, which is my condition, is a dangerous and slippery thing; and the danger is not that I shall be laughed at (of which the fear would be childish), but that I shall miss the truth where I have most need to be sure of my footing, and drag my friends after me in my fall. And I pray Nemesis not to visit upon me the words which I am going to utter. For I do indeed believe that to be an involuntary homicide is a less crime than to be a deceiver about beauty or goodness or justice in the matter of laws. And that is a risk which I would rather run among enemies than among friends, and therefore you do well to encourage me.

Glaucon laughed and said: Well then, Socrates, in case you and your argument do us any serious injury you shall be acquitted beforehand of the homicide, and shall not be held to be a deceiver; take courage then and speak.

Well, I said, the law says that when a man is acquitted he is free from guilt, and what holds at law may hold in argument.

Then why should you mind?

Well, I replied, I suppose that I must retrace my steps and say what I perhaps ought to have said before in the proper place. The part of the men has been played out, and now properly enough comes the turn of the women. Of them I will proceed to speak, and the more readily since I am invited by you.

For men born and educated like our citizens, the only way, in my opinion, of arriving at a right conclusion about the possession and use of women and children is to follow the path on which we originally started, when we said that the men were to be the guardians and watchdogs of the herd.

True.

Let us further suppose the birth and education of our women to be subject to similar or nearly similar regulations; then we shall see whether the result accords with our design.

What do you mean?

What I mean may be put into the form of a question, I said: Are dogs divided into hes and shes, or do they both share equally in hunting and in keeping watch and in the other duties of dogs? or do we entrust to the males the entire and exclusive care of the flocks, while we leave the females at home, under the idea that the bearing and suckling their puppies is labour enough for them?

No, he said, they share alike; the only difference between them is that the males are stronger and the females weaker.

But can you use different animals for the same purpose, unless they are bred and fed in the same way?

You cannot.

Then, if women are to have the same duties as men, they must have the same nurture and education?

Yes.

The education which was assigned to the men was music and gymnastic.

Yes.

Then women must be taught music and gymnastic and also the art of war, which they must practise like the men?

That is the inference, I suppose.

I should rather expect, I said, that several of our proposals, if they are carried out, being unusual, may appear ridiculous.

No doubt of it.

Yes, and the most ridiculous thing of all will be the sight of women naked in the palaestra, exercising with the men, especially when they are no longer young; they certainly will not be a vision of beauty, any more than the enthusiastic old men who in spite of wrinkles and ugliness continue to frequent the gymnasia.

Yes, indeed, he said: according to present notions the proposal would be thought ridiculous.

But then, I said, as we have determined to speak our minds, we must not fear the jests of the wits which will be directed against this sort of innovation; how they will talk of women's attainments both in music and gymnastic, and above all about their wearing armour and riding upon horseback!

Very true, he replied.

Yet having begun we must go forward to the rough places of the law; at the same time begging of these gentlemen for once in their life to be serious. Not long ago, as we shall remind them, the Hellenes were of the opinion, which is still generally received among the barbarians, that the sight of a naked man was ridiculous and improper; and when first the Cretans and then the Lacedaemonians introduced the custom, the wits of that day might equally have ridiculed the innovation.

No doubt.

But when experience showed that to let all things be uncovered was far better than to cover them up, and the ludicrous effect to the outward eye vanished before the better principle which reason asserted, then the man was perceived to be a fool who directs the shafts of his ridicule at any other sight but that of folly and vice, or seriously inclines to weigh the beautiful by any other standard but that of the good.

Very true, he replied.

First, then, whether the question is to be put in jest or in earnest, let us come to an understanding about the nature of woman: Is she capable of sharing either wholly or partially in the actions of men, or not at all? And is the art of war one of those arts in which she can or can not share? That will be the best way of commencing the enquiry, and will probably lead to the fairest conclusion.

That will be much the best way.

Shall we take the other side first and begin by arguing against ourselves; in this manner the adversary's position will not be undefended.

Why not? he said.

Then let us put a speech into the mouths of our opponents. They will say: "Socrates and Glaucon, no adversary need convict you, for you yourselves, at the first foundation of the State, admitted the principle that everybody was to do the one work suited to his own nature." And certainly, if I am not mistaken, such an admission was made by us. "And do not the natures of men and women differ very much indeed?" And we shall reply: Of course they do. Then we shall be asked, "Whether the tasks assigned to men and to women should not be different, and such as are agreeable to their different natures?" Certainly they should. "But if so, have you not fallen into a serious inconsistency in saying that men and women, whose natures are so entirely different, ought to perform the same actions?"—What defence will you make for us, my good Sir, against any one who offers these objections?

That is not an easy question to answer when asked suddenly; and I shall and I do beg of you to draw out the case on our side.

These are the objections, Glaucon, and there are many others of a like kind, which I foresaw long ago; they made me afraid and reluctant to take in hand any law about the possession and nurture of women and children.

By Zeus, he said, the problem to be solved is anything but easy.

Why yes, I said, but the fact is that when a man is out of his depth, whether he has fallen into a little swimming bath or into mid ocean, he has to swim all the same.

Very true.

And must not we swim and try to reach the shore: we will hope that Arion's dolphin or some other miraculous help may save us?

I suppose so, he said.

Well then, let us see if any way of escape can be found. We acknowledged—did we not? that different natures ought to have different pursuits, and that men's and women's natures are different. And now what are we saying?—that different natures ought to have the same pursuits,—this is the inconsistency which is charged upon us.

Precisely.

Verily, Glaucon, I said, glorious is the power of the art of contradiction! Why do you say so?

Because I think that many a man falls into the practice against his will. When he thinks that he is reasoning he is really disputing, just because he cannot define and divide, and so know that of which he is speaking; and he will pursue a merely verbal opposition in the spirit of contention and not of fair discussion.

Yes, he replied, such is very often the case; but what has that to do with us and our argument?

A great deal; for there is certainly a danger of our getting unintentionally into a verbal opposition.

In what way?

Why we valiantly and pugnaciously insist upon the verbal truth, that different natures ought to have different pursuits, but we never considered at all what was the meaning of sameness or difference of nature, or why we distinguished them when we assigned different pursuits to different natures and the same to the same natures.

Why, no, he said, that was never considered by us.

I said: Suppose that by way of illustration we were to ask the question whether there is not an opposition in nature between bald men and hairy men; and if this is admitted by us, then, if bald men are cobblers, we should forbid the hairy men to be cobblers, and conversely?

That would be a jest, he said.

Yes, I said, a jest; and why? because we never meant when we constructed the State, that the opposition of natures should extend to every difference, but only to those differences which affected the pursuit in which the individual is engaged; we should have argued, for example, that a physician and one who is in mind a physician may be said to have the same nature.

True.

Whereas the physician and the carpenter have different natures?

Certainly.

And if, I said, the male and female sex appear to differ in their fitness for any art or pursuit, we should say that such pursuit or art ought to be assigned to one or the other of them; but if the difference consists only in women bearing and men begetting children, this does not amount to a proof that a woman differs from a man in respect of the sort of education she should receive; and we shall therefore continue to maintain that our guardians and their wives ought to have the same pursuits.

Very true, he said.

Next, we shall ask our opponent how, in reference to any of the pursuits or arts of civic life, the nature of a woman differs from that of a man?

That will be quite fair.

And perhaps he, like yourself, will reply that to give a sufficient answer on the instant is not easy; but after a little reflection there is no difficulty.

Yes, perhaps.

Suppose then that we invite him to accompany us in the argument, and then we may hope to show him that there is nothing peculiar in the constitution of women which would affect them in the administration of the State.

By all means.

Let us say to him: Come now, and we will ask you a question:— when you spoke of a nature gifted or not gifted in any respect, did you mean to say that one man will acquire a thing easily, another with difficulty; a little learning will lead the one to discover a great deal; whereas the other, after much study and application, no sooner learns than he forgets; or again, did you mean, that the one has a body which is a good servant to his mind, while the body of the other is a hindrance to him?—would not these be the sort of differences which distinguish the man gifted by nature from the one who is ungifted?

No one will deny that.

And can you mention any pursuit of mankind in which the male sex has not all these gifts and qualities in a higher degree than the female? Need I waste time in speaking of the art of weaving, and the management of pancakes and preserves, in which womankind does really appear to be great, and in which for her to be beaten by a man is of all things the most absurd?

You are quite right, he replied, in maintaining the general inferiority of the female sex: although many women are in many things superior to many men, yet on the whole what you say is true.

And if so, my friend, I said, there is no special faculty of administration in a state which a woman has because she is a woman, or which a man has by virtue of his sex, but the gifts of nature are alike diffused in both; all the pursuits of men are the pursuits of women also, but in all of them a woman is inferior to a man.

Very true.

Then are we to impose all our enactments on men and none of them on women?

That will never do.

One woman has a gift of healing, another not; one is a musician, and another has no music in her nature?

Very true.

And one woman has a turn for gymnastic and military exercises, and another is unwarlike and hates gymnastics?

Certainly.

And one woman is a philosopher, and another is an enemy of philosophy; one has spirit, and another is without spirit?

That is also true.

Then one woman will have the temper of a guardian, and another not. Was not the selection of the male guardians determined by differences of this sort?

Yes.

Men and women alike possess the qualities which make a guardian; they differ only in their comparative strength or weakness.

Obviously.

And those women who have such qualities are to be selected as the companions and colleagues of men who have similar qualities and whom they resemble in capacity and in character?

Very true.

And ought not the same natures to have the same pursuits?

They ought.

Then, as we were saying before, there is nothing unnatural in assigning music and gymnastic to the wives of the guardians—to that point we come round again.

Certainly not.

The law which we then enacted was agreeable to nature, and therefore not an impossibility or mere aspiration; and the contrary practice, which prevails at present, is in reality a violation of nature.

That appears to be true.

We had to consider, first, whether our proposals were possible, and secondly whether they were the most beneficial?

Yes.

And the possibility has been acknowledged?

Yes.

The very great benefit has next to be established?

Quite so.

You will admit that the same education which makes a man a good guardian will make a woman a good guardian; for their original nature is the same?

Yes.

I should like to ask you a question.

What is it?

Would you say that all men are equal in excellence, or is one man better than another?

The latter.

And in the commonwealth which we were founding do you conceive the guardians who have been brought up on our model system to be more perfect men, or the cobblers whose education has been cobbling?

What a ridiculous question!

You have answered me, I replied: Well, and may we not further say that our guardians are the best of our citizens?

By far the best.

And will not their wives be the best women?

Yes, by far the best.

And can there be anything better for the interests of the State than that the men and women of a State should be as good as possible?

There can be nothing better.

And this is what the arts of music and gymnastic, when present in such manner as we have described, will accomplish?

Certainly.

Then we have made an enactment not only possible but in the highest degree beneficial to the State?

True.

Then let the wives of our guardians strip, for their virtue will be their robe, and let them share in the toils of war and the defence of their country; only in the distribution of labours the lighter are to be assigned to the women, who are the weaker natures, but in other respects their duties are to be the same. And as for the man who laughs at naked women exercising their bodies from the best of motives, in his laughter he is plucking

'A fruit of unripe wisdom,' and he himself is ignorant of what he is laughing at, or what he is about;—for that is, and ever will be, the best of sayings, That the useful is the noble and the hurtful is the base.

Very true.

Here, then, is one difficulty in our law about women, which we may say that we have now escaped; the wave has not swallowed us up alive for enacting that the guardians of either sex should have all their pursuits in common; to the utility and also to the possibility of this arrangement the consistency of the argument with itself bears witness.

Yes, that was a mighty wave which you have escaped.

Yes, I said, but a greater is coming; you will not think much of this when you see the next.

Go on; let me see.

The law, I said, which is the sequel of this and of all that has preceded, is to the following effect,—'that the wives of our guardians are to be common, and their children are to be common, and no parent is to know his own child, nor any child his parent.'

Yes, he said, that is a much greater wave than the other; and the possibility as well as the utility of such a law are far more questionable.

I do not think, I said, that there can be any dispute about the very great utility of having wives and children in common; the possibility is quite another matter, and will be very much disputed.

I think that a good many doubts may be raised about both.

You imply that the two questions must be combined, I replied. Now I meant that you should admit the utility; and in this way, as I thought, I should escape from one of them, and then there would remain only the possibility.

But that little attempt is detected, and therefore you will please to give a defence of both.

Well, I said, I submit to my fate. Yet grant me a little favour: let me feast my mind with the dream as day dreamers are in the habit of feasting themselves when they are walking alone; for before they have discovered any means of effecting their wishes—that is a matter which never troubles them—they would rather not tire themselves by thinking about possibilities; but assuming that what they desire is already granted to them, they proceed with their plan, and delight in detailing what they mean to do when their wish has come true—that is a way which they have of not doing much good to a capacity which was never good for much. Now I myself am beginning to lose heart, and I should like, with your permission, to pass over the question of possibility at present. Assuming therefore the possibility of the proposal, I shall now proceed to enquire how the rulers will carry out these arrangements, and I shall demonstrate that our plan, if executed, will be of the greatest benefit to the State and to the guardians. First of all, then, if you have no objection, I will endeavour with your help to consider the advantages of the measure; and hereafter the question of possibility.

I have no objection; proceed.

First, I think that if our rulers and their auxiliaries are to be worthy of the name which they bear, there must be willingness to obey in the one and the power of command in the other; the guardians must themselves obey the laws, and they must also imitate the spirit of them in any details which are entrusted to their care.

That is right, he said.

You, I said, who are their legislator, having selected the men, will now select the women and give them to them;—they must be as far as possible of like natures with them; and they must live in common houses and meet at common meals. None of them will have anything specially his or her own; they will be together, and will be brought up together, and will associate at gymnastic exercises. And so they will be drawn by a necessity of their natures to have intercourse with each other—necessity is not too strong a word, I think?

Yes, he said;—necessity, not geometrical, but another sort of necessity which lovers know, and which is far more convincing and constraining to the mass of mankind.

True, I said; and this, Glaucon, like all the rest, must proceed after an orderly fashion; in a city of the blessed, licentiousness is an unholy thing which the rulers will forbid.

Yes, he said, and it ought not to be permitted.

Then clearly the next thing will be to make matrimony sacred in the highest degree, and what is most beneficial will be deemed sacred?

Exactly.

And how can marriages be made most beneficial?—that is a question which I put to you, because I see in your house dogs for hunting, and of the nobler sort of birds not a few. Now, I beseech you, do tell me, have you ever attended to their pairing and breeding?

In what particulars?

Why, in the first place, although they are all of a good sort, are not some better than others?

True.

And do you breed from them all indifferently, or do you take care to breed from the best only?

From the best.

And do you take the oldest or the youngest, or only those of ripe age?

I choose only those of ripe age.

And if care was not taken in the breeding, your dogs and birds would greatly deteriorate?

Certainly.

And the same of horses and animals in general?

Undoubtedly.

Good heavens! my dear friend, I said, what consummate skill will our rulers need if the same principle holds of the human species!

Certainly, the same principle holds; but why does this involve any particular skill?

Because, I said, our rulers will often have to practise upon the body corporate with medicines. Now you know that when patients do not require medicines, but have only to be put under a regimen, the inferior sort of practitioner is deemed to be good enough; but when medicine has to be given, then the doctor should be more of a man.

That is quite true, he said; but to what are you alluding?

I mean, I replied, that our rulers will find a considerable dose of falsehood and deceit necessary for the good of their subjects: we were saying that the use of all these things regarded as medicines might be of advantage.

And we were very right.

And this lawful use of them seems likely to be often needed in the regulations of marriages and births.

How so?

Why, I said, the principle has been already laid down that the best of either sex should be united with the best as often, and the inferior with the inferior, as seldom as possible; and that they should rear the offspring of the one sort of union, but not of the other, if the flock is to be maintained in first-rate condition. Now these goings on must be a secret which the rulers only know, or there will be a further danger of our herd, as the guardians may be termed, breaking out into rebellion.

Very true.

Had we not better appoint certain festivals at which we will bring together the brides and bridegrooms, and sacrifices will be offered and suitable hymeneal songs composed by our poets: the number of weddings is a matter which must be left to the discretion of the rulers, whose aim will be to preserve the average of population? There are many other things which they will have to consider, such as the effects of wars and diseases and any similar agencies, in order as far as this is possible to prevent the State from becoming either too large or too small.

Certainly, he replied.

We shall have to invent some ingenious kind of lots which the less worthy may draw on each occasion of our bringing them together, and then they will accuse their own ill-luck and not the rulers.

To be sure, he said.

And I think that our braver and better youth, besides their other honours and rewards, might have greater facilities of intercourse with women given them; their bravery will be a reason, and such fathers ought to have as many sons as possible.

True.

And the proper officers, whether male or female or both, for offices are to be held by women as well as by men—Yes—The proper officers will take the offspring of the good parents to the pen or fold, and there they will deposit them with certain nurses who dwell in a separate quarter; but the offspring of the inferior, or of the better when they chance to be deformed, will be put away in some mysterious, unknown place, as they should be.

Yes, he said, that must be done if the breed of the guardians is to be kept pure.

They will provide for their nurture, and will bring the mothers to the fold when they are full of milk, taking the greatest possible care that no mother recognises her own child; and other wet-nurses may be engaged if more are required. Care will also be taken that the process of suckling shall not be protracted too long; and the mothers will have no getting up at night or other trouble, but will hand over all this sort of thing to the nurses and attendants.

You suppose the wives of our guardians to have a fine easy time of it when they are having children.

Why, said I, and so they ought. Let us, however, proceed with our scheme. We were saying that the parents should be in the prime of life?

Very true.

And what is the prime of life? May it not be defined as a period of about twenty years in a woman's life, and thirty in a man's?

Which years do you mean to include?

A woman, I said, at twenty years of age may begin to bear children to the State, and continue to bear them until forty; a man may begin at five-and-twenty, when he has passed the point at which the pulse of life beats quickest, and continue to beget children until he be fifty-five.

Certainly, he said, both in men and women those years are the prime of physical as well as of intellectual vigour.

Any one above or below the prescribed ages who takes part in the public hymeneals shall be said to have done an unholy and unrighteous thing; the child of which he is the father, if it steals into life, will have been conceived under auspices very unlike the sacrifices and prayers, which at each hymeneal priestesses and priest and the whole city will offer, that the new generation may be better and more useful than their good and useful parents, whereas his child will be the offspring of darkness and strange lust.

Very true, he replied.

And the same law will apply to any one of those within the prescribed age who forms a connection with any woman in the prime of life without the sanction of the rulers; for we shall say that he is raising up a bastard to the State, uncertified and unconsecrated.

Very true, he replied.

This applies, however, only to those who are within the specified age: after that we allow them to range at will, except that a man may not marry his daughter or his daughter's daughter, or his mother or his mother's mother; and women, on the other hand, are prohibited from marrying their sons or fathers, or son's son or father's father, and so on in either direction. And we grant all this, accompanying the permission with strict orders to prevent any embryo which may come into being from seeing the light; and if any force a way to the birth, the parents must understand that the offspring of such an union cannot be maintained, and arrange accordingly.

That also, he said, is a reasonable proposition. But how will they know who are fathers and daughters, and so on?

They will never know. The way will be this:—dating from the day of the hymeneal, the bridegroom who was then married will call all the male children who are born in the seventh and tenth month afterwards his sons, and the female children his daughters, and they will call him father, and he will call their children his grandchildren, and they will call the elder generation grandfathers and grandmothers. All who were begotten at the time when their fathers and mothers came together will be called their brothers and sisters, and these, as I was saying, will be forbidden to inter-marry. This, however, is not to be understood as an absolute prohibition of the marriage of brothers and sisters; if the lot favours them, and they receive the sanction of the Pythian oracle, the law will allow them.

Quite right, he replied.

Such is the scheme, Glaucon, according to which the guardians of our State are to have their wives and families in common. And now you would have the argument show that this community is consistent with the rest of our polity, and also that nothing can be better—would you not?

Yes, certainly.

Shall we try to find a common basis by asking of ourselves what ought to be the chief aim of the legislator in making laws and in the organization of a State,—what is the greatest good, and what is the greatest evil, and then consider whether our previous description has the stamp of the good or of the evil?

By all means.

Can there be any greater evil than discord and distraction and plurality where unity ought to reign? or any greater good than the bond of unity?

There cannot.

And there is unity where there is community of pleasures and pains—where all the citizens are glad or grieved on the same occasions of joy and sorrow?

No doubt.

Yes; and where there is no common but only private feeling a State is disorganized—when you have one half of the world triumphing and the other plunged in grief at the same events happening to the city or the citizens?

Certainly.

Such differences commonly originate in a disagreement about the use of the terms 'mine' and 'not mine,' 'his' and 'not his.'

Exactly so.

And is not that the best-ordered State in which the greatest number of persons apply the terms 'mine' and 'not mine' in the same way to the same thing?

Quite true.

Or that again which most nearly approaches to the condition of the individual—as in the body, when but a finger of one of us is hurt, the whole frame, drawn towards the soul as a centre and forming one kingdom under the ruling power therein, feels the hurt and sympathizes all together with the part affected, and we say that the man has a pain in his finger; and the same expression is used about any other part of the body, which has a sensation of pain at suffering or of pleasure at the alleviation of suffering.

Very true, he replied; and I agree with you that in the best-ordered State there is the nearest approach to this common feeling which you describe.

Then when any one of the citizens experiences any good or evil, the whole State will make his case their own, and will either rejoice or sorrow with him?

Yes, he said, that is what will happen in a well-ordered State.

It will now be time, I said, for us to return to our State and see whether this or some other form is most in accordance with these fundamental principles.

Very good.

Our State like every other has rulers and subjects?

True.

All of whom will call one another citizens?

Of course.

But is there not another name which people give to their rulers in other States?

Generally they call them masters, but in democratic States they simply call them rulers.

And in our State what other name besides that of citizens do the people give the rulers?

They are called saviours and helpers, he replied.

And what do the rulers call the people?

Their maintainers and foster-fathers.

And what do they call them in other States?

Slaves.

And what do the rulers call one another in other States?

Fellow-rulers.

And what in ours?

Fellow-guardians.

Did you ever know an example in any other State of a ruler who would speak of one of his colleagues as his friend and of another as not being his friend?

Yes, very often.

And the friend he regards and describes as one in whom he has an interest, and the other as a stranger in whom he has no interest?

Exactly.

But would any of your guardians think or speak of any other guardian as a stranger?

Certainly he would not; for every one whom they meet will be regarded by them either as a brother or sister, or father or mother, or son or daughter, or as the child or parent of those who are thus connected with him.

Capital, I said; but let me ask you once more: Shall they be a family in name only; or shall they in all their actions be true to the name? For example, in the use of the word 'father,' would the care of a father be implied and the filial reverence and duty and obedience to him which the law commands; and is the violator of these duties to be regarded as an impious and unrighteous person who is not likely to receive much good either at the hands of God or of man? Are these to be or not to be the strains which the children will hear repeated in their ears by all the citizens about those who are intimated to them to be their parents and the rest of their kinsfolk?

These, he said, and none other; for what can be more ridiculous than for them to utter the names of family ties with the lips only and not to act in the spirit of them?

Then in our city the language of harmony and concord will be more often heard than in any other. As I was describing before, when any one is well or ill, the universal word will be 'with me it is well' or 'it is ill.'

Most true.

And agreeably to this mode of thinking and speaking, were we not saying that they will have their pleasures and pains in common?

Yes, and so they will.

And they will have a common interest in the same thing which they will alike call 'my own,' and having this common interest they will have a common feeling of pleasure and pain?

Yes, far more so than in other States.

And the reason of this, over and above the general constitution of the State, will be that the guardians will have a community of women and children?

That will be the chief reason.

And this unity of feeling we admitted to be the greatest good, as was implied in our own comparison of a well-ordered State to the relation of the body and the members, when affected by pleasure or pain?

That we acknowledged, and very rightly.

Then the community of wives and children among our citizens is clearly the source of the greatest good to the State?

Certainly.

And this agrees with the other principle which we were affirming,— that the guardians were not to have houses or lands or any other property; their pay was to be their food, which they were to receive from the other citizens, and they were to have no private expenses; for we intended them to preserve their true character of guardians.

Right, he replied.

Both the community of property and the community of families, as I am saying, tend to make them more truly guardians; they will not tear the city in pieces by differing about 'mine' and 'not mine;' each man dragging any acquisition which he has made into a separate house of his own, where he has a separate wife and children and private pleasures and pains; but all will be affected as far as may be by the same pleasures and pains because they are all of one opinion about what is near and dear to them, and therefore they all tend towards a common end.

Certainly, he replied.

And as they have nothing but their persons which they can call their own, suits and complaints will have no existence among them; they will be delivered from all those quarrels of which money or children or relations are the occasion.

Of course they will.

Neither will trials for assault or insult ever be likely to occur among them. For that equals should defend themselves against equals we shall maintain to be honourable and right; we shall make the protection of the person a matter of necessity.

That is good, he said.

Yes; and there is a further good in the law; viz. that if a man has a quarrel with another he will satisfy his resentment then and there, and not proceed to more dangerous lengths.

Certainly.

To the elder shall be assigned the duty of ruling and chastising the younger.

Clearly.

Nor can there be a doubt that the younger will not strike or do any other violence to an elder, unless the magistrates command him; nor will he slight him in any way. For there are two guardians, shame and fear, mighty to prevent him: shame, which makes men refrain from laying hands on those who are to them in the relation of parents; fear, that the injured one will be succoured by the others who are his brothers, sons, fathers.

That is true, he replied.

Then in every way the laws will help the citizens to keep the peace with one another?

Yes, there will be no want of peace.

And as the guardians will never quarrel among themselves there will be no danger of the rest of the city being divided either against them or against one another.

None whatever.

I hardly like even to mention the little meannesses of which they will be rid, for they are beneath notice: such, for example, as the flattery of the rich by the poor, and all the pains and pangs which men experience in bringing up a family, and in finding money to buy necessaries for their household, borrowing and then repudiating, getting how they can, and giving the money into the hands of women and slaves to keep—the many evils of so many kinds which people suffer in this way are mean enough and obvious enough, and not worth speaking of.

Yes, he said, a man has no need of eyes in order to perceive that.

And from all these evils they will be delivered, and their life will be blessed as the life of Olympic victors and yet more blessed.

How so?

The Olympic victor, I said, is deemed happy in receiving a part only of the blessedness which is secured to our citizens, who have won a more glorious victory and have a more complete maintenance at the public cost. For the victory which they have won is the salvation of the whole State; and the crown with which they and their children are crowned is the fulness of all that life needs; they receive rewards from the hands of their country while living, and after death have an honourable burial.

Yes, he said, and glorious rewards they are.

Do you remember, I said, how in the course of the previous discussion some one who shall be nameless accused us of making our guardians unhappy—they had nothing and might have possessed all things—to whom we replied that, if an occasion offered, we might perhaps hereafter consider this question, but that, as at present advised, we would make our guardians truly guardians, and that we were fashioning the State with a view to the greatest happiness, not of any particular class, but of the whole?

Yes, I remember.

And what do you say, now that the life of our protectors is made out to be far better and nobler than that of Olympic victors—is the life of shoemakers, or any other artisans, or of husbandmen, to be compared with it?

Certainly not.

At the same time I ought here to repeat what I have said elsewhere, that if any of our guardians shall try to be happy in such a manner that he will cease to be a guardian, and is not content with this safe and harmonious life, which, in our judgment, is of all lives the best, but infatuated by some youthful conceit of happiness which gets up into his head shall seek to appropriate the whole state to himself, then he will have to learn how wisely Hesiod spoke, when he said, "half is more than the whole."

If he were to consult me, I should say to him: Stay where you are, when you have the offer of such a life.

You agree then, I said, that men and women are to have a common way of life such as we have described—common education, common children; and they are to watch over the citizens in common whether abiding in the city or going out to war; they are to keep watch together, and to hunt together like dogs; and always and in all things, as far as they are able, women are to share with the men? And in so doing they will do what is best, and will not violate, but preserve the natural relation of the sexes.

I agree with you, he replied.

The enquiry, I said, has yet to be made, whether such a community be found possible—as among other animals, so also among men—and if possible, in what way possible?

You have anticipated the question which I was about to suggest.

There is no difficulty, I said, in seeing how war will be carried on by them.

How?

Why, of course they will go on expeditions together; and will take with them any of their children who are strong enough, that, after the manner of the artisan's child, they may look on at the work which they will have to do when they are grown up; and besides looking on they will have to help and be of use in war, and to wait upon their fathers and mothers. Did you never observe in the arts how the potters' boys look on and help, long before they touch the wheel?

Yes, I have.

And shall potters be more careful in educating their children and in giving them the opportunity of seeing and practising their duties than our guardians will be?

The idea is ridiculous, he said.

There is also the effect on the parents, with whom, as with other animals, the presence of their young ones will be the greatest incentive to valour.

That is quite true, Socrates; and yet if they are defeated, which may often happen in war, how great the danger is! the children will be lost as well as their parents, and the State will never recover.

True, I said; but would you never allow them to run any risk?

I am far from saying that.

Well, but if they are ever to run a risk should they not do so on some occasion when, if they escape disaster, they will be the better for it?

Clearly.

Whether the future soldiers do or do not see war in the days of their youth is a very important matter, for the sake of which some risk may fairly be incurred.

Yes, very important.

This then must be our first step,—to make our children spectators of war; but we must also contrive that they shall be secured against danger; then all will be well.

True.

Their parents may be supposed not to be blind to the risks of war, but to know, as far as human foresight can, what expeditions are safe and what dangerous?

That may be assumed.

And they will take them on the safe expeditions and be cautious about the dangerous ones?

True.

And they will place them under the command of experienced veterans who will be their leaders and teachers?

Very properly.

Still, the dangers of war cannot be always foreseen; there is a good deal of chance about them?

True.

Then against such chances the children must be at once furnished with wings, in order that in the hour of need they may fly away and escape.

What do you mean? he said.

I mean that we must mount them on horses in their earliest youth, and when they have learnt to ride, take them on horseback to see war: the horses must not be spirited and warlike, but the most tractable and yet the swiftest that can be had. In this way they will get an excellent view of what is hereafter to be their own business; and if there is danger they have only to follow their elder leaders and escape.

I believe that you are right, he said.

Next, as to war; what are to be the relations of your soldiers to one another and to their enemies? I should be inclined to propose that the soldier who leaves his rank or throws away his arms, or is guilty of any other act of cowardice, should be degraded into the rank of a husbandman or artisan. What do you think?

By all means, I should say.

And he who allows himself to be taken prisoner may as well be made a present of to his enemies; he is their lawful prey, and let them do what they like with him.

Certainly.

But the hero who has distinguished himself, what shall be done to him? In the first place, he shall receive honour in the army from his youthful comrades; every one of them in succession shall crown him. What do you say?

I approve.

And what do you say to his receiving the right hand of fellowship?

To that too, I agree.

But you will hardly agree to my next proposal.

What is your proposal?

That he should kiss and be kissed by them.

Most certainly, and I should be disposed to go further, and say: Let no one whom he has a mind to kiss refuse to be kissed by him while the expedition lasts. So that if there be a lover in the army, whether his love be youth or maiden, he may be more eager to win the prize of valour.

Capital, I said. That the brave man is to have more wives than others has been already determined: and he is to have first choices in such matters more than others, in order that he may have as many children as possible?

Agreed.

Again, there is another manner in which, according to Homer, brave youths should be honoured; for he tells how Ajax, after he had distinguished himself in battle, was rewarded with long chines, which seems to be a compliment appropriate to a hero in the flower of his age, being not only a tribute of honour but also a very strengthening thing.

Most true, he said.

Then in this, I said, Homer shall be our teacher; and we too, at sacrifices and on the like occasions, will honour the brave according to the measure of their valour, whether men or women, with hymns and those other distinctions which we were mentioning; also with 'seats of precedence, and meats and full cups;' and in honouring them, we shall be at the same time training them.

That, he replied, is excellent.

Yes, I said; and when a man dies gloriously in war shall we not say, in the first place, that he is of the golden race?

To be sure.

Nay, have we not the authority of Hesiod for affirming that when they are dead

'They are holy angels upon the earth, authors of good, averters of evil, the guardians of speech-gifted men'?

Yes; and we accept his authority.

We must learn of the god how we are to order the sepulture of divine and heroic personages, and what is to be their special distinction; and we must do as he bids?

By all means.

And in ages to come we will reverence them and kneel before their sepulchres as at the graves of heroes. And not only they but any who are deemed pre-eminently good, whether they die from age, or in any other way, shall be admitted to the same honours.

That is very right, he said.

Next, how shall our soldiers treat their enemies? What about this?

In what respect do you mean?

First of all, in regard to slavery? Do you think it right that Hellenes should enslave Hellenic States, or allow others to enslave them, if they can help? Should not their custom be to spare them, considering the danger which there is that the whole race may one day fall under the yoke of the barbarians?

To spare them is infinitely better.

Then no Hellene should be owned by them as a slave; that is a rule which they will observe and advise the other Hellenes to observe.

Certainly, he said; they will in this way be united against the barbarians and will keep their hands off one another.

Next as to the slain; ought the conquerors, I said, to take anything but their armour? Does not the practice of despoiling an enemy afford an excuse for not facing the battle? Cowards skulk about the dead, pretending that they are fulfilling a duty, and many an army before now has been lost from this love of plunder.

Very true.

And is there not illiberality and avarice in robbing a corpse, and also a degree of meanness and womanishness in making an enemy of the dead body when the real enemy has flown away and left only his fighting gear behind him,—is not this rather like a dog who cannot get at his assailant, quarrelling with the stones which strike him instead?

Very like a dog, he said.

Then we must abstain from spoiling the dead or hindering their burial?

Yes, he replied, we most certainly must.

Neither shall we offer up arms at the temples of the gods, least of all the arms of Hellenes, if we care to maintain good feeling with other Hellenes; and, indeed, we have reason to fear that the offering of spoils taken from kinsmen may be a pollution unless commanded by the god himself?

Very true.

Again, as to the devastation of Hellenic territory or the burning of houses, what is to be the practice?

May I have the pleasure, he said, of hearing your opinion?

Both should be forbidden, in my judgment; I would take the annual produce and no more. Shall I tell you why?

Pray do.

Why, you see, there is a difference in the names 'discord' and 'war,' and I imagine that there is also a difference in their natures; the one is expressive of what is internal and domestic, the other of what is external and foreign; and the first of the two is termed discord, and only the second, war.

That is a very proper distinction, he replied.

And may I not observe with equal propriety that the Hellenic race is all united together by ties of blood and friendship, and alien and strange to the barbarians?

Very good, he said.

And therefore when Hellenes fight with barbarians and barbarians with Hellenes, they will be described by us as being at war when they fight, and by nature enemies, and this kind of antagonism should be called war; but when Hellenes fight with one another we shall say that Hellas is then in a state of disorder and discord, they being by nature friends; and such enmity is to be called discord.

I agree.

Consider then, I said, when that which we have acknowledged to be discord occurs, and a city is divided, if both parties destroy the lands and burn the houses of one another, how wicked does the strife appear! No true lover of his country would bring himself to tear in pieces his own nurse and mother: There might be reason in the conqueror depriving the conquered of their harvest, but still they would have the idea of peace in their hearts and would not mean to go on fighting for ever.

Yes, he said, that is a better temper than the other.

And will not the city, which you are founding, be an Hellenic city?

It ought to be, he replied.

Then will not the citizens be good and civilized?

Yes, very civilized.

And will they not be lovers of Hellas, and think of Hellas as their own land, and share in the common temples?

Most certainly.

And any difference which arises among them will be regarded by them as discord only—a quarrel among friends, which is not to be called a war?

Certainly not.

Then they will quarrel as those who intend some day to be reconciled?

Certainly.

They will use friendly correction, but will not enslave or destroy their opponents; they will be correctors, not enemies?

Just so.

And as they are Hellenes themselves they will not devastate Hellas, nor will they burn houses, nor ever suppose that the whole population of a city—men, women, and children—are equally their enemies, for they know that the guilt of war is always confined to a few persons and that the many are their friends. And for all these reasons they will be unwilling to waste their lands and rase their houses; their enmity to them will only last until the many innocent sufferers have compelled the guilty few to give satisfaction?

I agree, he said, that our citizens should thus deal with their Hellenic enemies; and with barbarians as the Hellenes now deal with one another.

Then let us enact this law also for our guardians:—that they are neither to devastate the lands of Hellenes nor to burn their houses.

Agreed; and we may agree also in thinking that these, like all our previous enactments, are very good.

But still I must say, Socrates, that if you are allowed to go on in this way you will entirely forget the other question which at the commencement of this discussion you thrust aside:—Is such an order of things possible, and how, if at all? For I am quite ready to acknowledge that the plan which you propose, if only feasible, would do all sorts of good to the State. I will add, what you have omitted, that your citizens will be the bravest of warriors, and will never leave their ranks, for they will all know one another, and each will call the other father, brother, son; and if you suppose the women to join their armies, whether in the same rank or in the rear, either as a terror to the enemy, or as auxiliaries in case of need, I know that they will then be absolutely invincible; and there are many domestic advantages which might also be mentioned and which I also fully acknowledge: but, as I admit all these advantages and as many more as you please, if only this State of yours were to come into existence, we need say no more about them; assuming then the existence of the State, let us now turn to the question of possibility and ways and means—the rest may be left.

If I loiter for a moment, you instantly make a raid upon me, I said, and have no mercy; I have hardly escaped the first and second waves, and you seem not to be aware that you are now bringing upon me the third, which is the greatest and heaviest. When you have seen and heard the third wave, I think you will be more considerate and will acknowledge that some fear and hesitation was natural respecting a proposal so extraordinary as that which I have now to state and investigate.

The more appeals of this sort which you make, he said, the more determined are we that you shall tell us how such a State is possible: speak out and at once.

Let me begin by reminding you that we found our way hither in the search after justice and injustice.

True, he replied; but what of that?

I was only going to ask whether, if we have discovered them, we are to require that the just man should in nothing fail of absolute justice; or may we be satisfied with an approximation, and the attainment in him of a higher degree of justice than is to be found in other men?

The approximation will be enough.

We were enquiring into the nature of absolute justice and into the character of the perfectly just, and into injustice and the perfectly unjust, that we might have an ideal. We were to look at these in order that we might judge of our own happiness and unhappiness according to the standard which they exhibited and the degree in which we resembled them, but not with any view of showing that they could exist in fact.

True, he said.

Would a painter be any the worse because, after having delineated with consummate art an ideal of a perfectly beautiful man, he was unable to show that any such man could ever have existed?

He would be none the worse.

Well, and were we not creating an ideal of a perfect State?

To be sure.

And is our theory a worse theory because we are unable to prove the possibility of a city being ordered in the manner described?

Surely not, he replied.

That is the truth, I said. But if, at your request, I am to try and show how and under what conditions the possibility is highest, I must ask you, having this in view, to repeat your former admissions.

What admissions?

I want to know whether ideals are ever fully realized in language? Does not the word express more than the fact, and must not the actual, whatever a man may think, always, in the nature of things, fall short of the truth? What do you say?

I agree.

Then you must not insist on my proving that the actual State will in every respect coincide with the ideal: if we are only able to discover how a city may be governed nearly as we proposed, you will admit that we have discovered the possibility which you demand; and will be contented. I am sure that I should be contented—will not you?

Yes, I will.

Let me next endeavour to show what is that fault in States which is the cause of their present maladministration, and what is the least change which will enable a State to pass into the truer form; and let the change, if possible, be of one thing only, or, if not, of two; at any rate, let the changes be as few and slight as possible.

Certainly, he replied.

I think, I said, that there might be a reform of the State if only one change were made, which is not a slight or easy though still a possible one.

What is it? he said.

Now then, I said, I go to meet that which I liken to the greatest of the waves; yet shall the word be spoken, even though the wave break and drown me in laughter and dishonour; and do you mark my words.

Proceed.

I said: 'Until philosophers are kings, or the kings and princes of this world have the spirit and power of philosophy, and political greatness and wisdom meet in one, and those commoner natures who pursue either to the exclusion of the other are compelled to stand aside, cities will never have rest from their evils,—nor the human race, as I believe,—and then only will this our State have a possibility of life and behold the light of day.' Such was the thought, my dear Glaucon, which I would fain have uttered if it had not seemed too extravagant; for to be convinced that in no other State can there be happiness private or public is indeed a hard thing.

Socrates, what do you mean? I would have you consider that the word which you have uttered is one at which numerous persons, and very respectable persons too, in a figure pulling off their coats all in a moment, and seizing any weapon that comes to hand, will run at you might and main, before you know where you are, intending to do heaven knows what; and if you don't prepare an answer, and put yourself in motion, you will be 'pared by their fine wits,' and no mistake.

You got me into the scrape, I said.

And I was quite right; however, I will do all I can to get you out of it; but I can only give you good-will and good advice, and, perhaps, I may be able to fit answers to your questions better than another—that is all. And now, having such an auxiliary, you must do your best to show the unbelievers that you are right.

I ought to try, I said, since you offer me such invaluable assistance. And I think that, if there is to be a chance of our escaping, we must explain to them whom we mean when we say that philosophers are to rule in the State; then we shall be able to defend ourselves: There will be discovered to be some natures who ought to study philosophy and to be leaders in the State; and others who are not born to be philosophers, and are meant to be followers rather than leaders.

Then now for a definition, he said.

Follow me, I said, and I hope that I may in some way or other be able to give you a satisfactory explanation.

Proceed.

I dare say that you remember, and therefore I need not remind you, that a lover, if he is worthy of the name, ought to show his love, not to some one part of that which he loves, but to the whole.

I really do not understand, and therefore beg of you to assist my memory.

Another person, I said, might fairly reply as you do; but a man of pleasure like yourself ought to know that all who are in the flower of youth do somehow or other raise a pang or emotion in a lover's breast, and are thought by him to be worthy of his affectionate regards. Is not this a way which you have with the fair: one has a snub nose, and you praise his charming face; the hook-nose of another has, you say, a royal look; while he who is neither snub nor hooked has the grace of regularity: the dark visage is manly, the fair are children of the gods; and as to the sweet 'honey pale,' as they are called, what is the very name but the invention of a lover who talks in diminutives, and is not averse to paleness if appearing on the cheek of youth? In a word, there is no excuse which you will not make, and nothing which you will not say, in order not to lose a single flower that blooms in the spring-time of youth.

If you make me an authority in matters of love, for the sake of the argument, I assent.

And what do you say of lovers of wine? Do you not see them doing the same? They are glad of any pretext of drinking any wine.

Very good.

And the same is true of ambitious men; if they cannot command an army, they are willing to command a file; and if they cannot be honoured by really great and important persons, they are glad to be honoured by lesser and meaner people,—but honour of some kind they must have.

Exactly.

Once more let me ask: Does he who desires any class of goods, desire the whole class or a part only?

The whole.

And may we not say of the philosopher that he is a lover, not of a part of wisdom only, but of the whole?

Yes, of the whole.

And he who dislikes learning, especially in youth, when he has no power of judging what is good and what is not, such an one we maintain not to be a philosopher or a lover of knowledge, just as he who refuses his food is not hungry, and may be said to have a bad appetite and not a good one?

Very true, he said.

Whereas he who has a taste for every sort of knowledge and who is curious to learn and is never satisfied, may be justly termed a philosopher? Am I not right?

Glaucon said: If curiosity makes a philosopher, you will find many a strange being will have a title to the name. All the lovers of sights have a delight in learning, and must therefore be included. Musical amateurs, too, are a folk strangely out of place among philosophers, for they are the last persons in the world who would come to anything like a philosophical discussion, if they could help, while they run about at the Dionysiac festivals as if they had let out their ears to hear every chorus; whether the performance is in town or country—that makes no difference—they are there. Now are we to maintain that all these and any who have similar tastes, as well as the professors of quite minor arts, are philosophers?

Certainly not, I replied; they are only an imitation.

He said: Who then are the true philosophers?

Those, I said, who are lovers of the vision of truth.

That is also good, he said; but I should like to know what you mean?

To another, I replied, I might have a difficulty in explaining; but I am sure that you will admit a proposition which I am about to make.

What is the proposition?

That since beauty is the opposite of ugliness, they are two?

Certainly.

And inasmuch as they are two, each of them is one?

True again.

And of just and unjust, good and evil, and of every other class, the same remark holds: taken singly, each of them is one; but from the various combinations of them with actions and things and with one another, they are seen in all sorts of lights and appear many?

Very true.

And this is the distinction which I draw between the sight-loving, art-loving, practical class and those of whom I am speaking, and who are alone worthy of the name of philosophers.

How do you distinguish them? he said.

The lovers of sounds and sights, I replied, are, as I conceive, fond of fine tones and colours and forms and all the artificial products that are made out of them, but their mind is incapable of seeing or loving absolute beauty.

True, he replied.

Few are they who are able to attain to the sight of this.

Very true.

And he who, having a sense of beautiful things has no sense of absolute beauty, or who, if another lead him to a knowledge of that beauty is unable to follow—of such an one I ask, Is he awake or in a dream only? Reflect: is not the dreamer, sleeping or waking, one who likens dissimilar things, who puts the copy in the place of the real object?

I should certainly say that such an one was dreaming.

But take the case of the other, who recognises the existence of absolute beauty and is able to distinguish the idea from the objects which participate in the idea, neither putting the objects in the place of the idea nor the idea in the place of the objects—is he a dreamer, or is he awake?

He is wide awake.

And may we not say that the mind of the one who knows has knowledge, and that the mind of the other, who opines only, has opinion?

Certainly.

But suppose that the latter should quarrel with us and dispute our statement, can we administer any soothing cordial or advice to him, without revealing to him that there is sad disorder in his wits?

We must certainly offer him some good advice, he replied.

Come, then, and let us think of something to say to him. Shall we begin by assuring him that he is welcome to any knowledge which he may have, and that we are rejoiced at his having it? But we should like to ask him a question: Does he who has knowledge know something or nothing? (You must answer for him.)

I answer that he knows something.

Something that is or is not?

Something that is; for how can that which is not ever be known?

And are we assured, after looking at the matter from many points of view, that absolute being is or may be absolutely known, but that the utterly non-existent is utterly unknown?

Nothing can be more certain.

Good. But if there be anything which is of such a nature as to be and not to be, that will have a place intermediate between pure being and the absolute negation of being?

Yes, between them.

And, as knowledge corresponded to being and ignorance of necessity to not-being, for that intermediate between being and not-being there has to be discovered a corresponding intermediate between ignorance and knowledge, if there be such?

Certainly.

Do we admit the existence of opinion?

Undoubtedly.

As being the same with knowledge, or another faculty?

Another faculty.

Then opinion and knowledge have to do with different kinds of matter corresponding to this difference of faculties?

Yes.

And knowledge is relative to being and knows being. But before I proceed further I will make a division.

What division?

I will begin by placing faculties in a class by themselves: they are powers in us, and in all other things, by which we do as we do. Sight and hearing, for example, I should call faculties. Have I clearly explained the class which I mean?

Yes, I quite understand.

Then let me tell you my view about them. I do not see them, and therefore the distinctions of figure, colour, and the like, which enable me to discern the differences of some things, do not apply to them. In speaking of a faculty I think only of its sphere and its result; and that which has the same sphere and the same result I call the same faculty, but that which has another sphere and another result I call different. Would that be your way of speaking?

Yes.

And will you be so very good as to answer one more question? Would you say that knowledge is a faculty, or in what class would you place it?

Certainly knowledge is a faculty, and the mightiest of all faculties.

And is opinion also a faculty?

Certainly, he said; for opinion is that with which we are able to form an opinion.

And yet you were acknowledging a little while ago that knowledge is not the same as opinion?

Why, yes, he said: how can any reasonable being ever identify that which is infallible with that which errs?

An excellent answer, proving, I said, that we are quite conscious of a distinction between them.

Yes.

Then knowledge and opinion having distinct powers have also distinct spheres or subject-matters?

That is certain.

Being is the sphere or subject-matter of knowledge, and knowledge is to know the nature of being?

Yes.

And opinion is to have an opinion?

Yes.

And do we know what we opine? or is the subject-matter of opinion the same as the subject-matter of knowledge?

Nay, he replied, that has been already disproven; if difference in faculty implies difference in the sphere or subject-matter, and if, as we were saying, opinion and knowledge are distinct faculties, then the sphere of knowledge and of opinion cannot be the same.

Then if being is the subject-matter of knowledge, something else must be the subject-matter of opinion?

Yes, something else.

Well then, is not-being the subject-matter of opinion? or, rather, how can there be an opinion at all about not-being? Reflect: when a man has an opinion, has he not an opinion about something? Can he have an opinion which is an opinion about nothing?

Impossible.

He who has an opinion has an opinion about some one thing?

Yes.

And not-being is not one thing but, properly speaking, nothing?

True.

Of not-being, ignorance was assumed to be the necessary correlative; of being, knowledge?

True, he said.

Then opinion is not concerned either with being or with not-being?

Not with either.

And can therefore neither be ignorance nor knowledge?

That seems to be true.

But is opinion to be sought without and beyond either of them, in a greater clearness than knowledge, or in a greater darkness than ignorance?

In neither.

Then I suppose that opinion appears to you to be darker than knowledge, but lighter than ignorance?

Both; and in no small degree.

And also to be within and between them?

Yes.

Then you would infer that opinion is intermediate?

No question.

But were we not saying before, that if anything appeared to be of a sort which is and is not at the same time, that sort of thing would appear also to lie in the interval between pure being and absolute not-being; and that the corresponding faculty is neither knowledge nor ignorance, but will be found in the interval between them?

True.

And in that interval there has now been discovered something which we call opinion?

There has.

Then what remains to be discovered is the object which partakes equally of the nature of being and not-being, and cannot rightly be termed either, pure and simple; this unknown term, when discovered, we may truly call the subject of opinion, and assign each to their proper faculty,—the extremes to the faculties of the extremes and the mean to the faculty of the mean.

True.

This being premised, I would ask the gentleman who is of opinion that there is no absolute or unchangeable idea of beauty—in whose opinion the beautiful is the manifold—he, I say, your lover of beautiful sights, who cannot bear to be told that the beautiful is one, and the just is one, or that anything is one—to him I would appeal, saying, Will you be so very kind, sir, as to tell us whether, of all these beautiful things, there is one which will not be found ugly; or of the just, which will not be found unjust; or of the holy, which will not also be unholy?

No, he replied; the beautiful will in some point of view be found ugly; and the same is true of the rest.

And may not the many which are doubles be also halves?—doubles, that is, of one thing, and halves of another?

Quite true.

And things great and small, heavy and light, as they are termed, will not be denoted by these any more than by the opposite names?

True; both these and the opposite names will always attach to all of them.

And can any one of those many things which are called by particular names be said to be this rather than not to be this?

He replied: They are like the punning riddles which are asked at feasts or the children's puzzle about the eunuch aiming at the bat, with what he hit him, as they say in the puzzle, and upon what the bat was sitting. The individual objects of which I am speaking are also a riddle, and have a double sense: nor can you fix them in your mind, either as being or not-being, or both, or neither.

Then what will you do with them? I said. Can they have a better place than between being and not-being? For they are clearly not in greater darkness or negation than not-being, or more full of light and existence than being.

That is quite true, he said.

Thus then we seem to have discovered that the many ideas which the multitude entertain about the beautiful and about all other things are tossing about in some region which is half-way between pure being and pure not-being?

We have.

Yes; and we had before agreed that anything of this kind which we might find was to be described as matter of opinion, and not as matter of knowledge; being the intermediate flux which is caught and detained by the intermediate faculty.

Quite true.

Then those who see the many beautiful, and who yet neither see absolute beauty, nor can follow any guide who points the way thither; who see the many just, and not absolute justice, and the like,—such persons may be said to have opinion but not knowledge?

That is certain.

But those who see the absolute and eternal and immutable may be said to know, and not to have opinion only?

211

Neither can that be denied.

The one love and embrace the subjects of knowledge, the other those of opinion? The latter are the same, as I dare say you will remember, who listened to sweet sounds and gazed upon fair colours, but would not tolerate the existence of absolute beauty.

Yes, I remember.

Shall we then be guilty of any impropriety in calling them lovers of opinion rather than lovers of wisdom, and will they be very angry with us for thus describing them?

I shall tell them not to be angry; no man should be angry at what is true.

But those who love the truth in each thing are to be called lovers of wisdom and not lovers of opinion.

Assuredly.

# BOOK VI

And thus, Glaucon, after the argument has gone a weary way, the true and the false philosophers have at length appeared in view.

I do not think, he said, that the way could have been shortened.

I suppose not, I said; and yet I believe that we might have had a better view of both of them if the discussion could have been confined to this one subject and if there were not many other questions awaiting us, which he who desires to see in what respect the life of the just differs from that of the unjust must consider.

And what is the next question? he asked.

Surely, I said, the one which follows next in order. Inasmuch as philosophers only are able to grasp the eternal and unchangeable, and those who wander in the region of the many and variable are not philosophers, I must ask you which of the two classes should be the rulers of our State?

And how can we rightly answer that question?

Whichever of the two are best able to guard the laws and institutions of our State—let them be our guardians.

Very good.

Neither, I said, can there be any question that the guardian who is to keep anything should have eyes rather than no eyes?

There can be no question of that.

And are not those who are verily and indeed wanting in the knowledge of the true being of each thing, and who have in their souls no clear pattern, and are unable as with a painter's eye to look at the absolute truth and to that original to repair, and having perfect vision of the other world to order the laws about beauty, goodness, justice in this, if not already ordered, and to guard and preserve the order of them—are not such persons, I ask, simply blind?

Truly, he replied, they are much in that condition.

And shall they be our guardians when there are others who, besides being their equals in experience and falling short of them in no particular of virtue, also know the very truth of each thing?

There can be no reason, he said, for rejecting those who have this greatest of all great qualities; they must always have the first place unless they fail in some other respect.

Suppose then, I said, that we determine how far they can unite this and the other excellences.

By all means.

In the first place, as we began by observing, the nature of the philosopher has to be ascertained. We must come to an understanding about him, and, when we have done so, then, if I am not mistaken, we shall also acknowledge that such an union of qualities is possible, and that those in whom they are united, and those only, should be rulers in the State.

What do you mean?

Let us suppose that philosophical minds always love knowledge of a sort which shows them the eternal nature not varying from generation and corruption.

Agreed.

And further, I said, let us agree that they are lovers of all true being; there is no part whether greater or less, or more or less honourable, which they are willing to renounce; as we said before of the lover and the man of ambition.

True.

And if they are to be what we were describing, is there not another quality which they should also possess?

What quality?

Truthfulness: they will never intentionally receive into their mind falsehood, which is their detestation, and they will love the truth.

Yes, that may be safely affirmed of them.

'May be,' my friend, I replied, is not the word; say rather 'must be affirmed:' for he whose nature is amorous of anything cannot help loving all that belongs or is akin to the object of his affections.

Right, he said.

And is there anything more akin to wisdom than truth?

How can there be?

Can the same nature be a lover of wisdom and a lover of falsehood?

Never.

The true lover of learning then must from his earliest youth, as far as in him lies, desire all truth?

Assuredly.

But then again, as we know by experience, he whose desires are strong in one direction will have them weaker in others; they will be like a stream which has been drawn off into another channel.

True.

He whose desires are drawn towards knowledge in every form will be absorbed in the pleasures of the soul, and will hardly feel bodily pleasure—I mean, if he be a true philosopher and not a sham one.

That is most certain.

Such an one is sure to be temperate and the reverse of covetous; for the motives which make another man desirous of having and spending, have no place in his character.

Very true.

Another criterion of the philosophical nature has also to be considered.

What is that?

There should be no secret corner of illiberality; nothing can be more antagonistic than meanness to a soul which is ever longing after the whole of things both divine and human.

Most true, he replied.

Then how can he who has magnificence of mind and is the spectator of all time and all existence, think much of human life?

He cannot.

Or can such an one account death fearful?

No indeed.

Then the cowardly and mean nature has no part in true philosophy?

Certainly not.

Or again: can he who is harmoniously constituted, who is not covetous or mean, or a boaster, or a coward—can he, I say, ever be unjust or hard in his dealings?

Impossible.

Then you will soon observe whether a man is just and gentle, or rude and unsociable; these are the signs which distinguish even in youth the philosophical nature from the unphilosophical.

True.

There is another point which should be remarked.

What point?

Whether he has or has not a pleasure in learning; for no one will love that which gives him pain, and in which after much toil he makes little progress.

Certainly not.

And again, if he is forgetful and retains nothing of what he learns, will he not be an empty vessel?

That is certain.

Labouring in vain, he must end in hating himself and his fruitless occupation? Yes.

Then a soul which forgets cannot be ranked among genuine philosophic natures; we must insist that the philosopher should have a good memory?

Certainly.

And once more, the inharmonious and unseemly nature can only tend to disproportion?

Undoubtedly.

And do you consider truth to be akin to proportion or to disproportion?

To proportion.

Then, besides other qualities, we must try to find a naturally well-proportioned and gracious mind, which will move spontaneously towards the true being of everything.

Certainly.

Well, and do not all these qualities, which we have been enumerating, go together, and are they not, in a manner, necessary to a soul, which is to have a full and perfect participation of being?

They are absolutely necessary, he replied.

And must not that be a blameless study which he only can pursue who has the gift of a good memory, and is quick to learn,—noble, gracious, the friend of truth, justice, courage, temperance, who are his kindred?

The god of jealousy himself, he said, could find no fault with such a study.

And to men like him, I said, when perfected by years and education, and to these only you will entrust the State.

Here Adeimantus interposed and said: To these statements, Socrates, no one can offer a reply; but when you talk in this way, a strange feeling passes over the minds of your hearers: They fancy that they are led astray a little at each step in the argument, owing to their own want of skill in asking and answering questions; these littles accumulate, and at the end of the discussion they are found to have sustained a mighty overthrow and all their former notions appear to be turned upside down. And as unskilful players of draughts are at last shut up by their more skilful adversaries and have no piece to move, so they too find themselves shut up at last; for they have nothing to say in this new game of which words are the counters; and yet all the time they are in the right. The observation is suggested to me by what is now occurring. For any one of us might say, that although in words he is not able to meet you at each step of the argument, he sees as a fact that the votaries of philosophy, when they carry on the study, not only in youth as a part of education, but as the pursuit of their maturer years, most of them become strange monsters, not to say utter rogues, and that those who may be considered the best of them are made useless to the world by the very study which you extol.

Well, and do you think that those who say so are wrong?

I cannot tell, he replied; but I should like to know what is your opinion.

Hear my answer; I am of opinion that they are quite right.

Then how can you be justified in saying that cities will not cease from evil until philosophers rule in them, when philosophers are acknowledged by us to be of no use to them?

You ask a question, I said, to which a reply can only be given in a parable.

Yes, Socrates; and that is a way of speaking to which you are not at all accustomed, I suppose.

I perceive, I said, that you are vastly amused at having plunged me into such a hopeless discussion; but now hear the parable, and then you will be still more amused at the meagreness of my imagination: for the manner in which the best men are treated in their own States is so grievous that no single thing on earth is comparable to it; and therefore, if I am to plead their cause, I must have recourse to fiction, and put together a figure made up of many things, like the fabulous unions of goats and stags which are found in pictures. Imagine then a fleet or a ship in which there is a captain who is taller and stronger than any of the crew, but he is a little deaf and has a similar infirmity in sight, and his knowledge of navigation is not much better. The sailors are quarrelling with one another about the steering—every one is of opinion that he has a right to steer, though he has never learned the art of navigation and cannot tell who taught him or when he learned, and will further assert that it cannot be taught, and they are ready to cut in pieces any one who says the contrary. They throng about the captain, begging and praying him to commit the helm to them; and if at any time they do not prevail, but others are preferred to them, they kill the others or throw them overboard, and having first chained up the noble captain's senses with drink or some narcotic drug, they mutiny and take possession of the ship and make free with the stores; thus, eating and drinking, they proceed on their voyage in such manner as might be expected of them. Him who is their partisan and cleverly aids them in their plot for getting the ship out of the captain's hands into their own whether by force or persuasion, they compliment with the name of sailor, pilot, able seaman, and abuse the other sort of man, whom they call a good-for-nothing; but that the true pilot must pay attention to the year and seasons and sky and stars and winds, and whatever else belongs to his art, if he intends to be really qualified for the command of a ship, and that he must and will be the steerer, whether other people like or not—the possibility of this union of authority with the steerer's art has never seriously entered into their thoughts or been made part of their calling. Now in vessels which are in a state of mutiny and by sailors who are mutineers, how will the true pilot be regarded? Will he not be called by them a prater, a star-gazer, a good-for-nothing?

Of course, said Adeimantus.

Then you will hardly need, I said, to hear the interpretation of the figure, which describes the true philosopher in his relation to the State; for you understand already.

Certainly.

Then suppose you now take this parable to the gentleman who is surprised at finding that philosophers have no honour in their cities; explain it to him and try to convince him that their having honour would be far more extraordinary.

I will.

Say to him, that, in deeming the best votaries of philosophy to be useless to the rest of the world, he is right; but also tell him to attribute their uselessness to the fault of those who will not use them, and not to themselves. The pilot should not humbly beg the sailors to be commanded by him—that is not the order of nature; neither are 'the wise to go to the doors of the rich'—the ingenious author of this saying told a lie—but the truth is, that, when a man is ill, whether he be rich or poor, to the physician he must go, and he who wants to be governed, to him who is able to govern. The ruler who is good for anything ought not to beg his subjects to be ruled by him; although the present governors of mankind are of a different stamp; they may be justly compared to the mutinous sailors, and the true helmsmen to those who are called by them good-for-nothings and star-gazers.

Precisely so, he said.

For these reasons, and among men like these, philosophy, the noblest pursuit of all, is not likely to be much esteemed by those of the opposite faction; not that the greatest and most lasting injury is done to her by her opponents, but by her own professing followers, the same of whom you suppose the accuser to say, that the greater number of them are arrant rogues, and the best are useless; in which opinion I agreed.

Yes.

And the reason why the good are useless has now been explained?

True.

Then shall we proceed to show that the corruption of the majority is also unavoidable, and that this is not to be laid to the charge of philosophy any more than the other?

By all means.

And let us ask and answer in turn, first going back to the description of the gentle and noble nature. Truth, as you will remember, was his leader, whom he followed always and in all things; failing in this, he was an impostor, and had no part or lot in true philosophy.

Yes, that was said.

Well, and is not this one quality, to mention no others, greatly at variance with present notions of him?

Certainly, he said.

And have we not a right to say in his defence, that the true lover of knowledge is always striving after being—that is his nature; he will not rest in the multiplicity of individuals which is an appearance only, but will go on—the keen edge will not be blunted, nor the force of his desire abate until he have attained the knowledge of the true nature of every essence by a sympathetic and kindred power in the soul, and by that power drawing near and mingling and becoming incorporate with very being, having begotten mind and truth, he will have knowledge and will live and grow truly, and then, and not till then, will he cease from his travail.

Nothing, he said, can be more just than such a description of him.

And will the love of a lie be any part of a philosopher's nature? Will he not utterly hate a lie?

He will.

And when truth is the captain, we cannot suspect any evil of the band which he leads?

Impossible.

Justice and health of mind will be of the company, and temperance will follow after?

True, he replied.

Neither is there any reason why I should again set in array the philosopher's virtues, as you will doubtless remember that courage, magnificence, apprehension, memory, were his natural gifts. And you objected that, although no one could deny what I then said, still, if you leave words and look at facts, the persons who are thus described are some of them manifestly useless, and the greater number utterly depraved; we were then led to enquire into the grounds of these accusations, and have now arrived at the point of asking why are the majority bad, which question of necessity brought us back to the examination and definition of the true philosopher.

Exactly.

And we have next to consider the corruptions of the philosophic nature, why so many are spoiled and so few escape spoiling—I am speaking of those who were said to be useless but not wicked—and, when we have done with them, we will speak of the imitators of philosophy, what manner of men are they who aspire after a profession which is above them and of which they are unworthy, and then, by their manifold inconsistencies, bring upon philosophy, and upon all philosophers, that universal reprobation of which we speak.

What are these corruptions? he said.

I will see if I can explain them to you. Every one will admit that a nature having in perfection all the qualities which we required in a philosopher, is a rare plant which is seldom seen among men.

Rare indeed.

And what numberless and powerful causes tend to destroy these rare natures!

What causes?

In the first place there are their own virtues, their courage, temperance, and the rest of them, every one of which praiseworthy qualities (and this is a most singular circumstance) destroys and distracts from philosophy the soul which is the possessor of them.

That is very singular, he replied.

Then there are all the ordinary goods of life—beauty, wealth, strength, rank, and great connections in the State—you understand the sort of things—these also have a corrupting and distracting effect.

I understand; but I should like to know more precisely what you mean about them.

Grasp the truth as a whole, I said, and in the right way; you will then have no difficulty in apprehending the preceding remarks, and they will no longer appear strange to you.

And how am I to do so? he asked.

Why, I said, we know that all germs or seeds, whether vegetable or animal, when they fail to meet with proper nutriment or climate or soil, in proportion to their vigour, are all the more sensitive to the want of a suitable environment, for evil is a greater enemy to what is good than to what is not.

Very true.

There is reason in supposing that the finest natures, when under alien conditions, receive more injury than the inferior, because the contrast is greater.

Certainly.

And may we not say, Adeimantus, that the most gifted minds, when they are ill-educated, become pre-eminently bad? Do not great crimes and the spirit of pure evil spring out of a fulness of nature ruined by education rather than from any inferiority, whereas weak natures are scarcely capable of any very great good or very great evil?

There I think that you are right.

And our philosopher follows the same analogy—he is like a plant which, having proper nurture, must necessarily grow and mature into all virtue, but, if sown and planted in an alien soil, becomes the most noxious of all weeds, unless he be preserved by some divine power. Do you really think, as people so often say, that our youth are corrupted by Sophists, or that private teachers of the art corrupt them in any degree worth speaking of? Are not the public who say these things the greatest of all Sophists? And do they not educate to perfection young and old, men and women alike, and fashion them after their own hearts?

When is this accomplished? he said.

When they meet together, and the world sits down at an assembly, or in a court of law, or a theatre, or a camp, or in any other popular resort, and there is a great uproar, and they praise some things which are being said or done, and blame other things, equally exaggerating both, shouting and clapping their hands, and the echo of the rocks and the place in which they are assembled redoubles the sound of the praise or blame—at such a time will not a young man's heart, as they say, leap within him? Will any private training enable him to stand firm against the overwhelming flood of popular opinion? or will he be carried away by the stream? Will he not have the notions of good and evil which the public in general have—he will do as they do, and as they are, such will he be?

Yes, Socrates; necessity will compel him.

And yet, I said, there is a still greater necessity, which has not been mentioned.

What is that?

The gentle force of attainder or confiscation or death, which, as you are aware, these new Sophists and educators, who are the public, apply when their words are powerless.

Indeed they do; and in right good earnest.

Now what opinion of any other Sophist, or of any private person, can be expected to overcome in such an unequal contest?

None, he replied.

No, indeed, I said, even to make the attempt is a great piece of folly; there neither is, nor has been, nor is ever likely to be, any different type of character which has had no other training in virtue but that which is supplied by public opinion—I speak, my friend, of human virtue only; what is more than human, as the proverb says, is not included: for I would not have you ignorant that, in the present evil state of governments, whatever is saved and comes to good is saved by the power of God, as we may truly say.

I quite assent, he replied.

Then let me crave your assent also to a further observation.

What are you going to say?

Why, that all those mercenary individuals, whom the many call Sophists and whom they deem to be their adversaries, do, in fact, teach nothing but the opinion of the many, that is to say, the opinions of their assemblies; and this is their wisdom. I might compare them to a man who should study the tempers and desires of a mighty strong beast who is fed by him—he would learn how to approach and handle him, also at what times and from what causes he is dangerous or the reverse, and what is the meaning of his several cries, and by what sounds, when another utters them, he is soothed or infuriated; and you may suppose further, that when, by continually attending upon him, he has become perfect in all this, he calls his knowledge wisdom, and makes of it a system or art, which he proceeds to teach, although he has no real notion of what he means by the principles or passions of which he is speaking, but calls this honourable and that dishonourable, or good or evil, or just or unjust, all in accordance with the tastes and tempers of the great brute. Good he pronounces to be that in which the beast delights and evil to be that which he dislikes; and he can give no other account of them except that the just and noble are the necessary, having never himself seen, and having no power of explaining to others the nature of either, or the difference between them, which is immense. By heaven, would not such an one be a rare educator?

Indeed he would.

And in what way does he who thinks that wisdom is the discernment of the tempers and tastes of the motley multitude, whether in painting or music, or, finally, in politics, differ from him whom I have been describing? For when a man consorts with the many, and exhibits to them his poem or other work of art or the service which he has done the State, making them his judges when he is not obliged, the so-called necessity of Diomede will oblige him to produce whatever they praise. And yet the reasons are utterly ludicrous which they give in confirmation of their own notions about the honourable and good. Did you ever hear any of them which were not?

No, nor am I likely to hear.

You recognise the truth of what I have been saying? Then let me ask you to consider further whether the world will ever be induced to believe in the existence of absolute beauty rather than of the many beautiful, or of the absolute in each kind rather than of the many in each kind?

Certainly not.

Then the world cannot possibly be a philosopher?

Impossible.

And therefore philosophers must inevitably fall under the censure of the world?

They must.

And of individuals who consort with the mob and seek to please them?

That is evident.

Then, do you see any way in which the philosopher can be preserved in his calling to the end? and remember what we were saying of him, that he was to have quickness and memory and courage and magnificence— these were admitted by us to be the true philosopher's gifts.

Yes.

Will not such an one from his early childhood be in all things first among all, especially if his bodily endowments are like his mental ones?

Certainly, he said.

And his friends and fellow-citizens will want to use him as he gets older for their own purposes?

No question.

Falling at his feet, they will make requests to him and do him honour and flatter him, because they want to get into their hands now, the power which he will one day possess.

That often happens, he said.

And what will a man such as he is be likely to do under such circumstances, especially if he be a citizen of a great city, rich and noble, and a tall proper youth? Will he not be full of boundless aspirations, and fancy himself able to manage the affairs of Hellenes and of barbarians, and having got such notions into his head will he not dilate and elevate himself in the fulness of vain pomp and senseless pride?

To be sure he will.

Now, when he is in this state of mind, if some one gently comes to him and tells him that he is a fool and must get understanding, which can only be got by slaving for it, do you think that, under such adverse circumstances, he will be easily induced to listen?

Far otherwise.

And even if there be some one who through inherent goodness or natural reasonableness has had his eyes opened a little and is humbled and taken captive by philosophy, how will his friends behave when they think that they are likely to lose the advantage which they were hoping to reap from his companionship? Will they not do and say anything to prevent him from yielding to his better nature and to render his teacher powerless, using to this end private intrigues as well as public prosecutions?

There can be no doubt of it.

And how can one who is thus circumstanced ever become a philosopher?

Impossible.

Then were we not right in saying that even the very qualities which make a man a philosopher may, if he be ill-educated, divert him from philosophy, no less than riches and their accompaniments and the other so-called goods of life?

We were quite right.

Thus, my excellent friend, is brought about all that ruin and failure which I have been describing of the natures best adapted to the best of all pursuits; they are natures which we maintain to be rare at any time; this being the class out of which come the men who are the authors of the greatest evil to States and individuals; and also of the greatest good when the tide carries them in that direction; but a small man never was the doer of any great thing either to individuals or to States.

That is most true, he said.

And so philosophy is left desolate, with her marriage rite incomplete: for her own have fallen away and forsaken her, and while they are leading a false and unbecoming life, other unworthy persons, seeing that she has no kinsmen to be her protectors, enter in and dishonour her; and fasten upon her the reproaches which, as you say, her reprovers utter, who affirm of her votaries that some are good for nothing, and that the greater number deserve the severest punishment.

That is certainly what people say.

Yes; and what else would you expect, I said, when you think of the puny creatures who, seeing this land open to them—a land well stocked with fair names and showy titles—like prisoners running out of prison into a sanctuary, take a leap out of their trades into philosophy; those who do so being probably the cleverest hands at their own miserable crafts? For, although philosophy be in this evil case, still there remains a dignity about her which is not to be found in the arts. And many are thus attracted by her whose natures are imperfect and whose souls are maimed and disfigured by their meannesses, as their bodies are by their trades and crafts. Is not this unavoidable?

Yes.

Are they not exactly like a bald little tinker who has just got out of durance and come into a fortune; he takes a bath and puts on a new coat, and is decked out as a bridegroom going to marry his master's daughter, who is left poor and desolate?

A most exact parallel.

What will be the issue of such marriages? Will they not be vile and bastard?

There can be no question of it.

And when persons who are unworthy of education approach philosophy and make an alliance with her who is in a rank above them what sort of ideas and opinions are likely to be generated? Will they not be sophisms captivating to the ear, having nothing in them genuine, or worthy of or akin to true wisdom?

No doubt, he said.

Then, Adeimantus, I said, the worthy disciples of philosophy will be but a small remnant: perchance some noble and well-educated person, detained by exile in her service, who in the absence of corrupting influences remains devoted to her; or some lofty soul born in a mean city, the politics of which he contemns and neglects; and there may be a gifted few who leave the arts, which they justly despise, and come to her;—or peradventure there are some who are restrained by our friend Theages' bridle; for everything in the life of Theages conspired to divert him from philosophy; but ill-health kept him away from politics. My own case of the internal sign is hardly worth mentioning, for rarely, if ever, has such a monitor been given to any other man. Those who belong to this small class have tasted how sweet and blessed a possession philosophy is, and have also seen enough of the madness of the multitude; and they know that no politician is honest, nor is there any champion of justice at whose side they may fight and be saved. Such an one may be compared to a man who has fallen among wild beasts—he will not join in the wickedness of his fellows, but neither is he able singly to resist all their fierce natures, and therefore seeing that he would be of no use to the State or to his friends, and reflecting that he would have to throw away his life without doing any good either to himself or others, he holds his peace, and goes his own way. He is like one who, in the storm of dust and sleet which the driving wind hurries along, retires under the shelter of a wall; and seeing the rest of mankind full of wickedness, he is content, if only he can live his own life and be pure from evil or unrighteousness, and depart in peace and good-will, with bright hopes.

Yes, he said, and he will have done a great work before he departs.

A great work—yes; but not the greatest, unless he find a State suitable to him; for in a State which is suitable to him, he will have a larger growth and be the saviour of his country, as well as of himself.

The causes why philosophy is in such an evil name have now been sufficiently explained: the injustice of the charges against her has been shown—is there anything more which you wish to say?

Nothing more on that subject, he replied; but I should like to know which of the governments now existing is in your opinion the one adapted to her.

Not any of them, I said; and that is precisely the accusation which I bring against them—not one of them is worthy of the philosophic nature, and hence that nature is warped and estranged;—as the exotic seed which is sown in a foreign land becomes denaturalized, and is wont to be overpowered and to lose itself in the new soil, even so this growth of philosophy, instead of persisting, degenerates and receives another character. But if philosophy ever finds in the State that perfection which she herself is, then will be seen that she is in truth divine, and that all other things, whether natures of men or institutions, are but human;— and now, I know, that you are going to ask, What that State is: No, he said; there you are wrong, for I was going to ask another question—whether it is the State of which we are the founders and inventors, or some other?

Yes, I replied, ours in most respects; but you may remember my saying before, that some living authority would always be required in the State having the same idea of the constitution which guided you when as legislator you were laying down the laws.

That was said, he replied.

Yes, but not in a satisfactory manner; you frightened us by interposing objections, which certainly showed that the discussion would be long and difficult; and what still remains is the reverse of easy.

What is there remaining?

The question how the study of philosophy may be so ordered as not to be the ruin of the State: All great attempts are attended with risk; 'hard is the good,' as men say.

Still, he said, let the point be cleared up, and the enquiry will then be complete.

I shall not be hindered, I said, by any want of will, but, if at all, by a want of power: my zeal you may see for yourselves; and please to remark in what I am about to say how boldly and unhesitatingly I declare that States should pursue philosophy, not as they do now, but in a different spirit.

In what manner?

At present, I said, the students of philosophy are quite young; beginning when they are hardly past childhood, they devote only the time saved from moneymaking and housekeeping to such pursuits; and even those of them who are reputed to have most of the philosophic spirit, when they come within sight of the great difficulty of the subject, I mean dialectic, take themselves off. In after life when invited by some one else, they may, perhaps, go and hear a lecture, and about this they make much ado, for philosophy is not considered by them to be their proper business: at last, when they grow old, in most cases they are extinguished more truly than Heracleitus' sun, inasmuch as they never light up again. (Heraclitus said that the sun was extinguished every evening and relighted every morning.)

But what ought to be their course?

Just the opposite. In childhood and youth their study, and what philosophy they learn, should be suited to their tender years: during this period while they are growing up towards manhood, the chief and special care should be given to their bodies that they may have them to use in the service of philosophy; as life advances and the intellect begins to mature, let them increase the gymnastics of the soul; but when the strength of our citizens fails and is past civil and military duties, then let them range at will and engage in no serious labour, as we intend them to live happily here, and to crown this life with a similar happiness in another.

How truly in earnest you are, Socrates! he said; I am sure of that; and yet most of your hearers, if I am not mistaken, are likely to be still more earnest in their opposition to you, and will never be convinced; Thrasymachus least of all.

Do not make a quarrel, I said, between Thrasymachus and me, who have recently become friends, although, indeed, we were never enemies; for I shall go on striving to the utmost until I either convert him and other men, or do something which may profit them against the day when they live again, and hold the like discourse in another state of existence.

You are speaking of a time which is not very near.

Rather, I replied, of a time which is as nothing in comparison with eternity. Nevertheless, I do not wonder that the many refuse to believe; for they have never seen that of which we are now speaking realized; they have seen only a conventional imitation of philosophy, consisting of words artificially brought together, not like these of ours having a natural unity. But a human being who in word and work is perfectly moulded, as far as he can be, into the proportion and likeness of virtue—such a man ruling in a city which bears the same image, they have never yet seen, neither one nor many of them—do you think that they ever did?

No indeed.

No, my friend, and they have seldom, if ever, heard free and noble sentiments; such as men utter when they are earnestly and by every means in their power seeking after truth for the sake of knowledge, while they look coldly on the subtleties of controversy, of which the end is opinion and strife, whether they meet with them in the courts of law or in society.

They are strangers, he said, to the words of which you speak.

And this was what we foresaw, and this was the reason why truth forced us to admit, not without fear and hesitation, that neither cities nor States nor individuals will ever attain perfection until the small class of philosophers whom we termed useless but not corrupt are providentially compelled, whether they will or not, to take care of the State, and until a like necessity be laid on the State to obey them; or until kings, or if not kings, the sons of kings or princes, are divinely inspired with a true love of true philosophy. That either or both of these alternatives are impossible, I see no reason to affirm: if they were so, we might indeed be justly ridiculed as dreamers and visionaries. Am I not right?

Quite right.

If then, in the countless ages of the past, or at the present hour in some foreign clime which is far away and beyond our ken, the perfected philosopher is or has been or hereafter shall be compelled by a superior power to have the charge of the State, we are ready to assert to the death, that this our constitution has been, and is—yea, and will be whenever the Muse of Philosophy is queen. There is no impossibility in all this; that there is a difficulty, we acknowledge ourselves.

My opinion agrees with yours, he said.

But do you mean to say that this is not the opinion of the multitude? I should imagine not, he replied.

O my friend, I said, do not attack the multitude: they will change their minds, if, not in an aggressive spirit, but gently and with the view of soothing them and removing their dislike of over-education, you show them your philosophers as they really are and describe as you were just now doing their character and profession, and then mankind will see that he of whom you are speaking is not such as they supposed—if they view him in this new light, they will surely change their notion of him, and answer in another strain. Who can be at enmity with one who loves them, who that is himself gentle and free from envy will be jealous of one in whom there is no jealousy? Nay, let me answer for you, that in a few this harsh temper may be found but not in the majority of mankind.

I quite agree with you, he said.

And do you not also think, as I do, that the harsh feeling which the many entertain towards philosophy originates in the pretenders, who rush in uninvited, and are always abusing them, and finding fault with them, who make persons instead of things the theme of their conversation? and nothing can be more unbecoming in philosophers than this.

It is most unbecoming.

For he, Adeimantus, whose mind is fixed upon true being, has surely no time to look down upon the affairs of earth, or to be filled with malice and envy, contending against men; his eye is ever directed towards things fixed and immutable, which he sees neither injuring nor injured by one another, but all in order moving according to reason; these he imitates, and to these he will, as far as he can, conform himself. Can a man help imitating that with which he holds reverential converse?

Impossible.

And the philosopher holding converse with the divine order,

becomes orderly and divine, as far as the nature of man allows; but like every one else, he will suffer from detraction.

Of course.

And if a necessity be laid upon him of fashioning, not only himself, but human nature generally, whether in States or individuals, into that which he beholds elsewhere, will he, think you, be an unskilful artificer of justice, temperance, and every civil virtue?

Anything but unskilful.

And if the world perceives that what we are saying about him is the truth, will they be angry with philosophy? Will they disbelieve us, when we tell them that no State can be happy which is not designed by artists who imitate the heavenly pattern?

They will not be angry if they understand, he said. But how will they draw out the plan of which you are speaking?

They will begin by taking the State and the manners of men, from which, as from a tablet, they will rub out the picture, and leave a clean surface. This is no easy task. But whether easy or not, herein will lie the difference between them and every other legislator,—they will have nothing to do either with individual or State, and will inscribe no laws, until they have either found, or themselves made, a clean surface.

They will be very right, he said.

Having effected this, they will proceed to trace an outline of the constitution?

No doubt.

And when they are filling in the work, as I conceive, they will often turn their eyes upwards and downwards: I mean that they will first look at absolute justice and beauty and temperance, and again at the human copy; and will mingle and temper the various elements of life into the image of a man; and this they will conceive according to that other image, which, when existing among men, Homer calls the form and likeness of God.

Very true, he said.

And one feature they will erase, and another they will put in, until they have made the ways of men, as far as possible, agreeable to the ways of God?

Indeed, he said, in no way could they make a fairer picture.

And now, I said, are we beginning to persuade those whom you described as rushing at us with might and main, that the painter of constitutions is such an one as we are praising; at whom they were so very indignant because to his hands we committed the State; and are they growing a little calmer at what they have just heard?

Much calmer, if there is any sense in them.

Why, where can they still find any ground for objection? Will they doubt that the philosopher is a lover of truth and being?

They would not be so unreasonable.

Or that his nature, being such as we have delineated, is akin to the highest good?

Neither can they doubt this.

But again, will they tell us that such a nature, placed under favourable circumstances, will not be perfectly good and wise if any ever was? Or will they prefer those whom we have rejected?

Surely not.

Then will they still be angry at our saying, that, until philosophers bear rule, States and individuals will have no rest from evil, nor will this our imaginary State ever be realized?

I think that they will be less angry.

Shall we assume that they are not only less angry but quite gentle, and that they have been converted and for very shame, if for no other reason, cannot refuse to come to terms?

By all means, he said.

Then let us suppose that the reconciliation has been effected. Will any one deny the other point, that there may be sons of kings or princes who are by nature philosophers?

Surely no man, he said.

And when they have come into being will any one say that they must of necessity be destroyed; that they can hardly be saved is not denied even by us; but that in the whole course of ages no single one of them can escape—who will venture to affirm this?

Who indeed!

But, said I, one is enough; let there be one man who has a city obedient to his will, and he might bring into existence the ideal polity about which the world is so incredulous.

Yes, one is enough.

The ruler may impose the laws and institutions which we have been describing, and the citizens may possibly be willing to obey them?

Certainly.

And that others should approve, of what we approve, is no miracle or impossibility?

I think not.

But we have sufficiently shown, in what has preceded, that all this, if only possible, is assuredly for the best.

We have.

And now we say not only that our laws, if they could be enacted, would be for the best, but also that the enactment of them, though difficult, is not impossible.

Very good.

And so with pain and toil we have reached the end of one subject, but more remains to be discussed;—how and by what studies and pursuits will the saviours of the constitution be created, and at what ages are they to apply themselves to their several studies?

Certainly.

I omitted the troublesome business of the possession of women, and the procreation of children, and the appointment of the rulers, because I knew that the perfect State would be eyed with jealousy and was difficult of attainment; but that piece of cleverness was not of much service to me, for I had to discuss them all the same. The women and children are now disposed of, but the other question of the rulers must be investigated from the very beginning. We were saying, as you will remember, that they were to be lovers of their country, tried by the test of pleasures and pains, and neither in hardships, nor in dangers, nor at any other critical moment were to lose their patriotism—he was to be rejected who failed, but he who always came forth pure, like gold tried in the refiner's fire, was to be made a ruler, and to receive honours and rewards in life and after death. This was the sort of thing which was being said, and then the argument turned aside and veiled her face; not liking to stir the question which has now arisen.

I perfectly remember, he said.

Yes, my friend, I said, and I then shrank from hazarding the bold word; but now let me dare to say—that the perfect guardian must be a philosopher.

Yes, he said, let that be affirmed.

And do not suppose that there will be many of them; for the gifts which were deemed by us to be essential rarely grow together; they are mostly found in shreds and patches.

What do you mean? he said.

You are aware, I replied, that quick intelligence, memory, sagacity, cleverness, and similar qualities, do not often grow together, and that persons who possess them and are at the same time high-spirited and magnanimous are not so constituted by nature as to live orderly and in a peaceful and settled manner; they are driven any way by their impulses, and all solid principle goes out of them.

Very true, he said.

On the other hand, those steadfast natures which can better be depended upon, which in a battle are impregnable to fear and immovable, are equally immovable when there is anything to be learned; they are always in a torpid state, and are apt to yawn and go to sleep over any intellectual toil.

Quite true.

And yet we were saying that both qualities were necessary in those to whom the higher education is to be imparted, and who are to share in any office or command.

Certainly, he said.

And will they be a class which is rarely found?

Yes, indeed.

Then the aspirant must not only be tested in those labours and dangers and pleasures which we mentioned before, but there is another kind of probation which we did not mention—he must be exercised also in many kinds of knowledge, to see whether the soul will be able to endure the highest of all, or will faint under them, as in any other studies and exercises.

Yes, he said, you are quite right in testing him. But what do you mean by the highest of all knowledge?

You may remember, I said, that we divided the soul into three parts; and distinguished the several natures of justice, temperance, courage, and wisdom?

Indeed, he said, if I had forgotten, I should not deserve to hear more.

And do you remember the word of caution which preceded the discussion of them?

To what do you refer?

We were saying, if I am not mistaken, that he who wanted to see them in their perfect beauty must take a longer and more circuitous way, at the end of which they would appear; but that we could add on a popular exposition of them on a level with the discussion which had preceded. And you replied that such an exposition would be enough for you, and so the enquiry was continued in what to me seemed to be a very inaccurate manner; whether you were satisfied or not, it is for you to say.

Yes, he said, I thought and the others thought that you gave us a fair measure of truth.

But, my friend, I said, a measure of such things which in any degree falls short of the whole truth is not fair measure; for nothing imperfect is the measure of anything, although persons are too apt to be contented and think that they need search no further.

Not an uncommon case when people are indolent.

Yes, I said; and there cannot be any worse fault in a guardian of the State and of the laws.

True.

The guardian then, I said, must be required to take the longer circuit, and toil at learning as well as at gymnastics, or he will never reach the highest knowledge of all which, as we were just now saying, is his proper calling.

What, he said, is there a knowledge still higher than this—higher than justice and the other virtues?

Yes, I said, there is. And of the virtues too we must behold not the outline merely, as at present—nothing short of the most finished picture should satisfy us. When little things are elaborated with an infinity of pains, in order that they may appear in their full beauty and utmost clearness, how ridiculous that we should not think the highest truths worthy of attaining the highest accuracy!

A right noble thought; but do you suppose that we shall refrain from asking you what is this highest knowledge?

Nay, I said, ask if you will; but I am certain that you have heard the answer many times, and now you either do not understand me or, as I rather think, you are disposed to be troublesome; for you have often been told that the idea of good is the highest knowledge, and that all other things become useful and advantageous only by their use of this. You can hardly be ignorant that of this I was about to speak, concerning which, as you have often heard me say, we know so little; and, without which, any other knowledge or possession of any kind will profit us nothing. Do you think that the possession of all other things is of any value if we do not possess the good? or the knowledge of all other things if we have no knowledge of beauty and goodness?

Assuredly not.

You are further aware that most people affirm pleasure to be the good, but the finer sort of wits say it is knowledge?

Yes.

And you are aware too that the latter cannot explain what they mean by knowledge, but are obliged after all to say knowledge of the good?

How ridiculous!

Yes, I said, that they should begin by reproaching us with our ignorance of the good, and then presume our knowledge of it—for the good they define to be knowledge of the good, just as if we understood them when they use the term 'good'—this is of course ridiculous.

Most true, he said.

And those who make pleasure their good are in equal perplexity; for they are compelled to admit that there are bad pleasures as well as good.

Certainly.

And therefore to acknowledge that bad and good are the same?

True.

There can be no doubt about the numerous difficulties in which this question is involved.

There can be none.

Further, do we not see that many are willing to do or to have or to seem to be what is just and honourable without the reality; but no one is satisfied with the appearance of good—the reality is what they seek; in the case of the good, appearance is despised by every one.

Very true, he said.

Of this then, which every soul of man pursues and makes the end of all his actions, having a presentiment that there is such an end, and yet hesitating because neither knowing the nature nor having the same assurance of this as of other things, and therefore losing whatever good there is in other things,—of a principle such and so great as this ought the best men in our State, to whom everything is entrusted, to be in the darkness of ignorance?

Certainly not, he said.

I am sure, I said, that he who does not know how the beautiful and the just are likewise good will be but a sorry guardian of them; and I suspect that no one who is ignorant of the good will have a true knowledge of them.

That, he said, is a shrewd suspicion of yours.

And if we only have a guardian who has this knowledge our State will be perfectly ordered?

Of course, he replied; but I wish that you would tell me whether you conceive this supreme principle of the good to be knowledge or pleasure, or different from either?

Aye, I said, I knew all along that a fastidious gentleman like you would not be contented with the thoughts of other people about these matters.

True, Socrates; but I must say that one who like you has passed a lifetime in the study of philosophy should not be always repeating the opinions of others, and never telling his own.

Well, but has any one a right to say positively what he does not know?

Not, he said, with the assurance of positive certainty; he has no right to do that: but he may say what he thinks, as a matter of opinion.

And do you not know, I said, that all mere opinions are bad, and the best of them blind? You would not deny that those who have any true notion without intelligence are only like blind men who feel their way along the road?

Very true.

And do you wish to behold what is blind and crooked and base, when others will tell you of brightness and beauty?

Still, I must implore you, Socrates, said Glaucon, not to turn away just as you are reaching the goal; if you will only give such an explanation of the good as you have already given of justice and temperance and the other virtues, we shall be satisfied.

Yes, my friend, and I shall be at least equally satisfied, but I cannot help fearing that I shall fail, and that my indiscreet zeal will bring ridicule upon me. No, sweet sirs, let us not at present ask what is the actual nature of the good, for to reach what is now in my thoughts would be an effort too great for me. But of the child of the good who is likest him, I would fain speak, if I could be sure that you wished to hear—otherwise, not.

By all means, he said, tell us about the child, and you shall remain in our debt for the account of the parent.

I do indeed wish, I replied, that I could pay, and you receive, the account of the parent, and not, as now, of the offspring only; take, however, this latter by way of interest, and at the same time have a care that I do not render a false account, although I have no intention of deceiving you.

Yes, we will take all the care that we can: proceed.

Yes, I said, but I must first come to an understanding with you, and remind you of what I have mentioned in the course of this discussion, and at many other times.

What?

The old story, that there is a many beautiful and a many good, and so of other things which we describe and define; to all of them the term 'many' is applied.

True, he said.

And there is an absolute beauty and an absolute good, and of other things to which the term 'many' is applied there is an absolute; for they may be brought under a single idea, which is called the essence of each.

Very true.

The many, as we say, are seen but not known, and the ideas are known but not seen.

Exactly.

And what is the organ with which we see the visible things?

The sight, he said.

And with the hearing, I said, we hear, and with the other senses perceive the other objects of sense?

True.

But have you remarked that sight is by far the most costly and complex piece of workmanship which the artificer of the senses ever contrived?

No, I never have, he said.

Then reflect; has the ear or voice need of any third or additional nature in order that the one may be able to hear and the other to be heard?

Nothing of the sort.

No, indeed, I replied; and the same is true of most, if not all, the other senses—you would not say that any of them requires such an addition?

Certainly not.

But you see that without the addition of some other nature there is no seeing or being seen?

How do you mean?

Sight being, as I conceive, in the eyes, and he who has eyes wanting to see; colour being also present in them, still unless there be a third nature specially adapted to the purpose, the owner of the eyes will see nothing and the colours will be invisible.

Of what nature are you speaking?

Of that which you term light, I replied.

True, he said.

Noble, then, is the bond which links together sight and visibility, and great beyond other bonds by no small difference of nature; for light is their bond, and light is no ignoble thing?

Nay, he said, the reverse of ignoble.

And which, I said, of the gods in heaven would you say was the lord of this element? Whose is that light which makes the eye to see perfectly and the visible to appear?

You mean the sun, as you and all mankind say.

May not the relation of sight to this deity be described as follows?
How?

Neither sight nor the eye in which sight resides is the sun?
No.

Yet of all the organs of sense the eye is the most like the sun?

By far the most like.

And the power which the eye possesses is a sort of effluence which is dispensed from the sun?

Exactly.

Then the sun is not sight, but the author of sight who is recognised by sight?

True, he said.

And this is he whom I call the child of the good, whom the good begat in his own likeness, to be in the visible world, in relation to sight and the things of sight, what the good is in the intellectual world in relation to mind and the things of mind: Will you be a little more explicit? he said.

Why, you know, I said, that the eyes, when a person directs them towards objects on which the light of day is no longer shining, but the moon and stars only, see dimly, and are nearly blind; they seem to have no clearness of vision in them?

Very true.

But when they are directed towards objects on which the sun shines, they see clearly and there is sight in them?

Certainly.

And the soul is like the eye: when resting upon that on which truth and being shine, the soul perceives and understands, and is radiant with intelligence; but when turned towards the twilight of becoming and perishing, then she has opinion only, and goes blinking about, and is first of one opinion and then of another, and seems to have no intelligence?

Just so.

Now, that which imparts truth to the known and the power of knowing to the knower is what I would have you term the idea of good, and this you will deem to be the cause of science, and of truth in so far as the latter becomes the subject of knowledge; beautiful too, as are both truth and knowledge, you will be right in esteeming this other nature as more beautiful than either; and, as in the previous instance, light and sight may be truly said to be like the sun, and yet not to be the sun, so in this other sphere, science and truth may be deemed to be like the good, but not the good; the good has a place of honour yet higher.

What a wonder of beauty that must be, he said, which is the author of science and truth, and yet surpasses them in beauty; for you surely cannot mean to say that pleasure is the good?

God forbid, I replied; but may I ask you to consider the image in another point of view?

In what point of view?

You would say, would you not, that the sun is not only the author of visibility in all visible things, but of generation and nourishment and growth, though he himself is not generation?

Certainly.

In like manner the good may be said to be not only the author of knowledge to all things known, but of their being and essence, and yet the good is not essence, but far exceeds essence in dignity and power.

Glaucon said, with a ludicrous earnestness: By the light of heaven, how amazing!

Yes, I said, and the exaggeration may be set down to you; for you made me utter my fancies.

And pray continue to utter them; at any rate let us hear if there is anything more to be said about the similitude of the sun.

Yes, I said, there is a great deal more.

Then omit nothing, however slight.

I will do my best, I said; but I should think that a great deal will have to be omitted.

I hope not, he said.

You have to imagine, then, that there are two ruling powers, and that one of them is set over the intellectual world, the other over the visible. I do not say heaven, lest you should fancy that I am playing upon the name ('ourhanoz, orhatoz'). May I suppose that you have this distinction of the visible and intelligible fixed in your mind?

I have.

Now take a line which has been cut into two unequal parts, and divide each of them again in the same proportion, and suppose the two main divisions to answer, one to the visible and the other to the intelligible, and then compare the subdivisions in respect of their clearness and want of clearness, and you will find that the first section in the sphere of the visible consists of images. And by images I mean, in the first place, shadows, and in the second place, reflections in water and in solid, smooth and polished bodies and the like: Do you understand?

Yes, I understand.

Imagine, now, the other section, of which this is only the resemblance, to include the animals which we see, and everything that grows or is made.

Very good.

Would you not admit that both the sections of this division have different degrees of truth, and that the copy is to the original as the sphere of opinion is to the sphere of knowledge?

Most undoubtedly.

Next proceed to consider the manner in which the sphere of the intellectual is to be divided.

In what manner?

244

Thus:—There are two subdivisions, in the lower of which the soul uses the figures given by the former division as images; the enquiry can only be hypothetical, and instead of going upwards to a principle descends to the other end; in the higher of the two, the soul passes out of hypotheses, and goes up to a principle which is above hypotheses, making no use of images as in the former case, but proceeding only in and through the ideas themselves.

I do not quite understand your meaning, he said.

Then I will try again; you will understand me better when I have made some preliminary remarks. You are aware that students of geometry, arithmetic, and the kindred sciences assume the odd and the even and the figures and three kinds of angles and the like in their several branches of science; these are their hypotheses, which they and every body are supposed to know, and therefore they do not deign to give any account of them either to themselves or others; but they begin with them, and go on until they arrive at last, and in a consistent manner, at their conclusion?

Yes, he said, I know.

And do you not know also that although they make use of the visible forms and reason about them, they are thinking not of these, but of the ideals which they resemble; not of the figures which they draw, but of the absolute square and the absolute diameter, and so on—the forms which they draw or make, and which have shadows and reflections in water of their own, are converted by them into images, but they are really seeking to behold the things themselves, which can only be seen with the eye of the mind?

That is true.

And of this kind I spoke as the intelligible, although in the search after it the soul is compelled to use hypotheses; not ascending to a first principle, because she is unable to rise above the region of hypothesis, but employing the objects of which the shadows below are resemblances in their turn as images, they having in relation to the shadows and reflections of them a greater distinctness, and therefore a higher value.

I understand, he said, that you are speaking of the province of geometry and the sister arts.

And when I speak of the other division of the intelligible, you will understand me to speak of that other sort of knowledge which reason herself attains by the power of dialectic, using the hypotheses not as first principles, but only as hypotheses—that is to say, as steps and points of departure into a world which is above hypotheses, in order that she may soar beyond them to the first principle of the whole; and clinging to this and then to that which depends on this, by successive steps she descends again without the aid of any sensible object, from ideas, through ideas, and in ideas she ends.

I understand you, he replied; not perfectly, for you seem to me to be describing a task which is really tremendous; but, at any rate, I understand you to say that knowledge and being, which the science of dialectic contemplates, are clearer than the notions of the arts, as they are termed, which proceed from hypotheses only: these are also contemplated by the understanding, and not by the senses: yet, because they start from hypotheses and do not ascend to a principle, those who contemplate them appear to you not to exercise the higher reason upon them, although when a first principle is added to them they are cognizable by the higher reason. And the habit which is concerned with geometry and the cognate sciences I suppose that you would term understanding and not reason, as being intermediate between opinion and reason.

You have quite conceived my meaning, I said; and now, corresponding to these four divisions, let there be four faculties in the soul—reason answering to the highest, understanding to the second, faith (or conviction) to the third, and perception of shadows to the last—and let there be a scale of them, and let us suppose that the several faculties have clearness in the same degree that their objects have truth.

I understand, he replied, and give my assent, and accept your arrangement.

# BOOK VII

And now, I said, let me show in a figure how far our nature is enlightened or unenlightened:—Behold! human beings living in a underground den, which has a mouth open towards the light and reaching all along the den; here they have been from their childhood, and have their legs and necks chained so that they cannot move, and can only see before them, being prevented by the chains from turning round their heads. Above and behind them a fire is blazing at a distance, and between the fire and the prisoners there is a raised way; and you will see, if you look, a low wall built along the way, like the screen which marionette players have in front of them, over which they show the puppets.

I see.

And do you see, I said, men passing along the wall carrying all sorts of vessels, and statues and figures of animals made of wood and stone and various materials, which appear over the wall? Some of them are talking, others silent.

You have shown me a strange image, and they are strange prisoners.

Like ourselves, I replied; and they see only their own shadows, or the shadows of one another, which the fire throws on the opposite wall of the cave?

True, he said; how could they see anything but the shadows if they were never allowed to move their heads?

And of the objects which are being carried in like manner they would only see the shadows?

Yes, he said.

And if they were able to converse with one another, would they not suppose that they were naming what was actually before them?

Very true.

And suppose further that the prison had an echo which came from the other side, would they not be sure to fancy when one of the passers-by spoke that the voice which they heard came from the passing shadow?

No question, he replied.

To them, I said, the truth would be literally nothing but the shadows of the images.

That is certain.

And now look again, and see what will naturally follow if the prisoners are released and disabused of their error. At first, when any of them is liberated and compelled suddenly to stand up and turn his neck round and walk and look towards the light, he will suffer sharp pains; the glare will distress him, and he will be unable to see the realities of which in his former state he had seen the shadows; and then conceive some one saying to him, that what he saw before was an illusion, but that now, when he is approaching nearer to being and his eye is turned towards more real existence, he has a clearer vision,—what will be his reply? And you may further imagine that his instructor is pointing to the objects as they pass and requiring him to name them,—will he not be perplexed? Will he not fancy that the shadows which he formerly saw are truer than the objects which are now shown to him?

Far truer.

And if he is compelled to look straight at the light, will he not have a pain in his eyes which will make him turn away to take refuge in the objects of vision which he can see, and which he will conceive to be in reality clearer than the things which are now being shown to him?

True, he said.

And suppose once more, that he is reluctantly dragged up a steep and rugged ascent, and held fast until he is forced into the presence of the sun himself, is he not likely to be pained and irritated? When he approaches the light his eyes will be dazzled, and he will not be able to see anything at all of what are now called realities.

Not all in a moment, he said.

He will require to grow accustomed to the sight of the upper world. And first he will see the shadows best, next the reflections of men and other objects in the water, and then the objects themselves; then he will gaze upon the light of the moon and the stars and the spangled heaven; and he will see the sky and the stars by night better than the sun or the light of the sun by day?

Certainly.

Last of all he will be able to see the sun, and not mere reflections of him in the water, but he will see him in his own proper place, and not in another; and he will contemplate him as he is.

Certainly.

He will then proceed to argue that this is he who gives the season and the years, and is the guardian of all that is in the visible world, and in a certain way the cause of all things which he and his fellows have been accustomed to behold?

Clearly, he said, he would first see the sun and then reason about him.

And when he remembered his old habitation, and the wisdom of the den and his fellow-prisoners, do you not suppose that he would felicitate himself on the change, and pity them?

Certainly, he would.

And if they were in the habit of conferring honours among themselves on those who were quickest to observe the passing shadows and to remark which of them went before, and which followed after, and which were together; and who were therefore best able to draw conclusions as to the future, do you think that he would care for such honours and glories, or envy the possessors of them? Would he not say with Homer, "Better to be the poor servant of a poor master," and to endure anything, rather than think as they do and live after their manner?

Yes, he said, I think that he would rather suffer anything than entertain these false notions and live in this miserable manner.

Imagine once more, I said, such an one coming suddenly out of the sun to be replaced in his old situation; would he not be certain to have his eyes full of darkness?

To be sure, he said.

And if there were a contest, and he had to compete in measuring the shadows with the prisoners who had never moved out of the den, while his sight was still weak, and before his eyes had become steady (and the time which would be needed to acquire this new habit of sight might be very considerable), would he not be ridiculous? Men would say of him that up he went and down he came without his eyes; and that it was better not even to think of ascending; and if any one tried to loose another and lead him up to the light, let them only catch the offender, and they would put him to death.

No question, he said.

This entire allegory, I said, you may now append, dear Glaucon, to the previous argument; the prison-house is the world of sight, the light of the fire is the sun, and you will not misapprehend me if you interpret the journey upwards to be the ascent of the soul into the intellectual world according to my poor belief, which, at your desire, I have expressed—whether rightly or wrongly God knows. But, whether true or false, my opinion is that in the world of knowledge the idea of good appears last of all, and is seen only with an effort; and, when seen, is also inferred to be the universal author of all things beautiful and right, parent of light and of the lord of light in this visible world, and the immediate source of reason and truth in the intellectual; and that this is the power upon which he who would act rationally either in public or private life must have his eye fixed.

I agree, he said, as far as I am able to understand you.

Moreover, I said, you must not wonder that those who attain to this beatific vision are unwilling to descend to human affairs; for

their souls are ever hastening into the upper world where they desire
to dwell; which desire of theirs is very natural, if our allegory may
be trusted.

Yes, very natural.

And is there anything surprising in one who passes from divine
contemplations to the evil state of man, misbehaving himself in a
ridiculous manner; if, while his eyes are blinking and before he has
become accustomed to the surrounding darkness, he is compelled to
fight in courts of law, or in other places, about the images or the shadows
of images of justice, and is endeavouring to meet the conceptions of
those who have never yet seen absolute justice?

Anything but surprising, he replied.

Any one who has common sense will remember that the
bewilderments of the eyes are of two kinds, and arise from two
causes, either from coming out of the light or from going into the
light, which is true of the mind's eye, quite as much as of the bodily
eye; and he who remembers this when he sees any one whose vision
is perplexed and weak, will not be too ready to laugh; he will first ask
whether that soul of man has come out of the brighter life, and is
unable to see because unaccustomed to the dark, or having turned
from darkness to the day is dazzled by excess of light. And he will
count the one happy in his condition and state of being, and he will
pity the other; or, if he have a mind to laugh at the soul which comes
from below into the light, there will be more reason in this than in
the laugh which greets him who returns from above out of the light
into the den.

That, he said, is a very just distinction.

But then, if I am right, certain professors of education must be
wrong when they say that they can put a knowledge into the soul which
was not there before, like sight into blind eyes.

They undoubtedly say this, he replied.

Whereas, our argument shows that the power and capacity of
learning exists in the soul already; and that just as the eye was unable
to turn from darkness to light without the whole body, so too the

instrument of knowledge can only by the movement of the whole soul be turned from the world of becoming into that of being, and learn by degrees to endure the sight of being, and of the brightest and best of being, or in other words, of the good.

Very true.

And must there not be some art which will effect conversion in the easiest and quickest manner; not implanting the faculty of sight, for that exists already, but has been turned in the wrong direction, and is looking away from the truth?

Yes, he said, such an art may be presumed.

And whereas the other so-called virtues of the soul seem to be akin to bodily qualities, for even when they are not originally innate they can be implanted later by habit and exercise, the virtue of wisdom more than anything else contains a divine element which always remains, and by this conversion is rendered useful and profitable; or, on the other hand, hurtful and useless. Did you never observe the narrow intelligence flashing from the keen eye of a clever rogue—how eager he is, how clearly his paltry soul sees the way to his end; he is the reverse of blind, but his keen eye-sight is forced into the service of evil, and he is mischievous in proportion to his cleverness?

Very true, he said.

But what if there had been a circumcision of such natures in the days of their youth; and they had been severed from those sensual pleasures, such as eating and drinking, which, like leaden weights, were attached to them at their birth, and which drag them down and turn the vision of their souls upon the things that are below—if, I say, they had been released from these impediments and turned in the opposite direction, the very same faculty in them would have seen the truth as keenly as they see what their eyes are turned to now.

Very likely.

Yes, I said; and there is another thing which is likely, or rather a necessary inference from what has preceded, that neither the uneducated and uninformed of the truth, nor yet those who never make an end of their education, will be able ministers of State; not the former, because they have no single aim of duty which is the rule of all their actions, private as well as public; nor the latter, because they will not act at all except upon compulsion, fancying that they are already dwelling apart in the islands of the blest.

Very true, he replied.

Then, I said, the business of us who are the founders of the State will be to compel the best minds to attain that knowledge which we have already shown to be the greatest of all—they must continue to ascend until they arrive at the good; but when they have ascended and seen enough we must not allow them to do as they do now.

What do you mean?

I mean that they remain in the upper world: but this must not be allowed; they must be made to descend again among the prisoners in the den, and partake of their labours and honours, whether they are worth having or not.

But is not this unjust? he said; ought we to give them a worse life, when they might have a better?

You have again forgotten, my friend, I said, the intention of the legislator, who did not aim at making any one class in the State happy above the rest; the happiness was to be in the whole State, and he held the citizens together by persuasion and necessity, making them benefactors of the State, and therefore benefactors of one another; to this end he created them, not to please themselves, but to be his instruments in binding up the State.

True, he said, I had forgotten.

Observe, Glaucon, that there will be no injustice in compelling our philosophers to have a care and providence of others; we shall explain to them that in other States, men of their class are not obliged to share in the toils of politics: and this is reasonable, for they grow up at their own sweet will, and the government would rather not have them. Being self-taught, they cannot be expected to show any gratitude for a culture which they have never received. But we have brought you into the world to be rulers of the hive, kings of yourselves and of the other citizens, and have educated you far better and more perfectly than they have been educated, and you are better able to share in the double duty. Wherefore each of you, when his turn comes, must go down to the general underground abode, and get the habit of seeing in the dark. When you have acquired the habit, you will see ten thousand times better than the inhabitants of the den, and you will know what the several images are, and what they represent, because you have seen the beautiful and just and good in their truth. And thus our State, which is also yours, will be a reality, and not a dream only, and will be administered in a spirit unlike that of other States, in which men fight with one another about shadows only and are distracted in the struggle for power, which in their eyes is a great good. Whereas the truth is that the State in which the rulers are most reluctant to govern is always the best and most quietly governed, and the State in which they are most eager, the worst.

Quite true, he replied.

And will our pupils, when they hear this, refuse to take their turn at the toils of State, when they are allowed to spend the greater part of their time with one another in the heavenly light?

Impossible, he answered; for they are just men, and the commands which we impose upon them are just; there can be no doubt that every one of them will take office as a stern necessity, and not after the fashion of our present rulers of State.

Yes, my friend, I said; and there lies the point. You must contrive for your future rulers another and a better life than that of a ruler, and then you may have a well-ordered State; for only in the State which offers this, will they rule who are truly rich, not in silver and gold, but in virtue and wisdom, which are the true blessings of life. Whereas if they go to the administration of public affairs, poor and hungering after their own private advantage, thinking that hence they are to snatch the chief good, order there can never be; for they will be fighting about office, and the civil and domestic broils which thus arise will be the ruin of the rulers themselves and of the whole State.

Most true, he replied.

And the only life which looks down upon the life of political ambition is that of true philosophy. Do you know of any other?

Indeed, I do not, he said.

And those who govern ought not to be lovers of the task? For, if they are, there will be rival lovers, and they will fight.

No question.

Who then are those whom we shall compel to be guardians? Surely they will be the men who are wisest about affairs of State, and by whom the State is best administered, and who at the same time have other honours and another and a better life than that of politics?

They are the men, and I will choose them, he replied.

And now shall we consider in what way such guardians will be produced, and how they are to be brought from darkness to light,—as some are said to have ascended from the world below to the gods?

By all means, he replied.

The process, I said, is not the turning over of an oyster-shell (In allusion to a game in which two parties fled or pursued according as an oyster-shell which was thrown into the air fell with the dark or light side uppermost.), but the turning round of a soul passing from a day which is little better than night to the true day of being, that is, the ascent from below, which we affirm to be true philosophy?

Quite so.

And should we not enquire what sort of knowledge has the power of effecting such a change?

Certainly.

What sort of knowledge is there which would draw the soul from becoming to being? And another consideration has just occurred to me: You will remember that our young men are to be warrior athletes?

Yes, that was said.

Then this new kind of knowledge must have an additional quality?

What quality?

Usefulness in war.

Yes, if possible.

There were two parts in our former scheme of education, were there not?

Just so.

There was gymnastic which presided over the growth and decay of the body, and may therefore be regarded as having to do with generation and corruption?

True.

Then that is not the knowledge which we are seeking to discover?

No.

But what do you say of music, which also entered to a certain extent into our former scheme?

Music, he said, as you will remember, was the counterpart of gymnastic, and trained the guardians by the influences of habit, by harmony making them harmonious, by rhythm rhythmical, but not giving them science; and the words, whether fabulous or possibly true, had kindred elements of rhythm and harmony in them. But in music there was nothing which tended to that good which you are now seeking.

You are most accurate, I said, in your recollection; in music there certainly was nothing of the kind. But what branch of knowledge is there, my dear Glaucon, which is of the desired nature; since all the useful arts were reckoned mean by us?

Undoubtedly; and yet if music and gymnastic are excluded, and the arts are also excluded, what remains?

Well, I said, there may be nothing left of our special subjects; and then we shall have to take something which is not special, but of universal application.

What may that be?

A something which all arts and sciences and intelligences use in common, and which every one first has to learn among the elements of education.

What is that?

The little matter of distinguishing one, two, and three—in a word, number and calculation:—do not all arts and sciences necessarily partake of them?

Yes.

Then the art of war partakes of them?

To be sure.

Then Palamedes, whenever he appears in tragedy, proves Agamemnon ridiculously unfit to be a general. Did you never remark how he declares that he had invented number, and had numbered the ships and set in array the ranks of the army at Troy; which implies that they had never been numbered before, and Agamemnon must be supposed literally to have been incapable of counting his own feet— how could he if he was ignorant of number? And if that is true, what sort of general must he have been?

I should say a very strange one, if this was as you say.

Can we deny that a warrior should have a knowledge of arithmetic?

Certainly he should, if he is to have the smallest understanding of military tactics, or indeed, I should rather say, if he is to be a man at all.

I should like to know whether you have the same notion which I have of this study?

What is your notion?

It appears to me to be a study of the kind which we are seeking, and which leads naturally to reflection, but never to have been rightly used; for the true use of it is simply to draw the soul towards being.

Will you explain your meaning? he said.

I will try, I said; and I wish you would share the enquiry with me, and say 'yes' or 'no' when I attempt to distinguish in my own mind what branches of knowledge have this attracting power, in order that we may have clearer proof that arithmetic is, as I suspect, one of them.

Explain, he said.

I mean to say that objects of sense are of two kinds; some of them do not invite thought because the sense is an adequate judge of them; while in the case of other objects sense is so untrustworthy that further enquiry is imperatively demanded.

You are clearly referring, he said, to the manner in which the senses are imposed upon by distance, and by painting in light and shade.

No, I said, that is not at all my meaning.

Then what is your meaning?

When speaking of uninviting objects, I mean those which do not pass from one sensation to the opposite; inviting objects are those which do; in this latter case the sense coming upon the object, whether at a distance or near, gives no more vivid idea of anything in particular than of its opposite. An illustration will make my meaning clearer:—here are three fingers—a little finger, a second finger, and a middle finger.

Very good.

You may suppose that they are seen quite close: And here comes the point.

What is it?

Each of them equally appears a finger, whether seen in the middle or at the extremity, whether white or black, or thick or thin— it makes no difference; a finger is a finger all the same. In these cases a man is not compelled to ask of thought the question what is a finger? for the sight never intimates to the mind that a finger is other than a finger.

True.

And therefore, I said, as we might expect, there is nothing here which invites or excites intelligence.

There is not, he said.

But is this equally true of the greatness and smallness of the fingers? Can sight adequately perceive them? and is no difference made by the circumstance that one of the fingers is in the middle and another at the extremity? And in like manner does the touch adequately perceive the qualities of thickness or thinness, of softness or hardness? And so of the other senses; do they give perfect intimations of such matters? Is not their mode of operation on this wise—the sense which is concerned with the quality of hardness is necessarily concerned also with the quality of softness, and only intimates to the soul that the same thing is felt to be both hard and soft?

You are quite right, he said.

And must not the soul be perplexed at this intimation which the sense gives of a hard which is also soft? What, again, is the meaning of light and heavy, if that which is light is also heavy, and that which is heavy, light?

Yes, he said, these intimations which the soul receives are very curious and require to be explained.

Yes, I said, and in these perplexities the soul naturally summons to her aid calculation and intelligence, that she may see whether the several objects announced to her are one or two.

True.

And if they turn out to be two, is not each of them one and different?

Certainly.

And if each is one, and both are two, she will conceive the two as in a state of division, for if there were undivided they could only be conceived of as one?

True.

The eye certainly did see both small and great, but only in a confused manner; they were not distinguished.

Yes.

Whereas the thinking mind, intending to light up the chaos, was compelled to reverse the process, and look at small and great as separate and not confused.

Very true.

Was not this the beginning of the enquiry 'What is great?' and 'What is small?'

Exactly so.

And thus arose the distinction of the visible and the intelligible.

Most true.

This was what I meant when I spoke of impressions which invited the intellect, or the reverse—those which are simultaneous with opposite impressions, invite thought; those which are not simultaneous do not.

I understand, he said, and agree with you.

And to which class do unity and number belong?

I do not know, he replied.

Think a little and you will see that what has preceded will supply the answer; for if simple unity could be adequately perceived by the sight or by any other sense, then, as we were saying in the case of the finger, there would be nothing to attract towards being; but when there is some contradiction always present, and one is the reverse of one and involves the conception of plurality, then thought begins to be aroused within us, and the soul perplexed and wanting to arrive at a decision asks 'What is absolute unity?' This is the way in which the study of the one has a power of drawing and converting the mind to the contemplation of true being.

And surely, he said, this occurs notably in the case of one; for we see the same thing to be both one and infinite in multitude?

Yes, I said; and this being true of one must be equally true of all number?

Certainly.

And all arithmetic and calculation have to do with number?

Yes.

And they appear to lead the mind towards truth?

Yes, in a very remarkable manner.

Then this is knowledge of the kind for which we are seeking, having a double use, military and philosophical; for the man of war must learn the art of number or he will not know how to array his troops, and the philosopher also, because he has to rise out of the sea of change and lay hold of true being, and therefore he must be an arithmetician.

That is true.

And our guardian is both warrior and philosopher?

Certainly.

Then this is a kind of knowledge which legislation may fitly prescribe; and we must endeavour to persuade those who are to be the principal men of our State to go and learn arithmetic, not as amateurs, but they must carry on the study until they see the nature of numbers with the mind only; nor again, like merchants or retail-traders, with a view to buying or selling, but for the sake of their military use, and of the soul herself; and because this will be the easiest way for her to pass from becoming to truth and being.

That is excellent, he said.

Yes, I said, and now having spoken of it, I must add how charming the science is! and in how many ways it conduces to our desired end, if pursued in the spirit of a philosopher, and not of a shopkeeper!

How do you mean?

I mean, as I was saying, that arithmetic has a very great and elevating effect, compelling the soul to reason about abstract number, and rebelling against the introduction of visible or tangible objects into the argument. You know how steadily the masters of the art repel and ridicule any one who attempts to divide absolute unity when he is calculating, and if you divide, they multiply (Meaning either (1) that they integrate the number because they deny the possibility of fractions; or (2) that division is regarded by them as a process of multiplication, for the fractions of one continue to be units.), taking care that one shall continue one and not become lost in fractions.

That is very true.

Now, suppose a person were to say to them: O my friends, what are these wonderful numbers about which you are reasoning, in which, as you say, there is a unity such as you demand, and each unit is equal, invariable, indivisible,—what would they answer?

They would answer, as I should conceive, that they were speaking of those numbers which can only be realized in thought.

Then you see that this knowledge may be truly called necessary, necessitating as it clearly does the use of the pure intelligence in the attainment of pure truth?

Yes; that is a marked characteristic of it.

And have you further observed, that those who have a natural talent for calculation are generally quick at every other kind of knowledge; and even the dull, if they have had an arithmetical training, although they may derive no other advantage from it, always become much quicker than they would otherwise have been.

Very true, he said.

And indeed, you will not easily find a more difficult study, and not many as difficult.

You will not.

And, for all these reasons, arithmetic is a kind of knowledge in which the best natures should be trained, and which must not be given up.

I agree.

Let this then be made one of our subjects of education. And next, shall we enquire whether the kindred science also concerns us?

You mean geometry?

Exactly so.

Clearly, he said, we are concerned with that part of geometry which relates to war; for in pitching a camp, or taking up a position, or closing or extending the lines of an army, or any other military manoeuvre, whether in actual battle or on a march, it will make all the difference whether a general is or is not a geometrician.

Yes, I said, but for that purpose a very little of either geometry or calculation will be enough; the question relates rather to the greater and more advanced part of geometry—whether that tends in any degree to make more easy the vision of the idea of good; and thither, as I was saying, all things tend which compel the soul to turn her gaze towards that place, where is the full perfection of being, which she ought, by all means, to behold.

True, he said.

Then if geometry compels us to view being, it concerns us; if becoming only, it does not concern us?

Yes, that is what we assert.

Yet anybody who has the least acquaintance with geometry will not deny that such a conception of the science is in flat contradiction to the ordinary language of geometricians.

How so?

They have in view practice only, and are always speaking, in a narrow and ridiculous manner, of squaring and extending and applying and the like—they confuse the necessities of geometry with those of daily life; whereas knowledge is the real object of the whole science.

Certainly, he said.

Then must not a further admission be made?

What admission?

That the knowledge at which geometry aims is knowledge of the eternal, and not of aught perishing and transient.

That, he replied, may be readily allowed, and is true.

Then, my noble friend, geometry will draw the soul towards truth, and create the spirit of philosophy, and raise up that which is now unhappily allowed to fall down.

Nothing will be more likely to have such an effect.

Then nothing should be more sternly laid down than that the inhabitants of your fair city should by all means learn geometry. Moreover the science has indirect effects, which are not small.

Of what kind? he said.

There are the military advantages of which you spoke, I said; and in all departments of knowledge, as experience proves, any one who has studied geometry is infinitely quicker of apprehension than one who has not.

Yes indeed, he said, there is an infinite difference between them.

Then shall we propose this as a second branch of knowledge which our youth will study?

Let us do so, he replied.

And suppose we make astronomy the third—what do you say?

I am strongly inclined to it, he said; the observation of the seasons and of months and years is as essential to the general as it is to the farmer or sailor.

I am amused, I said, at your fear of the world, which makes you guard against the appearance of insisting upon useless studies; and I quite admit the difficulty of believing that in every man there is an eye of the soul which, when by other pursuits lost and dimmed, is by these purified and re-illumined; and is more precious far than ten thousand bodily eyes, for by it alone is truth seen. Now there are two classes of persons: one class of those who will agree with you and will take your words as a revelation; another class to whom they will be utterly unmeaning, and who will naturally deem them to be idle tales, for they see no sort of profit which is to be obtained from them. And therefore you had better decide at once with which of the two you are proposing to argue. You will very likely say with neither, and that your chief aim in carrying on the argument is your own improvement; at the same time you do not grudge to others any benefit which they may receive.

I think that I should prefer to carry on the argument mainly on my own behalf.

Then take a step backward, for we have gone wrong in the order of the sciences.

What was the mistake? he said.

After plane geometry, I said, we proceeded at once to solids in revolution, instead of taking solids in themselves; whereas after the second dimension the third, which is concerned with cubes and dimensions of depth, ought to have followed.

That is true, Socrates; but so little seems to be known as yet about these subjects.

Why, yes, I said, and for two reasons:—in the first place, no government patronises them; this leads to a want of energy in the pursuit of them, and they are difficult; in the second place, students cannot learn them unless they have a director. But then a director can hardly be found, and even if he could, as matters now stand, the students, who are very conceited, would not attend to him. That, however, would be otherwise if the whole State became the director of these studies and gave honour to them; then disciples would want to come, and there would be continuous and earnest search, and discoveries would be made; since even now, disregarded as they are by the world, and maimed of their fair proportions, and although none of their votaries can tell the use of them, still these studies force their way by their natural charm, and very likely, if they had the help of the State, they would some day emerge into light.

Yes, he said, there is a remarkable charm in them. But I do not clearly understand the change in the order. First you began with a geometry of plane surfaces?

Yes, I said.

And you placed astronomy next, and then you made a step backward?

Yes, and I have delayed you by my hurry; the ludicrous state of solid geometry, which, in natural order, should have followed, made me pass over this branch and go on to astronomy, or motion of solids.

True, he said.

Then assuming that the science now omitted would come into existence if encouraged by the State, let us go on to astronomy, which will be fourth.

The right order, he replied. And now, Socrates, as you rebuked the vulgar manner in which I praised astronomy before, my praise shall be given in your own spirit. For every one, as I think, must see that astronomy compels the soul to look upwards and leads us from this world to another.

Every one but myself, I said; to every one else this may be clear, but not to me.

And what then would you say?

I should rather say that those who elevate astronomy into philosophy appear to me to make us look downwards and not upwards.

What do you mean? he asked.

You, I replied, have in your mind a truly sublime conception of our knowledge of the things above. And I dare say that if a person were to throw his head back and study the fretted ceiling, you would still think that his mind was the percipient, and not his eyes. And you are very likely right, and I may be a simpleton: but, in my opinion, that knowledge only which is of being and of the unseen can make the soul look upwards, and whether a man gapes at the heavens or blinks on the ground, seeking to learn some particular of sense, I would deny that he can learn, for nothing of that sort is matter of science; his soul is looking downwards, not upwards, whether his way to knowledge is by water or by land, whether he floats, or only lies on his back.

I acknowledge, he said, the justice of your rebuke. Still, I should like to ascertain how astronomy can be learned in any manner more conducive to that knowledge of which we are speaking?

I will tell you, I said: The starry heaven which we behold is wrought upon a visible ground, and therefore, although the fairest and most perfect of visible things, must necessarily be deemed inferior far to the true motions of absolute swiftness and absolute slowness, which are relative to each other, and carry with them that which is contained in them, in the true number and in every true figure. Now, these are to be apprehended by reason and intelligence, but not by sight.

True, he replied.

The spangled heavens should be used as a pattern and with a view to that higher knowledge; their beauty is like the beauty of figures or pictures excellently wrought by the hand of Daedalus, or some other great artist, which we may chance to behold; any geometrician who saw them would appreciate the exquisiteness of their workmanship, but he would never dream of thinking that in them he could find the true equal or the true double, or the truth of any other proportion.

No, he replied, such an idea would be ridiculous.

And will not a true astronomer have the same feeling when he looks at the movements of the stars? Will he not think that heaven and the things in heaven are framed by the Creator of them in the most perfect manner? But he will never imagine that the proportions of night and day, or of both to the month, or of the month to the year, or of the stars to these and to one another, and any other things that are material and visible can also be eternal and subject to no deviation—that would be absurd; and it is equally absurd to take so much pains in investigating their exact truth.

I quite agree, though I never thought of this before.

Then, I said, in astronomy, as in geometry, we should employ problems, and let the heavens alone if we would approach the subject in the right way and so make the natural gift of reason to be of any real use.

That, he said, is a work infinitely beyond our present astronomers.

Yes, I said; and there are many other things which must also have a similar extension given to them, if our legislation is to be of any value. But can you tell me of any other suitable study?

No, he said, not without thinking.

Motion, I said, has many forms, and not one only; two of them are obvious enough even to wits no better than ours; and there are others, as I imagine, which may be left to wiser persons.

But where are the two?

There is a second, I said, which is the counterpart of the one already named.

And what may that be?

The second, I said, would seem relatively to the ears to be what the first is to the eyes; for I conceive that as the eyes are designed to look up at the stars, so are the ears to hear harmonious motions; and these are sister sciences—as the Pythagoreans say, and we, Glaucon, agree with them?

Yes, he replied.

But this, I said, is a laborious study, and therefore we had better go and learn of them; and they will tell us whether there are any other applications of these sciences. At the same time, we must not lose sight of our own higher object.

What is that?

There is a perfection which all knowledge ought to reach, and which our pupils ought also to attain, and not to fall short of, as I was saying that they did in astronomy. For in the science of harmony, as you probably know, the same thing happens. The teachers of harmony compare the sounds and consonances which are heard only, and their labour, like that of the astronomers, is in vain.

Yes, by heaven! he said; and 'tis as good as a play to hear them talking about their condensed notes, as they call them; they put their ears close alongside of the strings like persons catching a sound from their neighbour's wall—one set of them declaring that they distinguish an intermediate note and have found the least interval

267

which should be the unit of measurement; the others insisting that the two sounds have passed into the same—either party setting their ears before their understanding.

You mean, I said, those gentlemen who tease and torture the strings and rack them on the pegs of the instrument: I might carry on the metaphor and speak after their manner of the blows which the plectrum gives, and make accusations against the strings, both of backwardness and forwardness to sound; but this would be tedious, and therefore I will only say that these are not the men, and that I am referring to the Pythagoreans, of whom I was just now proposing to enquire about harmony. For they too are in error, like the astronomers; they investigate the numbers of the harmonies which are heard, but they never attain to problems—that is to say, they never reach the natural harmonies of number, or reflect why some numbers are harmonious and others not.

That, he said, is a thing of more than mortal knowledge.

A thing, I replied, which I would rather call useful; that is, if sought after with a view to the beautiful and good; but if pursued in any other spirit, useless.

Very true, he said.

Now, when all these studies reach the point of inter-communion and connection with one another, and come to be considered in their mutual affinities, then, I think, but not till then, will the pursuit of them have a value for our objects; otherwise there is no profit in them.

I suspect so; but you are speaking, Socrates, of a vast work.

What do you mean? I said; the prelude or what? Do you not know that all this is but the prelude to the actual strain which we have to learn? For you surely would not regard the skilled mathematician as a dialectician?

Assuredly not, he said; I have hardly ever known a mathematician who was capable of reasoning.

But do you imagine that men who are unable to give and take a reason will have the knowledge which we require of them?

Neither can this be supposed.

And so, Glaucon, I said, we have at last arrived at the hymn of dialectic. This is that strain which is of the intellect only, but which the faculty of sight will nevertheless be found to imitate; for sight, as you may remember, was imagined by us after a while to behold the real animals and stars, and last of all the sun himself. And so with dialectic; when a person starts on the discovery of the absolute by the light of reason only, and without any assistance of sense, and perseveres until by pure intelligence he arrives at the perception of the absolute good, he at last finds himself at the end of the intellectual world, as in the case of sight at the end of the visible.

Exactly, he said.

Then this is the progress which you call dialectic?

True.

But the release of the prisoners from chains, and their translation from the shadows to the images and to the light, and the ascent from the underground den to the sun, while in his presence they are vainly trying to look on animals and plants and the light of the sun, but are able to perceive even with their weak eyes the images in the water (which are divine), and are the shadows of true existence (not shadows of images cast by a light of fire, which compared with the sun is only an image)—this power of elevating the highest principle in the soul to the contemplation of that which is best in existence, with which we may compare the raising of that faculty which is the very light of the body to the sight of that which is brightest in the material and visible world— this power is given, as I was saying, by all that study and pursuit of the arts which has been described.

I agree in what you are saying, he replied, which may be hard to believe, yet, from another point of view, is harder still to deny. This, however, is not a theme to be treated of in passing only, but will have to be discussed again and again. And so, whether our conclusion be true or false, let us assume all this, and proceed at once from the prelude or preamble to the chief strain (A play upon the Greek word, which means both 'law' and 'strain.'), and describe that in like manner. Say, then, what is the nature and what are the divisions of dialectic, and what are the paths which lead thither; for these paths will also lead to our final rest.

Dear Glaucon, I said, you will not be able to follow me here, though I would do my best, and you should behold not an image only but the absolute truth, according to my notion. Whether what I told you would or would not have been a reality I cannot venture to say; but you would have seen something like reality; of that I am confident.

Doubtless, he replied.

But I must also remind you, that the power of dialectic alone can reveal this, and only to one who is a disciple of the previous sciences.

Of that assertion you may be as confident as of the last.

And assuredly no one will argue that there is any other method of comprehending by any regular process all true existence or of ascertaining what each thing is in its own nature; for the arts in general are concerned with the desires or opinions of men, or are cultivated with a view to production and construction, or for the preservation of such productions and constructions; and as to the mathematical sciences which, as we were saying, have some apprehension of true being—geometry and the like—they only dream about being, but never can they behold the waking reality so long as they leave the hypotheses which they use unexamined, and are unable to give an account of them. For when a man knows not his own first principle, and when the conclusion and intermediate steps are also constructed out of he knows not what, how can he imagine that such a fabric of convention can ever become science?

Impossible, he said.

Then dialectic, and dialectic alone, goes directly to the first principle and is the only science which does away with hypotheses in order to make her ground secure; the eye of the soul, which is literally buried in an outlandish slough, is by her gentle aid lifted upwards; and she uses as handmaids and helpers in the work of conversion, the sciences which we have been discussing. Custom terms them sciences, but they ought to have some other name, implying greater clearness than opinion and less clearness than science: and this, in our previous sketch, was called understanding. But why should we dispute about names when we have realities of such importance to consider?

Why indeed, he said, when any name will do which expresses the thought of the mind with clearness?

At any rate, we are satisfied, as before, to have four divisions; two for intellect and two for opinion, and to call the first division science, the second understanding, the third belief, and the fourth perception of shadows, opinion being concerned with becoming, and intellect with being; and so to make a proportion:—As being is to becoming, so is pure intellect to opinion. And as intellect is to opinion, so is science to belief, and understanding to the perception of shadows.

But let us defer the further correlation and subdivision of the subjects of opinion and of intellect, for it will be a long enquiry, many times longer than this has been.

As far as I understand, he said, I agree.

And do you also agree, I said, in describing the dialectician as one who attains a conception of the essence of each thing? And he who does not possess and is therefore unable to impart this conception, in whatever degree he fails, may in that degree also be said to fail in intelligence? Will you admit so much?

Yes, he said; how can I deny it?

And you would say the same of the conception of the good? Until the person is able to abstract and define rationally the idea of good, and unless he can run the gauntlet of all objections, and is ready to disprove them, not by appeals to opinion, but to absolute truth, never faltering at any step of the argument—unless he can do all this, you would say that he knows neither the idea of good nor any other good; he apprehends only a shadow, if anything at all, which is given by opinion and not by science;—dreaming and slumbering in this life, before he is well awake here, he arrives at the world below, and has his final quietus.

In all that I should most certainly agree with you.

And surely you would not have the children of your ideal State, whom you are nurturing and educating—if the ideal ever becomes a reality—you would not allow the future rulers to be like posts (Literally 'lines,' probably the starting-point of a race-course.), having no reason in them, and yet to be set in authority over the highest matters?

Certainly not.

Then you will make a law that they shall have such an education as will enable them to attain the greatest skill in asking and answering questions?

Yes, he said, you and I together will make it.

Dialectic, then, as you will agree, is the coping-stone of the sciences, and is set over them; no other science can be placed higher—the nature of knowledge can no further go?

I agree, he said.

But to whom we are to assign these studies, and in what way they are to be assigned, are questions which remain to be considered.

Yes, clearly.

You remember, I said, how the rulers were chosen before?

Certainly, he said.

The same natures must still be chosen, and the preference again given to the surest and the bravest, and, if possible, to the fairest; and, having noble and generous tempers, they should also have the natural gifts which will facilitate their education.

And what are these?

Such gifts as keenness and ready powers of acquisition; for the mind more often faints from the severity of study than from the severity of gymnastics: the toil is more entirely the mind's own, and is not shared with the body.

Very true, he replied.

Further, he of whom we are in search should have a good memory, and be an unwearied solid man who is a lover of labour in any line; or he will never be able to endure the great amount of bodily exercise and to go through all the intellectual discipline and study which we require of him.

Certainly, he said; he must have natural gifts.

The mistake at present is, that those who study philosophy have no vocation, and this, as I was before saying, is the reason why she has fallen into disrepute: her true sons should take her by the hand and not bastards.

What do you mean?

In the first place, her votary should not have a lame or halting industry—I mean, that he should not be half industrious and half idle: as, for example, when a man is a lover of gymnastic and hunting, and all other bodily exercises, but a hater rather than a lover of the labour of learning or listening or enquiring. Or the occupation to which he devotes himself may be of an opposite kind, and he may have the other sort of lameness.

Certainly, he said.

And as to truth, I said, is not a soul equally to be deemed halt and lame which hates voluntary falsehood and is extremely indignant at herself and others when they tell lies, but is patient of involuntary falsehood, and does not mind wallowing like a swinish beast in the mire of ignorance, and has no shame at being detected?

To be sure.

And, again, in respect of temperance, courage, magnificence, and every other virtue, should we not carefully distinguish between the true son and the bastard? for where there is no discernment of such qualities states and individuals unconsciously err; and the state makes a ruler, and the individual a friend, of one who, being defective in some part of virtue, is in a figure lame or a bastard.

That is very true, he said.

All these things, then, will have to be carefully considered by us; and if only those whom we introduce to this vast system of education and training are sound in body and mind, justice herself will have nothing to say against us, and we shall be the saviours of the constitution and of the State; but, if our pupils are men of another stamp, the reverse will happen, and we shall pour a still greater flood of ridicule on philosophy than she has to endure at present.

That would not be creditable.

Certainly not, I said; and yet perhaps, in thus turning jest into earnest I am equally ridiculous.

In what respect?

I had forgotten, I said, that we were not serious, and spoke with too much excitement. For when I saw philosophy so undeservedly trampled under foot of men I could not help feeling a sort of indignation at the authors of her disgrace: and my anger made me too vehement.

Indeed! I was listening, and did not think so.

But I, who am the speaker, felt that I was. And now let me remind you that, although in our former selection we chose old men, we must not do so in this. Solon was under a delusion when he said that a man when he grows old may learn many things—for he can no more learn much than he can run much; youth is the time for any extraordinary toil.

Of course.

And, therefore, calculation and geometry and all the other elements of instruction, which are a preparation for dialectic, should be presented to the mind in childhood; not, however, under any notion of forcing our system of education.

Why not?

Because a freeman ought not to be a slave in the acquisition of knowledge of any kind. Bodily exercise, when compulsory, does no harm to the body; but knowledge which is acquired under compulsion obtains no hold on the mind.

Very true.

Then, my good friend, I said, do not use compulsion, but let early education be a sort of amusement; you will then be better able to find out the natural bent.

That is a very rational notion, he said.

Do you remember that the children, too, were to be taken to see the battle on horseback; and that if there were no danger they were to be brought close up and, like young hounds, have a taste of blood given them?

Yes, I remember.

The same practice may be followed, I said, in all these things—labours, lessons, dangers—and he who is most at home in all of them ought to be enrolled in a select number.

At what age?

At the age when the necessary gymnastics are over: the period whether of two or three years which passes in this sort of training is useless for any other purpose; for sleep and exercise are unpropitious to learning; and the trial of who is first in gymnastic exercises is one of the most important tests to which our youth are subjected.

Certainly, he replied.

After that time those who are selected from the class of twenty years old will be promoted to higher honour, and the sciences which they learned without any order in their early education will now be brought together, and they will be able to see the natural relationship of them to one another and to true being.

Yes, he said, that is the only kind of knowledge which takes lasting root.

Yes, I said; and the capacity for such knowledge is the great criterion of dialectical talent: the comprehensive mind is always the dialectical.

I agree with you, he said.

These, I said, are the points which you must consider; and those who have most of this comprehension, and who are most steadfast in their learning, and in their military and other appointed duties, when they have arrived at the age of thirty have to be chosen by you out of the select class, and elevated to higher honour; and you will have to prove them by the help of dialectic, in order to learn which of them is able to give up the use of sight and the other senses, and in company with truth to attain absolute being: And here, my friend, great caution is required.

Why great caution?

Do you not remark, I said, how great is the evil which dialectic has introduced?

What evil? he said.

The students of the art are filled with lawlessness.

Quite true, he said.

Do you think that there is anything so very unnatural or inexcusable in their case? or will you make allowance for them?

In what way make allowance?

I want you, I said, by way of parallel, to imagine a supposititious son who is brought up in great wealth; he is one of a great and numerous family, and has many flatterers. When he grows up to manhood, he learns that his alleged are not his real parents; but who the real are he is unable to discover. Can you guess how he will be likely to behave towards his flatterers and his supposed parents, first of all during the period when he is ignorant of the false relation, and then again when he knows? Or shall I guess for you?

If you please.

Then I should say, that while he is ignorant of the truth he will be likely to honour his father and his mother and his supposed relations more than the flatterers; he will be less inclined to neglect them when in need, or to do or say anything against them; and he will be less willing to disobey them in any important matter.

He will.

But when he has made the discovery, I should imagine that he would diminish his honour and regard for them, and would become more devoted to the flatterers; their influence over him would greatly increase; he would now live after their ways, and openly associate with them, and, unless he were of an unusually good disposition, he would trouble himself no more about his supposed parents or other relations.

Well, all that is very probable. But how is the image applicable to the disciples of philosophy?

In this way: you know that there are certain principles about justice and honour, which were taught us in childhood, and under their parental authority we have been brought up, obeying and honouring them.

That is true.

There are also opposite maxims and habits of pleasure which flatter and attract the soul, but do not influence those of us who have any sense of right, and they continue to obey and honour the maxims of their fathers.

True.

Now, when a man is in this state, and the questioning spirit asks what is fair or honourable, and he answers as the legislator has taught him, and then arguments many and diverse refute his words, until he is driven into believing that nothing is honourable any more than dishonourable, or just and good any more than the reverse, and so of all the notions which he most valued, do you think that he will still honour and obey them as before?

Impossible.

And when he ceases to think them honourable and natural as heretofore, and he fails to discover the true, can he be expected to pursue any life other than that which flatters his desires?

He cannot.

And from being a keeper of the law he is converted into a breaker of it?

Unquestionably.

Now all this is very natural in students of philosophy such as I have described, and also, as I was just now saying, most excusable.

Yes, he said; and, I may add, pitiable.

Therefore, that your feelings may not be moved to pity about our citizens who are now thirty years of age, every care must be taken in introducing them to dialectic.

Certainly.

There is a danger lest they should taste the dear delight too early; for youngsters, as you may have observed, when they first get the taste in their mouths, argue for amusement, and are always contradicting and refuting others in imitation of those who refute them; like puppy-dogs, they rejoice in pulling and tearing at all who come near them.

Yes, he said, there is nothing which they like better.

And when they have made many conquests and received defeats at the hands of many, they violently and speedily get into a way of not believing anything which they believed before, and hence, not only they, but philosophy and all that relates to it is apt to have a bad name with the rest of the world.

Too true, he said.

But when a man begins to get older, he will no longer be guilty of such insanity; he will imitate the dialectician who is seeking for truth, and not the eristic, who is contradicting for the sake of amusement; and the greater moderation of his character will increase instead of diminishing the honour of the pursuit.

Very true, he said.

And did we not make special provision for this, when we said that the disciples of philosophy were to be orderly and steadfast, not, as now, any chance aspirant or intruder?

Very true.

Suppose, I said, the study of philosophy to take the place of gymnastics and to be continued diligently and earnestly and exclusively for twice the number of years which were passed in bodily exercise— will that be enough?

Would you say six or four years? he asked.

Say five years, I replied; at the end of the time they must be sent down again into the den and compelled to hold any military or other office which young men are qualified to hold: in this way they will get their experience of life, and there will be an opportunity of trying whether, when they are drawn all manner of ways by temptation, they will stand firm or flinch.

And how long is this stage of their lives to last?

Fifteen years, I answered; and when they have reached fifty years of age, then let those who still survive and have distinguished themselves in every action of their lives and in every branch of knowledge come at last to their consummation: the time has now arrived at which they must raise the eye of the soul to the universal light which lightens all things, and behold the absolute good; for that is the pattern according to which they are to order the State and the lives of individuals, and the remainder of their own lives also; making philosophy their chief pursuit, but, when their turn comes, toiling also at politics and ruling for the public good, not as though they were performing some heroic action, but simply as a matter of duty; and when they have brought up in each generation others like themselves and left them in their place to be governors of the State, then they will depart to the Islands of the Blest and dwell there; and the city will give them public memorials and sacrifices and honour them, if the Pythian oracle consent, as demigods, but if not, as in any case blessed and divine.

You are a sculptor, Socrates, and have made statues of our governors faultless in beauty.

Yes, I said, Glaucon, and of our governesses too; for you must not suppose that what I have been saying applies to men only and not to women as far as their natures can go.

There you are right, he said, since we have made them to share in all things like the men.

Well, I said, and you would agree (would you not?) that what has been said about the State and the government is not a mere dream, and although difficult not impossible, but only possible in the way which has been supposed; that is to say, when the true philosopher kings are born in a State, one or more of them, despising the honours of this present world which they deem mean and worthless, esteeming above all things right and the honour that springs from right, and regarding justice as the greatest and most necessary of all things, whose ministers they are, and whose principles will be exalted by them when they set in order their own city?

How will they proceed?

They will begin by sending out into the country all the inhabitants of the city who are more than ten years old, and will take possession of their children, who will be unaffected by the habits of their parents; these they will train in their own habits and laws, I mean in the laws which we have given them: and in this way the State and constitution of which we were speaking will soonest and most easily attain happiness, and the nation which has such a constitution will gain most.

Yes, that will be the best way. And I think, Socrates, that you have very well described how, if ever, such a constitution might come into being.

Enough then of the perfect State, and of the man who bears its image—there is no difficulty in seeing how we shall describe him.

There is no difficulty, he replied; and I agree with you in thinking that nothing more need be said.

# BOOK VIII

And so, Glaucon, we have arrived at the conclusion that in the perfect State wives and children are to be in common; and that all education and the pursuits of war and peace are also to be common, and the best philosophers and the bravest warriors are to be their kings?

That, replied Glaucon, has been acknowledged.

Yes, I said; and we have further acknowledged that the governors, when appointed themselves, will take their soldiers and place them in houses such as we were describing, which are common to all, and contain nothing private, or individual; and about their property, you remember what we agreed?

Yes, I remember that no one was to have any of the ordinary possessions of mankind; they were to be warrior athletes and guardians, receiving from the other citizens, in lieu of annual payment, only their maintenance, and they were to take care of themselves and of the whole State.

True, I said; and now that this division of our task is concluded, let us find the point at which we digressed, that we may return into the old path.

There is no difficulty in returning; you implied, then as now, that you had finished the description of the State: you said that such a State was good, and that the man was good who answered to it, although, as now appears, you had more excellent things to relate both of State and man. And you said further, that if this was the true form, then the others were false; and of the false forms, you said, as I remember, that there were four principal ones, and that their defects, and the defects of the individuals corresponding to them, were worth examining. When we had seen all the individuals, and finally agreed as to who was the best and who was the worst of them, we were to consider whether the best was not also the happiest, and the worst the most miserable. I asked you what were the four forms of government of which you spoke, and then Polemarchus and Adeimantus put in their word; and you began again, and have found your way to the point at which we have now arrived.

Your recollection, I said, is most exact.

Then, like a wrestler, he replied, you must put yourself again in the same position; and let me ask the same questions, and do you give me the same answer which you were about to give me then.

Yes, if I can, I will, I said.

I shall particularly wish to hear what were the four constitutions of which you were speaking.

That question, I said, is easily answered: the four governments of which I spoke, so far as they have distinct names, are, first, those of Crete and Sparta, which are generally applauded; what is termed oligarchy comes next; this is not equally approved, and is a form of government which teems with evils: thirdly, democracy, which naturally follows oligarchy, although very different: and lastly comes tyranny, great and famous, which differs from them all, and is the fourth and worst disorder of a State. I do not know, do you? of any other constitution which can be said to have a distinct character. There are lordships and principalities which are bought and sold, and some other intermediate forms of government. But these are nondescripts and may be found equally among Hellenes and among barbarians.

Yes, he replied, we certainly hear of many curious forms of government which exist among them.

Do you know, I said, that governments vary as the dispositions of men vary, and that there must be as many of the one as there are of the other? For we cannot suppose that States are made of 'oak and rock,' and not out of the human natures which are in them, and which in a figure turn the scale and draw other things after them?

Yes, he said, the States are as the men are; they grow out of human characters.

Then if the constitutions of States are five, the dispositions of individual minds will also be five?

Certainly.

Him who answers to aristocracy, and whom we rightly call just and good, we have already described.

We have.

Then let us now proceed to describe the inferior sort of natures, being the contentious and ambitious, who answer to the Spartan polity; also the oligarchical, democratical, and tyrannical. Let us place the most just by the side of the most unjust, and when we see them we shall be able to compare the relative happiness or unhappiness of him who leads a life of pure justice or pure injustice. The enquiry will then be completed. And we shall know whether we ought to pursue injustice, as Thrasymachus advises, or in accordance with the conclusions of the argument to prefer justice.

Certainly, he replied, we must do as you say.

Shall we follow our old plan, which we adopted with a view to clearness, of taking the State first and then proceeding to the individual, and begin with the government of honour?—I know of no name for such a government other than timocracy, or perhaps timarchy. We will compare with this the like character in the individual; and, after that, consider oligarchy and the oligarchical man; and then again we will turn our attention to democracy and the democratical man; and lastly, we will go and view the city of tyranny, and once more take a look into the tyrant's soul, and try to arrive at a satisfactory decision.

That way of viewing and judging of the matter will be very suitable.

First, then, I said, let us enquire how timocracy (the government of honour) arises out of aristocracy (the government of the best).

Clearly, all political changes originate in divisions of the actual governing power; a government which is united, however small, cannot be moved.

Very true, he said.

In what way, then, will our city be moved, and in what manner will the two classes of auxiliaries and rulers disagree among themselves or with one another? Shall we, after the manner of Homer, pray the Muses to tell us 'how discord first arose'? Shall we imagine them in solemn mockery, to play and jest with us as if we were children, and to address us in a lofty tragic vein, making believe to be in earnest?

How would they address us?

After this manner:—A city which is thus constituted can hardly be shaken; but, seeing that everything which has a beginning has also an end, even a constitution such as yours will not last for ever, but will in time be dissolved. And this is the dissolution:—In plants that grow in the earth, as well as in animals that move on the earth's surface, fertility and sterility of soul and body occur when the circumferences of the circles of each are completed, which in short-lived existences pass over a short space, and in long-lived ones over a long space. But to the knowledge of human fecundity and sterility all the wisdom and education of your rulers will not attain; the laws which regulate them will not be discovered by an intelligence which is alloyed with sense, but will escape them, and they will bring children into the world when they ought not. Now that which is of divine birth has a period which is contained in a perfect number (i.e. a cyclical number, such as 6, which is equal to the sum of its divisors 1, 2, 3, so that when the circle or time represented by 6 is completed, the lesser times or rotations represented by 1, 2, 3 are also completed.), but the period of human birth is comprehended in a number in which first increments by involution and evolution (or squared and cubed) obtaining three intervals and four terms of like and unlike, waxing and waning numbers, make all the terms commensurable and agreeable to one another. (Probably the numbers 3, 4, 5, 6 of which the three first = the sides of the Pythagorean triangle. The terms will then be 3 cubed, 4 cubed, 5 cubed, which together = 6 cubed = 216.)

The base of these (3) with a third added (4) when combined with five (20) and raised to the third power furnishes two harmonies; the first a square which is a hundred times as great (400 = 4 x 100) (Or the first a square which is 100 x 100 = 10,000. The whole number will then be 17,500 = a square of 100, and an oblong of 100 by 75.), and the other a figure having one side equal to the former, but oblong, consisting of a hundred numbers squared upon rational diameters of a square (i.e. omitting fractions), the side of which is five (7 x 7 = 49 x 100 = 4900), each of them being less by one (than the perfect square which includes the fractions, sc. 50) or less by (Or, 'consisting of two numbers squared upon irrational diameters,' etc. = 100. For other explanations of the passage see Introduction.) two perfect squares of irrational diameters (of a square the side of which is five = 50 + 50 = 100); and a hundred cubes of three (27 x 100 = 2700 + 4900 + 400 = 8000). Now this number represents a geometrical figure which has control over the good and evil of births. For when your guardians are ignorant of the law of births, and unite bride and bridegroom out of season, the children will not be goodly or fortunate. And though only the best of them will be appointed by their predecessors, still they will be unworthy to hold their fathers' places, and when they come into power as guardians, they will soon be found to fail in taking care of us, the Muses, first by under-valuing music; which neglect will soon extend to gymnastic; and hence the young men of your State will be less cultivated. In the succeeding generation rulers will be appointed who have lost the guardian power of testing the metal of your different races, which, like Hesiod's, are of gold and silver and brass and iron. And so iron will be mingled with silver, and brass with gold, and hence there will arise dissimilarity and inequality and irregularity, which always and in all places are causes of hatred and war. This the Muses affirm to be the stock from which discord has sprung, wherever arising; and this is their answer to us.

Yes, and we may assume that they answer truly.

Why, yes, I said, of course they answer truly; how can the Muses speak falsely?

And what do the Muses say next?

When discord arose, then the two races were drawn different ways: the iron and brass fell to acquiring money and land and houses and gold and silver; but the gold and silver races, not wanting money but having the true riches in their own nature, inclined towards virtue and the ancient order of things. There was a battle between them, and at last they agreed to distribute their land and houses among individual owners; and they enslaved their friends and maintainers, whom they had formerly protected in the condition of freemen, and made of them subjects and servants; and they themselves were engaged in war and in keeping a watch against them.

I believe that you have rightly conceived the origin of the change.

And the new government which thus arises will be of a form intermediate between oligarchy and aristocracy?

Very true.

Such will be the change, and after the change has been made, how will they proceed? Clearly, the new State, being in a mean between oligarchy and the perfect State, will partly follow one and partly the other, and will also have some peculiarities.

True, he said.

In the honour given to rulers, in the abstinence of the warrior class from agriculture, handicrafts, and trade in general, in the institution of common meals, and in the attention paid to gymnastics and military training—in all these respects this State will resemble the former.

True.

But in the fear of admitting philosophers to power, because they are no longer to be had simple and earnest, but are made up of mixed elements; and in turning from them to passionate and less complex characters, who are by nature fitted for war rather than peace; and in the value set by them upon military stratagems and contrivances, and in the waging of everlasting wars—this State will be for the most part peculiar.

Yes.

Yes, I said; and men of this stamp will be covetous of money, like those who live in oligarchies; they will have, a fierce secret longing after gold and silver, which they will hoard in dark places, having magazines and treasuries of their own for the deposit and concealment of them; also castles which are just nests for their eggs, and in which they will spend large sums on their wives, or on any others whom they please.

That is most true, he said.

And they are miserly because they have no means of openly acquiring the money which they prize; they will spend that which is another man's on the gratification of their desires, stealing their pleasures and running away like children from the law, their father: they have been schooled not by gentle influences but by force, for they have neglected her who is the true Muse, the companion of reason and philosophy, and have honoured gymnastic more than music.

Undoubtedly, he said, the form of government which you describe is a mixture of good and evil.

Why, there is a mixture, I said; but one thing, and one thing only, is predominantly seen,—the spirit of contention and ambition; and these are due to the prevalence of the passionate or spirited element.

Assuredly, he said.

Such is the origin and such the character of this State, which has been described in outline only; the more perfect execution was not required, for a sketch is enough to show the type of the most perfectly just and most perfectly unjust; and to go through all the States and all the characters of men, omitting none of them, would be an interminable labour.

Very true, he replied.

Now what man answers to this form of government-how did he come into being, and what is he like?

I think, said Adeimantus, that in the spirit of contention which characterises him, he is not unlike our friend Glaucon.

Perhaps, I said, he may be like him in that one point; but there are other respects in which he is very different.

In what respects?

He should have more of self-assertion and be less cultivated, and yet a friend of culture; and he should be a good listener, but no speaker. Such a person is apt to be rough with slaves, unlike the educated man, who is too proud for that; and he will also be courteous to freemen, and remarkably obedient to authority; he is a lover of power and a lover of honour; claiming to be a ruler, not because he is eloquent, or on any ground of that sort, but because he is a soldier and has performed feats of arms; he is also a lover of gymnastic exercises and of the chase.

Yes, that is the type of character which answers to timocracy.

Such an one will despise riches only when he is young; but as he gets older he will be more and more attracted to them, because he has a piece of the avaricious nature in him, and is not single-minded towards virtue, having lost his best guardian.

Who was that? said Adeimantus.

Philosophy, I said, tempered with music, who comes and takes up her abode in a man, and is the only saviour of his virtue throughout life.

Good, he said.

Such, I said, is the timocratical youth, and he is like the timocratical State.

Exactly.

His origin is as follows:—He is often the young son of a brave father, who dwells in an ill-governed city, of which he declines the honours and offices, and will not go to law, or exert himself in any way, but is ready to waive his rights in order that he may escape trouble.

And how does the son come into being?

The character of the son begins to develope when he hears his mother complaining that her husband has no place in the government, of which the consequence is that she has no precedence among other women. Further, when she sees her husband not very eager about money, and instead of battling and railing in the law courts or assembly, taking whatever happens to him quietly; and when she observes that his thoughts always centre in himself, while he treats her with very considerable indifference, she is annoyed, and says to her son that his father is only half a man and far too easy-going: adding all the other complaints about her own ill-treatment which women are so fond of rehearsing.

Yes, said Adeimantus, they give us plenty of them, and their complaints are so like themselves.

And you know, I said, that the old servants also, who are supposed to be attached to the family, from time to time talk privately in the same strain to the son; and if they see any one who owes money to his father, or is wronging him in any way, and he fails to prosecute them, they tell the youth that when he grows up he must retaliate upon people of this sort, and be more of a man than his father. He has only to walk abroad and he hears and sees the same sort of thing: those who do their own business in the city are called simpletons, and held in no esteem, while the busy-bodies are honoured and applauded. The result is that the young man, hearing and seeing all these things—hearing, too, the words of his father, and having a nearer view of his way of life, and making comparisons of him and others—is drawn opposite ways: while his father is watering and nourishing the rational principle in his soul, the others are encouraging the passionate and appetitive; and he being not originally of a bad nature, but having kept bad company, is at last brought by their joint influence to a middle point, and gives up the kingdom which is within him to the middle principle of contentiousness and passion, and becomes arrogant and ambitious.

You seem to me to have described his origin perfectly.

Then we have now, I said, the second form of government and the second type of character?

We have.

Next, let us look at another man who, as Aeschylus says, "Is set over against another State;"

or rather, as our plan requires, begin with the State.

By all means.

I believe that oligarchy follows next in order.

And what manner of government do you term oligarchy?

A government resting on a valuation of property, in which the rich have power and the poor man is deprived of it.

I understand, he replied.

Ought I not to begin by describing how the change from timocracy to oligarchy arises?

Yes.

Well, I said, no eyes are required in order to see how the one passes into the other.

How?

The accumulation of gold in the treasury of private individuals is the ruin of timocracy; they invent illegal modes of expenditure; for what do they or their wives care about the law?

Yes, indeed.

And then one, seeing another grow rich, seeks to rival him, and thus the great mass of the citizens become lovers of money.

Likely enough.

And so they grow richer and richer, and the more they think of making a fortune the less they think of virtue; for when riches and virtue are placed together in the scales of the balance, the one always rises as the other falls.

True.

And in proportion as riches and rich men are honoured in the State, virtue and the virtuous are dishonoured.

Clearly.

And what is honoured is cultivated, and that which has no honour is neglected.

That is obvious.

And so at last, instead of loving contention and glory, men become lovers of trade and money; they honour and look up to the rich man, and make a ruler of him, and dishonour the poor man.

They do so.

They next proceed to make a law which fixes a sum of money as the qualification of citizenship; the sum is higher in one place and lower in another, as the oligarchy is more or less exclusive; and they allow no one whose property falls below the amount fixed to have any share in the government. These changes in the constitution they effect by force of arms, if intimidation has not already done their work.

Very true.

And this, speaking generally, is the way in which oligarchy is established.

Yes, he said; but what are the characteristics of this form of government, and what are the defects of which we were speaking?

First of all, I said, consider the nature of the qualification. Just think what would happen if pilots were to be chosen according to their property, and a poor man were refused permission to steer, even though he were a better pilot?

You mean that they would shipwreck?

Yes; and is not this true of the government of anything?

I should imagine so.

Except a city?—or would you include a city?

Nay, he said, the case of a city is the strongest of all, inasmuch as the rule of a city is the greatest and most difficult of all.

This, then, will be the first great defect of oligarchy?

Clearly.

And here is another defect which is quite as bad.

What defect?

The inevitable division: such a State is not one, but two States, the one of poor, the other of rich men; and they are living on the same spot and always conspiring against one another.

That, surely, is at least as bad.

Another discreditable feature is, that, for a like reason, they are incapable of carrying on any war. Either they arm the multitude, and then they are more afraid of them than of the enemy; or, if they do not call them out in the hour of battle, they are oligarchs indeed, few to fight as they are few to rule. And at the same time their fondness for money makes them unwilling to pay taxes.

How discreditable!

And, as we said before, under such a constitution the same persons have too many callings—they are husbandmen, tradesmen, warriors, all in one. Does that look well?

Anything but well.

There is another evil which is, perhaps, the greatest of all, and to which this State first begins to be liable.

What evil?

A man may sell all that he has, and another may acquire his property; yet after the sale he may dwell in the city of which he is no longer a part, being neither trader, nor artisan, nor horseman, nor hoplite, but only a poor, helpless creature.

Yes, that is an evil which also first begins in this State.

The evil is certainly not prevented there; for oligarchies have both the extremes of great wealth and utter poverty.

True.

But think again: In his wealthy days, while he was spending his money, was a man of this sort a whit more good to the State for the purposes of citizenship? Or did he only seem to be a member of the ruling body, although in truth he was neither ruler nor subject, but just a spendthrift?

As you say, he seemed to be a ruler, but was only a spendthrift.

May we not say that this is the drone in the house who is like the drone in the honeycomb, and that the one is the plague of the city as the other is of the hive?

Just so, Socrates.

And God has made the flying drones, Adeimantus, all without stings, whereas of the walking drones he has made some without stings but others have dreadful stings; of the stingless class are those who in their old age end as paupers; of the stingers come all the criminal class, as they are termed.

Most true, he said.

Clearly then, whenever you see paupers in a State, somewhere in that neighborhood there are hidden away thieves, and cut-purses and robbers of temples, and all sorts of malefactors.

Clearly.

Well, I said, and in oligarchical States do you not find paupers?

Yes, he said; nearly everybody is a pauper who is not a ruler.

And may we be so bold as to affirm that there are also many

criminals to be found in them, rogues who have stings, and whom the authorities are careful to restrain by force?

Certainly, we may be so bold.

The existence of such persons is to be attributed to want of education, ill-training, and an evil constitution of the State?

True.

Such, then, is the form and such are the evils of oligarchy; and there may be many other evils.

Very likely.

Then oligarchy, or the form of government in which the rulers are elected for their wealth, may now be dismissed. Let us next proceed to consider the nature and origin of the individual who answers to this State.

By all means.

Does not the timocratical man change into the oligarchical on this wise?

How?

A time arrives when the representative of timocracy has a son: at first he begins by emulating his father and walking in his footsteps, but presently he sees him of a sudden foundering against the State as upon a sunken reef, and he and all that he has is lost; he may have been a general or some other high officer who is brought to trial under a prejudice raised by informers, and either put to death, or exiled, or deprived of the privileges of a citizen, and all his property taken from him.

Nothing more likely.

And the son has seen and known all this—he is a ruined man, and his fear has taught him to knock ambition and passion headforemost from his bosom's throne; humbled by poverty he takes to money-making and by mean and miserly savings and hard work gets a fortune together. Is not such an one likely to seat the concupiscent and covetous element on the vacant throne and to suffer it to play the great king within him, girt with tiara and chain and scimitar?

Most true, he replied.

And when he has made reason and spirit sit down on the ground obediently on either side of their sovereign, and taught them to know their place, he compels the one to think only of how lesser sums may be turned into larger ones, and will not allow the other to worship and admire anything but riches and rich men, or to be ambitious of anything so much as the acquisition of wealth and the means of acquiring it.

Of all changes, he said, there is none so speedy or so sure as the conversion of the ambitious youth into the avaricious one.

And the avaricious, I said, is the oligarchical youth?

Yes, he said; at any rate the individual out of whom he came is like the State out of which oligarchy came.

Let us then consider whether there is any likeness between them.

Very good.

First, then, they resemble one another in the value which they set upon wealth?

Certainly.

Also in their penurious, laborious character; the individual only satisfies his necessary appetites, and confines his expenditure to them; his other desires he subdues, under the idea that they are unprofitable.

True.

He is a shabby fellow, who saves something out of everything and makes a purse for himself; and this is the sort of man whom the vulgar applaud. Is he not a true image of the State which he represents?

He appears to me to be so; at any rate money is highly valued by him as well as by the State.

You see that he is not a man of cultivation, I said.

I imagine not, he said; had he been educated he would never have made a blind god director of his chorus, or given him chief honour.

Excellent! I said. Yet consider: Must we not further admit that owing to this want of cultivation there will be found in him dronelike desires as of pauper and rogue, which are forcibly kept down by his general habit of life?

True.

Do you know where you will have to look if you want to discover his rogueries?

Where must I look?

You should see him where he has some great opportunity of acting dishonestly, as in the guardianship of an orphan.

Aye.

It will be clear enough then that in his ordinary dealings which give him a reputation for honesty he coerces his bad passions by an enforced virtue; not making them see that they are wrong, or taming them by reason, but by necessity and fear constraining them, and because he trembles for his possessions.

To be sure.

Yes, indeed, my dear friend, but you will find that the natural desires of the drone commonly exist in him all the same whenever he has to spend what is not his own.

Yes, and they will be strong in him too.

The man, then, will be at war with himself; he will be two men, and not one; but, in general, his better desires will be found to prevail over his inferior ones.

True.

For these reasons such an one will be more respectable than most people; yet the true virtue of a unanimous and harmonious soul will flee far away and never come near him.

I should expect so.

And surely, the miser individually will be an ignoble competitor in a State for any prize of victory, or other object of honourable ambition; he will not spend his money in the contest for glory; so afraid is he of awakening his expensive appetites and inviting them to help and join in the struggle; in true oligarchical fashion he fights with a small part only of his resources, and the result commonly is that he loses the prize and saves his money.

Very true.

Can we any longer doubt, then, that the miser and money-maker answers to the oligarchical State?

There can be no doubt.

Next comes democracy; of this the origin and nature have still to be considered by us; and then we will enquire into the ways of the democratic man, and bring him up for judgment.

That, he said, is our method.

Well, I said, and how does the change from oligarchy into democracy arise? Is it not on this wise?—The good at which such a State aims is to become as rich as possible, a desire which is insatiable?

What then?

The rulers, being aware that their power rests upon their wealth, refuse to curtail by law the extravagance of the spendthrift youth because they gain by their ruin; they take interest from them and buy up their estates and thus increase their own wealth and importance?

To be sure.

There can be no doubt that the love of wealth and the spirit of moderation cannot exist together in citizens of the same state to any considerable extent; one or the other will be disregarded.

That is tolerably clear.

And in oligarchical States, from the general spread of carelessness and extravagance, men of good family have often been reduced to beggary?

Yes, often.

And still they remain in the city; there they are, ready to sting and fully armed, and some of them owe money, some have forfeited their citizenship; a third class are in both predicaments; and they hate and conspire against those who have got their property, and against everybody else, and are eager for revolution.

That is true.

On the other hand, the men of business, stooping as they walk, and pretending not even to see those whom they have already ruined, insert their sting—that is, their money—into some one else who is not on his guard against them, and recover the parent sum many times over multiplied into a family of children: and so they make drone and pauper to abound in the State.

Yes, he said, there are plenty of them—that is certain.

The evil blazes up like a fire; and they will not extinguish it, either by restricting a man's use of his own property, or by another remedy: What other?

One which is the next best, and has the advantage of compelling the citizens to look to their characters:—Let there be a general rule that every one shall enter into voluntary contracts at his own risk, and there will be less of this scandalous money-making, and the evils of which we were speaking will be greatly lessened in the State.

Yes, they will be greatly lessened.

At present the governors, induced by the motives which I have named, treat their subjects badly; while they and their adherents, especially the young men of the governing class, are habituated to lead a life of luxury and idleness both of body and mind; they do nothing, and are incapable of resisting either pleasure or pain.

Very true.

They themselves care only for making money, and are as indifferent as the pauper to the cultivation of virtue.

Yes, quite as indifferent.

Such is the state of affairs which prevails among them. And often rulers and their subjects may come in one another's way, whether on a journey or on some other occasion of meeting, on a pilgrimage or a march, as fellow-soldiers or fellow-sailors; aye and they may observe the behaviour of each other in the very moment of danger—for where danger is, there is no fear that the poor will be despised by the rich—and very likely the wiry sunburnt poor man may be placed in battle at the side of a wealthy one who has never spoilt his complexion and has plenty of superfluous flesh—when he sees such an one puffing and at his wits'-end, how can he avoid drawing the conclusion that men like him are only rich because no one has the courage to despoil them? And when they meet in private will not people be saying to one another 'Our warriors are not good for much'?

Yes, he said, I am quite aware that this is their way of talking.

And, as in a body which is diseased the addition of a touch from without may bring on illness, and sometimes even when there is no external provocation a commotion may arise within—in the same way wherever there is weakness in the State there is also likely to be illness, of which the occasion may be very slight, the one party introducing from without their oligarchical, the other their democratical allies, and then the State falls sick, and is at war with herself; and may be at times distracted, even when there is no external cause.

Yes, surely.

And then democracy comes into being after the poor have conquered their opponents, slaughtering some and banishing some, while to the remainder they give an equal share of freedom and power; and this is the form of government in which the magistrates are commonly elected by lot.

Yes, he said, that is the nature of democracy, whether the revolution has been effected by arms, or whether fear has caused the opposite party to withdraw.

And now what is their manner of life, and what sort of a government have they? for as the government is, such will be the man.

Clearly, he said.

In the first place, are they not free; and is not the city full of freedom and frankness—a man may say and do what he likes?

'Tis said so, he replied.

And where freedom is, the individual is clearly able to order for himself his own life as he pleases?

Clearly.

Then in this kind of State there will be the greatest variety of human natures?

There will.

This, then, seems likely to be the fairest of States, being like an embroidered robe which is spangled with every sort of flower. And just as women and children think a variety of colours to be of all things most charming, so there are many men to whom this State, which is spangled with the manners and characters of mankind, will appear to be the fairest of States.

Yes.

Yes, my good Sir, and there will be no better in which to look for a government.

Why?

Because of the liberty which reigns there—they have a complete assortment of constitutions; and he who has a mind to establish a State, as we have been doing, must go to a democracy as he would to a bazaar at which they sell them, and pick out the one that suits him; then, when he has made his choice, he may found his State.

He will be sure to have patterns enough.

And there being no necessity, I said, for you to govern in this State, even if you have the capacity, or to be governed, unless you like, or go to war when the rest go to war, or to be at peace when others are at peace, unless you are so disposed—there being no necessity also, because some law forbids you to hold office or be a dicast, that you should not hold office or be a dicast, if you have a fancy—is not this a way of life which for the moment is supremely delightful?

For the moment, yes.

And is not their humanity to the condemned in some cases quite charming? Have you not observed how, in a democracy, many persons, although they have been sentenced to death or exile, just stay where they are and walk about the world—the gentleman parades like a hero, and nobody sees or cares?

Yes, he replied, many and many a one.

See too, I said, the forgiving spirit of democracy, and the 'don't care' about trifles, and the disregard which she shows of all the fine principles which we solemnly laid down at the foundation of the city— as when we said that, except in the case of some rarely gifted nature, there never will be a good man who has not from his childhood been used to play amid things of beauty and make of them a joy and a study—how grandly does she trample all these fine notions of ours under her feet, never giving a thought to the pursuits which make a statesman, and promoting to honour any one who professes to be the people's friend.

Yes, she is of a noble spirit.

These and other kindred characteristics are proper to democracy, which is a charming form of government, full of variety and disorder, and dispensing a sort of equality to equals and unequals alike.

We know her well.

Consider now, I said, what manner of man the individual is, or rather consider, as in the case of the State, how he comes into being.

Very good, he said.

Is not this the way—he is the son of the miserly and oligarchical father who has trained him in his own habits?

Exactly.

And, like his father, he keeps under by force the pleasures which are of the spending and not of the getting sort, being those which are called unnecessary?

Obviously.

Would you like, for the sake of clearness, to distinguish which are the necessary and which are the unnecessary pleasures?

I should.

Are not necessary pleasures those of which we cannot get rid, and of which the satisfaction is a benefit to us? And they are rightly called so, because we are framed by nature to desire both what is beneficial and what is necessary, and cannot help it.

True.

We are not wrong therefore in calling them necessary?

We are not.

And the desires of which a man may get rid, if he takes pains from his youth upwards—of which the presence, moreover, does no good, and in some cases the reverse of good—shall we not be right in saying that all these are unnecessary?

Yes, certainly.

Suppose we select an example of either kind, in order that we may have a general notion of them?

Very good.

Will not the desire of eating, that is, of simple food and

condiments, in so far as they are required for health and strength, be of the necessary class?

That is what I should suppose.

The pleasure of eating is necessary in two ways; it does us good and it is essential to the continuance of life?

Yes.

But the condiments are only necessary in so far as they are good for health?

Certainly.

And the desire which goes beyond this, of more delicate food, or other luxuries, which might generally be got rid of, if controlled and trained in youth, and is hurtful to the body, and hurtful to the soul in the pursuit of wisdom and virtue, may be rightly called unnecessary?

Very true.

May we not say that these desires spend, and that the others make money because they conduce to production?

Certainly.

And of the pleasures of love, and all other pleasures, the same holds good?

True.

And the drone of whom we spoke was he who was surfeited in pleasures and desires of this sort, and was the slave of the unnecessary desires, whereas he who was subject to the necessary only was miserly and oligarchical?

Very true.

Again, let us see how the democratical man grows out of the oligarchical: the following, as I suspect, is commonly the process.

What is the process?

When a young man who has been brought up as we were just now describing, in a vulgar and miserly way, has tasted drones' honey and has come to associate with fierce and crafty natures who are able to provide for him all sorts of refinements and varieties of pleasure—then, as you may imagine, the change will begin of the oligarchical principle within him into the democratical?

Inevitably.

And as in the city like was helping like, and the change was effected by an alliance from without assisting one division of the citizens, so too the young man is changed by a class of desires coming from without to assist the desires within him, that which is akin and alike again helping that which is akin and alike?

Certainly.

And if there be any ally which aids the oligarchical principle within him, whether the influence of a father or of kindred, advising or rebuking him, then there arises in his soul a faction and an opposite faction, and he goes to war with himself.

It must be so.

And there are times when the democratical principle gives way to the oligarchical, and some of his desires die, and others are banished; a spirit of reverence enters into the young man's soul and order is restored.

Yes, he said, that sometimes happens.

And then, again, after the old desires have been driven out, fresh ones spring up, which are akin to them, and because he their father does not know how to educate them, wax fierce and numerous.

Yes, he said, that is apt to be the way.

They draw him to his old associates, and holding secret intercourse with them, breed and multiply in him.

Very true.

At length they seize upon the citadel of the young man's soul, which they perceive to be void of all accomplishments and fair pursuits and true words, which make their abode in the minds of men who are dear to the gods, and are their best guardians and sentinels.

None better.

False and boastful conceits and phrases mount upwards and take their place.

They are certain to do so.

And so the young man returns into the country of the lotus-eaters, and takes up his dwelling there in the face of all men; and if any help be sent by his friends to the oligarchical part of him, the aforesaid vain conceits shut the gate of the king's fastness; and they will neither allow the embassy itself to enter, nor if private advisers offer the fatherly counsel of the aged will they listen to them or receive them. There is a battle and they gain the day, and then modesty, which they call silliness, is ignominiously thrust into exile by them, and temperance, which they nickname unmanliness, is trampled in the mire and cast forth; they persuade men that moderation and orderly expenditure are vulgarity and meanness, and so, by the help of a rabble of evil appetites, they drive them beyond the border.

Yes, with a will.

And when they have emptied and swept clean the soul of him who is now in their power and who is being initiated by them in great mysteries, the next thing is to bring back to their house insolence and anarchy and waste and impudence in bright array having garlands on their heads, and a great company with them, hymning their praises and calling them by sweet names; insolence they term breeding, and anarchy liberty, and waste magnificence, and impudence courage. And so the young man passes out of his original nature, which was trained in the school of necessity, into the freedom and libertinism of useless and unnecessary pleasures.

Yes, he said, the change in him is visible enough.

After this he lives on, spending his money and labour and time on unnecessary pleasures quite as much as on necessary ones; but if he be fortunate, and is not too much disordered in his wits, when years have elapsed, and the heyday of passion is over—supposing that he then re-admits into the city some part of the exiled virtues, and does not wholly give himself up to their successors—in that case he balances his pleasures and lives in a sort of equilibrium, putting the government of himself into the hands of the one which comes first and wins the turn; and when he has had enough of that, then into the hands of another; he despises none of them but encourages them all equally.

Very true, he said.

Neither does he receive or let pass into the fortress any true word of advice; if any one says to him that some pleasures are the satisfactions of good and noble desires, and others of evil desires, and that he ought to use and honour some and chastise and master the others—whenever this is repeated to him he shakes his head and says that they are all alike, and that one is as good as another.

Yes, he said; that is the way with him.

Yes, I said, he lives from day to day indulging the appetite of the hour; and sometimes he is lapped in drink and strains of the flute; then he becomes a water-drinker, and tries to get thin; then he takes a turn at gymnastics; sometimes idling and neglecting everything, then once more living the life of a philosopher; often he is busy with politics, and starts to his feet and says and does whatever comes into his head; and, if he is emulous of any one who is a warrior, off he is in that direction, or of men of business, once more in that. His life has neither law nor order; and this distracted existence he terms joy and bliss and freedom; and so he goes on.

Yes, he replied, he is all liberty and equality.

Yes, I said; his life is motley and manifold and an epitome of the lives of many;—he answers to the State which we described as fair and spangled. And many a man and many a woman will take him for their pattern, and many a constitution and many an example of manners is contained in him.

Just so.

Let him then be set over against democracy; he may truly be called the democratic man.

Let that be his place, he said.

Last of all comes the most beautiful of all, man and State alike, tyranny and the tyrant; these we have now to consider.

Quite true, he said.

Say then, my friend, In what manner does tyranny arise?—that it has a democratic origin is evident.

Clearly.

And does not tyranny spring from democracy in the same manner as democracy from oligarchy—I mean, after a sort?

How?

The good which oligarchy proposed to itself and the means by which it was maintained was excess of wealth—am I not right?

Yes.

And the insatiable desire of wealth and the neglect of all other things for the sake of money-getting was also the ruin of oligarchy?

True.

And democracy has her own good, of which the insatiable desire brings her to dissolution?

What good?

Freedom, I replied; which, as they tell you in a democracy, is the glory of the State—and that therefore in a democracy alone will the freeman of nature deign to dwell.

Yes; the saying is in every body's mouth.

I was going to observe, that the insatiable desire of this and the neglect of other things introduces the change in democracy, which occasions a demand for tyranny.

How so?

When a democracy which is thirsting for freedom has evil cup-bearers presiding over the feast, and has drunk too deeply of the strong wine of freedom, then, unless her rulers are very amenable and give a plentiful draught, she calls them to account and punishes them, and says that they are cursed oligarchs.

Yes, he replied, a very common occurrence.

Yes, I said; and loyal citizens are insultingly termed by her slaves who hug their chains and men of naught; she would have subjects who are like rulers, and rulers who are like subjects: these are men after her own heart, whom she praises and honours both in private and public. Now, in such a State, can liberty have any limit?

Certainly not.

By degrees the anarchy finds a way into private houses, and ends by getting among the animals and infecting them.

How do you mean?

I mean that the father grows accustomed to descend to the level of his sons and to fear them, and the son is on a level with his father, he having no respect or reverence for either of his parents; and this is his freedom, and the metic is equal with the citizen and the citizen with the metic, and the stranger is quite as good as either.

Yes, he said, that is the way.

And these are not the only evils, I said—there are several lesser ones: In such a state of society the master fears and flatters his scholars, and the scholars despise their masters and tutors; young and old are all alike; and the young man is on a level with the old, and is ready to compete with him in word or deed; and old men condescend to the young and are full of pleasantry and gaiety; they are loth to be thought morose and authoritative, and therefore they adopt the manners of the young.

Quite true, he said.

The last extreme of popular liberty is when the slave bought with money, whether male or female, is just as free as his or her purchaser; nor must I forget to tell of the liberty and equality of the two sexes in relation to each other.

Why not, as Aeschylus says, utter the word which rises to our lips?

That is what I am doing, I replied; and I must add that no one who does not know would believe, how much greater is the liberty which the animals who are under the dominion of man have in a democracy than in any other State: for truly, the she-dogs, as the proverb says, are as good as their she-mistresses, and the horses and asses have a way of marching along with all the rights and dignities of freemen; and they will run at any body who comes in their way if he does not leave the road clear for them: and all things are just ready to burst with liberty.

When I take a country walk, he said, I often experience what you describe. You and I have dreamed the same thing.

And above all, I said, and as the result of all, see how sensitive the citizens become; they chafe impatiently at the least touch of authority, and at length, as you know, they cease to care even for the laws, written or unwritten; they will have no one over them.

Yes, he said, I know it too well.

Such, my friend, I said, is the fair and glorious beginning out of which springs tyranny.

Glorious indeed, he said. But what is the next step?

The ruin of oligarchy is the ruin of democracy; the same disease magnified and intensified by liberty overmasters democracy—the truth being that the excessive increase of anything often causes a reaction in the opposite direction; and this is the case not only in the seasons and in vegetable and animal life, but above all in forms of government.

True.

The excess of liberty, whether in States or individuals, seems only to pass into excess of slavery.

Yes, the natural order.

And so tyranny naturally arises out of democracy, and the most aggravated form of tyranny and slavery out of the most extreme form of liberty?

As we might expect.

That, however, was not, as I believe, your question—you rather desired to know what is that disorder which is generated alike in oligarchy and democracy, and is the ruin of both?

Just so, he replied.

Well, I said, I meant to refer to the class of idle spendthrifts, of whom the more courageous are the leaders and the more timid the followers, the same whom we were comparing to drones, some stingless, and others having stings.

A very just comparison.

These two classes are the plagues of every city in which they are generated, being what phlegm and bile are to the body. And the good physician and lawgiver of the State ought, like the wise bee-master, to keep them at a distance and prevent, if possible, their ever coming in; and if they have anyhow found a way in, then he should have them and their cells cut out as speedily as possible.

Yes, by all means, he said.

Then, in order that we may see clearly what we are doing, let us imagine democracy to be divided, as indeed it is, into three classes; for in the first place freedom creates rather more drones in the democratic than there were in the oligarchical State.

That is true.

And in the democracy they are certainly more intensified.

How so?

Because in the oligarchical State they are disqualified and driven from office, and therefore they cannot train or gather strength; whereas in a democracy they are almost the entire ruling power, and while the keener sort speak and act, the rest keep buzzing about the bema and do not suffer a word to be said on the other side; hence in democracies almost everything is managed by the drones.

Very true, he said.

Then there is another class which is always being severed from the mass.

What is that?

They are the orderly class, which in a nation of traders is sure to be the richest.

Naturally so.

They are the most squeezable persons and yield the largest amount of honey to the drones.

Why, he said, there is little to be squeezed out of people who have little.

And this is called the wealthy class, and the drones feed upon them.

That is pretty much the case, he said.

The people are a third class, consisting of those who work with their own hands; they are not politicians, and have not much to live upon. This, when assembled, is the largest and most powerful class in a democracy.

True, he said; but then the multitude is seldom willing to congregate unless they get a little honey.

And do they not share? I said. Do not their leaders deprive the rich of their estates and distribute them among the people; at the same time taking care to reserve the larger part for themselves?

Why, yes, he said, to that extent the people do share.

And the persons whose property is taken from them are compelled to defend themselves before the people as they best can?

What else can they do?

And then, although they may have no desire of change, the others charge them with plotting against the people and being friends of oligarchy?

True.

And the end is that when they see the people, not of their own accord, but through ignorance, and because they are deceived by informers, seeking to do them wrong, then at last they are forced to become oligarchs in reality; they do not wish to be, but the sting of the drones torments them and breeds revolution in them.

That is exactly the truth.

Then come impeachments and judgments and trials of one another.

True.

The people have always some champion whom they set over them and nurse into greatness.

Yes, that is their way.

This and no other is the root from which a tyrant springs; when he first appears above ground he is a protector.

Yes, that is quite clear.

How then does a protector begin to change into a tyrant? Clearly when he does what the man is said to do in the tale of the Arcadian temple of Lycaean Zeus.

What tale?

The tale is that he who has tasted the entrails of a single human victim minced up with the entrails of other victims is destined to become a wolf. Did you never hear it?

Oh, yes.

And the protector of the people is like him; having a mob entirely at his disposal, he is not restrained from shedding the blood of kinsmen; by the favourite method of false accusation he brings them into court and murders them, making the life of man to disappear, and with unholy tongue and lips tasting the blood of his fellow citizens; some he kills and others he banishes, at the same time hinting at the abolition of debts and partition of lands: and after this, what will be his destiny? Must he not either perish at the hands of his enemies, or from being a man become a wolf—that is, a tyrant?

Inevitably.

This, I said, is he who begins to make a party against the rich?

The same.

After a while he is driven out, but comes back, in spite of his enemies, a tyrant full grown.

That is clear.

And if they are unable to expel him, or to get him condemned to death by a public accusation, they conspire to assassinate him.

Yes, he said, that is their usual way.

Then comes the famous request for a body-guard, which is the device of all those who have got thus far in their tyrannical career—"Let not the people's friend," as they say, "be lost to them."

Exactly.

The people readily assent; all their fears are for him—they have none for themselves.

Very true.

And when a man who is wealthy and is also accused of being an enemy of the people sees this, then, my friend, as the oracle said to Croesus, 'By pebbly Hermus' shore he flees and rests not, and is not ashamed to be a coward.'

And quite right too, said he, for if he were, he would never be ashamed again.

But if he is caught he dies.

Of course.

And he, the protector of whom we spoke, is to be seen, not 'larding the plain' with his bulk, but himself the overthrower of many, standing up in the chariot of State with the reins in his hand, no longer protector, but tyrant absolute.

No doubt, he said.

And now let us consider the happiness of the man, and also of the State in which a creature like him is generated.

Yes, he said, let us consider that.

At first, in the early days of his power, he is full of smiles, and he salutes every one whom he meets;—he to be called a tyrant, who is making promises in public and also in private! liberating debtors, and distributing land to the people and his followers, and wanting to be so kind and good to every one!

Of course, he said.

But when he has disposed of foreign enemies by conquest or treaty, and there is nothing to fear from them, then he is always stirring up some war or other, in order that the people may require a leader.

To be sure.

Has he not also another object, which is that they may be impoverished by payment of taxes, and thus compelled to devote themselves to their daily wants and therefore less likely to conspire against him?

Clearly.

And if any of them are suspected by him of having notions of freedom, and of resistance to his authority, he will have a good pretext for destroying them by placing them at the mercy of the enemy; and for all these reasons the tyrant must be always getting up a war.

He must.

Now he begins to grow unpopular.

A necessary result.

Then some of those who joined in setting him up, and who are in power, speak their minds to him and to one another, and the more courageous of them cast in his teeth what is being done.

Yes, that may be expected.

And the tyrant, if he means to rule, must get rid of them; he cannot stop while he has a friend or an enemy who is good for anything.

He cannot.

And therefore he must look about him and see who is valiant, who is high-minded, who is wise, who is wealthy; happy man, he is the enemy of them all, and must seek occasion against them whether he will or no, until he has made a purgation of the State.

Yes, he said, and a rare purgation.

Yes, I said, not the sort of purgation which the physicians make of the body; for they take away the worse and leave the better part, but he does the reverse.

If he is to rule, I suppose that he cannot help himself.

What a blessed alternative, I said:—to be compelled to dwell only with the many bad, and to be by them hated, or not to live at all!

Yes, that is the alternative.

And the more detestable his actions are to the citizens the more satellites and the greater devotion in them will he require?

Certainly.

And who are the devoted band, and where will he procure them?

They will flock to him, he said, of their own accord, if he pays them.

By the dog! I said, here are more drones, of every sort and from every land.

Yes, he said, there are.

But will he not desire to get them on the spot?

How do you mean?

He will rob the citizens of their slaves; he will then set them free and enrol them in his body-guard.

To be sure, he said; and he will be able to trust them best of all.

What a blessed creature, I said, must this tyrant be; he has put to death the others and has these for his trusted friends.

Yes, he said; they are quite of his sort.

Yes, I said, and these are the new citizens whom he has called into existence, who admire him and are his companions, while the good hate and avoid him.

Of course.

Verily, then, tragedy is a wise thing and Euripides a great tragedian.

Why so?

Why, because he is the author of the pregnant saying, 'Tyrants are wise by living with the wise;' and he clearly meant to say that they are the wise whom the tyrant makes his companions.

Yes, he said, and he also praises tyranny as godlike; and many other things of the same kind are said by him and by the other poets.

And therefore, I said, the tragic poets being wise men will forgive us and any others who live after our manner if we do not receive them into our State, because they are the eulogists of tyranny.

Yes, he said, those who have the wit will doubtless forgive us.

But they will continue to go to other cities and attract mobs, and hire voices fair and loud and persuasive, and draw the cities over to tyrannies and democracies.

Very true.

Moreover, they are paid for this and receive honour—the greatest honour, as might be expected, from tyrants, and the next greatest from democracies; but the higher they ascend our constitution hill, the more their reputation fails, and seems unable from shortness of breath to proceed further.

True.

But we are wandering from the subject: Let us therefore return and enquire how the tyrant will maintain that fair and numerous and various and ever-changing army of his.

If, he said, there are sacred treasures in the city, he will confiscate and spend them; and in so far as the fortunes of attainted persons may suffice, he will be able to diminish the taxes which he would otherwise have to impose upon the people.

And when these fail?

Why, clearly, he said, then he and his boon companions, whether male or female, will be maintained out of his father's estate.

You mean to say that the people, from whom he has derived his being, will maintain him and his companions?

Yes, he said; they cannot help themselves.

But what if the people fly into a passion, and aver that a grown-up son ought not to be supported by his father, but that the father should be supported by the son? The father did not bring him into being, or settle him in life, in order that when his son became a man he should himself be the servant of his own servants and should support him and his rabble of slaves and companions; but that his son should protect him, and that by his help he might be emancipated from the government of the rich and aristocratic, as they are termed. And so he bids him and his companions depart, just as any other father might drive out of the house a riotous son and his undesirable associates.

By heaven, he said, then the parent will discover what a monster he has been fostering in his bosom; and, when he wants to drive him out, he will find that he is weak and his son strong.

Why, you do not mean to say that the tyrant will use violence? What! beat his father if he opposes him?

Yes, he will, having first disarmed him.

Then he is a parricide, and a cruel guardian of an aged parent; and this is real tyranny, about which there can be no longer a mistake: as the saying is, the people who would escape the smoke which is the slavery of freemen, has fallen into the fire which is the tyranny of slaves. Thus liberty, getting out of all order and reason, passes into the harshest and bitterest form of slavery.

True, he said.

Very well; and may we not rightly say that we have sufficiently discussed the nature of tyranny, and the manner of the transition from democracy to tyranny?

Yes, quite enough, he said.

# BOOK IX

L ast of all comes the tyrannical man; about whom we have once more to ask, how is he formed out of the democratical? and how does he live, in happiness or in misery?

Yes, he said, he is the only one remaining.

There is, however, I said, a previous question which remains unanswered.

What question?

I do not think that we have adequately determined the nature and number of the appetites, and until this is accomplished the enquiry will always be confused.

Well, he said, it is not too late to supply the omission.

Very true, I said; and observe the point which I want to understand: Certain of the unnecessary pleasures and appetites I conceive to be unlawful; every one appears to have them, but in some persons they are controlled by the laws and by reason, and the better desires prevail over them—either they are wholly banished or they become few and weak; while in the case of others they are stronger, and there are more of them.

Which appetites do you mean?

I mean those which are awake when the reasoning and human and ruling power is asleep; then the wild beast within us, gorged with meat or drink, starts up and having shaken off sleep, goes forth to satisfy his desires; and there is no conceivable

315

folly or crime—not excepting incest or any other unnatural union, or parricide, or the eating of forbidden food—which at such a time, when he has parted company with all shame and sense, a man may not be ready to commit.

Most true, he said.

But when a man's pulse is healthy and temperate, and when before going to sleep he has awakened his rational powers, and fed them on noble thoughts and enquiries, collecting himself in meditation; after having first indulged his appetites neither too much nor too little, but just enough to lay them to sleep, and prevent them and their enjoyments and pains from interfering with the higher principle—which he leaves in the solitude of pure abstraction, free to contemplate and aspire to the knowledge of the unknown, whether in past, present, or future: when again he has allayed the passionate element, if he has a quarrel against any one—I say, when, after pacifying the two irrational principles, he rouses up the third, which is reason, before he takes his rest, then, as you know, he attains truth most nearly, and is least likely to be the sport of fantastic and lawless visions.

I quite agree.

In saying this I have been running into a digression; but the point which I desire to note is that in all of us, even in good men, there is a lawless wild-beast nature, which peers out in sleep. Pray, consider whether I am right, and you agree with me.

Yes, I agree.

And now remember the character which we attributed to the democratic man. He was supposed from his youth upwards to have been trained under a miserly parent, who encouraged the saving appetites in him, but discountenanced the unnecessary, which aim only at amusement and ornament?

True.

And then he got into the company of a more refined, licentious sort of people, and taking to all their wanton ways rushed into the opposite extreme from an abhorrence of his father's meanness. At last, being a better man than his corruptors, he was drawn in both directions until he halted midway and led a life, not of vulgar and slavish passion, but of what he deemed moderate indulgence in various pleasures. After this manner the democrat was generated out of the oligarch?

Yes, he said; that was our view of him, and is so still.

And now, I said, years will have passed away, and you must conceive this man, such as he is, to have a son, who is brought up in his father's principles.

I can imagine him.

Then you must further imagine the same thing to happen to the son which has already happened to the father:—he is drawn into a perfectly lawless life, which by his seducers is termed perfect liberty; and his father and friends take part with his moderate desires, and the opposite party assist the opposite ones. As soon as these dire magicians and tyrant-makers find that they are losing their hold on him, they contrive to implant in him a master passion, to be lord over his idle and spendthrift lusts—a sort of monstrous winged drone—that is the only image which will adequately describe him.

Yes, he said, that is the only adequate image of him.

And when his other lusts, amid clouds of incense and perfumes and garlands and wines, and all the pleasures of a dissolute life, now let loose, come buzzing around him, nourishing to the utmost the sting of desire which they implant in his drone-like nature, then at last this lord of the soul, having Madness for the captain of his guard, breaks out into a frenzy: and if he finds in himself any good opinions or appetites in process of formation, and there is in him any sense of shame remaining, to these better principles he puts an end, and casts them forth until he has purged away temperance and brought in madness to the full.

Yes, he said, that is the way in which the tyrannical man is generated.

And is not this the reason why of old love has been called a tyrant?

I should not wonder.

Further, I said, has not a drunken man also the spirit of a tyrant?

He has.

And you know that a man who is deranged and not right in his mind, will fancy that he is able to rule, not only over men, but also over the gods?

That he will.

And the tyrannical man in the true sense of the word comes into being when, either under the influence of nature, or habit, or both, he becomes drunken, lustful, passionate? O my friend, is not that so?

Assuredly.

Such is the man and such is his origin. And next, how does he live? Suppose, as people facetiously say, you were to tell me.

I imagine, I said, at the next step in his progress, that there will be feasts and carousals and revellings and courtezans, and all that sort of thing; Love is the lord of the house within him, and orders all the concerns of his soul.

That is certain.

Yes; and every day and every night desires grow up many and formidable, and their demands are many.

They are indeed, he said.

His revenues, if he has any, are soon spent.

True.

Then comes debt and the cutting down of his property.

Of course.

When he has nothing left, must not his desires, crowding in the nest like young ravens, be crying aloud for food; and he, goaded on by them, and especially by love himself, who is in a manner the captain of them, is in a frenzy, and would fain discover whom he can defraud or despoil of his property, in order that he may gratify them?

Yes, that is sure to be the case.

He must have money, no matter how, if he is to escape horrid pains and pangs.

He must.

And as in himself there was a succession of pleasures, and the new got the better of the old and took away their rights, so he being younger will claim to have more than his father and his mother, and if he has spent his own share of the property, he will take a slice of theirs.

No doubt he will.

And if his parents will not give way, then he will try first of all to cheat and deceive them.

Very true.

And if he fails, then he will use force and plunder them.

Yes, probably.

And if the old man and woman fight for their own, what then, my friend? Will the creature feel any compunction at tyrannizing over them?

Nay, he said, I should not feel at all comfortable about his parents.

But, O heavens! Adeimantus, on account of some new-fangled love of a harlot, who is anything but a necessary connection, can you believe that he would strike the mother who is his ancient friend and necessary to his very existence, and would place her under the authority of the other, when she is brought under the same roof with her; or that, under like circumstances, he would do the same to his withered old father, first and most indispensable of friends, for the sake of some newly-found blooming youth who is the reverse of indispensable?

Yes, indeed, he said; I believe that he would.

Truly, then, I said, a tyrannical son is a blessing to his father and mother.

He is indeed, he replied.

He first takes their property, and when that fails, and pleasures are beginning to swarm in the hive of his soul, then he breaks into a house, or steals the garments of some nightly wayfarer; next he proceeds to clear a temple. Meanwhile the old opinions which he had when a child, and which gave judgment about good and evil, are overthrown by those others which have just been emancipated, and are now the body-guard of love and share his empire. These in his democratic days, when he was still subject to the laws and to his father, were only let loose in the dreams of sleep. But now that he is under the dominion of love, he becomes always and in waking reality what he was then very rarely and in a dream only; he will commit the foulest murder, or eat forbidden food, or be guilty of any other horrid act. Love is his tyrant, and lives lordly in him and lawlessly, and being himself a king, leads him on, as a tyrant leads a State, to the performance of any reckless deed by which he can maintain himself and the rabble of his associates, whether those whom evil communications have brought in from without, or those whom he himself has allowed to break loose within him by reason of a similar evil nature in himself. Have we not here a picture of his way of life?

Yes, indeed, he said.

And if there are only a few of them in the State, and the rest of the people are well disposed, they go away and become the body-guard or mercenary soldiers of some other tyrant who may probably want them for a war; and if there is no war, they stay at home and do many little pieces of mischief in the city.

What sort of mischief?

For example, they are the thieves, burglars, cut-purses, foot-pads, robbers of temples, man-stealers of the community; or if they are able to speak they turn informers, and bear false witness, and take bribes.

A small catalogue of evils, even if the perpetrators of them are few in number.

Yes, I said; but small and great are comparative terms, and all these things, in the misery and evil which they inflict upon a State, do not come within a thousand miles of the tyrant; when this noxious class and their followers grow numerous and become conscious of their strength, assisted by the infatuation of the people, they choose from among themselves the one who has most of the tyrant in his own soul, and him they create their tyrant.

Yes, he said, and he will be the most fit to be a tyrant.

If the people yield, well and good; but if they resist him, as he began by beating his own father and mother, so now, if he has the power, he beats them, and will keep his dear old fatherland or motherland, as the Cretans say, in subjection to his young retainers whom he has introduced to be their rulers and masters. This is the end of his passions and desires.

Exactly.

When such men are only private individuals and before they get power, this is their character; they associate entirely with their own flatterers or ready tools; or if they want anything from anybody, they in their turn are equally ready to bow down before them: they profess every sort of affection for them; but when they have gained their point they know them no more.

Yes, truly.

They are always either the masters or servants and never the friends of anybody; the tyrant never tastes of true freedom or friendship.

Certainly not.

And may we not rightly call such men treacherous?

No question.

Also they are utterly unjust, if we were right in our notion of justice?

Yes, he said, and we were perfectly right.

Let us then sum up in a word, I said, the character of the worst man: he is the waking reality of what we dreamed.

Most true.

And this is he who being by nature most of a tyrant bears rule, and the longer he lives the more of a tyrant he becomes.

That is certain, said Glaucon, taking his turn to answer.

And will not he who has been shown to be the wickedest, be also the most miserable? and he who has tyrannized longest and most, most continually and truly miserable; although this may not be the opinion of men in general?

Yes, he said, inevitably.

And must not the tyrannical man be like the tyrannical State, and the democratical man like the democratical State; and the same of the others?

Certainly.

And as State is to State in virtue and happiness, so is man in relation to man?

To be sure.

Then comparing our original city, which was under a king, and the city which is under a tyrant, how do they stand as to virtue?

They are the opposite extremes, he said, for one is the very best and the other is the very worst.

There can be no mistake, I said, as to which is which, and therefore I will at once enquire whether you would arrive at a similar decision about their relative happiness and misery. And here we must not allow ourselves to be panic-stricken at the apparition of the tyrant, who is only a unit and may perhaps have a few retainers about him; but let us go as we ought into every corner of the city and look all about, and then we will give our opinion.

A fair invitation, he replied; and I see, as every one must, that a tyranny is the wretchedest form of government, and the rule of a king the happiest.

And in estimating the men too, may I not fairly make a like request, that I should have a judge whose mind can enter into and see through human nature? he must not be like a child who looks at the outside and is dazzled at the pompous aspect which the tyrannical nature assumes to the beholder, but let him be one who has a clear insight. May I suppose that the judgment is given in the hearing of us all by one who is able to judge, and has dwelt in the same place with him, and been present at his daily life and known him in his family relations, where he may be seen stripped of his tragedy attire, and again in the hour of public danger—he shall tell us about the happiness and misery of the tyrant when compared with other men?

That again, he said, is a very fair proposal.

Shall I assume that we ourselves are able and experienced judges and have before now met with such a person? We shall then have some one who will answer our enquiries.

By all means.

Let me ask you not to forget the parallel of the individual and the State; bearing this in mind, and glancing in turn from one to the other of them, will you tell me their respective conditions?

What do you mean? he asked.

Beginning with the State, I replied, would you say that a city which is governed by a tyrant is free or enslaved?

No city, he said, can be more completely enslaved.

And yet, as you see, there are freemen as well as masters in such a State?

Yes, he said, I see that there are—a few; but the people, speaking generally, and the best of them are miserably degraded and enslaved.

Then if the man is like the State, I said, must not the same rule prevail? his soul is full of meanness and vulgarity—the best elements in him are enslaved; and there is a small ruling part, which is also the worst and maddest.

Inevitably.

And would you say that the soul of such an one is the soul of a freeman, or of a slave?

He has the soul of a slave, in my opinion.

And the State which is enslaved under a tyrant is utterly incapable of acting voluntarily?

Utterly incapable.

And also the soul which is under a tyrant (I am speaking of the soul taken as a whole) is least capable of doing what she desires; there is a gadfly which goads her, and she is full of trouble and remorse?

Certainly.

And is the city which is under a tyrant rich or poor?

Poor.

And the tyrannical soul must be always poor and insatiable?

True.

And must not such a State and such a man be always full of fear?

Yes, indeed.

Is there any State in which you will find more of lamentation and sorrow and groaning and pain?

Certainly not.

And is there any man in whom you will find more of this sort of misery than in the tyrannical man, who is in a fury of passions and desires?

Impossible.

Reflecting upon these and similar evils, you held the tyrannical State to be the most miserable of States?

And I was right, he said.

Certainly, I said. And when you see the same evils in the tyrannical man, what do you say of him?

323

I say that he is by far the most miserable of all men.

There, I said, I think that you are beginning to go wrong.

What do you mean?

I do not think that he has as yet reached the utmost extreme of misery.

Then who is more miserable?

One of whom I am about to speak.

Who is that?

He who is of a tyrannical nature, and instead of leading a private life has been cursed with the further misfortune of being a public tyrant.

From what has been said, I gather that you are right.

Yes, I replied, but in this high argument you should be a little more certain, and should not conjecture only; for of all questions, this respecting good and evil is the greatest.

Very true, he said.

Let me then offer you an illustration, which may, I think, throw a light upon this subject.

What is your illustration?

The case of rich individuals in cities who possess many slaves: from them you may form an idea of the tyrant's condition, for they both have slaves; the only difference is that he has more slaves.

Yes, that is the difference.

You know that they live securely and have nothing to apprehend from their servants?

What should they fear?

Nothing. But do you observe the reason of this?

Yes; the reason is, that the whole city is leagued together for the protection of each individual.

Very true, I said. But imagine one of these owners, the master say of some fifty slaves, together with his family and property and slaves, carried off by a god into the wilderness, where there are no freemen to help him—will he not be in an agony of fear lest he and his wife and children should be put to death by his slaves?

Yes, he said, he will be in the utmost fear.

The time has arrived when he will be compelled to flatter divers of his slaves, and make many promises to them of freedom and other things, much against his will—he will have to cajole his own servants.

Yes, he said, that will be the only way of saving himself.

And suppose the same god, who carried him away, to surround him with neighbours who will not suffer one man to be the master of another, and who, if they could catch the offender, would take his life?

His case will be still worse, if you suppose him to be everywhere surrounded and watched by enemies.

And is not this the sort of prison in which the tyrant will be bound—he who being by nature such as we have described, is full of all sorts of fears and lusts? His soul is dainty and greedy, and yet alone, of all men in the city, he is never allowed to go on a journey, or to see the things which other freemen desire to see, but he lives in his hole like a woman hidden in the house, and is jealous of any other citizen who goes into foreign parts and sees anything of interest.

Very true, he said.

And amid evils such as these will not he who is ill-governed in his own person—the tyrannical man, I mean—whom you just now decided to be the most miserable of all—will not he be yet more miserable when, instead of leading a private life, he is constrained by fortune to be a public tyrant? He has to be master of others when he is not master of himself: he is like a diseased or paralytic man who is compelled to pass his life, not in retirement, but fighting and combating with other men.

Yes, he said, the similitude is most exact.

Is not his case utterly miserable? and does not the actual tyrant lead a worse life than he whose life you determined to be the worst?

Certainly.

He who is the real tyrant, whatever men may think, is the real slave, and is obliged to practise the greatest adulation and servility, and to be the flatterer of the vilest of mankind. He has desires which he is utterly unable to satisfy, and has more wants than any one, and is truly poor, if you know how to inspect the whole soul of him: all his life long he is beset with fear and is full of convulsions and distractions, even as the State which he resembles: and surely the resemblance holds?

Very true, he said.

Moreover, as we were saying before, he grows worse from having power: he becomes and is of necessity more jealous, more faithless, more unjust, more friendless, more impious, than he was at first; he is the purveyor and cherisher of every sort of vice, and the consequence is that he is supremely miserable, and that he makes everybody else as miserable as himself.

No man of any sense will dispute your words.

Come then, I said, and as the general umpire in theatrical contests proclaims the result, do you also decide who in your opinion is first in the scale of happiness, and who second, and in what order the others follow: there are five of them in all—they are the royal, timocratical, oligarchical, democratical, tyrannical.

The decision will be easily given, he replied; they shall be choruses coming on the stage, and I must judge them in the order in which they enter, by the criterion of virtue and vice, happiness and misery.

Need we hire a herald, or shall I announce, that the son of Ariston (the best) has decided that the best and justest is also the happiest, and that this is he who is the most royal man and king over himself; and that the worst and most unjust man is also the most miserable, and that this is he who being the greatest tyrant of himself is also the greatest tyrant of his State?

Make the proclamation yourself, he said.

And shall I add, "whether seen or unseen by gods and men"?

Let the words be added.

Then this, I said, will be our first proof; and there is another, which may also have some weight.

What is that?

The second proof is derived from the nature of the soul: seeing that the individual soul, like the State, has been divided by us into three principles, the division may, I think, furnish a new demonstration.

Of what nature?

It seems to me that to these three principles three pleasures correspond; also three desires and governing powers.

How do you mean? he said.

There is one principle with which, as we were saying, a man learns, another with which he is angry; the third, having many forms, has no special name, but is denoted by the general term appetitive, from the extraordinary strength and vehemence of the desires of eating and drinking and the other sensual appetites which are the main elements of it; also money-loving, because such desires are generally satisfied by the help of money.

That is true, he said.

If we were to say that the loves and pleasures of this third part were concerned with gain, we should then be able to fall back on a single notion; and might truly and intelligibly describe this part of the soul as loving gain or money.

I agree with you.

Again, is not the passionate element wholly set on ruling and conquering and getting fame?

True.

Suppose we call it the contentious or ambitious—would the term be suitable?

Extremely suitable.

On the other hand, every one sees that the principle of knowledge is wholly directed to the truth, and cares less than either of the others for gain or fame.

Far less.

'Lover of wisdom,' 'lover of knowledge,' are titles which we may fitly apply to that part of the soul?

Certainly.

One principle prevails in the souls of one class of men, another in others, as may happen?

Yes.

Then we may begin by assuming that there are three classes of men—lovers of wisdom, lovers of honour, lovers of gain?

Exactly.

And there are three kinds of pleasure, which are their several objects?

Very true.

Now, if you examine the three classes of men, and ask of them in turn which of their lives is pleasantest, each will be found praising his own and depreciating that of others: the money-maker will contrast the vanity of honour or of learning if they bring no money with the solid advantages of gold and silver?

True, he said.

And the lover of honour—what will be his opinion? Will he not think that the pleasure of riches is vulgar, while the pleasure of learning, if it brings no distinction, is all smoke and nonsense to him?

Very true.

And are we to suppose, I said, that the philosopher sets any value on other pleasures in comparison with the pleasure of knowing the truth, and in that pursuit abiding, ever learning, not so far indeed from the heaven of pleasure? Does he not call the other pleasures necessary, under the idea that if there were no necessity for them, he would rather not have them?

There can be no doubt of that, he replied.

Since, then, the pleasures of each class and the life of each are in dispute, and the question is not which life is more or less honourable, or better or worse, but which is the more pleasant or painless—how shall we know who speaks truly?

I cannot myself tell, he said.

Well, but what ought to be the criterion? Is any better than experience and wisdom and reason?

There cannot be a better, he said.

Then, I said, reflect. Of the three individuals, which has the greatest experience of all the pleasures which we enumerated? Has the lover of gain, in learning the nature of essential truth, greater experience of the pleasure of knowledge than the philosopher has of the pleasure of gain?

The philosopher, he replied, has greatly the advantage; for he has of necessity always known the taste of the other pleasures from his childhood upwards: but the lover of gain in all his experience has not of necessity tasted—or, I should rather say, even had he desired, could hardly have tasted—the sweetness of learning and knowing truth.

Then the lover of wisdom has a great advantage over the lover of gain, for he has a double experience?

Yes, very great.

Again, has he greater experience of the pleasures of honour, or the lover of honour of the pleasures of wisdom?

Nay, he said, all three are honoured in proportion as they attain their object; for the rich man and the brave man and the wise man alike have their crowd of admirers, and as they all receive honour they all have experience of the pleasures of honour; but the delight which is to be found in the knowledge of true being is known to the philosopher only.

His experience, then, will enable him to judge better than any one?

Far better.

And he is the only one who has wisdom as well as experience?

Certainly.

Further, the very faculty which is the instrument of judgment is not possessed by the covetous or ambitious man, but only by the philosopher?

What faculty?

Reason, with whom, as we were saying, the decision ought to rest.

Yes.

And reasoning is peculiarly his instrument?

Certainly.

If wealth and gain were the criterion, then the praise or blame of the lover of gain would surely be the most trustworthy?

Assuredly.

Or if honour or victory or courage, in that case the judgment of the ambitious or pugnacious would be the truest?

Clearly.

But since experience and wisdom and reason are the judges—The only inference possible, he replied, is that pleasures which are approved by the lover of wisdom and reason are the truest.

And so we arrive at the result, that the pleasure of the intelligent part of the soul is the pleasantest of the three, and that he of us in whom this is the ruling principle has the pleasantest life.

Unquestionably, he said, the wise man speaks with authority when he approves of his own life.

And what does the judge affirm to be the life which is next, and the pleasure which is next?

Clearly that of the soldier and lover of honour; who is nearer to himself than the money-maker.

Last comes the lover of gain?

Very true, he said.

Twice in succession, then, has the just man overthrown the unjust in this conflict; and now comes the third trial, which is dedicated to Olympian Zeus the saviour: a sage whispers in my ear that no pleasure except that of the wise is quite true and pure—all others are a shadow only; and surely this will prove the greatest and most decisive of falls?

Yes, the greatest; but will you explain yourself?

I will work out the subject and you shall answer my questions.

Proceed.

Say, then, is not pleasure opposed to pain?

True.

And there is a neutral state which is neither pleasure nor pain?

There is.

A state which is intermediate, and a sort of repose of the soul about either—that is what you mean?

Yes.

You remember what people say when they are sick?

What do they say?

That after all nothing is pleasanter than health. But then they never knew this to be the greatest of pleasures until they were ill.

Yes, I know, he said.

And when persons are suffering from acute pain, you must have heard them say that there is nothing pleasanter than to get rid of their pain?

I have.

And there are many other cases of suffering in which the mere rest and cessation of pain, and not any positive enjoyment, is extolled by them as the greatest pleasure?

Yes, he said; at the time they are pleased and well content to be at rest.

Again, when pleasure ceases, that sort of rest or cessation will be painful?

Doubtless, he said.

Then the intermediate state of rest will be pleasure and will also be pain?

So it would seem.

But can that which is neither become both?

I should say not.

And both pleasure and pain are motions of the soul, are they not?

Yes.

But that which is neither was just now shown to be rest and not motion, and in a mean between them?

Yes.

How, then, can we be right in supposing that the absence of pain is pleasure, or that the absence of pleasure is pain?

Impossible.

This then is an appearance only and not a reality; that is to say, the rest is pleasure at the moment and in comparison of what is painful, and painful in comparison of what is pleasant; but all these representations, when tried by the test of true pleasure, are not real but a sort of imposition?

That is the inference.

Look at the other class of pleasures which have no antecedent pains and you will no longer suppose, as you perhaps may at present, that pleasure is only the cessation of pain, or pain of pleasure.

What are they, he said, and where shall I find them?

There are many of them: take as an example the pleasures of smell, which are very great and have no antecedent pains; they come in a moment, and when they depart leave no pain behind them.

Most true, he said.

Let us not, then, be induced to believe that pure pleasure is the cessation of pain, or pain of pleasure.

No.

Still, the more numerous and violent pleasures which reach the soul through the body are generally of this sort—they are reliefs of pain.

That is true.

And the anticipations of future pleasures and pains are of a like nature?

Yes.

Shall I give you an illustration of them?

Let me hear.

You would allow, I said, that there is in nature an upper and lower and middle region?

I should.

And if a person were to go from the lower to the middle region, would he not imagine that he is going up; and he who is standing in the middle and sees whence he has come, would imagine that he is already in the upper region, if he has never seen the true upper world?

To be sure, he said; how can he think otherwise?

But if he were taken back again he would imagine, and truly imagine, that he was descending?

No doubt.

All that would arise out of his ignorance of the true upper and middle and lower regions?

Yes.

Then can you wonder that persons who are inexperienced in the truth, as they have wrong ideas about many other things, should also have wrong ideas about pleasure and pain and the intermediate state; so that when they are only being drawn towards the painful they feel pain and think the pain which they experience to be real, and in like manner, when drawn away from pain to the neutral or intermediate state, they firmly believe that they have reached the goal of satiety and pleasure; they, not knowing pleasure, err in contrasting pain with the absence of pain, which is like contrasting black with grey instead of white—can you wonder, I say, at this?

No, indeed; I should be much more disposed to wonder at the opposite.

Look at the matter thus:—Hunger, thirst, and the like, are inanitions of the bodily state?

Yes.

And ignorance and folly are inanitions of the soul?

True.

And food and wisdom are the corresponding satisfactions of either?

Certainly.

And is the satisfaction derived from that which has less or from that which has more existence the truer?

Clearly, from that which has more.

What classes of things have a greater share of pure existence in your judgment—those of which food and drink and condiments and all kinds of sustenance are examples, or the class which contains true opinion and knowledge and mind and all the different kinds of virtue? Put the question in this way:—Which has a more pure being—that which is concerned with the invariable, the immortal, and the true, and is of such a nature, and is found in such natures; or that which is concerned with and found in the variable and mortal, and is itself variable and mortal?

Far purer, he replied, is the being of that which is concerned with the invariable.

And does the essence of the invariable partake of knowledge in the same degree as of essence?

Yes, of knowledge in the same degree.

And of truth in the same degree?

Yes.

And, conversely, that which has less of truth will also have less of essence?

Necessarily.

Then, in general, those kinds of things which are in the service of the body have less of truth and essence than those which are in the service of the soul?

Far less.

And has not the body itself less of truth and essence than the soul?

Yes.

What is filled with more real existence, and actually has a more real existence, is more really filled than that which is filled with less real existence and is less real?

Of course.

And if there be a pleasure in being filled with that which is according to nature, that which is more really filled with more real being will more really and truly enjoy true pleasure; whereas that which participates in less real being will be less truly and surely satisfied, and will participate in an illusory and less real pleasure?

Unquestionably.

Those then who know not wisdom and virtue, and are always busy with gluttony and sensuality, go down and up again as far as the mean; and in this region they move at random throughout life, but they never pass into the true upper world; thither they neither look, nor do they ever find their way, neither are they truly filled with true being, nor do they taste of pure and abiding pleasure. Like cattle, with their eyes always looking down and their heads stooping to the earth, that is, to the dining-table, they fatten and feed and breed, and, in their excessive love of these delights, they kick and butt at one another with horns and hoofs which are made of iron; and they kill one another by reason of their insatiable lust. For they fill themselves with that which is not substantial, and the part of themselves which they fill is also unsubstantial and incontinent.

Verily, Socrates, said Glaucon, you describe the life of the many like an oracle.

Their pleasures are mixed with pains—how can they be otherwise? For they are mere shadows and pictures of the true, and are coloured by contrast, which exaggerates both light and shade, and so they implant in the minds of fools insane desires of themselves; and they are fought about as Stesichorus says that the Greeks fought about the shadow of Helen at Troy in ignorance of the truth.

Something of that sort must inevitably happen.

And must not the like happen with the spirited or passionate element of the soul? Will not the passionate man who carries his passion into action, be in the like case, whether he is envious and ambitious, or violent and contentious, or angry and discontented, if he be seeking to attain honour and victory and the satisfaction of his anger without reason or sense?

Yes, he said, the same will happen with the spirited element also.

Then may we not confidently assert that the lovers of money and honour, when they seek their pleasures under the guidance and in the company of reason and knowledge, and pursue after and win the pleasures which wisdom shows them, will also have the truest pleasures in the highest degree which is attainable to them, inasmuch as they follow truth; and they will have the pleasures which are natural to them, if that which is best for each one is also most natural to him?

Yes, certainly; the best is the most natural.

And when the whole soul follows the philosophical principle, and there is no division, the several parts are just, and do each of them their own business, and enjoy severally the best and truest pleasures of which they are capable?

Exactly.

But when either of the two other principles prevails, it fails in attaining its own pleasure, and compels the rest to pursue after a pleasure which is a shadow only and which is not their own?

True.

And the greater the interval which separates them from philosophy and reason, the more strange and illusive will be the pleasure?

Yes.

And is not that farthest from reason which is at the greatest distance from law and order?

Clearly.

And the lustful and tyrannical desires are, as we saw, at the greatest distance? Yes.

And the royal and orderly desires are nearest?

Yes.

Then the tyrant will live at the greatest distance from true or natural pleasure, and the king at the least?

Certainly.

But if so, the tyrant will live most unpleasantly, and the king most pleasantly?

Inevitably.

Would you know the measure of the interval which separates them?

Will you tell me?

There appear to be three pleasures, one genuine and two spurious: now the transgression of the tyrant reaches a point beyond the spurious; he has run away from the region of law and reason, and taken up his abode with certain slave pleasures which are his satellites, and the measure of his inferiority can only be expressed in a figure.

How do you mean?

I assume, I said, that the tyrant is in the third place from the oligarch; the democrat was in the middle?

Yes.

And if there is truth in what has preceded, he will be wedded to an image of pleasure which is thrice removed as to truth from the pleasure of the oligarch?

He will.

And the oligarch is third from the royal; since we count as one royal and aristocratical?

Yes, he is third.

Then the tyrant is removed from true pleasure by the space of a number which is three times three?

Manifestly.

The shadow then of tyrannical pleasure determined by the number of length will be a plane figure.

Certainly.

And if you raise the power and make the plane a solid, there is no difficulty in seeing how vast is the interval by which the tyrant is parted from the king.

Yes; the arithmetician will easily do the sum.

Or if some person begins at the other end and measures the interval by which the king is parted from the tyrant in truth of pleasure, he will find him, when the multiplication is completed, living 729 times more pleasantly, and the tyrant more painfully by this same interval.

What a wonderful calculation! And how enormous is the distance which separates the just from the unjust in regard to pleasure and pain!

Yet a true calculation, I said, and a number which nearly concerns human life, if human beings are concerned with days and nights and months and years. (729 NEARLY equals the number of days and nights in the year.)

Yes, he said, human life is certainly concerned with them.

Then if the good and just man be thus superior in pleasure to the evil and unjust, his superiority will be infinitely greater in propriety of life and in beauty and virtue?

Immeasurably greater.

Well, I said, and now having arrived at this stage of the argument, we may revert to the words which brought us hither: Was not some one saying that injustice was a gain to the perfectly unjust who was reputed to be just?

Yes, that was said.

Now then, having determined the power and quality of justice and injustice, let us have a little conversation with him.

What shall we say to him?

Let us make an image of the soul, that he may have his own words presented before his eyes.

Of what sort?

An ideal image of the soul, like the composite creations of ancient mythology, such as the Chimera or Scylla or Cerberus, and there are many others in which two or more different natures are said to grow into one.

There are said of have been such unions.

Then do you now model the form of a multitudinous, many-headed monster, having a ring of heads of all manner of beasts, tame and wild, which he is able to generate and metamorphose at will.

You suppose marvellous powers in the artist; but, as language is more pliable than wax or any similar substance, let there be such a model as you propose.

Suppose now that you make a second form as of a lion, and a third of a man, the second smaller than the first, and the third smaller than the second.

That, he said, is an easier task; and I have made them as you say.

And now join them, and let the three grow into one.

That has been accomplished.

Next fashion the outside of them into a single image, as of a man, so that he who is not able to look within, and sees only the outer hull, may believe the beast to be a single human creature.

I have done so, he said.

And now, to him who maintains that it is profitable for the human creature to be unjust, and unprofitable to be just, let us reply that, if he be right, it is profitable for this creature to feast the multitudinous monster and strengthen the lion and the lion-like qualities, but to starve and weaken the man, who is consequently liable to be dragged about at the mercy of either of the other two; and he is not to attempt to familiarize or harmonize them with one another—he ought rather to suffer them to fight and bite and devour one another.

Certainly, he said; that is what the approver of injustice says.

To him the supporter of justice makes answer that he should ever so speak and act as to give the man within him in some way or other the most complete mastery over the entire human creature. He should watch over the many-headed monster like a good husbandman, fostering and cultivating the gentle qualities, and preventing the wild ones from growing; he should be making the lion-heart his ally, and in common care of them all should be uniting the several parts with one another and with himself.

Yes, he said, that is quite what the maintainer of justice say.

And so from every point of view, whether of pleasure, honour, or advantage, the approver of justice is right and speaks the truth, and the disapprover is wrong and false and ignorant?

Yes, from every point of view.

Come, now, and let us gently reason with the unjust, who is not intentionally in error. "Sweet Sir," we will say to him, "what think you of things esteemed noble and ignoble? Is not the noble that which subjects the beast to the man, or rather to the god in man; and the ignoble that which subjects the man to the beast?" He can hardly avoid saying Yes— can he now?

Not if he has any regard for my opinion.

But, if he agree so far, we may ask him to answer another question: 'Then how would a man profit if he received gold and silver on the condition that he was to enslave the noblest part of him to the worst? Who can imagine that a man who sold his son or daughter into slavery for money, especially if he sold them into the hands of fierce and evil men, would be the gainer, however large might be the sum which he received? And will any one say that he is not a miserable caitiff who remorselessly sells his own divine being to that which is most godless and detestable? Eriphyle took the necklace as the price of her husband's life, but he is taking a bribe in order to compass a worse ruin.'

Yes, said Glaucon, far worse—I will answer for him.

Has not the intemperate been censured of old, because in him the huge multiform monster is allowed to be too much at large?

Clearly.

And men are blamed for pride and bad temper when the lion and serpent element in them disproportionately grows and gains strength?

Yes.

And luxury and softness are blamed, because they relax and weaken this same creature, and make a coward of him?

Very true.

And is not a man reproached for flattery and meanness who subordinates the spirited animal to the unruly monster, and, for the sake of money, of which he can never have enough, habituates him in the days of his youth to be trampled in the mire, and from being a lion to become a monkey?

True, he said.

And why are mean employments and manual arts a reproach? Only because they imply a natural weakness of the higher principle; the individual is unable to control the creatures within him, but has to court them, and his great study is how to flatter them.

Such appears to be the reason.

And therefore, being desirous of placing him under a rule like that of the best, we say that he ought to be the servant of the best, in whom the Divine rules; not, as Thrasymachus supposed, to the injury of the servant, but because every one had better be ruled by divine wisdom dwelling within him; or, if this be impossible, then by an external authority, in order that we may be all, as far as possible, under the same government, friends and equals.

True, he said.

And this is clearly seen to be the intention of the law, which is the ally of the whole city; and is seen also in the authority which we exercise over children, and the refusal to let them be free until we have established in them a principle analogous to the constitution of a state, and by cultivation of this higher element have set up in their hearts a guardian and ruler like our own, and when this is done they may go their ways.

Yes, he said, the purpose of the law is manifest.

From what point of view, then, and on what ground can we say that a man is profited by injustice or intemperance or other baseness, which will make him a worse man, even though he acquire money or power by his wickedness?

From no point of view at all.

What shall he profit, if his injustice be undetected and unpunished? He who is undetected only gets worse, whereas he who is detected and punished has the brutal part of his nature silenced and humanized; the gentler element in him is liberated, and his whole soul is perfected and ennobled by the acquirement of justice and temperance and wisdom, more than the body ever is by receiving gifts of beauty, strength and health, in proportion as the soul is more honourable than the body.

Certainly, he said.

To this nobler purpose the man of understanding will devote the energies of his life. And in the first place, he will honour studies which impress these qualities on his soul and will disregard others?

Clearly, he said.

In the next place, he will regulate his bodily habit and training, and so far will he be from yielding to brutal and irrational pleasures, that he will regard even health as quite a secondary matter; his first object will be not that he may be fair or strong or well, unless he is likely thereby to gain temperance, but he will always desire so to attemper the body as to preserve the harmony of the soul?

Certainly he will, if he has true music in him.

And in the acquisition of wealth there is a principle of order and harmony which he will also observe; he will not allow himself to be dazzled by the foolish applause of the world, and heap up riches to his own infinite harm?

Certainly not, he said.

He will look at the city which is within him, and take heed that no disorder occur in it, such as might arise either from superfluity or from want; and upon this principle he will regulate his property and gain or spend according to his means.

Very true.

And, for the same reason, he will gladly accept and enjoy such honours as he deems likely to make him a better man; but those, whether private or public, which are likely to disorder his life, he will avoid?

Then, if that is his motive, he will not be a statesman.

By the dog of Egypt, he will! in the city which is his own he certainly will, though in the land of his birth perhaps not, unless he have a divine call.

I understand; you mean that he will be a ruler in the city of which we are the founders, and which exists in idea only; for I do not believe that there is such an one anywhere on earth?

In heaven, I replied, there is laid up a pattern of it, methinks, which he who desires may behold, and beholding, may set his own house in order. But whether such an one exists, or ever will exist in fact, is no matter; for he will live after the manner of that city, having nothing to do with any other.

I think so, he said.

# BOOK X

O f the many excellences which I perceive in the order of
our State, there is none which upon reflection pleases
me better than the rule about poetry.

To what do you refer?

To the rejection of imitative poetry, which certainly ought
not to be received; as I see far more clearly now that the parts of
the soul have been distinguished.

What do you mean?

Speaking in confidence, for I should not like to have my
words repeated to the tragedians and the rest of the imitative
tribe—but I do not mind saying to you, that all poetical imitations
are ruinous to the understanding of the hearers, and that the
knowledge of their true nature is the only antidote to them.

Explain the purport of your remark.

Well, I will tell you, although I have always from my earliest
youth had an awe and love of Homer, which even now makes the
words falter on my lips, for he is the great captain and teacher of
the whole of that charming tragic company; but a man is not to
be reverenced more than the truth, and therefore I will speak out.

Very good, he said.

Listen to me then, or rather, answer me.

Put your question.

Can you tell me what imitation is? for I really do not know.

A likely thing, then, that I should know.

Why not? for the duller eye may often see a thing sooner than the keener.

Very true, he said; but in your presence, even if I had any faint notion, I could not muster courage to utter it. Will you enquire yourself?

Well then, shall we begin the enquiry in our usual manner: Whenever a number of individuals have a common name, we assume them to have also a corresponding idea or form:—do you understand me?

I do.

Let us take any common instance; there are beds and tables in the world—plenty of them, are there not?

Yes.

But there are only two ideas or forms of them—one the idea of a bed, the other of a table.

True.

And the maker of either of them makes a bed or he makes a table for our use, in accordance with the idea—that is our way of speaking in this and similar instances—but no artificer makes the ideas themselves: how could he?

Impossible.

And there is another artist,—I should like to know what you would say of him.

Who is he?

One who is the maker of all the works of all other workmen.

What an extraordinary man!

Wait a little, and there will be more reason for your saying so. For this is he who is able to make not only vessels of every kind, but plants and animals, himself and all other things—the earth and heaven, and the things which are in heaven or under the earth; he makes the gods also.

He must be a wizard and no mistake.

Oh! you are incredulous, are you? Do you mean that there is no such maker or creator, or that in one sense there might be a maker of all these things but in another not? Do you see that there is a way in which you could make them all yourself?

What way?

An easy way enough; or rather, there are many ways in which the feat might be quickly and easily accomplished, none quicker than that of turning a mirror round and round—you would soon enough make the sun and the heavens, and the earth and yourself, and other animals and plants, and all the other things of which we were just now speaking, in the mirror.

Yes, he said; but they would be appearances only.

Very good, I said, you are coming to the point now. And the painter too is, as I conceive, just such another—a creator of appearances, is he not?

Of course.

But then I suppose you will say that what he creates is untrue. And yet there is a sense in which the painter also creates a bed?

Yes, he said, but not a real bed.

And what of the maker of the bed? were you not saying that he too makes, not the idea which, according to our view, is the essence of the bed, but only a particular bed?

Yes, I did.

Then if he does not make that which exists he cannot make true existence, but only some semblance of existence; and if any one were to say that the work of the maker of the bed, or of any other workman, has real existence, he could hardly be supposed to be speaking the truth.

At any rate, he replied, philosophers would say that he was not speaking the truth.

No wonder, then, that his work too is an indistinct expression of truth.

No wonder.

Suppose now that by the light of the examples just offered we enquire who this imitator is?

If you please.

Well then, here are three beds: one existing in nature, which is made by God, as I think that we may say—for no one else can be the maker?

No.

There is another which is the work of the carpenter?

Yes.

And the work of the painter is a third?

Yes.

Beds, then, are of three kinds, and there are three artists who superintend them: God, the maker of the bed, and the painter?

Yes, there are three of them.

God, whether from choice or from necessity, made one bed in nature and one only; two or more such ideal beds neither ever have been nor ever will be made by God.

Why is that?

Because even if He had made but two, a third would still appear behind them which both of them would have for their idea, and that would be the ideal bed and not the two others.

Very true, he said.

God knew this, and He desired to be the real maker of a real bed, not a particular maker of a particular bed, and therefore He created a bed which is essentially and by nature one only.

So we believe.

Shall we, then, speak of Him as the natural author or maker of the bed?

Yes, he replied; inasmuch as by the natural process of creation He is the author of this and of all other things.

And what shall we say of the carpenter—is not he also the maker of the bed?

Yes.

But would you call the painter a creator and maker?

Certainly not.

Yet if he is not the maker, what is he in relation to the bed?

I think, he said, that we may fairly designate him as the imitator of that which the others make.

Good, I said; then you call him who is third in the descent from nature an imitator?

Certainly, he said.

And the tragic poet is an imitator, and therefore, like all other imitators, he is thrice removed from the king and from the truth?

That appears to be so.

Then about the imitator we are agreed. And what about the painter?—I would like to know whether he may be thought to imitate that which originally exists in nature, or only the creations of artists?

The latter.

As they are or as they appear? you have still to determine this.

What do you mean?

I mean, that you may look at a bed from different points of view, obliquely or directly or from any other point of view, and the bed will appear different, but there is no difference in reality. And the same of all things.

Yes, he said, the difference is only apparent.

Now let me ask you another question: Which is the art of painting designed to be—an imitation of things as they are, or as they appear—of appearance or of reality?

Of appearance.

Then the imitator, I said, is a long way off the truth, and can do all things because he lightly touches on a small part of them, and that part an image. For example: A painter will paint a cobbler, carpenter, or any other artist, though he knows nothing of their arts; and, if he is a good artist, he may deceive children or simple persons, when he shows them his picture of a carpenter from a distance, and they will fancy that they are looking at a real carpenter.

Certainly.

And whenever any one informs us that he has found a man who knows all the arts, and all things else that anybody knows, and every single thing with a higher degree of accuracy than any other man—whoever tells us this, I think that we can only imagine him to be a simple creature who is likely to have been deceived by some wizard or actor whom he met, and whom he thought all-knowing, because he himself was unable to analyse the nature of knowledge and ignorance and imitation.

Most true.

And so, when we hear persons saying that the tragedians, and Homer, who is at their head, know all the arts and all things human, virtue as well as vice, and divine things too, for that the good poet cannot compose well unless he knows his subject, and that he who has not this knowledge can never be a poet, we ought to consider whether here also there may not be a similar illusion. Perhaps they may have come across imitators and been deceived by them; they may not have remembered when they saw their works that these were but imitations thrice removed from the truth, and could easily be made without any knowledge of the truth, because they are appearances only and not realities? Or, after all, they may be in the right, and poets do really know the things about which they seem to the many to speak so well?

The question, he said, should by all means be considered.

Now do you suppose that if a person were able to make the original as well as the image, he would seriously devote himself to the image-making branch? Would he allow imitation to be the ruling principle of his life, as if he had nothing higher in him?

I should say not.

The real artist, who knew what he was imitating, would be interested in realities and not in imitations; and would desire to leave as memorials of himself works many and fair; and, instead of being the author of encomiums, he would prefer to be the theme of them.

Yes, he said, that would be to him a source of much greater honour and profit.

Then, I said, we must put a question to Homer; not about medicine, or any of the arts to which his poems only incidentally refer: we are not going to ask him, or any other poet, whether he has cured patients like Asclepius, or left behind him a school of medicine such as the Asclepiads were, or whether he only talks about medicine and other arts at second-hand; but we have a right to know respecting military tactics, politics, education, which are the chiefest and noblest subjects of his poems, and we may fairly ask him about them. 'Friend Homer,' then we say to him, 'if you are only in the second remove from truth in what you say of virtue, and not in the third—not an image maker or imitator—

and if you are able to discern what pursuits make men better or worse in private or public life, tell us what State was ever better governed by your help?' The good order of Lacedaemon is due to Lycurgus, and many other cities great and small have been similarly benefited by others; but who says that you have been a good legislator to them and have done them any good? Italy and Sicily boast of Charondas, and there is Solon who is renowned among us; but what city has anything to say about you?' Is there any city which he might name?

I think not, said Glaucon; not even the Homerids themselves pretend that he was a legislator.

Well, but is there any war on record which was carried on successfully by him, or aided by his counsels, when he was alive?

There is not.

Or is there any invention of his, applicable to the arts or to human life, such as Thales the Milesian or Anacharsis the Scythian, and other ingenious men have conceived, which is attributed to him?

There is absolutely nothing of the kind.

But, if Homer never did any public service, was he privately a guide or teacher of any? Had he in his lifetime friends who loved to associate with him, and who handed down to posterity an Homeric way of life, such as was established by Pythagoras who was so greatly beloved for his wisdom, and whose followers are to this day quite celebrated for the order which was named after him?

Nothing of the kind is recorded of him. For surely, Socrates, Creophylus, the companion of Homer, that child of flesh, whose name always makes us laugh, might be more justly ridiculed for his stupidity, if, as is said, Homer was greatly neglected by him and others in his own day when he was alive?

Yes, I replied, that is the tradition. But can you imagine, Glaucon, that if Homer had really been able to educate and improve mankind—if he had possessed knowledge and not been a mere imitator—can you imagine, I say, that he would not have had many followers, and been honoured and loved by them? Protagoras of Abdera, and Prodicus of Ceos, and a host of others, have only to whisper to their contemporaries:

349

'You will never be able to manage either your own house or your own State until you appoint us to be your ministers of education'—and this ingenious device of theirs has such an effect in making men love them that their companions all but carry them about on their shoulders. And is it conceivable that the contemporaries of Homer, or again of Hesiod, would have allowed either of them to go about as rhapsodists, if they had really been able to make mankind virtuous? Would they not have been as unwilling to part with them as with gold, and have compelled them to stay at home with them? Or, if the master would not stay, then the disciples would have followed him about everywhere, until they had got education enough?

Yes, Socrates, that, I think, is quite true.

Then must we not infer that all these poetical individuals, beginning with Homer, are only imitators; they copy images of virtue and the like, but the truth they never reach? The poet is like a painter who, as we have already observed, will make a likeness of a cobbler though he understands nothing of cobbling; and his picture is good enough for those who know no more than he does, and judge only by colours and figures.

Quite so.

In like manner the poet with his words and phrases may be said to lay on the colours of the several arts, himself understanding their nature only enough to imitate them; and other people, who are as ignorant as he is, and judge only from his words, imagine that if he speaks of cobbling, or of military tactics, or of anything else, in metre and harmony and rhythm, he speaks very well—such is the sweet influence which melody and rhythm by nature have. And I think that you must have observed again and again what a poor appearance the tales of poets make when stripped of the colours which music puts upon them, and recited in simple prose.

Yes, he said.

They are like faces which were never really beautiful, but only blooming; and now the bloom of youth has passed away from them?

Exactly.

Here is another point: The imitator or maker of the image knows nothing of true existence; he knows appearances only. Am I not right?

Yes.

Then let us have a clear understanding, and not be satisfied with half an explanation.

Proceed.

Of the painter we say that he will paint reins, and he will paint a bit?

Yes.

And the worker in leather and brass will make them?

Certainly.

But does the painter know the right form of the bit and reins? Nay, hardly even the workers in brass and leather who make them; only the horseman who knows how to use them—he knows their right form.

Most true.

And may we not say the same of all things?

What?

That there are three arts which are concerned with all things: one which uses, another which makes, a third which imitates them?

Yes.

And the excellence or beauty or truth of every structure, animate or inanimate, and of every action of man, is relative to the use for which nature or the artist has intended them.

True.

Then the user of them must have the greatest experience of them, and he must indicate to the maker the good or bad qualities which develop themselves in use; for example, the flute-player will tell the flute-maker which of his flutes is satisfactory to the performer; he will tell him how he ought to make them, and the other will attend to his instructions?

Of course.

The one knows and therefore speaks with authority about the goodness and badness of flutes, while the other, confiding in him, will do what he is told by him?

True.

The instrument is the same, but about the excellence or badness of it the maker will only attain to a correct belief; and this he will gain from him who knows, by talking to him and being compelled to hear what he has to say, whereas the user will have knowledge?

True.

But will the imitator have either? Will he know from use whether or no his drawing is correct or beautiful? or will he have right opinion from being compelled to associate with another who knows and gives him instructions about what he should draw?

Neither.

Then he will no more have true opinion than he will have knowledge about the goodness or badness of his imitations?

I suppose not.

The imitative artist will be in a brilliant state of intelligence about his own creations?

Nay, very much the reverse.

And still he will go on imitating without knowing what makes a thing good or bad, and may be expected therefore to imitate only that which appears to be good to the ignorant multitude?

Just so.

Thus far then we are pretty well agreed that the imitator has no knowledge worth mentioning of what he imitates. Imitation is only a kind of play or sport, and the tragic poets, whether they write in Iambic or in Heroic verse, are imitators in the highest degree?

Very true.

And now tell me, I conjure you, has not imitation been shown by us to be concerned with that which is thrice removed from the truth?

Certainly.

And what is the faculty in man to which imitation is addressed?

What do you mean?

I will explain: The body which is large when seen near, appears small when seen at a distance?

True.

And the same object appears straight when looked at out of the water, and crooked when in the water; and the concave becomes convex, owing to the illusion about colours to which the sight is liable.

Thus every sort of confusion is revealed within us; and this is that weakness of the human mind on which the art of conjuring and of deceiving by light and shadow and other ingenious devices imposes, having an effect upon us like magic.

True.

And the arts of measuring and numbering and weighing come to the rescue of the human understanding—there is the beauty of them—and the apparent greater or less, or more or heavier, no longer have the mastery over us, but give way before calculation and measure and weight?

Most true.

And this, surely, must be the work of the calculating and rational principle in the soul?

To be sure.

And when this principle measures and certifies that some things are equal, or that some are greater or less than others, there occurs an apparent contradiction?

True.

But were we not saying that such a contradiction is impossible—the same faculty cannot have contrary opinions at the same time about the same thing?

Very true.

Then that part of the soul which has an opinion contrary to measure is not the same with that which has an opinion in accordance with measure?

True.

And the better part of the soul is likely to be that which trusts to measure and calculation?

Certainly.

And that which is opposed to them is one of the inferior principles of the soul?

No doubt.

This was the conclusion at which I was seeking to arrive when I said that painting or drawing, and imitation in general, when doing their own proper work, are far removed from truth, and the companions and friends and associates of a principle within us which is equally removed from reason, and that they have no true or healthy aim.

Exactly.

The imitative art is an inferior who marries an inferior, and has inferior offspring.

Very true.

And is this confined to the sight only, or does it extend to the hearing also, relating in fact to what we term poetry?

Probably the same would be true of poetry.

Do not rely, I said, on a probability derived from the analogy of painting; but let us examine further and see whether the faculty with which poetical imitation is concerned is good or bad.

By all means.

We may state the question thus:—Imitation imitates the actions of men, whether voluntary or involuntary, on which, as they imagine, a good or bad result has ensued, and they rejoice or sorrow accordingly. Is there anything more?

No, there is nothing else.

But in all this variety of circumstances is the man at unity with himself—or rather, as in the instance of sight there was confusion and opposition in his opinions about the same things, so here also is there not strife and inconsistency in his life? Though I need hardly raise the question again, for I remember that all this has been already admitted; and the soul has been acknowledged by us to be full of these and ten thousand similar oppositions occurring at the same moment?

And we were right, he said.

Yes, I said, thus far we were right; but there was an omission which must now be supplied.

What was the omission?

Were we not saying that a good man, who has the misfortune to lose his son or anything else which is most dear to him, will bear the loss with more equanimity than another?

Yes.

But will he have no sorrow, or shall we say that although he cannot help sorrowing, he will moderate his sorrow?

The latter, he said, is the truer statement.

Tell me: will he be more likely to struggle and hold out against his sorrow when he is seen by his equals, or when he is alone?

It will make a great difference whether he is seen or not.

When he is by himself he will not mind saying or doing many things which he would be ashamed of any one hearing or seeing him do?

True.

There is a principle of law and reason in him which bids him resist, as well as a feeling of his misfortune which is forcing him to indulge his sorrow?

True.

But when a man is drawn in two opposite directions, to and from the same object, this, as we affirm, necessarily implies two distinct principles in him?

Certainly.

One of them is ready to follow the guidance of the law?

How do you mean?

The law would say that to be patient under suffering is best, and that we should not give way to impatience, as there is no knowing whether such things are good or evil; and nothing is gained by impatience; also, because no human thing is of serious importance, and grief stands in the way of that which at the moment is most required.

What is most required? he asked.

That we should take counsel about what has happened, and when the dice have been thrown order our affairs in the way which reason deems best; not, like children who have had a fall, keeping hold of the part struck and wasting time in setting up a howl, but always accustoming the soul forthwith to apply a remedy, raising up that which is sickly and fallen, banishing the cry of sorrow by the healing art.

Yes, he said, that is the true way of meeting the attacks of fortune.

Yes, I said; and the higher principle is ready to follow this suggestion of reason?

Clearly.

And the other principle, which inclines us to recollection of our troubles and to lamentation, and can never have enough of them, we may call irrational, useless, and cowardly?

Indeed, we may.

And does not the latter—I mean the rebellious principle—furnish a great variety of materials for imitation? Whereas the wise and calm temperament, being always nearly equable, is not easy to imitate or to appreciate when imitated, especially at a public festival when a promiscuous crowd is assembled in a theatre. For the feeling represented is one to which they are strangers.

Certainly.

Then the imitative poet who aims at being popular is not by nature made, nor is his art intended, to please or to affect the rational principle in the soul; but he will prefer the passionate and fitful temper, which is easily imitated?

Clearly.

And now we may fairly take him and place him by the side of the painter, for he is like him in two ways: first, inasmuch as his creations have an inferior degree of truth—in this, I say, he is like him; and he is also like him in being concerned with an inferior part of the soul; and therefore we shall be right in refusing to admit him into a well-ordered State, because he awakens and nourishes and strengthens the feelings and impairs the reason. As in a city when the evil are permitted to have authority and the good are put out of the way, so in the soul of man, as we maintain, the imitative poet implants an evil constitution, for he indulges the irrational nature which has no discernment of greater and less, but thinks the same thing at one time great and at another small—he is a manufacturer of images and is very far removed from the truth.

Exactly.

But we have not yet brought forward the heaviest count in our accusation:—the power which poetry has of harming even the good (and there are very few who are not harmed), is surely an awful thing?

Yes, certainly, if the effect is what you say.

Hear and judge: The best of us, as I conceive, when we listen to a passage of Homer, or one of the tragedians, in which he represents some pitiful hero who is drawling out his sorrows in a long oration, or weeping, and smiting his breast—the best of us, you know, delight in giving way to sympathy, and are in raptures at the excellence of the poet who stirs our feelings most.

Yes, of course I know.

But when any sorrow of our own happens to us, then you may observe that we pride ourselves on the opposite quality—we would fain be quiet and patient; this is the manly part, and the other which delighted us in the recitation is now deemed to be the part of a woman.

Very true, he said.

Now can we be right in praising and admiring another who is doing that which any one of us would abominate and be ashamed of in his own person?

No, he said, that is certainly not reasonable.

Nay, I said, quite reasonable from one point of view.

What point of view?

If you consider, I said, that when in misfortune we feel a natural hunger and desire to relieve our sorrow by weeping and lamentation, and that this feeling which is kept under control in our own calamities is satisfied and delighted by the poets;—the better nature in each of us, not having been sufficiently trained by reason or habit, allows the sympathetic element to break loose because the sorrow is another's; and the spectator fancies that there can be no disgrace to himself in praising and pitying any one who comes telling him what a good man he is, and making a fuss about his troubles; he thinks that the pleasure is a gain, and why should he be supercilious and lose this and the poem too? Few persons ever reflect, as I should imagine, that from the evil of other men something of evil is communicated to themselves. And so the feeling of sorrow which has gathered strength at the sight of the misfortunes of others is with difficulty repressed in our own.

How very true!

And does not the same hold also of the ridiculous? There are jests which you would be ashamed to make yourself, and yet on the comic stage, or indeed in private, when you hear them, you are greatly amused by them, and are not at all disgusted at their unseemliness;—the case of pity is repeated;—there is a principle in human nature which is disposed to raise a laugh, and this which you once restrained by reason, because you were afraid of being thought a buffoon, is now let out again; and having stimulated the risible faculty at the theatre, you are betrayed unconsciously to yourself into playing the comic poet at home.

Quite true, he said.

And the same may be said of lust and anger and all the other affections, of desire and pain and pleasure, which are held to be inseparable from every action—in all of them poetry feeds and waters the passions instead of drying them up; she lets them rule, although they ought to be controlled, if mankind are ever to increase in happiness and virtue.

I cannot deny it.

Therefore, Glaucon, I said, whenever you meet with any of the eulogists of Homer declaring that he has been the educator of Hellas, and that he is profitable for education and for the ordering of human things, and that you should take him up again and again and get to know him and regulate your whole life according to him, we may love and honour those who say these things—they are excellent people, as far as their lights extend; and we are ready to acknowledge that Homer is the greatest of poets and first of tragedy writers; but we must remain firm in our conviction that hymns to the gods and praises of famous men are the only poetry which ought to be admitted into our State. For if you go beyond this and allow the honeyed muse to enter, either in epic or lyric verse, not law and the reason of mankind, which by common consent have ever been deemed best, but pleasure and pain will be the rulers in our State.

That is most true, he said.

And now since we have reverted to the subject of poetry, let this our defence serve to show the reasonableness of our former judgment in sending away out of our State an art having the tendencies which we have described; for reason constrained us. But that she may not impute to us any harshness or want of politeness, let us tell her that there is an ancient quarrel between philosophy and poetry; of which there are many proofs, such as the saying of 'the yelping hound howling at her lord,' or of one 'mighty in the vain talk of fools,' and 'the mob of sages circumventing Zeus,' and the 'subtle thinkers who are beggars after all'; and there are innumerable other signs of ancient enmity between them. Notwithstanding this, let us assure our sweet friend and the sister arts of imitation, that if she will only prove her title to exist in a well-ordered State we shall be delighted to receive her—we are very conscious of her charms; but we may not on that account betray the truth. I dare say, Glaucon, that you are as much charmed by her as I am, especially when she appears in Homer?

Yes, indeed, I am greatly charmed.

Shall I propose, then, that she be allowed to return from exile, but upon this condition only—that she make a defence of herself in lyrical or some other metre?

Certainly.

And we may further grant to those of her defenders who are lovers of poetry and yet not poets the permission to speak in prose on her behalf: let them show not only that she is pleasant but also useful to States and to human life, and we will listen in a kindly spirit; for if this can be proved we shall surely be the gainers—I mean, if there is a use in poetry as well as a delight?

Certainly, he said, we shall be the gainers.

If her defence fails, then, my dear friend, like other persons who are enamoured of something, but put a restraint upon themselves when they think their desires are opposed to their interests, so too must we after the manner of lovers give her up, though not without a struggle. We too are inspired by that love of poetry which the education of noble States has implanted in us, and therefore we would have her appear at her best and truest; but so long as she is unable to make good her defence, this argument of ours shall be a charm to us, which we will repeat to ourselves while we listen to her strains; that we may not fall away into the childish love of her which captivates the many. At all events we are well aware that poetry being such as we have described is not to be regarded seriously as attaining to the truth; and he who listens to her, fearing for the safety of the city which is within him, should be on his guard against her seductions and make our words his law.

Yes, he said, I quite agree with you.

Yes, I said, my dear Glaucon, for great is the issue at stake, greater than appears, whether a man is to be good or bad. And what will any one be profited if under the influence of honour or money or power, aye, or under the excitement of poetry, he neglect justice and virtue?

Yes, he said; I have been convinced by the argument, as I believe that any one else would have been.

And yet no mention has been made of the greatest prizes and rewards which await virtue.

What, are there any greater still? If there are, they must be of an inconceivable greatness.

Why, I said, what was ever great in a short time? The whole period of three score years and ten is surely but a little thing in comparison with eternity?

Say rather 'nothing,' he replied.

And should an immortal being seriously think of this little space rather than of the whole?

Of the whole, certainly. But why do you ask?

Are you not aware, I said, that the soul of man is immortal and imperishable?

He looked at me in astonishment, and said: No, by heaven: And are you really prepared to maintain this?

Yes, I said, I ought to be, and you too—there is no difficulty in proving it.

I see a great difficulty; but I should like to hear you state this argument of which you make so light.

Listen then.

I am attending.

There is a thing which you call good and another which you call evil?

360

Yes, he replied.

Would you agree with me in thinking that the corrupting and destroying element is the evil, and the saving and improving element the good?

Yes.

And you admit that every thing has a good and also an evil; as ophthalmia is the evil of the eyes and disease of the whole body; as mildew is of corn, and rot of timber, or rust of copper and iron: in everything, or in almost everything, there is an inherent evil and disease?

Yes, he said.

And anything which is infected by any of these evils is made evil, and at last wholly dissolves and dies?

True.

The vice and evil which is inherent in each is the destruction of each; and if this does not destroy them there is nothing else that will; for good certainly will not destroy them, nor again, that which is neither good nor evil.

Certainly not.

If, then, we find any nature which having this inherent corruption cannot be dissolved or destroyed, we may be certain that of such a nature there is no destruction?

That may be assumed.

Well, I said, and is there no evil which corrupts the soul?

Yes, he said, there are all the evils which we were just now passing in review: unrighteousness, intemperance, cowardice, ignorance.

But does any of these dissolve or destroy her?—and here do not let us fall into the error of supposing that the unjust and foolish man, when he is detected, perishes through his own injustice, which is an evil of the soul. Take the analogy of the body: The evil of the body is a disease which wastes and reduces and annihilates the body; and all the things of which we were just now speaking come to annihilation through their own corruption attaching to them and inhering in them and so destroying them. Is not this true?

Yes.

Consider the soul in like manner. Does the injustice or other evil which exists in the soul waste and consume her? Do they by attaching to the soul and inhering in her at last bring her to death, and so separate her from the body?

Certainly not.

And yet, I said, it is unreasonable to suppose that anything can perish from without through affection of external evil which could not be destroyed from within by a corruption of its own?

It is, he replied.

Consider, I said, Glaucon, that even the badness of food, whether staleness, decomposition, or any other bad quality, when confined to the actual food, is not supposed to destroy the body; although, if the badness of food communicates corruption to the body, then we should say that the body has been destroyed by a corruption of itself, which is disease, brought on by this; but that the body, being one thing, can be destroyed by the badness of food, which is another, and which does not engender any natural infection—this we shall absolutely deny?

Very true.

And, on the same principle, unless some bodily evil can produce an evil of the soul, we must not suppose that the soul, which is one thing, can be dissolved by any merely external evil which belongs to another?

Yes, he said, there is reason in that.

Either, then, let us refute this conclusion, or, while it remains unrefuted, let us never say that fever, or any other disease, or the knife put to the throat, or even the cutting up of the whole body into the minutest pieces, can destroy the soul, until she herself is proved to become more unholy or unrighteous in consequence of these things being done to the body; but that the soul, or anything else if not destroyed by an internal evil, can be destroyed by an external one, is not to be affirmed by any man.

And surely, he replied, no one will ever prove that the souls of men become more unjust in consequence of death.

But if some one who would rather not admit the immortality of the soul boldly denies this, and says that the dying do really become more evil and unrighteous, then, if the speaker is right, I suppose that injustice, like disease, must be assumed to be fatal to the unjust, and that those who take this disorder die by the natural inherent power of destruction which evil has, and which kills them sooner or later, but in quite another way from that in which, at present, the wicked receive death at the hands of others as the penalty of their deeds?

Nay, he said, in that case injustice, if fatal to the unjust, will not be so very terrible to him, for he will be delivered from evil. But I rather suspect the opposite to be the truth, and that injustice which, if it have the power, will murder others, keeps the murderer alive—aye, and well awake too; so far removed is her dwelling-place from being a house of death.

True, I said; if the inherent natural vice or evil of the soul is unable to kill or destroy her, hardly will that which is appointed to be the destruction of some other body, destroy a soul or anything else except that of which it was appointed to be the destruction.

Yes, that can hardly be.

But the soul which cannot be destroyed by an evil, whether inherent or external, must exist for ever, and if existing for ever, must be immortal?

Certainly.

That is the conclusion, I said; and, if a true conclusion, then the souls must always be the same, for if none be destroyed they will not diminish in number. Neither will they increase, for the increase of the immortal natures must come from something mortal, and all things would thus end in immortality.

Very true.

But this we cannot believe—reason will not allow us—any more than we can believe the soul, in her truest nature, to be full of variety and difference and dissimilarity.

What do you mean? he said.

The soul, I said, being, as is now proven, immortal, must be the fairest of compositions and cannot be compounded of many elements?

Certainly not.

Her immortality is demonstrated by the previous argument, and there are many other proofs; but to see her as she really is, not as we now behold her, marred by communion with the body and other miseries, you must contemplate her with the eye of reason, in her original purity; and then her beauty will be revealed, and justice and injustice and all the things which we have described will be manifested more clearly. Thus far, we have spoken the truth concerning her as she appears at present, but we must remember also that we have seen her only in a condition which may be compared to that of the sea-god Glaucus, whose original image can hardly be discerned because his natural members are broken off and crushed and damaged by the waves in all sorts of ways, and incrustations have grown over them of seaweed and shells and stones, so that he is more like some monster than he is to his own natural form. And the soul which we behold is in a similar condition, disfigured by ten thousand ills. But not there, Glaucon, not there must we look.

Where then?

At her love of wisdom. Let us see whom she affects, and what society and converse she seeks in virtue of her near kindred with the immortal and eternal and divine; also how different she would become if wholly following this superior principle, and borne by a divine impulse out of the ocean in which she now is, and disengaged from the stones and shells and things of earth and rock which in wild variety spring up around her because she feeds upon earth, and is overgrown by the good things of this life as they are termed: then you would see her as she is, and know whether she have one shape only or many, or what her nature is. Of her affections and of the forms which she takes in this present life I think that we have now said enough.

True, he replied.

And thus, I said, we have fulfilled the conditions of the argument; we have not introduced the rewards and glories of justice, which, as you were saying, are to be found in Homer and Hesiod; but justice in her own nature has been shown to be best for the soul in her own nature. Let a man do what is just, whether he have the ring of Gyges or not, and even if in addition to the ring of Gyges he put on the helmet of Hades.

Very true.

And now, Glaucon, there will be no harm in further enumerating how many and how great are the rewards which justice and the other virtues procure to the soul from gods and men, both in life and after death.

Certainly not, he said.

Will you repay me, then, what you borrowed in the argument?

What did I borrow?

The assumption that the just man should appear unjust and the unjust just: for you were of opinion that even if the true state of the case could not possibly escape the eyes of gods and men, still this admission ought to be made for the sake of the argument, in order that pure justice might be weighed against pure injustice. Do you remember?

I should be much to blame if I had forgotten.

Then, as the cause is decided, I demand on behalf of justice that the estimation in which she is held by gods and men and which we acknowledge to be her due should now be restored to her by us; since she has been shown to confer reality, and not to deceive those who truly possess her, let what has been taken from her be given back, that so she may win that palm of appearance which is hers also, and which she gives to her own.

The demand, he said, is just.

In the first place, I said—and this is the first thing which you will have to give back—the nature both of the just and unjust is truly known to the gods.

Granted.

And if they are both known to them, one must be the friend and the other the enemy of the gods, as we admitted from the beginning?

True.

And the friend of the gods may be supposed to receive from them all things at their best, excepting only such evil as is the necessary consequence of former sins?

Certainly.

Then this must be our notion of the just man, that even when he is in poverty or sickness, or any other seeming misfortune, all things will in the end work together for good to him in life and death: for the gods have a care of any one whose desire is to become just and to be like God, as far as man can attain the divine likeness, by the pursuit of virtue?

Yes, he said; if he is like God he will surely not be neglected by him.

And of the unjust may not the opposite be supposed?

Certainly.

Such, then, are the palms of victory which the gods give the just?

That is my conviction.

And what do they receive of men? Look at things as they really are, and you will see that the clever unjust are in the case of runners, who run well from the starting-place to the goal but not back again from the goal: they go off at a great pace, but in the end only look foolish, slinking away with their ears draggling on their shoulders, and without a crown; but the true runner comes to the finish and receives the prize and is crowned. And this is the way with the just; he who endures to the end of every action and occasion of his entire life has a good report and carries off the prize which men have to bestow.

True.

And now you must allow me to repeat of the just the blessings which you were attributing to the fortunate unjust. I shall say of them, what you were saying of the others, that as they grow older, they become rulers in their own city if they care to be; they marry whom they like and give in marriage to whom they will; all that you said of the others I now say of these. And, on the other hand, of the unjust I say that the greater number, even though they escape in their youth, are found out at last and look foolish at the end of their course, and when they come to be old and miserable are flouted alike by stranger and citizen; they are beaten and then come those things unfit for ears polite, as you truly term them; they will be racked and have their eyes burned out, as you were saying. And you may suppose that I have repeated the remainder of your tale of horrors. But will you let me assume, without reciting them, that these things are true?

Certainly, he said, what you say is true.

These, then, are the prizes and rewards and gifts which are bestowed upon the just by gods and men in this present life, in addition to the other good things which justice of herself provides.

Yes, he said; and they are fair and lasting.

And yet, I said, all these are as nothing either in number or greatness in comparison with those other recompenses which await both just and unjust after death. And you ought to hear them, and then both just and unjust will have received from us a full payment of the debt which the argument owes to them.

Speak, he said; there are few things which I would more gladly hear.

Well, I said, I will tell you a tale; not one of the tales which Odysseus tells to the hero Alcinous, yet this too is a tale of a hero, Er the son of Armenius, a Pamphylian by birth. He was slain in battle, and ten days afterwards, when the bodies of the dead were taken up already in a state of corruption, his body was found unaffected by decay, and carried away home to be buried. And on the twelfth day, as he was lying on the funeral pile, he returned to life and told them what he had seen in the other world. He said that when his soul left the body he went on a journey with a great company, and that they came to a mysterious place at which there were two openings in the earth; they were near together, and over against them were two other openings in the heaven above. In the intermediate space there were judges seated, who commanded the just, after they had given judgment on them and had bound their sentences in front of them, to ascend by the heavenly way on the right hand; and in like manner the unjust were bidden by them to descend by the lower way on the left hand; these also bore the symbols of their deeds, but fastened on their backs. He drew near, and they told him that he was to be the messenger who would carry the report of the other world to men, and they bade him hear and see all that was to be heard and seen in that place. Then he beheld and saw on one side the souls departing at either opening of heaven and earth when sentence had been given on them; and at the two other openings other souls, some ascending out of the earth dusty and worn with travel, some descending out of heaven clean and bright. And arriving ever and anon they seemed to have come from a long journey, and they went forth with gladness into the meadow, where they encamped as at a festival; and those who knew one another embraced and conversed, the souls which came from earth curiously enquiring about the things above, and the souls which came from heaven about the things beneath. And they told one another of what had happened by the way, those from below weeping and sorrowing at the remembrance of the things which they had endured and seen in their journey beneath the earth (now the journey lasted a thousand years), while those from above were describing heavenly delights and visions of inconceivable beauty. The story, Glaucon, would take too long to tell; but the sum was this:—He said that for every wrong which they had done to any one they suffered tenfold; or once in a hundred years—such being reckoned to be the length of man's life, and the penalty being thus paid ten times in a thousand years. If, for example, there were any who had been the cause of many deaths, or had betrayed or enslaved cities or armies, or been guilty of any other evil behaviour, for each and all of their offences they received punishment ten times over, and the rewards of beneficence and justice and holiness were in the same proportion. I need hardly repeat what he said concerning young children dying almost as soon as they were born. Of piety and impiety to gods and parents, and of murderers, there were retributions other and greater far which he described. He mentioned that he was present when one of the spirits asked another, 'Where is Ardiaeus the Great?' (Now this Ardiaeus lived a thousand years before the time of Er: he had been the tyrant of some city of Pamphylia, and had murdered his aged father and his elder brother, and was said to have committed many other abominable crimes.) The answer of the other spirit was: 'He comes not hither and will never come. And this,' said he, 'was one of the dreadful sights which we ourselves witnessed. We were at the mouth of the cavern, and, having completed all our experiences, were about to reascend, when of a sudden Ardiaeus appeared and several others, most of whom were tyrants; and there were also besides the tyrants private individuals who had been great criminals: they were just, as they fancied, about to return into the upper world, but the mouth, instead of admitting them, gave a roar, whenever any of these incurable sinners or some one who had not been sufficiently punished tried to ascend; and then wild men of fiery aspect, who were standing by and heard the sound, seized and carried them off; and Ardiaeus and others they bound head and foot and hand, and threw them down and flayed them with scourges, and dragged them along the road at the side, carding them on thorns like wool, and declaring to the passers-by what were their crimes, and that they were being taken away to be cast into hell.' And of all the many terrors which they had endured, he said that there was none like the terror which each of them felt at that moment, lest they should hear the voice; and when there was silence, one by one they ascended with exceeding joy. These, said Er, were the penalties and retributions, and there were blessings as great.

Now when the spirits which were in the meadow had tarried seven days, on the eighth they were obliged to proceed on their journey, and, on the fourth day after, he said that they came to a place where they could see from above a line of light, straight as a column, extending right through the whole heaven and through the earth, in colour resembling the rainbow, only brighter and purer; another day's journey brought them to the place, and there, in the midst of the light, they saw the ends of the chains of heaven let down from above: for this light is the belt of heaven, and holds together the circle of the universe, like the under-girders of a trireme. From these ends is extended the spindle of Necessity, on which all the revolutions turn. The shaft and hook of this spindle are made of steel, and the whorl is made partly of steel and also partly of other materials. Now the whorl is in form like the whorl used on earth; and the description of it implied that there is one large hollow whorl which is quite scooped out, and into this is fitted another lesser one, and another, and another, and four others, making eight in all, like vessels which fit into one another; the whorls show their edges on the upper side, and on their lower side all together form one continuous whorl. This is pierced by the spindle, which is driven home through the centre of the eighth. The first and outermost whorl has the rim broadest, and the seven inner whorls are narrower, in the following proportions—the sixth is next to the first in size, the fourth next to the sixth; then comes the eighth; the seventh is fifth, the fifth is sixth, the third is seventh, last and eighth comes the second. The largest (or fixed stars) is spangled, and the seventh (or sun) is brightest; the eighth (or moon) coloured by the reflected light of the seventh; the second and fifth (Saturn and Mercury) are in colour like one another, and yellower than the preceding; the third (Venus) has the whitest light; the fourth (Mars) is reddish; the sixth (Jupiter) is in whiteness second. Now the whole spindle has the same motion; but, as the whole revolves in one direction, the seven inner circles move slowly in the other, and of these the swiftest is the eighth; next in swiftness are the seventh, sixth, and fifth, which move together; third in swiftness appeared to move according to the law of this reversed motion the fourth; the third appeared fourth and the second fifth. The spindle turns on the knees of Necessity; and on the upper surface of each circle is a siren, who goes round with them, hymning a single tone or note. The eight together form one harmony; and round about, at equal intervals, there is another band, three in number, each sitting upon her throne: these are the Fates, daughters of Necessity, who are clothed in white robes and have chaplets upon their heads, Lachesis and Clotho and Atropos, who accompany with their voices the harmony of the sirens—Lachesis singing of the past, Clotho of the present, Atropos of the future; Clotho from time to time assisting with a touch of her right hand the revolution of the outer circle of the whorl or spindle, and Atropos with her left hand touching and guiding the inner ones, and Lachesis laying hold of either in turn, first with one hand and then with the other.

When Er and the spirits arrived, their duty was to go at once to Lachesis; but first of all there came a prophet who arranged them in order; then he took from the knees of Lachesis lots and samples of lives, and having mounted a high pulpit, spoke as follows: "Hear the word of Lachesis, the daughter of Necessity. Mortal souls, behold a new cycle of life and mortality. Your genius will not be allotted to you, but you will choose your genius; and let him who draws the first lot have the first choice, and the life which he chooses shall be his destiny. Virtue is free, and as a man honours or dishonours her he will have more or less of her; the responsibility is with the chooser—God is justified." When the Interpreter had thus spoken he scattered lots indifferently among them all, and each of them took up the lot which fell near him, all but Er himself (he was not allowed), and each as he took his lot perceived the number which he had obtained. Then the Interpreter placed on the ground before them the samples of lives; and there were many more lives than the souls present, and they were of all sorts. There were lives of every animal and of man in every condition. And there were tyrannies among them, some lasting out the tyrant's life, others which broke off in the middle and came to an end in poverty and exile and beggary; and there were lives of famous men, some who were famous for their form and beauty as well as for their strength and success in games, or, again, for their birth and the qualities of their ancestors; and some who were the reverse of famous for the opposite qualities. And of women likewise; there was not, however, any definite character in them, because the soul, when choosing a new life, must of necessity become different. But there was every other quality, and the all mingled with one another, and also with elements of wealth and poverty, and disease and health; and there were mean states also. And here, my dear Glaucon, is the supreme peril of our human state; and therefore the utmost care should be taken. Let each one of us leave every other kind of knowledge and seek and follow one thing only, if peradventure he may be able to learn and may find some one who will make him able to learn and discern between good and evil, and so to choose always and everywhere the better life as he has opportunity. He should consider the bearing of all these things which have been mentioned severally and collectively upon virtue; he should know what the effect of beauty is when combined with poverty or wealth in a particular soul, and what are the good and evil consequences of noble and humble birth, of private and public station, of strength and weakness, of cleverness and dullness, and of all the natural and acquired gifts of the soul, and the operation of them when conjoined; he will then look at the nature of the soul, and from the consideration of all these qualities he will be able to determine which is the better and which is the worse; and so he will choose, giving the name of evil to the life which will make his soul more unjust, and good to the life which will make his soul more just; all else he will disregard. For we have seen and know that this is the best choice both in life and after death. A man must take with him into the world below an adamantine faith in truth and right, that there too he may be undazzled by the desire of wealth or the other allurements of evil, lest, coming upon tyrannies and similar villainies, he do irremediable wrongs to others and suffer yet worse himself; but let him know how to choose the mean and avoid the extremes on either side, as far as possible, not only in this life but in all that which is to come. For this is the way of happiness.

And according to the report of the messenger from the other world this was what the prophet said at the time: "Even for the last comer, if he chooses wisely and will live diligently, there is appointed a happy and not undesirable existence. Let not him who chooses first be careless, and let not the last despair." And when he had spoken, he who had the first choice came forward and in a moment chose the greatest tyranny; his mind having been darkened by folly and sensuality, he had not thought out the whole matter before he chose, and did not at first sight perceive that he was fated, among other evils, to devour his own children. But when he had time to reflect, and saw what was in the lot, he began to beat his breast and lament over his choice, forgetting the proclamation of the prophet; for, instead of throwing the blame of his misfortune on himself, he accused chance and the gods, and everything rather than himself. Now he was one of those who came from heaven, and in a former life had dwelt in a well-ordered State, but his virtue was a matter of habit only, and he had no philosophy. And it was true of others who were similarly overtaken, that the greater number of them came from heaven and therefore they had never been schooled by trial, whereas the pilgrims who came from earth having themselves suffered and seen others suffer, were not in a hurry to choose. And owing to this inexperience of theirs, and also because the lot was a chance, many of the souls exchanged a good destiny for an evil or an evil for a good. For if a man had always on his arrival in this world dedicated himself from the first to sound philosophy, and had been moderately fortunate in the number of the lot, he might, as the messenger reported, be happy here, and also his journey to another life and return to this, instead of being rough and underground, would be smooth and heavenly. Most curious, he said, was the spectacle—sad and laughable and strange; for the choice of the souls was in most cases based on their experience of a previous life. There he saw the soul which had once been Orpheus choosing the life of a swan out of enmity to the race of women, hating to be born of a woman because they had been his murderers; he beheld also the soul of Thamyras choosing the life of a nightingale; birds, on the other hand, like the swan and other musicians, wanting to be men. The soul which obtained the twentieth lot chose the life of a lion, and this was the soul of Ajax the son of Telamon, who would not be a man, remembering the injustice which was done him in the judgment about the arms. The next was Agamemnon, who took the life of an eagle, because, like Ajax, he hated human nature by reason of his sufferings. About the middle came the lot of Atalanta; she, seeing the great fame of an athlete, was unable to resist the temptation: and after her there followed the soul of Epeus the son of Panopeus passing into the nature of a woman cunning in the arts; and far away among the last who chose, the soul of the jester Thersites was putting on the form of a monkey. There came also the soul of Odysseus having yet to make a choice, and his lot happened to be the last of them all. Now the recollection of former toils had disenchanted him of ambition, and he went about for a considerable time in search of the life of a private man who had no cares; he had some difficulty in finding this, which was lying about and had been neglected by everybody else; and when he saw it, he said that he would have done the same had his lot been first instead of last, and that he was delighted to have it. And not only did men pass into animals, but I must also mention that there were animals tame and wild who changed into one another and into corresponding human natures—the good into the gentle and the evil into the savage, in all sorts of combinations.

All the souls had now chosen their lives, and they went in the order of their choice to Lachesis, who sent with them the genius whom they had severally chosen, to be the guardian of their lives and the fulfiller of the choice: this genius led the souls first to Clotho, and drew them within the revolution of the spindle impelled by her hand, thus ratifying the destiny of each; and then, when they were fastened to this, carried them to Atropos, who spun the threads and made them irreversible, whence without turning round they passed beneath the throne of Necessity; and when they had all passed, they marched on in a scorching heat to the plain of Forgetfulness, which was a barren waste destitute of trees and verdure; and then towards evening they encamped by the river of Unmindfulness, whose water no vessel can hold; of this they were all obliged to drink a certain quantity, and those who were not saved by wisdom drank more than was necessary; and each one as he drank forgot all things. Now after they had gone to rest, about the middle of the night there was a thunderstorm and earthquake, and then in an instant they were driven upwards in all manner of ways to their birth, like stars shooting. He himself was hindered from drinking the water. But in what manner or by what means he returned to the body he could not say; only, in the morning, awaking suddenly, he found himself lying on the pyre.

And thus, Glaucon, the tale has been saved and has not perished, and will save us if we are obedient to the word spoken; and we shall pass safely over the river of Forgetfulness and our soul will not be defiled. Wherefore my counsel is, that we hold fast ever to the heavenly way and follow after justice and virtue always, considering that the soul is immortal and able to endure every sort of good and every sort of evil. Thus shall we live dear to one another and to the gods, both while remaining here and when, like conquerors in the games who go round to gather gifts, we receive our reward. And it shall be well with us both in this life and in the pilgrimage of a thousand years which we have been describing.

# POLITICS

# Aristotle

# INTRODUCTION

*P*olitics of Aristotle is the second part of a treatise of which the *Ethics* is the first part. It looks back to the *Ethics* as the *Ethics* looks forward to *Politics*. For Aristotle did not separate, as we are inclined to do, the spheres of the statesman and the moralist. In the Ethics he has described the character necessary for the good life, but that life is for him essentially to be lived in society, and when in the last chapters of the Ethics he comes to the practical application of his inquiries, that finds expression not in moral exhortations addressed to the individual but in a description of the legislative opportunities of the statesman. It is the legislator's task to frame a society which shall make the good life possible. Politics for Aristotle is not a struggle between individuals or classes for power, nor a device for getting done such elementary tasks as the maintenance of order and security without too great encroachments on individual liberty. The state is "a community of well-being in families and aggregations of families for the sake of a perfect and self-sufficing life." The legislator is a craftsman whose material is society and whose aim is the good life.

In an early dialogue of Plato's, the *Protagoras*, Socrates asks Protagoras why it is not as easy to find teachers of virtue as it is to find teachers of swordsmanship, riding, or any other art. Protagoras' answer is that there are no special teachers of virtue, because virtue is taught by the whole community. Plato and Aristotle both accept the view of moral education implied in this answer. In a passage of *The Republic* (492 b) Plato repudiates the notion that the sophists have a corrupting moral influence upon young men. The public themselves, he says, are the real sophists and the most complete and thorough educators. No private education can hold out against the irresistible force of public opinion and the ordinary moral standards of society. But that makes it all the more essential that public opinion and social environment should not be left to grow up at haphazard as they ordinarily do, but should be made by the wise legislator the expression of the good and be informed in all their details by his knowledge. The legislator is the only possible teacher of virtue.

Such a programme for a treatise on government might lead us to expect in *Politics* mainly a description of a Utopia or ideal state which might inspire poets or philosophers but have little direct effect upon political institutions. Plato's *Republic* is obviously impracticable, for its author had turned away in despair from existing politics. He has no proposals, in that dialogue at least, for making the best of things as they are. The first lesson his philosopher has to learn is to turn away from this world of becoming and decay, and to look upon the unchanging eternal world of ideas. Thus his ideal city is, as he says, a pattern laid up in heaven by which the just man may rule his life, a pattern therefore in the meantime for the individual and not for the statesman. It is a city, he admits in the Laws, for gods or the children of gods, not for men as they are.

Aristotle has none of the high enthusiasm or poetic imagination of Plato. He is even unduly impatient of Plato's idealism, as is shown by the criticisms in the second book. But he has a power to see the possibilities of good in things that are imperfect, and the patience of the true politician who has learned that if he would make men what they ought to be, he must take them as he finds them. His ideal is constructed not of pure reason or poetry, but from careful and sympathetic study of a wide range of facts. His criticism of Plato in the light of history, in Book II. chap, v., though as a criticism it is curiously inept, reveals his own attitude admirably: "Let us remember that we should not disregard the experience of ages; in the multitude of years, these things, if they were good, would certainly not have been unknown; for almost everything has been found out, although sometimes they are not put together; in other cases men do not use the knowledge which they have." Aristotle in his Constitutions had made a study of one hundred and fifty-eight constitutions of the states of his day, and the fruits of that study are seen in the continual reference to concrete political experience, which makes *Politics* in some respects a critical history of the workings of the institutions of the Greek city state. In Books IV., V., and VI. the ideal state seems far away, and we find a dispassionate survey of imperfect states, the best ways of preserving them, and an analysis of the causes of their instability. It is as though Aristotle were saying: "I have shown you the proper and normal type of constitution, but if you will not have it and insist on living under a perverted form, you may as well know how to make the best of it." In this way *Politics*, though it defines the state in the light of its ideal, discusses states and institutions as they are. Ostensibly it is merely a continuation of the Ethics, but it comes to treat political questions from a purely political standpoint.

This combination of idealism and respect for the teachings of experience constitutes in some ways the strength and value of *Politics*, but it also makes it harder to follow. The large nation states to which we are accustomed make it difficult for us to think that the state could be constructed and modelled to express the good life. We can appreciate Aristotle's critical analysis of constitutions, but find it hard to take seriously his advice to the legislator. Moreover, the idealism and the empiricism of *Politics* are never really reconciled by Aristotle himself.

It may help to an understanding of *Politics* if something is said on those two points.

We are accustomed since the growth of the historical method to the belief that states are "not made but grow," and are apt to be impatient with the belief which Aristotle and Plato show in the powers of the lawgiver. But however true the maxim may be of the modern nation state, it was not true of the much smaller and more self-conscious Greek city. When Aristotle talks of the legislator, he is not talking in the air. Students of the Academy had been actually called on to give new constitutions to Greek states. For the Greeks the constitution was not merely as it is so often with us, a matter of political machinery. It was regarded as a way of life. Further, the constitution within the framework of which the ordinary process of administration and passing of decrees went on, was always regarded as the work of a special man or body of men, the lawgivers. If we study Greek history, we find that the position of the legislator corresponds to that assigned to him by Plato and Aristotle. All Greek states, except those perversions which Aristotle criticises as being "above law," worked under rigid constitutions, and the constitution was only changed when the whole people gave a commission to a lawgiver to draw up a new one. Such was the position of the AEsumnetes, whom Aristotle describes in Book III. chap, xiv., in earlier times, and of the pupils of the Academy in the fourth century. The lawgiver was not an ordinary politician. He was a state doctor, called in to prescribe for an ailing constitution. So Herodotus recounts that when the people of Cyrene asked the oracle of Delphi to help them in their dissensions, the oracle told them to go to Mantinea, and the Mantineans lent them Demonax, who acted as a "setter straight" and drew up a new constitution for Cyrene. So again the Milesians, Herodotus tells us, were long troubled by civil discord, till they asked help from Paros, and the Parians sent ten commissioners who gave Miletus a new constitution. So the Athenians, when they were founding their model new colony at Thurii, employed Hippodamus of Miletus, whom Aristotle mentions in Book II, as the best expert in town-planning, to plan the streets of the city, and Protagoras as the best expert in law-making, to give the city its laws. In the Laws Plato represents one of the persons of the dialogue as having been asked by the people of Gortyna to draw up laws for a colony which they were founding. The situation described must have occurred frequently in actual life. The Greeks thought administration should be democratic and law-making the work of experts. We think more naturally of law-making as the special right of the people and administration as necessarily confined to experts.

Aristotle's *Politics*, then, is a handbook for the legislator, the expert who is to be called in when a state wants help. We have called him a state doctor. It is one of the most marked characteristics of Greek political theory that Plato and Aristotle think of the statesman as one who has knowledge of what ought to be done, and can help those who call him in to prescribe for them, rather than one who has power to control the forces of society. The desire of society for the statesman's advice is taken for granted, Plato in *The Republic* says that a good constitution is only possible when the ruler does not want to rule; where men contend for power, where they have not learnt to distinguish between the art of getting hold of the helm of state and the art of steering, which alone is statesmanship, true politics is impossible.

With this position much that Aristotle has to say about government is in agreement. He assumes the characteristic Platonic view that all men seek the good, and go wrong through ignorance, not through evil will, and so he naturally regards the state as a community which exists for the sake of the good life. It is in the state that that common seeking after the good which is the profoundest truth about men and nature becomes explicit and knows itself. The state is for Aristotle prior to the family and the village, although it succeeds them in time, for only when the state with its conscious organisation is reached can man understand the secret of his past struggles after something he knew not what. If primitive society is understood in the light of the state, the state is understood in the light of its most perfect form, when the good after which all societies are seeking is realised in its perfection. Hence for Aristotle as for Plato, the natural state or the state as such is the ideal state, and the ideal state is the starting-point of political inquiry.

In accordance with the same line of thought, imperfect states, although called perversions, are regarded by Aristotle as the result rather of misconception and ignorance than of perverse will. They all represent, he says, some kind of justice. Oligarchs and democrats go wrong in their conception of the good. They have come short of the perfect state through misunderstanding of the end or through ignorance of the proper means to the end. But if they are states at all, they embody some common conception of the good, some common aspirations of all their members.

The Greek doctrine that the essence of the state consists in community of purpose is the counterpart of the notion often held in modern times that the essence of the state is force. The existence of force is for Plato and Aristotle a sign not of the state but of the state's failure. It comes from the struggle between conflicting misconceptions of the good. In so far as men conceive the good rightly they are united. The state represents their common agreement, force their failure to make that agreement complete. The cure, therefore, of political ills is knowledge of the good life, and the statesman is he who has such knowledge, for that alone can give men what they are always seeking.

If the state is the organisation of men seeking a common good, power and political position must be given to those who can forward this end. This is the principle expressed in Aristotle's account of political justice, the principle of "tools to those who can use them." As the aim of the state is differently conceived, the qualifications for government will vary. In the ideal state power will be given to the man with most knowledge of the good; in other states to the men who are most truly capable of achieving that end which the citizens have set themselves to pursue. The justest distribution of political power is that in which there is least waste of political ability.

Further, the belief that the constitution of a state is only the outward expression of the common aspirations and beliefs of its members, explains the paramount political importance which Aristotle assigns to education. It is the great instrument by which the legislator can ensure that the future citizens of his state will share those common beliefs which make the state possible. The Greeks with their small states had a far clearer apprehension than we can have of the dependence of a constitution upon the people who have to work it.

Such is in brief the attitude in which Aristotle approaches political problems, but in working out its application to men and institutions as they are, Aristotle admits certain compromises which are not really consistent with it.

1. Aristotle thinks of membership of a state as community in pursuit of the good. He wishes to confine membership in it to those who are capable of that pursuit in the highest and most explicit manner. His citizens, therefore, must be men of leisure, capable of rational thought upon the end of life. He does not recognise the significance of that less conscious but deep-seated membership of the state which finds its expression in loyalty and patriotism. His definition of citizen

includes only a small part of the population of any Greek city. He is forced to admit that the state is not possible without the co-operation of men whom he will not admit to membership in it, either because they are not capable of sufficient rational appreciation of political ends, like the barbarians whom he thought were natural slaves, or because the leisure necessary for citizenship can only be gained by the work of the artisans who by that very work make themselves incapable of the life which they make possible for others. "The artisan only attains excellence in proportion as he becomes a slave," and the slave is only a living instrument of the good life. He exists for the state, but the state does not exist for him.

2. Aristotle in his account of the ideal state seems to waver between two ideals. There is the ideal of an aristocracy and the ideal of what he calls constitutional government, a mixed constitution. The principle of "tools to those who can use them" ought to lead him, as it does Plato, to an aristocracy. Those who have complete knowledge of the good must be few, and therefore Plato gave entire power in his state into the hands of the small minority of philosopher guardians. It is in accordance with this principle that Aristotle holds that kingship is the proper form of government when there is in the state one man of transcendent virtue. At the same time, Aristotle always holds that absolute government is not properly political, that government is not like the rule of a shepherd over his sheep, but the rule of equals over equals. He admits that the democrats are right in insisting that equality is a necessary element in the state, though he thinks they do not admit the importance of other equally necessary elements. Hence he comes to say that ruling and being ruled over by turns is an essential feature of constitutional government, which he admits as an alternative to aristocracy. The end of the state, which is to be the standard of the distribution of political power, is conceived sometimes as a good for the apprehension and attainment of which "virtue" is necessary and sufficient (this is the principle of aristocracy), and sometimes as a more complex good, which needs for its attainment not only "virtue" but wealth and equality. This latter conception is the principle on which the mixed constitution is based.

This in its distribution of political power gives some weight to "virtue," some to wealth, and some to mere number. But the principle of "ruling and being ruled by turns" is not really compatible with an unmodified principle of "tools to those who can use them." Aristotle is right in seeing that political government demands equality, not in the sense that all members of the state should be equal in ability or should have equal power, but in the sense that none of them can properly be regarded simply as tools with which the legislator works, that each has a right to say what will be made of his own life. The analogy between the legislator and the craftsman on which Plato insists, breaks down because the legislator is dealing with men like himself, men who can to some extent conceive their own end in life and cannot be treated merely as means to the end of the legislator. The sense of the value of "ruling and being ruled in turn" is derived from the experience that the ruler may use his power to subordinate the lives of the citizens of the state not to the common good but to his own private purposes. In modern terms, it is a simple, rough-and-ready attempt to solve that constant problem of politics, how efficient government is to be combined with popular control. This problem arises from the imperfection of human nature, apparent in rulers as well as in ruled, and if the principle which attempts to solve it be admitted as a principle of importance in the formation of the best constitution, then the starting-point of politics will be man's actual imperfection, not his ideal nature. Instead, then, of beginning with a state which would express man's ideal nature, and adapting it as well as may be to man's actual shortcomings from that ideal, we must recognise that the state and all political machinery are as much the expression of man's weakness as of his ideal possibilities. The state is possible only because men have common aspirations, but government, and political power, the existence of officials who are given authority to act in the name of the whole state, are necessary because men's community is imperfect, because man's social nature expresses itself in conflicting ways, in the clash of interests, the rivalry of parties, and the struggle of classes, instead of in the united seeking after a common good. Plato and Aristotle were familiar with the legislator who was called in by the whole people, and they tended therefore to take the general will or common consent of the people for granted. Most political questions are concerned with the construction and expression of the general will, and with attempts to ensure that the political machinery made to express the general will shall not be exploited for private or sectional ends.

Aristotle's mixed constitution springs from a recognition of sectional interests in the state. For the proper relation between the claims of "virtue," wealth, and numbers is to be based not upon their relative importance in the good life, but upon the strength of the parties which they represent. The mixed constitution is practicable in a state where the middle class is strong, as only the middle class can mediate between the rich and the poor. The mixed constitution will be stable if it represents the actual balance of power between different classes in the state. When we come to Aristotle's analysis of existing constitutions, we find that while he regards them as imperfect approximations to the ideal, he also thinks of them as the result of the struggle between classes. Democracy, he explains, is the government not of the many but of the poor; oligarchy a government not of the few but of the rich. And each class is thought of, not as trying to express an ideal, but as struggling to acquire power or maintain its position. If ever the class existed in unredeemed nakedness, it was in the Greek cities of the fourth century, and its existence is abundantly recognised by Aristotle. His account of the causes of revolutions in Book V. shows how far were the existing states of Greece from the ideal with which he starts. His analysis of the facts forces him to look upon them as the scene of struggling factions. The causes of revolutions are not described as primarily changes in the conception of the common good, but changes in the military or economic power of the several classes in the state. The aim which he sets before oligarchs or democracies is not the good life, but simple stability or permanence of the existing constitution.

With this spirit of realism which pervades Books IV, V, and VI the idealism of Books I, II, VII, and VIII is never reconciled. Aristotle is content to call existing constitutions perversions of the true form.

But we cannot read *Politics* without recognising and profiting from the insight into the nature of the state which is revealed throughout. Aristotle's failure does not lie in this, that he is both idealist and realist, but that he keeps these two tendencies too far apart. He thinks too much of his ideal state, as something to be reached once for all by knowledge, as a fixed type to which actual states approximate or from which they are perversions. But if we are to think of actual politics as intelligible in the light of the ideal, we must think of that ideal as progressively revealed in history, not as something to be discovered by turning our back on experience and having recourse to abstract reasoning. If we stretch forward from what exists to an ideal, it is to a better which may be in its turn transcended, not to a single immutable best. Aristotle found in the society of his time men who were not capable of political reflection, and who, as he thought, did their best work under superintendence. He therefore called them natural slaves. For, according to Aristotle, that is a man's natural condition in which he does his best work. But Aristotle also thinks of nature as something fixed and immutable; and therefore sanctions the institution of slavery, which assumes that what men are that they will always be, and sets up an artificial barrier to their ever becoming anything else. We see in Aristotle's defence of slavery how the conception of nature as the ideal can have a debasing influence upon views of practical politics. His high ideal of citizenship offers to those who can satisfy its claims the prospect of a fair life; those who fall short are deemed to be different in nature and shut out entirely from approach to the ideal.

A. D. LINDSAY

# BOOK I

## CHAPTER

### I

As we see that every city is a society, and every society is established for some good purpose; for an apparent good is the spring of all human actions; it is evident that this is the principle upon which they are every one founded, and this is more especially true of that which has for its object the best possible, and is itself the most excellent, and comprehends all the rest. Now this is called a city, and the society thereof a political society; for those who think that the principles of a political, a regal, a family, and a herile government are the same are mistaken, while they suppose that each of these differ in the numbers to whom their power extends, but not in their constitution: so that with them a herile government is one composed of a very few, a domestic of more, a civil and a regal of still more, as if there was no difference between a large family and a small city, or that a regal government and a political one are the same, only that in the one a single person is continually at the head of public affairs; in the other, that each member of the state has in his turn a share in the government, and is at one time a magistrate, at another a private person, according to the rules of political science. But now this is not true, as will be evident to any one who will consider this question in the most approved method. As, in an inquiry into every other subject, it is necessary to separate the different parts of which it is compounded, till we arrive at their first elements, which are the most minute parts thereof; so by the same proceeding we shall acquire a knowledge of the primary parts of a city and see wherein they differ from each other, and whether the rules of art will give us any assistance in examining into each of these things which are mentioned.

## CHAPTER

## II

Now if in this particular science any one would attend to its original seeds, and their first shoot, he would then as in others have the subject perfectly before him; and perceive, in the first place, that it is requisite that those should be joined together whose species cannot exist without each other, as the male and the female, for the business of propagation; and this not through choice, but by that natural impulse which acts both upon plants and animals also, for the purpose of their leaving behind them others like themselves. It is also from natural causes that some beings command and others obey, that each may obtain their mutual safety; for a being who is endowed with a mind capable of reflection and forethought is by nature the superior and governor, whereas he whose excellence is merely corporeal is formect to be a slave; whence it follows that the different state of master and slave is equally advantageous to both. But there is a natural difference between a female and a slave: for nature is not like the artists who make the Delphic swords for the use of the poor, but for every particular purpose she has her separate instruments, and thus her ends are most complete, for whatsoever is employed on one subject only, brings that one to much greater perfection than when employed on many; and yet among the barbarians, a female and a slave are upon a level in the community, the reason for which is, that amongst them there are none qualified by nature to govern, therefore their society can be nothing but between slaves of different sexes. For which reason the poets say, it is proper for the Greeks to govern the barbarians, as if a barbarian and a slave were by nature one. Now of these two societies the domestic is the first, and Hesiod is right when he says, "First a house, then a wife, then an ox for the plough," for the poor man has always an ox before a household slave. That society then which nature has established for daily support is the domestic, and those who compose it are called by Charondas *homosipuoi*, and by Epimenides the Cretan *homokapnoi*; but the society of many families, which was first instituted for their lasting, mutual advantage, is called a village, and a village is most naturally composed of the descendants of one family, whom some persons call homogalaktes, the children and the children's children thereof: for which reason cities were originally governed by kings, as the barbarian states now are, which are composed of those who had before submitted to kingly government; for every family is governed by the elder, as are the branches thereof, on account of their relationship thereunto, which is what Homer says, "Each one ruled his wife and child;" and in this scattered manner they formerly lived. And the opinion which universally prevails, that the gods themselves are subject to kingly government, arises from hence, that all men formerly were, and many are so now; and as they imagined themselves to be made in the likeness of the gods, so they supposed their manner of life must needs be the same. And when many villages so entirely join themselves together as in every respect to form but one society, that society is a city, and contains in itself, if I may so speak, the end and perfection of government: first founded that we might live, but continued that we may live happily. For which reason every city must be allowed to be the work of nature, if we admit that the original society between male and female is; for to this as their end all subordinate societies tend, and the end of everything is the nature of it. For what every being is in its most perfect state, that certainly is the nature of that being, whether it be a man, a horse, or a house: besides, whatsoever produces the final cause and the end which we desire, must be best; but a government complete in itself is that final cause and what is best. Hence it is evident that a city is a natural production, and that man is naturally a political animal, and that whosoever is naturally and not accidentally unfit for society, must be either inferior or superior to man: thus the man in Homer, who is reviled for being "without society, without law, without family." Such a one must naturally be of a quarrelsome disposition, and as solitary as the birds. The gift of speech also evidently proves that man is a more social animal than the bees, or any of the herding cattle: for nature, as we say, does nothing in vain, and man is the only animal who enjoys it. Voice indeed, as being the token of pleasure and pain, is imparted to others also, and thus much their nature is capable of, to perceive pleasure and pain, and to impart these sensations to others; but it is by speech that we are enabled to express what is useful for us, and what is hurtful, and of course what is just and what is unjust: for in this particular man differs from other animals, that he alone has a perception of good and evil, of just and unjust, and it is a participation of these common sentiments which forms a family and a city. Besides, the notion of a city naturally precedes that of a family or an individual, for the whole must necessarily be prior to the parts, for if you take away the whole man, you cannot say a foot or a hand remains, unless by equivocation, as supposing a hand of stone to be made, but that would only be a dead one; but everything is understood to be this or that by its energic qualities and powers, so that when these no longer remain, neither can that be said to be the same, but something of the same name. That a city then precedes an individual is plain, for if an individual is not in himself sufficient to compose a perfect government, he is to a city as other parts are to a whole; but he that is incapable of society, or so complete in himself as not to want it, makes no part of a city, as a beast or a god. There is then in all persons a natural impetus to associate with each other in this manner, and he who first founded civil society was the cause of the greatest good; for as by the completion of it man is the most excellent of all living beings, so without law and justice he would be the worst of all, for nothing is so difficult to subdue as injustice in arms: but these arms man is born with, namely, prudence and valour, which he may apply to the most opposite purposes, for he who abuses them will be the most wicked, the most cruel, the most lustful, and most gluttonous being imaginable; for justice is a political virtue, by the rules of it the state is regulated, and these rules are the criterion of what is right.

# CHAPTER

## III

Since it is now evident of what parts a city is composed, it will be necessary to treat first of family government, for every city is made up of families, and every family has again its separate parts of which it is composed. When a family is complete, it consists of freemen and slaves; but as in every subject we should begin with examining into the smallest parts of which it consists, and as the first and smallest parts of a family are the master and slave, the husband and wife, the father and child, let us first inquire into these three, what each of them may be, and what they ought to be; that is to say, the herile, the nuptial, and the paternal. Let these then be considered as the three distinct parts of a family: some think that the providing what is necessary for the family is something different from the government of it, others that this is the greatest part of it; it shall be considered separately; but we will first speak of a master and a slave, that we may both understand the nature of those things which are absolutely necessary, and also try if we can learn anything better on this subject than what is already known. Some persons have thought that the power of the master over his slave originates from his superior knowledge, and that this knowledge is the same in the master, the magistrate, and the king, as we have already said; but others think that herile government is contrary to nature, and that it is the law which makes one man a slave and another free, but that in nature there is no difference; for which reason that power cannot be founded in justice, but in force.

# CHAPTER

## IV

Since then a subsistence is necessary in every family, the means of procuring it certainly makes up part of the management of a family, for without necessaries it is impossible to live, and to live well. As in all arts which are brought to perfection it is necessary that they should have their proper instruments if they would complete their works, so is it in the art of managing a family: now of instruments some of them are alive, others inanimate; thus with respect to the pilot of the ship, the tiller is without life, the sailor is alive; for a servant is as an instrument in many arts. Thus property is as an instrument to living; an estate is a multitude of instruments; so a slave is an animated instrument, but every one that can minister of himself is more valuable than any other instrument; for if every instrument, at command, or from a preconception of its master's will, could accomplish its work (as the story goes of the statues of Daedalus; or what the poet tells us of the tripods of Vulcan, "that they moved of their own accord into the assembly of the gods"), the shuttle would then weave, and the lyre play of itself; nor would the architect want servants, or the master slaves. Now what are generally called instruments are the efficients of something else, but possessions are what we simply use: thus with a shuttle we make something else for our use; but we only use a coat, or a bed: since then making and using differ from each other in species, and they both require their instruments, it is necessary that these should be different from each other. Now life is itself what we use, and not what we employ as the efficient of something else; for which reason the services of a slave are for use. A possession may be considered in the same nature as a part of anything; now a part is not only a part of something, but also is nothing else; so is a possession; therefore a master is only the master of the slave, but no part of him; but the slave is not only the slave of the master, but nothing else but that. This fully explains what is the nature of a slave, and what are his capacities; for that being who by nature is nothing of himself, but totally another's, and is a man, is a slave by nature; and that man who is the property of another, is his mere chattel, though he continues a man; but a chattel is an instrument for use, separate from the body.

# CHAPTER

## V

But whether any person is such by nature, and whether it is advantageous and just for any one to be a slave or no, or whether all slavery is contrary to nature, shall be considered hereafter; not that it is difficult to determine it upon general principles, or to understand it from matters of fact; for that some should govern, and others be governed, is not only necessary but useful, and from the hour of their birth some are marked out for those purposes, and others for the other, and there are many species of both sorts. And the better those are who are governed the better also is the government, as for instance of man, rather than the brute creation: for the more excellent the materials are with which the work is finished, the more excellent certainly is the work; and wherever there is a governor and a governed, there certainly is some work produced; for whatsoever is composed of many parts, which jointly become one, whether conjunct or separate, evidently show the marks of governing and governed; and this is true of every living thing in all nature; nay, even in some things which partake not of life, as in music; but this probably would be a disquisition too foreign to our present purpose. Every living thing in the first place is composed of soul and body, of these the one is by nature the governor, the other the governed; now if we would know what is natural, we ought to search for it in those subjects in which nature appears most perfect, and not in those which are corrupted; we should therefore examine into a man who is most perfectly formed both in soul and body, in whom this is evident, for in the depraved and vicious the body seems to rule rather than the soul, on account of their being corrupt and contrary to nature. We may then, as we affirm, perceive in an animal the first principles of herile and political government; for the soul governs the body as the master governs his slave; the mind governs the appetite with a political or a kingly power, which shows that it is both natural and advantageous that the body should be governed by the soul, and the pathetic part by the mind, and that part which is possessed of reason; but to have no ruling power, or an improper one, is hurtful to all; and this holds true not only of man, but of other animals also, for tame animals are naturally better than wild ones, and it is advantageous that both should be under subjection to man; for this is productive of their common safety: so is it naturally with the male and the female; the one is superior, the other inferior; the one governs, the other is governed; and the same rule must necessarily hold good with respect to all mankind. Those men therefore who are as much inferior to others as the body is to the soul, are to be thus disposed of, as the proper use of them is their bodies, in which their excellence consists; and if what I have said be true, they are slaves by nature, and it is advantageous to them to be always under government. He then is by nature formed a slave who is qualified to become the chattel of another person, and on that account is so, and who has just reason enough to know that there is such a faculty, without being indued with the use of it; for other animals have no perception of reason, but are entirely guided by appetite, and indeed they vary very little in their use from each other; for the advantage which we receive, both from slaves and tame animals, arises from their bodily strength administering to our necessities; for it is the intention of nature to make the bodies of slaves and freemen different from each other, that the one should be robust for their necessary purposes, the others erect, useless indeed for what slaves are employed in, but fit for civil life, which is divided into the duties of war and peace; though these rules do not always take place, for slaves have sometimes the bodies of freemen, sometimes the souls; if then it is evident that if some bodies are as much more excellent than others as the statues of the gods excel the human form, every one will allow that the inferior ought to be slaves to the superior; and if this is true with respect to the body, it is still juster to determine in the same manner, when we consider the soul; though it is not so easy to perceive the beauty of the soul as it is of the body. Since then some men are slaves by nature, and others are freemen, it is clear that where slavery is advantageous to any one, then it is just to make him a slave.

## CHAPTER

## VI

But it is not difficult to perceive that those who maintain the contrary opinion have some reason on their side; for a man may become a slave two different ways; for he may be so by law also, and this law is a certain compact, by which whatsoever is taken in battle is adjudged to be the property of the conquerors: but many persons who are conversant in law call in question this pretended right, and say that it would be hard that a man should be compelled by violence to be the slave and subject of another who had the power to compel him, and was his superior in strength; and upon this subject, even of those who are wise, some think one way and some another; but the cause of this doubt and variety of opinions arises from hence, that great abilities, when accompanied with proper means, are generally able to succeed by force: for victory is always owing to a superiority in some advantageous circumstances; so that it seems that force never prevails but in consequence of great abilities. But still the dispute concerning the justice of it remains; for some persons think, that justice consists in benevolence, others think it just that the powerful should govern: in the midst of these contrary opinions, there are no reasons sufficient to convince us, that the right of being master and governor ought not to be placed with those who have the greatest abilities. Some persons, entirely resting upon the right which the law gives (for that which is legal is in some respects just), insist upon it that slavery occasioned by war is just, not that they say it is wholly so, for it may happen that the principle upon which the wars were commenced is unjust; moreover no one will say that a man who is unworthily in slavery is therefore a slave; for if so, men of the noblest families might happen to be slaves, and the descendants of slaves, if they should chance to be taken prisoners in war and sold: to avoid this difficulty they say that such persons should not be called slaves, but barbarians only should; but when they say this, they do nothing more than inquire who is a slave by nature, which was what we at first said; for we must acknowledge that there are some persons who, wherever they are, must necessarily be slaves, but others in no situation; thus also it is with those of noble descent: it is not only in their own country that they are Esteemed as such, but everywhere, but the barbarians are respected on this account at home only; as if nobility and freedom were of two sorts, the one universal, the other not so. Thus says the Helen of Theodectes:

"Who dares reproach me with the name of slave? When from the immortal gods, on either side, I draw my lineage."

Those who express sentiments like these, shew only that they distinguish the slave and the freeman, the noble and the ignoble from each other by their virtues and their vices; for they think it reasonable, that as a man begets a man, and a beast a beast, so from a good man, a good man should be descended; and this is what nature desires to do, but frequently cannot accomplish it. It is evident then that this doubt has some reason in it, and that these persons are not slaves, and those freemen, by the appointment of nature; and also that in some instances it is sufficiently clear, that it is advantageous to both parties for this man to be a slave, and that to be a master, and that it is right and just, that some should be governed, and others govern, in the manner that nature intended; of which sort of government is that which a master exercises over a slave. But to govern ill is disadvantageous to both; for the same thing is useful to the part and to the whole, to the body and to the soul; but the slave is as it were a part of the master, as if he were an animated part of his body, though separate. For which reason a mutual utility and friendship may subsist between the master and the slave, I mean when they are placed by nature in that relation to each other, for the contrary takes place amongst those who are reduced to slavery by the law, or by conquest.

# CHAPTER

# VII

It is evident from what has been said, that a herile and a political government are not the same, or that all governments are alike to each other, as some affirm; for one is adapted to the nature of freemen, the other to that of slaves. Domestic government is a monarchy, for that is what prevails in every house; but a political state is the government of free men and equals. The master is not so called from his knowing how to manage his slave, but because he is so; for the same reason a slave and a freeman have their respective appellations. There is also one sort of knowledge proper for a master, another for a slave; the slave's is of the nature of that which was taught by a slave at Syracuse; for he for a stipulated sum instructed the boys in all the business of a household slave, of which there are various sorts to be learnt, as the art of cookery, and other such-like services, of which some are allotted to some, and others to others; some employments being more honourable, others more necessary; according to the proverb, "One slave excels another, one master excels another:" in such-like things the knowledge of a slave consists. The knowledge of the master is to be able properly to employ his slaves, for the mastership of slaves is the employment, not the mere possession of them; not that this knowledge contains anything great or respectable; for what a slave ought to know how to do, that a master ought to know how to order; for which reason, those who have it in their power to be free from these low attentions, employ a steward for this business, and apply themselves either to public affairs or philosophy: the knowledge of procuring what is necessary for a family is different from that which belongs either to the master or the slave: and to do this justly must be either by war or hunting. And thus much of the difference between a master and a slave.

## CHAPTER

## VIII

As a slave is a particular species of property, let us by all means inquire into the nature of property in general, and the acquisition of money, according to the manner we have proposed. In the first place then, some one may doubt whether the getting of money is the same thing as economy, or whether it is a part of it, or something subservient to it; and if so, whether it is as the art of making shuttles is to the art of weaving, or the art of making brass to that of statue founding, for they are not of the same service; for the one supplies the tools, the other the matter: by the matter I mean the subject out of which the work is finished, as wool for the cloth and brass for the statue. It is evident then that the getting of money is not the same thing as economy, for the business of the one is to furnish the means of the other to use them; and what art is there employed in the management of a family but economy, but whether this is a part of it, or something of a different species, is a doubt; for if it is the business of him who is to get money to find out how riches and possessions may be procured, and both these arise from various causes, we must first inquire whether the art of husbandry is part of money-getting or something different, and in general, whether the same is not true of every acquisition and every attention which relates to provision. But as there are many sorts of provision, so are the methods of living both of man and the brute creation very various; and as it is impossible to live without food, the difference in that particular makes the lives of animals so different from each other. Of beasts, some live in herds, others separate, as is most convenient for procuring themselves food; as some of them live upon flesh, others on fruit, and others on whatsoever they light on, nature having so distinguished their course of life, that they can very easily procure themselves subsistence; and as the same things are not agreeable to all, but one animal likes one thing and another another, it follows that the lives of those beasts who live upon flesh must be different from the lives of those who live on fruits; so is it with men, their lives differ greatly from each other; and of all these the shepherd's is the idlest, for they live upon the flesh of tame animals, without any trouble, while they are obliged to change their habitations on account of their flocks, which they are compelled to follow, cultivating, as it were, a living farm. Others live exercising violence over living creatures, one pursuing this thing, another that, these preying upon men; those who live near lakes and marshes and rivers, or the sea itself, on fishing, while others are fowlers, or hunters of wild beasts; but the greater part of mankind live upon the produce of the earth and its cultivated fruits; and the manner in which all those live who follow the direction of nature, and labour for their own subsistence, is nearly the same, without ever thinking to procure any provision by way of exchange or merchandise, such are shepherds, husbandmen, robbers, fishermen, and hunters: some join different employments together, and thus live very agreeably; supplying those deficiencies which were wanting to make their subsistence depend upon themselves only: thus, for instance, the same person shall be a shepherd and a robber, or a husbandman and a hunter; and so with respect to the rest, they pursue that mode of life which necessity points out. This provision then nature herself seems to have furnished all animals with, as well immediately upon their first origin as also when they are arrived at a state of maturity; for at the first of these periods some of them are provided in the womb with proper nourishment, which continues till that which is born can get food for itself, as is the case with worms and birds; and as to those which bring forth their young alive, they have the means for their subsistence for a certain time within themselves, namely milk. It is evident then that we may conclude of those things that are, that plants are created for the sake of animals, and animals for the sake of men; the tame for our use and provision; the wild, at least the greater part, for our provision also, or for some other advantageous purpose, as furnishing us with clothes, and the like. As nature therefore makes nothing either imperfect or in vain, it necessarily follows that she has made all these things for men: for which reason what we gain in war is in a certain degree a natural acquisition; for hunting is a part of it, which it is necessary for us to employ against wild beasts; and those men who being intended by nature for slavery are unwilling to submit to it, on which occasion such a war is by nature just: that species of acquisition then only which is according to nature is part of economy; and this ought to be at hand, or if not, immediately procured, namely, what is necessary to be kept in store to live upon, and which are useful as well for the state as the family. And true riches seem to consist in these; and the acquisition of those possessions which are necessary for a happy life is not infinite; though Solon says otherwise in this verse:

"No bounds to riches can be fixed for man;"

for they may be fixed as in other arts; for the instruments of no art whatsoever are infinite, either in their number or their magnitude; but riches are a number of instruments in domestic and civil economy; it is therefore evident that the acquisition of certain things according to nature is a part both of domestic and civil economy, and for what reason.

# CHAPTER

## IX

There is also another species of acquisition which they particularly call pecuniary, and with great propriety; and by this indeed it seems that there are no bounds to riches and wealth. Now many persons suppose, from their near relation to each other, that this is one and the same with that we have just mentioned, but it is not the same as that, though not very different; one of these is natural, the other is not, but rather owing to some art and skill; we will enter into a particular examination of this subject. The uses of every possession are two, both dependent upon the thing itself, but not in the same manner, the one supposing an inseparable connection with it, the other not; as a shoe, for instance, which may be either worn, or exchanged for something else, both these are the uses of the shoe; for he who exchanges a shoe with some man who wants one, for money or provisions, uses the shoe as a shoe, but not according to the original intention, for shoes were not at first made to be exchanged. The same thing holds true of all other possessions; for barter, in general, had its original beginning in nature, some men having a surplus, others too little of what was necessary for them: hence it is evident, that the selling provisions for money is not according to the natural use of things; for they were obliged to use barter for those things which they wanted; but it is plain that barter could have no place in the first, that is to say, in family society; but must have begun when the number of those who composed the community was enlarged: for the first of these had all things in common; but when they came to be separated they were obliged to exchange with each other many different things which both parties wanted. Which custom of barter is still preserved amongst many barbarous nations, who procure one necessary with another, but never sell anything; as giving and receiving wine for corn and the like. This sort of barter is not contradictory to nature, nor is it any species of money-getting; but is necessary in procuring that subsistence which is so consonant thereunto. But this barter introduced the use of money, as might be expected; for a convenient place from whence to import what you wanted, or to export what you had a surplus of, being often at a great distance, money necessarily made its way into commerce; for it is not everything which is naturally most useful that is easiest of carriage; for which reason they invented something to exchange with each other which they should mutually give and take, that being really valuable itself, should have the additional advantage of being of easy conveyance, for the purposes of life, as iron and silver, or anything else of the same nature: and this at first passed in value simply according to its weight or size; but in process of time it had a certain stamp, to save the trouble of weighing, which stamp expressed its value.

Money then being established as the necessary medium of exchange, another species of money-getting soon took place, namely, by buying and selling, at probably first in a simple manner, afterwards with more skill and experience, where and how the greatest profits might be made. For which reason the art of money-getting seems to be chiefly conversant about trade, and the business of it to be able to tell where the greatest profits can be made, being the means of procuring abundance of wealth and possessions: and thus wealth is very often supposed to consist in the quantity of money which any one possesses, as this is the medium by which all trade is conducted and a fortune made, others again regard it as of no value, as being of none by nature, but arbitrarily made so by compact; so that if those who use it should alter their sentiments, it would be worth nothing, as being of no service for any necessary purpose. Besides, he who abounds in money often wants necessary food; and it is impossible to say that any person is in good circumstances when with all his possessions he may perish with hunger.

Like Midas in the fable, who from his insatiable wish had everything he touched turned into gold. For which reason others endeavour to procure other riches and other property, and rightly, for there are other riches and property in nature; and these are the proper objects of economy: while trade only procures money, not by all means, but by the exchange of it, and for that purpose it is this which it is chiefly employed about, for money is the first principle and the end of trade; nor are there any bounds to be set to what is thereby acquired. Thus also there are no limits to the art of medicine, with respect to the health which it attempts to procure; the same also is true of all other arts; no line can be drawn to terminate their bounds, the several professors of them being desirous to extend them as far as possible. (But still the means to be employed for that purpose are limited; and these are the limits beyond which the art cannot proceed.) Thus in the art of acquiring riches there are no limits, for the object of that is money and possessions; but economy has a boundary, though this has not: for acquiring riches is not the business of that, for which reason it should seem that some boundary should be set to riches, though we see the contrary to this is what is practised; for all those who get riches add to their money without end; the cause of which is the near connection of these two arts with each other, which sometimes occasions the one to change employments with the other, as getting of money is their common object: for economy requires the possession of wealth, but not on its own account but with another view, to purchase things necessary therewith; but the other procures it merely to increase it: so that some persons are confirmed in their belief, that this is the proper object of economy, and think that for this purpose money should be saved and hoarded up without end; the reason for which disposition is, that they are intent upon living, but not upon living well; and this desire being boundless in its extent, the means which they aim at for that purpose are boundless also; and those who propose to live well, often confine that to the enjoyment of the pleasures of sense; so that as this also seems to depend upon what a man has, all their care is to get money, and hence arises the other cause for this art; for as this enjoyment is excessive in its degree, they endeavour to procure means proportionate to supply it; and if they cannot do this merely by the art of dealing in money, they will endeavour to do it by other ways, and apply all their powers to a purpose they were not by nature intended for. Thus, for instance, courage was intended to inspire fortitude, not to get money by; neither is this the end of the soldier's or the physician's art, but victory and health. But such persons make everything subservient to money-getting, as if this was the only end; and to the end everything ought to refer.

We have now considered that art of money-getting which is not necessary, and have seen in what manner we became in want of it; and also that which is necessary, which is different from it; for that economy which is natural, and whose object is to provide food, is not like this unlimited in its extent, but has its bounds.

# CHAPTER

## X

We have now determined what was before doubtful, whether or no the art of getting money is his business who is at the head of a family or a state, and though not strictly so, it is however very necessary; for as a politician does not make men, but receiving them from the hand of nature employs them to proper purposes; thus the earth, or the sea, or something else ought to supply them with provisions, and this it is the business of the master of the family to manage properly; for it is not the weaver's business to make yarn, but to use it, and to distinguish what is good and useful from what is bad and of no service; and indeed some one may inquire why getting money should be a part of economy when the art of healing is not, as it is as requisite that the family should be in health as that they should eat, or have anything else which is necessary; and as it is indeed in some particulars the business both of the master of the family, and he to whom the government of the state is entrusted, to see after the health of those under their care, but in others not, but the physician's; so also as to money; in some respects it is the business of the master of the family, in others not, but of the servant; but as we have already said, it is chiefly nature's, for it is her part to supply her offspring with food; for everything finds nourishment left for it in what produced it; for which reason the natural riches of all men arise from fruits and animals. Now money-making, as we say, being twofold, it may be applied to two purposes, the service of the house or retail trade; of which the first is necessary and commendable, the other justly censurable; for it has not its origin in nature, but by it men gain from each other; for usury is most reasonably detested, as it is increasing our fortune by money itself, and not employing it for the purpose it was originally intended, namely exchange.

And this is the explanation of the name (TOKOS), which means the breeding of money. For as offspring resemble their parents, so usury is money bred of money. Whence of all forms of money-making it is most against nature.

# CHAPTER

## XI

Having already sufficiently considered the general principles of this subject, let us now go into the practical part thereof; the one is a liberal employment for the mind, the other necessary. These things are useful in the management of one's affairs; to be skilful in the nature of cattle, which are most profitable, and where, and how; as for instance, what advantage will arise from keeping horses, or oxen, or sheep, or any other live stock; it is also necessary to be acquainted with the comparative value of these things, and which of them in particular places are worth most; for some do better in one place, some in another. Agriculture also should be understood, and the management of arable grounds and orchards; and also the care of bees, and fish, and birds, from whence any profit may arise; these are the first and most proper parts of domestic management.

With respect to gaining money by exchange, the principal method of doing this is by merchandise, which is carried on in three different ways, either by sending the commodity for sale by sea or by land, or else selling it on the place where it grows; and these differ from each other in this, that the one is more profitable, the other safer. The second method is by usury. The third by receiving wages for work done, and this either by being employed in some mean art, or else in mere bodily labour. There is also a third species of improving a fortune, that is something between this and the first; for it partly depends upon nature, partly upon exchange; the subject of which is, things that are immediately from the earth, or their produce, which, though they bear no fruit, are yet useful, such as selling of timber and the whole art of metallurgy, which includes many different species, for there are various sorts of things dug out of the earth.

These we have now mentioned in general, but to enter into particulars concerning each of them, though it might be useful to the artist, would be tiresome to dwell on. Now of all the works of art, those are the most excellent wherein chance has the least to do, and those are the meanest which deprave the body, those the most servile in which bodily strength alone is chiefly wanted, those most illiberal which require least skill; but as there are books written on these subjects by some persons, as by Chares the Panian, and Apollodorus the Lemnian, upon husbandry and planting; and by others on other matters, let those who have occasion consult them thereon; besides, every person should collect together whatsoever he hears occasionally mentioned, by means of which many of those who aimed at making a fortune have succeeded in their intentions; for all these are useful to those who make a point of getting money, as in the contrivance of Thales the Milesian (which was certainly a gainful one, but as it was his it was attributed to his wisdom, though the method he used was a general one, and would universally succeed), when they reviled him for his poverty, as if the study of philosophy was useless: for they say that he, perceiving by his skill in astrology that there would be great plenty of olives that year, while it was yet winter, having got a little money, he gave earnest for all the oil works that were in Miletus and Chios, which he hired at a low price, there being no one to bid against him; but when the season came for making oil, many persons wanting them, he all at once let them upon what terms he pleased; and raising a large sum of money by that means, convinced them that it was easy for philosophers to be rich if they chose it, but that that was not what they aimed at; in this manner is Thales said to have shown his wisdom. It indeed is, as we have said, generally gainful for a person to contrive to make a monopoly of anything; for which reason some cities also take this method when they want money, and monopolise their commodities. There was a certain person in Sicily who laid out a sum of money which was deposited in his hand in buying up all the iron from the iron merchants; so that when the dealers came from the markets to purchase, there was no one had any to sell but himself; and though he put no great advance upon it, yet by laying out fifty talents he made an hundred. When Dionysius heard this he permitted him to take his money with him, but forbid him to continue any longer in Sicily, as being one who contrived means for getting money inconsistent with his affairs. This man's view and Thales's was exactly the same; both of them contrived to procure a monopoly for themselves: it is useful also for politicians to understand these things, for many states want to raise money and by such means, as well as private families, nay more so; for which reason some persons who are employed in the management of public affairs confine themselves to this province only.

# CHAPTER

## XII

There are then three parts of domestic government, the masters, of which we have already treated, the fathers, and the husbands; now the government of the wife and children should both be that of free persons, but not the same; for the wife should be treated as a citizen of a free state, the children should be under kingly power; for the male is by nature superior to the female, except when something happens contrary to the usual course of nature, as is the elder and perfect to the younger and imperfect. Now in the generality of free states, the governors and the governed alternately change place; for an equality without any preference is what nature chooses; however, when one governs and another is governed, she endeavours that there should be a distinction between them in forms, expressions, and honours; according to what Amasis said of his laver. This then should be the established rule between the man and the woman. The government of children should be kingly; for the power of the father over the child is founded in affection and seniority, which is a species of kingly government; for which reason Homer very properly calls Jupiter "the father of gods and men," who was king of both these; for nature requires that a king should be of the same species with those whom he governs, though superior in some particulars, as is the case between the elder and the younger, the father and the son.

# CHAPTER

## XIII

I t is evident then that in the due government of a family, greater attention should be paid to the several members of it and their virtues than to the possessions or riches of it; and greater to the freemen than the slaves: but here some one may doubt whether there is any other virtue in a slave than his organic services, and of higher estimation than these, as temperance, fortitude, justice, and such-like habits, or whether they possess only bodily qualities: each side of the question has its difficulties; for if they possess these virtues, wherein do they differ from freemen? And that they do not, since they are men, and partakers of reason, is absurd. Nearly the same inquiry may be made concerning a woman and a child, whether these also have their proper virtues; whether a woman ought to be temperate, brave, and just, and whether a child is temperate or no; and indeed this inquiry ought to be general, whether the virtues of those who, by nature, either govern or are governed, are the same or different; for if it is necessary that both of them should partake of the fair and good, why is it also necessary that, without exception, the one should govern, the other always be governed? For this cannot arise from their possessing these qualities in different degrees; for to govern, and to be governed, are things different in species, but more or less are not. And yet it is wonderful that one party ought to have them, and the other not; for if he who is to govern should not be temperate and just, how can he govern well? Or if he is to be governed, how can he be governed well? For he who is intemperate and a coward will never do what he ought: it is evident then that both parties ought to be virtuous; but there is a difference between them, as there is between those who by nature command and who by nature obey, and this originates in the soul; for in this nature has planted the governing and submitting principle, the virtues of which we say are different, as are those of a rational and an irrational being. It is plain then that the same principle may be extended farther, and that there are in nature a variety of things which govern and are governed; for a freeman is governed in a different manner from a slave, a male from a female, and a man from a child: and all these have parts of mind within them, but in a different manner. Thus a slave can have no power of determination, a woman but a weak one, a child an imperfect one. Thus also must it necessarily be with respect to moral virtues; all must be supposed to possess them, but not in the same manner, but as is best suited to every one's employment; on which account he who is to govern ought to be perfect in moral virtue, for his business is entirely that of an architect, and reason is the architect; while others want only that portion of it which may be sufficient for their station; from whence it is evident, that although moral virtue is common to all those we have spoken of, yet the temperance of a man and a woman are not the same, nor their courage, nor their justice, though Socrates thought otherwise; for the courage of the man consists in commanding, the woman's in obeying; and the same is true in other particulars: and this will be evident to those who will examine different virtues separately; for those who use general terms deceive themselves when they say, that virtue consists in a good disposition of mind, or doing what is right, or something of this sort. They do much better who enumerate the different virtues as Georgias did, than those who thus define them; and as Sophocles speaks of a woman, we think of all persons, that their virtues should be applicable to their characters, for says he,

"Silence is a woman's ornament,"

but it is not a man's; and as a child is incomplete, it is evident that his virtue is not to be referred to himself in his present situation, but to that in which he will be complete, and his preceptor. In like manner the virtue of a slave is to be referred to his master; for we laid it down as a maxim, that the use of a slave was to employ him in what you wanted; so that it is clear enough that few virtues are wanted in his station, only that he may not neglect his work through idleness or fear: some person may question if what I have said is true, whether virtue is not necessary for artificers in their calling, for they often through idleness neglect their work, but the difference between them is very great; for a slave is connected with you for life, but the artificer not so nearly: as near therefore as the artificer approaches to the situation of a slave, just so much ought he to have of the virtues of one; for a mean artificer is to a certain point a slave; but then a slave is one of those things which are by nature what they are, but this is not true of a shoemaker, or any other artist. It is evident then that a slave ought to be trained to those virtues which are proper for his situation by his master; and not by him who has the power of a master, to teach him any particular art. Those therefore are in the wrong who would deprive slaves of reason, and say that they have only to follow their orders; for slaves want more instruction than children, and thus we determine this matter. It is necessary, I am sensible, for every one who treats upon government, to enter particularly into the relations of husband and wife, and of parent and child, and to show what are the virtues of each and their respective connections with each other; what is right and what is wrong; and how the one ought to be followed, and the other avoided. Since then every family is part of a city, and each of those individuals is part of a family, and the virtue of the parts ought to correspond to the virtue of the whole; it is necessary, that both the wives and children of the community should be instructed correspondent to the nature thereof, if it is of consequence to the virtue of the state, that the wives and children therein should be virtuous, and of consequence it certainly is, for the wives are one half of the free persons; and of the children the succeeding citizens are to be formed. As then we have determined these points, we will leave the rest to be spoken to in another place, as if the subject was now finished; and beginning again anew, first consider the sentiments of those who have treated of the most perfect forms of government.

# BOOK II

## CHAPTER

### I

Since then we propose to inquire what civil society is of all others best for those who have it in their power to live entirely as they wish, it is necessary to examine into the polity of those states which are allowed to be well governed; and if there should be any others which some persons have described, and which appear properly regulated, to note what is right and useful in them; and when we point out wherein they have failed, let not this be imputed to an affectation of wisdom, for it is because there are great defects in all those which are already established, that I have been induced to undertake this work. We will begin with that part of the subject which naturally presents itself first to our consideration. The members of every state must of necessity have all things in common, or some things common, and not others, or nothing at all common. To have nothing in common is evidently impossible, for society itself is one species of community; and the first thing necessary thereunto is a common place of habitation, namely the city, which must be one, and this every citizen must have a share in. But in a government which is to be well founded, will it be best to admit of a community in everything which is capable thereof, or only in some particulars, but in others not? For it is possible that the citizens may have their wives, and children, and goods in common, as in Plato's Commonwealth; for in that Socrates affirms that all these particulars ought to be so. Which then shall we prefer? The custom which is already established, or the laws which are proposed in that treatise?

## CHAPTER

## II

Now as a community of wives is attended with many other difficulties, so neither does the cause for which he would frame his government in this manner seem agreeable to reason, nor is it capable of producing that end which he has proposed, and for which he says it ought to take place; nor has he given any particular directions for putting it in practice. Now I also am willing to agree with Socrates in the principle which he proceeds upon, and admit that the city ought to be one as much as possible; and yet it is evident that if it is contracted too much, it will be no longer a city, for that necessarily supposes a multitude; so that if we proceed in this manner, we shall reduce a city to a family, and a family to a single person: for we admit that a family is one in a greater degree than a city, and a single person than a family; so that if this end could be obtained, it should never be put in practice, as it would annihilate the city; for a city does not only consist of a large number of inhabitants, but there must also be different sorts; for were they all alike, there could be no city; for a confederacy and a city are two different things; for a confederacy is valuable from its numbers, although all those who compose it are men of the same calling; for this is entered into for the sake of mutual defence, as we add an additional weight to make the scale go down. The same distinction prevails between a city and a nation when the people are not collected into separate villages, but live as the Arcadians. Now those things in which a city should be one are of different sorts, and in preserving an alternate reciprocation of power between these, the safety thereof consists (as I have already mentioned in my treatise on Morals), for amongst freemen and equals this is absolutely necessary; for all cannot govern at the same time, but either by the year, or according to some other regulation or time, by which means every one in his turn will be in office; as if the shoemakers and carpenters should exchange occupations, and not always be employed in the same calling. But as it is evidently better, that these should continue to exercise their respective trades; so also in civil society, where it is possible, it would be better that the government should continue in the same hands; but where it is not (as nature has made all men equal, and therefore it is just, be the administration good or bad, that all should partake of it), there it is best to observe a rotation, and let those who are their equals by turns submit to those who are at that time magistrates, as they will, in their turns, alternately be governors and governed, as if they were different men: by the same method different persons will execute different offices. From hence it is evident, that a city cannot be one in the manner that some persons propose; and that what has been said to be the greatest good which it could enjoy, is absolutely its destruction, which cannot be: for the good of anything is that which preserves it. For another reason also it is clear, that it is not for the best to endeavour to make a city too much one, because a family is more sufficient in itself than a single person, a city than a family; and indeed Plato supposes that a city owes its existence to that sufficiency in themselves which the members of it enjoy. If then this sufficiency is so desirable, the less the city is one the better.

# CHAPTER

## III

**B**ut admitting that it is most advantageous for a city to be one as much as possible, it does not seem to follow that this will take place by permitting all at once to say this is mine, and this is not mine (though this is what Socrates regards as a proof that a city is entirely one), for the word All is used in two senses; if it means each individual, what Socrates proposes will nearly take place; for each person will say, this is his own son, and his own wife, and his own property, and of everything else that may happen to belong to him, that it is his own. But those who have their wives and children in common will not say so, but all will say so, though not as individuals; therefore, to use the word all is evidently a fallacious mode of speech; for this word is sometimes used distributively, and sometimes collectively, on account of its double meaning, and is the cause of inconclusive syllogisms in reasoning. Therefore for all persons to say the same thing was their own, using the word all in its distributive sense, would be well, but is impossible: in its collective sense it would by no means contribute to the concord of the state. Besides, there would be another inconvenience attending this proposal, for what is common to many is taken least care of; for all men regard more what is their own than what others share with them in, to which they pay less attention than is incumbent on every one: let me add also, that every one is more negligent of what another is to see to, as well as himself, than of his own private business; as in a family one is often worse served by many servants than by a few. Let each citizen then in the state have a thousand children, but let none of them be considered as the children of that individual, but let the relation of father and child be common to them all, and they will all be neglected. Besides, in consequence of this, whenever any citizen behaved well or ill, every person, be the number what it would, might say, this is my son, or this man's or that; and in this manner would they speak, and thus would they doubt of the whole thousand, or of whatever number the city consisted; and it would be uncertain to whom each child belonged, and when it was born, who was to take care of it: and which do you think is better, for every one to say this is mine, while they may apply it equally to two thousand or ten thousand; or as we say, this is mine in our present forms of government, where one man calls another his son, another calls that same person his brother, another nephew, or some other relation, either by blood or marriage, and first extends his care to him and his, while another regards him as one of the same parish and the same tribe; and it is better for any one to be a nephew in his private capacity than a son after that manner. Besides, it will be impossible to prevent some persons from suspecting that they are brothers and sisters, fathers and mothers to each other; for, from the mutual likeness there is between the sire and the offspring, they will necessarily conclude in what relation they stand to each other, which circumstance, we are informed by those writers who describe different parts of the world, does sometimes happen; for in Upper Africa there are wives in common who yet deliver their children to their respective fathers, being guided by their likeness to them. There are also some mares and cows which naturally bring forth their young so like the male, that we can easily distinguish by which of them they were impregnated: such was the mare called Just, in Pharsalia.

## CHAPTER

## IV

Besides, those who contrive this plan of community cannot easily avoid the following evils; namely, blows, murders involuntary or voluntary, quarrels, and reproaches, all which it would be impious indeed to be guilty of towards our fathers and mothers, or those who are nearly related to us; though not to those who are not connected to us by any tie of affinity: and certainly these mischiefs must necessarily happen oftener amongst those who do not know how they are connected to each other than those who do; and when they do happen, if it is among the first of these, they admit of a legal expiation, but amongst the latter that cannot be done. It is also absurd for those who promote a community of children to forbid those who love each other from indulging themselves in the last excesses of that passion, while they do not restrain them from the passion itself, or those intercourses which are of all things most improper, between a Father and a son, a brother and a brother, and indeed the thing itself is most absurd. It is also ridiculous to prevent this intercourse between the nearest relations, for no other reason than the violence of the pleasure, while they think that the relation of father and daughter, the brother and sister, is of no consequence at all. It seems also more advantageous for the state, that the husbandmen should have their wives and children in common than the military, for there will be less affection among them in that case than when otherwise; for such persons ought to be under subjection, that they may obey the laws, and not seek after innovations. Upon the whole, the consequences of such a law as this would be directly contrary to those things which good laws ought to establish, and which Socrates endeavoured to establish by his regulations concerning women and children: for we think that friendship is the greatest good which can happen to any city, as nothing so much prevents seditions: and amity in a city is what Socrates commends above all things, which appears to be, as indeed he says, the effect of friendship; as we learn from Aristophanes in the Erotics, who says, that those who love one another from the excess of that passion, desire to breathe the same soul, and from being two to be blended into one: from whence it would necessarily follow, that both or one of them must be destroyed. But now in a city which admits of this community, the tie of friendship must, from that very cause, be extremely weak, when no father can say, this is my son; or son, this is my father; for as a very little of what is sweet, being mixed with a great deal of water is imperceptible after the mixture, so must all family connections, and the names they go by, be necessarily disregarded in such a community, it being then by no means necessary that the father should have any regard for him he called a son, or the brothers for those they call brothers. There are two things which principally inspire mankind with care and love of their offspring, knowing it is their own, and what ought to be the object of their affection, neither of which can take place in this sort of community. As for exchanging the children of the artificers and husbandmen with those of the military, and theirs reciprocally with these, it will occasion great confusion in whatever manner it shall be done; for of necessity, those who carry the children must know from whom they took and to whom they gave them; and by this means those evils which I have already mentioned will necessarily be the more likely to happen, as blows, incestuous love, murders, and the like; for those who are given from their own parents to other citizens, the military, for instance, will not call them brothers, sons, fathers, or mothers. The same thing would happen to those of the military who were placed among the other citizens; so that by this means every one would be in fear how to act in consequence of consanguinity. And thus let us determine concerning a community of wives and children.

# CHAPTER

# V

We proceed next to consider in what manner property should be regulated in a state which is formed after the most perfect mode of government, whether it should be common or not; for this may be considered as a separate question from what had been determined concerning wives and children; I mean, whether it is better that these should be held separate, as they now everywhere are, or that not only possessions but also the usufruct of them should be in common; or that the soil should have a particular owner, but that the produce should be brought together and used as one common stock, as some nations at present do; or on the contrary, should the soil be common, and should it also be cultivated in common, while the produce is divided amongst the individuals for their particular use, which is said to be practised by some barbarians; or shall both the soil and the fruit be common? When the business of the husbandman devolves not on the citizen, the matter is much easier settled; but when those labour together who have a common right of possession, this may occasion several difficulties; for there may not be an equal proportion between their labour and what they consume; and those who labour hard and have but a small proportion of the produce, will certainly complain of those who take a large share of it and do but little for that. Upon the whole, as a community between man and man so entire as to include everything possible, and thus to have all things that man can possess in common, is very difficult, so is it particularly so with respect to property; and this is evident from that community which takes place between those who go out to settle a colony; for they frequently have disputes with each other upon the most common occasions, and come to blows upon trifles: we find, too, that we oftenest correct those slaves who are generally employed in the common offices of the family: a community of property then has these and other inconveniences attending it.

But the manner of life which is now established, more particularly when embellished with good morals and a system of equal laws, is far superior to it, for it will have the advantage of both; by both I mean properties being common, and divided also; for in some respects it ought to be in a manner common, but upon the whole private: for every man's attention being employed on his own particular concerns, will prevent mutual complaints against each other; nay, by this means industry will be increased, as each person will labour to improve his own private property; and it will then be, that from a principle of virtue they will mutually perform good offices to each other, according to the proverb, "All things are common amongst friends;" and in some cities there are traces of this custom to be seen, so that it is not impracticable, and particularly in those which are best governed; some things are by this means in a manner common, and others might be so; for there, every person enjoying his own private property, some things he assists his friend with, others are considered as in common; as in Lacedaemon, where they use each other's slaves, as if they were, so to speak, their own, as they do their horses and dogs, or even any provision they may want in a journey.

It is evident then that it is best to have property private, but to make the use of it common; but how the citizens are to be brought to it is the particular business of the legislator. And also with respect to pleasure, it is unspeakable how advantageous it is, that a man should think he has something which he may call his own; for it is by no means to no purpose, that each person should have an affection for himself, for that is natural, and yet to be a self-lover is justly censured; for we mean by that, not one that simply loves himself, but one that loves himself more than he ought; in like manner we blame a money-lover, and yet both money and self is what all men love. Besides, it is very pleasing to us to oblige and assist our friends and companions, as well as those whom we are connected with by the rights of hospitality; and this cannot be done without the establishment of private property, which cannot take place with those who make a city too much one; besides, they prevent every opportunity of exercising two principal virtues, modesty and liberality. Modesty with respect to the female sex, for this virtue requires you to abstain from her who is another's; liberality, which depends upon private property, for without that no one can appear liberal, or do any generous action; for liberality consists in imparting to others what is our own.

This system of polity does indeed recommend itself by its good appearance and specious pretences to humanity; and when first proposed to any one, must give him great pleasure, as he will conclude it to be a wonderful bond of friendship, connecting all to all; particularly when any one censures the evils which are now to be found in society, as arising from properties not being common, I mean the disputes which happen between man and man, upon their different contracts with each other; those judgments which are passed in court in consequence of fraud, and perjury, and flattering the rich, none of which arise from properties being private, but from the vices of mankind. Besides, those who live in one general community, and have all things in common, oftener dispute with each other than those who have their property separate; from the very small number indeed of those who have their property in common, compared with those where it is appropriated, the instances of their quarrels are but few. It is also but right to mention, not only the inconveniences they are preserved from who live in a communion of goods, but also the advantages they are deprived of; for when the whole comes to be considered, this manner of life will be found impracticable.

We must suppose, then, that Socrates's mistake arose from the principle he set out with being false; we admit, indeed, that both a family and a city ought to be one in some particulars, but not entirely; for there is a point beyond which if a city proceeds in reducing itself to one, it will be no longer a city.

There is also another point at which it will still continue to be a city, but it will approach so near to not being one, that it will be worse than none; as if any one should reduce the voices of those who sing in concert to one, or a verse to a foot. But the people ought to be made one, and a community, as I have already said, by education; as property at Lacedaemon, and their public tables at Crete, were made common by their legislators. But yet, whosoever shall introduce any education, and think thereby to make his city excellent and respectable, will be absurd, while he expects to form it by such regulations, and not by manners, philosophy, and laws. And whoever would establish a government upon a community of goods, ought to know that he should consult the experience of many years, which would plainly enough inform him whether such a scheme is useful; for almost all things have already been found out, but some have been neglected, and others which have been known have not been put in practice. But this would be most evident, if any one could see such a government really established: for it would be impossible to frame such a city without dividing and separating it into its distinct parts, as public tables, wards, and tribes; so that here the laws will do nothing more than forbid the military to engage in agriculture, which is what the Lacedaemonians are at present endeavouring to do.

Nor has Socrates told us (nor is it easy to say) what plan of government should be pursued with respect to the individuals in the state where there is a community of goods established; for though the majority of his citizens will in general consist of a multitude of persons of different occupations, of those he has determined nothing; whether the property of the husbandman ought to be in common, or whether each person should have his share to himself; and also, whether their wives and children ought to be in common: for if all things are to be alike common to all, where will be the difference between them and the military, or what would they get by submitting to their government? And upon what principles would they do it, unless they should establish the wise practice of the Cretans? For they, allowing everything else to their slaves, forbid them only gymnastic exercises and the use of arms. And if they are not, but these should be in the same situation with respect to their property which they are in other cities, what sort of a community will there be? In one city there must of necessity be two, and those contrary to each other; for he makes the military the guardians of the state, and the husbandman, artisans, and others, citizens; and all those quarrels, accusations, and things of the like sort, which he says are the bane of other cities, will be found in his also: notwithstanding Socrates says they will not want many laws in consequence of their education, but such only as may be necessary for regulating the streets, the markets, and the like, while at the same time it is the education of the military only that he has taken any care of. Besides, he makes the husbandmen masters of property upon paying a tribute; but this would be likely to make them far more troublesome and high-spirited than the Helots, the Penestise, or the slaves which others employ; nor has he ever determined whether it is necessary to give any attention to them in these particulars, nor thought of what is connected therewith, their polity, their education, their laws; besides, it is of no little consequence, nor is it easy to determine, how these should be framed so as to preserve the community of the military.

Besides, if he makes the wives common, while the property continues separate, who shall manage the domestic concerns with the same care which the man bestows upon his fields? Nor will the inconvenience be remedied by making property as well as wives common; and it is absurd to draw a comparison from the brute creation, and say, that the same principle should regulate the connection of a man and a woman which regulates theirs amongst whom there is no family association.

It is also very hazardous to settle the magistracy as Socrates has done; for he would have persons of the same rank always in office, which becomes the cause of sedition even amongst those who are of no account, but more particularly amongst those who are of a courageous and warlike disposition; it is indeed evidently necessary that he should frame his community in this manner; for that golden particle which God has mixed up in the soul of man flies not from one to the other, but always continues with the same; for he says, that some of our species have gold, and others silver, blended in their composition from the moment of their birth: but those who are to be husbandmen and artists, brass and iron; besides, though he deprives the military of happiness, he says, that the legislator ought to make all the citizens happy; but it is impossible that the whole city can be happy, without all, or the greater, or some part of it be happy. For happiness is not like that numerical equality which arises from certain numbers when added together, although neither of them may separately contain it; for happiness cannot be thus added together, but must exist in every individual, as some properties belong to every integral; and if the military are not happy, who else are so? For the artisans are not, nor the multitude of those who are employed in inferior offices. The state which Socrates has described has all these defects, and others which are not of less consequence.

# CHAPTER

# VI

It is also nearly the same in the treatise upon Laws which was writ afterwards, for which reason it will be proper in this place to consider briefly what he has there said upon government, for Socrates has thoroughly settled but very few parts of it; as for instance, in what manner the community of wives and children ought to be regulated, how property should be established, and government conducted.

Now he divides the inhabitants into two parts, husbandmen and soldiers, and from these he select a third part who are to be senators and govern the city; but he has not said whether or no the husbandman and artificer shall have any or what share in the government, or whether they shall have arms, and join with the others in war, or not. He thinks also that the women ought to go to war, and have the same education as the soldiers; as to other particulars, he has filled his treatise with matter foreign to the purpose; and with respect to education, he has only said what that of the guards ought to be.

As to his book of Laws, laws are the principal thing which that contains, for he has there said but little concerning government; and this government, which he was so desirous of framing in such a manner as to impart to its members a more entire community of goods than is to be found in other cities, he almost brings round again to be the same as that other government which he had first proposed; for except the community of wives and goods, he has framed both his governments alike, for the education of the citizens is to be the same in both; they are in both to live without any servile employ, and their common tables are to be the same, excepting that in that he says the women should have common tables, and that there should be a thousand men-at-arms, in this, that there should be five thousand.

All the discourses of Socrates are masterly, noble, new, and inquisitive; but that they are all true it may probably be too much to say. For now with respect to the number just spoken of, it must be acknowledged that he would want the country of Babylonia for them, or some one like it, of an immeasurable extent, to support five thousand idle persons, besides a much greater number of women and servants. Every one, it is true, may frame an hypothesis as he pleases, but yet it ought to be possible. It has been said, that a legislator should have two things in view when he frames his laws, the country and the people. He will also do well, if he has some regard to the neighbouring states, if he intends that his community should maintain any political intercourse with them, for it is not only necessary that they should understand that practice of war which is adapted to their own country, but to others also; for admitting that any one chooses not this life either in public or private, yet there is not the less occasion for their being formidable to their enemies, not only when they invade their country, but also when they retire out of it.

It may also be considered whether the quantity of each person's property may not be settled in a different manner from what he has done it in, by making it more determinate; for he says, that every one ought to have enough whereon to live moderately, as if any one had said to live well, which is the most comprehensive expression. Besides, a man may live moderately and miserably at the same time; he had therefore better have proposed, that they should live both moderately and liberally; for unless these two conspire, luxury will come in on the one hand, or wretchedness on the other, since these two modes of living are the only ones applicable to the employment of our substance; for we cannot say with respect to a man's fortune, that he is mild or courageous, but we may say that he is prudent and liberal, which are the only qualities connected therewith.

It is also absurd to render property equal, and not to provide for the increasing number of the citizens; but to leave that circumstance uncertain, as if it would regulate itself according to the number of women who should happen to be childless, let that be what it would because this seems to take place in other cities; but the case would not be the same in such a state which he proposes and those which now actually unite; for in these no one actually wants, as the property is divided amongst the whole community, be their numbers what they will; but as it could not then be divided, the supernumeraries, whether they were many or few, would have nothing at all. But it is more necessary than even to regulate property, to take care that the increase of the people should not exceed a certain number; and in determining that, to take into consideration those children who will die, and also those women who will be barren; and to neglect this, as is done in several cities, is to bring certain poverty on the citizens; and poverty is the cause of sedition and evil. Now Phidon the Corinthian, one of the oldest legislators, thought the families and the number of the citizens should continue the same; although it should happen that all should have allotments at the first, disproportionate to their numbers.

In Plato's *Laws* it is however different; we shall mention hereafter what we think would be best in these particulars. He has also neglected in that treatise to point out how the governors are to be distinguished from the governed; for he says, that as of one sort of wool the warp ought to be made, and of another the woof, so ought some to govern, and others to be governed. But since he admits, that all their property may be increased fivefold, why should he not allow the same increase to the country? He ought also to consider whether his allotment of the houses will be useful to the community, for he appoints two houses to each person, separate from each other; but it is inconvenient for a person to inhabit two houses. Now he is desirous to have his whole plan of government neither a democracy nor an oligarchy, but something between both, which he calls a polity, for it is to be composed of men-at-arms. If Plato intended to frame a state in which more than in any other everything should be common, he has certainly given it a right name; but if he intended it to be the next in perfection to that which he had already framed, it is not so; for perhaps some persons will give the preference to the Lacedaemonian form of government, or some other which may more completely have attained to the aristocratic form.

Some persons say, that the most perfect government should be composed of all others blended together, for which reason they commend that of Lacedaemon; for they say, that this is composed of an oligarchy, a monarchy, and a democracy, their kings representing the monarchical part, the senate the oligarchical; and, that in the ephori may be found the democratical, as these are taken from the people. But some say, that in the ephori is absolute power, and that it is their common meal and daily course of life, in which the democratical form is represented. It is also said in this treatise of *Laws*, that the best form of government must, be one composed of a democracy and a tyranny; though such a mixture no one else would ever allow to be any government at all, or if it is, the worst possible; those propose what is much better who blend many governments together; for the most perfect is that which is formed of many parts. But now in this government of Plato's there are no traces of a monarchy, only of an oligarchy and democracy; though he seems to choose that it should rather incline to an oligarchy, as is evident from the appointment of the magistrates; for to choose them by lot is common to both; but that a man of fortune must necessarily be a member of the assembly, or to elect the magistrates, or take part in the management of public affairs, while others are passed over, makes the state incline to an oligarchy; as does the endeavouring that the greater part of the rich may be in office, and that the rank of their appointments may correspond with their fortunes.

The same principle prevails also in the choice of their senate; the manner of electing which is favourable also to an oligarchy; for all are obliged to vote for those who are senators of the first class, afterwards they vote for the same number out of the second, and then out of the third; but this compulsion to vote at the election of senators does not extend to the third and fourth classes and the first and second class only are obliged to vote for the fourth. By this means he says he shall necessarily have an equal number of each rank, but he is mistaken— for the majority will always consist of those of the first rank, and the most considerable people; and for this reason, that many of the commonalty not being obliged to it, will not attend the elections. From hence it is evident, that such a state will not consist of a democracy and a monarchy, and this will be further proved by what we shall say when we come particularly to consider this form of government.

There will also great danger arise from the manner of electing the senate, when those who are elected themselves are afterwards to elect others; for by this means, if a certain number choose to combine together, though not very considerable, the election will always fall according to their pleasure. Such are the things which Plato proposes concerning government in his book of *Laws*.

## CHAPTER

## VII

There are also some other forms of government, which have been proposed either by private persons, or philosophers, or politicians, all of which come much nearer to those which have been really established, or now exist, than these two of Plato's; for neither have they introduced the innovation of a community of wives and children, and public tables for the women, but have been contented to set out with establishing such rules as are absolutely necessary.

There are some persons who think, that the first object of government should be to regulate well everything relating to private property; for they say, that a neglect herein is the source of all seditions whatsoever. For this reason, Phaleas the Chalcedonian first proposed, that the fortunes of the citizens should be equal, which he thought was not difficult to accomplish when a community was first settled, but that it was a work of greater difficulty in one that had been long established; but yet that it might be effected, and an equality of circumstances introduced by these means, that the rich should give marriage portions, but never receive any, while the poor should always receive, but never give.

But Plato, in his treatise of *Laws*, thinks that a difference in circumstances should be permitted to a certain degree; but that no citizen should be allowed to possess more than five times as much as the lowest census, as we have already mentioned. But legislators who would establish this principle are apt to overlook what they ought to consider; that while they regulate the quantity of provisions which each individual shall possess, they ought also to regulate the number of his children; for if these exceed the allotted quantity of provision, the law must necessarily be repealed; and yet, in spite of the repeal, it will have the bad effect of reducing many from wealth to poverty, so difficult is it for innovators not to fall into such mistakes. That an equality of goods was in some degree serviceable to strengthen the bands of society, seems to have been known to some of the ancients; for Solon made a law, as did some others also, to restrain persons from possessing as much land as they pleased. And upon the same principle there are laws which forbid men to sell their property, as among the Locrians, unless they can prove that some notorious misfortune has befallen them. They were also to preserve their ancient patrimony, which custom being broken through by the Leucadians, made their government too democratic; for by that means it was no longer necessary to be possessed of a certain fortune to be qualified to be a magistrate. But if an equality of goods is established, this may be either too much, when it enables the people to live luxuriously, or too little, when it obliges them to live hard. Hence it is evident, that it is not proper for the legislator to establish an equality of circumstances, but to fix a proper medium. Besides, if any one should regulate the division of property in such a manner that there should be a moderate sufficiency for all, it would be of no use; for it is of more consequence that the citizen should entertain a similarity of sentiments than an equality of circumstances; but this can never be attained unless they are properly educated under the direction of the law. But probably Phaleas may say, that this in what he himself mentions; for he both proposes a equality of property and one plan of education in his city. But he should have said particularly what education he intended, nor is it of any service to have this to much one; for this education may be one, and yet such as will make the citizens over-greedy, to grasp after honours, or riches, or both. Besides, not only an inequality of possessions, but also of honours, will occasion seditions, but this upon contrary grounds;

for the vulgar will be seditious if there be an inequality of goods, by those of more elevated sentiments, if there is an equality of honours.

"When good and bad do equal honours share."

For men are not guilty of crimes for necessaries only (for which he thinks an equality of goods would be a sufficient remedy, as they would then have no occasion to steal cold or hunger), but that they may enjoy what they desire, and not wish for it in vain; for if their desire extend beyond the common necessaries of life, they were be wicked to gratify them; and not only so, but if their wishes point that way, they will do the same to enjoy those pleasures which are free from the alloy of pain. What remedy then shall we find for these three disorders. And first, to prevent stealing from necessity, let every one be supplied with a moderate subsistence, which may make the addition of his own industry necessary; second to prevent stealing to procure the luxuries of life, temperance be enjoined; and thirdly, let those who wish for pleasure in itself seek for it only in philosophy, all others want the assistance of men.

Since then men are guilty of the greatest crimes from ambition, and not from necessity, no one, for instance aims at being a tyrant to keep him from the cold, hence great honour is due to him who kills not a thief, but tyrant; so that polity which Phaleas establishes would only be salutary to prevent little crimes. He has also been very desirous to establish such rules as will conduce to perfect the internal policy of his state, and he ought also to have done the same with respect to its neighbours and all foreign nations; for the considerations of the military establishment should take place in planning every government, that it may not be unprovided in case of a war, of which he has said nothing; so also with respect to property, it ought not only to be adapted to the exigencies of the state, but also to such dangers as may arise from without.

Thus it should not be so much as to tempt those who are near, and more powerful to invade it, while those who possess it are not able to drive out the invaders, nor so little as that the state should not be able to go to war with those who are quite equal to itself, and of this he has determined nothing; it must indeed be allowed that it is advantageous to a community to be rather rich than poor; probably the proper boundary is this, not to possess enough to make it worth while for a more powerful neighbour to attack you, any more than he would those who had not so much as yourself; thus when Autophradatus proposed to besiege Atarneus, Eubulus advised him to consider what time it would require to take the city, and then would have him determine whether it would answer, for that he should choose, if it would even take less than he proposed, to quit the place; his saying this made Autophradatus reflect upon the business and give over the siege. There is, indeed, some advantage in an equality of goods amongst the citizens to prevent seditions; and yet, to say truth, no very great one; for men of great abilities will stomach their being put upon a level with the rest of the community. For which reason they will very often appear ready for every commotion and sedition; for the wickedness of mankind is insatiable. For though at first two oboli might be sufficient, yet when once it is become customary, they continually want something more, until they set no limits to their expectations; for it is the nature of our desires to be boundless, and many live only to gratify them. But for this purpose the first object is, not so much to establish an equality of fortune, as to prevent those who are of a good disposition from desiring more than their own, and those who are of a bad one from being able to acquire it; and this may be done if they are kept in an inferior station, and not exposed to injustice. Nor has he treated well the equality of goods, for he has extended his regulation only to land; whereas a man's substance consists not only in this, but also in slaves, cattle, money, and all that variety of things which fall under the name of chattels; now there must be either an equality established in all these, or some certain rule, or they must be left entirely at large. It appears too by his laws, that he intends to establish only a small state, as all the artificers are to belong to the public, and add nothing to the complement of citizens; but if all those who are to be employed in public works are to be the slaves of the public, it should be done in the same manner as it is at Epidamnum, and as Diophantus formerly regulated it at Athens. From these particulars any one may nearly judge whether Phaleas's community is well or ill established.

# CHAPTER

## VIII

Hippodamus, the son of Euruphon a Milesian, contrived the art of laying out towns, and separated the Pireus. This man was in other respects too eager after notice, and seemed to many to live in a very affected manner, with his flowing locks and his expensive ornaments, and a coarse warm vest which he wore, not only in the winter, but also in the hot weather. As he was very desirous of the character of a universal scholar, he was the first who, not being actually engaged in the management of public affairs, sat himself to inquire what sort of government was best; and he planned a state, consisting of ten thousand persons, divided into three parts, one consisting of artisans, another of husbandmen, and the third of soldiers; he also divided the lands into three parts, and allotted one to sacred purposes, another to the public, and the third to individuals. The first of these was to supply what was necessary for the established worship of the gods; the second was to be allotted to the support of the soldiery; and the third was to be the property of the husbandman. He thought also that there need only be three sorts of laws, corresponding to the three sorts of actions which can be brought, namely, for assault, trespasses, or death. He ordered also that there should be a particular court of appeal, into which all causes might be removed which were supposed to have been unjustly determined elsewhere; which court should be composed of old men chosen for that purpose. He thought also that they should not pass sentence by votes; but that every one should bring with him a tablet, on which he should write, that he found the party guilty, if it was so, but if not, he should bring a plain tablet; but if he acquitted him of one part of the indictment but not of the other, he should express that also on the tablet; for he disapproved of that general custom already established, as it obliges the judges to be guilty of perjury if they determined positively either on the one side or the other. He also made a law, that those should be rewarded who found out anything for the good of the city, and that the children of those who fell in battle should be educated at the public expense; which law had never been proposed by any other legislator, though it is at present in use at Athens as well as in other cities, he would have the magistrates chosen out of the people in general, by whom he meant the three parts before spoken of; and that those who were so elected should be the particular guardians of what belonged to the public, to strangers, and to orphans.

These are the principal parts and most worthy of notice in Hippodamus's plan. But some persons might doubt the propriety of his division of the citizens into three parts; for the artisans, the husbandmen, and the soldiers are to compose one community, where the husbandmen are to have no arms, and the artisans neither arms nor land, which would in a manner render them slaves to the soldiery. It is also impossible that the whole community should partake of all the honourable employments in it—for the generals and the guardians of the state must necessarily be appointed out of the soldiery, and indeed the most honourable magistrates; but as the two other parts will not have their share in the government, how can they be expected to have any affection for it? But it is necessary that the soldiery should be superior to the other two parts, and this superiority will not be easily gained without they are very numerous; and if they are so, why should the community consist of any other members? Why should any others have a right to elect the magistrates? Besides, of what use are the husbandmen to this community? Artisans, 'tis true, are necessary, for these every city wants, and they can live upon their business. If the husbandmen indeed furnished the soldiers with provisions, they would be properly part of the community; but these are supposed to have their private property, and to cultivate it for their own use. Moreover, if the soldiers themselves are to cultivate that common land which is appropriated for their support, there will be no distinction between the soldier and the husbandman, which the legislator intended there should be; and if there should be any others who are to cultivate the private property of the husbandman and the common lands of the military, there will be a fourth order in the state which will have no share in it, and always entertain hostile sentiments towards it. If any one should propose that the same persons should cultivate their own lands and the public ones also, then there would be a deficiency of provisions to supply two families, as the lands would not immediately yield enough for themselves and the soldiers also; and all these things would occasion great confusion.

Nor do I approve of his method of determining causes, when he would have the judge split the case which comes simply before him; and thus, instead of being a judge, become an arbitrator. Now when any matter is brought to arbitration, it is customary for many persons to confer together upon the business that is before them; but when a cause is brought before judges it is not so; and many legislators take care that the judges shall not have it in their power to communicate their sentiments to each other. Besides, what can prevent confusion on the bench when one judge thinks a fine should be different from what another has set it at; one proposing twenty minae, another ten, or be it more or less, another four, and another five; and it is evident, that in this manner they will differ from each other, while some will give the whole damages sued for, and others nothing; in this situation, how shall their determinations be settled? Besides, a judge cannot be obliged to perjure himself who simply acquits or condemns, if the action is fairly and justly brought; for he who acquits the party does not say that he ought not to pay any fine at all, but that he ought not to pay a fine of twenty minae. But he that condemns him is guilty of perjury if he sentences him to pay twenty minae while he believes the damages ought not to be so much.

Now with respect to these honours which he proposes to bestow on those who can give any information useful to the community, this, though very pleasing in speculation, is what the legislator should not settle, for it would encourage informers, and probably occasion commotions in the state. And this proposal of his gives rise also to further conjectures and inquiries; for some persons have doubted whether it is useful or hurtful to alter the established law of any country, if even for the better; for which reason one cannot immediately determine upon what he here says, whether it is advantageous to alter the law or not. We know, indeed, that it is possible to propose to new model both the laws and government as a common good; and since we have mentioned this subject, it may be very proper to enter into a few particulars concerning it, for it contains some difficulties, as I have already said, and it may appear better to alter them, since it has been found useful in other sciences.

Thus the science of physic is extended beyond its ancient bounds; so is the gymnastic, and indeed all other arts and powers; so that one may lay it down for certain that the same thing will necessarily hold good in the art of government. And it may also be affirmed, that experience itself gives a proof of this; for the ancient laws are too simple and barbarous; which allowed the Greeks to wear swords in the city, and to buy their wives of each other. And indeed all the remains of old laws which we have are very simple; for instance, a law in Cuma relative to murder. If any person who prosecutes another for murder can produce a certain number of witnesses to it of his own relations, the accused person shall be held guilty. Upon the whole, all persons ought to endeavour to follow what is right, and not what is established; and it is probable that the first men, whether they sprung out of the earth, or were saved from some general calamity, had very little understanding or knowledge, as is affirmed of these aborigines; so that it would be absurd to continue in the practice of their rules. Nor is it, moreover, right to permit written laws always to remain without alteration; for as in all other sciences, so in politics, it is impossible to express everything in writing with perfect exactness; for when we commit anything to writing we must use general terms, but in every action there is something particular to itself, which these may not comprehend; from whence it is evident, that certain laws will at certain times admit of alterations. But if we consider this matter in another point of view, it will appear to require great caution; for when the advantage proposed is trifling, as the accustoming the people easily to abolish their laws is of bad consequence, it is evidently better to pass over some faults which either the legislator or the magistrates may have committed; for the alterations will not be of so much service as a habit of disobeying the magistrates will be of disservice. Besides, the instance brought from the arts is fallacious; for it is not the same thing to alter the one as the other. For a law derives all its strength from custom, and this requires long time to establish; so that, to make it an easy matter to pass from the established laws to other new ones, is to weaken the power of laws. Besides, here is another question; if the laws are to be altered, are they all to be altered, and in every government or not, and whether at the pleasure of one person or many? All which particulars will make a great difference; for which reason we will at present drop the inquiry, to pursue it at some other time.

# CHAPTER

## IX

There are two considerations which offer themselves with respect to the government established at Lacedaemon and Crete, and indeed in almost all other states whatsoever; one is whether their laws do or do not promote the best establishment possible? The other is whether there is anything, if we consider either the principles upon which it is founded or the executive part of it, which prevents the form of government that they had proposed to follow from being observed; now it is allowed that in every well-regulated state the members of it should be free from servile labour; but in what manner this shall be effected is not so easy to determine; for the Penestse have very often attacked the Thessalians, and the Helots the Lacedaemonians, for they in a manner continually watch an opportunity for some misfortune befalling them. But no such thing has ever happened to the Cretans; the reason for which probably is, that although they are engaged in frequent wars with the neighbouring cities, yet none of these would enter into an alliance with the revolters, as it would be disadvantageous for them, who themselves also have their villains. But now there is perpetual enmity between the Lacedaemonians and all their neighbours, the Argives, the Messenians, and the Arcadians. Their slaves also first revolted from the Thessalians while they were engaged in wars with their neighbours the Acheans, the Perrabeans, and the Magnesians. It seems to me indeed, if nothing else, yet something very troublesome to keep upon proper terms with them; for if you are remiss in your discipline they grow insolent, and think themselves upon an equality with their masters; and if they are hardly used they are continually plotting against you and hate you. It is evident, then, that those who employ slaves have not as yet hit upon the right way of managing them.

As to the indulging of women in any particular liberties, it is hurtful to the end of government and the prosperity of the city; for as a man and his wife are the two parts of a family, if we suppose a city to be divided into two parts, we must allow that the number of men and women will be equal.

In whatever city then the women are not under good regulations, we must look upon one half of it as not under the restraint of law, as it there happened; for the legislator, desiring to make his whole city a collection of warriors with respect to the men, he most evidently accomplished his design; but in the meantime the women were quite neglected, for they live without restraint in every improper indulgence and luxury. So that in such a state riches will necessarily be in general esteem, particularly if the men are governed by their wives, which has been the case with many a brave and warlike people except the Celts, and those other nations, if there are any such, who openly practise pederasty. And the first mythologists seem not improperly to have joined Mars and Venus together; for all nations of this character are greatly addicted either to the love of women or of boys, for which reason it was thus at Lacedaemon; and many things in their state were done by the authority of the women. For what is the difference, if the power is in the hands of the women, or in the hands of those whom they themselves govern? It must turn to the same account. As this boldness of the women can be of no use in any common occurrences, if it was ever so, it must be in war; but even here we find that the Lacedaemonian women were of the greatest disservice, as was proved at the time of the Theban invasion, when they were of no use at all, as they are in other cities, but made more disturbance than even the enemy.

The origin of this indulgence which the Lacedaemonian women enjoy is easily accounted for, from the long time the men were absent from home upon foreign expeditions against the Argives, and afterwards the Arcadians and Messenians, so that, when these wars were at an end, their military life, in which there is no little virtue, prepared them to obey the precepts of their law-giver; but we are told, that when Lycurgus endeavoured also to reduce the women to an obedience to his laws, upon their refusal he declined it. It may indeed be said that the women were the causes of these things, and of course all the fault was theirs. But we are not now considering where the fault lies, or where it does not lie, but what is right and what is wrong; and when the manners of the women are not well regulated, as I have already said, it must not only occasion faults which are disgraceful to the state, but also increase the love of money. In the next place, fault may be found with his unequal division of property, for some will have far too much, others too little; by which means the land will come into few hands, which business is badly regulated by his laws. For he made it infamous for any one either to buy or sell their possessions, in which he did right; but he permitted any one that chose it to give them away, or bequeath them, although nearly the same consequences will arise from one practice as from the other. It is supposed that near two parts in five of the whole country is the property of women, owing to their being so often sole heirs, and having such large fortunes in marriage; though it would be better to allow them none, or a little, or a certain regulated proportion. Now every one is permitted to make a woman his heir if he pleases; and if he dies intestate, he who succeeds as heir at law gives it to whom he pleases. From whence it happens that although the country is able to support fifteen hundred horse and thirty thousand foot, the number does not amount to one thousand.

And from these facts it is evident, that this particular is badly regulated; for the city could not support one shock, but was ruined for want of men. They say, that during the reigns of their ancient kings they used to present foreigners with the freedom of their city, to prevent there being a want of men while they carried on long wars; it is also affirmed that the number of Spartans was formerly ten thousand; but be that as it will, an equality of property conduces much to increase the number of the people. The law, too, which he made to encourage population was by no means calculated to correct this inequality; for being willing that the Spartans should be as numerous as possible, to make them desirous of having large families he ordered that he who had three children should be excused the night-watch, and that he who had four should pay no taxes: though it is very evident, that while the land was divided in this manner, that if the people increased there must many of them be very poor.

Nor was he less blamable for the manner in which he constituted the ephori; for these magistrates take cognisance of things of the last importance, and yet they are chosen out of the people in general; so that it often happens that a very poor person is elected to that office, who, from that circumstance, is easily bought. There have been many instances of this formerly, as well as in the late affair at Andros. And these men, being corrupted with money, went as far as they could to ruin the city: and, because their power was too great and nearly tyrannical, their kings were obliged to natter them, which contributed greatly to hurt the state; so that it altered from an aristocracy to a democracy. This magistracy is indeed the great support of the state; for the people are easy, knowing that they are eligible to the first office in it; so that, whether it took place by the intention of the legislator, or whether it happened by chance, this is of great service to their affairs; for it is necessary that every member of the state should endeavour that each part of the government should be preserved, and continue the same. And upon this principle their kings have always acted, out of regard to their honour; the wise and good from their attachment to the senate, a seat wherein they consider as the reward of virtue; and the common people, that they may support the ephori, of whom they consist. And it is proper that these magistrates should be chosen out of the whole community, not as the custom is at present, which is very ridiculous. The ephori are the supreme judges in causes of the last consequence; but as it is quite accidental what sort of persons they may be, it is not right that they should determine according to their own opinion, but by a written law or established custom. Their way of life also is not consistent with the manners of the city, for it is too indulgent; whereas that of others is too severe; so that they cannot support it, but are obliged privately to act contrary to law, that they may enjoy some of the pleasures of sense. There are also great defects in the institution of their senators. If indeed they were fitly trained to the practice of every human virtue, every one would readily admit that they would be useful to the government; but still it might be debated whether they should be continued judges for life, to determine points of the greatest moment, since the mind has its old age as well as the body; but as they are so brought up, that even the legislator could not depend upon them as good men, their power must be inconsistent with the safety of the state: for it is known that the members of that body have been guilty both of bribery and partiality in many public affairs; for which reason it had been much better if they had been made answerable for their conduct, which they are not. But it may be said the ephori seem to have a check upon all the magistrates. They have indeed in this particular very great power; but I affirm that they should not be entrusted with this control in the manner they are. Moreover, the mode of choice which they make use of at the election of their senators is very childish. Nor is it right for any one to solicit for a place he is desirous of; for every person, whether he chooses it or not, ought to execute any office he is fit for. But his intention was evidently the same in this as in the other parts of his government. For making his citizens ambitious after honours, with men of that disposition he has filled his senate, since no others will solicit for that office; and yet the principal part of those crimes which men are deliberately guilty of arise from ambition and avarice.

We will inquire at another time whether the office of a king is useful to the state: thus much is certain, that they should be chosen from a consideration of their conduct and not as they are now. But that the legislator himself did not expect to make all his citizens honourable and completely virtuous is evident from this, that he distrusts them as not being good men; for he sent those upon the same embassy that were at variance with each other; and thought, that in the dispute of the kings the safety of the state consisted. Neither were their common meals at first well established: for these should rather have been provided at the public expense, as at Crete, where, as at Lacedaemon, every one was obliged to buy his portion, although he might be very poor, and could by no means bear the expense, by which means the contrary happened to what the legislator desired: for he intended that those public meals should strengthen the democratic part of his government: but this regulation had quite the contrary effect, for those who were very poor could not take part in them; and it was an observation of their forefathers, that the not allowing those who could not contribute their proportion to the common tables to partake of them, would be the ruin of the state. Other persons have censured his laws concerning naval affairs, and not without reason, as it gave rise to disputes. For the commander of the fleet is in a manner set up in opposition to the kings, who are generals of the army for life.

There is also another defect in his laws worthy of censure, which Plato has given in his book of Laws; that the whole constitution was calculated only for the business of war: it is indeed excellent to make them conquerors; for which reason the preservation of the state depended thereon. The destruction of it commenced with their victories: for they knew not how to be idle, or engage in any other employment than war. In this particular also they were mistaken, that though they rightly thought, that those things which are the objects of contention amongst mankind are better procured by virtue than vice, yet they wrongfully preferred the things themselves to virtue. Nor was the public revenue well managed at Sparta, for the state was worth nothing while they were obliged to carry on the most extensive wars, and the subsidies were very badly raised; for as the Spartans possessed a large extent of country, they were not exact upon each other as to what they paid in. And thus an event contrary to the legislator's intention took place; for the state was poor, the individuals avaricious. Enough of the Lacedaemonian government; for these seem the chief defects in it.

# CHAPTER

# X

The government of Crete bears a near resemblance to this, in some few particulars it is not worse, but in general it is far inferior in its contrivance. For it appears and is allowed in many particulars the constitution of Lacedaemon was formed in imitation of that of Crete; and in general most new things are an improvement upon the old. For they say, that when Lycurgus ceased to be guardian to King Charilles he went abroad and spent a long time with his relations in Crete, for the Lycians are a colony of the Lacedaemonians; and those who first settled there adopted that body of laws which they found already established by the inhabitants; in like manner also those who now live near them have the very laws which Minos first drew up.

This island seems formed by nature to be the mistress of Greece, for it is entirely surrounded by a navigable ocean which washes almost all the maritime parts of that country, and is not far distant on the one side from Peloponnesus, on the other, which looks towards Asia, from Triopium and Rhodes. By means of this situation Minos acquired the empire of the sea and the islands; some of which he subdued, in others planted colonies: at last he died at Camicus while he was attacking Sicily. There is this analogy between the customs of the Lacedaemonians and the Cretans, the Helots cultivate the grounds for the one, the domestic slaves for the other. Both states have their common meals, and the Lacedaemonians called these formerly not *psiditia* but *andpia*, as the Cretans do; which proves from whence the custom arose. In this particular their governments are also alike: the ephori have the same power with those of Crete, who are called *kosmoi*; with this difference only, that the number of the one is five, of the other ten. The senators are the same as those whom the Cretans call the council. There was formerly also a kingly power in Crete; but it was afterwards dissolved, and the command of their armies was given to the *kosmoi*. Every one also has a vote in their public assembly; but this has only the power of confirming what has already passed the council and the *kosmoi*.

The Cretans conducted their public meals better than the Lacedaemonians, for at Lacedaemon each individual was obliged to furnish what was assessed upon him; which if he could not do, there was a law which deprived him of the rights of a citizen, as has been already mentioned: but in Crete they were furnished by the community; for all the corn and cattle, taxes and contributions, which the domestic slaves were obliged to furnish, were divided into parts and allotted to the gods, the exigencies of the state, and these public meals; so that all the men, women, and children were maintained from a common stock. The legislator gave great attention to encourage a habit of eating sparingly, as very useful to the citizens. He also endeavoured, that his community might not be too populous, to lessen the connection with women, by introducing the love of boys: whether in this he did well or ill we shall have some other opportunity of considering. But that the public meals were better ordered at Crete than at Lacedaemon is very evident.

The institution of the *kosmoi*, was still worse than that of the ephori: for it contained all the faults incident to that magistracy and some peculiar to itself; for in both cases it is uncertain who will be elected: but the Lacedaemonians have this advantage which the others have not, that as all are eligible, the whole community have a share in the highest honours, and therefore all desire to preserve the state: whereas among the Cretans the *kosmoi* are not chosen out of the people in general, but out of some certain families, and the senate out of the *kosmoi*. And the same observations which may be made on the senate at Lacedaemon may be applied to these; for their being under no control, and their continuing for life, is an honour greater than they merit; and to have their proceedings not regulated by a written law, but left to their own discretion, is dangerous. (As to there being no insurrections, although the people share not in the management of public affairs, this is no proof of a well-constituted government, as the *kosmoi* have no opportunity of being bribed like the ephori, as they live in an island far from those who would corrupt them.) But the method they take to correct that fault is absurd, impolitic, and tyrannical: for very often either their fellow-magistrates or some private persons conspire together and turn out the *kosmoi*. They are also permitted to resign their office before their time is elapsed, and if all this was done by law it would be well, and not at the pleasure of the individuals, which is a bad rule to follow. But what is worst of all is, that general confusion which those who are in power introduce to impede the ordinary course of justice; which sufficiently shows what is the nature of the government, or rather lawless force: for it is usual with the principal persons amongst them to collect together some of the common people and their friends, and then revolt and set up for themselves, and come to blows with each other. And what is the difference, if a state is dissolved at once by such violent means, or if it gradually so alters in process of time as to be no longer the same constitution? A state like this would ever be exposed to the invasions of those who were powerful and inclined to attack it; but, as has been already mentioned, its situation preserves it, as it is free from the inroads of foreigners; and for this reason the family slaves still remain quiet at Crete, while the Helots are perpetually revolting: for the Cretans take no part in foreign affairs, and it is but lately that any foreign troops have made an attack upon the island; and their ravages soon proved the ineffectualness of their laws. And thus much for the government of Crete.

# CHAPTER

# XI

The government of Carthage seems well established, and in many respects superior to others; in some particulars it bears a near resemblance to the Lacedaemonians; and indeed these three states, the Cretans, the Lacedaemonians and the Carthaginians are in some things very like each other, in others they differ greatly. Amongst many excellent constitutions this may show how well their government is framed, that although the people are admitted to a share in the administration, the form of it remains unaltered, without any popular insurrections, worth notice, on the one hand, or degenerating into a tyranny on the other. Now the Carthaginians have these things in common with the Lacedaemonians: public tables for those who are connected together by the tie of mutual friendship, after the manner of their Phiditia; they have also a magistracy, consisting of an hundred and four persons, similar to the ephori, or rather selected with more judgment; for amongst the Lacedaemonians, all the citizens are eligible, but amongst the Carthaginians, they are chosen out of those of the better sort: there is also some analogy between the king and the senate in both these governments, though the Carthaginian method of appointing their kings is best, for they do not confine themselves to one family; nor do they permit the election to be at large, nor have they any regard to seniority; for if amongst the candidates there are any of greater merit than the rest, these they prefer to those who may be older; for as their power is very extensive, if they are persons of no account, they may be very hurtful to the state, as they have always been to the Lacedaemonians; also the greater part of those things which become reprehensible by their excess are common to all those governments which we have described.

Now of those principles on which the Carthaginians have established their mixed form of government, composed of an aristocracy and democracy, some incline to produce a democracy, others an oligarchy: for instance, if the kings and the senate are unanimous upon any point in debate, they can choose whether they will bring it before the people or no; but if they disagree, it is to these they must appeal, who are not only to hear what has been approved of by the senate, but are finally to determine upon it; and whosoever chooses it, has a right to speak against any matter whatsoever that may be proposed, which is not permitted in other cases. The five, who elect each other, have very great and extensive powers; and these choose the hundred, who are magistrates of the highest rank: their power also continues longer than any other magistrates, for it commences before they come into office, and is prolonged after they are out of it; and in this particular the state inclines to an oligarchy: but as they are not elected by lot, but by suffrage, and are not permitted to take money, they are the greatest supporters imaginable of an aristocracy.

The determining all causes by the same magistrates, and not orae in one court and another in another, as at Lacedaemon, has the same influence. The constitution of Carthage is now shifting from an aristocracy to an oligarchy, in consequence of an opinion which is favourably entertained by many, who think that the magistrates in the community ought not to be persons of family only, but of fortune also; as it is impossible for those who are in bad circumstances to support the dignity of their office, or to be at leisure to apply to public business. As choosing men of fortune to be magistrates make a state incline to an oligarchy, and men of abilities to an aristocracy, so is there a third method of proceeding which took place in the polity of Carthage; for they have an eye to these two particulars when they elect their officers, particularly those of the highest rank, their kings and their generals. It must be admitted, that it was a great fault in their legislator not to guard against the constitution's degenerating from an aristocracy; for this is a most necessary thing to provide for at first, that those citizens who have the best abilities should never be obliged to do anything unworthy their character, but be always at leisure to serve the public, not only when in office, but also when private persons; for if once you are obliged to look among the wealthy, that you may have men at leisure to serve you, your greatest offices, of king and general, will soon become venal; in consequence of which, riches will be more honourable than virtue and a love of money be the ruling principle in the city-for what those who have the chief power regard as honourable will necessarily be the object which the citizens in general will aim at; and where the first honours are not paid to virtue, there the aristocratic form of government cannot flourish: for it is reasonable to conclude, that those who bought their places should generally make an advantage of what they laid out their money for; as it is absurd to suppose, that if a man of probity who is poor should be desirous of gaining something, a bad man should not endeavour to do the same, especially to reimburse himself; for which reason the magistracy should be formed of those who are most able to support an aristocracy. It would have been better for the legislature to have passed over the poverty of men of merit, and only to have taken care to have ensured them sufficient leisure, when in office, to attend to public affairs.

It seems also improper, that one person should execute several offices, which was approved of at Carthage; for one business is best done by one person; and it is the duty of the legislator to look to this, and not make the same person a musician and a shoemaker: so that where the state is not small it is more politic and more popular to admit many persons to have a share in the government; for, as I just now said, it is not only more usual, but everything is better and sooner done, when one thing only is allotted to one person: and this is evident both in the army and navy, where almost every one, in his turn, both commands and is under command. But as their government inclines to an oligarchy, they avoid the ill effects of it by always appointing some of the popular party to the government of cities to make their fortunes. Thus they consult this fault in their constitution and render it stable; but this is depending on chance; whereas the legislator ought to frame his government, that there the no room for insurrections. But now, if there should be any general calamity, and the people should revolt from their rulers, there is no remedy for reducing them to obedience by the laws. And these are the particulars of the Lacedaemonian, the Cretan, and the Carthaginian governments which seem worthy of commendation.

# CHAPTER

## XII

Some of those persons who have written upon government had never any share in public affairs, but always led a private life. Everything worthy of notice in their works we have already spoke to. Others were legislators, some in their own cities, others were employed in regulating the governments of foreign states. Some of them only composed a body of laws; others formed the constitution also, as Lycurgus; and Solon, who did both. The Lacedaemonians have been already mentioned. Some persons think that Solon was an excellent legislator, who could dissolve a pure oligarchy, and save the people from that slavery which hung over them, and establish the ancient democratic form of government in his country; wherein every part of it was so framed as to be well adapted to the whole. In the senate of Areopagus an oligarchy was preserved; by the manner of electing their magistrates, an aristocracy; and in their courts of justice, a democracy.

Solon seems not to have altered the established form of government, either with respect to the senate or the mode of electing their magistrates; but to have raised the people to great consideration in the state by allotting the supreme judicial department to them; and for this some persons blame him, as having done what would soon overturn that balance of power he intended to establish; for by trying all causes whatsoever before the people, who were chosen by lot to determine them, it was necessary to flatter a tyrannical populace who had got this power; which contributed to bring the government to that pure democracy it now is.

Both Ephialtes and Pericles abridged the power of the Areopagites, the latter of whom introduced the method of paying those who attended the courts of justice: and thus every one who aimed at being popular proceeded increasing the power of the people to what we now see it. But it is evident that this was not Solon's intention, but that it arose from accident; for the people being the cause of the naval victory over the Medes, assumed greatly upon it, and enlisted themselves under factious demagogues, although opposed by the better part of the citizens. He thought it indeed most necessary to entrust the people with the choice of their magistrates and the power of calling them to account; for without that they must have been slaves and enemies to the other citizens: but he ordered them to elect those only who were persons of good account and property, either out of those who were worth five hundred medimns, or those who were called *xeugitai*, or those of the third census, who were called horsemen.

As for those of the fourth, which consisted of mechanics, they were incapable of any office. Zaleucus was the legislator of the Western Locrians, as was Charondas, the Catanean, of his own cities, and those also in Italy and Sicily which belonged to the Calcidians. Some persons endeavour to prove that Onomacritus, the Locrian, was the first person of note who drew up laws; and that he employed himself in that business while he was at Crete, where he continued some time to learn the prophetic art: and they say, that Thales was his companion; and that Lycurgus and Zaleucus were the scholars of Thales, and Charondas of Zaleucus; but those who advance this, advance what is repugnant to chronology. Philolaus also, of the family of the Bacchiades, was a Theban legislator. This man was very fond of Diocles, a victor in the Olympic games, and when he left his country from a disgust at an improper passion which his mother Alithoe had entertained for him, and settled at Thebes, Philolaus followed him, where they both died, and where they still show their tombs placed in view of each other, but so disposed, that one of them looks towards Corinth, the other does not; the reason they give for this is, that Diodes, from his detestation of his mother's passion, would have his tomb so placed that no one could see Corinth from it; but Philolaus chose that it might be seen from his: and this was the cause of their living at Thebes.

As Philolaus gave them laws concerning many other things, so did he upon adoption, which they call adoptive laws; and this he in particular did to preserve the number of families. Charondas did nothing new, except in actions for perjury, which he was the first person who took into particular consideration. He also drew up his laws with greater elegance and accuracy than even any of our present legislators. Philolaus introduced the law for the equal distribution of goods; Plato that for the community of women, children, and goods, and also for public tables for the women; and one concerning drunkenness, that they might observe sobriety in their symposiums. He also made a law concerning their warlike exercises; that they should acquire a habit of using both hands alike, as it was necessary that one hand should be as useful as the other.

As for Draco's laws, they were published when the government was already established, and they have nothing particular in them worth mentioning, except their severity on account of the enormity of their punishments. Pittacus was the author of some laws, but never drew up any form of government; one of which was this, that if a drunken man beat any person he should be punished more than if he did it when sober; for as people are more apt to be abusive when drunk than sober, he paid no consideration to the excuse which drunkenness might claim, but regarded only the common benefit. Andromadas Regmus was also a lawgiver to the Thracian talcidians. There are some laws of his concerning murders and heiresses extant, but these contain nothing that any one can say is new and his own. And thus much for different sorts of governments, as well those which really exist as those which different persons have proposed.

# BOOK III

## CHAPTER

### I

Every one who inquires into the nature of government, and what are its different forms, should make this almost his first question, What is a city? For upon this there is a dispute: for some persons say the city did this or that, while others say, not the city, but the oligarchy, or the tyranny. We see that the city is the only object which both the politician and legislator have in view in all they do: but government is a certain ordering of those who inhabit a city. As a city is a collective body, and, like other wholes, composed of many parts, it is evident our first inquiry must be, what a citizen is: for a city is a certain number of citizens. So that we must consider whom we ought to call citizen, and who is one; for this is often doubtful: for every one will not allow that this character is applicable to the same person; for that man who would be a citizen in a republic would very often not be one in an oligarchy. We do not include in this inquiry many of those who acquire this appellation out of the ordinary way, as honorary persons, for instance, but those only who have a natural right to it.

Now it is not residence which constitutes a man a citizen; for in this sojourners and slaves are upon an equality with him; nor will it be sufficient for this purpose, that you have the privilege of the laws, and may plead or be impleaded, for this all those of different nations, between whom there is a mutual agreement for that purpose, are allowed; although it very often happens, that sojourners have not a perfect right therein without the protection of a patron, to whom they are obliged to apply, which shows that their share in the community is incomplete. In like manner, with respect to boys who are not yet enrolled, or old men who are past war, we admit that they are in some respects citizens, but not completely so, but with some exceptions, for these are not yet arrived to years of maturity, and those are past service; nor is there any difference between them. But what we mean is sufficiently intelligible and clear, we want a complete citizen, one in whom there is no deficiency to be corrected to make him so. As to those who are banished, or infamous, there may be the same objections made and the same answer given. There is nothing that more characterises a complete citizen than having a share in the judicial and executive part of the government.

With respect to offices, some are fixed to a particular time, so that no person is, on any account, permitted to fill them twice; or else not till some certain period has intervened; others are not fixed, as a juryman's, and a member of the general assembly: but probably some one may say these are not offices, nor have the citizens in these capacities any share in the government; though surely it is ridiculous to say that those who have the principal power in the state bear no office in it. But this objection is of no weight, for it is only a dispute about words; as there is no general term which can be applied both to the office of a juryman and a member of the assembly. For the sake of distinction, suppose we call it an indeterminate office: but I lay it down as a maxim, that those are citizens who could exercise it. Such then is the description of a citizen who comes nearest to what all those who are called citizens are. Every one also should know, that of the component parts of those things which differ from each other in species, after the first or second remove, those which follow have either nothing at all or very little common to each.

Now we see that governments differ from each other in their form, and that some of them are defective, others as excellent as possible: for it is evident, that those which have many deficiencies and degeneracies in them must be far inferior to those which are without such faults. What I mean by degeneracies will be hereafter explained. Hence it is clear that the office of a citizen must differ as governments do from each other: for which reason he who is called a citizen has, in a democracy, every privilege which that station supposes. In other forms of government he may enjoy them; but not necessarily: for in some states the people have no power; nor have they any general assembly, but a few select men.

The trial also of different causes is allotted to different persons; as at Lacedaemon all disputes concerning contracts are brought before some of the ephori: the senate are the judges in cases of murder, and so on; some being to be heard by one magistrate, others by another: and thus at Carthage certain magistrates determine all causes. But our former description of a citizen will admit of correction; for in some governments the office of a juryman and a member of the general assembly is not an indeterminate one; but there are particular persons appointed for these purposes, some or all of the citizens being appointed jurymen or members of the general assembly, and this either for all causes and all public business whatsoever, or else for some particular one: and this may be sufficient to show what a citizen is; for he who has a right to a share in the judicial and executive part of government in any city, him we call a citizen of that place; and a city, in one word, is a collective body of such persons sufficient in themselves to all the purposes of life.

# CHAPTER

## II

In common use they define a citizen to be one who is sprung from citizens on both sides, not on the father's or the mother's only. Others carry the matter still further, and inquire how many of his ancestors have been citizens, as his grandfather, great-grandfather, etc., but some persons have questioned how the first of the family could prove themselves citizens, according to this popular and careless definition. Gorgias of Leontium, partly entertaining the same doubt, and partly in jest, says, that as a mortar is made by a mortar-maker, so a citizen is made by a citizen-maker, and a Larisssean by a Larisssean-maker. This is indeed a very simple account of the matter; for if citizens are so, according to this definition, it will be impossible to apply it to the first founders or first inhabitants of states, who cannot possibly claim in right either of their father or mother. It is probably a matter of still more difficulty to determine their rights as citizens who are admitted to their freedom after any revolution in the state. As, for instance, at Athens, after the expulsion of the tyrants, when Clisthenes enrolled many foreigners and city-slaves amongst the tribes; and the doubt with respect to them was, not whether they were citizens or no, but whether they were legally so or not. Though indeed some persons may have this further doubt, whether a citizen can be a citizen when he is illegally made; as if an illegal citizen, and one who is no citizen at all, were in the same predicament: but since we see some persons govern unjustly, whom yet we admit to govern, though not justly, and the definition of a citizen is one who exercises certain offices, for such a one we have defined a citizen to be, it is evident, that a citizen illegally created yet continues to be a citizen, but whether justly or unjustly so belongs to the former inquiry.

# CHAPTER

## III

I t has also been doubted what was and what was not the act of
the city; as, for instance, when a democracy arises out of an
aristocracy or a tyranny; for some persons then refuse to fulfil
their contracts; as if the right to receive the money was in the tyrant
and not in the state, and many other things of the same nature; as
if any covenant was founded for violence and not for the common
good. So in like manner, if anything is done by those who have the
management of public affairs where a democracy is established, their
actions are to be considered as the actions of the state, as well as in
the oligarchy or tyranny.

And here it seems very proper to consider this question, When shall
we say that a city is the same, and when shall we say that it is different?

It is but a superficial mode of examining into this question to begin
with the place and the people; for it may happen that these may be
divided from that, or that some one of them may live in one place, and
some in another (but this question may be regarded as no very knotty
one; for, as a city may acquire that appellation on many accounts, it
may be solved many ways); and in like manner, when men inhabit one
common place, when shall we say that they inhabit the same city, or that
the city is the same? For it does not depend upon the walls; for I can
suppose Peloponnesus itself surrounded with a wall, as Babylon was,
and every other place, which rather encircles many nations than one city,
and that they say was taken three days when some of the inhabitants
knew nothing of it: but we shall find a proper time to determine this
question; for the extent of a city, how large it should be, and whether
it should consist of more than one people, these are particulars that
the politician should by no means be unacquainted with. This, too, is
a matter of inquiry, whether we shall say that a city is the same while
it is inhabited by the same race of men, though some of them are

perpetually dying, others coming into the world, as we say that a river or a fountain is the same, though the waters are continually changing; or when a revolution takes place shall we say the men are the same, but the city is different: for if a city is a community, it is a community of citizens; but if the mode of government should alter, and become of another sort, it would seem a necessary consequence that the city is not the same; as we regard the tragic chorus as different from the comic, though it may probably consist of the same performers: thus every other community or composition is said to be different if the species of composition is different; as in music the same hands produce different harmony, as the Doric and Phrygian. If this is true, it is evident, that when we speak of a city as being the same we refer to the government there established; and this, whether it is called by the same name or any other, or inhabited by the same men or different. But whether or no it is right to dissolve the community when the constitution is altered is another question.

## CHAPTER

## IV

What has been said, it follows that we should consider whether the same virtues which constitute a good man make a valuable citizen, or different; and if a particular inquiry is necessary for this matter we must first give a general description of the virtues of a good citizen; for as a sailor is one of those who make up a community, so is a citizen, although the province of one sailor may be different from another's (for one is a rower, another a steersman, a third a boatswain, and so on, each having their several appointments), it is evident that the most accurate description of any one good sailor must refer to his peculiar abilities, yet there are some things in which the same description may be applied to the whole crew, as the safety of the ship is the common business of all of them, for this is the general centre of all their cares: so also with respect to citizens, although they may in a few particulars be very different, yet there is one care common to them all, the safety of the community, for the community of the citizens composes the state; for which reason the virtue of a citizen has necessarily a reference to the state. But if there are different sorts of governments, it is evident that those actions which constitute the virtue of an excellent citizen in one community will not constitute it in another; wherefore the virtue of such a one cannot be perfect: but we say, a man is good when his virtues are perfect; from whence it follows, that an excellent citizen does not possess that virtue which constitutes a good man. Those who are any ways doubtful concerning this question may be convinced of the truth of it by examining into the best formed states: for, if it is impossible that a city should consist entirely of excellent citizens (while it is necessary that every one should do well in his calling, in which consists his excellence, as it is impossible that all the citizens should have the same qualifications) it is impossible that the virtue of a citizen and a good man should be the same; for all should possess the virtue of an excellent citizen: for from hence necessarily arise the perfection of the city: but that every one should possess the virtue of a good man is impossible without all the citizens in a well-regulated state were necessarily virtuous. Besides, as a city is composed of dissimilar parts, as an animal is of life and body; the soul of reason and appetite; a family of a man and his wife—property of a master and a slave; in the same manner, as a city is composed of all these and many other very different parts, it necessarily follows that the virtue of all the citizens cannot be the same; as the business of him who leads the band is different from the other dancers. From all which proofs it is evident that the virtues of a citizen cannot be one and the same. But do we never find those virtues united which constitute a good man and excellent citizen? For we say, such a one is an excellent magistrate and a prudent and good man; but prudence is a necessary qualification for all those who engage in public affairs. Nay, some persons affirm that the education of those who are intended to command should, from the beginning, be different from other citizens, as the children of kings are generally instructed in riding and warlike exercises; and thus Euripides says:

". . . No showy arts Be mine, but teach me what the state requires."

As if those who are to rule were to have an education peculiar to themselves. But if we allow, that the virtues of a good man and a good magistrate may be the same, and a citizen is one who obeys the magistrate, it follows that the virtue of the one cannot in general be the same as the virtue of the other, although it may be true of some particular citizen; for the virtue of the magistrate must be different from the virtue of the citizen. For which reason Jason declared that was he deprived of his kingdom he should pine away with regret, as not knowing how to live a private man. But it is a great recommendation to know how to command as well as to obey; and to do both these things well is the virtue of an accomplished citizen. If then the virtue of a good man consists only in being able to command, but the virtue of a good citizen renders him equally fit for the one as well as the other, the commendation of both of them is not the same. It appears, then, that both he who commands and he who obeys should each of them learn their separate business: but that the citizen should be master of and take part in both these, as any one may easily perceive; in a family government there is no occasion for the master to know how to perform the necessary offices, but rather to enjoy the labour of others; for to do the other is a servile part. I mean by the other, the common family business of the slave.

There are many sorts of slaves; for their employments are various: of these the handicraftsmen are one, who, as their name imports, get their living by the labour of their hands, and amongst these all mechanics are included; for which reasons such workmen, in some states, were not formerly admitted into any share in the government; till at length democracies were established: it is not therefore proper for any man of honour, or any citizen, or any one who engages in public affairs, to learn these servile employments without they have occasion for them for their own use; for without this was observed the distinction between a master and a slave would be lost. But there is a government of another sort, in which men govern those who are their equals in rank, and freemen, which we call a political government, in which men learn to command by first submitting to obey, as a good general of horse, or a commander-in-chief, must acquire a knowledge of their duty by having been long under the command of another, and the like in every appointment in the army: for well is it said, no one knows how to command who has not himself been under command of another. The virtues of those are indeed different, but a good citizen must necessarily be endowed with them; he ought also to know in what manner freemen ought to govern, as well as be governed: and this, too, is the duty of a good man. And if the temperance and justice of him who commands is different from his who, though a freeman, is under command, it is evident that the virtues of a good citizen cannot be the same as justice, for instance but must be of a different species in these two different situations, as the temperance and courage of a man and a woman are different from each other; for a man would appear a coward who had only that courage which would be graceful in a woman, and a woman would be thought a talker who should take as large a part in the conversation as would become a man of consequence.

The domestic employments of each of them are also different; it is the man's business to acquire subsistence, the woman's to take care of it. But direction and knowledge of public affairs is a virtue peculiar to those who govern, while all others seem to be equally requisite for both parties; but with this the governed have no concern, it is theirs to entertain just notions: they indeed are like flute-makers, while those who govern are the musicians who play on them. And thus much to show whether the virtue of a good man and an excellent citizen is the same, or if it is different, and also how far it is the same, and how far different.

# CHAPTER

## V

**B**ut with respect to citizens there is a doubt remaining, whether those only are truly so who are allowed to share in the government, or whether the mechanics also are to be considered as such? For if those who are not permitted to rule are to be reckoned among them, it is impossible that the virtue of all the citizens should be the same, for these also are citizens; and if none of them are admitted to be citizens, where shall they be ranked? For they are neither sojourners nor foreigners? Or shall we say that there will no inconvenience arise from their not being citizens, as they are neither slaves nor freedmen: for this is certainly true, that all those are not citizens who are necessary to the existence of a city, as boys are not citizens in the same manner that men are, for those are perfectly so, the others under some conditions; for they are citizens, though imperfect ones: for in former times among some people the mechanics were either slaves or foreigners, for which reason many of them are so now: and indeed the best regulated states will not permit a mechanic to be a citizen; but if it be allowed them, we cannot then attribute the virtue we have described to every citizen or freeman, but to those only who are disengaged from servile offices. Now those who are employed by one person in them are slaves; those who do them for money are mechanics and hired servants: hence it is evident on the least reflection what is their situation, for what I have said is fully explained by appearances. Since the number of communities is very great, it follows necessarily that there will be many different sorts of citizens, particularly of those who are governed by others, so that in one state it may be necessary to admit mechanics and hired servants to be citizens, but in others it may be impossible; as particularly in an aristocracy, where honours are bestowed on virtue and dignity: for it is impossible for one who lives the life of a mechanic or hired servant to acquire the practice of virtue. In an oligarchy also hired servants are not admitted to be citizens; because there a man's right to bear any office is regulated by his fortune; but mechanics are, for many citizens are very rich.

There was a law at Thebes that no one could have a share in the government till he had been ten years out of trade. In many states the law invites strangers to accept the freedom of the city; and in some democracies the son of a free-woman is himself free. The same is also observed in many others with respect to natural children; but it is through want of citizens regularly born that they admit such: for these laws are always made in consequence of a scarcity of inhabitants; so, as their numbers increase, they first deprive the children of a male or female slave of this privilege, next the child of a free-woman, and last of all they will admit none but those whose fathers and mothers were both free.

That there are many sorts of citizens, and that he may be said to be as completely who shares the honours of the state, is evident from what has been already said. Thus Achilles, in Homer, complains of Agamemnon's treating him like an unhonoured stranger; for a stranger or sojourner is one who does not partake of the honours of the state: and whenever the right to the freedom of the city is kept obscure, it is for the sake of the inhabitants. From what has been said it is plain whether the virtue of a good man and an excellent citizen is the same or different: and we find that in some states it is the same, in others not; and also that this is not true of each citizen, but of those only who take the lead, or are capable of taking the lead, in public affairs, either alone or in conjunction with others.

# CHAPTER

## VI

Having established these points, we proceed next to consider whether one form of government only should be established, or more than one; and if more, how many, and of what sort, and what are the differences between them. The form of government is the ordering and regulating of the city, and all the offices in it, particularly those wherein the supreme power is lodged; and this power is always possessed by the administration; but the administration itself is that particular form of government which is established in any state: thus in a democracy the supreme power is lodged in the whole people; on the contrary, in an oligarchy it is in the hands of a few. We say then, that the form of government in these states is different, and we shall find the same thing hold good in others. Let us first determine for whose sake a city is established; and point out the different species of rule which man may submit to in social life.

I have already mentioned in my treatise on the management of a family, and the power of the master, that man is an animal naturally formed for society, and that therefore, when he does not want any foreign assistance, he will of his own accord desire to live with others; not but that mutual advantage induces them to it, as far as it enables each person to live more agreeably; and this is indeed the great object not only to all in general, but also to each individual: but it is not merely matter of choice, but they join in society also, even that they may be able to live, which probably is not without some share of merit, and they also support civil society, even for the sake of preserving life, without they are grievously overwhelmed with the miseries of it: for it is very evident that men will endure many calamities for the sake of living, as being something naturally sweet and desirable. It is easy to point out the different modes of government, and we have already settled them in our exoteric discourses. The power of the master, though by nature equally serviceable, both to the master and to the slave, yet nevertheless has for its object the benefit of the master, while the benefit of the slave arises accidentally; for if the slave is destroyed, the power of the master is at an end: but the authority which a man has over his wife, and children, and his family, which we call domestic government, is either for the benefit of those who are under subjection, or else for the common benefit of the whole: but its particular object is the benefit of the governed, as we see in other arts; in physic, for instance, and the gymnastic exercises, wherein, if any benefit arise to the master, it is accidental; for nothing forbids the master of the exercises from sometimes being himself one of those who exercises, as the steersman is always one of the sailors; but both the master of the exercises and the steersman consider the good of those who are under their government. Whatever good may happen to the steersman when he is a sailor, or to the master of the exercises when he himself makes one at the games, is not intentional, or the object of their power; thus in all political governments which are established to preserve and defend the equality of the citizens it is held right to rule by turns. Formerly, as was natural, every one expected that each of his fellow citizens should in his turn serve the public, and thus administer to his private good, as he himself when in office had done for others; but now every one is desirous of being continually in power, that he may enjoy the advantage which he makes of public business and being in office; as if places were a never-failing remedy for every complaint, and were on that account so eagerly sought after.

It is evident, then, that all those governments which have a common good in view are rightly established and strictly just, but those who have in view only the good of the rulers are all founded on wrong principles, and are widely different from what a government ought to be, for they are tyranny over slaves, whereas a city is a community of freemen.

# CHAPTER

## VII

Having established these particulars, we come to consider next the different number of governments which there are, and what they are; and first, what are their excellencies: for when we have determined this, their defects will be evident enough.

It is evident that every form of government or administration, for the words are of the same import, must contain a supreme power over the whole state, and this supreme power must necessarily be in the hands of one person, or a few, or many; and when either of these apply their power for the common good, such states are well governed; but when the interest of the one, the few, or the many who enjoy this power is alone consulted, then ill; for you must either affirm that those who make up the community are not citizens, or else let these share in the advantages of government. We usually call a state which is governed by one person for the common good, a kingdom; one that is governed by more than one, but by a few only, an aristocracy; either because the government is in the hands of the most worthy citizens, or because it is the best form for the city and its inhabitants. When the citizens at large govern for the public good, it is called a state; which is also a common name for all other governments, and these distinctions are consonant to reason; for it will not be difficult to find one person, or a very few, of very distinguished abilities, but almost impossible to meet with the majority of a people eminent for every virtue; but if there is one common to a whole nation it is valour; for this is created and supported by numbers: for which reason in such a state the profession of arms will always have the greatest share in the government.

Now the corruptions attending each of these governments are these; a kingdom may degenerate into a tyranny, an aristocracy into an oligarchy, and a state into a democracy. Now a tyranny is a monarchy where the good of one man only is the object of government, an oligarchy considers only the rich, and a democracy only the poor; but neither of them have a common good in view.

# CHAPTER

# VIII

I t will be necessary to enlarge a little more upon the nature of each of these states, which is not without some difficulty, for he who would enter into a philosophical inquiry into the principles of them, and not content himself with a superficial view of their outward conduct, must pass over and omit nothing, but explain the true spirit of each of them. A tyranny then is, as has been said, a monarchy, where one person has an absolute and despotic power over the whole community and every member therein: an oligarchy, where the supreme power of the state is lodged with the rich: a democracy, on the contrary, is where those have it who are worth little or nothing. But the first difficulty that arises from the distinctions which we have laid down is this, should it happen that the majority of the inhabitants who possess the power of the state (for this is a democracy) should be rich, the question is, how does this agree with what we have said? The same difficulty occurs, should it ever happen that the poor compose a smaller part of the people than the rich, but from their superior abilities acquire the supreme power; for this is what they call an oligarchy; it should seem then that our definition of the different states was not correct: nay, moreover, could any one suppose that the majority of the people were poor, and the minority rich, and then describe the state in this manner, that an oligarchy was a government in which the rich, being few in number, possessed the supreme power, and that a democracy was a state in which the poor, being many in number, possessed it, still there will be another difficulty; for what name shall we give to those states we have been describing? I mean, that in which the greater number are rich, and that in which the lesser number are poor (where each of these possess the supreme power), if there are no other states than those we have described. It seems therefore evident to reason, that whether the supreme power is vested in the hands of many or few may be a matter of accident; but that it is clear enough, that when it is in the hands of the few, it will be a government of the rich; when in the hands of the many, it will be a government of the poor; since in all countries there are many poor and few rich: it is not therefore the cause that has been already assigned (namely, the number of people in power) that makes the difference between the two governments; but an oligarchy and democracy differ in this from each other, in the poverty of those who govern in the one, and the riches of those who govern in the other; for when the government is in the hands of the rich, be they few or be they more, it is an oligarchy; when it is in the hands of the poor, it is a democracy: but, as we have already said, the one will be always few, the other numerous, but both will enjoy liberty; and from the claims of wealth and liberty will arise continual disputes with each other for the lead in public affairs.

# CHAPTER

# IX

Let us first determine what are the proper limits of an oligarchy and a democracy, and what is just in each of these states; for all men have some natural inclination to justice; but they proceed therein only to a certain degree; nor can they universally point out what is absolutely just; as, for instance, what is equal appears just, and is so; but not to all; only among those who are equals: and what is unequal appears just, and is so; but not to all, only amongst those who are unequals; which circumstance some people neglect, and therefore judge ill; the reason for which is, they judge for themselves, and every one almost is the worst judge in his own cause. Since then justice has reference to persons, the same distinctions must be made with respect to persons which are made with respect to things, in the manner that I have already described in my Ethics.

As to the equality of the things, these they agree in; but their dispute is concerning the equality of the persons, and chiefly for the reason above assigned; because they judge ill in their own cause; and also because each party thinks, that if they admit what is right in some particulars, they have done justice on the whole: thus, for instance, if some persons are unequal in riches, they suppose them unequal in the whole; or, on the contrary, if they are equal in liberty, they suppose them equal in the whole: but what is absolutely just they omit; for if civil society was founded for the sake of preserving and increasing property, every one's right in the city would be equal to his fortune; and then the reasoning of those who insist upon an oligarchy would be valid; for it would not be right that he who contributed one mina should have an equal share in the hundred along with him who brought in all the rest, either of the original money or what was afterwards acquired.

Nor was civil society founded merely to preserve the lives of its members; but that they might live well: for otherwise a state might be composed of slaves, or the animal creation: but this is not so; for these have no share in the happiness of it; nor do they live after their own choice; nor is it an alliance mutually to defend each other from injuries, or for a commercial intercourse: for then the Tyrrhenians and Carthaginians, and all other nations between whom treaties of commerce subsist, would be citizens of one city; for they have articles to regulate their exports and imports, and engagements for mutual protection, and alliances for mutual defence; but yet they have not all the same magistrates established among them, but they are different among the different people; nor does the one take any care, that the morals of the other should be as they ought, or that none of those who have entered into the common agreements should be unjust, or in any degree vicious, only that they do not injure any member of the confederacy. But whosoever endeavours to establish wholesome laws in a state, attends to the virtues and the vices of each individual who composes it; from whence it is evident, that the first care of him who would found a city, truly deserving that name, and not nominally so, must be to have his citizens virtuous; for otherwise it is merely an alliance for self-defence; differing from those of the same cast which are made between different people only in place: for law is an agreement and a pledge, as the sophist Lycophron says, between the citizens of their intending to do justice to each other, though not sufficient to make all the citizens just and good: and that this is faact is evident, for could any one bring different places together, as, for instance, enclose Megara and Corinth in a wall, yet they would not be one city, not even if the inhabitants intermarried with each other, though this inter-community contributes much to make a place one city. Besides, could we suppose a set of people to live separate from each other, but within such a distance as would admit of an intercourse, and that there were laws subsisting between each party, to prevent their injuring one another in their mutual dealings, supposing one a carpenter, another a husbandman, shoemaker, and the like, and that their numbers were ten thousand, still all that they would have together in common would be a tariff for trade, or an alliance for mutual defence, but not the same city. And why? Not because their mutual intercourse is not near enough, for even if persons so situated should come to one place, and every one should live in his own house as in his native city, and there should be alliances subsisting between each party to mutually assist and prevent any injury being done to the other, still they would not be admitted to be a city by those who think correctly, if they preserved the same customs when they were together as when they were separate.

It is evident, then, that a city is not a community of place; nor established for the sake of mutual safety or traffic with each other; but that these things are the necessary consequences of a city, although they may all exist where there is no city: but a city is a society of people joining together with their families and their children to live agreeably for the sake of having their lives as happy and as independent as possible: and for this purpose it is necessary that they should live in one place and intermarry with each other: hence in all cities there are family-meetings, clubs, sacrifices, and public entertainments to promote friendship; for a love of sociability is friendship itself; so that the end then for which a city is established is, that the inhabitants of it may live happy, and these things are conducive to that end: for it is a community of families and villages for the sake of a perfect independent life; that is, as we have already said, for the sake of living well and happily. It is not therefore founded for the purpose of men's merely living together, but for their living as men ought; for which reason those who contribute most to this end deserve to have greater power in the city than those who are their equals in family and freedom, but their inferiors in civil virtue, or those who excel them in wealth but are below them in worth. It is evident from what has been said, that in all disputes upon government each party says something that is just.

# CHAPTER

## X

It may also be a doubt where the supreme power ought to be lodged. Shall it be with the majority, or the wealthy, with a number of proper persons, or one better than the rest, or with a tyrant? But whichever of these we prefer some difficulty will arise. For what? Shall the poor have it because they are the majority? They may then divide among themselves, what belongs to the rich: nor is this unjust; because truly it has been so judged by the supreme power. But what avails it to point out what is the height of injustice if this is not? Again, if the many seize into their own hands everything which belongs to the few, it is evident that the city will be at an end. But virtue will never destroy what is virtuous; nor can what is right be the ruin of the state: therefore such a law can never be right, nor can the acts of a tyrant ever be wrong, for of necessity they must all be just; for he, from his unlimited power, compels every one to obey his command, as the multitude oppress the rich. Is it right then that the rich, the few, should have the supreme power? And what if they be guilty of the same rapine and plunder the possessions of the majority, that will be as right as the other: but that all things of this sort are wrong and unjust is evident. Well then, these of the better sort shall have it: but must not then all the other citizens live unhonoured, without sharing the offices of the city; for the offices of a city are its honours, and if one set of men are always in power, it is evident that the rest must be without honour. Well then, let it be with one person of all others the fittest for it: but by this means the power will be still more contracted, and a greater number than before continue unhonoured. But some one may say, that it is wrong to let man have the supreme power and not the law, as his soul is subject to so many passions. But if this law appoints an aristocracy, or a democracy, how will it help us in our present doubts? For those things will happen which we have already mentioned.

## CHAPTER

## XI

Other particulars we will consider separately; but it seems proper to prove, that the supreme power ought to be lodged with the many, rather than with those of the better sort, who are few; and also to explain what doubts (and probably just ones) may arise: now, though not one individual of the many may himself be fit for the supreme power, yet when these many are joined together, it does not follow but they may be better qualified for it than those; and this not separately, but as a collective body; as the public suppers exceed those which are given at one person's private expense: for, as they are many, each person brings in his share of virtue and wisdom; and thus, coming together, they are like one man made up of a multitude, with many feet, many hands, and many intelligences: thus is it with respect to the manners and understandings of the multitude taken together; for which reason the public are the best judges of music and poetry; for some understand one part, some another, and all collectively the whole; and in this particular men of consequence differ from each of the many; as they say those who are beautiful do from those who are not so, and as fine pictures excel any natural objects, by collecting the several beautiful parts which were dispersed among different originals into one, although the separate parts, as the eye or any other, might be handsomer than in the picture.

But if this distinction is to be made between every people and every general assembly, and some few men of consequence, it may be doubtful whether it is true; nay, it is clear enough that, with respect to a few, it is not; since the same conclusion might be applied even to brutes: and indeed wherein do some men differ from brutes? Not but that nothing prevents what I have said being true of the people in some states. The doubt then which we have lately proposed, with all its consequences, may be settled in this manner; it is necessary that the freemen who compose the bulk of the people should have absolute power in some things; but as they are neither men of property, nor act uniformly upon principles of virtue, it is not safe to trust them with the first offices in the state, both on account of their iniquity and their ignorance; from the one of which they will do what is wrong, from the other they will mistake: and yet it is dangerous to allow them no power or share in the government; for when there are many poor people who are incapable of acquiring the honours of their country, the state must necessarily have many enemies in it; let them then be permitted to vote in the public assemblies and to determine causes; for which reason Socrates, and some other legislators, gave them the power of electing the officers of the state, and also of inquiring into their conduct when they came out of office, and only prevented their being magistrates by themselves; for the multitude when they are collected together have all of them sufficient understanding for these purposes, and, mixing among those of higher rank, are serviceable to the city, as some things, which alone are improper for food, when mixed with others make the whole more wholesome than a few of them would be.

But there is a difficulty attending this form of government, for it seems, that the person who himself was capable of curing any one who was then sick, must be the best judge whom to employ as a physician; but such a one must be himself a physician; and the same holds true in every other practice and art: and as a physician ought to give an account of his practice to a physician, so ought it to be in other arts: those whose business is physic may be divided into three sorts, the first of these is he who makes up the medicines; the second prescribes, and is to the other as the architect is to the mason; the third is he who understands the science, but never practises it: now these three distinctions may be found in those who understand all other arts; nor have we less opinion of their judgment who are only instructed in the principles of the art than of those who practise it: and with respect to elections the same method of proceeding seems right; for to elect a proper person in any science is the business of those who are skilful therein; as in geometry, of geometricians; in steering, of steersmen: but if some individuals should know something of particular arts and works, they do not know more than the professors of them: so that even upon this principle neither the election of magistrates, nor the censure of their conduct, should be entrusted to the many.

But probably all that has been here said may not be right; for, to resume the argument I lately used, if the people are not very brutal indeed, although we allow that each individual knows less of these affairs than those who have given particular attention to them, yet when they come together they will know them better, or at least not worse; besides, in some particular arts it is not the workman only who is the best judge; namely, in those the works of which are understood by those who do not profess them: thus he who builds a house is not the only judge of it, for the master of the family who inhabits it is a better; thus also a steersman is a better judge of a tiller than he who made it; and he who gives an entertainment than the cook. What has been said seems a sufficient solution of this difficulty; but there is another that follows: for it seems absurd that the power of the state should be lodged with those who are but of indifferent morals, instead of those who are of excellent characters. Now the power of election and censure are of the utmost consequence, and this, as has been said, in some states they entrust to the people; for the general assembly is the supreme court of all, and they have a voice in this, and deliberate in all public affairs, and try all causes, without any objection to the meanness of their circumstances, and at any age: but their treasurers, generals, and other great officers of state are taken from men of great fortune and worth. This difficulty also may be solved upon the same principle; and here too they may be right, for the power is not in the man who is member of the assembly, or council, but the assembly itself, and the council, and the people, of which each individual of the whole community are the parts, I mean as senator, adviser, or judge; for which reason it is very right, that the many should have the greatest powers in their own hands; for the people, the council, and the judges are composed of them, and the property of all these collectively is more than the property of any person or a few who fill the great offices of the state: and thus I determine these points.

The first question that we stated shows plainly, that the supreme power should be lodged in laws duly made and that the magistrate or magistrates, either one or more, should be authorised to determine those cases which the laws cannot particularly speak to, as it is impossible for them, in general language, to explain themselves upon everything that may arise: but what these laws are which are established upon the best foundations has not been yet explained, but still remains a matter of some question: but the laws of every state will necessarily be like every state, either trifling or excellent, just or unjust; for it is evident, that the laws must be framed correspondent to the constitution of the government; and, if so, it is plain, that a well-formed government will have good laws, a bad one, bad ones.

# CHAPTER

## XII

Since in every art and science the end aimed at is always good, so particularly in this, which is the most excellent of all, the founding of civil society, the good wherein aimed at is justice; for it is this which is for the benefit of all. Now, it is the common opinion, that justice is a certain equality; and in this point all the philosophers are agreed when they treat of morals: for they say what is just, and to whom; and that equals ought to receive equal: but we should know how we are to determine what things are equal and what unequal; and in this there is some difficulty, which calls for the philosophy of the politician. Some persons will probably say, that the employments of the state ought to be given according to every particular excellence of each citizen, if there is no other difference between them and the rest of the community, but they are in every respect else alike: for justice attributes different things to persons differing from each other in their character, according to their respective merits. But if this is admitted to be true, complexion, or height, or any such advantage will be a claim for a greater share of the public rights. But that this is evidently absurd is clear from other arts and sciences; for with respect to musicians who play on the flute together, the best flute is not given to him who is of the best family, for he will play never the better for that, but the best instrument ought to be given to him who is the best artist.

If what is now said does not make this clear, we will explain it still further: if there should be any one, a very excellent player on the flute, but very deficient in family and beauty, though each of them are more valuable endowments than a skill in music, and excel this art in a higher degree than that player excels others, yet the best flutes ought to be given to him; for the superiority in beauty and fortune should have a reference to the business in hand; but these have none. Moreover, according to this reasoning, every possible excellence might come in comparison with every other; for if bodily strength might dispute the point with riches or liberty, even any bodily strength might do it; so that if one person excelled in size more than another did in virtue, and his size was to qualify him to take place of the other's virtue, everything must then admit of a comparison with each other; for if such a size is greater than virtue by so much, it is evident another must be equal to it: but, since this is impossible, it is plain that it would be contrary to common sense to dispute a right to any office in the state from every superiority whatsoever: for if one person is slow and the other swift, neither is the one better qualified nor the other worse on that account, though in the gymnastic races a difference in these particulars would gain the prize; but a pretension to the offices of the state should be founded on a superiority in those qualifications which are useful to it: for which reason those of family, independency, and fortune, with great propriety, contend with each other for them; for these are the fit persons to fill them: for a city can no more consist of all poor men than it can of all slaves But if such persons are requisite, it is evident that those also who are just and valiant are equally so; for without justice and valour no state can be supported, the former being necessary for its existence, the latter for its happiness.

# CHAPTER

# XIII

It seems, then, requisite for the establishment of a state, that all, or at least many of these particulars should be well canvassed and inquired into; and that virtue and education may most justly claim the right of being considered as the necessary means of making the citizens happy, as we have already said. As those who are equal in one particular are not therefore equal in all, and those who are unequal in one particular are not therefore unequal in all, it follows that all those governments which are established upon a principle which supposes they are, are erroneous.

We have already said, that all the members of the community will dispute with each other for the offices of the state; and in some particulars justly, but not so in general; the rich, for instance, because they have the greatest landed property, and the ultimate right to the soil is vested in the community; and also because their fidelity is in general most to be depended on. The freemen and men of family will dispute the point with each other, as nearly on an equality; for these latter have a right to a higher regard as citizens than obscure persons, for honourable descent is everywhere of great esteem: nor is it an improper conclusion, that the descendants of men of worth will be men of worth themselves; for noble birth is the fountain of virtue to men of family: for the same reason also we justly say, that virtue has a right to put in her pretensions. Justice, for instance, is a virtue, and so necessary to society, that all others must yield her the precedence.

Let us now see what the many have to urge on their side against the few; and they may say, that if, when collectively taken, they are compared with them, they are stronger, richer, and better than they are. But should it ever happen that all these should inhabit the same city, I mean the good, the rich, the noble, as well as the many, such as usually make up the community, I ask, will there then be any reason to dispute concerning who shall govern, or will there not? For in every community which we have mentioned there is no dispute where the supreme power should be placed; for as these differ from each other, so do those in whom that is placed; for in one state the rich enjoy it, in others the meritorious, and thus each according to their separate manners. Let us however consider what is to be done when all these happen at the same time to inhabit the same city. If the virtuous should be very few in number, how then shall we act? Shall we prefer the virtuous on account of their abilities, if they are capable of governing the city? Or should they be so many as almost entirely to compose the state?

There is also a doubt concerning the pretensions of all those who claim the honours of government: for those who found them either on fortune or family have nothing which they can justly say in their defence; since it is evident upon their principle, that if any one person can be found richer than all the rest, the right of governing all these will be justly vested in this one person. In the same manner, one man who is of the best family will claim it from those who dispute the point upon family merit: and probably in an aristocracy the same dispute might arise on the score of virtue, if there is one man better than all the other men of worth who are in the same community; it seems just, by the same reasoning, that he should enjoy the supreme power. And upon this principle also, while the many suppose they ought to have the supreme command, as being more powerful than the few, if one or more than one, though a small number should be found stronger than themselves, these ought rather to have it than they.

All these things seem to make it plain, that none of these principles are justly founded on which these persons would establish their right to the supreme power; and that all men whatsoever ought to obey them: for with respect to those who claim it as due to their virtue or their fortune, they might have justly some objection to make; for nothing hinders but that it may sometimes happen, that the many may be better or richer than the few, not as individuals, but in their collective capacity.

As to the doubt which some persons have proposed and objected, we may answer it in this manner; it is this, whether a legislator, who would establish the most perfect system of laws, should calculate them for the use of the better part of the citizens, or the many, in the circumstances we have already mentioned? The rectitude of anything consists in its equality; that therefore which is equally right will be advantageous to the whole state, and to every member of it in common.

Now, in general, a citizen is one who both shares in the government and also in his turn submits to be governed; their condition, it is true, is different in different states: the best is that in which a man is enabled to choose and to persevere in a course of virtue during his whole life, both in his public and private state. But should there be one person, or a very few, eminent for an uncommon degree of virtue, though not enough to make up a civil state, so that the virtue of the many, or their political abilities, should be too inferior to come in comparison with theirs, if more than one; or if but one, with his only; such are not to be considered as part of the city; for it would be doing them injustice to rate them on a level with those who are so far their inferiors in virtue and political abilities, that they appear to them like a god amongst men. From whence it is evident, that a system of laws must be calculated for those who are equal to each other in nature and power. Such men, therefore, are not the object of law; for they are themselves a law: and it would be ridiculous in any one to endeavour to include them in the penalties of a law: for probably they might say what Antisthenes tells us the lions did to the hares when they demanded to be admitted to an equal share with them in the government. And it is on this account that democratic states have established the ostracism; for an equality seems the principal object of their government. For which reason they compel all those who are very eminent for their power, their fortune, their friendships, or any other cause which may give them too great weight in the government, to submit to the ostracism, and leave the city for a stated time; as the fabulous histories relate the Argonauts served Hercules, for they refused to take him with them in the ship Argo on account of his superior valour. For which reason those who hate a tyranny and find fault with the advice which Periander gave to Thrasybulus, must not think there was nothing to be said in its defence; for the story goes, that Periander said nothing to the messenger in answer to the business he was consulted about, but striking off those ears of corn which were higher than the rest, reduced the whole crop to a level; so that the messenger, without knowing the cause of what was done, related the fact to Thrasybulus, who understood by it that he must take off all the principal men in the city. Nor is this serviceable to tyrants only; nor is it tyrants only who do it; for the same thing is practised both in oligarchies and democracies: for the ostracism has in a manner nearly the same power, by restraining and banishing those who are too great; and what is done in one city is done also by those who have the supreme power in separate states; as the Athenians with respect to the Samians, the Chians, and the Lesbians; for when they suddenly acquired the superiority over all Greece, they brought the other states into subjection, contrary to the treaties which subsisted between them. The King of Persia also very often reduces the Medes and Babylonians when they assume upon their former power: and this is a principle which all governments whatsoever keep in their eye; even those which are best administered, as well as those which are not, do it; these for the sake of private utility, the others for the public good.

The same thing is to be perceived in the other arts and sciences; for a painter would not represent an animal with a foot disproportionally large, though he had drawn it remarkably beautiful; nor would the shipwright make the prow or any other part of the vessel larger than it ought to be; nor will the master of the band permit any who sings louder and better than the rest to sing in concert with them. There is therefore no reason that a monarch should not act in agreement with free states, to support his own power, if they do the same thing for the benefit of their respective communities; upon which account when there is any acknowledged difference in the power of the citizens, the reason upon which the ostracism is founded will be politically just; but it is better for the legislator so to establish his state at the beginning as not to want this remedy: but if in course of time such an inconvenience should arise, to endeavour to amend it by some such correction. Not that this was the use it was put to: for many did not regard the benefit of their respective communities, but made the ostracism a weapon in the hand of sedition.

It is evident, then, that in corrupt governments it is partly just and useful to the individual, though probably it is as clear that it is not entirely just: for in a well-governed state there may be great doubts about the use of it, not on account of the pre-eminence which one may have in strength, riches, or connection: but when the pre-eminence is virtue, what then is to be done? For it seems not right to turn out and banish such a one; neither does it seem right to govern him, for that would be like desiring to share the power with Jupiter and to govern him: nothing then remains but what indeed seems natural, and that is for all persons quietly to submit to the government of those who are thus eminently virtuous, and let them be perpetually kings in the separate states.

# CHAPTER

# XIV

What has been now said, it seems proper to change our subject and to inquire into the nature of monarchies; for we have already admitted them to be one of those species of government which are properly founded. And here let us consider whether a kingly government is proper for a city or a country whose principal object is the happiness of the inhabitants, or rather some other. But let us first determine whether this is of one kind only, or more; and it is easy to know that it consists of many different species, and that the forms of government are not the same in all: for at Sparta the kingly power seems chiefly regulated by the laws; for it is not supreme in all circumstances; but when the king quits the territories of the state he is their general in war; and all religious affairs are entrusted to him: indeed the kingly power with them is chiefly that of a general who cannot be called to an account for his conduct, and whose command is for life: for he has not the power of life and death, except as a general; as they frequently had in their expeditions by martial law, which we learn from Homer; for when Agamemnon is affronted in council, he restrains his resentment, but when he is in the field and armed with this power, he tells the Greeks:

"Whoe'er I know shall shun th' impending fight, To dogs and vultures soon shall be a prey; For death is mine . . ."

This, then, is one species of monarchical government in which the kingly power is in a general for life; and is sometimes hereditary, sometimes elective: besides, there is also another, which is to be met with among some of the barbarians, in which the kings are invested with powers nearly equal to a tyranny, yet are, in some respects, bound by the laws and the customs of their country; for as the barbarians are by nature more prone to slavery than the Greeks, and those in Asia more than those in Europe, they endure without murmuring a despotic government; for this reason their governments are tyrannies; but yet not liable to be overthrown, as being customary and according to law. Their guards also are such as are used in a kingly government, not a despotic one; for the guards of their kings are his citizens, but a tyrant's are foreigners. The one commands, in the manner the law directs, those who willingly obey; the other, arbitrarily, those who consent not. The one, therefore, is guarded by the citizens, the other against them.

These, then, are the two different sorts of these monarchies, and another is that which in ancient Greece they called *aesumnetes*; which is nothing more than an elective tyranny; and its difference from that which is to be found amongst the barbarians consists not in its not being according to law, but only in its not being according to the ancient customs of the country. Some persons possessed this power for life, others only for a particular time or particular purpose, as the people of Mitylene elected Pittacus to oppose the exiles, who were headed by Antimenides and Alcaeus the poet, as we learn from a poem of his; for he upbraids the Mitylenians for having chosen Pittacus for their tyrant, and with one voice extolling him to the skies who was the ruin of a rash and devoted people. These sorts of government then are, and ever were, despotic, on account of their being tyrannies; but inasmuch as they are elective, and over a free people, they are also kingly.

A fourth species of kingly government is that which was in use in the heroic times, when a free people submitted to a kingly government, according to the laws and customs of their country. For those who were at first of benefit to mankind, either in arts or arms, or by collecting them into civil society, or procuring them an establishment, became the kings of a willing people, and established an hereditary monarchy. They were particularly their generals in war, and presided over their sacrifices, excepting such only as belonged to the priests: they were also the supreme judges over the people; and in this case some of them took an oath, others did not; they did, the form of swearing was by their sceptre held out.

In ancient times the power of the kings extended to everything whatsoever, both civil, domestic, and foreign; but in after-times they relinquished some of their privileges, and others the people assumed, so that, in some states, they left their kings only the right of presiding over the sacrifices; and even those whom it were worth while to call by that name had only the right of being commander-in-chief in their foreign wars.

These, then, are the four sorts of kingdoms: the first is that of the heroic times; which was a government over a free people, with its rights in some particulars marked out; for the king was their general, their judge, and their high priest. The second, that of the barbarians; which is an hereditary despotic government regulated by laws: the third is that which they call aesumnetic, which is an elective tyranny. The fourth is the Lacedaemonian; and this, in few words, is nothing more than an hereditary generalship: and in these particulars they differ from each other. There is a fifth species of kingly government, which is when one person has a supreme power over all things whatsoever, in the manner that every state and every city has over those things which belong to the public: for as the master of a family is king in his own house, so such a king is master of a family in his own city or state.

# CHAPTER

## XV

**B**ut the different sorts of kingly governments may, if I may so say, be reduced to two; which we will consider more particularly. The last spoken of, and the Lacedaemonian, for the chief of the others are placed between these, which are as it were at the extremities, they having less power than an absolute government, and yet more than the Lacedaemonians; so that the whole matter in question may be reduced to these two points; the one is, whether it is advantageous to the citizens to have the office of general continue in one person for life, and whether it should be confined to any particular families or whether every one should be eligible: the other, whether it is advantageous for one person to have the supreme power over everything or not. But to enter into the particulars concerning the office of a Lacedaemonian general would be rather to frame laws for a state than to consider the nature and utility of its constitution, since we know that the appointing of a general is what is done in every state. Passing over this question then, we will proceed to consider the other part of their government, which is the polity of the state; and this it will be necessary to examine particularly into, and to go through such questions as may arise.

Now the first thing which presents itself to our consideration is this, whether it is best to be governed by a good man, or by good laws? Those who prefer a kingly government think that laws can only speak a general language, but cannot adapt themselves to particular circumstances; for which reason it is absurd in any science to follow written rule; and even in Egypt the physician was allowed to alter the mode of cure which the law prescribed to him, after the fourth day; but if he did it sooner it was at his own peril: from whence it is evident, on the very same account, that a government of written laws is not the best; and yet general reasoning is necessary to all those who are to govern, and it will be much more perfect in those who are entirely free from passions than in those to whom they are natural. But now this is a quality which laws possess; while the other is natural to the human soul. But some one will say in answer to this, that man will be a better judge of particulars. It will be necessary, then, for a king to be a lawgiver, and that his laws should be published, but that those should have no authority which are absurd, as those which are not, should. But whether is it better for the community that those things which cannot possibly come under the cognisance of the law either at all or properly should be under the government of every worthy citizen, as the present method is, when the public community, in their general assemblies, act as judges and counsellors, where all their determinations are upon particular cases, for one individual, be he who he will, will be found, upon comparison, inferior to a whole people taken collectively: but this is what a city is, as a public entertainment is better than one man's portion: for this reason the multitude judge of many things better than any one single person. They are also less liable to corruption from their numbers, as water is from its quantity: besides, the judgment of an individual must necessarily be perverted if he is overcome by anger or any other passion; but it would be hard indeed if the whole community should be misled by anger. Moreover, let the people be free, and they will do nothing but in conformity to the law, except only in those cases which the law cannot speak to. But though what I am going to propose may not easily be met with, yet if the majority of the state should happen to be good men, should they prefer one uncorrupt governor or many equally good, is it not evident that they should choose the many? But there may be divisions among these which cannot happen when there is but one. In answer to this it may be replied that all their souls will be as much animated with virtue as this one man's.

If then a government of many, and all of them good men, compose an aristocracy, and the government of one a kingly power, it is evident that the people should rather choose the first than the last; and this whether the state is powerful or not, if many such persons so alike can be met with: and for this reason probable it was, that the first governments were generally monarchies; because it was difficult to find a number of persons eminently virtuous, more particularly as the world was then divided into small communities; besides, kings were appointed in return for the benefits they had conferred on mankind; but such actions are peculiar to good men: but when many persons equal in virtue appeared at the time, they brooked not a superiority, but sought after an equality and established a free state; but after this, when they degenerated, they made a property of the public; which probably gave rise to oligarchies; for they made wealth meritorious, and the honours of government were reserved for the rich: and these afterwards turned to tyrannies and these in their turn gave rise to democracies; for the power of the tyrants continually decreasing, on account of their rapacious avarice, the people grew powerful enough to frame and establish democracies: and as cities after that happened to increase, probably it was not easy for them to be under any other government than a democracy. But if any person prefers a kingly government in a state, what is to be done with the king's children? Is the family also to reign? But should they have such children as some persons usually have, it will be very detrimental. It may be said, that then the king who has it in his power will never permit such children to succeed to his kingdom. But it is not easy to trust to that; for it is very hard and requires greater virtue than is to be met with in human nature. There is also a doubt concerning the power with which a king should be entrusted: whether he should be allowed force sufficient to compel those who do not choose to be obedient to the laws, and how he is to support his government? For if he is to govern according to law and do nothing of his own will which is contrary thereunto, at the same time it will be necessary to protect that power with which he guards the law, This matter however may not be very difficult to determine; for he ought to have a proper power, and such a one is that which will be sufficient to make the king superior to any one person or even a large part of the community, but inferior to the whole, as the ancients always appointed guards for that person whom they created aesumnetes or tyrant; and some one advised the Syracusians, when Dionysius asked for guards, to allow him such.

# CHAPTER

## XVI

We will next consider the absolute monarch that we have just mentioned, who does everything according to his own will: for a king governing under the direction of laws which he is obliged to follow does not of himself create any particular species of government, as we have already said: for in every state whatsoever, either aristocracy or democracy, it is easy to appoint a general for life; and there are many who entrust the administration of affairs to one person only; such is the government at Dyrrachium, and nearly the same at Opus. As for an absolute monarchy as it is called, that is to say, when the whole state is wholly subject to the will of one person, namely the king, it seems to many that it is unnatural that one man should have the entire rule over his fellow citizens when the state consists of equals: for nature requires that the same right and the same rank should necessarily take place amongst all those who are equal by nature: for as it would be hurtful to the body for those who are of different constitutions to observe the same regimen, either of diet or clothing, so is it with respect to the honours of the state as hurtful, that those who are equal in merit should be unequal in rank; for which reason it is as much a man's duty to submit to command as to assume it, and this also by rotation; for this is law, for order is law; and it is more proper that law should govern than any one of the citizens: upon the same principle, if it is advantageous to place the supreme power in some particular persons, they should be appointed to be only guardians, and the servants of the laws, for the supreme power must be placed somewhere; but they say, that it is unjust that where all are equal one person should continually enjoy it. But it seems unlikely that man should be able to adjust that which the law cannot determine; it may be replied, that the law having laid down the best rules possible, leaves the adjustment and application of particulars to the discretion of the magistrate; besides, it allows anything to be altered which experience proves may be better established. Moreover, he who would place the supreme power in mind, would place it in God and the laws; but he who entrusts man with it, gives it to a wild beast, for such his appetites sometimes make him; for passion influences those who are in power, even the very best of men: for which reason law is reason without desire.

The instance taken from the arts seems fallacious: wherein it is said to be wrong for a sick person to apply for a remedy to books, but that it would be far more eligible to employ those who are skilful in physic; for these do nothing contrary to reason from motives of friendship but earn their money by curing the sick, whereas those who have the management of public affairs do many things through hatred or favour. And, as a proof of what we have advanced, it may be observed, that whenever a sick person suspects that his physician has been persuaded by his enemies to be guilty of any foul practice to him in his profession, he then rather chooses to apply to books for his cure: and not only this but even physicians themselves when they are ill call in other physicians: and those who teach others the gymnastic exercises, exercise with those of the same profession, as being incapable from self-partiality to form a proper judgment of what concerns themselves. From whence it is evident, that those who seek for what is just, seek for a mean; now law is a mean. Moreover; the moral law is far superior and conversant with far superior objects than the written law; for the supreme magistrate is safer to be trusted to than the one, though he is inferior to the other. But as it is impossible that one person should have an eye to everything himself, it will be necessary that the supreme magistrate should employ several subordinate ones under him; why then should not this be done at first, instead of appointing one person in this manner? Besides, if, according to what has been already said, the man of worth is on that account fit to govern, two men of worth are certainly better than one: as, for instance, in Homer, "Let two together go:" and also Agamemnon's wish; "Were ten such faithful counsel mine!" Not but that there are even now some particular magistrates invested with supreme power to decide, as judges, those things which the law cannot, as being one of those cases which comes not properly under its jurisdiction; for of those which can there is no doubt: since then laws comprehend some things, but not all, it is necessary to enquire and consider which of the two is preferable, that the best man or the best law should govern; for to reduce every subject which can come under the deliberation of man into a law is impossible.

No one then denies, that it is necessary that there should be some person to decide those cases which cannot come under the cognisance of a written law: but we say, that it is better to have many than one; for though every one who decides according to the principles of the law decides justly; yet surely it seems absurd to suppose, that one person can see better with two eyes, and hear better with two ears, or do better with two hands and two feet, than many can do with many: for we see that absolute monarchs now furnish themselves with many eyes and ears and hands and feet; for they entrust those who are friends to them and their government with part of their power; for if they are not friends to the monarch, they will not do what he chooses; but if they are friends to him, they are friends also to his government: but a friend is an equal and like his friend: if then he thinks that such should govern, he thinks that his equal also should govern. These are nearly the objections which are usually made to a kingly power.

# CHAPTER

# XVII

Probably what we have said may be true of some persons, but not of others; for some men are by nature formed to be under the government of a master; others, of a king; others, to be the citizens of a free state, just and useful; but a tyranny is not according to nature, nor the other perverted forms of government; for they are contrary to it. But it is evident from what has been said, that among equals it is neither advantageous nor right that one person should be lord over all where there are no established laws, but his will is the law; or where there are; nor is it right that one who is good should have it over those who are good; or one who is not good over those who are not good; nor one who is superior to the rest in worth, except in a particular manner, which shall be described, though indeed it has been already mentioned. But let us next determine what people are best qualified for a kingly government, what for an aristocratic, and what for a democratic. And, first, for a kingly; and it should be those who are accustomed by nature to submit the civil government of themselves to a family eminent for virtue: for an aristocracy, those who are naturally framed to bear the rule of free men, whose superior virtue makes them worthy of the management of others: for a free state, a war-like people, formed by nature both to govern and be governed by laws which admit the poorest citizen to share the honours of the commonwealth according to his worth. But whenever a whole family or any one of another shall happen so far to excel in virtue as to exceed all other persons in the community, then it is right that the kingly power should be in them, or if it is an individual who does so, that he should be king and lord of all; for this, as we have just mentioned, is not only correspondent to that principle of right which all founders of all states, whether aristocracies, oligarchies, or democracies, have a regard to (for in placing the supreme power they all think it right to fix it to excellence, though not the same); but it is also agreeable to what has been already said; as it would not be right to kill, or banish, or ostracise such a one for his superior merit. Nor would it be proper to let him have the supreme power only in turn; for it is contrary to nature that what is highest should ever be lowest: but this would be the case should such a one ever be governed by others. So that there can nothing else be done but to submit, and permit him continually to enjoy the supreme power. And thus much with respect to kingly power in different states, and whether it is or is not advantageous to them, and to what, and in what manner.

# CHAPTER

## XVIII

Since then we have said that there are three sorts of regular governments, and of these the best must necessarily be that which is administered by the best men (and this must be that which happens to have one man, or one family, or a number of persons excelling all the rest in virtue, who are able to govern and be governed in such a manner as will make life most agreeable, and we have already shown that the virtue of a good man and of a citizen in the most perfect government will be the same), it is evident, that in the same manner, and for those very qualities which would procure a man the character of good, any one would say, that the government of a state was a well-established aristocracy or kingdom; so that it will be found to be education and morals that are almost the whole which go to make a good man, and the same qualities will make a good citizen or good king.

These particulars being treated of, we will now proceed to consider what sort of government is best, how it naturally arises, and how it is established; for it is necessary to make a proper inquiry concerning this.

# BOOK IV

## CHAPTER

### I

In every art and science which is not conversant in parts but in some one genus in which it is complete, it is the business of that art alone to determine what is fitted to its particular genus; as what particular exercise is fitted to a certain particular body, and suits it best: for that body which is formed by nature the most perfect and superior to others necessarily requires the best exercise-and also of what one kind that must be which will suit the generality; and this is the business of the gymnastic arts: and although any one should not desire to acquire an exact knowledge and skill in these exercises, yet it is not, on that account, the less necessary that he who professes to be a master and instruct the youth in them should be perfect therein: and we see that this is what equally befalls the healing, shipbuilding, cloth-making, and indeed all other arts; so that it evidently belongs to the same art to find out what kind of government is best, and would of all others be most correspondent to our wish, while it received no molestation from without: and what particular species of it is adapted to particular persons; for there are many who probably are incapable of enjoying the best form: so that the legislator, and he who is truly a politician, ought to be acquainted not only with that which is most perfect imaginable, but also that which is the best suited to any given circumstances. There is, moreover, a third sort, an imaginary one, and he ought, if such a one should be presented to his consideration, to be able to discern what sort of one it would be at the beginning; and, when once established, what would be the proper means to preserve it a long time. I mean, for instance, if a state should happen not to have the best form of government, or be deficient in what was necessary, or not receive every advantage possible, but something less. And, besides all this, it is necessary to know what sort of government is best fitting for all cities: for most of those writers who have treated this subject, however speciously they may handle other parts of it, have failed in describing the practical parts: for it is not enough to be able to perceive what is best without it is what can be put in practice. It should also be simple, and easy for all to attain to. But some seek only the most subtile forms of government. Others again, choosing rather to treat of what is common, censure those under which they live, and extol the excellence of a particular state, as the Lacedaemonian, or some other: but every legislator ought to establish such a form of government as from the present state and disposition of the people who are to receive it they will most readily submit to and persuade the community to partake of: for it is not a business of less trouble to correct the mistakes of an established government than to form a new one; as it is as difficult to recover what we have forgot as to learn anything afresh. He, therefore, who aspires to the character of a legislator, ought, besides all we have already said, to be able to correct the mistakes of a government already established, as we have before mentioned. But this is impossible to be done by him who does not know how many different forms of government there are: some persons think that there is only one species both of democracy and oligarchy; but this is not true: so that every one should be acquainted with the difference of these governments, how great they are, and whence they arise; and should have equal knowledge to perceive what laws are best, and what are most suitable to each particular government:

for all laws are, and ought to be, framed agreeable to the state that is to be governed by them, and not the state to the laws: for government is a certain ordering in a state which particularly respects the magistrates in what manner they shall be regulated, and where the supreme power shall be placed; and what shall be the final object which each community shall have in view; but the laws are something different from what regulates and expresses the form of the constitution—it is their office to direct the conduct of the magistrate in the execution of his office and the punishment of offenders. From whence it is evident, that the founders of laws should attend both to the number and the different sorts of government; for it is impossible that the same laws should be calculated for all sorts of oligarchies and all sorts of democracies, for of both these governments there are many species, not one only.

# CHAPTER

# II

Since, then, according to our first method in treating of the different forms of government, we have divided those which are regular into three sorts, the kingly, the aristocratical, the free states, and shown the three excesses which these are liable to: the kingly, of becoming tyrannical; the aristocratical, oligarchical; and the free state, democratical: and as we have already treated of the aristocratical and kingly; for to enter into an inquiry what sort of government is best is the same thing as to treat of these two expressly; for each of them desires to be established upon the principles of virtue: and as, moreover, we have already determined wherein a kingly power and an aristocracy differ from each other, and when a state may be said to be governed by a king, it now remains that we examine into a free state, and also these other governments, an oligarchy, a democracy, and a tyranny; and it is evident of these three excesses which must be the worst of all, and which next to it; for, of course, the excesses of the best and most holy must be the worst; for it must necessarily happen either that the name of king only will remain, or else that the king will assume more power than belongs to him, from whence tyranny will arise, the worst excess imaginable, a government the most contrary possible to a free state. The excess next hurtful is an oligarchy; for an aristocracy differs much from this sort of government: that which is least so is a democracy. This subject has been already treated of by one of those writers who have gone before me, though his sentiments are not the same as mine: for he thought, that of all excellent constitutions, as a good oligarchy or the like, a democracy was the worst, but of all bad ones, the best.

Now I affirm, that all these states have, without exception, fallen into excess; and also that he should not have said that one oligarchy was better than another, but that it was not quite so bad. But this question we shall not enter into at present. We shall first inquire how many different sorts of free states there are; since there are many species of democracies and oligarchies; and which of them is the most comprehensive, and most desirable after the best form of government; or if there is any other like an aristocracy, well established; and also which of these is best adapted to most cities, and which of them is preferable for particular persons: for, probably, some may suit better with an oligarchy than a democracy, and others better with a democracy than an oligarchy; and afterwards in what manner any one ought to proceed who desires to establish either of these states, I mean every species of democracy, and also of oligarchy. And to conclude, when we shall have briefly gone through everything that is necessary, we will endeavour to point out the sources of corruption, and stability, in government, as well those which are common to all as those which are peculiar to each state, and from what causes they chiefly arise.

# CHAPTER

# III

The reason for there being many different sorts of governments is this, that each state consists of a great number of parts; for, in the first place, we see that all cities are made up of families: and again, of the multitude of these some must be rich, some poor, and others in the middle station; and that, both of the rich and poor, some will be used to arms, others not. We see also, that some of the common people are husbandmen, others attend the market, and others are artificers. There is also a difference between the nobles in their wealth, and the dignity in which they live: for instance, in the number of horses they breed; for this cannot be supported without a large fortune: for which reason, in former times, those cities whose strength consisted in horse became by that means oligarchies; and they used horse in their expeditions against the neighbouring cities; as the Eretrians the Chalcidians, the Magnetians, who lived near the river Meander, and many others in Asia. Moreover, besides the difference of fortune, there is that which arises from family and merit; or, if there are any other distinctions which make part of the city, they have been already mentioned in treating of an aristocracy, for there we considered how many parts each city must necessarily be composed of; and sometimes each of these have a share in the government, sometimes a few, sometimes more.

It is evident then, that there must be many forms of government, differing from each other in their particular constitution: for the parts of which they are composed each differ from the other. For government is the ordering of the magistracies of the state; and these the community share between themselves, either as they can attain them by force, or according to some common equality which there is amongst them, as poverty, wealth, or something which they both partake of. There must therefore necessarily be as many different forms of governments as there are different ranks in the society, arising from the superiority of some over others, and their different situations. And these seem chiefly to be two, as they say, of the winds: namely, the north and the south; and all the others are declinations from these. And thus in politics, there is the government of the many and the government of the few; or a democracy and an oligarchy: for an aristocracy may be considered as a species of oligarchy, as being also a government of the few; and what we call a free state may be considered as a democracy: as in the winds they consider the west as part of the north, and the east as part of the south: and thus it is in music, according to some, who say there are only two species of it, the Doric and the Phrygian, and all other species of composition they call after one of these names; and many people are accustomed to consider the nature of government in the same light; but it is both more convenient and more correspondent to truth to distinguish governments as I have done, into two species: one, of those which are established upon proper principles; of which there may be one or two sorts: the other, which includes all the different excesses of these; so that we may compare the best form of government to the most harmonious piece of music; the oligarchic and despotic to the more violent tunes; and the democratic to the soft and gentle airs.

## CHAPTER

## IV

We ought not to define a democracy as some do, who say simply, that it is a government where the supreme power is lodged in the people; for even in oligarchies the supreme power is in the majority. Nor should they define an oligarchy a government where the supreme power is in the hands of a few: for let us suppose the number of a people to be thirteen hundred, and that of these one thousand were rich, who would not permit the three hundred poor to have any share in the government, although they were free, and their equal in everything else; no one would say, that this government was a democracy. In like manner, if the poor, when few in number, should acquire the power over the rich, though more than themselves, no one would say, that this was an oligarchy; nor this, when the rest who are rich have no share in the administration. We should rather say, that a democracy is when the supreme power is in the hands of the freemen; an oligarchy, when it is in the hands of the rich: it happens indeed that in the one case the many will possess it, in the other the few; because there are many poor and few rich. And if the power of the state was to be distributed according to the size of the citizens, as they say it is in Ethiopia, or according to their beauty, it would be an oligarchy: for the number of those who are large and beautiful is small.

Nor are those things which we have already mentioned alone sufficient to describe these states; for since there are many species both of a democracy and an oligarchy, the matter requires further consideration; as we cannot admit, that if a few persons who are free possess the supreme power over the many who are not free, that this government is a democracy: as in Apollonia, in Ionia, and in Thera: for in each of these cities the honours of the state belong to some few particular families, who first founded the colonies. Nor would the rich, because they are superior in numbers, form a democracy, as formerly at Colophon; for there the majority had large possessions before the Lydian war: but a democracy is a state where the freemen and the poor, being the majority, are invested with the power of the state. An oligarchy is a state where the rich and those of noble families, being few, possess it.

We have now proved that there are various forms of government and have assigned a reason for it; and shall proceed to show that there are even more than these, and what they are, and why; setting out with the principle we have already laid down. We admit that every city consists not of one, but many parts: thus, if we should endeavour to comprehend the different species of animals we should first of all note those parts which every animal must have, as a certain sensorium, and also what is necessary to acquire and retain food, as a mouth and a belly; besides certain parts to enable it to move from place to place. If, then, these are the only parts of an animal and there are differences between them; namely, in their various sorts of stomachs, bellies, and sensoriums: to which we must add their motive powers; the number of the combinations of all these must necessarily make up the different species of animals. For it is not possible that the same kind of animal should have any very great difference in its mouth or ears; so that when all these are collected, who happen to have these things similar in all, they make up a species of animals of which there are as many as there are of these general combinations of necessary parts.

The same thing is true of what are called states; for a city is not made of one but many parts, as has already been often said; one of which is those who supply it with provisions, called husbandmen, another called mechanics, whose employment is in the manual arts, without which the city could not be inhabited; of these some are busied about what is absolutely necessary, others in what contribute to the elegancies and pleasures of life; the third sort are your exchange-men, I mean by these your buyers, sellers, merchants, and victuallers; the fourth are your hired labourers or workmen; the fifth are the men-at-arms, a rank not less useful than the other, without you would have the community slaves to every invader; but what cannot defend itself is unworthy of the name of a city; for a city is self-sufficient, a slave not. So that when Socrates, in Plato's Republic, says that a city is necessarily composed of four sorts of people, he speaks elegantly but not correctly, and these are, according to him, weavers, husbandmen, shoe-makers, and builders; he then adds, as if these were not sufficient, smiths, herdsmen for what cattle are necessary, and also merchants and victuallers, and these are by way of appendix to his first list; as if a city was established for necessity, and not happiness, or as if a shoe-maker and a husbandman were equally useful. He reckons not the military a part before the increase of territory and joining to the borders of the neighbouring powers will make war necessary: and even amongst them who compose his four divisions, or whoever have any connection with each other, it will be necessary to have some one to distribute justice, and determine between man and man. If, then, the mind is a more valuable part of man than the body, every one would wish to have those things more regarded in his city which tend to the advantage of these than common matters, such are war and justice; to which may be added council, which is the business of civil wisdom (nor is it of any consequence whether these different employments are filled by different persons or one, as the same man is oftentimes both a soldier and a husbandman): so that if both the judge and the senator are parts of the city, it necessarily follows that the soldier must be so also. The seventh sort are those who serve the public in expensive employments at their own charge: these are called the rich. The eighth are those who execute the different offices of the state, and without these it could not possibly subsist: it is therefore necessary that there should be some persons capable of governing and filling the places in the city; and this either for life or in rotation: the office of senator, and judge, of which we have already sufficiently treated, are the only ones remaining. If, then, these things are necessary for a state, that it may be happy and just, it follows that the citizens who engage in public affairs should be men of abilities therein. Several persons think, that different employments may be allotted to the same person; as a soldier's, a husbandman's, and an artificer's; as also that others may be both senators and judges.

Besides, every one supposes himself a man of political abilities, and that he is qualified for almost every department in the state. But the same person cannot at once be poor and rich: for which reason the most obvious division of the city is into two parts, the poor and rich; moreover, since for the generality the one are few, the other many, they seem of all the parts of a city most contrary to each other; so that as the one or the other prevail they form different states; and these are the democracy and the oligarchy.

But that there are many different states, and from what causes they arise, has been already mentioned: and that there are also different species both of democracies and oligarchies we will now show. Though this indeed is evident from what we have already said: there are also many different sorts of common people, and also of those who are called gentlemen. Of the different sorts of the first are husbandmen, artificers, exchange-men, who are employed in buying and selling, seamen, of which some are engaged in war, some in traffic, some in carrying goods and passengers from place to place, others in fishing, and of each of these there are often many, as fishermen at Tarentum and Byzantium, masters of galleys at Athens, merchants at AEgina and Chios, those who let ships on freight at Tenedos; we may add to these those who live by their manual labour and have but little property; so that they cannot live without some employ: and also those who are not free-born on both sides, and whatever other sort of common people there may be. As for gentlemen, they are such as are distinguished either by their fortune, their birth, their abilities, or their education, or any such-like excellence which is attributed to them.

The most pure democracy is that which is so called principally from that equality which prevails in it: for this is what the law in that state directs; that the poor shall be in no greater subjection than the rich; nor that the supreme power shall be lodged with either of these, but that both shall share it. For if liberty and equality, as some persons suppose, are chiefly to be found in a democracy, it must be most so by every department of government being alike open to all; but as the people are the majority, and what they vote is law, it follows that such a state must be a democracy. This, then, is one species thereof. Another is, when the magistrates are elected by a certain census; but this should be but small, and every one who was included in it should be eligible, but as soon as he was below it should lose that right. Another sort is, in which every citizen who is not infamous has a share in the government, but where the government is in the laws. Another, where every citizen without exception has this right. Another is like these in other particulars, but there the people govern, and not the law: and this takes place when everything is determined by a majority of votes, and not by a law; which happens when the people are influenced by the demagogues: for where a democracy is governed by stated laws there is no room for them, but men of worth fill the first offices in the state: but where the power is not vested in the laws, there demagogues abound: for there the people rule with kingly power: the whole composing one body; for they are supreme, not as individuals but in their collective capacity.

Homer also discommends the government of many; but whether he means this we are speaking of, or where each person exercises his power separately, is uncertain. When the people possess this power they desire to be altogether absolute, that they may not be under the control of the law, and this is the time when flatterers are held in repute. Nor is there any difference between such a people and monarchs in a tyranny: for their manners are the same, and they both hold a despotic power over better persons than themselves. For their decrees are like the others' edicts; their demagogues like the others' flatterers: but their greatest resemblance consists in the mutual support they give to each other, the flatterer to the tyrant, the demagogue to the people: and to them it is owing that the supreme power is lodged in the votes of the people, and not in the laws; for they bring everything before them, as their influence is owing to their being supreme whose opinions they entirely direct; for these are they whom the multitude obey. Besides, those who accuse the magistrates insist upon it, that the right of determining on their conduct lies in the people, who gladly receive their complaints as the means of destroying all their offices.

Any one, therefore, may with great justice blame such a government as being a democracy, and not a free state; for where the government is not in the laws, then there is no free state, for the law ought to be supreme over all things; and particular incidents which arise should be determined by the magistrates or the state. If, therefore, a democracy is to be reckoned a free state, it is evident that any such establishment which centres all power in the votes of the people cannot, properly speaking, be a democracy: for their decrees cannot be general in their extent. Thus, then, we may describe the several species of democracies.

# CHAPTER

## V

Of the different species of oligarchies one is, when the right to the offices is regulated by a certain census; so that the poor, although the majority, have no share in it; while all those who are included therein take part in the management of public affairs. Another sort is, when the magistrates are men of very small fortune, who upon any vacancy do themselves fill it up: and if they do this out of the community at large, the state approaches to an aristocracy; if out of any particular class of people, it will be an oligarchy. Another sort of oligarchy is, when the power is an hereditary nobility. The fourth is, when the power is in the same hands as the other, but not under the control of law; and this sort of oligarchy exactly corresponds to a tyranny in monarchies, and to that particular species of democracies which I last mentioned in treating of that state: this has the particular name of a dynasty. These are the different sorts of oligarchies and democracies.

It should also be known, that it often happens that a free state, where the supreme power is in the laws, may not be democratic, and yet in consequence of the established manners and customs of the people, may be governed as if it was; so, on the other hand, where the laws may countenance a more democratic form of government, these may make the state inclining to an oligarchy; and this chiefly happens when there has been any alteration in the government; for the people do not easily change, but love their own ancient customs; and it is by small degrees only that one thing takes place of another; so that the ancient laws will remain, while the power will be in the hands of those who have brought about a revolution in the state.

# CHAPTER

# VI

It is evident from what has been said, that there are as many different sorts of democracies and oligarchies as I have reckoned up: for, of necessity, either all ranks of the people which I have enumerated must have a share in the government, or some only, and others not; for when the husbandmen, and those only who possess moderate fortunes, have the supreme power, they will govern according to law; for as they must get their livings by their employs, they have but little leisure for public business: they will therefore establish proper laws, and never call public assemblies but when there is a necessity for them; and they will readily let every one partake with them in the administration of public affairs as soon as they possess that fortune which the law requires for their qualification: every one, therefore, who is qualified will have his share in the government: for to exclude any would be to make the government an oligarchy, and for all to have leisure to attend without they had a subsistence would be impossible: for these reasons, therefore, this government is a species of democracy. Another species is distinguished by the mode of electing their magistrates, in which every one is eligible, to whose birth there are no objections, provided he is supposed to have leisure to attend: for which reason in such a democracy the supreme power will be vested in the laws, as there will be nothing paid to those who go to the public assemblies. A third species is where every freeman has a right to a share in the government, which he will not accept for the cause already assigned; for which reason here also the supreme power will be in the law. The fourth species of democracy, the last which was established in order of time, arose when cities were greatly enlarged to what they were at first, and when the public revenue became something considerable; for then the populace, on account of their numbers, were admitted to share in the management of public affairs, for then even the poorest people were at leisure to attend to them, as they received wages for so doing; nay, they were more so than others, as they were not hindered by having anything of their own to mind, as the rich had; for which reason these last very often did not frequent the public assemblies and the courts of justice: thus the supreme power was lodged in the poor, and not in the laws. These are the different sorts of democracies, and such are the causes which necessarily gave birth to them.

The first species of oligarchy is, when the generality of the state are men of moderate and not too large property; for this gives them leisure for the management of public affairs: and, as they are a numerous body, it necessarily follows that the supreme power must be in the laws, and not in men; for as they are far removed from a monarchical government, and have not sufficient fortune to neglect their private affairs, while they are too many to be supported by the public, they will of course determine to be governed by the laws, and not by each other. But if the men of property in the state are but few, and their property is large, then an oligarchy of the second sort will take place; for those who have most power will think that they have a right to lord it over the others; and, to accomplish this, they will associate to themselves some who have an inclination for public affairs, and as they are not powerful enough to govern without law, they will make a law for that purpose. And if those few who have large fortunes should acquire still greater power, the oligarchy will then alter into one of the third sort; for they will get all the offices of the state into their own hands by a law which directs the son to succeed upon the death of his father; and, after that, when, by means of their increasing wealth and powerful connections, they extend still further their oppression, a monarchical dynasty will directly succeed wherein men will be supreme, and not the law; and this is the fourth species of an oligarchy correspondent to the last-mentioned class of democracies.

# CHAPTER

# VII

There are besides two other states, a democracy and an oligarchy, one of which all speak of, and it is always esteemed a species of the four sorts; and thus they reckon them up; a monarchy, an oligarchy, a democracy, and this fourth which they call an aristocracy. There is also a fifth, which bears a name that is also common to the other four, namely, a state: but as this is seldom to be met with, it has escaped those who have endeavoured to enumerate the different sorts of governments, which they fix at four only, as does Plato in his Republic.

An aristocracy, of which I have already treated in the first book, is rightly called so; for a state governed by the best men, upon the most virtuous principles, and not upon any hypothesis, which even good men may propose, has alone a right to be called an aristocracy, for it is there only that a man is at once a good man and a good citizen; while in other states men are good only relative to those states. Moreover, there are some other states which are called by the same name, that differ both from oligarchies and free states, wherein not only the rich but also the virtuous have a share in the administration; and have therefore acquired the name of aristocracies; for in those governments wherein virtue is not their common care, there are still men of worth and approved goodness. Whatever state, then, like the Carthaginians, favours the rich, the virtuous, and the citizens at large, is a sort of aristocracy: when only the two latter are held in esteem, as at Lacedaemon, and the state is jointly composed of these, it is a virtuous democracy. These are the two species of aristocracies after the first, which is the best of all governments. There is also a third, which is, whenever a free state inclines to the dominion of a few.

# CHAPTER

## VIII

It now remains for us to treat of that government which is particularly called a free state, and also of a tyranny; and the reason for my choosing to place that free state here is, because this, as well as those aristocracies already mentioned, although they do not seem excesses, yet, to speak true, they have all departed from what a perfect government is. Nay, they are deviations both of them equally from other forms, as I said at the beginning. It is proper to mention a tyranny the last of all governments, for it is of all others the least like one: but as my intention is to treat of all governments in general, for this reason that also, as I have said, will be taken into consideration in its proper place.

I shall now inquire into a free state and show what it is; and we shall the better understand its positive nature as we have already described an oligarchy and a democracy; for a free state is indeed nothing more than a mixture of them, and it has been usual to call those which incline most to a democracy, a free state; those which incline most to an oligarchy, an aristocracy, because those who are rich are generally men of family and education; besides, they enjoy those things which others are often guilty of crimes to procure: for which reason they are regarded as men of worth and honour and note.

Since, then, it is the genius of an aristocracy to allot the larger part of the government to the best citizens, they therefore say, that an oligarchy is chiefly composed of those men who are worthy and honourable: now it seems impossible that where the government is in the hands of the good, there the laws should not be good, but bad; or, on the contrary, that where the government is in the hands of the bad, there the laws should be good; nor is a government well constituted because the laws are, without at the same time care is taken that they are observed; for to enforce obedience to the laws which it makes is one proof of a good constitution in the state-another is, to have laws well calculated for those who are to abide by them; for if they are improper they must be obeyed: and this may be done two ways, either by their being the best relative to the particular state, or the best absolutely. An aristocracy seems most likely to confer the honours of the state on the virtuous; for virtue is the object of an aristocracy, riches of an oligarchy, and liberty of a democracy; for what is approved of by the majority will prevail in all or in each of these three different states; and that which seems good to most of those who compose the community will prevail: for what is called a state prevails in many communities, which aim at a mixture of rich and poor, riches and liberty: as for the rich, they are usually supposed to take the place of the worthy and honourable. As there are three things which claim an equal rank in the state, freedom, riches, and virtue (for as for the fourth, rank, it is an attendant on two of the others, for virtue and riches are the origin of family), it is evident, that the conjuncture of the rich and the poor make up a free state; but that all three tend to an aristocracy more than any other, except that which is truly so, which holds the first rank.

We have already seen that there are governments different from a monarchy, a democracy, and an oligarchy; and what they are, and wherein they differ from each other; and also aristocracies and states properly so called, which are derived from them; and it is evident that these are not much unlike each other.

# CHAPTER

## IX

We shall next proceed to show how that government which is peculiarly called a state arises alongside of democracy and oligarchy, and how it ought to be established; and this will at the same time show what are the proper boundaries of both these governments, for we must mark out wherein they differ from one another, and then from both these compose a state of such parts of each of them as will show from whence they were taken.

There are three different ways in which two states may be blended and joined together; for, in the first place, all those rules may be adopted which the laws of each of them have ordered; as for instance in the judicial department, for in an oligarchy the rich are fined if they do not come to the court as jurymen, but the poor are not paid for their attendance; but in democracies they are, while the rich are not fined for their neglect. Now these things, as being common to both, are fit to be observed in a free state which is composed of both. This, then, is one way in which they may be joined together. In the second place, a medium may be taken between the different methods which each state observes; for instance, in a democracy the right to vote in the public assembly is either confined by no census at all, or limited by a very small one; in an oligarchy none enjoy it but those whose census is high: therefore, as these two practices are contrary to each other, a census between each may be established in such a state. In the third place, different laws of each community may be adopted; as, for instance, as it seems correspondent to the nature of a democracy, that the magistrates should be chosen by lot, but an aristocracy by vote, and in the one state according to a census, but not in the other: let, then, an aristocracy and a free state copy something from each of them; let them follow an oligarchy in choosing their magistrates by vote, but a democracy in not admitting of any census, and thus blend together the different customs of the two governments. But the best proof of a happy mixture of a democracy and an oligarchy is this, when a person may properly call the same state a democracy and an oligarchy. It is evident that those who speak of it in this manner are induced to it because both these governments are there well blended together: and indeed this is common to all mediums, that the extremes of each side should be discerned therein, as at Lacedaemon; for many affirm that it is a democracy from the many particulars in which it follows that form of government; as for instance, in the first place, in the bringing up of their children, for the rich and poor are brought up in the same manner;

and their education is such that the children of the poor may partake of it; and the same rules are observed when they are youths and men, there is no distinction between a rich person and a poor one; and in their public tables the same provision is served to all. The rich also wear only such clothes as the poorest man is able to purchase. Moreover, with respect to two magistracies of the highest rank, one they have a right to elect to, the other to fill; namely, the senate and the ephori. Others consider it as an oligarchy, the principles of which it follows in many things, as in choosing all their officers by vote, and not by lot; in there being but a few who have a right to sit in judgment on capital causes and the like. Indeed, a state which is well composed of two others ought to resemble them both, and neither, Such a state ought to have its means of preservation in itself, and not without; and when I say in itself, I do not mean that it should owe this to the forbearance of their neighbours, for this may happen to a bad government, but to every member of the community's not being willing that there should be the least alteration in their constitution. Such is the method in which a free state or aristocracy ought to be established.

# CHAPTER

# X

It now remains to treat of a tyranny; not that there is much to be said on that subject, but as it makes part of our plan, since we enumerated it amongst our different sorts of governments. In the beginning of this work we inquired into the nature of kingly government, and entered into a particular examination of what was most properly called so, and whether it was advantageous to a state or not, and what it should be, and how established; and we divided a tyranny into two pieces when we were upon this subject, because there is something analogous between this and a kingly government, for they are both of them established by law; for among some of the barbarians they elect a monarch with absolute power, and formerly among the Greeks there were some such, whom they called sesumnetes. Now these differ from each other; for some possess only kingly power regulated by law, and rule those who voluntarily submit to their government; others rule despotically according to their own will. There is a third species of tyranny, most properly so called, which is the very opposite to kingly power; for this is the government of one who rules over his equals and superiors without being accountable for his conduct, and whose object is his own advantage, and not the advantage of those he governs; for which reason he rules by compulsion, for no freemen will ever willingly submit to such a government. These are the different species of tyrannies, their principles, and their causes.

# CHAPTER

## XI

We proceed now to inquire what form of government and what manner of life is best for communities in general, not adapting it to that superior virtue which is above the reach of the vulgar, or that education which every advantage of nature and fortune only can furnish, nor to those imaginary plans which may be formed at pleasure; but to that mode of life which the greater part of mankind can attain to, and that government which most cities may establish: for as to those aristocracies which we have now mentioned, they are either too perfect for a state to support, or one so nearly alike to that state we now going to inquire into, that we shall treat of them both as one.

The opinions which we form upon these subjects must depend upon one common principle: for if what I have said in my treatise on Morals is true, a happy life must arise from an uninterrupted course of virtue; and if virtue consists in a certain medium, the middle life must certainly be the happiest; which medium is attainable by every one. The boundaries of virtue and vice in the state must also necessarily be the same as in a private person; for the form of government is the life of the city. In every city the people are divided into three sorts; the very rich, the very poor, and those who are between them. If this is universally admitted, that the mean is best, it is evident that even in point of fortune mediocrity is to be preferred; for that state is most submissive to reason; for those who are very handsome, or very strong, or very noble, or very rich; or, on the contrary; those who are very poor, or very weak, or very mean, with difficulty obey it; for the one are capricious and greatly flagitious, the other rascally and mean, the crimes of each arising from their different excesses: nor will they go through the different offices of the state; which is detrimental to it: besides, those who excel in strength, in riches, or friends, or the like, neither know how nor are willing to submit to command: and this begins at home when they are boys; for there they are brought up too delicately to be accustomed to obey their preceptors: as for the very poor, their general and excessive want of what the rich enjoy reduces them to a state too mean: so that the one know not how to command, but to be commanded as slaves, the others know not how to submit to any command, nor to command themselves but with despotic power.

A city composed of such men must therefore consist of slaves and masters, not freemen; where one party must hate, and the other despise, where there could be no possibility of friendship or political community: for community supposes affection; for we do not even on the road associate with our enemies. It is also the genius of a city to be composed as much as possible of equals; which will be most so when the inhabitants are in the middle state: from whence it follows, that that city must be best framed which is composed of those whom we say are naturally its proper members. It is men of this station also who will be best assured of safety and protection; for they will neither covet what belongs to others, as the poor do; nor will others covet what is theirs, as the poor do what belongs to the rich; and thus, without plotting against any one, or having any one plot against them, they will live free from danger: for which reason Phocylides wisely wishes for the middle state, as being most productive of happiness. It is plain, then, that the most perfect political community must be amongst those who are in the middle rank, and those states are best instituted wherein these are a larger and more respectable part, if possible, than both the other; or, if that cannot be, at least than either of them separate; so that being thrown into the balance it may prevent either scale from preponderating.

It is therefore the greatest happiness which the citizens can enjoy to possess a moderate and convenient fortune; for when some possess too much, and others nothing at all, the government must either be in the hands of the meanest rabble or else a pure oligarchy; or, from the excesses of both, a tyranny; for this arises from a headstrong democracy or an oligarchy, but very seldom when the members of the community are nearly on an equality with each other. We will assign a reason for this when we come to treat of the alterations which different states are likely to undergo. The middle state is therefore best, as being least liable to those seditions and insurrections which disturb the community; and for the same reason extensive governments are least liable to these inconveniences; for there those in a middle state are very numerous, whereas in small ones it is easy to pass to the two extremes, so as hardly to have any in a medium remaining, but the one half rich, the other poor: and from the same principle it is that democracies are more firmly established and of longer continuance than oligarchies; but even in those when there is a want of a proper number of men of middling fortune, the poor extend their power too far, abuses arise, and the government is soon at an end.

We ought to consider as a proof of what I now advance, that the best lawgivers themselves were those in the middle rank of life, amongst whom was Solon, as is evident from his poems, and Lycurgus, for he was not a king, and Charondas, and indeed most others. What has been said will show us why of so many free states some have changed to democracies, others to oligarchies: for whenever the number of those in the middle state has been too small, those who were the more numerous, whether the rich or the poor, always overpowered them and assumed to themselves the administration of public affairs; from hence arose either a democracy or an oligarchy. Moreover, when in consequence of their disputes and quarrels with each other, either the rich get the better of the poor, or the poor of the rich, neither of them will establish a free state; but, as the record of their victory, one which inclines to their own principles, and form either a democracy or an oligarchy.

Those who made conquests in Greece, having all of them an eye to the respective forms of government in their own cities, established either democracies or oligarchies, not considering what was serviceable to the state, but what was similar to their own; for which reason a government has never been established where the supreme power has been placed amongst those of the middling rank, or very seldom; and, amongst a few, one man only of those who have yet been conquerors has been persuaded to give the preference to this order of men: it is indeed an established custom with the inhabitants of most cities not to desire an equality, but either to aspire to govern, or when they are conquered, to submit.

Thus we have shown what the best state is, and why. It will not be difficult to perceive of the many states which there are, for we have seen that there are various forms both of democracies and oligarchies, to which we should give the first place, to which the second, and in the same manner the next also; and to observe what are the particular excellences and defects of each, after we have first described the best possible; for that must be the best which is nearest to this, that worst which is most distant from the medium, without any one has a particular plan of his own which he judges by. I mean by this, that it may happen, that although one form of government may be better than another, yet there is no reason to prevent another from being preferable thereunto in particular circumstances and for particular purposes.

# CHAPTER

## XII

After what has been said, it follows that we should now show what particular form of government is most suitable for particular persons; first laying this down as a general maxim, that that party which desires to support the actual administration of the state ought always to be superior to that which would alter it. Every city is made up of quality and quantity: by quality I mean liberty, riches, education, and family, and by quantity its relative populousness: now it may happen that quality may exist in one of those parts of which the city is composed, and quantity in another; thus the number of the ignoble may be greater than the number of those of family, the number of the poor than that of the rich; but not so that the quantity of the one shall overbalance the quality of the other; those must be properly adjusted to each other; for where the number of the poor exceeds the proportion we have mentioned, there a democracy will rise up, and if the husbandry should have more power than others, it will be a democracy of husbandmen; and the democracy will be a particular species according to that class of men which may happen to be most numerous: thus, should these be the husbandmen, it will be of these, and the best; if of mechanics and those who hire themselves out, the worst possible: in the same manner it may be of any other set between these two. But when the rich and the noble prevail more by their quality than they are deficient in quantity, there an oligarchy ensues; and this oligarchy may be of different species, according to the nature of the prevailing party. Every legislator in framing his constitution ought to have a particular regard to those in the middle rank of life; and if he intends an oligarchy, these should be the object of his laws; if a democracy, to these they should be entrusted; and whenever their number exceeds that of the two others, or at least one of them, they give stability to the constitution; for there is no fear that the rich and the poor should agree to conspire together against them, for neither of these will choose to serve the other. If any one would choose to fix the administration on the widest basis, he will find none preferable to this; for to rule by turns is what the rich and the poor will not submit to, on account of their hatred to each other. It is, moreover, allowed that an arbitrator is the most proper person for both parties to trust to; now this arbitrator is the middle rank.

Those who would establish aristocratical governments are mistaken not only in giving too much power to the rich, but also in deceiving the common people; for at last, instead of an imaginary good, they must feel a real evil, for the encroachments of the rich are more destructive to the state than those of the poor.

# CHAPTER

# XIII

There are five particulars in which, under fair pretences, the rich craftily endeavour to undermine the rights of the people, these are their public assemblies, their offices of state, their courts of justice, their military power, and their gymnastic exercises. With respect to their public assemblies, in having them open to all, but in fining the rich only, or others very little, for not attending; with respect to offices, in permitting the poor to swear off, but not granting this indulgence to those who are within the census; with respect to their courts of justice, in fining the rich for non-attendance, but the poor not at all, or those a great deal, and these very little, as was done by the laws of Charondas. In some places every citizen who was enrolled had a right to attend the public assemblies and to try causes; which if they did not do, a very heavy fine was laid upon them; that through fear of the fine they might avoid being enrolled, as they were then obliged to do neither the one nor the other. The same spirit of legislation prevailed with respect to their bearing arms and their gymnastic exercises; for the poor are excused if they have no arms, but the rich are fined; the same method takes place if they do not attend their gymnastic exercises, there is no penalty on one, but there is on the other: the consequence of which is, that the fear of this penalty induces the rich to keep the one and attend the other, while the poor do neither. These are the deceitful contrivances of oligarchical legislators.

The contrary prevails in a democracy; for there they make the poor a proper allowance for attending the assemblies and the courts, but give the rich nothing for doing it: whence it is evident, that if any one would properly blend these customs together, they must extend both the pay and the fine to every member of the community, and then every one would share in it, whereas part only now do. The citizens of a free state ought to consist of those only who bear arms: with respect to their census it is not easy to determine exactly what it ought to be, but the rule that should direct upon this subject should be to make it as extensive as possible, so that those who are enrolled in it make up a greater part of the people than those who are not; for those who are poor, although they partake not of the offices of the state, are willing to live quiet, provided that no one disturbs them in their property: but this is not an easy matter; for it may not always happen, that those who are at the head of public affairs are of a humane behaviour. In time of war the poor are accustomed to show no alacrity without they have provisions found them; when they have, then indeed they are willing to fight.

In some governments the power is vested not only in those who bear arms, but also in those who have borne them. Among the Malienses the state was composed of these latter only, for all the officers were soldiers who had served their time. And the first states in Greece which succeeded those where kingly power was established, were governed by the military. First of all the horse, for at that time the strength and excellence of the army depended on the horse, for as to the heavy-armed foot they were useless without proper discipline; but the art of tactics was not known to the ancients, for which reason their strength lay in their horse: but when cities grew larger, and they depended more on their foot, greater numbers partook of the freedom of the city; for which reason what we call republics were formerly called democracies. The ancient governments were properly oligarchies or kingdoms; for on account of the few persons in each state, it would have been impossible to have found a sufficient number of the middle rank; so these being but few, and those used to subordination, they more easily submitted to be governed.

We have now shown why there are many sorts of governments, and others different from those we have treated of: for there are more species of democracies than one, and the like is true of other forms, and what are their differences, and whence they arise; and also of all others which is the best, at least in general; and which is best suited for particular people.

## CHAPTER

## XIV

We will now proceed to make some general reflections upon the governments next in order, and also to consider each of them in particular; beginning with those principles which appertain to each: now there are three things in all states which a careful legislator ought well to consider, which are of great consequence to all, and which properly attended to the state must necessarily be happy; and according to the variation of which the one will differ from the other. The first of these is the public assembly; the second the officers of the state, that is, who they ought to be, and with what power they should be entrusted, and in what manner they should be appointed; the third, the judicial department.

Now it is the proper business of the public assembly to determine concerning war and peace, making or breaking off alliances, to enact laws, to sentence to death, banishment, or confiscation of goods, and to call the magistrates to account for their behaviour when in office.

Now these powers must necessarily be entrusted to the citizens in general, or all of them to some; either to one magistrate or more; or some to one, and some to another, or some to all, but others to some: to entrust all to all is in the spirit of a democracy, for the people aim at equality. There are many methods of delegating these powers to the citizens at large, one of which is to let them execute them by turn, and not altogether, as was done by Tellecles, the Milesian, in his state. In others the supreme council is composed of the different magistrates, and they succeed to the offices of the community by proper divisions of tribes, wards, and other very small proportions, till every one in his turn goes through them: nor does the whole community ever meet together, without it is when new laws are enacted, or some national affair is debated, or to hear what the magistrates have to propose to them. Another method is for the people to meet in a collective body, but only for the purpose of holding the comitia, making laws, determining concerning war or peace, and inquiring into the conduct of their magistrates, while the remaining part of the public business is conducted by the magistrates, who have their separate departments, and are chosen out of the whole community either by vote or ballot. Another method is for the people in general to meet for the choice of the magistrates, and to examine into their conduct; and also to deliberate concerning war and alliances, and to leave other things to the magistrates, whoever happen to be chosen, whose particular employments are such as necessarily require persons well skilled therein. A fourth method is for every person to deliberate upon every subject in public assembly, where the magistrates can determine nothing of themselves, and have only the privilege of giving their opinions first; and this is the method of the most pure democracy, which is analogous to the proceedings in a dynastic oligarchy and a tyrannic monarchy.

These, then, are the methods in which public business is conducted in a democracy. When the power is in the hands of part of the community only, it is an oligarchy and this also admits of different customs; for whenever the officers of the state are chosen out of those who have a moderate fortune, and these from that circumstance are many, and when they depart not from that line which the law has laid down, but carefully follow it, and when all within the census are eligible, certainly it is then an oligarchy, but founded on true principles of government from its moderation. When the people in general do not partake of the deliberative power, but certain persons chosen for that purpose, who govern according to law; this also, like the first, is an oligarchy. When those who have the deliberative power elect each other, and the son succeeds to the father, and when they can supersede the laws, such a government is of necessity a strict oligarchy. When some persons determine on one thing, and others on another, as war and peace, and when all inquire into the conduct of their magistrates, and other things are left to different officers, elected either by vote or lot, then the government is an aristocracy or a free state. When some are chosen by vote and others by lot, and these either from the people in general, or from a certain number elected for that purpose, or if both the votes and the lots are open to all, such a state is partly an aristocracy, partly a free government itself. These are the different methods in which the deliberative power is vested in different states, all of whom follow some regulation here laid down. It is advantageous to a democracy, in the present sense of the word, by which I mean a state wherein the people at large have a supreme power, even over the laws, to hold frequent public assemblies; and it will be best in this particular to imitate the example of oligarchies in their courts of justice; for they fine those who are appointed to try causes if they do not attend, so should they reward the poor for coming to the public assemblies: and their counsels will be best when all advise with each other, the citizens with the nobles, the nobles with the citizens. It is also advisable when the council is to be composed of part of the citizens, to elect, either by vote or lot, an equal number of both ranks. It is also proper, if the common people in the state are very numerous, either not to pay every one for his attendance, but such a number only as will make them equal to the nobles, or to reject many of them by lot.

In an oligarchy they should either call up some of the common people to the council, or else establish a court, as is done in some other states, whom they call pre-advisers or guardians of the laws, whose business should be to propose first what they should afterwards enact. By this means the people would have a place in the administration of public affairs, without having it in their power to occasion any disorder in the government. Moreover, the people may be allowed to have a vote in whatever bill is proposed, but may not themselves propose anything contrary thereto; or they may give their advice, while the power of determining may be with the magistrates only. It is also necessary to follow a contrary practice to what is established in democracies, for the people should be allowed the power of pardoning, but not of condemning, for the cause should be referred back again to the magistrates: whereas the contrary takes place in republics; for the power of pardoning is with the few, but not of condemning, which is always referred to the people at large. And thus we determine concerning the deliberative power in any state, and in whose hands it shall be.

## CHAPTER

## XV

We now proceed to consider the choice of magistrates; for this branch of public business contains many different Parts, as how many there shall be, what shall be their particular office, and with respect to time how long each of them shall continue in place; for some make it six months, others shorter, others for a year, others for a much longer time; or whether they should be perpetual or for a long time, or neither; for the same person may fill the same office several times, or he may not be allowed to enjoy it even twice, but only once: and also with respect to the appointment of magistrates, who are to be eligible, who is to choose them, and in what manner; for in all these particulars we ought properly to distinguish the different ways which may be followed; and then to show which of these is best suited to such and such governments.

Now it is not easy to determine to whom we ought properly to give the name of magistrate, for a government requires many persons in office; but every one of those who is either chosen by vote or lot is not to be reckoned a magistrate. The priests, for instance, in the first place; for these are to be considered as very different from civil magistrates: to these we may add the choregi and heralds; nay, even ambassadors are elected: there are some civil employments which belong to the citizens; and these are either when they are all engaged in one thing, as when as soldiers they obey their general, or when part of them only are, as in governing the women or educating the youth; and also some economic, for they often elect corn-meters: others are servile, and in which, if they are rich, they employ slaves. But indeed they are most properly called magistrates, who are members of the deliberative council, or decide causes, or are in some command, the last more especially, for to command is peculiar to magistrates. But to speak truth, this question is of no great consequence, nor is it the province of the judges to decide between those who dispute about words; it may indeed be an object of speculative inquiry; but to inquire what officers are necessary in a state, and how many, and what, though not most necessary, may yet be advantageous in a well-established government, is a much more useful employment, and this with respect to all states in general, as well as to small cities.

In extensive governments it is proper to allot one employment to one person, as there are many to serve the public in so numerous a society, where some may be passed over for a long time, and others never be in office but once; and indeed everything is better done which has the whole attention of one person, than when that attention is divided amongst many; but in small states it is necessary that a few of the citizens should execute many employments; for their numbers are so small it will not be convenient to have many of them in office at the same time; for where shall we find others to succeed them in turn? Small states will sometimes want the same magistrates and the same laws as large ones; but the one will not want to employ them so often as the other; so that different charges may be intrusted to the same person without any inconvenience, for they will not interfere with each other, and for want of sufficient members in the community it will be necessary. If we could tell how many magistrates are necessary in every city, and how many, though not necessary, it is yet proper to have, we could then the better know how many different offices one might assign to one magistrate. It is also necessary to know what tribunals in different places should have different things under their jurisdiction, and also what things should always come under the cognisance of the same magistrate; as, for instance, decency of manners, shall the clerk of the market take cognisance of that if the cause arises in the market, and another magistrate in another place, or the same magistrate everywhere: or shall there be a distinction made of the fact, or the parties? As, for instance, in decency of manners, shall it be one cause when it relates to a man, another when it relates to a woman?

In different states shall the magistrates be different or the same? I mean, whether in a democracy, an oligarchy, an aristocracy, and a monarchy, the same persons shall have the same power? Or shall it vary according to the different formation of the government? As in an aristocracy the offices of the state are allotted to those who are well educated; in an oligarchy to those who are rich; in a democracy to the freemen? Or shall the magistrates differ as the communities differ? For it may happen that the very same may be sometimes proper, sometimes otherwise: in this state it may be necessary that the magistrate have great powers, in that but small. There are also certain magistrates peculiar to certain states—as the pre-advisers are not proper in a democracy, but a senate is; for one such order is necessary, whose business shall be to consider beforehand and prepare those bills which shall be brought before the people that they may have leisure to attend to their own affairs; and when these are few in number the state inclines to an oligarchy. The pre-advisers indeed must always be few for they are peculiar to an oligarchy: and where there are both these offices in the same state, the pre-adviser's is superior to the senator's, the one having only a democratical power, the other an oligarchical: and indeed the power of the senate is lost in those democracies, in which the people, meeting in one public assembly, take all the business into their own hands; and this is likely to happen either when the community in general are in easy circumstances, or when they are paid for their attendance; for they are then at leisure often to meet together and determine everything for themselves. A magistrate whose business is to control the manners of the boys, or women, or who takes any department similar to this, is to be found in an aristocracy, not in a democracy; for who can forbid the wives of the poor from appearing in public? Neither is such a one to be met with in an oligarchy; for the women there are too delicate to bear control. And thus much for this subject. Let us endeavour to treat at large of the establishment of magistrates, beginning from first principles. Now, they differ from each other in three ways, from which, blended together, all the varieties which can be imagined arise. The first of these differences is in those who appoint the magistrates, the second consists in those who are appointed, the third in the mode of appointment; and each of these three differ in three manners; for either all the citizens may appoint collectively, or some out of their whole body, or some out of a particular order in it, according to fortune, family, or virtue, or some other rule (as at Megara, where the right of election was amongst those who had returned together to their country, and had reinstated themselves by force of arms) and this either by vote or lot. Again, these several modes may be differently formed together, as some magistrates may be chosen by part of the community, others by the whole; some out of part, others out of the whole; some by vote, others by lot: and each of these different modes admit of a four-fold subdivision; for either all may elect all by vote or by lot; and when all elect, they may either proceed without any distinction, or they may elect by a certain division of tribes, wards, or companies, till they have gone through the whole community: and some magistrates may be elected one way, and others another. Again, if some magistrates are elected either by vote or lot of all the citizens, or by the vote of some and the lot of some, or some one way and some another; that is to say, some by the vote of all, others by the lot of all, there will then be twelve different methods of electing the magistrates, without blending the two together. Of these there are two adapted to a democracy; namely, to have all the magistrates chosen out of all the people, either by vote or lot, or both; that is to say, some of them by lot, some by vote. In a free state the whole community should not elect at the same time, but some out of the whole, or out of some particular rank; and this either by lot, or vote, or both: and they should elect either out of the whole community, or out of some particular persons in it, and this both by lot and vote. In an oligarchy it is proper to choose some magistrates out of the whole body of the citizens, some by vote, some by lot, others by both: by lot is most correspondent to that form of government. In a free aristocracy, some magistrates should be chosen out of the community in general, others out of a particular rank, or these by choice, those by lot. In a pure oligarchy, the magistrates should be chosen out of certain ranks, and by certain persons, and some of those by lot, others by both methods; but to choose them out of the whole community is not correspondent to the nature of this government. It is proper in an aristocracy for the whole community to elect their magistrates out of particular persons, and this by vote. These then are all the different ways of electing of magistrates; and they have been allotted according to the nature of the different communities; but what mode of proceeding is proper for different communities, or how the offices ought to be established, or with what powers shall be particularly explained. I mean by the powers of a magistrate, what should be his particular province, as the management of the finances or the laws of the state; for different magistrates have different powers, as that of the general of the army differs from the clerk of the market.

# CHAPTER

# XVI

Of the three parts of which a government is formed, we now come to consider the judicial; and this also we shall divide in the same manner as we did the magisterial, into three parts. Of whom the judges shall consist, and for what causes, and how. When I say of whom, I mean whether they shall be the whole people, or some particulars; by for what causes I mean, how many different courts shall be appointed; by how, whether they shall be elected by vote or lot. Let us first determine how many different courts there ought to be. Now these are eight. The first of these is the court of inspection over the behaviour of the magistrates when they have quitted their office; the second is to punish those who have injured the public; the third is to take cognisance of those causes in which the state is a party; the fourth is to decide between magistrates and private persons, who appeal from a fine laid upon them; the fifth is to determine disputes which may arise concerning contracts of great value; the sixth is to judge between foreigners, and of murders, of which there are different species; and these may all be tried by the same judges or by different ones; for there are murders of malice prepense and of chance-medley; there is also justifiable homicide, where the fact is admitted, and the legality of it disputed.

There is also another court called at Athens the Court of Phreattae, which determines points relating to a murder committed by one who has run away, to decide whether he shall return; though such an affair happens but seldom, and in very large cities; the seventh, to determine causes wherein strangers are concerned, and this whether they are between stranger and stranger or between a stranger and a citizen. The eighth and last is for small actions, from one to five drachma's, or a little more; for these ought also to be legally determined, but not to be brought before the whole body of the judges. But without entering into any particulars concerning actions for murder, and those wherein strangers are the parties, let us particularly treat of those courts which have the jurisdiction of those matters which more particularly relate to the affairs of the community and which if not well conducted occasion seditions and commotions in the state. Now, of necessity, either all persons must have a right to judge of all these different causes, appointed for that purpose, either by vote or lot, or all of all, some of them by vote, and others by lot, or in some causes by vote, in others by lot. Thus there will be four sorts of judges. There will be just the same number also if they are chosen out of part of the people only; for either all the judges must be chosen out of that part either by vote or lot, or some by lot and some by vote, or the judges in particular causes must be chosen some by vote, others by lot; by which means there will be the same number of them also as was mentioned. Besides, different judges may be joined together; I mean those who are chosen out of the whole people or part of them or both; so that all three may sit together in the same court, and this either by vote, lot, or both. And thus much for the different sorts of judges. Of these appointments that which admits all the community to be judges in all causes is most suitable to a democracy; the second, which appoints that certain persons shall judge all causes, to an oligarchy; the third, which appoints the whole community to be judges in some causes, but particular persons in others, to an aristocracy or free state.

# BOOK V

## CHAPTER

## I

W e have now gone through those particulars we proposed to speak of; it remains that we next consider from what causes and how alterations in government arise, and of what nature they are, and to what the destruction of each state is owing; and also to what form any form of polity is most likely to shift into, and what are the means to be used for the general preservation of governments, as well as what are applicable to any partictular state; and also of the remedies which are to be applied either to all in general, or to any one considered separately, when they are in a state of corruption: and here we ought first to lay down this principle, that there are many governments, all of which approve of what is just and what is analogically equal; and yet have failed from attaining thereunto, as we have already mentioned; thus democracies have arisen from supposing that those who are equal in one thing are so in every other circumstance; as, because they are equal in liberty, they are equal in everything else; and oligarchies, from supposing that those who are unequal in one thing are unequal in all; that when men are so in point of fortune, that inequality extends to everything else. Hence it follows, that those who in some respects are equal with others think it right to endeavour to partake of an equality with them in everything; and those who are superior to others endeavour to get still more; and it is this more which is the inequality: thus most states, though they have some notion of what is just, yet are almost totally wrong; and, upon this account, when either party has not that share in the administration which answers to his expectations, he becomes seditious: but those who of all others have the greatest right to be so are the last that are; namely, those who excel in virtue; for they alone can be called generally superior. There are, too, some persons of distinguished families who, because they are so, disdain to be on an equality with others, for those esteem themselves noble who boast of their ancestors' merit and fortune: these, to speak truth, are the origin and fountain from whence seditions arise. The alterations which men may propose to make in governments are two; for either they may change the state already established into some other, as when they propose to erect an oligarchy where there is a democracy; or a democracy, or free state, where there is an oligarchy, or an aristocracy from these, or those from that; or else, when they have no objection to the established government, which they like very well, but choose to have the sole management in it themselves; either in the hands of a few or one only. They will also raise commotions concerning the degree in which they would have the established power; as if, for instance, the government is an oligarchy, to have it more purely so, and in the same manner if it is a democracy, or else to have it less so; and, in like manner, whatever may be the nature of the government, either to extend or contract its powers; or else to make some alterations in some parts of it; as to establish or abolish a particular magistracy, as some persons say Lysander endeavoured to abolish the kingly power in Sparta; and Pausanias that of the ephori. Thus in Epidamnus there was an alteration in one part of the constitution, for instead of the philarchi they established a senate. It is also necessary for all the magistrates at Athens; to attend in the court of the Helisea when any new magistrate is created: the power of the archon also in that state partakes of the nature of an oligarchy: inequality is always the occasion of sedition, but not when those who are unequal are treated in a different manner correspondent to that inequality. Thus kingly power is unequal when exercised over equals. Upon the whole, those who aim after an equality are the cause of seditions. Equality is twofold, either in number or value. Equality in number is when two things contain the same parts or the same quantity; equality in value is by proportion as two exceeds one, and three two by the same number-thus by proportion four exceeds two, and two one in the same degree, for two is the same part of four that one is of two; that is to say, half. Now, all agree in what is absolutely and simply just; but, as we have already said they dispute concerning proportionate value; for some persons, if they are equal in one respect, think themselves equal in all; others, if they are superior in one thing, think they may claim the superiority in all; from whence chiefly arise two sorts of governments, a democracy and an oligarchy; for nobility and virtue are to be found only amongst a few; the contrary amongst the many; there being in no place a hundred of the first to be met with, but enough of the last everywhere. But to establish a government entirely upon either of these equalities is wrong, and this the example of those so established makes evident, for none of them have been stable; and for this reason, that it is impossible that whatever is wrong at the first and in its principles should not at last meet with a bad end: for which reason in some things an equality of numbers ought to take place, in others an equality in value. However, a democracy is safer and less liable to sedition than an oligarchy; for in this latter it may arise from two causes, for either the few in power may conspire against each other or against the people; but in a democracy only one; namely, against the few who aim at exclusive power; but there is no instance worth speaking of, of a sedition of the people against themselves. Moreover, a government composed of men of moderate fortunes comes much nearer to a democracy than an oligarchy, and is the safest of all such states.

# CHAPTER

## II

Since we are inquiring into the causes of seditions and revolutions in governments, we must begin entirely with the first principles from whence they arise. Now these, so to speak, are nearly three in number; which we must first distinguish in general from each other, and endeavour to show in what situation people are who begin a sedition; and for what causes; and thirdly, what are the beginnings of political troubles and mutual quarrels with each other. Now that cause which of all others most universally inclines men to desire to bring about a change in government is that which I have already mentioned; for those who aim at equality will be ever ready for sedition, if they see those whom they esteem their equals possess more than they do, as well as those also who are not content with equality but aim at superiority, if they think that while they deserve more than, they have only equal with, or less than, their inferiors. Now, what they aim at may be either just or unjust; just, when those who are inferior are seditious, that they may be equal; unjust, when those who are equal are so, that they may be superior. These, then, are the situations in which men will be seditious: the causes for which they will be so are profit and honour; and their contrary: for, to avoid dishonour or loss of fortune by mulcts, either on their own account or their friends, they will raise a commotion in the state. The original causes which dispose men to the things which I have mentioned are, taken in one manner, seven in number, in another they are more; two of which are the same with those that have been already mentioned: but influencing in a different manner; for profit and honour sharpen men against each other; not to get the possession of them for themselves (which was what I just now supposed), but when they see others, some justly, others unjustly, engrossing them. The other causes are haughtiness, fear, eminence, contempt, disproportionate increase in some part of the state. There are also other things which in a different manner will occasion revolutions in governments; as election intrigues, neglect, want of numbers, a too great dissimilarity of circumstances.

## CHAPTER

## III

What influence ill-treatment and profit have for this purpose, and how they may be the causes of sedition, is almost self-evident; for when the magistrates are haughty and endeavour to make greater profits than their office gives them, they not only occasion seditions amongst each other, but against the state also who gave them their power; and this their avarice has two objects, either private property or the property of the state. What influence honours have, and how they may occasion sedition, is evident enough; for those who are themselves unhonoured while they see others honoured, will be ready for any disturbance: and these things are done unjustly when any one is either honoured or discarded contrary to their deserts, justly when they are according to them. Excessive honours are also a cause of sedition when one person or more are greater than the state and the power of the government can permit; for then a monarchy or a dynasty is usually established: on which account the ostracism was introduced in some places, as at Argos and Athens: though it is better to guard against such excesses in the founding of a state, than when they have been permitted to take place, to correct them afterward. Those who have been guilty of crimes will be the cause of sedition, through fear of punishment; as will those also who expect an injury, that they may prevent it; as was the case at Rhodes, when the nobles conspired against the people on account of the decrees they expected would pass against them. Contempt also is a cause of sedition and conspiracies; as in oligarchies, where there are many who have no share in the administration. The rich also even in democracies, despising the disorder and anarchy which will arise, hope to better themselves by the same means which happened at Thebes after the battle of Oenophyta, where, in consequence of bad administration, the democracy was destroyed; as it was at Megara, where the power of the people was lost through anarchy and disorder; the same thing happened at Syracuse before the tyranny of Gelon; and at Rhodes there was the same sedition before the popular government was overthrown. Revolutions in state will also arise from a disproportionate increase; for as the body consists of many parts, it ought to increase proportion-ably to preserve its symmetry, which would otherwise be destroyed; as if the foot was to be four cubits long, and the rest of the body but two palms; it might otherwise be changed into an animal of a different form, if it increase beyond proportion not only in quantity, but also in disposition of parts; so also a city consists of parts, some of which may often increase without notice, as the number of poor in democracies and free states. They will also sometimes happen by accident, as at Tarentum, a little after the Median war, where so many of the nobles were killed in a battle by the Iapygi, that from a free state the government was turned into a democracy; and at Argos, where so many of the citizens were killed by Cleomenes the Spartan, that they were obliged to admit several husbandmen to the freedom of the state: and at Athens, through the unfortunate event of the infantry battles, the number of the nobles was reduced by the soldiers being chosen from the list of citizens in the Lacedaemonian wars. Revolutions also sometimes take place in a democracy, though seldomer; for where the rich grow numerous or properties increase, they become oligarchies or dynasties. Governments also sometimes alter without seditions by a combination of the meaner people; as at Hersea: for which purpose they changed the mode of election from votes to lots, and thus got themselves chosen: and by negligence, as when the citizens admit those who are not friends to the constitution into the chief offices of the state, which happened at Orus, when the oligarchy of the archons was put an end to at the election of Heracleodorus, who changed that form of government into a democratic free state. By little and little, I mean by this, that very often great alterations silently take place in the form of government from people's overlooking small matters; as at Ambracia, where the census was originally small, but at last became nothing at all, as if a little and nothing at all were nearly or entirely alike. That state also is liable to seditions which is composed of different nations, till their differences are blended together and undistinguishable; for as a city cannot be composed of every multitude, so neither can it in every given time; for which reason all those republics which have hitherto been originally composed of different people or afterwards admitted their neighbours to the freedom of their city, have been most liable to revolutions; as when the Achaeans joined with the Traezenians in founding Sybaris; for soon after, growing more powerful than the Traezenians, they expelled them from the city; from whence came the proverb of Sybarite wickedness: and again, disputes from a like cause happened at Thurium between the Sybarites and those who had joined with them in building the city; for they assuming upon these, on account of the country being their own, were driven out. And at Byzantium the new citizens, being detected in plots against the state, were driven out of the city by force of arms. The Antisseans also, having taken in those who were banished from Chios, afterwards did the same thing; and also the Zancleans, after having taken in the people of Samos. The Appolloniats, in the Euxine Sea, having admitted their sojourners to the freedom of their city, were troubled with seditions: and the Syracusians, after the expulsion of their tyrants, having enrolled strangers and mercenaries amongst their citizens, quarrelled with each other and came to an open rupture: and the people of Amphipolis, having taken in a colony of Chalcidians, were the greater part of them driven out of the city by them. Many persons occasion seditions in oligarchies because they think themselves ill-used in not sharing the honours of the state with their equals, as I have already mentioned; but in democracies the principal people do the same because they have not more than an equal share with others who are not equal to them. The situation of the place will also sometimes occasion disturbances in the state when the ground is not well adapted for one city; as at Clazomene, where the people who lived in that part of the town called Chytrum quarrelled with them who lived in the island, and the Colophonians with the Notians. At Athens too the disposition of the citizens is not the same, for those who live in the Piraeus are more attached to a popular government than those who live in the city properly so called; for as the interposition of a rivulet, however small, will occasion the line of the phalanx to fluctuate, so any trifling disagreement will be the cause of seditions; but they will not so soon flow from anything else as from the disagreement between virtue and vice, and next to that between poverty and riches, and so on in order, one cause having more influence than another; one of which that I last mentioned.

## CHAPTER

## IV

But seditions in government do not arise for little things, but from them; for their immediate cause is something of moment. Now, trifling quarrels are attended with the greatest consequences when they arise between persons of the first distinction in the state, as was the case with the Syracusians in a remote period; for a revolution in the government was brought about by a quarrel between two young men who were in office, upon a love affair; for one of them being absent, the other seduced his mistress; he in his turn, offended with this, persuaded his friend's wife to come and live with him; and upon this the whole city took part either with the one or the other, and the government was overturned: therefore every one at the beginning of such disputes ought to take care to avoid the consequences; and to smother up all quarrels which may happen to arise amongst those in power, for the mischief lies in the beginning; for the beginning is said to be half of the business, so that what was then but a little fault will be found afterwards to bear its full proportion to what follows. Moreover, disputes between men of note involve the whole city in their consequences; in Hestiaea, after the Median war: two brothers having a dispute about their paternal estate; he who was the poorer, from the other's having concealed part of the effects, and some money which his father had found, engaged the popular party on his side, while the other, who was rich, the men of fashion. And at Delphos, a quarrel about a wedding was the beginning of all the seditions that afterwards arose amongst them; for the bridegroom, being terrified by some unlucky omen upon waiting upon the bride, went away without marrying her; which her relations resenting, contrived secretly to convey some sacred money into his pocket while he was sacrificing, and then killed him as an impious person. At Mitylene also, a dispute, which arose concerning a right of heritage, was the beginning of great evils, and a war with the Athenians, in which Paches took their city, for Timophanes, a man of fortune, leaving two daughters, Doxander, who was circumvented in procuring them in marriage for his two sons, began a sedition, and excited the Athenians to attack them, being the host of that state. There was also a dispute at Phocea, concerning a right of inheritance, between Mnasis, the father of Mnasis, and Euthucrates, the father of Onomarchus, which brought on the Phoceans the sacred war. The government too of Epidamnus was changed from a quarrel that arose from an intended marriage; for a certain man having contracted his daughter in marriage, the father of the young person to whom she was contracted, being archon, punishes him, upon which account he, resenting the affront, associated himself with those who were excluded from any share in the government, and brought about a revolution. A government may be changed either into an oligarchy, democracy, or a free state; when the magistrates, or any part of the city acquire great credit, or are increased in power, as the court of Areopagus at Athens, having procured great credit during the Median war, added firmness to their administration; and, on the other hand, the maritime force, composed of the commonalty, having gained the victory at Salamis, by their power at sea, got the lead in the state, and strengthened the popular party: and at Argos, the nobles, having gained great credit by the battle of Mantinea against the Lacedaemonians, endeavoured to dissolve the democracy. And at Syracuse, the victory in their war with the Athenians being owing to the common people, they changed their free state into a democracy: and at Chalcis, the people having taken off the tyrant Phocis, together with the nobles, immediately seized the government: and at Ambracia also the people, having expelled the tyrant Periander, with his party, placed the supreme power in themselves. And this in general ought to be known, that whosoever has been the occasion of a state being powerful, whether private persons, or magistrates, a certain tribe, or any particular part of the citizens, or the multitude, be they who they will, will be the cause of disputes in the state. For either some persons, who envy them the honours they have acquired, will begin to be seditious, or they, on account of the dignity they have acquired, will not be content with their former equality. A state is also liable to commotions when those parts of it which seem to be opposite to each other approach to an equality, as the rich and the common people; so that the part which is between them both is either nothing at all, or too little to be noticed; for if one party is so much more powerful than the other, as to be evidently stronger, that other will not be willing to hazard the danger: for which reason those who are superior in excellence and virtue will never be the cause of seditions; for they will be too few for that purpose when compared to the many. In general, the beginning and the causes of seditions in all states are such as I have now described, and revolutions therein are brought about in two ways, either by violence or fraud: if by violence, either at first by compelling them to submit to the change when it is made. It may also be brought about by fraud in two different ways, either when the people, being at first deceived, willingly consent to an alteration in their government, and are afterwards obliged by force to abide by it: as, for instance, when the four hundred imposed upon the people by telling them that the king of Persia would supply them with money for the war against the Lacedaemonians; and after they had been guilty of this falsity, they endeavoured to keep possession of the supreme power; or when they are at first persuaded and afterwards consent to be governed: and by one of these methods which I have mentioned are all revolutions in governments brought about.

# CHAPTER

# V

We ought now to inquire into those events which will arise from these causes in every species of government. Democracies will be most subject to revolutions from the dishonesty of their demagogues; for partly, by informing against men of property, they induce them to join together through self-defence, for a common fear will make the greatest enemies unite; and partly by setting the common people against them: and this is what any one may continually see practised in many states. In the island of Cos, for instance, the democracy was subverted by the wickedness of the demagogues, for the nobles entered into a combination with each other. And at Rhodes the demagogues, by distributing of bribes, prevented the people from paying the trierarchs what was owing to them, who were obliged by the number of actions they were harassed with to conspire together and destroy the popular state. The same thing was brought about at Heraclea, soon after the settlement of the city, by the same persons; for the citizens of note, being ill treated by them, quitted the city, but afterwards joining together they returned and overthrew the popular state. Just in the same manner the democracy was destroyed in Megara; for there the demagogues, to procure money by confiscations, drove out the nobles, till the number of those who were banished was considerable, who, returning, got the better of the people in a battle, and established an oligarchy. The like happened at Cume, during the time of the democracy, which Thrasymachus destroyed; and whoever considers what has happened in other states may perceive the same revolutions to have arisen from the same causes. The demagogues, to curry favour with the people, drive the nobles to conspire together, either by dividing their estates, or obliging them to spend them on public services, or by banishing them, that they may confiscate the fortunes of the wealthy. In former times, when the same person was both demagogue and general, the democracies were changed into tyrannies; and indeed most of the ancient tyrannies arose from those states: a reason for which then subsisted, but not now; for at that time the demagogues were of the soldiery; for they were not then powerful by their eloquence; but, now the art of oratory is cultivated, the able speakers are at present the demagogues; but, as they are unqualified to act in a military capacity, they cannot impose themselves on the people as tyrants, if we except in one or two trifling instances. Formerly, too, tyrannies were more common than now, on account of the very extensive powers with which some magistrates were entrusted: as the prytanes at Miletus; for they were supreme in many things of the last consequence; and also because at that time the cities were not of that very great extent, the people in general living in the country, and being employed in husbandry, which gave them, who took the lead in public affairs, an opportunity, if they had a turn for war, to make themselves tyrants; which they all did when they had gained the confidence of the people; and this confidence was their hatred to the rich. This was the case of Pisistratus at Athens, when he opposed the Pediaci: and of Theagenes in Megara, who slaughtered the cattle belonging to the rich, after he had seized those who kept them by the riverside. Dionysius also, for accusing Daphnseus and the rich, was thought worthy of being raised to a tyranny, from the confidence which the people had of his being a popular man in consequence of these enmities. A government shall also alter from its ancient and approved democratic form into one entirely new, if there is no census to regulate the election of magistrates; for, as the election is with the people, the demagogues who are desirous of being in office, to flatter them, will endeavour with all their power to make the people superior even to the laws. To prevent this entirely, or at least in a great measure, the magistrates should be elected by the tribes, and not by the people at large. These are nearly the revolutions to which democracies are liable, and also the causes from whence they arise.

# CHAPTER

## VI

There are two things which of all others most evidently occasion a revolution in an oligarchy; one is, when the people are ill used, for then every individual is ripe for sedition; more particularly if one of the oligarchy should happen to be their leader; as Lygdamis, at Naxus, who was afterwards tyrant of that island. Seditions also which arise from different causes will differ from each other; for sometimes a revolution is brought about by the rich who have no share in the administration, which is in the hands of a very few indeed: and this happened at Massilia, Ister, Heraclea, and other cities; for those who had no share in the government ceased not to raise disputes till they were admitted to it: first the elder brothers, and then the younger also: for in some places the father and son are never in office at the same time; in others the elder and younger brother: and where this is observed the oligarchy partakes something of a free state. At Ister it was changed into a democracy; in Heraclea, instead of being in the hands of a few, it consisted of six hundred. At Cnidus the oligarchy was destroyed by the nobles quarrelling with each other, because the government was in the hands of so few: for there, as we have just mentioned, if the father was in office, the son could not; or, if there were many brothers, the eldest only; for the people, taking advantage of their disputes, elected one of the nobles for their general, and got the victory: for where there are seditions government is weak. And formerly at Erithria, during the oligarchy of the Basilides, although the state flourished greatly under their excellent management, yet because the people were displeased that the power should be in the hands of so few, they changed the government. Oligarchies also are subject to revolutions, from those who are in office therein, from the quarrels of the demagogues with each other. The demagogues are of two sorts; one who flatter the few when they are in power: for even these have their demagogues; such was

Charicles at Athens, who had great influence over the thirty; and, in the same manner, Phrynichus over the four hundred. The others are those demagogues who have a share in the oligarchy, and flatter the people: such were the state-guardians at Larissa, who flattered the people because they were elected by them. And this will always happen in every oligarchy where the magistrates do not elect themselves, but are chosen out of men either of great fortune or certain ranks, by the soldiers or by the people; as was the custom at Abydos. And when the judicial department is not in the hands of the supreme power, the demagogues, favouring the people in their causes, overturn the government; which happened at Heraclea in Pontus: and also when some desire to contract the power of the oligarchy into fewer hands; for those who endeavour to support an equality are obliged to apply to the people for assistance. An oligarchy is also subject to revolutions when the nobility spend their fortunes by luxury; for such persons are desirous of innovations, and either endeavour to be tyrants themselves or to support others in being so, as Hypparinus supported Dionysius of Syracuse. And at Amphipolis one Cleotimus collected a colony of Chalcidians, and when they came set them to quarrel with the rich: and at AEgina a certain person who brought an action against Chares attempted on that account to alter the government. Sometimes they will try to raise commotions, sometimes they will rob the public, and then quarrel with each other, or else fight with those who endeavour to detect them; which was the case at Apollonia in Pontus. But if the members of an oligarchy agree among themselves the state is not very easily destroyed without some external force. Pharsalus is a proof of this, where, though the place is small, yet the citizens have great power, from the prudent use they make of it. An oligarchy also will be destroyed when they create another oligarchy under it; that is, when the management of public affairs is in the hands of a few, and not equally, but when all of them do not partake of the supreme power, as happened once at Elis, where the supreme power in general was in the hands of a very few out of whom a senate was chosen, consisting but of ninety, who held their places for life; and their mode of election was calculated to preserve the power amongst each other's families, like the senators at Lacedaemon. An oligarchy is liable to a revolution both in time of war and peace; in war, because through a distrust in the citizens the government is obliged to employ mercenary troops, and he to whom they give the command of the army will very often assume the tyranny, as Timophanes did at Corinth; and if they appoint more than one general, they will very probably establish a dynasty: and sometimes, through fear of this, they are forced to let the people in general have some share in the government, because they are obliged to employ them. In peace, from their want of confidence in each other, they will entrust the guardianship of the state to mercenaries and their general, who will be an arbiter between them, and sometimes become master of both, which happened at Larissa, when Simos and the Aleuadae had the chief power. The same thing happened at Abydos, during the time of the political clubs, of which Iphiades' was one. Commotions also will happen in an oligarchy from one party's overbearing and insulting another, or from their quarrelling about their law-suits or marriages. How their marriages, for instance, will have that effect has been already shown: and in Eretria, Diagoras destroyed the oligarchy of the knights upon the same account. A sedition also arose at Heraclea, from a certain person being condemned by the court; and at Thebes, in consequence of a man's being guilty of adultery; the punishment indeed which Eurytion suffered at Heraclea was just, yet it was illegally executed: as was that at Thebes upon Archias; for their enemies endeavoured to have them publicly bound in the pillory. Many revolutions also have been brought about in oligarchies by those who could not brook the despotism which those persons assumed who were in power, as at Cnidus and Chios. Changes also may happen by accident in what we call a free state and in an oligarchy; wheresoever the senators, judges, and magistrates are chosen according to a certain census; for it often happens that the highest census is fixed at first; so that a few only could have a share in the government, in an oligarchy, or in a free state those of moderate fortunes only; when the city grows rich, through peace or some other happy cause, it becomes so little that every one's fortune is equal to the census, so that the whole community may partake of all the honours of government; and this change sometimes happens by little and little, and insensible approaches, sometimes quicker. These are the revolutions and seditions that arise in oligarchies, and the causes to which they are owing: and indeed both democracies and oligarchies sometimes alter, not into governments of a contrary form, but into those of the same government; as, for instance, from having the supreme power in the law to vest it in the ruling party, or the contrariwise.

# CHAPTER

# VII

Commotions also arise in aristocracies, from there being so few persons in power (as we have already observed they do in oligarchies, for in this particular an aristocracy is most near an oligarchy, for in both these states the administration of public affairs is in the hands of a few; not that this arises from the same cause in both, though herein they chiefly seem alike): and these will necessarily be most likely to happen when the generality of the people are high-spirited and think themselves equal to each other in merit; such were those at Lacedasmon, called the Partheniae (for these were, as well as others, descendants of citizens), who being detected in a conspiracy against the state, were sent to found Tarentum. They will happen also when some great men are disgraced by those who have received higher honours than themselves, to whom they are no ways inferior in abilities, as Lysander by the kings: or when an ambitious man cannot get into power, as Cinadon, who, in the reign of Agesilaus, was chief in a conspiracy against the Spartans: and also when some are too poor and others too rich, which will most frequently happen in time of war; as at Lacedaemon during the Messenian war, which is proved by a poem of Tyrtaeus, called "Eunomia;" for some persons being reduced thereby, desired that the lands might be divided: and also when some person of very high rank might still be higher if he could rule alone, which seemed to be Pausanias's intention at Lacedaemon, when he was their general in the Median war, and Anno's at Carthage. But free states and aristocracies are mostly destroyed from want of a fixed administration of public affairs; the cause of which evil arises at first from want of a due mixture of the democratic and the oligarchic parts in a free state; and in an aristocracy from the same causes, and also from virtue not being properly joined to power; but chiefly from the two first, I mean the undue mixture of the democratic and oligarchic parts; for these two are what all free states endeavour to blend together, and many of those which we call aristocracies, in this particular these states differ from each other, and on this account the one of them is less stable than the other, for that state which inclines most to an oligarchy is called an aristocracy, and that which inclines most to a democracy is called a free state; on which account this latter is more secure than the former, for the wider the foundation the securer the building, and it is ever best to live where equality prevails. But the rich, if the community gives them rank, very often endeavour to insult and tyrannise over others. On the whole, whichever way a government inclines, in that it will settle, each party supporting their own. Thus a free state will become a democracy; an aristocracy an oligarchy; or the contrary, an aristocracy may change into a democracy (for the poor, if they think themselves injured, directly take part with the contrary side) and a free state into an oligarchy. The only firm state is that where every one enjoys that equality he has a right to and fully possesses what is his own. And what I have been speaking of happened to the Thurians; for the magistrates being elected according to a very high census, it was altered to a lower, and they were subdivided into more courts, but in consequence of the nobles possessing all the land, contrary to law; the state was too much of an oligarchy, which gave them an opportunity of encroaching greatly on the rest of the people; but these, after they had been well inured to war, so far got the better of their guards as to expel every one out of the country who possessed more than he ought. Moreover, as all aristocracies are free oligarchies, the nobles therein endeavour to have rather too much power, as at Lacedaemon, where property is now in the hands of a few, and the nobles have too much liberty to do as they please and make such alliances as they please. Thus the city of the Locrians was ruined from an alliance with Dionysius; which state was neither a democracy nor well-tempered aristocracy. But an aristocracy chiefly approaches to a secret change by its being destroyed by degrees, as we have already said of all governments in general; and this happens from the cause of the alteration being trifling; for whenever anything which in the least regards the state is treated with contempt, after that something else, and this of a little more consequence, will be more easily altered, until the whole fabric of government is entirely subverted, which happened in the government of Thurium; for the law being that they should continue soldiers for five years, some young men of a martial disposition, who were in great esteem amongst their officers, despising those who had the management of public affairs, and imagining they could easily accomplish their intention, first endeavoured to abolish this law, with a view of having it lawful to continue the same person perpetually in the military, perceiving that the people would readily appoint them. Upon this, the magistrates who are called counselors first joined together with an intention to oppose it but were afterwards induced to agree to it, from a belief that if that law was not repealed they would permit the management of all other public affairs to remain in their hands; but afterwards, when they endeavoured to restrain some fresh alterations that were making, they found that they could do nothing, for the whole form of government was altered into a dynasty of those who first introduced the innovations. In short, all governments are liable to be destroyed either from within or from without; from without when they have for their neighbour a state whose policy is contrary to theirs, and indeed if it has great power the same thing will happen if it is not their neighbour; of which both the Athenians and the Lacedaemonians are a proof; for the one, when conquerors everywhere destroyed the oligarchies; the other the democracies. These are the chief causes of revolutions and dissensions in governments.

# CHAPTER

# VIII

We are now to consider upon what the preservation of governments in general and of each state in particular depends; and, in the first place, it is evident that if we are right in the causes we have assigned for their destruction, we know also the means of their preservation; for things contrary produce contraries: but destruction and preservation are contrary to each other. In well-tempered governments it requires as much care as anything whatsoever, that nothing be done contrary to law: and this ought chiefly to be attended to in matters of small consequence; for an illegality that approaches insensibly, approaches secretly, as in a family small expenses continually repeated consume a man's income; for the understanding is deceived thereby, as by this false argument; if every part is little, then the whole is little: now, this in one sense is true, in another is false, for the whole and all the parts together are large, though made up of small parts. The first therefore of anything is what the state ought to guard against. In the next place, no credit ought to be given to those who endeavour to deceive the people with false pretences; for they will be confuted by facts. The different ways in which they will attempt to do this have been already mentioned. You may often perceive both aristocracies and oligarchies continuing firm, not from the stability of their forms of government, but from the wise conduct of the magistrates, both towards those who have a part in the management of public affairs, and those also who have not: towards those who have not, by never injuring them; and also introducing those who are of most consequence amongst them into office; nor disgracing those who are desirous of honour; or encroaching on the property of individuals; towards those who have, by behaving to each other upon an equality; for that equality which the favourers of a democracy desire to have established in the state is not only just, but convenient also, amongst those who are of the same rank: for which reason, if the administration is in the hands of many, those rules which are established in democracies will be very useful; as to let no one continue in office longer than six months: that all those who are of the same rank may have their turn; for between these there is a sort of democracy: for which reason demagogues are most likely to arise up amongst them, as we have already mentioned: besides, by this means both aristocracies and democracies will be the less liable to be corrupted into dynasties, because it will not be so easy for those who are magistrates for a little to do as much mischief as they could in a long time: for it is from hence that tyrannies arise in democracies and oligarchies; for either those who are most powerful in each state establish a tyranny, as the demagogues in the one, the dynasties in the other, or the chief magistrates who have been long in power. Governments are sometimes preserved not only by having the means of their corruption at a great distance, but also by its being very near them; for those who are alarmed at some impending evil keep a stricter hand over the state; for which reason it is necessary for those who have the guardianship of the constitution to be able to awaken the fears of the people, that they may preserve it, and not like a night-guard to be remiss in protecting the state, but to make the distant danger appear at hand. Great care ought also to be used to endeavour to restrain the quarrels and disputes of the nobles by laws, as well as to prevent those who are not already engaged in them from taking a part therein; for to perceive an evil at its very first approach is not the lot of every one, but of the politician. To prevent any alteration taking place in an oligarchy or free state on account of the census, if that happens to continue the same while the quantity of money is increased, it will be useful to take a general account of the whole amount of it in former times, to compare it with the present, and to do this every year in those cities where the census is yearly, in larger communities once in three or five years; and if the whole should be found much larger or much less than it was at the time when the census was first established in the state, let there be a law either to extend or contract it, doing both these according to its increase or decrease; if it increases making the census larger, if it decreases smaller: and if this latter is not done in oligarchies and free states, you will have a dynasty arise in the one, an oligarchy in the other: if the former is not, free states will be changed into democracies, and oligarchies into free states or democracies. It is a general maxim in democracies, oligarchies, monarchies, and indeed in all governments, not to let any one acquire a rank far superior to the rest of the community, but rather to endeavour to confer moderate honours for a continuance than great ones for a short time; for these latter spoil men, for it is not every one who can bear prosperity: but if this rule is not observed, let not those honours which were conferred all at once be all at once taken away, but rather by degrees. But, above all things, let this regulation be made by the law, that no one shall have too much power, either by means of his fortune or friends; but if he has, for his excess therein, let it be contrived that he shall quit the country. Now, as many persons promote innovations, that they may enjoy their own particular manner of living, there ought to be a particular officer to inspect the manners of every one, and see that these are not contrary to the genius of the state in which he lives, whether it may be an oligarchy, a democracy, or any other form of government; and, for the same reason, those should be guarded against who are most prosperous in the city: the means of doing which is by appointing those who are otherwise to the business and the offices of the state. I mean, to oppose men of account to the common people, the poor to the rich, and to blend both these into one body, and to increase the numbers of those who are in the middle rank; and this will prevent those seditions which arise from an inequality of condition. But above all, in every state it is necessary, both by the laws and every other method possible, to prevent those who are employed by the public from being venal, and this particularly in an oligarchy; for then the people will not be so much displeased from seeing themselves excluded from a share in the government (nay, they will rather be glad to have leisure to attend their private affairs) as at suspecting that the officers of the state steal the public money, then indeed they are afflicted with double concern, both because they are deprived of the honours of the state, and pillaged by those who enjoy them. There is one method of blending together a democracy and an aristocracy, if office brought no profit; by which means both the rich and the poor will enjoy what they desire; for to admit all to a share in the government is democratical; that the rich should be in office is aristocratical. This must be done by letting no public employment whatsoever be attended with any emolument; for the poor will not desire to be in office when they can get nothing by it, but had rather attend to their own affairs: but the rich will choose it, as they want nothing of the community. Thus the poor will increase their fortunes by being wholly employed in their own concerns; and the principal part of the people will not be governed by the lower sort. To prevent the exchequer from being defrauded, let all public money be delivered out openly in the face of the whole city, and let copies of the accounts be deposited in the different wards tribes, and divisions. But, as the magistrates are to execute their offices without any advantages, the law ought to provide proper honours for those who execute them well. In democracies also it is necessary that the rich should be protected, by not permitting their lands to be divided, nor even the produce of them, which in some states is done unperceivably. It would be also better if the people would prevent them when they offer to exhibit a number of unnecessary and yet expensive public entertainments of plays, music, processions, and the like. In an oligarchy it is necessary to take great care of the poor, and allot them public employments which are gainful; and, if any of the rich insult them, to let their punishment be severer than if they insulted one of their own rank; and to let estates pass by affinity, and not gift: nor to permit any person to have more than one; for by this means property will be more equally divided, and the greater part of the poor get into better circumstances. It is also serviceable in a democracy and an oligarchy to allot those who take no part in public affairs an equality or a preference in other things; the rich in a democracy, to the poor in an oligarchy: but still all the principal offices in the state to be filled only by those who are best qualified to discharge them.

# CHAPTER

# IX

There are three qualifications necessary for those who fill the first departments in government; first of all, an affection for the established constitution; second place, abilities every way completely equal to the business of their office; in the third, virtue and justice correspondent to the nature of that particular state they are placed in; for if justice is not the same in all states, it is evident that there must be different species thereof. There may be some doubt, when all these qualifications do not in the same persons, in what manner the choice shall be made; as for instance, suppose that one person is an accomplished general, but a bad man and no friend to the constitution; another is just and a friend to it, which shall one prefer? We should then consider of two qualities, which of them the generality possess in a greater degree, which in a less; for which reason in the choice of a general we should regard his courage more than his virtue as the more uncommon quality; as there are fewer capable of conducting an army than there are good men: but, to protect the state or manage the finances, the contrary rule should be followed; for these require greater virtue than the generality are possessed of, but only that knowledge which is common to all. It may be asked, if a man has abilities equal to his appointment in the state, and is affectionate to the constitution, what occasion is there for being virtuous, since these two things alone are sufficient to enable him to be useful to the public? It is, because those who possess those qualities are often deficient in prudence; for, as they often neglect their own affairs, though they know them and love themselves, so nothing will prevent their serving the public in the same manner. In short, whatsoever the laws contain which we allow to be useful to the state contributes to its preservation: but its first and principal support is (as has been often insisted upon) to have the number of those who desire to preserve it greater than those who wish to destroy it. Above all things that ought not to be forgotten which many governments now corrupted neglect; namely, to preserve a mean. For many things seemingly favourable to a democracy destroy a democracy, and many things seemingly favourable to an oligarchy destroy an oligarchy. Those who think this the only virtue extend it to excess, not considering that as a nose which varies a little from perfect straightness, either towards a hook nose or a flat one, may yet be beautiful and agreeable to look at; but if this particularity is extended beyond measure, first of all the properties of the part is lost, but at last it can hardly be admitted to be a nose at all, on account of the excess of the rise or sinking: thus it is with other parts of the human body; so also the same thing is true with respect to states; for both an oligarchy and a democracy may something vary from their most perfect form and yet be well constituted; but if any one endeavours to extend either of them too far, at first he will make the government the worse for it, but at last there will be no government at all remaining. The lawgiver and the politician therefore should know well what preserves and what destroys a democracy or an oligarchy, for neither the one nor the other can possibly continue without rich and poor: but that whenever an entire equality of circumstances prevails, the state must necessarily become of another form; so that those who destroy these laws, which authorise an inequality in property, destroy the government. It is also an error in democracies for the demagogues to endeavour to make the common people superior to the laws; and thus by setting them at variance with the rich, dividing one city into two; whereas they ought rather to speak in favour of the rich. In oligarchies, on the contrary, it is wrong to support those who are in administration against the people. The oaths also which they take in an oligarchy ought to be contrary to what they now are; for, at present, in some places they swear, "I will be adverse to the common people, and contrive all I can against them;" whereas they ought rather to suppose and pretend the contrary; expressing in their oaths, that they will not injure the people. But of all things which I have mentioned, that which contributes most to preserve the state is, what is now most despised, to educate your children for the state; for the most useful laws, and most approved by every statesman, will be of no service if the citizens are not accustomed to and brought up in the principles of the constitution; of a democracy, if that is by law established; of an oligarchy, if that is; for if there are bad morals in one man, there are in the city. But to educate a child fit for the state, it must not be done in the manner which would please either those who have the power in an oligarchy or those who desire a democracy, but so as they may be able to conduct either of these forms of governments. But now the children of the magistrates in an oligarchy are brought up too delicately, and the children of the poor hardy with exercise and labour; so that they are both desirous of and able to promote innovations. In democracies of the purest form they pursue a method which is contrary to their welfare; the reason of which is, that they define liberty wrong: now, there are two things which seem to be the objects of a democracy, that the people in general should possess the supreme power, and all enjoy freedom; for that which is just seems to be equal, and what the people think equal, that is a law: now, their freedom and equality consists in every one's doing what they please: that is in such a democracy every one may live as he likes; "as his inclination guides," in the words of Euripides: but this is wrong, for no one ought to think it slavery to live in subjection to government, but protection. Thus I have mentioned the causes of corruption in different states, and the means of their preservation.

# CHAPTER

# X

It now remains that we speak of monarchies, their causes of corruption, and means of preservation; and indeed almost the same things which have been said of other governments happen to kingdoms and tyrannies; for a kingdom partakes of an aristocracy, a tyranny of the worst species of an oligarchy and democracy; for which reason it is the worst that man can submit to, as being composed of two, both of which are bad, and collectively retains all the corruptions and all the defects of both these states. These two species of monarchies arise from principles contrary to each other: a kingdom is formed to protect the better sort of people against the multitude, and kings are appointed out of those, who are chosen either for their superior virtue and actions flowing from virtuous principles, or else from their noble descent; but a tyrant is chosen out of the meanest populace; an enemy to the better sort, that the common people may not be oppressed by them. That this is true experience convinces us; for the generality of tyrants were indeed mere demagogues, who gained credit with the people by oppressing the nobles. Some tyrannies were established in this manner after the cities were considerably enlarged—others before that time, by kings who exceeded the power which their country allowed them, from a desire of governing despotically: others were founded by those who were elected to the superior offices in the state; for formerly the people appointed officers for life, who came to be at the head of civil and religious affairs, and these chose one out of their body in whom the supreme power over all the magistrates was placed. By all these means it was easy to establish a tyranny, if they chose it; for their power was ready at hand, either by their being kings, or else by enjoying the honours of the state; thus Phidon at Argos and other tyrants enjoyed originally the kingly power; Phalaris and others in Ionia, the honours of the state. Pansetius at Leontium, Cypselus at Corinth, Pisistratus at Athens, Dionysius at Syracuse, and others, acquired theirs by having been demagogues. A kingdom, as we have said, partakes much of the nature of an aristocracy, and is bestowed according to worth, as either virtue, family, beneficent actions, or these joined with power; for those who have been benefactors to cities and states, or have it in their powers to be so, have acquired this honour, and those who have prevented a people from falling into slavery by war, as Codrus, or those who have freed them from it, as Cyrus, or the founders of cities, or settlers of colonies, as the kings of Sparta, Macedon, and Molossus. A king desires to be the guardian of his people, that those who have property may be secure in the possession of it, and that the people in general meet with no injury; but a tyrant, as has been often said, has no regard to the common good, except for his own advantage; his only object is pleasure, but a king's is virtue: what a tyrant therefore is ambitious of engrossing is wealth, but a king rather honour. The guards too of a king are citizens, a tyrant's foreigners.

That a tyranny contains all that is bad both in a democracy and an oligarchy is evident; with an oligarchy it has for its end gain, as the only means of providing the tyrant with guards and the luxuries of life; like that it places no confidence in the people; and therefore deprives them of the use of arms: it is also common to them both to persecute the populace, to drive them out of the city and their own habitations. With a democracy it quarrels with the nobles, and destroys them both publicly and privately, or drives them into banishment, as rivals and an impediment to the government; hence naturally arise conspiracies both amongst those who desire to govern and those who desire not to be slaves; hence arose Periander's advice to Thrasybulus to take off the tallest stalks, hinting thereby, that it was necessary to make away with the eminent citizens. We ought then in reason, as has been already said, to account for the changes which arise in a monarchy from the same causes which produce them in other states: for, through injustice received, fear, and contempt, many of those who are under a monarchical government conspire against it; but of all species of injustice, injurious contempt has most influence on them for that purpose: sometimes it is owing to their being deprived of their private fortunes. The dissolution too of a kingdom and a tyranny are generally the same; for monarchs abound in wealth and honour, which all are desirous to obtain. Of plots: some aim at the life of those who govern, others at their government; the first arises from hatred to their persons; which hatred may be owing to many causes, either of which will be sufficient to excite their anger, and the generality of those who are under the influence of that passion will join in a conspiracy, not for the sake of their own advancement, but for revenge. Thus the plot against the children of Pisistratus arose from their injurious treatment of Harmodius's sister, and insulting him also; for Harmodius resenting the injury done to his sister, and Aristogiton the injury done to Harmodius. Periander the tyrant of Ambracia also lost his life by a conspiracy, for some improper liberties he took with a boy in his cups: and Philip was slain by Pausanias for neglecting to revenge him of the affront he had received from Attains; as was Amintas the Little by Darda, for insulting him on account of his age; and the eunuch by Evagoras the Cyprian in revenge for having taken his son's wife away from him . . .

Many also who have had their bodies scourged with stripes have, through resentment, either killed those who caused them to be inflicted or conspired against them, even when they had kingly power, as at Mitylene Megacles, joining with his friends, killed the Penthelidee, who used to go about striking those they met with clubs. Thus, in later times, Smendes killed Penthilus for whipping him and dragging him away from his wife. Decamnichus also was the chief cause of the conspiracy against Archelaus, for he urged others on: the occasion of his resentment was his having delivered him to Euripides the poet to be scourged; for Euripides was greatly offended with him for having said something of the foulness of his breath. And many others have been killed or conspired against on the same account. Fear too is a cause which produces the same effects, as well in monarchies as in other states: thus Artabanes conspired against Xerxes through fear of punishment for having hanged Darius according to his orders, whom he supposed he intended to pardon, as the order was given at supper-time. Some kings also have been dethroned and killed in consequence of the contempt they were held in by the people; as some one conspired against Sardanapalus, having seen him spinning with his wife, if what is related of him is true, or if not of him, it may very probably be true of some one else. Dion also conspired against Dionysius the Younger, seeing his subjects desirous of a conspiracy, and that he himself was always drunk: and even a man's friends will do this if they despise him; for from the confidence he places in them, they think that they shall not be found out. Those also who think they shall gain his throne will conspire against a king through contempt; for as they are powerful themselves, and despise the danger, on account of their own strength, they will readily attempt it. Thus a general at the head of his army will endeavour to dethrone the monarch, as Cyrus did Astyages, despising both his manner of life and his forces; his forces for want of action, his life for its effeminacy: thus Suthes, the Thracian, who was general to Amadocus, conspired against him. Sometimes more than one of these causes will excite men to enter into conspiracies, as contempt and desire of gain; as in the instance of Mithridates against Ariobarzanes. Those also who are of a bold disposition, and have gained military honours amongst kings, will of all others be most like to engage in sedition; for strength and courage united inspire great bravery: whenever, therefore, these join in one person, he will be very ready for conspiracies, as he will easily conquer. Those who conspire against a tyrant through love of glory and honour have a different motive in view from what I have already mentioned; for, like all others who embrace danger, they have only glory and honour in view, and think, not as some do, of the wealth and pomp they may acquire, but engage in this as they would in any other noble action, that they may be illustrious and distinguished, and destroy a tyrant, not to succeed in his tyranny, but to acquire renown. No doubt but the number of those who act upon this principle is small, for we must suppose they regard their own safety as nothing in case they should not succeed, and must embrace the opinion of Dion (which few can do) when he made war upon Dionysius with a very few troops; for he said, that let the advantage he made be ever so little it would satisfy him to have gained it; and that, should it be his lot to die the moment he had gained footing in his country, he should think his death sufficiently glorious. A tyranny also is exposed to the same destruction as all other states are, from too powerful neighbours: for it is evident, that an opposition of principles will make them desirous of subverting it; and what they desire, all who can, do: and there is a principle of opposition in one state to another, as a democracy against a tyranny, as says Hesiod, "a potter against a potter;" for the extreme of a democracy is a tyranny; a kingly power against an aristocracy, from their different forms of government—for which reason the Lacedaemonians destroyed many tyrannies; as did the Syracusians during the prosperity of their state. Nor are they only destroyed from without, but also from within, when those who have no share in the power bring about a revolution, as happened to Gelon, and lately to Dionysius; to the first, by means of Thrasybulus, the brother of Hiero, who nattered Gelon's son, and induced him to lead a life of pleasure, that he himself might govern; but the family joined together and endeavoured to support the tyranny and expel Thrasybulus; but those whom they made of their party seized the opportunity and expelled the whole family. Dion made war against his relation Dionysius, and being assisted by the people, first expelled and then killed him. As there are two causes which chiefly induce men to conspire against tyrants, hatred and contempt, one of these, namely hatred, seems inseparable from them. Contempt also is often the cause of their destruction: for though, for instance, those who raised themselves to the supreme power generally preserved it; but those who received it from them have, to speak truth, almost immediately all of them lost it; for, falling into an effeminate way of life, they soon grew despicable, and generally fell victims to conspiracies. Part of their hatred may be very fitly ascribed to anger; for in some cases this is their motive to action: for it is often a cause which impels them to act more powerfully than hatred, and they proceed with greater obstinacy against those whom they attack, as this passion is not under the direction of reason. Many persons also indulge this passion through contempt; which occasioned the fall of the Pisistratidae and many others. But hatred is more powerful than anger; for anger is accompanied with grief, which prevents the entrance of reason; but hatred is free from it. In short, whatever causes may be assigned as the destruction of a pure oligarchy unmixed with any other government and an extreme democracy, the same may be applied to a tyranny; for these are divided tyrannies.

Kingdoms are seldom destroyed by any outward attack; for which reason they are generally very stable; but they have many causes of subversion within; of which two are the principal; one is when those who are in power excite a sedition, the other when they endeavour to establish a tyranny by assuming greater power than the law gives them. A kingdom, indeed, is not what we ever see erected in our times, but rather monarchies and tyrannies; for a kingly government is one that is voluntarily submitted to, and its supreme power admitted upon great occasions: but where many are equal, and there are none in any respect so much better than another as to be qualified for the greatness and dignity of government over them, then these equals will not willingly submit to be commanded; but if any one assumes the government, either by force or fraud, this is a tyranny. To what we have already said we shall add, the causes of revolutions in an hereditary kingdom. One of these is, that many of those who enjoy it are naturally proper objects of contempt only: another is, that they are insolent while their power is not despotic; but they possess kingly honours only. Such a state is soon destroyed; for a king exists but while the people are willing to obey, as their submission to him is voluntary, but to a tyrant involuntary. These and such-like are the causes of the destruction of monarchies.

# CHAPTER

# XI

Monarchies, in a word, are preserved by means contrary to what I have already mentioned as the cause of their destruction; but to speak to each separately: the stability of a kingdom will depend upon the power of the king's being kept within moderate bounds; for by how much the less extensive his power is, by so much the longer will his government continue; for he will be less despotic and more upon an equality of condition with those he governs; who, on that account, will envy him the less.

It was on this account that the kingdom of the Molossi continued so long; and the Lacedaemonians from their government's being from the beginning divided into two parts, and also by the moderation introduced into the other parts of it by Theopompus, and his establishment of the ephori; for by taking something from the power he increased the duration of the kingdom, so that in some measure he made it not less, but bigger; as they say he replied to his wife, who asked him if he was not ashamed to deliver down his kingdom to his children reduced from what he received it from his ancestors? No, says he, I give it him more lasting. Tyrannies are preserved two ways most opposite to each other, one of which is when the power is delegated from one to the other, and in this manner many tyrants govern in their states. Report says that Periander founded many of these. There are also many of them to be met with amongst the Persians. What has been already mentioned is as conducive as anything can be to preserve a tyranny; namely, to keep down those who are of an aspiring disposition, to take off those who will not submit, to allow no public meals, no clubs, no education, nothing at all, but to guard against everything that gives rise to high spirits or mutual confidence; nor to suffer the learned meetings of those who are at leisure to hold conversation with each other; and to endeavour by every means possible to keep all the people strangers to each other; for knowledge increases mutual confidence; and to oblige all strangers to appear in public, and to live near the city-gate, that all their actions may be sufficiently seen; for those who are kept like slaves seldom entertain any noble thoughts: in short, to imitate everything which the Persians and barbarians do, for they all contribute to support slavery; and to endeavour to know what every one who is under their power does and says; and for this purpose to employ spies: such were those women whom the Syracusians called potagogides Hiero also used to send out listeners wherever there was any meeting or conversation; for the people dare not speak with freedom for fear of such persons; and if any one does, there is the less chance of its being concealed; and to endeavour that the whole community should mutually accuse and come to blows with each other, friend with friend, the commons with the nobles, and the rich with each other. It is also advantageous for a tyranny that all those who are under it should be oppressed with poverty, that they may not be able to compose a guard; and that, being employed in procuring their daily bread, they may have no leisure to conspire against their tyrants. The Pyramids of Egypt are a proof of this, and the

votive edifices of the Cyposelidse, and the temple of Jupiter Olympus,
built by the Pisistratidae, and the works of Polycrates at Samos; for all
these produced one end, the keeping the people poor. It is necessary
also to multiply taxes, as at Syracuse; where Dionysius in the space of
five years collected all the private property of his subjects into his own
coffers. A tyrant also should endeavour to engage his subjects in a war,
that they may have employment and continually depend upon their
general. A king is preserved by his friends, but a tyrant is of all persons
the man who can place no confidence in friends, as every one has it in
his desire and these chiefly in their power to destroy him. All these
things also which are done in an extreme democracy should be done in
a tyranny, as permitting great licentiousness to the women in the house,
that they may reveal their husbands' secrets; and showing great
indulgence to slaves also for the same reason; for slaves and women
conspire not against tyrants: but when they are treated with kindness,
both of them are abettors of tyrants, and extreme democracies also; and
the people too in such a state desire to be despotic. For which reason
flatterers are in repute in both these: the demagogue in the democracy,
for he is the proper flatterer of the people; among tyrants, he who will
servilely adapt himself to their humours; for this is the business of
flatterers. And for this reason tyrants always love the worst of wretches,
for they rejoice in being flattered, which no man of a liberal spirit will
submit to; for they love the virtuous, but flatter none. Bad men too are
fit for bad purposes; "like to like," as the proverb says. A tyrant also
should show no favour to a man of worth or a freeman; for he should
think, that no one deserved to be thought these but himself; for he who
supports his dignity, and is a friend to freedom, encroaches upon the
superiority and the despotism of the tyrant: such men, therefore, they
naturally hate, as destructive to their government. A tyrant also should
rather admit strangers to his table and familiarity than citizens, as these
are his enemies, but the others have no design against him. These and
such-like are the supports of a tyranny, for it comprehends whatsoever
is wicked. But all these things may be comprehended in three divisions,
for there are three objects which a tyranny has in view; one of which is,

that the citizens should be of poor abject dispositions; for such men never propose to conspire against any one. The second is, that they should have no confidence in each other; for while they have not this, the tyrant is safe enough from destruction. For which reason they are always at enmity with those of merit, as hurtful to their government; not only as they scorn to be governed despotically, but also because they can rely upon each other's fidelity, and others can rely upon theirs, and because they will not inform against their associates, nor any one else. The third is, that they shall be totally without the means of doing anything; for no one undertakes what is impossible for him to perform: so that without power a tyranny can never be destroyed. These, then, are the three objects which the inclinations of tyrants desire to see accomplished; for all their tyrannical plans tend to promote one of these three ends, that their people may neither have mutual confidence, power, nor spirit. This, then, is one of the two methods of preserving tyrannies: the other proceeds in a way quite contrary to what has been already described, and which may be discerned from considering to what the destruction of a kingdom is owing; for as one cause of that is, making the government approach near to a tyranny, so the safety of a tyranny consists in making the government nearly kingly; preserving only one thing, namely power, that not only the willing, but the unwilling also, must be obliged to submit; for if this is once lost, the tyranny is at an end. This, then, as the foundation, must be preserved: in other particulars carefully do and affect to seem like a king; first, appear to pay a great attention to what belongs to the public; nor make such profuse presents as will offend the people; while they are to supply the money out of the hard labour of their own hands, and see it given in profusion to mistresses, foreigners, and fiddlers; keeping an exact account both of what you receive and pay; which is a practice some tyrants do actually follow, by which means they seem rather fathers of families than tyrants: nor need you ever fear the want of money while you have the supreme power of the state in your own hands. It is also much better for those tyrants who quit their kingdom to do this than to leave behind them money they have hoarded up; for their regents will be much less desirous of making innovations, and they are more to be dreaded by absent tyrants than the citizens; for such of them as he suspects he takes with him, but these regents must be left behind. He should also endeavour to appear to collect such taxes and require such services as the exigencies of the state demand, that whenever they are wanted they may be ready in time of war; and particularly to take care that he appear to collect and keep them not as his own property, but the public's. His appearance also should not be severe, but respectable, so that he should inspire those who approach him with veneration and not fear; but this will not be easily accomplished if he is despised. If, therefore, he will not take the pains to acquire any other, he ought to endeavour to be a man of political abilities, and to fix that opinion of himself in the judgment of his subjects. He should also take care not to appear to be guilty of the least offence against modesty, nor to suffer it in those under him: nor to permit the women of his family to treat others haughtily; for the haughtiness of women has been the ruin of many tyrants. With respect to the pleasures of sense, he ought to do directly contrary to the practice of some tyrants at present; for they do not only continually indulge themselves in them for many days together, but they seem also to desire to have other witnesses of it, that they may wonder at their happiness; whereas he ought really to be moderate in these, and, if not, to appear to others to avoid them—for it is not the sober man who is exposed either to plots or contempt, but the drunkard; not the early riser, but the sluggard. His conduct in general should also be contrary to what is reported of former tyrants; for he ought to improve and adorn his city, so as to seem a guardian and not a tyrant; and, moreover, always to seem particularly attentive to the worship of the gods; for from persons of such a character men entertain less fears of suffering anything illegal while they suppose that he who governs them is religious and reverences the gods; and they will be less inclined to raise insinuations against such a one, as being peculiarly under their protection: but this must be so done as to give no occasion for any suspicion of hypocrisy. He should also take care to show such respect to men of merit in every particular, that they should not think they could be treated with greater distinction by their fellow citizens in a free state. He should also let all honours flow immediately from himself, but every censure from his subordinate officers and judges. It is also a common protection of all monarchies not to make one person too great, or, certainly, not many; for they will support each other: but, if it is necessary to entrust any large powers to one person, to take care that it is not one of an ardent spirit; for this disposition is upon every opportunity most ready for a revolution: and, if it should seem necessary to deprive any one of his power, to do it by degrees, and not reduce him all at once. It is also necessary to abstain from all kinds of insolence; more particularly from corporal punishment; which you must be most cautious never to exercise over those who have a delicate sense of honour; for, as those who love money are touched to the quick when anything affects their property, so are men of honour and principle when they receive any disgrace: therefore, either never employ personal punishment, or, if you do, let it be only in the manner in which a father would correct his son, and not with contempt; and, upon the whole, make amends for any seeming disgrace by bestowing greater honours. But of all persons who are most likely to entertain designs against the person of a tyrant, those are chiefly to be feared and guarded against who regard as nothing the loss of their own lives, so that they can but accomplish their purpose: be very careful therefore of those who either think themselves affronted, or those who are dear to them; for those who are excited by anger to revenge regard as nothing their own persons: for, as Heraclitus says, it is dangerous to fight with an angry man who will purchase with his life the thing he aims at. As all cities are composed of two sorts of persons, the rich and the poor, it is necessary that both these should find equal protection from him who governs them, and that the one party should not have it in their power to injure the other; but that the tyrant should attach to himself that party which is the most powerful; which, if he does, he will have no occasion either to make his slaves free, or to deprive citizens of their arms; for the strength of either of the parties added to his own forces will render him superior to any conspiracy. It would be superfluous to go through all particulars; for the rule of conduct which the tyrant ought to pursue is evident enough, and that is, to affect to appear not the tyrant, but the king; the guardian of those he governs, not their plunderer, but their protector, and to affect the middle rank in life, not one superior to all others: he should, therefore, associate his nobles with him and soothe his people; for his government will not only be necessarily more honourable and worthy of imitation, as it will be over men of worth, and not abject wretches who perpetually both hate and fear him; but it will be also more durable. Let him also frame his life so that his manners may be consentaneous to virtue, or at least let half of them be so, that he may not be altogether wicked, but only so in part.

# CHAPTER

# XII

Indeed an oligarchy and a tyranny are of all governments of the shortest duration. The tyranny of Orthagoras and his family at Sicyon, it is true, continued longer than any other: the reason for which was, that they used their power with moderation, and were in many particulars obedient to the laws; and, as Clisthenes was an able general, he never fell into contempt, and by the care he took that in many particulars his government should be popular. He is reported also to have presented a person with a crown who adjudged the victory to another; and some say that it is the statue of that judge which is placed in the forum.

They say also, that Pisistratus submitted to be summoned into the court of the Areopagites. The second that we shall mention is the tyranny of the Cypselidæ, at Corinth, which continued seventy-seven years and six months; for Cypselus was tyrant there thirty years, Periander forty-four, and Psammetichus, the son of Georgias, three years; the reason for which was, that Cypselus was a popular man, and governed without guards. Periander indeed ruled like a tyrant, but then he was an able general. The third was that of the Pisistradidae at Athens; but it was not continual: for Pisistratus himself was twice expelled; so that out of thirty-three years he was only fifteen in power, and his son eighteen; so that the whole time was thirty-three years. Of the rest we shall mention that of Hiero, and Gelo at Syracuse; and this did not continue long, for both their reigns were only eighteen years; for Gelo died in the eighth year of his tyranny, and Hiero in his tenth. Thrasybulus fell in his eleventh month, and many other tyrannies have continued a very short time. We have now gone through the general cases of corruption and means of preservation both in free states and monarchies. In Plato's Republic, Socrates is introduced treating upon the changes which different governments are liable to: but his discourse is faulty; for he does not particularly mention what changes the best and first governments are liable to; for he only assigns the general cause, of nothing being immutable, but that in time everything will alter [***tr.: text is unintelligible here***] he conceives that nature will then produce bad men, who will not submit to education, and in this, probably, he is not wrong; for it is certain that there are some persons whom it is impossible by any education to make good men; but why should this change be more peculiar to what he calls the best-formed government, than to all other forms, and indeed to all other things that exist? And in respect to his assigned time, as the cause of the alteration of all things, we find that those which did not begin to exist at the same time cease to be at the same time; so that, if anything came into beginning the day before the solstice, it must alter at the same time. Besides, why should such a form of government be changed into the Lacedaemonian? For, in general, when governments alter, they alter into the contrary species to what they before were, and not into one like their former. And this reasoning holds true of other changes; for he says, that from the Lacedaemonian form it changes into an oligarchy, and from thence into a democracy, and from a democracy into a tyranny: and sometimes a contrary change takes place, as from a democracy into an oligarchy, rather than into a monarchy. With respect to a tyranny he neither says whether there will be any change in it; or if not, to what cause it will be owing; or if there is, into what other state it will alter: but the reason of this is, that a tyranny is an indeterminate government; and, according to him, every state ought to alter into the first, and most perfect, thus the continuity and circle would be preserved. But one tyranny often changed into another; as at Syria, from Myron's to Clisthenes'; or into an oligarchy, as was Antileo's at Chalcas; or into a democracy, as was Gelo's at Syracuse; or into an aristocracy, as was Charilaus's at Lacedaemon, and at Carthage. An oligarchy is also changed into a tyranny; such was the rise of most of the ancient tyrannies in Sicily; at Leontini, into the tyranny of Panaetius; at Gela, into that of Cleander; at Rhegium into that of Anaxilaus; and the like in many other cities. It is absurd also to suppose, that a state is changed into an oligarchy because those who are in power are avaricious and greedy of money, and not because those who are by far richer than their fellow citizens think it unfair that those who have nothing should have an equal share in the rule of the state with themselves, who possess so much-for in many oligarchies it is not allowable to be employed in money-getting, and there are many laws to prevent it. But in Carthage, which is a democracy, money-getting is creditable, and yet their form of government remains unaltered. It is also absurd to say, that in an oligarchy there are two cities, one of the poor and another of the rich; for why should this happen to them more than to the Lacedaemonians, or any other state where all possess not equal property, or where all are not equally good? For though no one member of the community should be poorer than he was before, yet a democracy might nevertheless change into an oligarchy; if the rich should be more powerful than the poor, and the one too negligent, and the other attentive: and though these changes are owing to many causes, yet he mentions but one only, that the citizens become poor by luxury, and paying interest-money; as if at first they were all rich, or the greater part of them: but this is not so, but when some of those who have the principal management of public affairs lose their fortunes, they will endeavour to bring about a revolution; but when others do, nothing of consequence will follow, nor when such states do alter is there any more reason for their altering into a democracy than any other. Besides, though some of the members of the community may not have spent their fortunes, yet if they share not in the honours of the state, or if they are ill-used and insulted, they will endeavour to raise seditions, and bring about a revolution, that they may be allowed to do as they like; which, Plato says, arises from too much liberty. Although there are many oligarchies and democracies, yet Socrates, when he is treating of the changes they may undergo, speaks of them as if there was but one of each sort.

# BOOK VI

## CHAPTER

### I

We have already shown what is the nature of the supreme council in the state, and wherein one may differ from another, and how the different magistrates should be regulated; and also the judicial department, and what is best suited to what state; and also to what causes both the destruction and preservation of governments are owing.

As there are very many species of democracies, as well as of other states, it will not be amiss to consider at the same time anything which we may have omitted to mention concerning either of them, and to allot to each that mode of conduct which is peculiar to and advantageous for them; and also to inquire into the combinations of all these different modes of government which we have mentioned; for as these are blended together the government is altered, as from an aristocracy to be an oligarchy, and from a free state to be a democracy. Now, I mean by those combinations of government (which I ought to examine into, but have not yet done), namely, whether the deliberative department and the election of magistrates is regulated in a manner correspondent to an oligarchy, or the judicial to an aristocracy, or the deliberative part only to an oligarchy, and the election of magistrates to an aristocracy, or whether, in any other manner, everything is not regulated according to the nature of the government. But we will first consider what particular sort of democracy is fitted to a particular city, and also what particular oligarchy to a particular people; and of other states, what is advantageous to what. It is also necessary to show clearly, not only which of these governments is best for a state, but also how it ought to be established there, and other things we will treat of briefly.

And first, we will speak of a democracy; and this will at the same time show clearly the nature of its opposite which some persons call an oligarchy; and in doing this we must examine into all the parts of a democracy, and everything that is connected therewith; for from the manner in which these are compounded together different species of democracies arise: and hence it is that they are more than one, and of various natures. Now, there are two causes which occasion there being so many democracies; one of which is that which we have already mentioned; namely, there being different sorts of people; for in one country the majority are husbandmen, in another mechanics, and hired servants; if the first of these is added to the second, and the third to both of them, the democracy will not only differ in the particular of better or worse, but in this, that it will be no longer the same government; the other is that which we will now speak of. The different things which are connected with democracies and seem to make part of these states, do, from their being joined to them, render them different from others: this attending a few, that more, and another all. It is necessary that he who would found any state which he may happen to approve of, or correct one, should be acquainted with all these particulars. All founders of states endeavour to comprehend within their own plan everything of nearly the same kind with it; but in doing this they err, in the manner I have already described in treating of the preservation and destruction of governments. I will now speak of these first principles and manners, and whatever else a democratical state requires.

# CHAPTER

## II

Now the foundation of a democratical state is liberty, and people have been accustomed to say this as if here only liberty was to be found; for they affirm that this is the end proposed by every democracy. But one part of liberty is to govern and be governed alternately; for, according to democratical justice, equality is measured by numbers, and not by worth: and this being just, it is necessary that the supreme power should be vested in the people at large; and that what the majority determine should be final: so that in a democracy the poor ought to have more power than the rich, as being the greater number; for this is one mark of liberty which all framers of a democracy lay down as a criterion of that state; another is, to live as every one likes; for this, they say, is a right which liberty gives, since he is a slave who must live as he likes not. This, then, is another criterion of a democracy. Hence arises the claim to be under no command whatsoever to any one, upon any account, any otherwise than by rotation, and that just as far only as that person is, in his turn, under his also. This also is conducive to that equality which liberty demands. These things being premised, and such being the government, it follows that such rules as the following should be observed in it, that all the magistrates should be chosen out of all the people, and all to command each, and each in his turn all: that all the magistrates should be chosen by lot, except to those offices only which required some particular knowledge and skill: that no census, or a very small one, should be required to qualify a man for any office: that none should be in the same employment twice, or very few, and very seldom, except in the army: that all their appointments should be limited to a very short time, or at least as many as possible: that the whole community should be qualified to judge in all causes whatsoever, let the object be ever so extensive, ever so interesting, or of ever so high a nature; as at Athens, where the people at large judge the magistrates when they come out of office, and decide concerning public affairs as well as private contracts: that the supreme power should be in the public assembly; and that no magistrate should be allowed any discretionary power but in a few instances, and of no consequence to public business. Of all magistrates a senate is best suited to a democracy, where the whole community is not paid for giving their attendance; for in that case it loses its power; for then the people will bring all causes before them, by appeal, as we have already mentioned in a former book. In the next place, there should, if possible, be a fund to pay all the citizens—who have any share in the management of public affairs, either as members of the assembly, judges, and magistrates; but if this cannot be done, at least the magistrates, the judges the senators, and members of the supreme assembly, and also those officers who are obliged to eat at a common table ought to be paid. Moreover, as an oligarchy is said to be a government of men of family, fortune, and education; so, on the contrary, a democracy is a government in the hands of men of no birth, indigent circumstances, and mechanical employments. In this state also no office should be for life; and, if any such should remain after the government has been long changed into a democracy, they should endeavour by degrees to diminish the power; and also elect by lot instead of vote. These things, then, appertain to all democracies; namely, to be established on that principle of justice which is homogeneous to those governments; that is, that all the members of the state, by number, should enjoy an equality, which seems chiefly to constitute a democracy, or government of the people: for it seems perfectly equal that the rich should have no more share in the government than the poor, nor be alone in power; but that all should be equal, according to number; for thus, they think, the equality and liberty of the state best preserved.

# CHAPTER

## III

In the next place we must inquire how this equality is to be procured. Shall the qualifications be divided so that five hundred rich should be equal to a thousand poor, or shall the thousand have equal power with the five hundred? Or shall we not establish our equality in this manner? But divide indeed thus, and afterwards taking an equal number both out of the five hundred and the thousand, invest them with the power of creating the magistrates and judges. Is this state then established according to perfect democratical justice, or rather that which is guided by numbers only? For the defenders of a democracy say, that that is just which the majority approve of: but the favourers of an oligarchy say, that that is just which those who have most approve of; and that we ought to be directed by the value of property. Both the propositions are unjust; for if we agree with what the few propose we erect a tyranny: for if it should happen that an individual should have more than the rest who are rich, according to oligarchical justice, this man alone has a right to the supreme power; but if superiority of numbers is to prevail, injustice will then be done by confiscating the property of the rich, who are few, as we have already said. What then that equality is, which both parties will admit, must be collected from the definition of right which is common to them both; for they both say that what the majority of the state approves of ought to be established. Be it so; but not entirely: but since a city happens to be made up of two different ranks of people, the rich and the poor, let that be established which is approved of by both these, or the greater part: but should there be opposite sentiments, let that be established which shall be approved of by the greater part: but let this be according to the census; for instance, if there should be ten of the rich and twenty of the poor, and six of the first and fifteen of the last should agree upon any measure, and the remaining four of the rich should join with the remaining five of the poor in opposing it, that party whose census when added together should determine which opinion should be law, and should these happen to be equal, it should be regarded as a case similar to an assembly or court of justice dividing equally upon any question that comes before them, who either determine it by lot or some such method. But although, with respect to what is equal and just, it may be very difficult to establish the truth, yet it is much easier to do than to persuade those who have it in their power to encroach upon others to be guided thereby; for the weak always desire what is equal and just, but the powerful pay no regard thereunto.

## CHAPTER

## IV

There are four kinds of democracies. The best is that which is composed of those first in order, as we have already said, and this also is the most ancient of any. I call that the first which every one would place so, was he to divide the people; for the best part of these are the husbandmen. We see, then, that a democracy may be framed where the majority live by tillage or pasturage; for, as their property is but small, they will not be at leisure perpetually to hold public assemblies, but will be continually employed in following their own business, not having otherwise the means of living; nor will they be desirous of what another enjoys, but will rather like to follow their own business than meddle with state affairs and accept the offices of government, which will be attended with no great profit; for the major part of mankind are rather desirous of riches than honour (a proof of this is, that they submitted to the tyrannies in ancient times, and do now submit to the oligarchies, if no one hinders them in their usual occupations, or deprives them of their property; for some of them soon get rich, others are removed from poverty); besides, their having the right of election and calling their magistrates to account for their conduct when they come out of office, will satisfy their desire of honours, if any of them entertain that passion: for in some states, though the commonalty have not the right of electing the magistrates, yet it is vested in part of that body chosen to represent them: and it is sufficient for the people at large to possess the deliberative power: and this ought to be considered as a species of democracy; such was that formerly at Mantinsea: for which reason it is proper for the democracy we have been now treating of to have a power (and it has been usual for them to have it) of censuring their magistrates when out of office, and sitting in judgment upon all causes: but that the chief magistrates should be elected, and according to a certain census, which should vary with the rank of their office, or else not by a census, but according to their abilities for their respective appointments. A state thus constituted must be well constituted; for the magistracies will be always filled with the best men with the approbation of the people; who will not envy their superiors: and these and the nobles should be content with this part in the administration; for they will not be governed by their inferiors. They will be also careful to use their power with moderation, as there are others to whom full power is delegated to censure their conduct; for it is very serviceable to the state to have them dependent upon others, and not to be permitted to do whatsoever they choose; for with such a liberty there would be no check to that evil particle there is in every one: therefore it is necessary and most for the benefit of the state that the offices thereof should be filled by the principal persons in it, whose characters are unblemished, and that the people are not oppressed. It is now evident that this is the best species of democracy, and on what account; because the people are such and have such powers as they ought to have. To establish a democracy of husbandmen some of those laws which were observed in many ancient states are universally useful; as, for instance, on no account to permit any one to possess more than a certain quantity of land, or within a certain distance from the city. Formerly also, in some states, no one was allowed to sell their original lot of land. They also mention a law of one Oxylus, which forbade any one to add to their patrimony by usury. We ought also to follow the law of the

Aphutaeans, as useful to direct us in this particular we are now speaking of; for they having but very little ground, while they were a numerous people, and at the same time were all husbandmen, did not include all their lands within the census, but divided them in such a manner that, according to the census, the poor had more power than the rich. Next to the commonalty of husbandmen is one of shepherds and herdsmen; for they have many things in common with them, and, by their way of life, are excellently qualified to make good soldiers, stout in body, and able to continue in the open air all night. The generality of the people of whom other democracies are composed are much worse than these; for their lives are wretched nor have they any business with virtue in anything they do; these are your mechanics, your exchange-men, and hired servants; as all these sorts of men frequent the exchange and the citadel, they can readily attend the public assembly; whereas the husbandmen, being more dispersed in the country, cannot so easily meet together; nor are they equally desirous of doing it with these others! When a country happens to be so situated that a great part of the land lies at a distance from the city, there it is easy to establish a good democracy or a free state for the people in general will be obliged to live in the country; so that it will be necessary in such a democracy, though there may be an exchange-mob at hand, never to allow a legal assembly without the inhabitants of the country attend. We have shown in what manner the first and best democracy ought to be established, and it will be equally evident as to the rest, for from these we should proceed as a guide, and always separate the meanest of the people from the rest. But the last and worst, which gives to every citizen without distinction a share in every part of the administration, is what few citizens can bear, nor is it easy to preserve for any long time, unless well supported by laws and manners. We have already noticed almost every cause that can destroy either this or any other state. Those who have taken the lead in such a democracy have endeavoured to support it, and make the people powerful by collecting together as many persons as they could and giving them their freedom, not only legitimately but naturally born, and also if either of their parents were citizens, that is to say, if either their father or mother; and this method is better suited to this state than any other: and thus the demagogues have usually managed. They ought, however, to take care, and do this no longer than the common people are superior to the nobles and those of the middle rank, and then stop; for, if they proceed still further, they will make the state disorderly, and the nobles will ill brook the power of the common people, and be full of resentment against it; which was the cause of an insurrection at Cyrene: for a little evil is overlooked, but when it becomes a great one it strikes the eye. It is, moreover, very useful in such a state to do as Clisthenes did at Athens, when he was desirous of increasing the power of the people, and as those did who established the democracy in Cyrene; that is, to institute many tribes and fraternities, and to make the religious rites of private persons few, and those common; and every means is to be contrived to associate and blend the people together as much as possible; and that all former customs be broken through. Moreover, whatsoever is practised in a tyranny seems adapted to a democracy of this species; as, for instance, the licentiousness of the slaves, the women, and the children; for this to a certain degree is useful in such a state; and also to overlook every one's living as they choose; for many will support such a government: for it is more agreeable to many to live without any control than as prudence would direct.

# CHAPTER

# V

It is also the business of the legislator and all those who would support a government of this sort not to make it too great a work, or too perfect; but to aim only to render it stable: for, let a state be constituted ever so badly, there is no difficulty in its continuing a few days: they should therefore endeavour to procure its safety by all those ways which we have described in assigning the causes of the preservation and destruction of governments; avoiding what is hurtful, and by framing such laws, written and unwritten, as contain those things which chiefly tend to the preservation of the state; nor to suppose that that is useful either for a democratic or an oligarchic form of government which contributes to make them more purely so, but what will contribute to their duration: but our demagogues at present, to flatter the people, occasion frequent confiscations in the courts; for which reason those who have the welfare of the state really at heart should act directly opposite to what they do, and enact a law to prevent forfeitures from being divided amongst the people or paid into the treasury, but to have them set apart for sacred uses: for those who are of a bad disposition would not then be the less cautious, as their punishment would be the same; and the community would not be so ready to condemn those whom they sat in judgment on when they were to get nothing by it: they should also take care that the causes which are brought before the public should be as few as possible, and punish with the utmost severity those who rashly brought an action against any one; for it is not the commons but the nobles who are generally prosecuted: for in all things the citizens of the same state ought to be affectionate to each other, at least not to treat those who have the chief power in it as their enemies. Now, as the democracies which have been lately established are very numerous, and it is difficult to get the common people to attend the public assemblies without they are paid for it, this, when there is not a sufficient public revenue, is fatal to the nobles; for the deficiencies therein must be necessarily made up by taxes, confiscations, and fines imposed by corrupt courts of justice: which things have already destroyed many democracies. Whenever, then, the revenues of the state are small, there should be but few public assemblies and but few courts of justice: these, however, should have very extensive jurisdictions, but should continue sitting a few days only, for by this means the rich would not fear the expense, although they should receive nothing for their attendance, though the poor did; and judgment also would be given much better; for the rich will not choose to be long absent from their own affairs, but will willingly be so for a short time: and, when there are sufficient revenues, a different conduct ought to be pursued from what the demagogues at present follow; for now they divide the surplus of the public money amongst the poor; these receive it and again want the same supply, while the giving it is like pouring water into a sieve: but the true patriot in a democracy ought to take care that the majority of the community are not too poor, for this is the cause of rapacity in that government; he therefore should endeavour that they may enjoy perpetual plenty; and as this also is advantageous to the rich, what can be saved out of the public money should be put by, and then divided at once amongst the poor, if possible, in such a quantity as may enable every one of them to purchase a little field, and, if that cannot be done, at least to give each of them enough to procure the implements of trade and husbandry; and if there is not enough for all to receive so much at once, then to divide it according to tribes or any other allotment. In the meantime let the rich pay them for necessary services, but not be obliged to find them in useless amusements. And something like this was the manner in which they managed at Carthage, and preserved the affections of the people; for by continually sending some of their community into colonies they procured plenty. It is also worthy of a sensible and generous nobility to divide the poor amongst them, and supplying them with what is necessary, induce them to work; or to imitate the conduct of the people at Tarentum: for they, permitting the poor to partake in common of everything which is needful for them, gain the affections of the commonalty. They have also two different ways of electing their magistrates; for some are chosen by vote, others by lot; by the last, that the people at large may have some share in the administration; by the former, that the state may be well governed: the same may be accomplished if of the same magistrates you choose some by vote, others by lot. And thus much for the manner in which democracies ought to be established.

# CHAPTER

## VI

What has been already said will almost of itself sufficiently show how an oligarchy ought to be founded; for he who would frame such a state should have in his view a democracy to oppose it; for every species of oligarchy should be founded on principles diametrically opposite to some species of democracy.

The first and best-framed oligarchy is that which approaches near to what we call a free state; in which there ought to be two different census, the one high, the other low: from those who are within the latter the ordinary officers of the state ought to be chosen; from the former the supreme magistrates: nor should any one be excluded from a part of the administration who was within the census; which should be so regulated that the commonalty who are included in it should by means thereof be superior to those who have no share in the government; for those who are to have the management of public affairs ought always to be chosen out of the better sort of the people. Much in the same manner ought that oligarchy to be established which is next in order: but as to that which is most opposite to a pure democracy, and approaches nearest to a dynasty and a tyranny, as it is of all others the worst, so it requires the greatest care and caution to preserve it: for as bodies of sound and healthy constitutions and ships which are well manned and well found for sailing can bear many injuries without perishing, while a diseased body or a leaky ship with an indifferent crew cannot support the least shock; so the worst-established governments want most looking after. A number of citizens is the preservation of a democracy; for these are opposed to those rights which are founded in rank: on the contrary, the preservation of an oligarchy depends upon the due regulation of the different orders in the society.

# CHAPTER

# VII

As the greater part of the community are divided into four sorts of people; husbandmen, mechanics, traders, and hired servants; and as those who are employed in war may likewise be divided into four; the horsemen, the heavy-armed soldier, the light-armed, and the sailor, where the nature of the country can admit a great number of horse; there a powerful oligarchy may be easily established: for the safety of the inhabitants depends upon a force of that sort; but those who can support the expense of horsemen must be persons of some considerable fortune. Where the troops are chiefly heavy-armed, there an oligarchy, inferior in power to the other, may be established; for the heavy-armed are rather made up of men of substance than the poor: but the light-armed and the sailors always contribute to support a democracy: but where the number of these is very great and a sedition arises, the other parts of the community fight at a disadvantage; but a remedy for this evil is to be learned from skilful generals, who always mix a proper number of light-armed soldiers with their horse and heavy-armed: for it is with those that the populace get the better of the men of fortune in an insurrection; for these being lighter are easily a match for the horse and the heavy-armed: so that for an oligarchy to form a body of troops from these is to form it against itself: but as a city is composed of persons of different ages, some young and some old, the fathers should teach their sons, while they were very young, a light and easy exercise; but, when they are grown up, they should be perfect in every warlike exercise. Now, the admission of the people to any share in the government should either be (as I said before) regulated by a census, or else, as at Thebes, allowed to those who for a certain time have ceased from any mechanic employment, or as at Massalia, where they are chosen according to their worth, whether citizens or foreigners. With respect to the magistrates of the highest rank which it may be necessary to have in a state, the services they are bound to do the public should be expressly laid down, to prevent the common people from being desirous of accepting their employments, and also to induce them to regard their magistrates with favour when they know what a price they pay for their honours. It is also necessary that the magistrates, upon entering into their offices, should make magnificent sacrifices and erect some public structure, that the people partaking of the entertainment, and seeing the city ornamented with votive gifts in their temples and public structures, may see with pleasure the stability of the government: add to this also, that the nobles will have their generosity recorded: but now this is not the conduct which those who are at present at the head of an oligarchy pursue, but the contrary; for they are not more desirous of honour than of gain; for which reason such oligarchies may more properly be called little democracies. Thus we have explained on what principles a democracy and an oligarchy ought to be established.

## CHAPTER

## VIII

After what has been said I proceed next to treat particularly of the magistrates; of what nature they should be, how many, and for what purpose, as I have already mentioned: for without necessary magistrates no state can exist, nor without those which contribute to its dignity and good order can exist happily: now it is necessary that in small states the magistrates should be few; in a large one, many: also to know well what offices may be joined together, and what ought to be separated. The first thing necessary is to establish proper regulators in the markets; for which purpose a certain magistrate should be appointed to inspect their contracts and preserve good order; for of necessity, in almost every city there must be both buyers and sellers to supply each other's mutual wants: and this is what is most productive of the comforts of life; for the sake of which men seem to have joined together in one community. A second care, and nearly related to the first, is to have an eye both to the public and private edifices in the city, that they may be an ornament; and also to take care of all buildings which are likely to fall: and to see that the highways are kept in proper repair; and also that the landmarks between different estates are preserved, that there may be no disputes on that account; and all other business of the same nature. Now, this business may be divided into several branches, over each of which in populous cities they appoint a separate person; one to inspect the buildings, another the fountains, another the harbours; and they are called the inspectors of the city. A third, which is very like the last, and conversant nearly about the same objects, only in the country, is to take care of what is done out of the city. The officers who have this employment we call inspectors of the lands, or inspectors of the woods; but the business of all three of them is the same. There must also be other officers appointed to receive the public revenue and to deliver it out to those who are in the different departments of the state: these are called receivers or quaestors. There must also be another, before whom all private contracts and sentences of courts should be enrolled, as well as proceedings and declarations. Sometimes this employment is divided amongst many, but there is one supreme over the rest; these are called proctors, notaries, and the like. Next to these is an officer whose business is of all others the most necessary, and yet most difficult; namely, to take care that sentence is executed upon those who are condemned; and that every one pays the fines laid on him; and also to have the charge of those who are in prison. This office is very disagreeable on account of the odium attending it, so that no one will engage therein without it is made very profitable, or, if they do, will they be willing to execute it according to law; but it is most necessary, as it is of no service to pass judgment in any cause without that judgment is carried into execution: for without this human society could not subsist: for which reason it is best that this office should not be executed by one person, but by some of the magistrates of the other courts. In like manner, the taking care that those fines which are ordered by the judges are levied should be divided amongst different persons. And as different magistrates judge different causes, let the causes of the young be heard by the young: and as to those which are already brought to a hearing, let one person pass sentence, and another see it executed: as, for instance, let the magistrates who have the care of the public buildings execute the sentence which the inspectors of the markets have passed, and the like in other cases: for by so much the less odium attends those who carry the laws into execution, by so much the easier will they be properly put in force: therefore for the same persons to pass the sentence and to execute it will subject them to general hatred; and if they pass it upon all, they will be considered as the enemies of all. Thus one person has often the custody of the prisoner's body, while another sees the sentence against him executed, as the eleven did at Athens: for which reason it is prudent to separate these offices, and to give great attention thereunto as equally necessary with anything we have already mentioned; for it will certainly happen that men of character will decline accepting this office, and worthless persons cannot properly be entrusted with it, as having themselves rather an occasion for a guard than being qualified to guard others. This, therefore, ought by no means to be a separate office from others; nor should it be continually allotted to any individuals, but the young men; where there is a city-guard, the youths ought in turns to take these offices upon them. These, then, as the most necessary magistrates, ought to be first mentioned: next to these are others no less necessary, but of much higher rank, for they ought to be men of great skill and fidelity. These are they who have the guard of the city, and provide everything that is necessary for war; whose business it is, both in war and peace, to defend the walls and the gates, and to take care to muster and marshal the citizens. Over all these there are sometimes more officers, sometimes fewer: thus in little cities there is only one whom they call either general or polemarch; but where there are horse and light-armed troops, and bowmen, and sailors, they sometimes put distinct commanders over each of these; who again have others under them, according to their different divisions; all of which join together to make one military body: and thus much for this department. Since some of the magistrates, if not all, have business with the public money, it is necessary that there should be other officers, whose employment should be nothing else than to take an account of what they have, and correct any mismanagement therein. But besides all these magistrates there is one who is supreme over them all, who very often has in his own power the disposal of the public revenue and taxes; who presides over the people when the supreme power is in them; for there must be some magistrate who has a power to summon them together, and to preside as head of the state. These are sometimes called preadvisers; but where there are many, more properly a council. These are nearly the civil magistrates which are requisite to a government: but there are other persons whose business is confined to religion; as the priests, and those who are to take care of the temples, that they are kept in proper repair, or, if they fall down, that they may be rebuilt; and whatever else belongs to public worship. This charge is sometimes entrusted to one person, as in very small cities: in others it is delegated to many, and these distinct from the priesthood, as the builders or keepers of holy places, and officers of the sacred revenue. Next to these are those who are appointed to have the general care of all those public sacrifices to the tutelar god of the state, which the laws do not entrust to the priests: and these in different states have different appellations. To enumerate in few words the different departments of all those magistrates who are necessary: these are either religion, war, taxes, expenditures, markets, public buildings, harbours, highways. Belonging to the courts of justice there are scribes to enroll private contracts; and there must also be guards set over the prisoners, others to see the law is executed, council on either side, and also others to watch over the conduct of those who are to decide the causes. Amongst the magistrates also may finally be reckoned those who are to give their advice in public affairs. But separate states, who are peculiarly happy and have leisure to attend to more minute particulars, and are very attentive to good order, require particular magistrates for themselves; such as those who have the government of the women; who are to see the laws are executed; who take care of the boys and preside over their education. To these may be added those who have the care of their gymnastic exercises, their theatres, and every other public spectacle which there may happen to be. Some of these, however, are not of general use; as the governors of the women: for the poor are obliged to employ their wives and children in servile offices for want of slaves. As there are three magistrates to whom some states entrust the supreme power; namely, guardians of the laws, preadvisers, and senators; guardians of the laws suit best to an aristocracy, preadvisers to an oligarchy, and a senate to a democracy. And thus much briefly concerning all magistrates.

# BOOK VII

## CHAPTER

### I

He who proposes to make that inquiry which is necessary concerning what government is best, ought first to determine what manner of living is most eligible; for while this remains uncertain it will also be equally uncertain what government is best: for, provided no unexpected accidents interfere, it is highly probable, that those who enjoy the best government will live the most happily according to their circumstances; he ought, therefore, first to know what manner of life is most desirable for all; and afterwards whether this life is the same to the man and the citizen, or different. As I imagine that I have already sufficiently shown what sort of life is best in my popular discourses on that subject, I think I may very properly repeat the same here; as most certainly no one ever called in question the propriety of one of the divisions; namely, that as what is good, relative to man, may be divided into three sorts, what is external, what appertains to the body, and what to the soul, it is evident that all these must conspire to make a man happy: for no one would say that a man was happy who had no fortitude, no temperance, no justice, no prudence;

but was afraid of the flies that flew round him: nor would abstain from the meanest theft if he was either hungry or dry, or would murder his dearest friend for a farthing; and also was in every particular as wanting in his understanding as an infant or an idiot. These truths are so evident that all must agree to them; though some may dispute about the quantity and the degree: for they may think, that a very little virtue is sufficient for happiness; but for riches, property, power, honour, and all such things, they endeavour to increase them without bounds: but to such we reply, that it is easy to prove from what experience teaches us in these cases, that these external goods produce not virtue, but virtue them. As to a happy life, whether it is to be found in pleasure or virtue or both, certain it is, that those whose morals are most pure, and whose understandings are best cultivated, will enjoy more of it, although their fortune is but moderate than those do who own an exuberance of wealth, are deficient in those; and this utility any one who reflects may easily convince himself of; for whatsoever is external has its boundary, as a machine, and whatsoever is useful in its excess is either necessarily hurtful, or at best useless to the possessor; but every good quality of the soul the higher it is in degree, so much the more useful it is, if it is permitted on this subject to use the word useful as well as noble. It is also very evident, that the accidents of each subject take place of each other, as the subjects themselves, of which we allow they are accidents, differ from each other in value; so that if the soul is more noble than any outward possession, as the body, both in itself and with respect to us, it must be admitted of course that the best accidents of each must follow the same analogy. Besides, it is for the sake of the soul that these things are desirable; and it is on this account that wise men should desire them, not the soul for them. Let us therefore be well assured, that every one enjoys as much happiness as he possesses virtue and wisdom, and acts according to their dictates; since for this we have the example of GOD Himself, *who is completely happy, not from any external good, but in Himself, and because such is His nature. For good fortune is something different from happiness, as every good which depends not on the mind is owing to chance or fortune; but it is not from fortune that any one is wise and just: hence it follows, that that city is happiest which is the best and acts best: for no one can do well who acts not well; nor can the deeds either of man or city be praiseworthy without virtue and wisdom; for whatsoever is just, or wise, or prudent in a man, the same things are just, wise, and prudent in a city.*

Thus much by way of introduction; for I could not but just touch upon this subject, though I could not go through a complete investigation of it, as it properly belongs to another question: let us at present suppose so much, that a man's happiest life, both as an individual and as a citizen, is a life of virtue, accompanied with those enjoyments which virtue usually procures. If there are any who are not convinced by what I have said, their doubts shall be answered hereafter, at present we shall proceed according to our intended method.

# CHAPTER

## II

It now remains for us to say whether the happiness of any individual man and the city is the same or different: but this also is evident; for whosoever supposes that riches will make a person happy, must place the happiness of the city in riches if it possesses them; those who prefer a life which enjoys a tyrannic power over others will also think, that the city which has many others under its command is most happy: thus also if any one approves a man for his virtue, he will think the most worthy city the happiest: but here there are two particulars which require consideration, one of which is, whether it is the most eligible life to be a member of the community and enjoy the rights of a citizen, or whether to live as a stranger, without interfering in public affairs; and also what form of government is to be preferred, and what disposition of the state is best; whether the whole community should be eligible to a share in the administration, or only the greater part, and some only: as this, therefore, is a subject of political examination and speculation, and not what concerns the individual, and the first of these is what we are at present engaged in, the one of these I am not obliged to speak to, the other is the proper business of my present design. It is evident that government must be the best which is so established, that every one therein may have it in his power to act virtuously and live happily: but some, who admit that a life of virtue is most eligible, still doubt which is preferable a public life of active virtue, or one entirely disengaged from what is without and spent in contemplation; which some say is the only one worthy of a philosopher; and one of these two different modes of life both now and formerly seem to have been chosen by all those who were the most virtuous men; I mean the public or philosophic. And yet it is of no little consequence on which side the truth lies; for a man of sense must naturally incline to the better choice; both as an individual and a citizen. Some think that a tyrannic government over those near us is the greatest injustice; but that a political one is not unjust: but that still is a restraint on the pleasures and tranquillity of life. Others hold the quite contrary opinion, and think that a public and active life is the only life for man: for that private persons have no opportunity of practising any one virtue, more than they have who are engaged in public life the management of the state. These are their sentiments; others say, that a tyrannical and despotical mode of government is the only happy one; for even amongst some free states the object of their laws seems to be to tyrannise over their neighbours: so that the generality of political institutions, wheresoever dispersed, if they have any one common object in view, have all of them this, to conquer and govern. It is evident, both from the laws of the Lacedaemonians and Cretans, as well as by the manner in which they educated their children, that all which they had in view was to make them soldiers: besides, among all nations, those who have power enough and reduce others to servitude are honoured on that account; as were the Scythians, Persians, Thracians, and Gauls: with some there are laws to heighten the virtue of courage; thus they tell us that at Carthage they allowed every person to wear as many rings for distinction as he had served campaigns. There was also a law in Macedonia, that a man who had not himself killed an enemy should be obliged to wear a halter; among the Scythians, at a festival, none were permitted to drink out of the cup was carried about who had not done the same thing. Among the Iberians, a warlike nation, they fixed as many columns upon a man's tomb as he had slain enemies: and among different nations different things of this sort prevail, some of them established by law, others by custom. Probably it may seem too absurd to those who are willing to take this subject into their consideration to inquire whether it is the business of a legislator to be able to point out by what means a state may govern and tyrannise over its neighbours, whether they will, or will not: for how can that belong either to the politician or legislator which is unlawful? For that cannot be lawful which is done not only justly, but unjustly also: for a conquest may be unjustly made. But we see nothing of this in the arts: for it is the business neither of the physician nor the pilot to use either persuasion or force, the one to his patients, the other to his passengers: and yet many seem to think a despotic government is a political one, and what they would not allow to be just or proper, if exercised over themselves, they will not blush to exercise over others; for they endeavour to be wisely governed themselves, but think it of no consequence whether others are so or not: but a despotic power is absurd, except only where nature has framed the one party for dominion, the other for subordination; and therefore no one ought to assume it over all in general, but those only which are the proper objects thereof: thus no one should hunt men either for food or sacrifice, but what is fit for those purposes, and these are wild animals which are eatable.

Now a city which is well governed might be very happy in itself while it enjoyed a good system of laws, although it should happen to be so situated as to have no connection with any other state, though its constitution should not be framed for war or conquest; for it would then have no occasion for these. It is evident therefore that the business of war is to be considered as commendable, not as a final end, but as the means of procuring it. It is the duty of a good legislator to examine carefully into his state; and the nature of the people, and how they may partake of every intercourse, of a good life, and of the happiness which results from it: and in this respect some laws and customs differ from others. It is also the duty of a legislator, if he has any neighbouring states to consider in what manner he shall oppose each of them, or what good offices he shall show them. But what should be the final end of the best governments will be considered hereafter.

# CHAPTER

## III

We will now speak to those who, while they agree that a life of virtue is most eligible, yet differ in the use of it addressing ourselves to both these parties; for there are some who disapprove of all political governments, and think that the life of one who is really free is different from the life of a citizen, and of all others most eligible: others again think that the citizen is the best; and that it is impossible for him who does nothing to be well employed; but that virtuous activity and happiness are the same thing. Now both parties in some particulars say what is right, in others what is wrong, thus, that the life of a freeman is better than the life of a slave is true, for a slave, as a slave, is employed in nothing honourable; for the common servile employments which he is commanded to perform have nothing virtuous in them; but, on the other hand, it is not true that a submission to all sorts of governments is slavery; for the government of freemen differs not more from the government of slaves than slavery and freedom differ from each other in their nature; and how they do has been already mentioned. To prefer doing of nothing to virtuous activity is also wrong, for happiness consists in action, and many noble ends are produced by the actions of the just and wise. From what we have already determined on this subject, some one probably may think, that supreme power is of all things best, as that will enable a man to command very many useful services from others; so that he who can obtain this ought not to give it up to another, but rather to seize it: and, for this purpose, the father should have no attention or regard for the son, or the son for the father, or friend for friend; for what is best is most eligible: but to be a member of the community and be in felicity is best. What these persons advance might probably be true, if the supreme good was certainly theirs who plunder and use violence to others: but it is most unlikely that it should be so; for it is a mere supposition: for it does not follow that their actions are honourable who thus assume the supreme power over others, without they were by nature as superior to them as a man to a woman, a father to a child, a master to a slave: so that he who so far forsakes the paths of virtue can never return back from whence he departed from them: for amongst equals whatever is fair and just ought to be reciprocal; for this is equal and right; but that equals should not partake of what is equal, or like to like, is contrary to nature: but whatever is contrary to nature is not right; therefore, if there is any one superior to the rest of the community in virtue and abilities for active life, him it is proper to follow, him it is right to obey, but the one alone will not do, but must be joined to the other also: and, if we are right in what we have now said, it follows that happiness consists in virtuous activity, and that both with respect to the community as well as the individual an active life is the happiest: not that an active life must necessarily refer to other persons, as some think, or that those studies alone are practical which are pursued to teach others what to do; for those are much more so whose final object is in themselves, and to improve the judgment and understanding of the man; for virtuous activity has an end, therefore is something practical; nay, those who contrive the plan which others follow are more particularly said to act, and are superior to the workmen who execute their designs. But it is not necessary that states which choose to have no intercourse with others should remain inactive; for the several members thereof may have mutual intercourse with each other; for there are many opportunities for this among the different citizens; the same thing is true of every individual: for, was it otherwise, neither could the Deity nor the universe be perfect; to neither of whom can anything external separately exist. Hence it is evident that that very same life which is happy for each individual is happy also for the state and every member of it.

# CHAPTER

## IV

A s I have now finished what was introductory to this subject, and considered at large the nature of other states, it now remains that I should first say what ought to be the establishment of a city which one should form according to one's wish; for no good state can exist without a moderate proportion of what is necessary. Many things therefore ought to be forethought of as desirable, but none of them such as are impossible: I mean relative to the number of citizens and the extent of the territory: for as other artificers, such as the weaver and the shipwright, ought to have such materials as are fit for their work, since so much the better they are, by so much superior will the work itself necessarily be; so also ought the legislator and politician endeavour to procure proper materials for the business they have in hand. Now the first and principal instrument of the politician is the number of the people; he should therefore know how many, and what they naturally ought to be: in like manner the country, how large, and what it is. Most persons think that it is necessary for a city to be large to be happy: but, should this be true, they cannot tell what is a large one and what a small one; for according to the multitude of the inhabitants they estimate the greatness of it; but they ought rather to consider its strength than its numbers; for a state has a certain object in view, and from the power which it has in itself of accomplishing it, its greatness ought to be estimated; as a person might say, that Hippocrates was a greater physician, though not a greater man, than one that exceeded him in the size of his body: but if it was proper to determine the strength of the city from the number of the inhabitants, it should never be collected from the multitude in general who may happen to be in it; for in a city there must necessarily be many slaves, sojourners, and foreigners; but from those who are really part of the city and properly constitute its members; a multitude of these is indeed a proof of a large city, but in a state where a large number of mechanics inhabit, and but few soldiers, such a state cannot be great; for the greatness of the city, and the number of men in it, are not the same thing. This too is evident from fact, that it is very difficult, if not impossible, to govern properly a very numerous body of men; for of all the states which appear well governed we find not one where the rights of a citizen are open to an indiscriminate multitude. And this is also evident from the nature of the thing; for as law is a certain order, so good law is of course a certain good order: but too large a multitude are incapable of this, unless under the government of that DIVINE POWER which comprehends the universe. Not but that, as quantity and variety are usually essential to beauty, the perfection of a city consists in the largeness of it as far as that largeness is consistent with that order already mentioned: but still there is a determinate size to all cities, as well as everything else, whether animals, plants, or machines, for each of these, if they are neither too little nor too big, have their proper powers; but when they have not their due growth, or are badly constructed, as a ship a span long is not properly a ship, nor one of two furlongs length, but when it is of a fit size; for either from its smallness or from its largeness it may be quite useless: so is it with a city; one that is too small has not in itself the power of self-defence, but this is essential to a city: one that is too large is capable of self-defence in what is necessary; but then it is a nation and not a city: for it will be very difficult to accommodate a form of government to it: for who would choose to be the general of such an unwieldy multitude, or who could be their herald but a stentor? The first thing therefore necessary is, that a city should consist of such numbers as will be sufficient to enable the inhabitants to live happily in their political community: and it follows, that the more the inhabitants exceed that necessary number the greater will the city be: but this must not be, as we have already said, without bounds; but what is its proper limit experience will easily show, and this experience is to be collected from the actions both of the governors and the governed. Now, as it belongs to the first to direct the inferior magistrates and to act as judges, it follows that they can neither determine causes with justice nor issue their orders with propriety without they know the characters of their fellow citizens: so that whenever this happens not to be done in these two particulars, the state must of necessity be badly managed; for in both of them it is not right to determine too hastily and without proper knowledge, which must evidently be the case where the number of the citizens is too many: besides, it is more easy for strangers and sojourners to assume the rights of citizens, as they will easily escape detection in so great a multitude. It is evident, then, that the best boundary for a city is that wherein the numbers are the greatest possible, that they may be the better able to be sufficient in themselves, while at the same time they are not too large to be under the eye and government of the magistrates. And thus let us determine the extent of a city.

## CHAPTER

## V

What we have said concerning a city may nearly be applied to a country; for as to what soil it should be, every one evidently will commend it if it is such as is sufficient in itself to furnish what will make the inhabitants happy; for which purpose it must be able to supply them with all the necessaries of life; for it is the having these in plenty, without any want, which makes them content. As to its extent, it should be such as may enable the inhabitants to live at their ease with freedom and temperance. Whether we have done right or wrong in fixing this limit to the territory shall be considered more minutely hereafter, when we come particularly to inquire into property, and what fortune is requisite for a man to live on, and how and in what manner they ought to employ it; for there are many doubts upon this question, while each party insists upon their own plan of life being carried to an excess, the one of severity, the other of indulgence. What the situation of the country should be it is not difficult to determine, in some particulars respecting that we ought to be advised by those who are skilful in military affairs. It should be difficult of access to an enemy, but easy to the inhabitants: and as we said, that the number of inhabitants ought to be such as can come under the eye of the magistrate, so should it be with the country; for then it is easily defended. As to the position of the city, if one could place it to one's wish, it is convenient to fix it on the seaside: with respect to the country, one situation which it ought to have has been already mentioned, namely, that it should be so placed as easily to give assistance to all places, and also to receive the necessaries of life from all parts, and also wood, or any other materials which may happen to be in the country.

# CHAPTER

# VI

But with respect to placing a city in the neighbourhood of the sea, there are some who have many doubts whether it is serviceable or hurtful to a well-regulated state; for they say, that the resort of persons brought up under a different system of government is disserviceable to the state, as well by impeding the laws as by their numbers; for a multitude of merchants must necessarily arise from their trafficking backward and forward upon the seas, which will hinder the well-governing of the city: but if this inconvenience should not arise, it is evident that it is better, both on account of safety and also for the easier acquisition of the necessaries of life, that both the city and the country should be near the sea; for it is necessary that those who are to sustain the attack of the enemy should be ready with their assistance both by land and by sea, and to oppose any inroad, both ways if possible but if not, at least where they are most powerful, which they may do while they possess both. A maritime situation is also useful for receiving from others what your own country will not produce, and exporting those necessaries of your own growth which are more than you have occasion for; but a city ought to traffic to supply its own wants, and not the wants of others; for those who themselves furnish an open market for every one, do it for the sake of gain; which it is not proper for a well-established state to do, neither should they encourage such a commerce. Now, as we see that many places and cities have docks and harbours lying very convenient for the city, while those who frequent them have no communication with the citadel, and yet they are not too far off, but are surrounded by walls and such-like fortifications, it is evident, that if any good arises from such an intercourse the city will receive it, but if anything hurtful, it will be easy to restrain it by a law declaring and deputing whom the state will allow to have an intercourse with each other, and whom not. As to a naval power, it is by no means doubtful that it is necessary to have one to a certain degree; and this not only for the sake of the city itself, but also because it may be necessary to appear formidable to some of the neighbouring states, or to be able to assist them as well by sea as by land; but to know how great that force should be, the health of the state should be inquired into, and if that appears vigorous and enables her to take the lead of other communities, it is necessary that her force should correspond with her actions. As for that multitude of people which a maritime power creates, they are by no means necessary to a state, nor ought they to make a part of the citizens; for the mariners and infantry, who have the command, are freemen, and upon these depends a naval engagement: but when there are many servants and husbandmen, there they will always have a number of sailors, as we now see happens to some states, as in Heraclea, where they man many triremes, though the extent of their city is much inferior to some others. And thus we determine concerning the country, the port, the city, the sea, and a maritime power: as to the number of the citizens, what that ought to be we have already said.

# CHAPTER

## VII

We now proceed to point out what natural disposition the members of the community ought to be of: but this any one will easily perceive who will cast his eye over the states of Greece, of all others the most celebrated, and also the other different nations of this habitable world. Those who live in cold countries, as the north of Europe, are full of courage, but wanting in understanding and the arts: therefore they are very tenacious of their liberty; but, not being politicians, they cannot reduce their neighbours under their power: but the Asiatics, whose understandings are quick, and who are conversant in the arts, are deficient in courage; and therefore are always conquered and the slaves of others: but the Grecians, placed as it were between these two boundaries, so partake of them both as to be at the same time both courageous and sensible; for which reason Greece continues free, and governed in the best manner possible, and capable of commanding the whole world, could they agree upon one system of policy. Now this is the difference between the Grecians and other nations, that the latter have but one of these qualities, whereas in the former they are both happily blended together. Hence it is evident, that those persons ought to be both sensible and courageous who will readily obey a legislator, the object of whose laws is virtue. As to what some persons say, that the military must be mild and tender to those they know, but severe and cruel to those they know not, it is courage which makes any one lovely; for that is the faculty of the soul which we most admire: as a proof of this, our resentment rises higher against our friends and acquaintance than against those we know not: for which reason Archilaus accusing his friends says very properly to himself, Shall my friends insult me? The spirit of freedom and command also is what all inherit who are of this disposition for courage is commanding and invincible. It also is not right for any one to say, that you should be severe to those you know not; for this behaviour is proper for no one: nor are those who are of a noble disposition harsh in their manners, excepting only to the wicked; and when they are particularly so, it is, as has been already said, against their friends, when they think they have injured them; which is agreeable to reason: for when those who think they ought to receive a favour from any one do not receive it, beside the injury done them, they consider what they are deprived of: hence the saying, "Cruel are the wars of brothers;" and this, "Those who have greatly loved do greatly hate." And thus we have nearly determined how many the inhabitants of a city ought to be, and what their natural disposition, and also the country how large, and of what sort is necessary; I say nearly, because it is needless to endeavour at as great accuracy in those things which are the objects of the senses as in those which are inquired into by the understanding only.

## CHAPTER

## VIII

As in natural bodies those things are not admitted to be parts of them without which the whole would not exist, so also it is evident that in a political state everything that is necessary thereunto is not to be considered as a part of it, nor any other community from whence one whole is made; for one thing ought to be common and the same to the community, whether they partake of it equally or unequally, as, for instance, food, land, or the like; but when one thing is for the benefit of one person, and another for the benefit of another, in this there is nothing like a community, excepting that one makes it and the other uses it; as, for instance, between any instrument employed in making any work, and the workmen, as there is nothing common between the house and the builder, but the art of the builder is employed on the house. Thus property is necessary for states, but property is no part of the state, though many species of it have life; but a city is a community of equals, for the purpose of enjoying the best life possible: but the happiest life is the best which consists in the perfect practice of virtuous energies: as therefore some persons have great, others little or no opportunity of being employed in these, it is evident that this is the cause of the difference there is between the different cities and communities there are to be found; for while each of these endeavour to acquire what is best by various and different means, they give rise to different modes of living and different forms of government. We are now to consider what those things are without which a city cannot possibly exist; for what we call parts of the city must of necessity inhere in it: and this we shall plainly understand, if we know the number of things necessary to a city: first, the inhabitants must have food: secondly, arts, for many instruments are necessary in life: thirdly, arms, for it is necessary that the community should have an armed force within themselves, both to support their government against those of their own body who might refuse obedience to it, and also to defend it from those who might attempt to attack it from without: fourthly, a certain revenue, as well for the internal necessities of the state as for the business of war: fifthly, which is indeed the chief concern, a religious establishment: sixthly in order, but first of all in necessity, a court to determine both criminal and civil causes. These things are absolutely necessary, so to speak, in every state; for a city is a number of people not accidentally met together, but with a purpose of ensuring to themselves sufficient independency and self-protection; and if anything necessary for these purposes is wanting, it is impossible that in such a situation these ends can be obtained. It is necessary therefore that a city should be capable of acquiring all these things: for this purpose a proper number of husbandmen are necessary to procure food, also artificers and soldiers, and rich men, and priests and judges, to determine what is right and proper.

# CHAPTER

## IX

Having determined thus far, it remains that we consider whether all these different employments shall be open to all; for it is possible to continue the same persons always husbandmen, artificers, judges, or counsellors; or shall we appoint different persons to each of those employments which we have already mentioned; or shall some of them be appropriated to particulars, and others of course common to all? But this does not take place in every state, for, as we have already said, it is possible that all may be common to all, or not, but only common to some; and this is the difference between one government and another: for in democracies the whole community partakes of everything, but in oligarchies it is different.

Since we are inquiring what is the best government possible, and it is admitted to be that in which the citizens are happy; and that, as we have already said, it is impossible to obtain happiness without virtue; it follows, that in the best-governed states, where the citizens are really men of intrinsic and not relative goodness, none of them should be permitted to exercise any mechanic employment or follow merchandise, as being ignoble and destructive to virtue; neither should they be husbandmen, that they may be at leisure to improve in virtue and perform the duty they owe to the state. With respect to the employments of a soldier, a senator, and a judge, which are evidently necessary to the community, shall they be allotted to different persons, or shall the same person execute both? This question, too, is easily answered: for in some cases the same persons may execute them, in others they should be different, where the different employments require different abilities, as when courage is wanting for one, judgment for the other, there they should be allotted to different persons; but when it is evident, that it is impossible to oblige those who have arms in their hands, and can insist on their own terms, to be always under command; there these different employments should be trusted to one person; for those who have arms in their hands have it in their option whether they will or will not assume the supreme power: to these two (namely, those who have courage and judgment) the government must be entrusted; but not in the same manner, but as nature directs; what requires courage to the young, what requires judgment to the old; for with the young is courage, with the old is wisdom: thus each will be allotted the part they are fit for according to their different merits. It is also necessary that the landed property should belong to these men; for it is necessary that the citizens should be rich, and these are the men proper for citizens; for no mechanic ought to be admitted to the rights of a citizen, nor any other sort of people whose employment is not entirely noble, honourable, and virtuous; this is evident from the principle we at first set out with; for to be happy it is necessary to be virtuous; and no one should say that a city is happy while he considers only one part of its citizens, but for that purpose he ought to examine into all of them. It is evident, therefore, that the landed property should belong to these, though it may be necessary for them to have husbandmen, either slaves, barbarians, or servants. There remains of the different classes of the people whom we have enumerated, the priests, for these evidently compose a rank by themselves; for neither are they to be reckoned amongst the husbandmen nor the mechanics; for reverence to the gods is highly becoming every state: and since the citizens have been divided into orders, the military and the council, and it is proper to offer due worship to the gods, and since it is necessary that those who are employed in their service should have nothing else to do, let the business of the priesthood be allotted to those who are in years. We have now shown what is necessary to the existence of a city, and of what parts it consists, and that husbandmen, mechanic, and mercenary servants are necessary to a city; but that the parts of it are soldiers and sailors, and that these are always different from those, but from each other only occasionally.

# CHAPTER

## X

I t seems neither now nor very lately to have been known to those philosophers who have made politics their study, that a city ought to be divided by families into different orders of men; and that the husbandmen and soldiers should be kept separate from each other; which custom is even to this day preserved in Egypt and in Crete; also Sesostris having founded it in Egypt, Minos in Crete. Common meals seem also to have been an ancient regulation, and to have been established in Crete during the reign of Minos, and in a still more remote period in Italy; for those who are the best judges in that country say that one Italus being king of AEnotria., from whom the people, changing their names, were called Italians instead of AEnotrians, and that part of Europe was called Italy which is bounded by the Scylletic Gulf on the one side and the Lametic on the other, the distance between which is about half a day's journey. This Italus, they relate, made the AEnotrians, who were formerly shepherds, husbandmen, and gave them different laws from what they had before, and to have been the first who established common meals, for which reason some of his descendants still use them, and observe some of his laws. The Opici inhabit that part which lies towards the Tyrrhenian Sea, who both now are and formerly were called Ausonians. The Chones inhabited the part toward Iapigia and the Ionian Sea which is called Syrtis. These Chones were descended from the AEnotrians. Hence arose the custom of common meals, but the separation of the citizens into different families from Egypt: for the reign of Sesostris is of much higher antiquity than that of Minos. As we ought to think that most other things were found out in a long, nay, even in a boundless time (reason teaching us that want would make us first invent that which was necessary, and, when that was obtained, then those things which were requisite for the conveniences and ornament of life), so should we conclude the same with respect to a political state;

now everything in Egypt bears the marks of the most remote antiquity, for these people seem to be the most ancient of all others, and to have acquired laws and political order; we should therefore make a proper use of what is told us of them, and endeavour to find out what they have omitted. We have already said, that the landed property ought to belong to the military and those who partake of the government of the state; and that therefore the husbandmen should be a separate order of people; and how large and of what nature the country ought to be: we will first treat of the division of the land, and of the husbandmen, how many and of what sort they ought to be; since we by no means hold that property ought to be common, as some persons have said, only thus far, in friendship, it should be their custom to let no citizen want subsistence. As to common meals, it is in general agreed that they are proper in well-regulated cities; my reasons for approving of them shall be mentioned hereafter: they are what all the citizens ought to partake of; but it will not be easy for the poor, out of what is their own, to furnish as much as they are ordered to do, and supply their own house besides. The expense also of religious worship should be defrayed by the whole state. Of necessity therefore the land ought to be divided into two parts, one of which should belong to the community in general, the other to the individuals separately; and each of these parts should again be subdivided into two: half of that which belongs to the public should be appropriated to maintain the worship of the gods, the other half to support the common meals. Half of that which belongs to the individuals should be at the extremity of the country, the other half near the city, so that these two portions being allotted to each person, all would partake of land in both places, which would be both equal and right; and induce them to act in concert with greater harmony in any war with their neighbours: for when the land is not divided in this manner, one party neglects the inroads of the enemy on the borders, the other makes it a matter of too much consequence and more than is necessary; for which reason in some places there is a law which forbids the inhabitants of the borders to have any vote in the council when they are debating upon a war which is made against them as their private interest might prevent their voting impartially. Thus therefore the country ought to be divided and for the reasons before mentioned. Could one have one's choice, the husbandmen should by all means be slaves, not of the same nation, or men of any spirit; for thus they would be laborious in their business, and safe from attempting any novelties: next to these barbarian servants are to be preferred, similar in natural disposition to these we have already mentioned. Of these, let those who are to cultivate the private property of the individual belong to that individual, and those who are to cultivate the public territory belong to the public. In what manner these slaves ought to be used, and for what reason it is very proper that they should have the promise of their liberty made them, as a reward for their services, shall be mentioned hereafter.

# CHAPTER

## XI

We have already mentioned, that both the city and all the country should communicate both with the sea and the continent as much as possible. There are these four things which we should be particularly desirous of in the position of the city with respect to itself: in the first place, health is to be consulted as the first thing necessary: now a city which fronts the east and receives the winds which blow from thence is esteemed most healthful; next to this that which has a northern position is to be preferred, as best in winter. It should next be contrived that it may have a proper situation for the business of government and for defence in war: that in war the citizens may have easy access to it; but that it may be difficult of access to, and hardly to be taken by, the enemy. In the next place particularly, that there may be plenty of water, and rivers near at hand: but if those cannot be found, very large cisterns must be prepared to save rain-water, so that there may be no want of it in case they should be driven into the town in time of war. And as great care should be taken of the health of the inhabitants, the first thing to be attended to is, that the city should have a good situation and a good position; the second is, that they may have good water to drink; and this not be negligently taken care of; for what we chiefly and most frequently use for the support of the body must principally influence the health of it; and this influence is what the air and water naturally have: for which reason in all wise governments the waters ought to be appropriated to different purposes, and if they are not equally good, and if there is not a plenty of necessary water, that which is to drink should be separated from that which is for other uses. As to fortified places, what is proper for some governments is not proper for all; as, for instance, a lofty citadel is proper for a monarchy and an oligarchy; a city built upon a plain suits a democracy; neither of these for an aristocracy, but rather many strong places. As to the form of private houses, those are thought to be best and most useful for their different purposes which are distinct and separate from each other, and built in the modern manner, after the plan of Hippodamus: but for safety in time of war, on the contrary, they should be built as they formerly were; for they were such that strangers could not easily find their way out of them, and the method of access to them such as an enemy could with difficulty find out if he proposed to besiege them. A city therefore should have both these sorts of buildings, which may easily be contrived if any one will so regulate them as the planters do their rows of vines; not that the buildings throughout the city should be detached from each other, only in some parts of it; thus elegance and safety will be equally consulted. With respect to walls, those who say that a courageous people ought not to have any, pay too much respect to obsolete notions; particularly as we may see those who pride themselves therein continually confuted by facts. It is indeed disreputable for those who are equal, or nearly so, to the enemy, to endeavour to take refuge within their walls—but since it very often happens, that those who make the attack are too powerful for the bravery and courage of those few who oppose them to resist, if you would not suffer the calamities of war and the insolence of the enemy, it must be thought the part of a good soldier to seek for safety under the shelter and protection of walls more especially since so many missile weapons and machines have been most ingeniously invented to besiege cities with. Indeed to neglect surrounding a city with a wall would be similar to choosing a country which is easy of access to an enemy, or levelling the eminences of it; or as if an individual should not have a wall to his house lest it should be thought that the owner of it was a coward: nor should this be left unconsidered, that those who have a city surrounded with walls may act both ways, either as if it had or as if it had not; but where it has not they cannot do this. If this is true, it is not only necessary to have walls, but care must be taken that they may be a proper ornament to the city, as well as a defence in time of war; not only according to the old methods, but the modern improvements also: for as those who make offensive war endeavour by every way possible to gain advantages over their adversaries, so should those who are upon the defensive employ all the means already known, and such new ones as philosophy can invent, to defend themselves: for those who are well prepared are seldom first attacked.

# CHAPTER

# XII

As the citizens in general are to eat at public tables in certain companies, and it is necessary that the walls should have bulwarks and towers in proper places and at proper distances, it is evident that it will be very necessary to have some of these in the towers; let the buildings for this purpose be made the ornaments of the walls. As to temples for public worship, and the hall for the public tables of the chief magistrates, they ought to be built in proper places, and contiguous to each other, except those temples which the law or the oracle orders to be separate from all other buildings; and let these be in such a conspicuous eminence, that they may have every advantage of situation, and in the neighbourhood of that part of the city which is best fortified. Adjoining to this place there ought to be a large square, like that which they call in Thessaly The Square of Freedom, in which nothing is permitted to be bought or sold; into which no mechanic nor husbandman, nor any such person, should be permitted to enter, unless commanded by the magistrates. It will also be an ornament to this place if the gymnastic exercises of the elders are performed in it. It is also proper, that for performing these exercises the citizens should be divided into distinct classes, according to their ages, and that the young persons should have proper officers to be with them, and that the seniors should be with the magistrates; for having them before their eyes would greatly inspire true modesty and ingenuous fear. There ought to be another square separate from this for buying and selling, which should be so situated as to be commodious for the reception of goods both by sea and land. As the citizens may be divided into magistrates and priests, it is proper that the public tables of the priests should be in buildings near the temples. Those of the magistrates who preside over contracts, indictments, and such-like, and also over the markets, and the public streets near the square, or some public way, I mean the square where things are bought and sold; for I intended the other for those who are at leisure, and this for necessary business. The same order which I have directed here should be observed also in the country; for there also their magistrates such as the surveyors of the woods and overseers of the grounds, must necessarily have their common tables and their towers, for the purpose of protection against an enemy. There ought also to be temples erected at proper places, both to the gods and the heroes; but it is unnecessary to dwell longer and most minutely on these particulars—for it is by no means difficult to plan these things, it is rather so to carry them into execution; for the theory is the child of our wishes, but the practical part must depend upon fortune; for which reason we shall decline saying anything farther upon these subjects.

# CHAPTER

# XIII

We will now show of what numbers and of what sort of people a government ought to consist, that the state may be happy and well administered. As there are two particulars on which the excellence and perfection of everything depend, one of these is, that the object and end proposed should be proper; the other, that the means to accomplish it should be adapted to that purpose; for it may happen that these may either agree or disagree with each other; for the end we propose may be good, but in taking the means to obtain it we may err; at other times we may have the right and proper means in our power, but the end may be bad, and sometimes we may mistake in both; as in the art of medicine the physician does not sometimes know in what situation the body ought to be, to be healthy; nor what to do to procure the end he aims at. In every art and science, therefore, we should be master of this knowledge, namely, the proper end, and the means to obtain it. Now it is evident that all persons are desirous to live well and be happy; but that some have the means thereof in their own power, others not; and this either through nature or fortune; for many ingredients are necessary to a happy life; but fewer to those who are of a good than to those who are of a bad disposition. There are others who continually have the means of happiness in their own power, but do not rightly apply them. Since we propose to inquire what government is best, namely, that by which a state may be best administered, and that state is best administered where the people are the happiest, it is evident that happiness is a thing we should not be unacquainted with. Now, I have already said in my treatise on Morals (if I may here make any use of what I have there shown), that happiness consists in the energy and perfect practice of virtue; and this not relatively, but simply; I mean by relatively, what is necessary in some certain circumstances; by simply, what is good and fair in itself: of the first sort are just punishments, and restraints in a just cause; for they arise from virtue and are necessary, and on that account are virtuous; though it is more desirable that neither any state nor any individual should stand in need of them; but those actions which are intended either to procure honour or wealth are simply good; the others eligible only to remove an evil; these, on the contrary, are the foundation and means of relative good. A worthy man indeed will bear poverty, disease, and other unfortunate accidents with a noble mind; but happiness consists in the contrary to these (now we have already determined in our treatise on Morals, that he is a man of worth who considers what is good because it is virtuous as what is simply good; it is evident, therefore, that all the actions of such a one must be worthy and simply good): this has led some persons to conclude, that the cause of happiness was external goods; which would be as if any one should suppose that the playing well upon the lyre was owing to the instrument, and not to the art. It necessarily follows from what has been said, that some things should be ready at hand and others procured by the legislator; for which reason in founding a city we earnestly wish that there may be plenty of those things which are supposed to be under the dominion of fortune (for some things we admit her to be mistress over); but for a state to be worthy and great is not only the work of fortune but of knowledge and judgment also. But for a state to be worthy it is necessary that those citizens which are in the administration should be worthy also; but as in our city every citizen is to be so, we must consider how this may be accomplished; for if this is what every one could be, and not some individuals only, it would be more desirable; for then it would follow, that what might be done by one might be done by all. Men are worthy and good three ways; by nature, by custom, by reason. In the first place, a man ought to be born a man, and not any other animal; that is to say, he ought to have both a body and soul; but it avails not to be only born with some things, for custom makes great alterations; for there are some things in nature capable of alteration either way which are fixed by custom, either for the better or the worse. Now, other animals live chiefly a life of nature; and in very few things according to custom; but man lives according to reason also, which he alone is endowed with; wherefore he ought to make all these accord with each other; for if men followed reason, and were persuaded that it was best to obey her, they would act in many respects contrary to nature and custom. What men ought naturally to be, to make good members of a community, I have already determined; the rest of this discourse therefore shall be upon education; for some things are acquired by habit, others by hearing them.

## CHAPTER

## XIV

As every political community consists of those who govern and of those who are governed, let us consider whether during the continuance of their lives they ought to be the same persons or different; for it is evident that the mode of education should be adapted to this distinction. Now, if one man differed from another as much, as we believe, the gods and heroes differ from men: in the first place, being far their superiors in body; and, secondly, in the soul: so that the superiority of the governors over the governed might be evident beyond a doubt, it is certain that it would be better for the one always to govern, the other always to be governed: but, as this is not easy to obtain, and kings are not so superior to those they govern as Scylax informs us they are in India, it is evident that for many reasons it is necessary that all in their turns should both govern and be governed: for it is just that those who are equal should have everything alike; and it is difficult for a state to continue which is founded in injustice; for all those in the country who are desirous of innovation will apply themselves to those who are under the government of the rest, and such will be their numbers in the state, that it will be impossible for the magistrates to get the better of them. But that the governors ought to excel the governed is beyond a doubt; the legislator therefore ought to consider how this shall be, and how it may be contrived that all shall have their equal share in the administration. Now, with respect to this it will be first said, that nature herself has directed us in our choice, laying down the selfsame thing when she has made some young, others old: the first of whom it becomes to obey, the latter to command; for no one when he is young is offended at his being under government, or thinks himself too good for it; more especially when he considers that he himself shall receive the same honours which he pays when he shall arrive at a proper age. In some respects it must be acknowledged that the governors and the governed are the same, in others they are different; it is therefore necessary that their education should be in some respect the same, in others different: as they say, that he will be a good governor who has first learnt to obey. Now of governments, as we have already said, some are instituted for the sake of him who commands; others for him who obeys: of the first sort is that of the master over the servant; of the latter, that of freemen over each other. Now some things which are commanded differ from others; not in the business, but in the end proposed thereby: for which reason many works, even of a servile nature, are not disgraceful for young freemen to perform; for many things which are ordered to be done are not honourable or dishonourable so much in their own nature as in the end which is proposed, and the reason for which they are undertaken. Since then we have determined, that the virtue of a good citizen and good governor is the same as of a good man; and that every one before he commands should have first obeyed, it is the business of the legislator to consider how his citizens may be good men, what education is necessary to that purpose, and what is the final object of a good life. The soul of man may be divided into two parts; that which has reason in itself, and that which hath not, but is capable of obeying its dictates: and according to the virtues of these two parts a man is said to be good: but of those virtues which are the ends, it will not be difficult for those to determine who adopt the division I have already given; for the inferior is always for the sake of the superior; and this is equally evident both in the works of art as well as in those of nature; but that is superior which has reason. Reason itself also is divided into two parts, in the manner we usually divide it; the theoretic and the practical; which division therefore seems necessary for this part also: the same analogy holds good with respect to actions; of which those which are of a superior nature ought always to be chosen by those who have it in their power; for that is always most eligible to every one which will procure the best ends. Now life is divided into labour and rest, war and peace; and of what we do the objects are partly necessary and useful, partly noble: and we should give the same preference to these that we do to the different parts of the soul and its actions, as war to procure peace; labour, rest; and the useful, the noble. The politician, therefore, who composes a body of laws ought to extend his views to everything; the different parts of the soul and their actions; more particularly to those things which are of a superior nature and ends; and, in the same manner, to the lives of men and their different actions.

They ought to be fitted both for labour and war, but rather for rest and peace; and also to do what is necessary and useful, but rather what is fair and noble. It is to those objects that the education of the children ought to tend, and of all the youths who want instruction. All the Grecian states which now seem best governed, and the legislators who founded those states, appear not to have framed their polity with a view to the best end, or to every virtue, in their laws and education; but eagerly to have attended to what is useful and productive of gain: and nearly of the same opinion with these are some persons who have written lately, who, by praising the Lacedaemonian state, show they approve of the intention of the legislator in making war and victory the end of his government. But how contrary to reason this is, is easily proved by argument, and has already been proved by facts (but as the generality of men desire to have an extensive command, that they may have everything desirable in the greater abundance; so Thibron and others who have written on that state seem to approve of their legislator for having procured them an extensive command by continually enuring them to all sorts of dangers and hardships): for it is evident, since the Lacedemonians have now no hope that the supreme power will be in their own hand, that neither are they happy nor was their legislator wise. This also is ridiculous, that while they preserved an obedience to their laws, and no one opposed their being governed by them, they lost the means of being honourable: but these people understand not rightly what sort of government it is which ought to reflect honour on the legislator; for a government of freemen is nobler than despotic power, and more consonant to virtue. Moreover, neither should a city be thought happy, nor should a legislator be commended, because he has so trained the people as to conquer their neighbours; for in this there is a great inconvenience: since it is evident that upon this principle every citizen who can will endeavour to procure the supreme power in his own city; which crime the Lacedaemonians accuse Pausanias of, though he enjoyed such great honours.

Such reasoning and such laws are neither political, useful nor true: but a legislator ought to instil those laws on the minds of men which are most useful for them, both in their public and private capacities. The rendering a people fit for war, that they may enslave their inferiors ought not to be the care of the legislator; but that they may not themselves be reduced to slavery by others. In the next place, he should take care that the object of his government is the safety of those who are under it, and not a despotism over all: in the third place, that those only are slaves who are fit to be only so. Reason indeed concurs with experience in showing that all the attention which the legislator pays to the business of war, and all other rules which he lays down, should have for their object rest and peace; since most of those states (which we usually see) are preserved by war; but, after they have acquired a supreme power over those around them, are ruined; for during peace, like a sword, they lose their brightness: the fault of which lies in the legislator, who never taught them how to be at rest.

# CHAPTER

## XV

As there is one end common to a man both as an individual and a citizen, it is evident that a good man and a good citizen must have the same object in view; it is evident that all the virtues which lead to rest are necessary; for, as we have often said, the end of war is peace, of labour, rest; but those virtues whose object is rest, and those also whose object is labour, are necessary for a liberal life and rest; for we want a supply of many necessary things that we may be at rest. A city therefore ought to be temperate, brave, and patient; for, according to the proverb, "Rest is not for slaves;" but those who cannot bravely face danger are the slaves of those who attack them. Bravery, therefore, and patience are necessary for labour, philosophy for rest, and temperance and justice in both; but these chiefly in time of peace and rest; for war obliges men to be just and temperate; but the enjoyment of pleasure, with the rest of peace, is more apt to produce insolence; those indeed who are easy in their circumstances, and enjoy everything that can make them happy, have great occasion for the virtues of temperance and justice. Thus if there are, as the poets tell us, any inhabitants in the happy isles, to these a higher degree of philosophy, temperance, and justice will be necessary, as they live at their ease in the full plenty of every sensual pleasure. It is evident, therefore, that these virtues are necessary in every state that would be happy or worthy; for he who is worthless can never enjoy real good, much less is he qualified to be at rest; but can appear good only by labour and being at war, but in peace and at rest the meanest of creatures. For which reason virtue should not be cultivated as the Lacedaemonians did; for they did not differ from others in their opinion concerning the supreme good, but in imagining this good was to be procured by a particular virtue; but since there are greater goods than those of war, it is evident that the enjoyment of those which are valuable in themselves should be desired, rather than those virtues which are useful in war; but how and by what means this is to be acquired is now to be considered. We have already assigned three causes on which it will depend; nature, custom, and reason, arid shown what sort of men nature must produce for this purpose; it remains then that we determine which we shall first begin by in education, reason or custom, for these ought always to preserve the most entire harmony with each other; for it may happen that reason may err from the end proposed, and be corrected by custom. In the first place, it is evident that in this as in other things, its beginning or production arises from some principle, and its end also arises from another principle, which is itself an end. Now, with us, reason and intelligence are the end of nature; our production, therefore, and our manners ought to be accommodated to both these. In the next place, as the soul and the body are two distinct things, so also we see that the soul is divided into two parts, the reasoning and not-reasoning, with their habits which are two in number, one belonging to each, namely appetite and intelligence; and as the body is in production before the soul, so is the not-reasoning part of the soul before the reasoning; and this is evident; for anger, will and desire are to be seen in children nearly as soon as they are born; but reason and intelligence spring up as they grow to maturity. The body, therefore, necessarily demands our care before the soul; next the appetites for the sake of the mind; the body for the sake of the soul.

# CHAPTER

# XVI

If then the legislator ought to take care that the bodies of the children are as perfect as possible, his first attention ought to be given to matrimony; at what time and in what situation it is proper that the citizens should engage in the nuptial contract. Now, with respect to this alliance, the legislator ought both to consider the parties and their time of life, that they may grow old at the same part of time, and that their bodily powers may not be different; that is to say, the man being able to have children, but the woman too old to bear them; or, on the contrary, the woman be young enough to produce children, but the man too old to be a father; for from such a situation discords and disputes continually arise. In the next place, with respect to the succession of children, there ought not to be too great an interval of time between them and their parents; for when there is, the parent can receive no benefit from his child's affection, or the child any advantage from his father's protection; neither should the difference in years be too little, as great inconveniences may arise from it; as it prevents that proper reverence being shown to a father by a boy who considers him as nearly his equal in age, and also from the disputes it occasions in the economy of the family. But, to return from this digression, care ought to be taken that the bodies of the children may be such as will answer the expectations of the legislator; this also will be affected by the same means. Since season for the production of children is determined (not exactly, but to speak in general), namely, for the man till seventy years, and the woman till fifty, the entering into the marriage state, as far as time is concerned, should be regulated by these periods. It is extremely bad for the children when the father is too young; for in all animals whatsoever the parts of the young are imperfect, and are more likely to be productive of females than males, and diminutive also in size; the same thing of course necessarily holds true in men; as a proof of this you may see in those cities where the men and women usually marry very young, the people in general are very small and ill framed; in child-birth also the women suffer more, and many of them die. And thus some persons tell us the oracle of Traezenium should be explained, as if it referred to the many women who were destroyed by too early marriages, and not their gathering their fruits too soon. It is also conducive to temperance not to marry too soon; for women who do so are apt to be intemperate. It also prevents the bodies of men from acquiring their full size if they marry before their growth is completed; for this is the determinate period, which prevents any further increase; for which reason the proper time for a woman to marry is eighteen, for a man thirty-seven, a little more or less; for when they marry at that time their bodies are in perfection, and they will also cease to have children at a proper time; and moreover with respect to the succession of the children, if they have them at the time which may reasonably be expected, they will be just arriving into perfection when their parents are sinking down under the load of seventy years. And thus much for the time which is proper for marriage; but moreover a proper season of the year should be observed, as many persons do now, and appropriate the winter for this business. The married couple ought also to regard the precepts of physicians and naturalists, each of whom have treated on these subjects. What is the fit disposition of the body will be better mentioned when we come to speak of the education of the child; we will just slightly mention a few particulars. Now, there is no occasion that any one should have the habit of body of a wrestler to be either a good citizen, or to enjoy a good constitution, or to be the father of healthy children; neither should he be infirm or too much dispirited by misfortunes, but between both these. He ought to have a habit of labour, but not of too violent labour; nor should that be confined to one object only, as the wrestler's is; but to such things as are proper for freemen. These things are equally necessary both for men and women. Women with child should also take care that their diet is not too sparing, and that they use sufficient exercise; which it will be easy for the legislator to effect if he commands them once every day to repair to the worship of the gods who are supposed to preside over matrimony. But, contrary to what is proper for the body, the mind ought to be kept as tranquil as possible; for as plants partake of the nature of the soil, so does the child receive much of the disposition of the mother. With respect to the exposing or bringing up of children, let it be a law, that nothing imperfect or maimed shall be brought up,.......... As the proper time has been pointed out for a man and a woman to enter into the marriage state, so also let us determine how long it is advantageous for the community that they should have children; for as the children of those who are too young are imperfect both in body and mind, so also those whose parents are too old are weak in both: while therefore the body continues in perfection, which (as some poets say, who reckon the different periods of life by sevens) is till fifty years, or four or five more, the children may be equally perfect; but when the parents are past that age it is better they should have no more. With respect to any connection between a man and a woman, or a woman and a man, when either of the parties are betrothed, let it be held in utter detestation on any pretext whatsoever; but should any one be guilty of such a thing after the marriage is consummated, let his infamy be as great as his guilt deserves.

## CHAPTER

## XVII

When a child is born it must be supposed that the strength of its body will depend greatly upon the quality of its food. Now whoever will examine into the nature of animals, and also observe those people who are very desirous their children should acquire a warlike habit, will find that they feed them chiefly with milk, as being best accommodated to their bodies, but without wine, to prevent any distempers: those motions also which are natural to their age are very serviceable; and to prevent any of their limbs from being crooked, on account of their extreme ductility, some people even now use particular machines that their bodies may not be distorted. It is also useful to enure them to the cold when they are very little; for this is very serviceable for their health; and also to enure them to the business of war; for which reason it is customary with many of the barbarians to dip their children in rivers when the water is cold; with others to clothe them very slightly, as among the Celts; for whatever it is possible to accustom children to, it is best to accustom them to it at first, but to do it by degrees: besides, boys have naturally a habit of loving the cold, on account of the heat. These, then, and such-like things ought to be the first object of our attention: the next age to this continues till the child is five years old; during which time it is best to teach him nothing at all, not even necessary labour, lest it should hinder his growth; but he should be accustomed to use so much motion as not to acquire a lazy habit of body; which he will get by various means and by play also: his play also ought to be neither illiberal nor too laborious nor lazy. Their governors and preceptors also should take care what sort of tales and stories it may be proper for them to hear; for all these ought to pave the way for their future instruction: for which reason the generality of their play should be imitations of what they are afterwards to do seriously. They too do wrong who forbid by laws the disputes between boys and their quarrels, for they contribute to increase their growth—as they are a sort of exercise to the body: for the struggles of the heart and the compression of the spirits give strength to those who labour, which happens to boys in their disputes. The preceptors also ought to have an eye upon their manner of life, and those with whom they converse; and to take care that they are never in the company of slaves. At this time and till they are seven years old it is necessary that they should be educated at home. It is also very proper to banish, both from their hearing and sight, everything which is illiberal and the like. Indeed it is as much the business of the legislator as anything else, to banish every indecent expression out of the state: for from a permission to speak whatever is shameful, very quickly arises the doing it, and this particularly with young people: for which reason let them never speak nor hear any such thing: but if it appears that any freeman has done or said anything that is forbidden before he is of age to be thought fit to partake of the common meals, let him be punished by disgrace and stripes; but if a person above that age does so, let him be treated as you would a slave, on account of his being infamous. Since we forbid his speaking everything which is forbidden, it is necessary that he neither sees obscene stories nor pictures; the magistrates therefore are to take care that there are no statues or pictures of anything of this nature, except only to those gods to whom the law permits them, and to which the law allows persons of a certain age to pay their devotions, for themselves, their wives, and children. It should also be illegal for young persons to be present either at iambics or comedies before they are arrived at that age when they are allowed to partake of the pleasures of the table: indeed a good education will preserve them from all the evils which attend on these things. We have at present just touched upon this subject; it will be our business hereafter, when we properly come to it, to determine whether this care of children is unnecessary, or, if necessary, in what manner it must be done; at present we have only mentioned it as necessary. Probably the saying of Theodoras, the tragic actor, was not a bad one: That he would permit no one, not even the meanest actor, to go upon the stage before him, that he might first engage the ear of the audience. The same thing happens both in our connections with men and things: what we meet with first pleases best; for which reason children should be kept strangers to everything which is bad, more particularly whatsoever is loose and offensive to good manners. When five years are accomplished, the two next may be very properly employed in being spectators of those exercises they will afterwards have to learn. There are two periods into which education ought to be divided, according to the age of the child; the one is from his being seven years of age to the time of puberty; the other from thence till he is one-and-twenty: for those who divide ages by the number seven are in general wrong: it is much better to follow the division of nature; for every art and every instruction is intended to complete what nature has left defective: we must first consider if any regulation whatsoever is requisite for children; in the next place, if it is advantageous to make it a common care, or that every one should act therein as he pleases, which is the general practice in most cities; in the third place, what it ought to be.

# BOOK VIII

## CHAPTER

### I

No one can doubt that the magistrate ought greatly to interest himself in the care of youth; for where it is neglected it is hurtful to the city, for every state ought to be governed according to its particular nature; for the form and manners of each government are peculiar to itself; and these, as they originally established it, so they usually still preserve it. For instance, democratic forms and manners a democracy; oligarchic, an oligarchy: but, universally, the best manners produce the best government. Besides, as in every business and art there are some things which men are to learn first and be made accustomed to, which are necessary to perform their several works; so it is evident that the same thing is necessary in the practice of virtue. As there is one end in view in every city, it is evident that education ought to be one and the same in each; and that this should be a common care, and not the individual's, as it now is, when every one takes care of his own children separately; and their instructions are particular also, each person teaching them as they please; but what ought to be engaged in ought to be common to all. Besides, no one ought to think that any citizen belongs to him in particular, but to the state in general; for each one is a part of the state, and it is the natural duty of each part to regard the good of the whole: and for this the Lacedaemonians may be praised; for they give the greatest attention to education, and make it public. It is evident, then, that there should be laws concerning education, and that it should be public.

## CHAPTER

## II

What education is, and how children ought to be instructed, is what should be well known; for there are doubts concerning the business of it, as all people do not agree in those things they would have a child taught, both with respect to their improvement in virtue and a happy life: nor is it clear whether the object of it should be to improve the reason or rectify the morals. From the present mode of education we cannot determine with certainty to which men incline, whether to instruct a child in what will be useful to him in life; or what tends to virtue, and what is excellent: for all these things have their separate defenders. As to virtue, there is no particular in which they all agree: for as all do not equally esteem all virtues, it reasonably follows that they will not cultivate the same. It is evident that what is necessary ought to be taught to all: but that which is necessary for one is not necessary for all; for there ought to be a distinction between the employment of a freeman and a slave. The first of these should be taught everything useful which will not make those who know it mean. Every work is to be esteemed mean, and every art and every discipline which renders the body, the mind, or the understanding of freemen unfit for the habit and practice of virtue: for which reason all those arts which tend to deform the body are called mean, and all those employments which are exercised for gain; for they take off from the freedom of the mind and render it sordid. There are also some liberal arts which are not improper for freemen to apply to in a certain degree; but to endeavour to acquire a perfect skill in them is exposed to the faults I have just mentioned; for there is a great deal of difference in the reason for which any one does or learns anything: for it is not illiberal to engage in it for one's self, one's friend, or in the cause of virtue; while, at the same time, to do it for the sake of another may seem to be acting the part of a servant and a slave. The mode of instruction which now prevails seems to partake of both parts.

# CHAPTER

# III

There are four things which it is usual to teach children—reading, gymnastic exercises, and music, to which (in the fourth place) some add painting. Reading and painting are both of them of singular use in life, and gymnastic exercises, as productive of courage. As to music, some persons may doubt, as most persons now use it for the sake of pleasure: but those who originally made it part of education did it because, as has been already said, nature requires that we should not only be properly employed, but to be able to enjoy leisure honourably: for this (to repeat what I have already said) is of all things the principal. But, though both labour and rest are necessary, yet the latter is preferable to the first; and by all means we ought to learn what we should do when at rest: for we ought not to employ that time at play; for then play would be the necessary business of our lives. But if this cannot be, play is more necessary for those who labour than those who are at rest: for he who labours requires relaxation; which play will supply: for as labour is attended with pain and continued exertion, it is necessary that play should be introduced, under proper regulations, as a medicine: for such an employment of the mind is a relaxation to it, and eases with pleasure. Now rest itself seems to partake of pleasure, of happiness, and an agreeable life: but this cannot be theirs who labour, but theirs who are at rest; for he who labours, labours for the sake of some end which he has not: but happiness is an end which all persons think is attended with pleasure and not with pain: but all persons do not agree in making this pleasure consist in the same thing; for each one has his particular standard, correspondent to his own habits; but the best man proposes the best pleasure, and that which arises from the noblest actions. But it is evident, that to live a life of rest there are some things which a man must learn and be instructed in; and that the object of this learning and this instruction centres in their acquisition: but the learning and instruction which is given for labour has for its object other things; for which reason the ancients made music a part of education; not as a thing necessary, for it is not of that nature, nor as a thing useful, as reading, in the common course of life, or for managing of a family, or for learning anything as useful in public life. Painting also seems useful to enable a man to judge more accurately of the productions of the finer arts: nor is it like the gymnastic exercises, which contribute to health and strength; for neither of these things do we see produced by music; there remains for it then to be the employment of our rest, which they had in view who introduced it; and, thinking it a proper employment for freemen, to them they allotted it; as Homer sings:

"How right to call Thalia to the feast:"

and of some others he says:

"The bard was call'd, to ravish every ear:"

and, in another place, he makes Ulysses say the happiest part of man's life is

"When at the festal board, in order plac'd, They hear the song."

It is evident, then, that there is a certain education in which a child may be instructed, not as useful nor as necessary, but as noble and liberal: but whether this is one or more than one, and of what sort they are, and how to be taught, shall be considered hereafter: we are now got so far on our way as to show that we have the testimony of the ancients in our favour, by what they have delivered down upon education—for music makes this plain. Moreover, it is necessary to instruct children in what is useful, not only on account of its being useful in itself, as, for instance, to learn to read, but also as the means of acquiring other different sorts of instruction: thus they should be instructed in painting, not only to prevent their being mistaken in purchasing pictures, or in buying or selling of vases, but rather as it makes them judges of the beauties of the human form; for to be always hunting after the profitable ill agrees with great and freeborn souls. As it is evident whether a boy should be first taught morals or reasoning, and whether his body or his understanding should be first cultivated, it is plain that boys should be first put under the care of the different masters of the gymnastic arts, both to form their bodies and teach them their exercises.

# CHAPTER

# IV

Now those states which seem to take the greatest care of their children's education, bestow their chief attention on wrestling, though it both prevents the increase of the body and hurts the form of it. This fault the Lacedaemonians did not fall into, for they made their children fierce by painful labour, as chiefly useful to inspire them with courage: though, as we have already often said, this is neither the only thing nor the principal thing necessary to attend to; and even with respect to this they may not thus attain their end; for we do not find either in other animals, or other nations, that courage necessarily attends the most cruel, but rather the milder, and those who have the dispositions of lions: for there are many people who are eager both to kill men and to devour human flesh, as the Achaeans and Heniochi in Pontus, and many others in Asia, some of whom are as bad, others worse than these, who indeed live by tyranny, but are men of no courage. Nay, we know that the Lacedaemonians themselves, while they continued those painful labours, and were superior to all others (though now they are inferior to many, both in war and gymnastic exercises), did not acquire their superiority by training their youth to these exercises, but because those who were disciplined opposed those who were not disciplined at all. What is fair and honourable ought then to take place in education of what is fierce and cruel: for it is not a wolf, nor any other wild beast, which will brave any noble danger, but rather a good man. So that those who permit boys to engage too earnestly in these exercises, while they do not take care to instruct them in what is necessary to do, to speak the real truth, render them mean and vile, accomplished only in one duty of a citizen, and in every other respect, as reason evinces, good for nothing. Nor should we form our judgments from past events, but from what we see at present: for now they have rivals in their mode of education, whereas formerly they had not. That gymnastic exercises are useful, and in what manner, is admitted; for during youth it is very proper to go through a course of those which are most gentle, omitting that violent diet and those painful exercises which are prescribed as necessary; that they may not prevent the growth of the body: and it is no small proof that they have this effect, that amongst the Olympic candidates we can scarce find two or three who have gained a victory both when boys and men: because the necessary exercises they went through when young deprived them of their strength. When they have allotted three years from the time of puberty to other parts of education, they are then of a proper age to submit to labour and a regulated diet; for it is impossible for the mind and body both to labour at the same time, as they are productive of contrary evils to each other; the labour of the body preventing the progress of the mind, and the mind of the body.

# CHAPTER

## V

With respect to music we have already spoken a little in a doubtful manner upon this subject. It will be proper to go over again more particularly what we then said, which may serve as an introduction to what any other person may choose to offer thereon; for it is no easy matter to distinctly point out what power it has, nor on what accounts one should apply it, whether as an amusement and refreshment, as sleep or wine; as these are nothing serious, but pleasing, and the killers of care, as Euripides says; for which reason they class in the same order and use for the same purpose all these, namely, sleep, wine, and music, to which some add dancing; or shall we rather suppose that music tends to be productive of virtue, having a power, as the gymnastic exercises have to form the body in a certain way, to influence the manners so as to accustom its professors to rejoice rightly? Or shall we say, that it is of any service in the conduct of life, and an assistant to prudence? For this also is a third property which has been attributed to it. Now that boys are not to be instructed in it as play is evident; for those who learn don't play, for to learn is rather troublesome; neither is it proper to permit boys at their age to enjoy perfect leisure; for to cease to improve is by no means fit for what is as yet imperfect; but it may be thought that the earnest attention of boys in this art is for the sake of that amusement they will enjoy when they come to be men and completely formed; but, if this is the case, why are they themselves to learn it, and not follow the practice of the kings of the Medes and Persians, who enjoy the pleasure of music by hearing others play, and being shown its beauties by them; for of necessity those must be better skilled therein who make this science their particular study and business, than those who have only spent so much time at it as was sufficient just to learn the principles of it. But if this is a reason for a child's being taught anything, they ought also to learn the art of cookery, but this is absurd. The same doubt occurs if music has a power of improving the manners; for why should they on this account themselves learn it, and not reap every advantage of regulating the passions or forming a judgment on the merits of the performance by hearing others, as the Lacedaemonians; for they, without having ever learnt music, are yet able to judge accurately what is good and what is bad; the same reasoning may be applied if music is supposed to be the amusement of those who live an elegant and easy life, why should they learn themselves, and not rather enjoy the benefit of others' skill. Let us here consider what is our belief of the immortal gods in this particular. Now we find the poets never represent Jupiter himself as singing and playing; nay, we ourselves treat the professors of these arts as mean people, and say that no one would practise them but a drunkard or a buffoon. But probably we may consider this subject more at large hereafter. The first question is, whether music is or is not to make a part of education? And of those three things which have been assigned as its proper employment, which is the right? Is it to instruct, to amuse, or to employ the vacant hours of those who live at rest? Or may not all three be properly allotted to it? For it appears to partake of them all; for play is necessary for relaxation, and relaxation pleasant, as it is a medicine for that uneasiness which arises from labour. It is admitted also that a happy life must be an honourable one, and a pleasant one too, since happiness consists in both these; and we all agree that music is one of the most pleasing things, whether alone or accompanied with a voice; as Musseus says, "Music's the sweetest joy of man;" for which reason it is justly admitted into every company and every happy life, as having the power of inspiring joy. So that from this any one may suppose that it is necessary to instruct young persons in it; for all those pleasures which are harmless are not only conducive to the final end of life, but serve also as relaxations; and, as men are but rarely in the attainment of that final end, they often cease from their labour and apply to amusement, with no further view than to acquire the pleasure attending it. It is therefore useful to enjoy such pleasures as these. There are some persons who make play and amusement their end, and probably that end has some pleasure annexed to it, but not what should be; but while men seek the one they accept the other for it; because there is some likeness in human actions to the end; for the end is pursued for the sake of nothing else that attends it; but for itself only; and pleasures like these are sought for, not on account of what follows them, but on account of what has gone before them, as labour and grief; for which reason they seek for happiness in these sort of pleasures; and that this is the reason any one may easily perceive. That music should be pursued, not on this account only, but also as it is very serviceable during the hours of relaxation from labour, probably no one doubts; we should also inquire whether besides this use it may not also have another of nobler nature—and we ought not only to partake of the common pleasure arising from it (which all have the sensation of, for music naturally gives pleasure, therefore the use of it is agreeable to all ages and all dispositions); but also to examine if it tends anything to improve our manners and our souls. And this will be easily known if we feel our dispositions any way influenced thereby; and that they are so is evident from many other instances, as well as the music at the Olympic games; and this confessedly fills the soul with enthusiasm; but enthusiasm is an affection of the soul which strongly agitates the disposition. Besides, all those who hear any imitations sympathise therewith; and this when they are conveyed even without rhythm or verse. Moreover, as music is one of those things which are pleasant, and as virtue itself consists in rightly enjoying, loving, and hating, it is evident that we ought not to learn or accustom ourselves to anything so much as to judge right and rejoice in honourable manners and noble actions. But anger and mildness, courage and modesty, and their contraries, as well as all other dispositions of the mind, are most naturally imitated by music and poetry; which is plain by experience, for when we hear these our very soul is altered; and he who is affected either with joy or grief by the imitation of any objects, is in very nearly the same situation as if he was affected by the objects themselves; thus, if any person is pleased with seeing a statue of any one on no other account but its beauty, it is evident that the sight of the original from

631

whence it was taken would also be pleasing; now it happens in the other senses there is no imitation of manners; that is to say, in the touch and the taste; in the objects of sight, a very little; for these are merely representations of things, and the perceptions which they excite are in a manner common to all. Besides, statues and paintings are not properly imitations of manners, but rather signs and marks which show the body is affected by some passion. However, the difference is not great, yet young men ought not to view the paintings of Pauso, but of Polygnotus, or any other painter or statuary who expresses manners. But in poetry and music there are imitations of manners; and this is evident, for different harmonies differ from each other so much by nature, that those who hear them are differently affected, and are not in the same disposition of mind when one is performed as when another is; the one, for instance, occasions grief and contracts the soul, as the mixed Lydian: others soften the mind, and as it were dissolve the heart: others fix it in a firm and settled state, such is the power of the Doric music only; while the Phrygian fills the soul with enthusiasm, as has been well described by those who have written philosophically upon this part of education; for they bring examples of what they advance from the things themselves. The same holds true with respect to rhythm; some fix the disposition, others occasion a change in it; some act more violently, others more liberally. From what has been said it is evident what an influence music has over the disposition of the mind, and how variously it can fascinate it: and if it can do this, most certainly it is what youth ought to be instructed in. And indeed the learning of music is particularly adapted to their disposition; for at their time of life they do not willingly attend to anything which is not agreeable; but music is naturally one of the most agreeable things; and there seems to be a certain connection between harmony and rhythm; for which reason some wise men held the soul itself to be harmony; others, that it contains it.

# CHAPTER

# VI

We will now determine whether it is proper that children should be taught to sing, and play upon any instrument, which we have before made a matter of doubt. Now, it is well known that it makes a great deal of difference when you would qualify any one in any art, for the person himself to learn the practical part of it; for it is a thing very difficult, if not impossible, for a man to be a good judge of what he himself cannot do. It is also very necessary that children should have some employment which will amuse them; for which reason the rattle of Archytas seems well contrived, which they give children to play with, to prevent their breaking those things which are about the house; for at their age they cannot sit still: this therefore is well adapted to infants, as instruction ought to be their rattle as they grow up; hence it is evident that they should be so taught music as to be able to practise it. Nor is it difficult to say what is becoming or unbecoming of their age, or to answer the objections which some make to this employment as mean and low. In the first place, it is necessary for them to practise, that they may be judges of the art: for which reason this should be done when they are young; but when they are grown older the practical part may be dropped; while they will still continue judges of what is excellent in the art, and take a proper pleasure therein, from the knowledge they acquired of it in their youth. As to the censure which some persons throw upon music, as something mean and low, it is not difficult to answer that, if we will but consider how far we propose those who are to be educated so as to become good citizens should be instructed in this art, and what music and what rhythms they should be acquainted with; and also what instruments they should play upon; for in these there is probably a difference. Such then is the proper answer to that censure: for it must be admitted, that in some cases nothing can prevent music being attended, to a certain degree, with the bad effects which are ascribed to it; it is therefore clear that the learning of it should never prevent the business of riper years; nor render the body effeminate, and unfit for the business of war or the state; but it should be practised by the young, judged of by the old. That children may learn music properly, it is necessary that they should not be employed in those parts of it which are the objects of dispute between the masters in that science; nor should they perform such pieces as are wondered at from the difficulty of their execution; and which, from being first exhibited in the public games, are now become a part of education; but let them learn so much of it as to be able to receive proper pleasure from excellent music and rhythms; and not that only which music must make all animals feel, and also slaves and boys, but more. It is therefore plain what instruments they should use; thus, they should never be taught to play upon the flute, or any other instrument which requires great skill, as the harp or the like, but on such as will make them good judges of music, or any other instruction: besides, the flute is not a moral instrument, but rather one that will inflame the passions, and is therefore rather to be used when the soul is to be animated than when instruction is intended. Let me add also, that there is something therein which is quite contrary to what education requires; as the player on the flute is prevented from speaking: for which reason our forefathers very properly forbade the use of it to youth and freemen, though they themselves at first used it; for when their riches procured them greater leisure, they grew more animated in the cause of virtue; and both before and after the Median war their noble actions so exalted their minds that they attended to every part of education; selecting no one in particular, but endeavouring to collect the whole: for which reason they introduced the flute also, as one of the instruments they were to learn to play on. At Lacedaemon the choregus himself played on the flute; and it was so common at Athens that almost every freeman understood it, as is evident from the tablet which Thrasippus dedicated when he was choregus; but afterwards they rejected it as dangerous; having become better judges of what tended to promote virtue and what did not. For the same reason many of the ancient instruments were thrown aside, as the dulcimer and the lyre; as also those which were to inspire those who played on them with pleasure, and which required a nice finger and great skill to play well on. What the ancients tell us, by way of fable, of the flute is indeed very rational; namely, that after Minerva had found it, she threw it away: nor are they wrong who say that the goddess disliked it for deforming the face of him who played thereon: not but that it is more probable that she rejected it as the knowledge thereof contributed nothing to the improvement of the mind. Now, we regard Minerva as the inventress of arts and sciences. As we disapprove of a child's being taught to understand instruments, and to play like a master (which we would have confined to those who are candidates for the prize in that science; for they play not to improve themselves in virtue, but to please those who hear them, and gratify their importunity); therefore we think the practice of it unfit for freemen; but then it should be confined to those who are paid for doing it; for it usually gives people sordid notions, for the end they have in view is bad: for the impertinent spectator is accustomed to make them change their music; so that the artists who attend to him regulate their bodies according to his motions.

# CHAPTER

# VII

We are now to enter into an inquiry concerning harmony and rhythm; whether all sorts of these are to be employed in education, or whether some peculiar ones are to be selected; and also whether we should give the same directions to those who are engaged in music as part of education, or whether there is something different from these two. Now, as all music consists in melody and rhythm, we ought not to be unacquainted with the power which each of these has in education; and whether we should rather choose music in which melody prevails, or rhythm: but when I consider how many things have been well written upon these subjects, not only by some musicians of the present age, but also by some philosophers who are perfectly skilled in that part of music which belongs to education; we will refer those who desire a very particular knowledge therein to those writers, and shall only treat of it in general terms, without descending to particulars. Melody is divided by some philosophers, whose notions we approve of, into moral, practical, and that which fills the mind with enthusiasm: they also allot to each of these a particular kind of harmony which naturally corresponds therewith: and we say that music should not be applied to one purpose only, but many; both for instruction and purifying the soul (now I use the word purifying at present without any explanation, but shall speak more at large of it in my Poetics); and, in the third place, as an agreeable manner of spending the time and a relaxation from the uneasiness of the mind. It is evident that all harmonies are to be used; but not for all purposes; but the most moral in education: but to please the ear, when others play, the most active and enthusiastic; for that passion which is to be found very strong in some souls is to be met with also in all; but the difference in different persons consists in its being in a less or greater degree, as pity, fear, and enthusiasm also; which latter is so powerful in some as to overpower the soul: and yet we see those persons, by the application of sacred music to soothe their mind, rendered as sedate and composed as if they had employed the art of the physician: and this must necessarily happen to the compassionate, the fearful, and all those who are subdued by their passions: nay, all persons, as far as they are affected with those passions, admit of the same cure, and are restored to tranquillity with pleasure. In the same manner, all music which has the power of purifying the soul affords a harmless pleasure to man. Such, therefore, should be the harmony and such the music which those who contend with each other in the theatre should exhibit: but as the audience is composed of two sorts of people, the free and the well-instructed, the rude the mean mechanics, and hired servants, and a long collection of the like, there must be some music and some spectacles to please and soothe them; for as their minds are as it were perverted from their natural habits, so also is there an unnatural harmony, and overcharged music which is accommodated to their taste: but what is according to nature gives pleasure to every one, therefore those who are to contend upon the theatre should be allowed to use this species of music. But in education ethic melody and ethic harmony should be used, which is the Doric, as we have already said, or any other which those philosophers who are skilful in that music which is to be employed in education shall approve of. But Socrates, in Plato's Republic, is very wrong when he permits only the Phrygian music to be used as well as the Doric, particularly as amongst other instruments he banishes the flute; for the Phrygian music has the same power in harmony as the flute has amongst the instruments; for they are both pathetic and raise the mind: and this the practice of the poets proves; for in their bacchanal songs, or whenever they describe any violent emotions of the mind, the flute is the instrument they chiefly use: and the Phrygian harmony is most suitable to these subjects. Now, that the dithyrambic measure is Phrygian is allowed by general consent; and those who are conversant in studies of this sort bring many proofs of it; as, for instance, when Philoxenus endeavoured to compose dithyrambic music for Doric harmony, he naturally fell back again into Phrygian, as being fittest for that purpose; as every one indeed agrees, that the Doric music is most serious, and fittest to inspire courage: and, as we always commend the middle as being between the two extremes, and the Doric has this relation with respect to other harmonies, it is evident that is what the youth ought to be instructed in. There are two things to be taken into consideration, both what is possible and what is proper; every one then should chiefly endeavour to attain those things which contain both these qualities: but this is to be regulated by different times of life; for instance, it is not easy for those who are advanced in years to sing such pieces of music as require very high notes, for nature points out to them those which are gentle and require little strength of voice (for which reason some who are skilful in music justly find fault with Socrates for forbidding the youth to be instructed in gentle harmony; as if, like wine, it would make them drunk, whereas the effect of that is to render men bacchanals, and not make them languid): these therefore are what should employ those who are grown old. Moreover, if there is any harmony which is proper for a child's age, as being at the same time elegant and instructive, as the Lydian of all others seems chiefly to be—These then are as it were the three boundaries of education, moderation, possibility, and decorum.

# THE
# ENCHIRIDION

# Epictetus

# INTRODUCTION

The little book by Epictetus called *Enchiridion* or "manual" has played a disproportionately large role in the rise of modern attitudes and modern philosophy. As soon as it had been translated into the vernacular languages, it became a bestseller among independent intellectuals, among anti-Christian thinkers, and among philosophers of a subjective cast. Montaigne had a copy of the *Enchiridion* among his books. Pascal violently rejected the megalomaniac pride of the Stoic philosopher. Frederick the Great carried the book with him on all campaigns. It was a source of inspiration and encouragement to Anthony, Earl of Shaftesbury, in the serious illness which ended only in his death; many pages of his diaries contain passages copied from the *Enchiridion*. It has been studied and widely quoted by Scottish philosophers like Francis Hutcheson, Adam Smith, and Adam Ferguson who valued Stoic moral philosophy for its reconciliation of social dependency and personal independence.

That there was a rebirth of Stoicism in the centuries of rebirth which marked the emergence of the modern age was not mere chance. Philosophical, moral, and social conditions of the time united to cause it. Roman Stoicism had been developed in times of despotism as a philosophy of lonely and courageous souls who had recognized the redeeming power of philosophical reason in all the moral and social purposes of life. Philosophy as a way of life makes men free. It is the last ditch stand of liberty in a world of servitude. Many elements in the new age led to thought which had structural affinity with Roman Stoicism. Modern times had created the independent thinker, the free intellectual in a secular civilization. Modern times had destroyed medieval liberties and had established the new despotism of the absolute state supported by ecclesiastical authority. Modern philosophies continued the basic trend in Stoicism in making the subjective consciousness the foundation of philosophy. The Stoic emphasis on moral problems was also appealing in an era of rapid transition when all the values which had previously been taken for granted were questioned and reconsidered.

While it is interesting to observe how varied were the effects produced by this small volume, this epitome of the Stoic system of moral philosophy, these effects seem still more remarkable when we consider that it was not intended to be a philosophical treatise on Stoicism for students. It was, rather, to be a guide for the advanced student of Stoicism to show him the best roads toward the goal of becoming a true philosopher. Thus, Epictetus and his *Enchiridion* have a unique position in Roman Stoicism. Seneca and Marcus Aurelius had selected Stoic philosophy as the most adequate system for expressing their existential problems of independence, solitude, and history. In this enterprise, Seneca made tremendous strides toward the insights of social psychology as a by-product of his consciousness of decadence (in this he was close to Nietzsche), but he was not primarily concerned with the unity of the Stoic system. Marcus Aurelius changed the philosophical doctrine into the regimen of the lonesome ruler. In contrast to both, Epictetus was teaching Stoic philosophy as a doctrine and as a way of life. The *Enchiridion* is a summary of theoretical and applied Stoicism.

Epictetus was the son of a woman slave, born between 50 and 60 A.D. at Hieropolis in Phrygia. We do not know how he came to Rome. He was there as slave to one of Nero's distinguished freedmen who served as the Emperor's secretary. While still in service, Epictetus took courses with Musonius Rufus, the fashionable Stoic philosopher, who was impressed by the sincere and dynamic personality of the young slave and trained him to be a Stoic philosopher. Epictetus became a free man and began teaching philosophy on street corners, in the market, but he was not successful. During the rule of Domitian, Epictetus with many other philosophers was exiled from Rome, probably between 89 and 92 A.D. He went to Nicopolis, across Actium in Epirus, where he conducted his own school. He was so well regarded and highly esteemed that he established the reputation of the place as the town of

Epictetus' school. Students came from Athens and Rome to attend his classes. Private citizens came to ask his advice and guidance. Some of his students returned to their homes to enter the traditional careers to which they were socially obligated. Others assumed the philosophic way of life in order to escape into the sphere of Stoic freedom.

Among the students was a young Roman, Flavius Arrian, who took courses at Nicopolis when Epictetus was already old. Flavius, who was born in 108 A.D., was one of the intimates of Hadrian, who made him consul in 130 A.D. He probably studied with Epictetus between the years 123 and 126 A.D. The informal philosophical talks which Epictetus had with his students fascinated him. Needless to say there were also systematic courses in the fields of philosophy. But it was the informal discourses which convinced Arrian that he had finally discovered a Stoic Socrates or a Stoic Diogenes, who was not merely teaching a doctrine, but also living the truth. Arrian recorded many of the discourses and informal conversations of Epictetus with his intimate students. He took them down in shorthand in order not to lose the ineffable liveliness, grace, and wit of the beloved teacher. Arrian retired into private life after the death of Hadrian in 138 A.D. and dedicated himself to his literary work. He published his notes on Epictetus' teaching under the title: *Discourses in Four Books*. The *Enchiridion*, which was also arranged by Arrian, is a brief summary of the basic ideas of Stoic philosophy and an introduction to the techniques required to transform Stoic philosophy into a way of life.

Thus, we do not have any original writings of Epictetus. Like G. H. Mead in recent times, he was completely dedicated to the human and intellectual problems of his students. He left it for them to preserve what they considered to be the lasting message of the teacher. In contrast to Seneca and Marcus Aurelius, Epictetus had no subjective approach to the Stoic doctrines. Moral philosophy was the center of his teaching, and epistemology was only instrumental. It is even permissible to say that he took physics or cosmology too lightly. If this is granted, we must admit that he is completely absorbed by the fundamentals of Stoic thought as presented in the *Enchiridion*. Epictetus' personality is totally integrated in the act of reasoning which establishes conformity with nature.

A remarkable difference between the *Discourses* and the *Enchiridion* should be mentioned. The *Discourses* are a living image of the teacher in action; they present the process of philosophizing, not the finished product. They show the enthusiastic and sober, the realistic and pathetic moralist in constantly changing perspectives determined by the changing students with their various concerns, problems, and questions; his teachings, his formulations, have direct reference to the various life situations in which the students should apply and practice the master's Stoic teaching. No human situation is omitted; as a guide to conduct, philosophy has relevance for all. Whether the students have to attend a dinner party, whether they are among competitors in a stadium or in a swimming pool, whether they have to present themselves at court or in an office, whether they are in the company of their mothers and sisters or of girl friends, in all human situations the philosopher knows the correct advice for the philosophical apprentice. Thus, in the *Discourses*, Arrian presents the unique individuality of the philosopher and of his applied moral method in living contact with various students in concrete situations. Epictetus as teacher anticipates very modern educational methods in his regard for the structure of situations and the changing perspectives in human relationships.

Nothing like this is revealed in the *Enchiridion*. Gone is the Stoic philosopher as living spirit. What remains is the living spirit of Stoicism. The *Enchiridion* is a manual for the combat officer. This analogy should be taken seriously. The Roman Stoics coined the formula: *Vivere militare!* (Life is being a soldier.) The student of philosophy is a private, the advancing Stoic is a non-commissioned officer, and the philosopher is the combat officer. For this reason all Roman Stoics apply metaphors and images derived from military life. Apprentice students of Stoicism are described as messengers, as scouts of God, as representatives of divine nature. The advancing student who is close to the goal of being a philosopher has the rank of an officer. He is already able to establish inner freedom and independence. He understands the basic Stoic truth of subjective consciousness, which is to distinguish what is in our power from what is not in our power. Not in our power are all the elements which constitute our environment, such as wealth, health, reputation, social prestige, power, the lives of those we love, and death. In our power are our thinking, our intentions, our desires, our decisions. These make it possible for us to control ourselves and to make of ourselves elements and parts of the universe of nature. This knowledge of ourselves makes us free in a world of dependencies. This superiority of our powers enables us to live in conformity with nature. The rational philosophy of control of Self and of adjustment to the Whole implies an asceticism of the emotional and the sensitive life. The philosopher must examine and control his passions, his love, his tenderness at all times in order always to be ready for the inevitable moment of farewell. The Stoics practiced a Jesuitism *avant la lettre*. They were able to live in the world as if they did not live in it. To the Stoic, life is a military camp, a play on the stage, a banquet to which we are invited. The *Enchiridion* briefly indicated the techniques which the philosopher should apply in acting well the diverse roles which God might assign to those whom he loves, the Stoic philosophers. From the rules of social conduct to the recommendations of sexual asceticism before marriage, and the method of true thinking, the advanced Stoic will find all principles of perfection and all precepts for realizing philosophical principles in his conduct in this tiny volume.

Thus the *Enchiridion* was liberating for all intellectuals who learned from it that there are philosophical ways of self-redemption. From its time, the secular thinker could feel jubilant because he was not in need of a divine grace. Epictetus had taught him that philosophical reason could make him free and that he was capable of redeeming himself by sound reasoning.

In the Stoic distinctions of personality and world, of I and mine, of subjective consciousness and the world of objects, of freedom and dependence, we find implicit the basic elements of modern philosophies of rationalism and of objective idealism or pantheism. For this reason there is a continuous renascence of Stoicism from Descartes, Grotius, and Bishop Butler, to Montesquieu, Adam Smith, and Kant. In this long development in modern times, the tiny *Enchiridion* of Epictetus played a remarkable part.

The translations of Epictetus and of all other Stoics had the widest effect on philosophers, theologians, and lay thinkers. They were studied by the clergy of the various Christian denominations, by the scientists who were striving for a natural religion, and by the independent philosophers who were eager to separate philosophy from religion. There were many outstanding bishops in the Catholic and Anglican Churches who were eager to transform the traditions of Roman Stoicism into Christian Stoicism. Among the Calvinistic denominations were many thinkers who were in sympathy with Stoic moral principles because of their praise of the austerity of life and of the control of passions. Likewise the adherents of natural religion were propagating Stoicism as the ideal pattern of universally valid and intelligible religion. Renascent Stoicism had three functions in the rise of the modern world. First, it reconciled Christian traditions to modern rationalistic philosophies; secondly, it established an ideal pattern of natural religion; and, thirdly, it opened the way for the autonomy of morals.

ALBERT SALOMON
The New School for Social Research
July, *1948*

# THE ENCHIRIDION

## I

There are things which are within our power, and there are things which are beyond our power. Within our power are opinion, aim, desire, aversion, and, in one word, whatever affairs are our own. Beyond our power are body, property, reputation, office, and, in one word, whatever are not properly our own affairs.

Now the things within our power are by nature free, unrestricted, unhindered; but those beyond our power are weak, dependent, restricted, alien. Remember, then, that if you attribute freedom to things by nature dependent and take what belongs to others for your own, you will be hindered, you will lament, you will be disturbed, you will find fault both with gods and men. But if you take for your own only that which is your own and view what belongs to others just as it really is, then no one will ever compel you, no one will restrict you; you will find fault with no one, you will accuse no one, you will do nothing against your will; no one will hurt you, you will not have an enemy, nor will you suffer any harm.

Aiming, therefore, at such great things, remember that you must not allow yourself any inclination, however slight, toward the attainment of the others; but that you must entirely quit some of them, and for the present postpone the rest. But if you would have these, and possess power and wealth likewise, you may miss the latter in seeking the former; and you will certainly fail of that by which alone happiness and freedom are procured.

Seek at once, therefore, to be able to say to every unpleasing semblance, "You are but a semblance and by no means the real thing." And then examine it by those rules which you have; and first and chiefly by this: whether it concerns the things which are within our own power or those which are not; and if it concerns anything beyond our power, be prepared to say that it is nothing to you.

## II

Remember that desire demands the attainment of that of which you are desirous; and aversion demands the avoidance of that to which you are averse; that he who fails of the object of his desires is disappointed; and he who incurs the object of his aversion is wretched. If, then, you shun only those undesirable things which you can control, you will never incur anything which you shun; but if you shun sickness, or death, or poverty, you will run the risk of wretchedness. Remove [the habit of] aversion, then, from all things that are not within our power, and apply it to things undesirable which are within our power. But for the present, altogether restrain desire; for if you desire any of the things not within our own power, you must necessarily be disappointed; and you are not yet secure of those which are within our power, and so are legitimate objects of desire.

Where it is practically necessary for you to pursue or avoid anything, do even this with discretion and gentleness and moderation.

## III

With regard to whatever objects either delight the mind or contribute to use or are tenderly beloved, remind yourself of what nature they are, beginning with the merest trifles: if you have a favorite cup, that it is but a cup of which you are fond of—for thus, if it is broken, you can bear it;

if you embrace your child or your wife, that you embrace a mortal—and thus, if either of them dies, you can bear it.

## IV

When you set about any action, remind yourself of what nature the action is. If you are going to bathe, represent to yourself the incidents usual in the bath—some persons pouring out, others pushing in, others scolding, others pilfering. And thus you will more safely go about this action if you say to yourself, "I will now go to bathe and keep my own will in harmony with nature." And so with regard to every other action. For thus, if any impediment arises in bathing, you will be able to say, "It was not only to bathe that I desired, but to keep my will in harmony with nature; and I shall not keep it thus if I am out of humor at things that happen."

## V

Men are disturbed not by things, but by the views which they take of things. Thus death is nothing terrible, else it would have appeared so to Socrates. But the terror consists in our notion of death, that it is terrible. When, therefore, we are hindered or disturbed, or grieved, let us never impute it to others, but to ourselves—that is, to our own views. It is the action of an uninstructed person to reproach others for his own misfortunes; of one entering upon instruction, to reproach himself; and one perfectly instructed, to reproach neither others nor himself.

## VI

Be not elated at any excellence not your own. If a horse should be elated, and say, "I am handsome," it might be endurable. But when you are elated and say, "I have a handsome horse," know that you are elated only on the merit of the horse. What then is your own? The use of the phenomena of existence. So that when you are in harmony with nature in this respect, you will be elated with some reason; for you will be elated at some good of your own.

# VII

As in a voyage, when the ship is at anchor, if you go on shore to get water, you may amuse yourself with picking up a shellfish or a truffle in your way, but your thoughts ought to be bent toward the ship, and perpetually attentive, lest the captain should call, and then you must leave all these things, that you may not have to be carried on board the vessel, bound like a sheep; thus likewise in life, if, instead of a truffle or shellfish, such a thing as a wife or a child be granted you, there is no objection; but if the captain calls, run to the ship, leave all these things, and never look behind. But if you are old, never go far from the ship, lest you should be missing when called for.

# VIII

Demand not that events should happen as you wish; but wish them to happen as they do happen, and you will go on well.

# IX

Sickness is an impediment to the body, but not to the will unless itself pleases. Lameness is an impediment to the leg, but not to the will; and say this to yourself with regard to everything that happens. For you will find it to be an impediment to something else, but not truly to yourself.

# X

Upon every accident, remember to turn toward yourself and inquire what faculty you have for its use. If you encounter a handsome person, you will find continence the faculty needed; if pain, then fortitude; if reviling, then patience. And when thus habituated, the phenomena of existence will not overwhelm you.

# XI

Never say of anything, "I have lost it," but, "I have restored it." Has your child died? It is restored. Has your wife died? She is restored. Has your estate been taken away? That likewise is restored. "But it was a bad man who took it." What is it to you by whose hands he who gave it has demanded it again? While he permits you to possess it, hold it as something not your own, as do travelers at an inn.

# XII

If you would improve, lay aside such reasonings as these: "If I neglect my affairs, I shall not have a maintenance; if I do not punish my servant, he will be good for nothing." For it were better to die of hunger, exempt from grief and fear, than to live in affluence with perturbation; and it is better that your servant should be bad than you unhappy.

Begin therefore with little things. Is a little oil spilled or a little wine stolen? Say to yourself, "This is the price paid for peace and tranquillity; and nothing is to be had for nothing." And when you call your servant, consider that it is possible he may not come at your call; or, if he does, that he may not do what you wish. But it is not at all desirable for him, and very undesirable for you, that it should be in his power to cause you any disturbance.

# XIII

If you would improve, be content to be thought foolish and dull with regard to externals. Do not desire to be thought to know anything; and though you should appear to others to be somebody, distrust yourself. For be assured, it is not easy at once to keep your will in harmony with nature and to secure externals; but while you are absorbed in the one, you must of necessity neglect the other.

## XIV

If you wish your children and your wife and your friends to live forever, you are foolish, for you wish things to be in your power which are not so, and what belongs to others to be your own. So likewise, if you wish your servant to be without fault, you are foolish, for you wish vice not to be vice but something else. But if you wish not to be disappointed in your desires, that is in your own power. Exercise, therefore, what is in your power. A man's master is he who is able to confer or remove whatever that man seeks or shuns. Whoever then would be free, let him wish nothing, let him decline nothing, which depends on others; else he must necessarily be a slave.

## XV

Remember that you must behave as at a banquet. Is anything brought round to you? Put out your hand and take a moderate share. Does it pass by you? Do not stop it. Is it not yet come? Do not yearn in desire toward it, but wait till it reaches you. So with regard to children, wife, office, riches; and you will some time or other be worthy to feast with the gods. And if you do not so much as take the things which are set before you, but are able even to forego them, then you will not only be worthy to feast with the gods, but to rule with them also. For, by thus doing, Diogenes and Heraclitus, and others like them, deservedly became divine, and were so recognized.

## XVI

When you see anyone weeping for grief, either that his son has gone abroad or that he has suffered in his affairs, take care not to be overcome by the apparent evil, but discriminate and be ready to say, "What hurts this man is not this occurrence itself—for another man might not be hurt by it—but the view he chooses to take of it." As far as conversation goes, however, do not disdain to accommodate yourself to him and, if need be, to groan with him. Take heed, however, not to groan inwardly, too.

## XVII

Remember that you are an actor in a drama of such sort as the Author chooses—if short, then in a short one; if long, then in a long one. If it be his pleasure that you should enact a poor man, or a cripple, or a ruler, or a private citizen, see that you act it well. For this is your business—to act well the given part, but to choose it belongs to another.

## XVIII

When a raven happens to croak unluckily, be not overcome by appearances, but discriminate and say, "Nothing is portended to *me*, either to my paltry body, or property, or reputation, or children, or wife. But to *me* all portents are lucky if I will. For whatsoever happens, it belongs to me to derive advantage therefrom."

## XIX

You can be unconquerable if you enter into no combat in which it is not in your own power to conquer. When, therefore, you see anyone eminent in honors or power, or in high esteem on any other account, take heed not to be bewildered by appearances and to pronounce him happy; for if the essence of good consists in things within our own power, there will be no room for envy or emulation. But, for your part, do not desire to be a general, or a senator, or a consul, but to be free; and the only way to this is a disregard of things which lie not within our own power.

# XX

Remember that it is not he who gives abuse or blows, who affronts, but the view we take of these things as insulting. When, therefore, anyone provokes you, be assured that it is your own opinion which provokes you. Try, therefore, in the first place, not to be bewildered by appearances. For if you once gain time and respite, you will more easily command yourself.

# XXI

Let death and exile, and all other things which appear terrible, be daily before your eyes, but death chiefly; and you will never entertain an abject thought, nor too eagerly covet anything.

# XXII

If you have an earnest desire toward philosophy, prepare yourself from the very first to have the multitude laugh and sneer, and say, "He is returned to us a philosopher all at once"; and, "Whence this supercilious look?" Now, for your part, do not have a supercilious look indeed, but keep steadily to those things which appear best to you, as one appointed by God to this particular station. For remember that, if you are persistent, those very persons who at first ridiculed will afterwards admire you. But if you are conquered by them, you will incur a double ridicule.

# XXIII

If you ever happen to turn your attention to externals, for the pleasure of anyone, be assured that you have ruined your scheme of life. Be content, then, in everything, with being a philosopher; and if you wish to seem so likewise to anyone, appear so to yourself, and it will suffice you.

## XXIV

Let not such considerations as these distress you: "I shall live in discredit and be nobody anywhere." For if discredit be an evil, you can no more be involved in evil through another than in baseness. Is it any business of yours, then, to get power or to be admitted to an entertainment? By no means. How then, after all, is this discredit? And how it is true that you will be nobody anywhere when you ought to be somebody in those things only which are within your own power, in which you may be of the greatest consequence? "But my friends will be unassisted." What do you mean by "unassisted"? They will not have money from you, nor will you make them Roman citizens. Who told you, then, that these are among the things within our own power, and not rather the affairs of others? And who can give to another the things which he himself has not? "Well, but get them, then, that we too may have a share." If I can get them with the preservation of my own honor and fidelity and self-respect, show me the way and I will get them; but if you require me to lose my own proper good, that you may gain what is no good, consider how unreasonable and foolish you are. Besides, which would you rather have, a sum of money or a faithful and honorable friend? Rather assist me, then, to gain this character than require me to do those things by which I may lose it. Well, but my country, say you, as far as depends upon me, will be unassisted. Here, again, what assistance is this you mean? It will not have porticos nor baths of your providing? And what signifies that? Why, neither does a smith provide it with shoes, nor a shoemaker with arms. It is enough if everyone fully performs his own proper business. And were you to supply it with another faithful and honorable citizen, would not he be of use to it? Yes. Therefore neither are you yourself useless to it. "What place, then," say you, "shall I hold in the state?" Whatever you can hold with the preservation of your fidelity and honor. But if, by desiring to be useful to that, you lose these, how can you serve your country when you have become faithless and shameless?

## XXV

Is anyone preferred before you at an entertainment, or in courtesies, or in confidential intercourse? If these things are good, you ought to rejoice that he has them; and if they are evil, do not be grieved that you have them not. And remember that you cannot be permitted to rival others in externals without using the same means to obtain them. For how can he who will not haunt the door of any man, will not attend him, will not praise him, have an equal share with him who does these things? You are unjust, then, and unreasonable if you are unwilling to pay the price for which these things are sold, and would have them for nothing. For how much are lettuces sold? An obulus, for instance. If another, then, paying an obulus, takes the lettuces, and you, not paying it, go without them, do not imagine that he has gained any advantage over you. For as he has the lettuces, so you have the obulus which you did not give. So, in the present case, you have not been invited to such a person's entertainment because you have not paid him the price for which a supper is sold. It is sold for praise; it is sold for attendance. Give him, then, the value if it be for your advantage. But if you would at the same time not pay the one, and yet receive the other, you are unreasonable and foolish. Have you nothing, then, in place of the supper? Yes, indeed, you have—not to praise him whom you do not like to praise; not to bear the insolence of his lackeys.

## XXVI

The will of nature may be learned from things upon which we are all agreed. As when our neighbor's boy has broken a cup, or the like, we are ready at once to say, "These are casualties that will happen"; be assured, then, that when your own cup is likewise broken, you ought to be affected just as when another's cup was broken. Now apply this to greater things. Is the child or wife of another dead? There is no one who would not say, "This is an accident of mortality." But if anyone's own child happens to die, it is immediately, "Alas! how wretched am I!" It should be always remembered how we are affected on hearing the same thing concerning others.

## XXVII

As a mark1 is not set up for the sake of missing the aim, so neither does the nature of evil exist in the world.

## XXVIII

If a person had delivered up your body to some passer-by, you would certainly be angry. And do you feel no shame in delivering up your own mind to any reviler, to be disconcerted and confounded?

## XXIX[2]

In every affair consider what precedes and what follows, and then undertake it. Otherwise you will begin with spirit, indeed, careless of the consequences, and when these are developed, you will shamefully desist. "I would conquer at the Olympic Games." But consider what precedes and what follows, and then, if it be for your advantage, engage in the affair. You must conform to rules, submit to a diet, refrain from dainties; exercise your body, whether you choose it or not, at a stated hour, in heat and cold; you must drink no cold water, and sometimes no wine—in a word, you must give yourself up to your trainer as to a physician. Then, in the combat, you may be thrown into a ditch, dislocate your arm, turn your ankle, swallow an abundance of dust, receive stripes [for negligence], and, after all, lose the victory.

When you have reckoned up all this, if your inclination still holds, set about the combat. Otherwise, take notice, you will behave like children who sometimes play wrestlers, sometimes gladiators, sometimes blow a trumpet, and sometimes act a tragedy, when they happen to have seen and admired these shows. Thus you too will be at one time a wrestler, and another a gladiator; now a philosopher, now an orator; but nothing in earnest. Like an ape you mimic all you see, and one thing after another is sure to please you, but is out of favor as soon as it becomes familiar. For you have never entered upon anything considerately; nor after having surveyed and tested the whole matter, but carelessly, and with a halfway zeal. Thus some, when they have seen a philosopher and heard a man speaking like Euphrates[3]—though, indeed, who can speak like him?—have a mind to be philosophers, too. Consider first, man, what the matter is, and what your own nature is able to bear. If you would be a wrestler, consider your shoulders, your back, your thighs; for different persons are made for different things. Do you think that you can act as you do and be a philosopher, that you can eat, drink, be angry, be discontented, as you are now? You must watch, you must labor, you must get the better of certain appetites, must quit your acquaintances, be despised by your servant, be laughed at by those you meet; come off worse than others in everything—in offices, in honors, before tribunals. When you have fully considered all these things, approach, if you please—that is, if, by parting with them, you have a mind to purchase serenity, freedom, and tranquillity. If not, do not come hither; do not, like children, be now a philosopher, then a publican, then an orator, and then one of Caesar's officers. These things are not consistent. You must be one man, either good or bad. You must cultivate either your own reason or else externals; apply yourself either to things within or without you—that is, be either a philosopher or one of the mob.

# XXX

Duties are universally measured by relations. Is a certain man your father? In this are implied taking care of him, submitting to him in all things, patiently receiving his reproaches, his correction. But he is a bad father. Is your natural tie, then, to a *good* father? No, but to a father. Is a brother unjust? Well, preserve your own just relation toward him. Consider not what *he* does, but what *you* are to do to keep your own will in a state conformable to nature, for another cannot hurt you unless you please. You will then be hurt when you consent to be hurt. In this manner, therefore, if you accustom yourself to contemplate the relations of neighbor, citizen, commander, you can deduce from each the corresponding duties.

# XXXI

Be assured that the essence of piety toward the gods lies in this—to form right opinions concerning them, as existing and as governing the universe justly and well. And fix yourself in this resolution, to obey them, and yield to them, and willingly follow them amidst all events, as being ruled by the most perfect wisdom. For thus you will never find fault with the gods, nor accuse them of neglecting you. And it is not possible for this to be affected in any other way than by withdrawing yourself from things which are not within our own power, and by making good or evil to consist only in those which are. For if you suppose any other things to be either good or evil, it is inevitable that, when you are disappointed of what you wish or incur what you would avoid, you should reproach and blame their authors. For every creature is naturally formed to flee and abhor things that appear hurtful and that which causes them; and to pursue and admire those which appear beneficial and that which causes them. It is impracticable, then, that one who supposes himself to be hurt should rejoice in the person who, as he thinks, hurts him, just as it is impossible to rejoice in the hurt itself. Hence, also, a father is reviled by his son when he does not impart the things which seem to be good; and this made Polynices and Eteocles[4] mutually enemies—that empire seemed good to both. On this account the husbandman reviles the gods; [and so do] the sailor, the merchant, or those who have lost wife or child. For where our interest is, there, too, is piety directed. So that whoever is careful to regulate his desires and aversions as he ought is thus made careful of piety likewise. But it also becomes incumbent on everyone to offer libations and sacrifices and first fruits, according to the customs of his country, purely, and not heedlessly nor negligently; not avariciously, nor yet extravagantly.

# XXXII

When you have recourse to divination, remember that you know not what the event will be, and you come to learn it of the diviner; but of what nature it is you knew before coming; at least, if you are of philosophic mind. For if it is among the things not within our own power, it can by no means be either good or evil. Do not, therefore, bring with you to the diviner either desire or aversion—else you will approach him trembling—but first clearly understand that every event is indifferent and nothing to *you*, of whatever sort it may be; for it will be in your power to make a right use of it, and this no one can hinder. Then come with confidence to the gods as your counselors; and afterwards, when any counsel is given you, remember what counselors you have assumed, and whose advice you will neglect if you disobey. Come to divination as Socrates prescribed, in cases of which the whole consideration relates to the event, and in which no opportunities are afforded by reason or any other art to discover the matter in view. When, therefore, it is our duty to share the danger of a friend or of our country, we ought not to consult the oracle as to whether we shall share it with them or not. For though the diviner should forewarn you that the auspices are unfavorable, this means no more than that either death or mutilation or exile is portended. But we have reason within us; and it directs us, even with these hazards, to stand by our friend and our country. Attend, therefore, to the greater diviner, the Pythian God, who once cast out of the temple him who neglected to save his friend.[5]

# XXXIII

Begin by prescribing to yourself some character and demeanor, such as you may preserve both alone and in company.

Be mostly silent, or speak merely what is needful, and in few words. We may, however, enter sparingly into discourse sometimes, when occasion calls for it; but let it not run on any of the common subjects, as gladiators, or horse races, or athletic champions, or food, or drink—the vulgar topics of conversation—and especially not on men, so as either to blame, or praise, or make comparisons. If you are able, then, by your own conversation, bring over that of your company to proper subjects; but if you happen to find yourself among strangers, be silent.

Let not your laughter be loud, frequent, or abundant.

Avoid taking oaths, if possible, altogether; at any rate, so far as you are able.

Avoid public and vulgar entertainments; but if ever an occasion calls you to them, keep your attention upon the stretch, that you may not imperceptibly slide into vulgarity. For be assured that if a person be ever so pure himself, yet, if his companion be corrupted, he who converses with him will be corrupted likewise.

Provide things relating to the body no further than absolute need requires, as meat, drink, clothing, house, retinue. But cut off everything that looks toward show and luxury.

Before marriage guard yourself with all your ability from unlawful intercourse with women; yet be not uncharitable or severe to those who are led into this, nor boast frequently that you yourself do otherwise.

If anyone tells you that a certain person speaks ill of you, do not make excuses about what is said of you, but answer: "He was ignorant of my other faults, else he would not have mentioned these alone."

It is not necessary for you to appear often at public spectacles; but if ever there is a proper occasion for you to be there, do not appear more solicitous for any other than for yourself—that is, wish things to be only just as they are, and only the best man to win; for thus nothing will go against you. But abstain entirely from acclamations and derision and violent emotions. And when you come away, do not discourse a great deal on what has passed and what contributes nothing to your own amendment. For it would appear by such discourse that you were dazzled by the show.

Be not prompt or ready to attend private recitations; but if you do attend, preserve your gravity and dignity, and yet avoid making yourself disagreeable.

When you are going to confer with anyone, and especially with one who seems your superior, represent to yourself how Socrates or Zeno[6] would behave in such a case, and you will not be at a loss to meet properly whatever may occur.

When you are going before anyone in power, fancy to yourself that you may not find him at home, that you may be shut out, that the doors may not be opened to you, that he may not notice you. If, with all this, it be your duty to go, bear what happens and never say to yourself, "It was not worth so much"; for this is vulgar, and like a man bewildered by externals.

In company, avoid a frequent and excessive mention of your own actions and dangers. For however agreeable it may be to yourself to allude to the risks you have run, it is not equally agreeable to others to hear your adventures. Avoid likewise an endeavor to excite laughter, for this may readily slide you into vulgarity, and, besides, may be apt to lower you in the esteem of your acquaintance. Approaches to indecent discourse are likewise dangerous. Therefore, when anything of this sort happens, use the first fit opportunity to rebuke him who makes advances that way, or, at least, by silence and blushing and a serious look show yourself to be displeased by such talk.

# XXXIV

If you are dazzled by the semblance of any promised pleasure, guard yourself against being bewildered by it; but let the affair wait your leisure, and procure yourself some delay. Then bring to your mind both points of time—that in which you shall enjoy the pleasure, and that in which you will repent and reproach yourself, after you have enjoyed it—and set before you, in opposition to these, how you will rejoice and applaud yourself if you abstain. And even though it should appear to you a seasonable gratification, take heed that its enticements and allurements and seductions may not subdue you, but set in opposition to this how much better it is to be conscious of having gained so great a victory.

# XXXV

When you do anything from a clear judgment that it ought to be done, never shrink from being seen to do it, even though the world should misunderstand it; for if you are not acting rightly, shun the action itself; if you are, why fear those who wrongly censure you?

# XXXVI

As the proposition, "either it is day or it is night," has much force in a disjunctive argument, but none at all in a conjunctive one, so, at a feast, to choose the largest share is very suitable to the bodily appetite, but utterly inconsistent with the social spirit of the entertainment. Remember, then, when you eat with another, not only the value to the body of those things which are set before you, but also the value of proper courtesy toward your host.

# XXXVII

If you have assumed any character beyond your strength, you have both demeaned yourself ill in that and quitted one which you might have supported.

# XXXVIII

As in walking you take care not to tread upon a nail, or turn your foot, so likewise take care not to hurt the ruling faculty of your mind. And if we were to guard against this in every action, we should enter upon action more safely.

# XXXIX

The body is to everyone the proper measure of its possessions, as the foot is of the shoe. If, therefore, you stop at this, you will keep the measure; but if you move beyond it, you must necessarily be carried forward, as down a precipice; as in the case of a shoe, if you go beyond its fitness to the foot, it comes first to be gilded, then purple, and then studded with jewels. For to that which once exceeds the fit measure there is no bound.

# XL

Women from fourteen years old are flattered by men with the title of mistresses. Therefore, perceiving that they are regarded only as qualified to give men pleasure, they begin to adorn themselves, and in that to place all their hopes. It is worth while, therefore, to try that they may perceive themselves honored only so far as they appear beautiful in their demeanor and modestly virtuous.

# XLI

It is a mark of want of intellect to spend much time in things relating to the body, as to be immoderate in exercises, in eating and drinking, and in the discharge of other animal functions. These things should be done incidentally and our main strength be applied to our reason.

# XLII

When any person does ill by you, or speaks ill of you, remember that he acts or speaks from an impression that it is right for him to do so. Now it is not possible that he should follow what appears right to you, but only what appears so to himself. Therefore, if he judges from false appearances, he is the person hurt, since he, too, is the person deceived. For if anyone takes a true proposition to be false, the proposition is not hurt, but only the man is deceived. Setting out, then, from these principles, you will meekly bear with a person who reviles you, for you will say upon every occasion, "It seemed so to him."

# XLIII

Everything has two handles: one by which it may be borne, another by which it cannot. If your brother acts unjustly, do not lay hold on the affair by the handle of his injustice, for by that it cannot be borne, but rather by the opposite—that he is your brother, that he was brought up with you; and thus you will lay hold on it as it is to be borne.

# XLIV

These reasonings have no logical connection: "I am richer than you, therefore I am your superior." "I am more eloquent than you, therefore I am your superior." The true logical connection is rather this: "I am richer than you, therefore my possessions must exceed yours." "I am more eloquent than you, therefore my style must surpass yours." But you, after all, consist neither in property nor in style.

# XLV

Does anyone bathe hastily? Do not say that he does it ill, but hastily. Does anyone drink much wine? Do not say that he does ill, but that he drinks a great deal. For unless you perfectly understand his motives, how should you know if he acts ill? Thus you will not risk yielding to any appearances but such as you fully comprehend.

# XLVI

Never proclaim yourself a philosopher, nor make much talk among the ignorant about your principles, but show them by actions. Thus, at an entertainment, do not discourse how people ought to eat, but eat as you ought. For remember that thus Socrates also universally avoided all ostentation. And when persons came to him and desired to be introduced by him to philosophers, he took them and introduced them; so well did he bear being overlooked. So if ever there should be among the ignorant any discussion of principles, be for the most part silent. For there is great danger in hastily throwing out what is undigested. And if anyone tells you that you know nothing, and you are not nettled at it, then you may be sure that you have really entered on your work. For sheep do not hastily throw up the grass to show the shepherds how much they have eaten, but, inwardly digesting their food, they produce it outwardly in wool and milk. Thus, therefore, do you not make an exhibition before the ignorant of your principles, but of the actions to which their digestion gives rise.

## XLVII

When you have learned to nourish your body frugally, do not pique yourself upon it; nor, if you drink water, be saying upon every occasion, "I drink water." But first consider how much more frugal are the poor than we, and how much more patient of hardship. If at any time you would inure yourself by exercise to labor and privation, for your own sake and not for the public, do not attempt great feats; but when you are violently thirsty, just rinse your mouth with water, and tell nobody.

## XLVIII

The condition and characteristic of a vulgar person is that he never looks for either help or harm from himself, but only from externals. The condition and characteristic of a philosopher is that he looks to himself for all help or harm. The marks of a proficient are that he censures no one, praises no one, blames no one, accuses no one; says nothing concerning himself as being anybody or knowing anything. When he is in any instance hindered or restrained, he accuses himself; and if he is praised, he smiles to himself at the person who praises him; and if he is censured, he makes no defense. But he goes about with the caution of a convalescent, careful of interference with anything that is doing well but not yet quite secure. He restrains desire; he transfers his aversion to those things only which thwart the proper use of our own will; he employs his energies moderately in all directions; if he appears stupid or ignorant, he does not care;

and, in a word, he keeps watch over himself as over an enemy and one in ambush.

## XLIX

When anyone shows himself vain on being able to understand and interpret the works of Chrysippus,⁷ say to yourself: "Unless Chrysippus had written obscurely, this person would have had nothing to be vain of. But what do I desire? To understand nature, and follow her. I ask, then, who interprets her; and hearing that Chrysippus does, I have recourse to him. I do not understand his writings. I seek, therefore, one to interpret *them.*" So far there is nothing to value myself upon. And when I find an interpreter, what remains is to make use of his instructions. This alone is the valuable thing. But if I admire merely the interpretation, what do I become more than a grammarian, instead of a philosopher, except, indeed, that instead of Homer I interpret Chrysippus? When anyone, therefore, desires me to read Chrysippus to him, I rather blush when I cannot exhibit actions that are harmonious and consonant with his discourse.

## L

Whatever rules you have adopted, abide by them as laws, and as if you would be impious to transgress them; and do not regard what anyone says of you, for this, after all, is no concern of yours. How long, then, will you delay to demand of yourself the noblest improvements, and in no instance to transgress the judgments of reason? You have received the philosophic principles with which you ought to be conversant; and you have been conversant with them. For what other master, then, do you wait as an excuse for this delay in self-reformation? You are no longer a boy but a grown man. If, therefore, you will be negligent and slothful, and always add procrastination to procrastination, purpose to purpose, and fix day after day in which you will attend to yourself, you will insensibly continue to accomplish nothing and, living and dying, remain of vulgar mind. This instant, then, think yourself worthy of living as a man grown up and a proficient. Let whatever appears to be the best be to you an inviolable law. And if any instance of pain or pleasure, glory or disgrace, be set before you, remember that now is the combat, now the Olympiad comes on, nor can it be put off; and that by one failure and defeat honor may be lost or—won. Thus Socrates became perfect, improving himself by everything, following reason alone. And though you are not yet a Socrates, you ought, however, to live as one seeking to be a Socrates.

# LI

The first and most necessary topic in philosophy is the practical application of principles, as, *We ought not to lie*; the second is that of demonstrations as, *Why it is that we ought not to lie*; the third, that which gives strength and logical connection to the other two, as, *Why this is a demonstration*. For what is demonstration? What is a consequence? What a contradiction? What truth? What falsehood? The third point is then necessary on account of the second; and the second on account of the first. But the most necessary, and that whereon we ought to rest, is the first. But we do just the contrary. For we spend all our time on the third point and employ all our diligence about that, and entirely neglect the first. Therefore, at the same time that we lie, we are very ready to show how it is demonstrated that lying is wrong.

Upon all occasions we ought to have these maxims ready at hand:

Conduct me, Zeus, and thou, O Destiny,
Wherever your decrees have fixed my lot.
I follow cheerfully; and, did I not,
Wicked and wretched, I must follow still.[8]

Who'er yields properly to Fate is deemed
Wise among men, and knows the laws of Heaven.[9]

And this third:
"O Crito, if it thus pleases the gods, thus let it be."[10] "Anytus and
Melitus may kill me indeed; but hurt me they cannot."[11]

# FOOTNOTES

[1] Happiness, the effect of virtue, is the mark which God has set up for us to aim at. Our missing it is no work of His; nor so properly anything real, as a mere negative and failure of our own.

[2] Chapter XV of the third book of the *Discourses*, which, with the exception of some very trifling differences, is the same as chapter XXIX of the *Enchiridion.*—Ed.

[3] Euphrates was a philosopher of Syria, whose character is described, with the highest encomiums, by Pliny the Younger, *Letters* I. 10.

[4] The two inimical sons of Oedipus, who killed each other in battle.—Ed.

[5] This refers to an anecdote given in full by Simplicius, in his commentary on this passage, of a man assaulted and killed on his way to consult the oracle, while his companion, deserting him, took refuge in the temple till cast out by the Deity.—Tr.

[6] Reference is to Zeno of Cyprus (335-263 B.C.), the founder of the Stoic school.—Ed.

[7] Chrysippus (*c.* 280-207 B.C.) was a Stoic philosopher who became head of the Stoa after Cleanthes. His works, which are lost, were most influential and were generally accepted as the authoritative interpretation of orthodox Stoic philosophy.—Ed.

[8] Cleanthes, in Diogenes Laertius, quoted also by Seneca, *Epistle* 107.

[9] Euripides, Fragments.

[10] Plato, *Crito*, Chap. XVII.

[11] Plato, *Apology*, Chap. XVIII.